BUSINESS, SOCIETY, AND GOVERNMENT ESSENTIALS

Understanding the interrelationship of business, society, and government is vital to working at any level in a company of any size. This text uses a case analysis approach to explore this interrelationship in today's high-tech global community.

The authors crystallize the complex array of issues that business leaders, managers, and employees face in market and nonmarket environments, from balancing stakeholder interests and dealing with government regulations to managing crises and making socially responsible and ethical decisions. Technical concepts come to life through a variety of cases and case questions, thought-provoking personal and professional applications, ethical dilemmas, and practical exercises. Furthermore, an appendix offers approaches to case analysis and includes a case analysis table that serves as a model for students and professors. With its thorough coverage of relevant issues and skill-building elements to stimulate critical thinking, this text will prepare students to understand and confront real-world business concerns.

Robert N. Lussier, PhD, professor of management at Springfield College, teaches business, society, and government. He has a national and international reputation as the author of more than 375 publications, including journal articles with public policy analysis and recommendations, as well as management, leadership, and human relations textbooks. More than one million students globally have used Lussier's books.

Herbert Sherman, PhD, professor of management and chair of the Management Science Department at Long Island University–Brooklyn campus, teaches courses in business strategy, business and society, and organizational behavior. He has published six books in the last eight years, several readers, more than 50 cases, and nearly 100 articles in strategic management, small business/entrepreneurship, and business ethics.

BUSINESS, SOCIETY, AND GOVERNMENT ESSENTIALS

Strategy and Applied Ethics
2nd Edition

Robert N. Lussier & Herbert Sherman

Routledge
Taylor & Francis Group

NEW YORK AND LONDON

Visit the companion website for this
title at **www.routledge.com/cw/lussier**

This edition first published 2014
by Routledge
711 Third Avenue, New York, NY 10017

Simultaneously published in the UK
by Routledge
2 Park Square, Milton Park, Abingdon, Oxon OX14 4RN

Routledge is an imprint of the Taylor & Francis Group, an informa business

First edition published by Waveland Press, 2008

Library of Congress Cataloging in Publication Data
Lussier, Robert N.
  Business, society, and government essentials : strategy and applied ethics /
  Robert N. Lussier & Herbert Sherman. — 2nd ed.
    p. cm.
  Includes bibliographical references and index.
  1. Social responsibility of business. 2. Corporations—Moral and ethical aspects.
  3. Business ethics. 4. Industrial policy. I. Sherman, Herbert. II. Title.
  HD60.L87 2013
  174'.4—dc23
  2012041545

ISBN: 978–0–415–62209–7
ISBN: 978–0–415–62210–3
ISBN: 978–0–203–10634–1

Typeset in Times New Roman
by Swales & Willis Ltd, Exeter, Devon

SUSTAINABLE
FORESTRY
INITIATIVE
Certified Chain of Custody
At Least 20% Certified Forest Content

www.sfiprogram.org
SFI-00712

Printed in the United States of America by Courier, Kendallville, Indiana

TABLE OF CONTENTS

PREFACE

RATIONALE AND UNIQUE FEATURES OF THE BOOK

After using other texts to teach courses on the interrelationship of business, society, and government (BSG), we were not completely satisfied that these texts met the needs of our students. Therefore, in an effort to meet our goals in teaching the course and to offer students a comprehensive text that is clearly written, we decided to write our own textbook that:

- has a **personalized, easy-to-read writing style**. By relating the material to students' personal and professional lives, the text engages students and encourages them to read the book.
- lets students realize that everyone who works for a large or a small company (not just top-level managers of major corporations), nonprofit, or the government **will face** several of the **issues** discussed in the text.
- starts with a **macro view** of business, society, and government, which is followed by a **micro view** that first focuses on business, next on society, and then on government.
- is designed around a **framework** that is based on the business, society, and government stakeholder environment and interrelationships, which integrate market and nonmarket strategies to meet the needs of the stakeholder, and include global contexts and technology and sustainability issues. The framework is illustrated in Model 1.1.

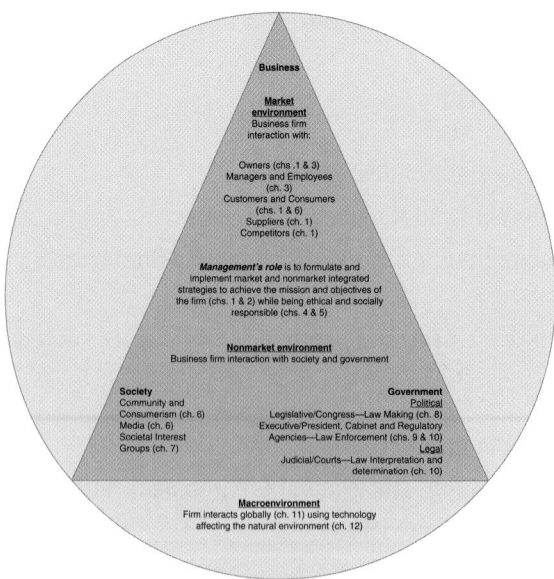

Model 1.1: The Business, Society, and Government Interrelationship Stakeholder Environment (from page 5).

■ takes an essentials approach. Traditional, comprehensive, and essential concepts are covered in **12 chapters**, thereby eliminating the need for instructors to assign multiple chapters per week or to select chapters to skip. This essentials approach also allows instructors to add their own material to the course without overburdening the students.

■ uses a **case study approach**, with a mix of small and large businesses to illustrate text concepts and facilitate an understanding of their application in the real world:

— Each chapter begins with a brief case and case questions. The questions are answered throughout the chapter to illustrate the application of the chapter concepts.

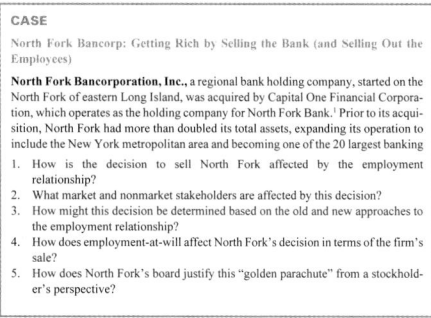

(see Case, page 77)

— The end-of-chapter cases are real-life situations that illustrate text concepts from the current and prior chapters. Questions at the end of these cases also bring in ethical considerations.

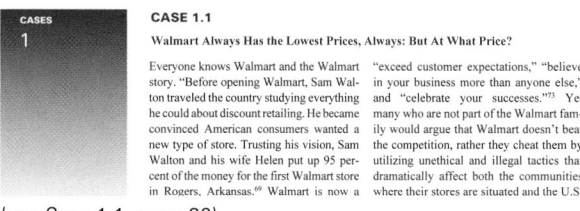

(see Case 1.1, page 30)

— An integrative comprehensive case that clearly illustrates the business, society, and government interrelationship for one small business is presented in parts at the end of each chapter.

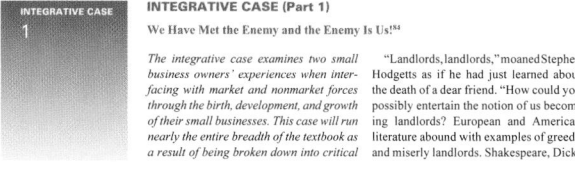

(see Integrative Case, page 32)

■ emphasizes an **applied ethics** approach by providing ethical guidelines throughout the text and by presenting *ethical dilemmas* and regular cases that have either an explicit or an implicit ethical component, which is particularly helpful in dealing with current issues.

— This approach is designed to develop and sharpen students' ability to make personal and professional ethical decisions.

— The two **ethical dilemma cases** within each chapter challenge readers to address an issue faced by a real-life organization. They ask: "Is the behavior in the case ethical?" and "What would you do in this situation?"

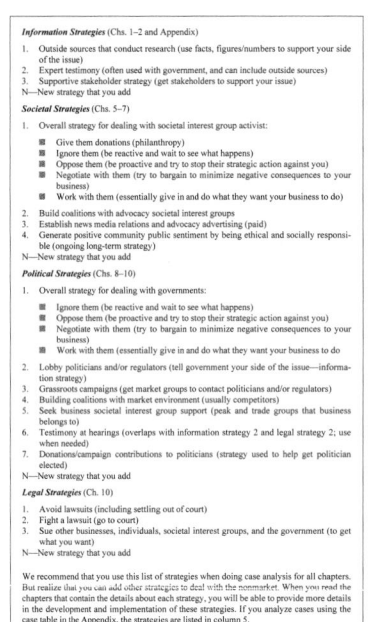

Figure 1.4: Nonmarket Strategies for Business (from page 22)

▪ uses a **strategy focus** by listing nonmarket strategies in Figure 1.4. The last section of Chapter 2 describes how to conduct a strategic analysis (5 Is) of issues, integrating market and nonmarket strategies and then discussing how businesses use the strategies in Chapters 3–12. Students are encouraged to use the strategic analysis, which is the basis for the unified case analysis form when conducting case studies.

▪ provides a **unified case analysis form** (a nine-column worksheet, which is contained in the Appendix at the end of the book) that can be used for all cases, with a clear focus on the BSG interrelationship. If students use the case analysis form when analyzing the alternative ways in which a case can be handled, they answer the question "Is this alternative strategy legal and ethical?" (Use of the case analysis form is optional.)

BLANK TABLE

BSG 5 Is Strategic Analysis: CASE _____ Ch. _____ Name _____ Date _____

Issue Identification [1] Write the problem issue {One issue per sheet} [Ch. 2]	Interested Strategic Stakeholders [2] {Bus, Soc, & Gov} For (+) or Against (–) Business or Neutral (=) {Model 1.1, p. 5} [Ch. 2, 1–10]	Incentive of Stakeholders [3] What can they gain or lose that will get them involved? Cost vs. Benefit (C > B, B > C) [Ch. 2]	Objective for issue and Information to be [4] used to meet objective Fact (F), Assumption, (A) {#s, outside sources} [Ch. 2]
Stage of Life Cycle {Figure 2.4 p. 53}			

Interaction Strategies:

Alternative strategic action [5] to meet the objective {Figure 1.4 p. 22} [Ch. 2, 1–10]	Market analysis [6] Market reactions (+, =, –) [Ch. 2]	Nonmkt analysis [7] Nonmarket reactions (+, =, –) [Ch. 2]	Select strategic action [8] Is it legal and ethical? Selected? (Y/N/Wait) [Chs. 1–10]	Implementation actions for each strategy [9] Urgency? {policies, procedures, rules} Evaluate results [Ch. 2, 1–10]

(see page 518)

PEDAGOGICAL FEATURES

▪ Each chapter begins with a list of *learning outcomes* (approximately eight per chapter), the last one being to define a list of *key terms*, which are explained within the chapter and part of a matching review in the chapter summary. Learning outcomes are listed in the text prior to the topic's coverage. Next are a *Chapter Outline* and

What's This Chapter About?, giving readers the topical highlights and a synopsis of the chapter's content.

> Learning Outcome 1: Describe stakeholder management and the need to balance stockholder and other stakeholder interests.

■ References are current with a good balance of research from concept-related journals (*Business & Society, Business and Society Review, Business Ethics Quarterly, Journal of Business Ethics*), general management research of the concepts (*Academy of Management—Journal, Review, Perspective, Learning & Education*), and popular press for current real-world examples (*BusinessWeek, Forbes, Fortune, Wall Street Journal*).

■ Multiple *current real business examples* of the concepts appear throughout each chapter. **Company names** are in bold to stand out.

■ *Personal and professional application* questions that motivate students to see how the text concepts relate to them appear throughout each chapter (249 total, averaging 21 per chapter).

> **Personal and Professional Applications**
>
> 1. Give examples of how society and government influenced a business you work(ed) for.

■ *Figures* and *diagrams* highlight main topics, offer additional details, and illustrate selected concepts.

■ Chapter *summaries* provide the *answers to the learning outcomes* and include a *key term* matching exercise.

■ Each chapter contains *review questions* (RQ) (related to chapter concepts) and *discussion/critical thinking questions* (DQ) that provide a ready means of knowledge retention and enrichment (an average of 17 RQ per chapter and 12 DQ per chapter).

■ *Application exercises* require students to find examples of businesses dealing with the chapter concepts. They may include online searching. (Forty of these questions are distributed among the 12 chapters.)

■ *Three cases* with questions appear at the end of each chapter. One of the three cases is an unfolding *comprehensive integrative case*.

■ *Websites* are listed throughout the text for students seeking additional information.

■ *Website* with quizzes, etc.

■ At least one *exercise* per chapter in the Instructor's Manual is based on one of the cases. Exercises will include one of the following: a role-playing exercise, an opinion survey with feedback, a paper simulation, an online exercise, an in-box/out-box exercise.

COURSES

This text is appropriate for the following courses: Business, Society, and Government; Business and Society; Business and Government; Business Ethics; Corporate Social Responsibility; Environment of Business; Social Issues in Management; Business and Public Policy; Public Affairs; Public Administration; strategy courses and nonbusiness courses, such as Political Science and Sociology that focus on the interrelationship among business, society, and government.

The book covers Association of Advance Collegiate Schools of Business (AACSB) topics including the influence of political, social, legal and regulatory, environmental, and technology issues; global issues; and ethics and the impact of diversity on organizations.

INSTRUCTOR'S MANUAL

Important instructional material completes this package for this course.

■ Answers to all review and case questions; a case analysis form with grading guidelines; and suggestions for case exercises—written by the authors
■ Test Bank, with traditional questions—written by Jimidene Murphy, Wharton County Junior College. PowerPoint slides for class lectures—developed by Charlie T. Cook, Jr., Shelton State Community College.
■ Website with quizzes, etc.
■ Case teaching notes developed by the authors to include one case per chapter that employs the nine-column case analysis, answers to all case questions, and teaching tips.
■ The files for the instructor's manual can be found on our site at www.routledge. com/cw/lussier

CHANGES IN THE SECOND EDITION

■ While maintaining the overall book structure, ethics is now a separate chapter with expanded coverage within the chapter and throughout the book, and prior Chapters 5 (Community and Consumerism) and 6 (Media and Advertising) are now combined.
■ A major new section in Chapter 12 describes sustainability with green management examples.
■ New government laws and regulations and agencies have been added including health and finance: The Patient Protection and Affordable Care Act of 2010 and the Dodd-Frank Wall Street Reform and Consumer Protection Act of 2009 with the new Consumer Financial Protection Bureau (CFPB).
■ The entire book has been completely updated with more than 90 percent of the references being new to this edition.
■ Virtually all of the cases have been either updated or replaced.
■ Most of the company, nongovernment organization (NGO), and government examples have been replaced with current examples.

STRUCTURE OF THE BOOK

The first part begins with a macro approach, laying the foundation for an understanding of the business, society, and government interrelationship. This is followed by a micro approach that provides more details of the interrelationships from the business perspective.

The second part focuses on the market environment of business with the need for a stakeholder approach to public affairs and issues management, and the relationship with employees, stockholders, and corporate governance, while being socially responsible.

The third part turns the focus to how the nonmarket society affects business and the need for business to be ethical in dealing with the community and consumers, and the role of the media and societal interest groups in developing nonmarket issues that business must deal with.

The fourth part also focuses on the nonmarket, but changes the focus to how the government affects business and the need for business to understand the laws and regulations and how to influence politicians and regulators to allow the business to compete effectively in the market environment.

The last part expands the business, society, and government interrelationship to the more complete global level and explores the effects of technology and the natural environment on business and the need for sustainable business practices.

Part 1

THE INTER-RELATIONSHIP OF BUSINESS, SOCIETY, AND GOVERNMENT

Chapter 1

THE BUSINESS, SOCIETY, AND GOVERNMENT ETHICAL INTERRELATIONSHIP STAKEHOLDER ENVIRONMENT

Learning Outcomes

In this chapter, you will find out the answers to these key questions:

▪ What is the course all about?
▪ How can taking this course benefit your personal and professional lives?
▪ How do business, society, and government influence each other and you?

After studying this chapter, you should be able to:

1. Characterize business, society, and government and explain their interrelationships
2. Differentiate the market and nonmarket environments and state how they influence each other
3. Explain the nonmarket society and government environments and how they affect business
4. Contrast the political and legal environments, briefly stating what each branch of government does, and summarize their balance of power
5. Discuss the role of business and its managers, including stakeholders
6. Define "strategy," differentiate market and nonmarket strategies, and describe the need to integrate them
7. Define the following key terms (in order of appearance in the chapter):

business	nonmarket society environment	lying
product	public sentiment	cheating
society	political environment	stealing
societal interest groups	legal environment	moral management
government	strategy	amoral managers
special interest groups	market strategies	values
social problems	nonmarket strategies	business ethics
market environment	ethics	stakeholders
nonmarket environment	honesty	

■ Chapter Outline

What's This Chapter About?[1]

This chapter presents basic concepts that are critical to understanding the course content, or what this book is all about. The other chapters in the book provide greater details and applications of these concepts.

This chapter covers three separate yet interrelated topics that build on each other. First, we discuss basic concepts and why you should study business, society, and government, or what's in it for you. Essentially, the book is about how business, society, and government interact and influence each other (and you), and strategies business use to deal with issues of society and government. Based on this foundation, we discuss the environment in which they interact. Our third section further builds on this material by discussing the role of business and its managers.

We end by pulling the chapter concepts, environment, and mangers' role together by describing a top management stakeholder approach, an applied ethics approach, and the structure of the book.

[1] Note that this is an important section to read before getting into the chapter because it briefly explains the topics of the chapter, why they are important, and how they are related.

CASE

When You DoubleClick Ethics, Does Google Twitter?

Google Inc. is one of the most popular and well-known companies in the world. According to Forbes' "World's Biggest Public Companies," Google ranked number 120 out of 2,000 firms worldwide. Ninety-nine percent of Google's revenue is derived from its advertising programs.[1] Google is famous for its search engine (with its biggest competitors in 2012 being Bing and Yahoo!), but recently it expanded its operations by entering several new industries including smartphones (the android software system—a market dominated by Apple), Internet connection software (Google Chrome in competition with Microsoft Explorer and Mozilla Firefox), as well as the social networking industry (Google+ to compete against Facebook and Twitter).

In 2004, Google acquired Keyhole, Inc., the developer of Earth Viewer, which gives a three-dimensional view of the Earth. Google renamed the service Google Earth in 2005. Two years later, Google bought the online video site YouTube for $1.65 billion in stock. On April 13, 2007, Google reached an agreement to acquire DoubleClick for $3.1 billion, giving Google access to valuable relationships with Web publishers and advertising agencies. On August 5, 2009, Google bought out its first public company, purchasing video software maker On2 Technologies for $106.5 million. Google also acquired Aardvark, a social network search engine, for $50 million.

In addition to the many companies Google has purchased, the company has partnered with other organizations for everything from research to advertising. In 2005, Google partnered with NASA Ames Research Center to build 1,000,000 square feet of offices. Google then entered into a partnership with Sun Microsystems in October 2005 to help share and distribute each other's technologies. The company also partnered with AOL of Time Warner to enhance each other's video search services. Google's 2005 partnerships also included financing the new top-level domain for mobile devices, along with other companies including Microsoft, Nokia, and Ericsson. Increasing its advertising reach even further, Google and Fox Interactive Media of News Corporation entered into a $900 million agreement to provide search and advertising facilities for the popular social networking site MySpace.[2]

Google's main slogan is "Don't be evil." Google prides itself in respect for the individual and honesty. Its code of conduct goes further to say that when it comes to its customers Google aims to build a good sense of trust and when it comes to competition, it maintains a fair playing field. Google believes that a company can make a profit by conducting business in a proper and polite manner without harming others.[3]

As a multinational firm, Google operates in numerous countries with differing laws and customs. One country that has proven to be a rather large obstacle for Google is China. In January of 2010 Google announced that it may withdraw from doing business with China after a highly sophisticated and targeted attack on its corporate infrastructure, originating from China, resulted in the theft of intellectual property.[4] Google is not the only company to encounter problems in its business relationship with China.[5]

Google, along with Facebook and Twitter, has also been accused of making Internet communications more complicated. The *New York Times* stated that Internet social networking sites (including Google+) and e-mail made managing communication more confusing.[6] However, findings from the 2011 Corporate Social Responsibility Index conducted by the Boston College Center for Corporate Citizenship and the Reputation Institute indicated that Google was ranked #2 among all firms in 2011. This study has been going on since 2008, when Google ranked #1. Rankings were #3 in 2009 and #10 in 2010.[7] The following questions are related to the Google case. Answers can be found within the chapter.

1. What are the main ethical issues when it comes to Google and the way they operate?
2. What are some of the social problems affecting Google?
3. Identify the key stakeholders in this case.
4. If you were the president of Google, what nonmarket actions would you take relative to the stakeholders addressed in question 3?

WHY STUDY BUSINESS, SOCIETY, AND GOVERNMENT?

The introductory Google case illustrates how businesses must interact with numerous organizations representing the government, other businesses, and the general society, rather than simply acting as independent entities. Let's begin with an example of how society and government affect business. Definitions of *business*, *society,* and *government* will help understand the ways in which you can and must sometimes interact with them. Our capitalist pluralistic society both highly influences and is influenced by business, society, and government, including the ways in which special interest groups function. The top management stakeholder approach and applied ethics approach provided at the end of the chapter offer a framework for analyzing situations and making decisions within the world we live.

How Government and Society Affect Business

Business interacts with society and the government and these external forces influence how business is operated.[8] Thus, it is important to understand the interrelationships among business, society, and government.[9] As one quick example, if the government lowers mortgage loan interest rates, society may buy more houses and realtors will sell more houses, but a change in mortgage rules could make it harder to buy or sell houses.[10] Model 1.1 provides an overview of the business, society, and government interrelationship. The Model is the foundational structure for the book and will be explained throughout this chapter and, as noted on the Model, throughout the book's 12 chapters.

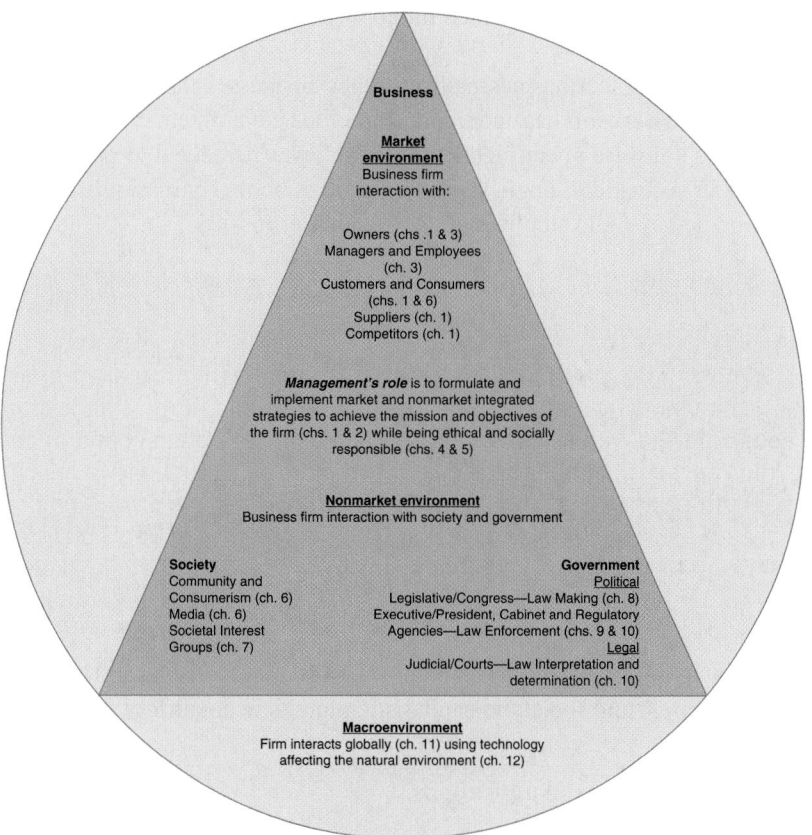

Business

Market environment
Business firm interaction with:

Owners (chs .1 & 3)
Managers and Employees (ch. 3)
Customers and Consumers (chs. 1 & 6)
Suppliers (ch. 1)
Competitors (ch. 1)

Management's role is to formulate and implement market and nonmarket integrated strategies to achieve the mission and objectives of the firm (chs. 1 & 2) while being ethical and socially responsible (chs. 4 & 5)

Nonmarket environment
Business firm interaction with society and government

Society
Community and Consumerism (ch. 6)
Media (ch. 6)
Societal Interest Groups (ch. 7)

Government
Political
Legislative/Congress—Law Making (ch. 8)
Executive/President, Cabinet and Regulatory Agencies—Law Enforcement (chs. 9 & 10)
Legal
Judicial/Courts—Law Interpretation and determination (ch. 10)

Macroenvironment
Firm interacts globally (ch. 11) using technology affecting the natural environment (ch. 12)

■ **Model 1.1:** The Business, Society, and Government Interrelationship Stakeholder Environment

Among other reasons, some people start their own business or become managers because they think they can run their business any way they want. However, this is only partly true. For example, if you want to start a restaurant and bar in your hometown, you will find that numerous local government regulations govern the location and operation of a restaurant. First, city government zoning restrictions will dictate where you can and can't locate your business, when you may open and must close your business, and the type of signage you must use.

At the state level, your business will first have to be registered and obtain a state tax ID number. For a restaurant or bar, you will need to meet state and federal employee safety and health standards, and if you want to serve alcohol you will need a state liquor license. If you don't adhere to these rules and regulations, the government can force you to close your business; yet meeting government regulations is not the only requirement for operating a successful business.

If one or more customers gets sick eating your food, is injured in a fall on your premises, or gets in an accident driving home drunk, your business may not only be liable under the law but negative publicity about your business and public sentiment could then turn against you, and sales could drop. Furthermore, organizations, including **Mothers Against Drunk Driving (MADD)**, and social trends toward healthier eating and dieting may affect your restaurant's drinking policy and food and beverage offerings.

Government and society can also help business. Without the infrastructure the government builds and supports, business would not be efficient. For example, the government has historically focused on creating and maintaining interstate communication and transportation systems, the basic necessities of free trade. The **U.S. Postal Service** was created to ensure the safe and reliable delivery of mail while the telephone service was originally created as a regulated monopoly (**AT&T**) to guarantee cost-effective telecommunications.

Government laws protect businesses from other businesses through regulating unfair business practices. **Microsoft** has undergone numerous government investigations related to their Windows software operating system, which was perceived to give preference to certain Microsoft software. **Google** started to digitize books, but lawsuits by publishers resulted in Google having to stop without copyright permission.[11]

Google Case Question 1: What are the main ethical issues when it comes to Google and the way they operate?

Google's motto of "Don't be evil" provides Google with a moral compass, yet its actions may not always follow that path. For example, Google aims to build a good sense of trust with its customers yet it has threatened to abandon customers in China because of intellectual property theft rather than build better security systems. Furthermore, the *New York Times* accused Google of making communication via the Internet more confusing for its customers. Google claims that it strives for a good and fair playing field when it comes to competition, yet Google was digitizing books without permission, a clear violation of copyright law.

As illustrated, to be successful in business, you need to understand and have good relations with government and society in capitalistic pluralistic countries.[12]

Personal and Professional Applications

1. Give examples of how society and government influenced a business you work(ed) for.

Learning Outcome 1: Characterize business, society, and government and explain their interrelationship.

Business, Society, and Government and Interactions with Them

As a foundation for discussions throughout this chapter and the textbook, we define and briefly explain what business, society, and government are and how you interact with them.

Business. *A business is a firm that sells a product for a profit. A product may be a good, a service, or both.* The three forms of business ownership are sole *proprietorships* owned by one person, *partnerships* owned by two or more people, and *corporations* owned by any number of stockholders.

A central theme of this book is that business should be responsible to society and government.[13] Successful businesses help, rather than hurt, society, and they operate within the government's laws and regulations.[14] The common term for this aspect of business behavior is "corporate social responsibility," which will be discussed in Chapter 4.

Society. *Society is the people, including interest groups, and the communities affected by business. Societal interest groups are nonprofit organizations that promote a cause.* We use societal interest groups as a broad term to clearly distinguish nonprofits from business and government. Societal interest groups include NGOs, public interest groups, advocacy groups, activist groups, civil society groups, online communities, and other nonprofit organizations, such as unions. Members of society unite because they represent a common cause or share common beliefs about an issue that is important to them. **Greenpeace, Common Cause, MADD,** and **People for the Ethical Treatment of Animals (PETA)** are purposeful organizations that are societal interest groups. NGOs often pressure business to conform to their interest.[15] On the other hand, they sometimes partner with business to meet their mutual interest.[16] As related to this course, *communities* are the areas in which people live and businesses operate.

Government. *Government includes the executive, legislative, and judicial branches at the local, county, state, federal, and international levels.* The government makes and enforces the laws, regulations, and rules that business and society should abide by. If people and businesses break the law, they can be punished, usually through the court system.

Some authors refer to society and government as a combined term "society." However, a distinct difference that you need to understand separates society and government, so we keep the terms separate throughout the book.

Interactions with Business, Society, and Government. This book relates to your personal and professional lives because everything we do affects, and is affected by, business, government, and society. This book also will teach you how to apply ethics in your personal and professional lives. Below are some examples of how you interact with business, society, and government.

■ Do you have, or did you ever have, a job working for a *business*? If yes, you are a part of the business community. Also, as part of the business community, you buy products from businesses.

■ Has business helped (e.g., sponsored a sports team) or in any way hurt your local community (e.g., caused pollution)?

■ Have you ever done volunteer work or received services from a *societal* nonprofit organization?

■ Was this local agency part of a larger regional or national organization or did it have international ties such as the **YMCA** and **UNICEF**?

■ Did you ever attend a *government* public school, community college, or state college or university?

■ Do you have a social security number, a driver's license, or a passport?

■ Did you know that you pay taxes when you fill up your gas tank? Most likely you pay sales and income tax to the government.

Personal and Professional Applications

2. Describe your personal interactions with business, society, and government.

Capitalism, Pluralism, and Special Interest Groups

Capitalism is a market economic system in which private individuals and corporations own the means of production and operate to make a profit with limited social intervention and government restraint. A capitalistic country can also be pluralistic. A *pluralistic* country has a political system that attempts to balance power between business, society, and government so that no one group dominates. At the same time, a pluralistic society has literally tens of thousands of special interest groups. *Special interest groups include any profit, nonprofit, or government organization that is working for its own best interest, sometimes at the expense of others.* In a *democracy* every person is free with equal right to participate in a system of government. The United States is a democracy, with capitalism and pluralism. One difference between an economic system and a political system is the medium of exchange. In an economic system, the medium of exchange is generally money and other assets. In a political system, the medium of exchange is generally favors, such as votes and special interest campaign contributions and lobbying, with expectations of helping the business with favorable legislation. This book will help you to better understand the balance of power and how special interest groups fight for power to get what they want. Chapter 7 focuses on societal special interest groups and the strategies they use to get what they want.

Personal and Professional Applications

3. Describe your view of our capitalist pluralistic market system and its special interest groups.

Factors Contributing to Special Interest Groups and Social Problems.

Some of the factors contributing to special interest groups and social problems include rising expectations, an entitlement mentality, the rights movement, and victimization. These four factors are separate, yet related, and they lead to criticism of business.

People have *rising expectations* that each generation should have a higher standard of living than the previous one, and that business and government should also strive and act to serve people better. Economic inequity and poverty are contributing factors to societal problems. *Social problems occur when society's expectations are not met by business and/or government.* These gaps between expectations and reality can occur in business ethics and social responsibility, jobs, medical insurance and health care costs that continue to increase, the environment, retirement and social security, and terrorism.

Entitlement mentality is the belief that we are owed something, such as a good job with benefits, medical insurance and good health care, a good education and retirement without having to work for it, just because we are a member of society or a particular group in that society.

The *rights movement* is based on the Bill of Rights, which were ratified as amendments to the U.S. Constitution in 1791. More recently, beginning with the Civil Rights cases of the 1950s, the U.S. Supreme Court has established rights for African, Hispanic, Asian, and Native Americans; women; the disabled and aged; and other minority groups. At the local, county, state, and federal level, certain special interest groups such as homosexuals, smokers and nonsmokers, obese people, AIDS victims, and illegal immigrants are seeking additional rights. The **United Nations (UN)** has a statement on Human Rights, and promotes human rights globally.

Victimization occurs when people believe they have been unfairly treated or hurt by business, societal institutions, or government. Victims have the "Don't blame me . . . it's not my fault" attitude and desire justice (usually in the form of compensation) for their injuries and loss of rights. Some people believe they have been victimized by the government's attempts to correct unfair treatment. Victimization occurs among all race, age, gender, and other social and economic classifications.

Google Case Question 2: What are some of the social problems affecting Google?

Many of Google's services are available to the public for free (i.e., Internet searches, Google+, and YouTube), yet some individuals seem to feel entitled to greater access to Google's proprietary technology and have pirated some of its intellectual property. Google's reaction to this piracy has been to announce a possible withdrawal from the China market, potentially negatively impacting millions of users. This withdrawal would seem to place corporate interests above those of consumers thereby challenging, and perhaps modifying, Google's ethics of "Do no evil."

Personal and Professional Applications

4. List some of your personal special interests.

5. State what you believe to be the most important social problems we have today. Do they relate to question 4?

6. Do you have rising expectations and an entitlement mentality, do you want special rights, and have you been victimized?

ETHICAL DILEMMA 1.1 Day Laborers—Are They the Newest and Oldest Victimized Class?

Day laborer is a term that generally refers to an individual (either unskilled or semi-skilled) who works and gets paid on a daily or short-term basis. To find work, day laborers often congregate on street corners and wait for employers to drive by and offer them work. The term also includes those who may be employed by temporary staffing agencies that assign them work on a daily basis with client employers. Day laborers have an informal relationship with the labor market, often working for different employers each day, being paid in cash, and lacking key benefits, such as health or unemployment insurance. However, day laborers, like many other workers in this country, may be eligible for wage and safety protections provided by federal law. Coverage does not depend on a worker's immigration status.

Because of day laborers' informal relationship with the labor market, congressional representatives, researchers, and advocacy groups have raised concerns that day laborers may be used for the most hazardous work but not paid appropriate wages or provided safe working conditions. However, little is actually known about who these day laborers are, what their working conditions are, or the extent to which protections afforded under federal wage and safety and health laws are enforced.[17]

Questions

1. Is it ethical for businesses to hire day workers, or are they victimizing them?
2. What impact do day workers have on business, government, and society?
3. Should government get involved? If so, what should it do?
4. Would you hire day workers? Why or why not?

How Special Interest Groups Affect Business. Let's illustrate how special interest groups affect business with an example. The East End of Long Island, New York, commonly called the Hamptons, combines the beauty of an oceanfront community with the glamor of movie stars and multimillionaires. Living in the Hamptons is considered desirable, and residential construction has continued at a rapid rate. Yet, this part of Long Island also possesses historical sites (Southampton was founded in 1640), numerous farms and vineyards, and an incredible array of natural wildlife.

Builders have met with tremendous opposition from individuals and groups who feel victimized by the construction. One such opposition NGO is the **Group of the South Fork**. Formed in 1972 in response to increasing construction of what has been called "McMansions" (look-alike homes that are 4,000 square feet or larger), the group is a volunteer-directed, professionally staffed, not-for-profit environmental advocacy organization established to protect the environment, the community's rural character, and the quality of life across the South Fork of Long Island's East End through public advocacy and public education. The group has successfully lobbied local and county legislators who have passed laws and regulations limiting growth. This legislation has negatively affected builders by establishing low-density housing, restricting property clearance, and setting aside hundreds of acres of prime real estate for historical preservation and conservancy.

Benefits to Your Personal and Professional Lives

Now that we have an understanding of what business, society, and government are all about and that these interrelated entities are important to you, let's focus on what this book has to offer you: it will help you to better understand how business, society, and government each work independently and interdependently with special interest groups, how they interact to shape the world we live in, and how they affect your personal and professional lives. Here are what business publications have to say about the importance of the topics of this book related to your career:

- ■ "Most companies could use help in broadening their relationships with government."[18]
- ■ "Understanding the intricacies of government could become as critical a path to the executive suite as mastering financial statements."[19]
- ■ "In looking at ideal preparation for a senior executive, you need to add an understanding of government regulatory issues."[20] In fact, the head of government relations, David Thodey, was promoted to CEO of **Telstra**.[21] Telstra, a telecommunications and information services company with businesses across Australia, Asia, North America, and Europe, has 39,000 employees and sales of $25 billion.[22]
- ■ Business schools are focusing more on teaching graduates to "better understand the role of regulatory agencies and governments."[23]
- ■ "What makes a CEO an MPV? . . . Skillfully managing relationships with government."[24]

Based on these statements, you can see why it is important to understand how government action impacts business and to be able to make smart, timely, and effective decisions.[25] Also, understanding the relationship between business and society,[26] and the business—government—society interface is essential.[27]

On a more general career and personal level, studying this book will improve your ability to: think critically; analyze issues you face; make better decisions; and communicate your ideas to others in your personal and professional lives.

In order to improve your abilities, you must read and understand the text and apply the concepts to the cases and exercises at the end of the chapters. You also need to apply the concepts to your personal and professional lives. As you may have already noticed, Personal and Professional Applications found within the chapters will help you apply the text's concepts.

Personal and Professional Applications

7.   Describe how this course can benefit you in your personal and professional lives.

THE BUSINESS, SOCIETY, AND GOVERNMENT ENVIRONMENT

Let's build on basic concepts from the first section of this chapter and discuss the environment in which business, society, and government interact. We use the term *environment* to mean the conditions that surround business, society, and government and that affect the way they operate and interact (we do not use *environment* to mean the natural world of people, animals, and plants). The environment is a configuration of influences that affect how businesses operate.[28] Of the multiple ways to classify the environment, you will learn the major ones in this section. We begin with the market environment, followed by the nonmarket two parts: society environment and government environment, and end with the global macroenvironment. Model 1.1 illustrates the environment.

Learning Outcome 2: Differentiate the market and nonmarket environments and state how they influence each other.

The Market Environment

The *market environment includes owners, employees, suppliers, customers, and competitors.* (See Model 1.1 and Figure 1.1.) Businesses operate in the *market environment*

Interaction	Stakeholders in the Market Environment		
Direct	*Suppliers*	**Business**	*Customers/Consumers*
	Distribution-Retailers/ Creditors	Owners/Stockholders Employees/Managers	Purchasers of the products/ Users of the products
Indirect		*Competitors*	

■ **Figure 1.1:** The Market Environment

through direct interactions with customers and suppliers, often through agreements, such as contracts.[29] Firms also compete for customers, so they indirectly interact with competitors. Businesses have owners and many, but not all, have employees who operate the firm. The interrelationship involves economic transactions and the exchange of property.

Owners/Stockholders. Proprietorships and partnerships have *owners* who are entitled to business profits or losses; they have no stockholders. Corporations are owned by one or more *stockholders*. Many, especially large corporations, sell company stock, creating owners with the anticipation of sharing in the profitability of the business through dividends and/or increased stock prices. Corporations can also be part owners of other businesses through buying stock or through other agreements. *Institutional investors*, including **TIAA-CREF** and **Fidelity**, that manage retirement and other funds, are also owners, often through mutual funds. Stockholders commonly vote for the corporation's board of directors, which in turn hires the top managers.

> **Personal and Professional Applications**
>
> 8.   Who are the owners of a business you work(ed) for?

Employees/Managers. All businesses have at least one owner who may also act as the manager and sole employee. *Employees* are paid for working. The owners of the firm can manage the business themselves or hire managers, who are also employees, to do the job for them. Employees may also own stock in a corporation.

    Managers are responsible to the owners/stockholders for the success of the business. They make decisions through planning, organizing, leading, and controlling the firm's resources. Today's successful manager realizes that without motivated employees to serve customers, the business will not be successful. You will learn more about stockholders and employees in Chapter 3.

Customers/Consumers. Without *customers* to buy your products, you don't have a business. A customer buys the product. A consumer uses the product. Thus, a customer is not necessarily the consumer, and vice versa. Who are **Coca-Cola**'s customers? Its retail customers buy its Coke products to sell to their customers, who may be the Coke consumers. *Consumers* use the product, or in this case, drink Coke products. You can be a consumer without being a customer—retailers and someone, a parent or friend, could have bought the Coke for you. So Coke focuses on both customers and consumers.[30] Businesses that don't meet customers' needs are not successful and usually go out of business. Also, consumers who are hurt by a product, such as tobacco, may sue the business.[31] We will discuss customers and consumers in Chapter 2 and societal consumerism in Chapter 6.

> **Personal and Professional Applications**
>
> 9. Who are the customers and consumers of the products of a business you work(ed) for?

Suppliers (Distribution-Retailers/Creditors). Businesses usually have *suppliers* to help them meet the needs of their customers. Suppliers often play a major role in the success of businesses. For example, **Ford Motor Company** manufactures automobiles with parts from more than 1,000 suppliers. Your **local Ford dealership** is a *retailer* who interacts with Ford Motor to buy and resell its cars. **Sprint Nextel** took a multibillion risk in teaming up with supplier **Apple** by agreeing to buy at least 30.5 million iPhones, primarily to get new profitable wireless customer phone contracts it couldn't get without the iPhone.[32] In addition, *wholesalers* sell to retailers, such as **Costco** and **BJ's**.

As you can see, we are talking about the business *distribution* system of getting products to consumers. For example, distribution could be from supplier to manufacturer to wholesaler to retailer to consumer; any level of the distribution system can be skipped; and suppliers can be used at all stages of the distribution system.

Many businesses have *creditors* who lend them money that is paid back with interest. For example, many firms get loans and have lines of credit with banks and financial institutions, such as **Bank of America** and **Citibank**.

> **Personal and Professional Applications**
>
> 10. Identify some of the major suppliers of a business you work(ed) for.

Competitors. Firms compete on numerous levels in order to maximize profits and mitigate future risks.[33] Businesses *compete* with other businesses for customers. Businesses may not interact directly with their competitors, and some interactions, like price fixing, are illegal. But competitor actions often have a direct effect on a business. For example, **Southwest Airlines** offered one-way airfares as low as $49, and major competitors were forced to follow suit.[34]

On the other hand, competitors sometimes help each other. The Japanese automakers got the productivity edge on U.S. automakers, but **Toyota** let **Ford**, **GM**, and **Chrysler** automakers visit their plants. In California, Toyota and GM formed a joint venture to make autos in the same plant. When the government is considering laws and regulations, like miles-per-gallon requirements and pollution standards, the automakers usually join forces to influence the outcome to their advantage or to minimize negative outcome to their business.

> **Personal and Professional Applications**
>
> 11. Identify some of the major competitors of a business you work(ed) for.

The Internal and External Environments. The *internal environment* includes the stakeholders within the business firm, such as owners/stockholders and employees/managers. The *external environment* includes the stakeholders outside of the business firm: customers, suppliers, competitors in the internal environment and nonmarket society, and government stakeholders. Managers are also responsible for the interactions with society and government, our next two topics.

Learning Outcome 3: Explain the nonmarket society and government environments and how they affect business.

The Nonmarket Society Environment

Business also operates in the *nonmarket environment, which includes interactions with society and government.* The nonmarket environment structures (via laws and regulations) how business operates in the market environment, and the positions of firms in the market, while being the source of business opportunities and threats. *The nonmarket society environment includes societal interest groups and communities and the news media.* (See Model 1.1 and Figure 1.2 for an illustration.)

Societal Interest Groups. Recall that we already defined society and societal interest groups along with a list of some nonprofit nongovernmental organizations (NGOs). Interest groups with a special interest or cause, including **MADD, American Association of Retired People (AARP), and PETA,** often pressure business and government to meet their social agenda.[35] They are called *activist* and *advocate groups.* MADD continues to pressure makers of alcohol, such as making sure advertising does not encourage teenage drinking or drinking and driving. Unions—including the **AFL-CIO**, **Teamsters**, and the **United Auto Workers (UAW)**—are NGOs that represent the interests of their members and workers in general and therefore are societal interest groups.[36] We discuss unions in Chapter 3.

On the other hand, business also has its nonprofit NGO societal interest groups to help represent its interaction with society and government, including general business interest (**Chamber of Commerce**, the **Business Roundtable**) and industry-specific associations and trade groups (the **National Association of Realtors** and the **American Council of Life Insurance**). In Chapter 7, you will learn more about societal interest groups and the strategies they use to influence business. In Chapters 8–10, you will learn how these groups affect government and the strategies that business interest groups use with society and government.

Personal and Professional Applications

12. What societal interest groups do/did you belong to?

Communities and News Media. As discussed, you are part of multiple communities. Communities are segments of society—people in a geographic area. With the Internet, online communities can have widely expanded geographic areas. Business has a social responsibility to communities,[37] which we will discuss later in this chapter and

Stakeholders in the Nonmarket Society Environment		
Societal Interest Groups	**Business** Owners/Shareholders Employees/Managers	*Communities and News Media*

■ **Figure 1.2:** The Nonmarket Society Environment

in Chapter 4. *The collective community develops public sentiment in favor of or against business, which influences business, societal interest groups, and government to take or not take specific action.* Unfortunately, public sentiment has been negative toward business recently, in large part because of such business debacles as **Enron** and **Tyco**.

The *news media* (audio-radio, print-newspapers and magazines, video-TV, and Internet) are the major means by which people in communities find out about what business and government are doing. Thus, the news media help shape public sentiment about both business and government. You most likely found out about the **WorldCom** and **Madoff** scandals and other major business events through the news media or from someone who did. So many businesses work hard to get good press and to avoid negative press.[38] The government also provides all types of reports, such as the census, and all types of statistics that are news, which are reported through various news media. Most, if not all, societal interest groups also provide news to its members. You will learn more about communities and the news media in Chapter 6.

Personal and Professional Applications
13. What is your sentiment toward business?
14. What is your primary medium for obtaining news?

Learning Outcome 4: Contrast the political and legal environments, briefly stating what each branch of government does, and summarize their balance of power.

The Nonmarket Government Environment

Government relations are important to business success, and the debate continues as to whether more or less government is better for business.[39] The *nonmarket government environment* has three branches of government that fall under one of two categories: *the political environment includes the executive and legislative branches of government; the legal environment includes the judicial branch of government.* The legislative and executive branches are known as the political environment because the president and members of Congress are elected; in the legal branch, most of the judges are appointed, so business has to interact differently with them.

Here we briefly discuss the legislative, executive, and judicial branches at the local, state, federal, and international levels. (See Model 1.1 and Figure 1.3 for an illustration.)

Political Lawmakers Legislative Branch /Congress	**Business** Owners/Shareholders Employees/Managers	*Political Law Enforcement* Executive Branch/President, Cabinet, and Regulatory Agencies
	Law Interpretation and Determination Judicial Branch/Courts	

■ **Figure 1.3:** The Nonmarket Government Environment

Legislative Branch. Simply put, at the federal and state levels, *Congress* makes the laws. The Senate and House of Representatives develop and vote on bills to become law. In Chapter 8 you will learn the details of lawmaking and strategies (in the form of lobbying) that businesses use to influence Congress to meet their special interests.[40] Federal laws overrule state laws, and states can't pass laws that supersede those made by the federal government.

Executive Branch. Simply for now, the *president* and the *cabinet* and *regulatory agencies* enforce the laws. They also have the power to make regulations (regulators interpret and implement laws enacted by Congress). For example, the **Food and Drug Administration (FDA)** regulates product safety, including labeling. The president appoints the cabinet heads and influences regulators' attitudes toward business. You will learn more about the executive branch and regulation in Chapter 9 and about antitrust laws in Chapter 10.

Judicial Branch. The courts *interpret* the legality of the laws passed by Congress, based on the Constitution and other criteria, and they *determine* the outcomes of court cases. For example, over 30 years ago, the **U.S. Supreme Court** decided that the law prohibiting abortion was unconstitutional and made abortion legal. More recently, the Massachusetts court, and other states, declared that same-sex marriage is legal in their state; however, many other states will not recognize this marriage. Court cases are often started at a lower-level court and can be appealed to higher-level courts—with the highest U.S. court being the Supreme Court, which can decide to hear or not hear cases. For example, Internet file sharing was brought to a few courts and appealed to the Supreme Court, which ruled that file-sharing firms may be liable for copyright infringement if their products encourage illegal swapping of songs and movies.[41] You will learn more about the judicial branch in Chapter 10.

Checks and Balances. The U.S. government is set up with a system of checks and balances so that no one branch has too much power. This approach is known as government pluralism. The president appoints the cabinet members, regulators, and Supreme Court justices and makes the federal government budget with the approval of Congress; the president can veto bills initiated by Congress. Congress makes the laws, with the president's approval, but can override a president's veto, approves Supreme Court nominations, may impeach and/or expel a president, and also has power over regulators. Appointed by the president for life, with the approval of Congress, the Supreme Court judges can declare laws unconstitutional while acting as the final authority on any case they choose to rule on. Their impact on business, government, and society therefore can be quite strong.

> **Personal and Professional Applications**
>
> 15. State your personal sentiment about business, society, and government.

The Global Macroenvironment

The *macroenvironment* includes the total environment of the business context. Thus, the macroenvironment includes the market and nonmarket society and government environments we already discussed, plus it goes beyond those environments to include the international, technological, and natural environments. (See Model 1.1.) The macroenvironment extends the domestic market and nonmarket environments to the global village, resulting in a very complex system. Thus, this book progresses from the market to the nonmarket environments to the macroenvironment.

The International Environment. Today's executives need to understand the international environment.[42] Since at least the early 1990s, for all larger businesses, the question hasn't been whether to go global, it's been how to best compete globally. Even small domestic businesses often compete with multinationals at home. Back in 1989, management guru Peter Drucker predicted that in five years there would be two kinds of managers—those who think globally in terms of a world economy and those who are unemployed; those who are unemployed deserve it.[43] He was right.

Many multinational companies, including **GE** and **FedEx**, conduct business in more than 100 countries. Each country has its own system of interactions among business, society, and government, with each country having its own culture, laws, and ways of doing business that sometimes conflict with the way things are done in the United States. When you think of the complexity of conducting business in so many countries, it's mind-boggling. It takes a large staff of professional managers at headquarters and in each country to be successful in all markets.

For example, **McDonald's** has restaurant locations in more than 100 countries/markets all over the world and allows its local franchises some latitude in offering menu items that are considered "local friendly." For example, the Big Mac in India is not made of beef, because the cow is sacred; instead, they offer a McVeggie.[44]

International interest groups include the **World Health Organization (WHO)**, which deals with health issues, and the **UN**, which deals primarily with global society issues and some business issues. More important to business, there is the **World Trade Organization (WTO)**, which develops rules for conducting international business. WTO rules apply only to its members, and the WTO doesn't have much power to force businesses from around the world to comply, like country governments. You will learn more about the global environment in Chapter 11.

The Technological Environment. *Technology* provides innovations of new and improved products and the processes for creating them. Information technology has increased the speed of business with overnight delivery, the fax machine, computers and the Internet, and smartphones, to make communicating globally in real time possible, and wireless continues to change the way we do business.[45] E-businesses, like **Amazon.com** and **eBay**, and technology-driven products, such as the Kindle, **Apple** iPhones and iPads, and **Microsoft** Xbox have created new markets and affected customer and consumer behavior. You will learn more about the technology environment in Chapter 12.

ETHICAL DILEMMA 1.2 Has DropBox Dropped the Ethical Ball on File Sharing?

The ability to share electronic files between users has been a controversial topic over the past 15 years. Napster was the first major online music service (originally a file-sharing service) to make a major impact on how people, especially university students, used the Internet. Its technology allowed music fans to easily share MP3-format song files with each other, thus leading to the music industry's accusations of massive copyright violations. Although the original service was shut down by court order, it paved the way for decentralized P2P file-sharing programs, which have been much harder to control.

BearShare followed on the heels of Napster and allowed individuals to create music, video, and other files on the Internet and make them available for speedy and easy access by other users of the software. Several record companies filed complaints against BearShare, claiming that "massive copyright infringement is the very purpose of the BearShare System and software. . . . Defendants know it; they encourage and contribute to it; and they readily could prevent it—but choose not to." The Supreme Court ruled in favor of record companies and against BearShare who ended up paying a $30 million settlement. Users of BearShare now have the opportunity to listen and download music to their computers for free, however they are not permitted or physically able to share that music with anyone else.

DropBox is the latest technology where any file saved to Dropbox is also instantly saved to the owner's computers, phones, and the Dropbox website and may be shared by allowing others access to the owner's folder. Dropbox works with Windows, Mac, Linux, iPad, iPhone, Android, and BlackBerry and allows the user, with subscription, to save up to 100 GBs of materials.[46]

How does DropBox handle the illegal file-sharing issue? Under user terms and conditions DropBox states that:

> Files and other content in the Services may be protected by intellectual property rights of others. Please do not copy, upload, download, or share files unless you have the right to do so. You, not Dropbox, will be fully responsible and liable for what you copy, share, upload, download, or otherwise use while using the Services.[47]

Questions

1. Was it ethical for Napster, BearShare, and DropBox to offer free technology for file sharing copyrighted material?
2. What is the impact of illegal file sharing on society?
3. Should the government get involved and actively monitor DropBox and other file-sharing services, and, if so, what should the government do?
4. DropBox places the responsibility of meeting copyright protection laws on the users of the service. Have they shirked their ethical and legal responsibility by creating a service that facilitates intellectual property theft?
5. Have you ever downloaded music or movies without paying? If so, would you do it again after reading this case?

The Natural Environment. Nature includes the air, water/sea life, land, plants/food, trees, animals, and so forth within our communities. Clearly, economic growth has put a strain on our natural resources and on the ability of the ecosystems to cleanse and regenerate.[48] Societal advocacy groups have pressured business to stop, or cut down on, polluting the natural environment, and the government has passed laws forcing business to cut pollution. Business has reacted to this pressure with positive policies toward the natural environment.[49] For example, automobile manufacturers **Toyota**, **Honda**, **Ford**, **GM**, and others have developed hybrid vehicles in order to reduce air pollution, increase gas efficiency, and increase vehicle acceleration. **Nissan** Leaf was the first all-electric car.[50] You will learn more about the natural environment in Chapter 12.

Personal and Professional Applications

16. Discuss how the international, technological, and natural environments have personally affected you and a business you work(ed) for.

Google Case Question 3: Identify the key stakeholders in this case.

The Market Environment
1. Customers: Internet consumers (those who use Internet services but do not pay for the services) and software and service purchasers.
2. Suppliers: Through partnerships Google has relationships with NASA Ames Research Center (for building space), Sun Microsystems (shared technology), and AOL (to enhance video search services).
3. Competitors: Facebook and Twitter (social networking); Apple (smartphone software); and Microsoft Explorer and Mozilla Firefox (Internet connectivity); Bing and Yahoo! (Internet search engines).
4. Employees: not mentioned.
5. Stockholders: not mentioned.

The Nonmarket Environment
Social
News Media: *New York Times.*
Social Interest Groups: Boston College Center for Corporate Citizenship, the Reputation Institute, unknown hackers from China.

Political
Regulatory/Law Enforcement Agencies: not mentioned.

Legal
Courts: not mentioned.

The Macroenvironment
1. International: China.
2. Societal: Popularity of social networks, the Internet, smartphones, and data theft.

THE ROLE OF BUSINESS AND ITS MANAGERS

Now that we have an overview of the interrelationship among business, society, and government and each one's environment, let's move ahead and focus on the role of business and its managers. In this section, we first describe the role of business and its responsibility to stakeholders. We then discuss the manager's role of integrating market and nonmarket strategies, along with a list of nonmarket strategies.

Learning Outcome 5: Discuss the role of business and its managers, including stakeholders.

The Role of Business and the Responsibility to be Ethical with Stakeholders

The role of business is to create value for its owners/stockholders and its other stakeholders. A stakeholder has a *stake* or, as we call it, a special *interest* in business activities because they are affected by business decisions or can affect business performance.[51] Take a look at Figures 1.1 to 1.3. The business, society, and government groups listed are common stakeholders, but they most likely will never all have an interest in every issue facing the business, and stakeholders can change based on the issue. Identifying stakeholders for specific issues is important.[52]

Corporate Social Responsibility. Business has a responsibility to be ethical with its stakeholders.[53] *Corporate social responsibility* (CSR) is the conscious effort to operate in a manner that balances stakeholder interests.[54] Business should try to meet societal expectations so that it doesn't contribute to social problems.[55] For example, managers are responsible for making a profit for the business owners, but at the same time, they also have a responsibility to offer customers safe products, not to hurt community environments, and to obey government laws and regulations including honest financial reporting.[56] More "pinstripes" are getting prison stripes these days as the government cracks down on corporate crime.[57] You will learn more about corporate social responsibility and ethics in Chapters 4 and 5, but stakeholder responsibility is interwoven throughout each chapter.

> Learning Outcome 6: Define "strategy," differentiate market and nonmarket strategies, and describe the need to integrate them.

The Role of Managers and Strategy

Here we discuss the manager's role and three nonmarket strategies.

Managers Integrate Market and Nonmarket Strategies. Managers' goal is to generate competitive advantage.[58] Therefore, they need to integrate market and nonmarket environment strategies to create value for stakeholders while being socially responsible.[59] Many successful firms develop CSR strategies.[60] *A strategy guides the firm's interactions with its stakeholders to achieve the firm's objectives. Market strategies are used to compete for customers with the help of suppliers.* Recall that owners and employees/managers are also part of the business internal environment.

We assume you have learned, or will learn, market strategies based on environmental analysis that includes the following: *corporate-level grand strategies*—growth (concentration, integration, diversification; mergers and acquisitions), stability, turnaround, and retrenchment; *business-level strategies*—adaptive strategies (prospecting, defending, analyzing), *competitive strategies* (diversification, cost leadership, focus), and *functional-level strategies* (operations, marketing, financing, and human resources).

> **Personal and Professional Applications**
>
> 17. Explain how a business you work(ed) for creates value for stakeholders.

Nonmarket Strategies. Our primary focus of the book is nonmarket strategies, because market strategies generate issues of special interest that are addressed in the nonmarket environment.[61] *Nonmarket strategies guide the firm's interactions with society and government stakeholders.* The firm conducts business in the market environment (although it can sell products to societal interest groups and the government, it doesn't conduct business in the nonmarket environment, yet it is affected by it) and seeks societal approval and follows government laws as it interacts with regulators.[62] Society and government structure the way business operates and competes in the market environment. Nonmarket strategies shape the nonmarket environment and affect the structure of the market environment and the position of the business in that market. The nonmarket also creates opportunities for and threats to the firm.

The Importance of the Nonmarket Environment. To be successful, the business must take advantage of market opportunities and avoid threats created by the nonmarket environment. Without a strategy to deal effectively with the nonmarket, you can't conduct business in the market environment. Consider the following example of nonmarket opportunity that turned into a threat. Some years ago in the state of Maine, the legal drinking age was lowered to 18. Entrepreneur Dick Peltier opened the **Peltier Bar** in Portland that targeted the 18- to 20-year-old age group, and the business was very profitable. However, a few years later, the state increased the legal drinking age back to 21. So Peltier virtually lost his business overnight.

Nonmarket strategies are more significant to some industries and businesses than others. Nonmarket strategies are as important as, and sometimes more important than, market strategies, such as when the government has great control over the market mechanisms (supply, demand, and price). For example, the highly regulated cable TV industry requires nonmarket strategies because cable service is a regulated monopoly where government grants monopoly power in a certain geographical area. Nonmarket strategies that are not integrated with a market strategy, however, will not be successful because if you don't deal effectively with the government, you will not be in the cable business.

Thus, managers are concerned about the interrelationships between the market and nonmarket environments and the integration of market and nonmarket strategies to manage issues effectively in both environments.[63] As an example of the need to integrate market and nonmarket strategies, recall that to operate a bar you need a government liquor license. Without a nonmarket strategy to get the license, or to stop it from being revoked, you don't have a business. A liquor license on its own, though, is not enough; the bar needs to compete successfully for customers in the market environment to be profitable.

Figure 1.4 lists nonmarket information, societal, political, and legal strategies used by business to achieve objectives. The strategies will be fully explained in Chapters 2–12, and the specific chapter(s) containing detailed coverage is/are listed next to the type of strategy. You will also learn strategies used by society and government when interacting with business in Chapter 7. Based on strategic action, businesses also develop policies, procedures, and rules to handle recurring issues.

Google Case Question 4: If you were the president of Google, what nonmarket actions would you take relative to the stakeholders addressed in question 3?

In answering this question, we will construct a table using the stakeholders from question 1 and the nonmarket strategies from Figure 1.4. The strategies run across the top of the table, while the stakeholders are listed in the first column.

Information Strategies (Chs. 1–2 and Appendix)

1. Outside sources that conduct research (use facts, figures/numbers to support your side of the issue)
2. Expert testimony (often used with government, and can include outside sources)
3. Supportive stakeholder strategy (get stakeholders to support your issue)
N—New strategy that you add

Societal Strategies (Chs. 5–7)

1. Overall strategy for dealing with societal interest group activist:

   ▪ Give them donations (philanthropy)
   ▪ Ignore them (be reactive and wait to see what happens)
   ▪ Oppose them (be proactive and try to stop their strategic action against you)
   ▪ Negotiate with them (try to bargain to minimize negative consequences to your business)
   ▪ Work with them (essentially give in and do what they want your business to do)

2. Build coalitions with advocacy societal interest groups
3. Establish news media relations and advocacy advertising (paid)
4. Generate positive community public sentiment by being ethical and socially responsible (ongoing long-term strategy)
N—New strategy that you add

Political Strategies (Chs. 8–10)

1. Overall strategy for dealing with governments:

   ▪ Ignore them (be reactive and wait to see what happens)
   ▪ Oppose them (be proactive and try to stop their strategic action against you)
   ▪ Negotiate with them (try to bargain to minimize negative consequences to your business)
   ▪ Work with them (essentially give in and do what they want your business to do

2. Lobby politicians and/or regulators (tell government your side of the issue—information strategy)
3. Grassroots campaigns (get market groups to contact politicians and/or regulators)
4. Building coalitions with market environment (usually competitors)
5. Seek business societal interest group support (peak and trade groups that business belongs to)
6. Testimony at hearings (overlaps with information strategy 2 and legal strategy 2; use when needed)
7. Donations/campaign contributions to politicians (strategy used to help get politician elected)
N—New strategy that you add

Legal Strategies (Ch. 10)

1. Avoid lawsuits (including settling out of court)
2. Fight a lawsuit (go to court)
3. Sue other businesses, individuals, societal interest groups, and the government (to get what you want)
N—New strategy that you add

We recommend that you use this list of strategies when doing case analysis for all chapters. But realize that you can add other strategies to deal with the nonmarket. When you read the chapters that contain the details about each strategy, you will be able to provide more details in the development and implementation of these strategies. If you analyze cases using the case table in the Appendix, the strategies are listed in column 5.

▪ **Figure 1.4:** Nonmarket Strategies for Business

■ Table 1.1: Nonmarket Strategies for Google by Stakeholder

Stakeholder	S1	S2	S3	S4	P1	P2	P3	P4	P5	P6	P7	L1	L2	L3
Internet Consumers in General				X								X		X
Software/Service Purchasers	X			X								X		X
Suppliers	X			X					X					
Competitors	X			X				X	X					
NY Times	X		X	X								X	X	X
Boston College Center and Reputation Institute	X	X	X	X								X	X	X
Unknown Hackers from China	X			X								X	X	
Chinese Consumers	X		X	X				X				X		X
Chinese Government					X	X					X			

S = Societal strategies corresponding to the strategy number in Figure 1.4
P = Political strategies corresponding to the strategy number in Figure 1.4
L = Legal strategies corresponding to the strategy number in Figure 1.4
X = States that the strategy from Figure 1.4 is used

Note: This multifaceted problem requires both market and nonmarket solutions per stakeholder; many of these strategies overlap with other nonmarket stakeholder strategies. Looking at Figure 1.4, you will see that the most often cited nonmarket strategies include operating in a way to gain community sentiment and to establish media and government relations. The CEO clearly needs to gain public support through media management and implement strategies to address the security problems in China.

OUR APPROACH TO THE BOOK AND CASES

In this final section, we present the top management stakeholder approach and the applied ethics approach to the book and cases; then we pull the chapter together to form a unifying structure for the book.

The Top Management Stakeholder Approach

Throughout this book, we focus on stakeholder management, the topic of our next chapter, or how you, as a top-level manager of a business of any size, can successfully interact with business, government, and society stakeholders to achieve financial success while being ethical and socially responsible. Therefore, the cases in this text generally place you in the position of a top-level business manager. The cases require critical thinking in your application of the text material to the business facing market and nonmarket issues. As the manager in charge, the cases ask you to make decisions regarding what strategies to use to deal with the nonmarket issues presented, and how you would implement the strategies.

Although we take a top-level management approach, you don't need to be a top manager to benefit from a better understanding of the issues facing top-level executives and the decisions they must make. We realize that most people never become top-level managers of major *Fortune 500* companies, yet many people work in small and medium-sized businesses where becoming a top-level manager is quite possible, as may happen if they start a business. The integrative cases at the end of each chapter put you in the role of a small business manager by asking you to analyze major issues discussed in each case through the eyes of two small business owners. Furthermore, the critical thinking skills you can develop through this course will help you to climb the corporate ladder by providing the necessary knowledge and understanding of the issues facing today's CEOs. You may also have the opportunity to give input to top-level managers who are making the decisions, and understanding their perspective will allow you to provide more salient advice. If you currently are a top-level executive or on your way to becoming one, congratulations.

If you choose to work for the government or a nonprofit interest NGO, this text will help you understand issues from the business perspective so that in your position, you'll know how to successfully interact with business. Conversely, you will also have the opportunity to see things from, or to take the side of, society or government.

> **Personal and Professional Applications**
>
> 18. Do the managers where you work(ed) use a stakeholder approach?
>
> 19. Do you want a career in business, societal interest groups, or the government?

The Applied Ethics Approach

Let's begin by defining some business ethics concepts. Because ethics is such an important topic, we devote the entire Chapter 5 to ethics.

Ethics and Morality. *Ethics is the moral standard of right and wrong that influences behavior.* Ethics is intended to provide rules of behavior without requiring government laws, regulation, and legal enforcement. Ethics includes judgments about behaviors and practices based on *moral* standards of what "society" believes are right and wrong.[64] Ethics are guidelines for our behavior. However, the degree of influence that ethical standards have over people does vary; some people are clearly more or less ethical than others. Some people consciously try to be ethical and others don't. How ethical are you? At the end of Chapter 5, an exercise gives you the opportunity to assess how ethical your behavior is.

Ethics allows us to judge whether our behavior (what we do and say) is appropriate and guides us in relating to others and how we expect them to relate to us. Moral standards are universal; morals are impartial, apply to everyone, and should take precedence over self-interest. For example, everyone is expected to be honest.

Honesty and Integrity. *Honesty indicates a tendency not to lie, cheat, or steal. Lying is making statements that one knows to be false or misleading. Misleading* is saying or not saying things to get others to believe something that is not true. *Cheating is breaking rules. Stealing is taking something that does not belong to the thief.* Thus, honesty is ethical and dishonesty is unethical behavior. People are often dishonest for personal gain.[65] For example, calling in sick when you are not sick and plan to spend the day doing other things (lying and cheating), and getting paid for not working (stealing), is dishonest. *Integrity* is about being honest with yourself and being honest with others.

Morality and Management. *Moral management includes moral, immoral, and amoral managers.* When *moral managers* judge a behavior to be ethically right, such as treating people with respect, they will engage in the behavior; when moral managers believe a behavior is unethical, such as lying, they will not engage in the behavior. Unfortunately, some *immoral managers* knowingly engage in unethical behavior to benefit themselves and their firms in some way. There are also *amoral managers. Amoral managers do not believe ethics applies to business, or they just don't think about ethics when it comes to their behavior and making decisions.* We will discuss reasons for unethical behavior later in Chapter 5. Moral managers take a stakeholder approach to management, immoral and amoral managers don't. Our focus is on developing moral managers who consider ethics when making personal and professional decisions.

Values. Values and ethics are different. American morality has been influenced by Judeo-Christian religious principles, primarily through the Bible, about right and wrong behavior.[66] Values vary among people, for example some people believe telling the truth is important while others think nothing of lying. So values are not universal, and businesses can't let their employees operate according to their own individual values. *Values are important desired behaviors.* Values are our most cherished beliefs.[67] Businesses use value statements, such as **Ford**'s slogan "Quality is job one" and **FedEx's** "People-Service-Profit" philosophy, to guide all employee behavior. Values are often stated in codes of ethics, which we will discuss later in Chapter 5.

Business Ethics. *Business ethics is the application of ethics to issues that arise in business.* In other words, business ethics is the process of determining what behavior is appropriate for an issue in a given business situation. Employees—not companies—make ethical or unethical decisions, and managers choose to be immoral, amoral, or moral. However, a business's reputation is based on the ethics of its employees and the CSR of its managers.[68]

Applied Ethics. In each and every chapter, and in every case, we give you the opportunity to apply ethics concepts to your personal and professional lives. The two ethical dilemma cases within the chapters ask you to apply ethics to the text concept using a real-life organization. They ask you, "Is the behavior in the case ethical?" and "What would you do in this situation?" The end-of-chapter cases include questions that also bring in ethical considerations. If you use the case table, presented in the Appendix, when analyzing the alternatives, you answer the question: "Is this alternative strategy legal and ethical?" So the applied ethics approach is designed to help develop your ability to make ethical decisions in your personal and professional lives.

Structure of the Book

We developed the Business, Society, and Government Interrelationship Stakeholder Environment Model 1.1 to put all three environment classification systems together with the manager's role into one unified framework—the framework that is also the structure for the book. Model 1.1 also provides an index by stating in which chapter, by number (Ch. #), the material for each stakeholder is discussed in greater detail. *Stakeholders are affected by the business and can affect firm performance.*

Tying Ethics and Stakeholders Together—Ethics Guidelines. Guidelines for ethical behaviors would include, as a bare minimum, being honest and trying to create a win-win situation for all stakeholders so that everyone gets a good deal whenever possible. Model 1.1 lists the most relevant stakeholders. The triangle represents the country level in which each group influences the other two, and the circle represents the larger global level of business, society, and government environments that affect the national triangle interrelationships. As you can see in Model 1.1, the primary focus is on the market and nonmarket societal and government environments, which are discussed in Chapters 2–10. In Chapters 11–12, we continue this focus but add the global macroenvironment, technology, and natural environments to the discussion. We don't include the international, technical, and natural environment in the triangle because we recognize that we live in a global environment and that technology and the natural environment are important pressing international issues for all countries. We recommend that you use Model 1.1 every time you conduct a case analysis to review major stakeholders and as an index to find out which chapters contain which details about the stakeholders. Note that the role of managers is listed between the market and nonmarket environments.

SUMMARY

The chapter summary is organized to answer the learning outcomes for Chapter 1.

1. **Characterize business, society and government and explain their interrelationships.**

   A *business* is a firm that sells a product for a profit. *Society* includes interest groups and the communities affected by business. *Government* includes the executive, legislative, and judicial branches at the local, state, federal, and international levels. They are all interrelated because the actions of each group affect the actions of the others.

2. **Differentiate the market and non-market environments and state how they influence each other.**

   The *market environment* includes owners, employees, suppliers, customers, and competitors, whereas the *nonmarket environment* includes interactions with society and government. Businesses compete for customers in the market environment to make a profit. The nonmarket environment structures (laws and regulations) how business operates in the market environment and the positions of firms in the market, and it creates opportunities for and threats to business. The market environment creates issues of special interest that are addressed in the nonmarket environment.

3. **Explain the nonmarket society and government environments and how they affect business.**

   The *nonmarket society environment* includes societal interest groups and communities, whereas the *nonmarket government environment* includes the executive, legislative, and judicial branches at the local, state, federal, and international levels. Social

interest group activists pressure business to meet their special interest. They commonly use community public sentiment and the news media to help them. The government creates and enforces the laws, rules, and regulations that firms must abide by when conducting business in the market environment.

4. **Contrast the political and legal environments, briefly stating what each branch of government does, and summarize their balance of power.**

   The *political environment* includes the government legislative branch, which initiates and passes the laws, and the executive branch, which enforces the laws and regulations, whereas the *legal environment* includes the judicial branch, which interprets and determines the laws. The government is pluralistic so that no one branch has too much power. The power of the president is checked by Congress whose members must approve presidential selections for cabinet positions, judicial appointments, and budget, and Congress has power over regulators. The power of Congress is checked by the president, who can veto its bills. The courts can change the laws and regulations made by Congress and executive-branch regulators.

5. **Discuss the role of business and its managers, including stakeholders.**

   The role of business is to create value for stakeholders, who are affected by the business and can affect firm performance. Thus, they have an interest in business activities. The role of managers is to integrate market and nonmarket environmental strategies ethically to create value for stakeholders.

6. **Define "strategy," differentiate market and nonmarket strategies,**

and describe the need to integrate them.

A strategy guides firm interactions with its stakeholders to achieve objectives. Market strategies are used to compete for customers with the help of suppliers to make a profit, whereas nonmarket strategies guide firm interactions with society and government stakeholders. Society and government create business opportunities and threats that require integrated strategies to guide firm interactions. Nonmarket strategies are used to affect the structure (laws and regulations) of the nonmarket environment that affect how business competes in the market environment. Thus, managers must integrate strategies to influence the nonmarket structure so that they can compete effectively in the market environment.

7. **Fill in the blank with the appropriate key term** (in order of appearance in the chapter):

_____ is a firm that sells a product for a profit.

_____ may be a good, a service or both.

_____ is the people, including interest groups, and the communities affected by business.

_____ are nonprofit organizations that promote a cause.

_____ includes the executive, legislative, and judicial branches at the local, county, state, federal, and international levels

_____ include any profit, nonprofit, or government organization that is working for its own best interest, sometimes at the expense of others.

_____ occur when society's expectations are not met by business and/or government; a gap between expectations and reality.

_____ includes owners, employees, suppliers, customers, and competitors.

_____ includes interactions with society and government.

_____ includes societal interest groups and communities with news media.

The collective community develops _____ in favor of or against business, which influences business, societal interest groups, and government to take or not take specific action.

_____ includes the executive and legislative branches of government.

_____ includes the judicial branch of government.

_____ guides firm interactions with its stakeholders to achieve the firm's objectives.

_____ are used to compete for customers with the help of suppliers.

_____ guide firm interactions with society and government stakeholders.

_____ is the moral standard of right and wrong that influences behavior.

_____ indicates a tendency not to lie, cheat, or steal.

_____ is making statements that one knows to be false or misleading.

_____ is breaking rules.

_____ is taking something that does not belong to the thief.

_____ includes moral, immoral, and amoral managers.

_____ do not believe ethics applies to business or they just don't think about ethics when they make decisions and behave.

_____ are important desired behaviors.

_____ is the application of ethics to issues that arise in business.

_____ are affected by the business and can affect firm performance.

KEY TERMS (IN ALPHABETICAL ORDER)

amoral managers (p. 24)
business (p. 7)
business ethics (p. 25)
cheating (p. 24)
ethics (p. 24)
government (p. 7)
honesty (p. 24)
legal environment (p. 15)
lying (p. 24)
market environment (p. 11)
market strategies (p. 20)
moral management (p. 24)
nonmarket environment (p. 14)

nonmarket society environment (p. 14)
nonmarket strategies (p. 20)
political environment (p. 15)
product (p. 7)
public sentiment (p. 15)
social problems (p. 8)
societal interest groups (p. 7)
society (p. 7)
special interest groups (p. 8)
stakeholders (p. 25)
stealing (p. 24)
strategy (p. 20)
values (p. 25)

REVIEW QUESTIONS

1 What are the three major components of this chapter and textbook?

2 What are the three branches of government?

3 What is the difference between capitalism, pluralism, and democracy?

4 What type of market systems does the United States have?

5 What are four factors contributing to special interests and social problems?

6 What is the relationship between social problems and special interest groups?

7 Which stakeholders are found in the market and nonmarket environments?

8 What is the difference between a customer and a consumer?

9 What is the difference between the political and legal environments?

10 Which stakeholders are found in the internal and external environments?

11 How is the book structured?

12 What is the role of business?

13 What is the role of managers?

14 What are the three nonmarket strategic areas?

DISCUSSION/CRITICAL THINKING QUESTIONS

Be sure to give a detailed explanation for your answer to each question.

1 What do you like and dislike about our pluralistic society?

2 How do special interest groups from business, society, and government help and hurt our country?

3 List some social problems related to business. Which is the most

important problem facing our country today?

4 Do societal interest groups help or hinder business?

5 Does the government have too much or too little power over business?

6 Is the market environment or the nonmarket environment more important?

7 Does business really care about stakeholders or just about making a profit?

8 Is this book more relevant to large or small business?

APPLICATION EXERCISES

1.1 DESCRIBE A BUSINESS'S ENVIRONMENT

Select a business, preferably one you work(ed) for, and provide the following information.

Market Environment. List the firm's specific:

Owners/stockholders
Managers/employee
Customers—Describe target market
Suppliers (distribution—retailers, creditors)
Competitors

Nonmarket Societal Environment. Do as follows and answer these questions.

Societal Interest groups—list any advocate groups the firm interacts with and any business/trade associations it belongs to.

Communities—Where does the business operate? What is the public sentiment toward the firm?

News Media—Has the firm had any positive or negative press?

Nonmarket Government Environment. Answer these questions.

Legislative—What laws affect the business?
Executive—What regulations affect the business?
Judicial—Has it been sued or sued others?

Other Environments. Answer these questions.

International—Does the business compete with foreign firms, and does it do business in other countries? If yes, list firms and countries.

Technological Environment—How does the firm use technology, and how has technology affected its competitiveness?

Natural Environment—Has the firm had any air, water, or land issues?

1.2 DESCRIBE A BUSINESS'S STRATEGIES

Select a business, preferably one you work(ed) for (it can be the same one used for Application 1.1) and answer the following questions.

Market Strategies.

Describe the primary market strategy the business uses.

Nonmarket Strategies.

Describe any nonmarket strategies (Figure 1.4) the business has used.

Explain the issue requiring the strategy.

Integrated Strategies.

Give an example of an integrated strategy used by the firm.

1.3 BUSINESS STRATEGY EXAMPLES

Identify the strategies of one to three major corporations you are interested in learning more about. You may want to visit the corporations' websites and surf the Web for information about the firms and/or go to the library to get this information. News media outlets are a good place to search.

CASE 1.1

Walmart Always Has the Lowest Prices, Always: But At What Price?

Everyone knows Walmart and the Walmart story. "Before opening Walmart, Sam Walton traveled the country studying everything he could about discount retailing. He became convinced American consumers wanted a new type of store. Trusting his vision, Sam Walton and his wife Helen put up 95 percent of the money for the first Walmart store in Rogers, Arkansas.[69] Walmart is now a global company with more than 2 million associates worldwide that generated about $421.85 billion in revenue, earning almost $16.39 billion in net income for 2011.[70]

Mr Walton's success came from understanding the customer. "The secret of successful retailing is to give your customers what they want . . . if you think about it from the point of view of the customer, you want everything: a wide assortment of good quality merchandise; the lowest possible prices; guaranteed satisfaction with what you buy; friendly, knowledgeable service; convenient hours; free parking; a pleasant shopping experience."[71]

Low prices and high-quality service—easy to say but very hard to do and remain profitable according to Michael Porter, a professor at Harvard University. A firm could not be all things to all people—what he calls being stuck in the middle.[72] And yet it appears that Walmart has done the impossible. They certainly have lower prices than their major competitors (Kmart, Target) and boast a much larger selection with more courteous service.

So how does Walmart do it? According to Sam Walton, following ten rules for making a business successful is the key. These rules include observations such as "exceed customer expectations," "believe in your business more than anyone else," and "celebrate your successes."[73] Yet many who are not part of the Walmart family would argue that Walmart doesn't beat the competition, rather they cheat them by utilizing unethical and illegal tactics that dramatically affect both the communities where their stores are situated and the U.S. national economy.

Walmart has been accused over the years of numerous illegal and unethical practices, including the hiring of illegal immigrants.[74] Walmart has also come under fire for sexual discrimination, when several women reported that Walmart "frequently pays its female workers less than their male counterparts for comparable jobs and bypasses women for key promotions."[75] Locking employees in company warehouses during inventory audits, predatory pricing policies (pricing below product costs in order to undermine competitors), and even the death of downtown America (specifically their small businesses) are among the complaints.[76]

Yet of all the charges leveled against Walmart, the one with the most far-reaching effects seems to deal with their treatment of their suppliers—those who provide the goods at very low costs. Walmart's practices have forced suppliers to lower prices, and therefore Walmart works with suppliers overseas who pay below the required minimum wage in their country. "Walmart is legendary for forcing its suppliers to redesign everything from their packaging to their computer systems. It is also legendary for quite straightforwardly telling them what it will pay for their goods."[77]

"Walmart's relentless pressure can crush the companies it does business with and force them to send jobs overseas. . . . Eighty-five percent of the stores' items are made overseas, often in Third World sweat-shops."[78] "By taking its orders abroad, Walmart has forced many U.S. manufacturers out of business"[79] and has cost many Americans good-paying jobs. These semi-skilled workers have had to pick up jobs in the service sector—in lower-paying jobs that might ironically include working at Walmart. Other retailers have followed Walmart's example in order to remain competitive and they, too, have lowered wages and put pressure on their suppliers, which, in turn, has created downward pressure on the U.S. economy in general.

Walmart is not only experiencing problems at home but abroad as well. One problem, "fraudulently labeled ordinary pork as a more expensive organic variety"[80] forced the closing of 13 stores in the city of Chongqing. Also, by taking business away from smaller companies, Walmart was viewed negatively by the Chinese public. These problems, as well as others, resulted in the resignations of top executives at Walmart China, including the president and chief executive, the senior vice president for human resources, the chief operating officer, and the chief financial officer.

Questions

1. Imagine that you are the president of a privately held U.S. publisher of children's books and were approached by Walmart to supply them with 2 million books per year. You currently produce a tenth of that amount at your plant located just outside Huntsville, Alabama. What are the issues you should consider in deciding whether to pursue this opportunity? How might your answer be different if you were a small operating unit of a major public international corporation?

2. As president of Walmart you have been asked at a press conference whether your firm has become the largest corporation in the world by following Sam Walton's ten rules of successful business or by clawing its way to the top on the backs of others, especially U.S. manufacturers. How would you react to this comment? Would your reaction be different in front of a group of potential investors? Current stockholders?

3. Walmart prides itself on customer service and providing the customers exactly what they want. As a potential customer of Walmart (if you're not one already), would you shop there given the information in this case? Why or why not?

CASE 1.2

The Recording Industry Association of America (RIAA) and File Sharing

The Recording Industry Association of America (RIAA®), a business societal interest group, "is the trade organization that supports and promotes the creative and financial vitality of the major music companies. Its members are the music labels that comprise the most vibrant record industry in the world. RIAA® members create, manufacture and/or distribute approximately 85% of all legitimate recorded music produced and sold in the United States. In support of this mission, the RIAA works to protect the intellectual property and First Amendment rights of artists and music labels; conduct consumer, industry and technical research; and monitor and review state and federal laws, regulations and policies. The RIAA® also certifies Gold®, Platinum®, Multi-Platinum™ and Diamond sales awards as well as Los Premios De Oro y Platino™, an award celebrating Latin music sales."[81]

In September 2005, RIAA announced a round of copyright infringement lawsuits against 757 individuals engaged in Internet theft, including computer network users at 17 different colleges. These 'John Doe' lawsuits cited individuals for illegally distributing copyrighted music on the Internet via unauthorized peer-to-peer services such as eDonkey, Grokster, Kazaa, and LimeWire. In a recent win for the RIAA on May 12, 2010, a U.S. federal court found LimeWire guilty and liable for copyright infringement. "The evidence demonstrates that [LimeWire] optimized LimeWire's features to ensure that users can download digital recordings, the majority of which are protected by copyright."[82] This was a huge win for the RIAA because LimeWire was a popular file-sharing system. LimeWire has had to change its operations based upon this ruling. Copyright infringements and overall protection has become a global problem for RIAA as well. On February 10, 2012, the International Intellectual Property Alliance (IIPA) found that several countries failed "to provide adequate and effective protection for U.S. Intellectual property."[83] The report's overall goal was to identify shortcomings within the international community and try to recommend a procedure to make the global outlook better while promoting opportunities between the United States and the global communities. The IIPA's report noted that China, Russia, and Canada were the worst offenders when it came to copyright protection because they did not provide clear regulations concerning copyright infringements. On the other hand, IIPA's report did show that some countries have made improvements in their regulations such as Spain, Italy, and the Ukraine. These countries have several new regulations concerning copyright infringement, including a judgment in the Ukraine against a well-known pirate service called ex.ua.

Questions

1. Given the earlier material on Napster, BearShare, and DropBox in this chapter, why do you think that manufacturers and distributors of sound formed the RIAA?

2. What market and nonmarket actions has RIAA taken on behalf of the sound recording industry?

3. If you were part of the IIPA, what recommendations would you make to countries to provide more effective regulations?

INTEGRATIVE CASE

1

INTEGRATIVE CASE (Part 1)

We Have Met the Enemy and the Enemy Is Us![84]

The integrative case examines two small business owners' experiences when interfacing with market and nonmarket forces through the birth, development, and growth of their small businesses. This case will run nearly the entire breadth of the textbook as a result of being broken down into critical incidents that align with material presented in the chapters. One case will appear at the end of each chapter (one incident per chapter). Each incident is applied to a standalone case that can be combined with the other related cases to provide continuity of learning as the text moves from one topic to another. Below is the first part of the integrative case.

"Landlords, landlords," moaned Stephen Hodgetts as if he had just learned about the death of a dear friend. "How could you possibly entertain the notion of us becoming landlords? European and American literature abound with examples of greedy and miserly landlords. Shakespeare, Dickens, Pushkin, Steinbeck, Alger Jr., the list goes on and on. These writers have sullied the rental profession and anyone who practices it. Why don't we just become money lenders and factory owners for God sake and change our names to Fagan and Shylock?"

It was August of 2002 and there seemed to be no help in sight for the ailing stock market. The Dow Jones had plummeted from over 10,000 in May to under 8,000 in August, a 20 percent drop.[85] Richard Davis and Stephen Hodgetts[86], long-time friends, colleagues, and coauthors, were commiserating their respective losses over a glass of fine wine. Both had taken major hits in their personal stock portfolios and retirement accounts that had lost at least a third of their value. For people on a fixed income, with at most 3 percent annual raises to look forward to the rest of their lives, the prospects for a comfortable retirement were looking dimmer and dimmer.

Davis had been hoping to teach only a few more years (he was in his late fifties) and had hoped to have built up a large enough nest egg to retire in comfort. Comfort meant living at his current standard of living, which meant at least one trip to Europe per year with his wife, Adrienne, and the wherewithal to be well stocked in good Merlots and Cabernets. Hodgetts, on the other hand, was in his late forties, yet he too dreamed of early retirement. He wanted to write his great novel, join Davis on his European adventures, and go on a cross-country speaking circuit.

In order to solve their financial woes, Davis proposed that they go into the rental business in order to increase their prospects for retirement. Hodgetts's reaction, to say the least, was quite extreme and quite negative.

"Calm down, Stephen. Besides, you're missing the point," replied Davis. "You have yet to hear me through. First of all landlords are not only a necessary evil, as you seem to infer, but play a critical role in our economy. Where would people live who could not afford homes of their own if there were no landlords willing to rent space for people to live in? Secondly, my idea is to not become just any type of landlord but to focus on those individuals who, given their economic situation, will take a long time to have or never have enough money for a down payment for a house. There are a number of people in this community who are economically stable enough to always pay their rent and their credit card bills but for some reason have had a bad credit history or cannot save enough money to even put 5 percent down on a home. We are going to help those people who cannot help themselves."

As Davis was talking, Hodgetts' face turned redder and redder as deep concern turned to anger. "Hold on!" Hodgetts bellowed. "You're suggesting that we're not going to be just any sort of landlord. No, no, that's not just good enough for Davis and Hodgetts. We're going to become the best type of landlords: SLUMLORDS!"

Questions

1. Hodgetts clearly feels that becoming a landlord is a dishonorable profession. What might be the source of this sentiment? Do other professions have similar reputations? If so, why?

2. What is your own opinion about landlords? How might these opinions affect your analysis of this case?

3. Assuming that Davis wanted to convince Hodgetts to join him in becoming a landlord, what market-based arguments could he employ? Nonmarket-based arguments?

REFERENCES AND NOTES

REFERENCES AND NOTES

1

REFERENCES AND NOTES

1 Google Annual Report, February 15, 2008.

2 http://en.wikipedia.org/wiki/Google (accessed January 24, 2012).

3 http://investor.google.com/corporate/code-of-conduct.html (accessed January 24, 2012).

4 http://googleblog.blogspot.com/2010/01/new-approach-to-china.html (accessed January 24, 2012).

5 J. Dean, "Ethical Conflicts for Firms in China," *Wall Street Journal* (January 13, 2010). http://online.wsj.com/ article/ SB126335402591827235.html.

6 N. Bilton, "Friend Me, Follow Me or Google Me?" *New York Times* (December 20, 2011). http://bits.blogs. nytimes.com /2011/12/20/friend-me-follow-me-google-me/?scp=3&sq=google&st=cse.

7 F. Reed, "Google Gets High Marks for Social Responsibility" (October 11, 2011). http://www.marketing pilgrim.com/2011/10/google-gets-high-marks-for-social-responsibility.html.

8 M. D. P. Lee, "Configuration of External Influences: The Combined Effects of Institutions and Stakeholders on Corporate Social Responsibility Strategies," *Journal of Business Ethics* 102(2) (2011): 281–298.

9 J. Marcus, E. C. Kurucz, and B. A. Colbert, "Conceptions of the Business-Society-Nature Interface: Implications for Management Scholarship," *Business & Society* 49(3) (2010): 402–438.

10 J. Revell, "The Newest Threat to Home Prices," *Fortune* (September 26, 2011): 82.

11 M. Orey, "Why Google Wants to Make Nice," *BusinessWeek* (May 11, 2009): 54–56.

12 N. M. Dahan, J. Doh, and H. Teegen, "Role of Nongovernmental Organizations in the Business—Government—Society Interface: Special Issue Overview and Introductory Essay," *Business & Society* 49(1) (2010): 20–34.

13 P. Schreck, "Reviewing the Business Case for Corporate Social Responsibility: New Evidence and Analysis," *Journal of Business Ethics* 103(2) (2011): 167–188.

14 W. R. Evans and W. D. Davis, "An Examination of Perceived Corporate Citizenship, Job Applicant Attraction, and CSR Work Role

Definition," *Business & Society* 50(3) (2011): 456–480.

15 M. D. P. Lee, "Configuration of External Influences: The Combined Effects of Institutions and Stakeholders on Corporate Social Responsibility Strategies," *Journal of Business Ethics* 102(2) (2011): 281–298.

16 D. Baur and G. Palazzo, "The Moral Legitimacy of NGOs as Partners of Corporations," *Business Ethics Quarterly* 21(4) (2011): 482–511.

17 U.S. Government Accounting Office, "Worker Protection: Labor's Efforts to Enforce Protections for Day Laborers Could Benefit from Better Data and Guidance," GAO-02-925, (September 2002): 1. http://www.gao.gov/new.items/d02925.pdf (accessed October 13, 2005).

18 G. Colvin, "Even All-Stars Need Awesome Coaches," *Fortune* (October 17, 2011): 33.

19 P. O'Connell and J. McGregor, "Managing Through the Economic Storm," *BusinessWeek* (June 29, 2009): 46–48.

20 P. O'Connell and J. McGregor, "Managing Through the Economic Storm," *BusinessWeek* (June 29, 2009): 46–48.

21 L. McFarland, "Australia's Telstra Names New Chief Amid Frayed Government Relations," *Wall Street Journal* (May 11, 2009): B2.

22 www.telstra.com (accessed November 16, 2011).

23 A. Lobb, A. Dizik, and J. Porter, "Lessons That Fit the Times," *Wall Street Journal* (August 20, 2009): B5.

24 G. Colvin, "What Makes a CEO an MPV?" *Fortune* (June 13, 2011): 27.

25 "What Is BGOV?" *BusinessWeek* (Spring 2011): B1.

26 J. Marcus, E. C. Kurucz, and B. A. Colbert, "Conceptions of the Business-Society-Nature Interface: Implications for Management Scholarship," *Business & Society* 49(3) (2010): 402–438.

27 N. M. Dahan, J. Doh, and H. Teegen, "Role of Nongovernmental Organizations in the Business—Government—Society Interface: Special Issue Overview and Introductory Essay," *Business & Society* 49(1) (2010): 20–34.

28 M. D. P. Lee, "Configuration of External Influences: The Combined Effects of

Institutions and Stakeholders on Corporate Social Responsibility Strategies," *Journal of Business Ethics* 102(2) (2011): 281–298.

29 B. Dyck, K. Walker, F. Starke, and K. Uggerslev, "Addressing Concerns Raised by Critics of Business Schools by Teaching Multiple Approaches to Management," *Business and Society Review* 116(1) (2011): 1–27.

30 Information taken from www.coca-cola.com (accessed October 14, 2011).

31 A. Armenakis and J. Wigand, "Stakeholder Actions and Their Impact on the Organizational Cultures of Two Tobacco Companies," *Business and Society Review* 115(2) (2010): 147–171.

32 J. S. Lublin and S. E. Ante, "Inside Sprint's Bet on iPhone," *Wall Street Journal* (October 4, 2011): A1–A2.

33 M. Rhee and M. E. Valdez, "Contextual Factors Surrounding Reputation Damage with Potential Implications for Reputation Repair," *Academy of Management Journal* 34(1) (2009): 146–168.

34 M. Estel, "Southwest Airlines CEO Flies Unchartered Skies," *Wall Street Journal* (March 25, 2009): B1.

35 M. D. P. Lee, "Configuration of External Influences: The Combined Effects of Institutions and Stakeholders on Corporate Social Responsibility Strategies," *Journal of Business Ethics* 102(2) (2011): 281–298.

36 M. Orey and J. Sasseen, "No Solidarity for Labor," *BusinessWeek* (June 15, 2009): 28–29.

37 P. Schreck, "Reviewing the Business Case for Corporate Social Responsibility: New Evidence and Analysis," *Journal of Business Ethics* 103(2) (2011): 167–188.

38 M. Rhee and M. E. Valdez, "Contextual Factors Surrounding Reputation Damage with Potential Implications for Reputation Repair," *Academy of Management Journal* 34(1) (2009): 146–168.

39 P. O'Connell and J. McGregor, "Managing Through the Economic Storm," *BusinessWeek* (June 29, 2009): 46–48.

40 R. Robin and B. Roth, "Lobbyists Set Their Sights on the Supercommittee," *BusinessWeek* (August 15–28, 2011): 25–26.

41 "The Supreme Court Ruled," *The Wall Street Journal* (June 28, 2005): 1.

42 G. Colvin, "What Makes a CEO an MPV?" *Fortune* (June 13, 2011): 27.

43 R. N. Lussier, R. W. Baeder, and J. Corman, "Measuring Global Practices: Global

Strategic Planning Through Company Situational Analysis," *Business Horizons* 37(5) (September–October 1994): 56–63.

44 http://www.mcdonaldsindia.com/menu.html (accessed October 14, 2011).

45 C. K. Ajemian and D. M. Reid, "Preventing Global Warming: The United States, China, and Intellectual Property," *Business and Society Review* 115(4) (2010): 417–436.

46 http://www.dropbox.com/features (accessed February 7, 2012).

47 http://www.dropbox.com/terms, July 6, 2011 (accessed February 7, 2012).

48 S. Sndhu, "Shifting Paradigms in Corporate Environmentalism: From Poachers to Gamekeepers," *Business and Society Review* 115(3) (2010): 285–310.

49 C. Dibrell, J. Craig, and E. Hansen, "Natural Environment, Market Orientation, and Firm Innovativeness: An Organizational Life Cycle Perspective," *Journal of Small Business Management* 49(3) (2011): 467–489.

50 A. Taylor, "The Great Electric Car Race," *Fortune* (September 26, 2011): 33.

51 A. Armenakis and J. Wigand, "Stakeholder Actions and Their Impact on the Organizational Cultures of Two Tobacco Companies," *Business and Society Review* 115(2) (2010): 147–171.

52 B. Dyck, K. Walker, F. Starke, and K. Uggerslev, "Addressing Concerns Raised by Critics of Business Schools by Teaching Multiple Approaches to Management," *Business and Society Review* 116(1) (2011): 1–27.

53 A. Arnaud, "Conceptualizing and Measuring Ethical Work Climate: Development and Validation of the Ethical Climate Index," *Business & Society* 49(2) (2010): 345–358.

54 C. H. Amato and L. H. Amato, "Corporate Commitment to Global Quality of Life Issues: Do Slack Resources, Industry Affiliations, and Multinational Headquarters Matter?" *Business & Society* 50(2) (2011): 388–416.

55 V. Pompe and M. Korthals, "Ethical Room for Maneuver: Playground for the Food Business," *Business and Society Review*, 115(3) (2010): 367–391.

56 C. L. Pearce and C. C. Manz, "Leadership Centrality and Corporate Social Ir-Responsibility (CSIR): The Potential Ameliorating Effects of Self and Shared Leadership on CSIR," *Journal of Business Ethics* 102(4) (2010): 563–579.

57 N. Easton and T. Demos, "The Business Guide to Congress," *Fortune* (May 11, 2009): 72–75.

58 M. Delmas, V. H. Hoffmann, and M. Kuss, "Under the Tip of the Iceberg: Absorptive Capacity, Environmental Strategy, and Competitive Advantage," *Business & Society* 50(1) (2011): 116–154.

59 T. Hahn, A. Kolk, and M. Winn, "A New Future for Business? Rethinking Management Theory and Business Strategy," *Business & Society* 49(3) (2010): 385–401.

60 M. Orlitzky, D. S. Siegel, and D. A. Waldman, "Strategic Corporate Social Responsibility and Environmental Sustainability," *Business & Society* 50(1) (2011): 6–27.

61 T. Hahn, A. Kolk, and M. Winn, "A New Future for Business? Rethinking Management Theory and Business Strategy," *Business & Society* 49(3) (2010): 385–401.

62 M. D. P. Lee, "Configuration of External Influences: The Combined Effects of Institutions and Stakeholders on Corporate Social Responsibility Strategies," *Journal of Business Ethics* 102(2) (2011): 281–298.

63 N. M. Dahan, J. Doh, and H. Teegen, "Role of Nongovernmental Organizations in the Business—Government— Society Interface: Special Issue Overview and Introductory Essay," *Business & Society* 49(1) (2010): 20–34.

64 M. J. O'Fallon and K. D. Butterfield, "Moral Differentiation: Exploring Boundaries of the 'Monkey See, Monkey Do' Perspective," *Journal of Business Ethics* 102(3) (2011): 379–399.

65 L. F. Ackert, B. K. Church, X. Kuang, and L. Qi, "Lying—An Experimental Investigation of the Role of Situational Factors," *Business Ethics Quarterly* 21(4) (2011): 605–632.

66 D. Bay, K. McKeage, and J. McKeage, "An Historical Perspective on the Interplay of Christian Thought and Business Ethics," *Business & Society* 49(4) (2010): 652–676.

67 Suggested by anonymous reviewer.

68 M. Rhee and M. E. Valdez, "Contextual Factors Surrounding Reputation Damage with Potential Implications for Reputation Repair," *Academy of Management Journal* 34(1) (2009): 146–168.

69 http://www.walmartstores.com/AboutUs/297.aspx (accessed June 20, 2012).

70 http://subscriber.hoovers.com/H/company360/financialSummary.html?companyId=11600000000000 (accessed June 20, 2012).

71 Ibid.

72 M. E. Porter, *Competitive Advantage: Creating and Sustaining Superior Performance* (New York: The Free Press, 1985).

73 http://www.walmartstores.com/wmstore/wmstores/Mainabout.jsp?BV_SessionID=@@@@0258870220 (accessed July 2, 2005).

74 http://moneycentral.msn.com/content/invest/extra/P112616.asp (accessed July 5, 2005).

75 http://www.cbsnews.com/stories/2003/10/23/national/main579655.shtml (accessed July 5, 2005).

76 http://www.pbs.org/itvs/storewars/story.html (accessed July 5, 2005).

77 C. Fishman, "The Wal-Mart You Don't Know," *Fast Company* (December 200): 68.

78 http://www.pbs.org/itvs/storewars/stores3.html (accessed July 5, 2005).

79 Ibid.

80 L. Burkitt, *Wall Street Journal* (Online) (October 17, 2011).

81 http://www.riaa.com/aboutus.php (accessed June 20, 2012).

82 http://news.cnet.com/8301-31001_3-20004811-261.html.

83 http://www.riaa.com/news_room.php?content_selector=newsandviews&news_year_filter=2012.

84 Adapted from H. Sherman and D. J. Rowley. "To Invest or Not to Invest, That Is the Question!," *Journal of the International Academy for Case Studies* 12(5) (2006): 45–52.

85 https://www.dwdean.com/DWDean/Secure/AuthFrame/frames.asp?ID=233&EXID=&Language=en&ENID=17425&Account=232016409&month=(accessed April 3, 2003).

86 Although the names of the characters in the case have been changed at their request, the case is factual in nature.

Part 2

BUSINESS

Chapter 2

STRATEGIC STAKEHOLDER AND ETHICAL PUBLIC AFFAIRS, ISSUES, AND CRISIS MANAGEMENT

Learning Outcomes

In this chapter, you will find out the answers to these key questions:

- How do you use a stakeholder approach to management?
- What are public affairs and how do you manage them?
- How do you conduct a strategic analysis to develop strategies for dealing with public affairs?

After studying this chapter, you should be able to:

1. Describe stakeholder management and the need to balance stockholder and other stakeholder interests
2. Differentiate public affairs management from issues management
3. Identify the three-phase process of issues management
4. Define *crisis* and discuss the four stages of crisis management, including the 3 As of crisis communication
5. List and briefly describe the 5 Is of strategic analysis
6. Categorize the issue life cycle stages with the strategic focus for each stage
7. Define the following key terms (in order of appearance in the chapter):

stakeholder management	crisis management stages	objectives
strategic stakeholders	3As of crisis	writing objectives
public affairs (PA)	communication	model
public affairs management	5 Is of strategic analysis	supportive information
issues management	issues to business	information strategies
issues management	issues life cycle	interaction strategies
process	strategic stakeholders	
crisis	with incentives	

■ Chapter Outline

The Strategic Stakeholder Approach to Management and Ethics
    From the Stockholder to the Stakeholder Approach
    Stakeholder Management and Ethics
    Balancing Owner and Other Stakeholder Interests

Public Affairs and Issues Management
    Public Affairs Activities and Functions
    Public Affairs Management
    Issues Management
    Issues Management Can Preclude Crisis Management

Crisis Management
    1. Developing the Crisis Team
    2. Planning—Risk Assessment, Monitoring, and Crisis Prevention
    3. Managing the Crisis—Communication
    4. Analyzing Post Crisis

Strategic Analysis: The 5 Is
    1. Issue Identification
    2. Interested Strategic Stakeholders
    3. Incentive of Stakeholders
    4. Information—Objectives
    5. Interaction Strategies

What's This Chapter About?

This chapter implements the basic concepts from Chapter 1 while presenting the strategy framework for the entire book with its case study approach. The four major concept sections are closely interrelated.

We begin with a discussion of the stakeholder approach to management and ethics. Next we discuss public affairs (how business interacts with stakeholders) and issues management (a public affairs management approach to interacting with stakeholders). Our third section extends issues management by describing how to identify and prevent potential crises and how to deal with crises that weren't prevented.

Our last section pulls the chapter together by presenting a five-stage strategic analysis for dealing with stakeholders. The 5 Is analysis presents a framework for critically thinking about issues and stakeholders in your personal and professional lives. It is a helpful guide in case analysis.

CASE

Can Philip Morris Now Take a Breath of Fresh Air?

Victory is sweet, but is it really? The Philip Morris USA (PM) division of the Altria Group had been bombarded for many years by class action suits alleging that they knew their tobacco-based products were a major contributor to cancer-related illness for their consumers. In November 1998, the industry settled with 46 states for a total of $40 billion. Beginning in 1999, Philip Morris spent about $100 million per year on a TV campaign attempting to mitigate the highly negative publicity.[1]

Despite the settlement and the advertising campaigns, the problem was far from over. In April 2003, PM lost a $10.1 billion class action suit dealing with the claim of false advertising of light cigarettes.[2] CEO Louis Camilleri threatened to take the firm into bankruptcy. Altria's future was in doubt, and investors who normally focused on high dividends dumped the stock, despite its generous 9.1 percent yield. Some continued to shun Altria, despite a dividend yield that remained above 4 percent in 2005 and a low of 14 times next year's expected earnings trading range. Some major mutual fund managers said they weren't willing to risk owning the stock and watching the company possibly lose its litigation battles.[3]

However, the air seemed to clear after a 2005 decision in which the Illinois Supreme Court threw out the $10.1 billion class action lawsuit. Analysts claimed the court ruling was a major victory for PM and the Altria Group.[4] At the investor conference, Camilleri said the company was optimistic about its legal prospects and looked toward a highly optimistic future for the firm. Altria, however, still faced numerous legal challenges.[5] In 2011, thinking that the air had finally cleared, Camilleri claimed that cigarettes, though harmful and addictive, are "'not that hard' to quit."[6] His comment caused an uproar with shareholders because it followed a statement on ABC News by a nurse within the tobacco industry that "tobacco kills more than 400,000 Americans and 5 million people worldwide each year." Many believed it was a questionable statement to make given that some studies showed it may be just as hard to quit smoking cigarettes as it is to quit certain illegal drugs. Camilleri in his statement also noted that the company was working toward making tobacco products more regulated so that more Americans can quit easier; yet many challenged this statement in light of continued cigarette advertisements indirectly targeting adolescents.

The following questions are related to the Philip Morris case. Answers can be found within the chapter.

1. Describe Altria Group's (PM's) approach to management as presented in this case; is it stockholder or stakeholder?
2. Who are some of the strategic/critical stakeholders in this case?
3. How does PM interact with its stakeholders in this case?
4. What are the key issues in this case for PM?
5. What stage of the issues life-cycle model does this case reflect?
6. What are the market reaction and consequences of PM's nonmarket strategy of continuing to directly fight lawsuits in the courts and in the news media?

THE STRATEGIC STAKEHOLDER APPROACH TO MANAGEMENT AND ETHICS

In this section, we discuss the change from the stockholder to stakeholder approach to management, explain what stakeholder management is, and describe the need to ethically balance owner and other stakeholder interests.

From the Stockholder to the Stakeholder Approach

The traditional *stockholder approach* to management focused on meeting the needs of the owners/stockholders and maximizing profits, without regard for other business stakeholders described in Chapter 1. The power of various stakeholders has risen over the years,[7] and the paradigm has shifted from the stockholder to the stakeholder approach to management.[8] The stakeholder approach of trying to create a win-win for all stakeholders has been justified as a necessary precondition to stockholder value maximization.[9] However, with multiple stakeholders with different interests, it is often difficult to create a win for all stakeholders. But a win-win is the ultimate goal.

Today, managers realize that generating long-term value depends on responding to critical stakeholders, so they are developing a stakeholder orientation.[10] Thus, to be successful and maximize profits, businesses are focusing on being ethical with critical stakeholders that directly affect business performance.[11] Stakeholder theory is a popular area of research.[12] In fact, research provides evidence that businesses using the stakeholder approach are more successful than those using the stockholder approach, and most successful large businesses use a stakeholder approach.[13] For example, **Shell Oil Company** integrated the stakeholder management approach into its business practice worldwide as a long-term comprehensive strategy.[14]

Personal and Professional Applications

1. The CEO of Land O' Lakes suggests that you should help others to get ahead in their career. Do you agree?

Philip Morris Case Question 1: Describe Altria Group's (PM's) approach to management as presented in this case; is it stockholder or stakeholder?

PM appears to be employing a stockholder approach by focusing on the needs of the owners/stockholders and maximizing profits without regard for any other business stakeholders, especially their customers who claim to have been injured by their products and lured into smoking light cigarettes through false advertising. Rather than discontinue manufacturing these products and/or settling injurious claims, PM chose to confront their consumers and detractors through the court system and in the media.

Learning Outcome 1: Describe stakeholder management and the need to balance stockholder and other stakeholder interests.

Stakeholder Management and Ethics

Stakeholder management is based on making decisions on specific issues in an ethical manner in ways that provide value to strategic stakeholders. Thus, stakeholder management includes being ethical by trying to create a win-win situation for strategic stakeholders.[15] It is common to differentiate between primary and secondary stakeholders. Thus, we refer to strategic stakeholders as primary, and other stakeholders as secondary. *Strategic stakeholders are critically affected by firm action, and/or they can affect firm performance.* Recall (Chapter 1) that stakeholders are affected by the business and can affect firm performance. The difference between primary and secondary stakeholders is the word "critical."

Critical refers to those stakeholder interests that have direct financial impact on the business (benefit or loss). Advocate interest groups and the government are critical stakeholders when they protect or hurt other stakeholders. All other stakeholders indirectly affected are stakeholders for the issue in question. So the business must focus more on strategic stakeholders because of their ability to help or hurt the firm, than on secondary stakeholders who have less impact.

Strategic also refers to developing a nonmarket strategy that can be integrated with the market strategy. Managers and firms can't give all stakeholders whatever they want because resources are limited, thus requiring the business to make choices as to which stakeholders' requests will be fulfilled and which will not. Sometimes the strategic answer to a specific stakeholder group's request, therefore, has to be no, especially when the stakeholder is a limited special interest person or group whose demand is not supported by the majority of the business stakeholders. Thus, strategic planning considers stakeholders.[16]

Personal and Professional Applications

2. Select a business you work(ed) for. Does it use a stockholder or a stakeholder approach?

Philip Morris Case Question 2: Who are some of the strategic/critical stakeholders in this case?

Besides the stockholders (including mutual fund managers), strategic/critical stakeholders include consumers (especially those engaged in class action suits), other litigants (the 48 states that settled), the tobacco industry, the various court systems, the Department of Justice, and the news media.

Balancing Owner and Other Stakeholder Interests

Managers, who are paid employees, are agents of owners/stockholders and they must look out for owners/stockholders' interests and make a profit; if they don't, they are often fired. Owners are usually strategic stakeholders, but other stakeholders vary by issue. Thus, managers need to balance the needs of owners and other stakeholders, attempting to ethically create value for both.[17] Notice that we said "try" to create value and win-win situations.

In reality, managers must make decisions that benefit (that is, produce positive circumstances while preventing negative consequences) business but don't necessarily benefit other stakeholders. For example, when a business or one of its units is not profitable, managers may implement layoffs, which is not beneficial to the employees and the community.

Successful top-level managers use the stakeholder approach to create a culture in which everyone in the organization focuses on stakeholders. Thus, they create a stakeholder corporation.[18] Successful companies today are assessing stakeholder management performance and so are organizations, including the **Dow Jones** Sustainability Indexes.[19]

Personal and Professional Applications

3. Give an example of a specific decision a business you work(ed) for that did *not* create value and a win-win situation for stakeholders. Be sure to identify the stakeholders and how they were hurt by the decision.

PUBLIC AFFAIRS AND ISSUES MANAGEMENT

This section broadens the discussion of stakeholder management and applies it to public affairs and issues management. We first discuss public affairs activities and functions, then managing public affairs, followed by issues management, which is part of public affairs management. We end by explaining how issues management helps the business prevent and prepare to manage crises.

Public Affairs Activities and Functions

Public affairs (PA) refers to how business interacts with stakeholders. It is also about firm stakeholder relationships.[20] PA is about dealing with relevant stakeholders regarding a current issue that needs to be addressed through nonmarket strategies. Many terms are used to refer to public affairs, which can make PA somewhat confusing. Different companies that perform the same PA activities and functions may use different terms, such as public relations, corporate relations, external affairs, public policy, corporate communications, or corporate social responsibility. Issues management and crisis management also refer to PA. See Figure 2.1 for a list of the PA activities and functions of 250 large and medium-sized U.S. companies ranked by use. Many firms hire public relations agencies to help them perform their PA functions; public relations firms offer, among other benefits, contacts and an independent view of the firm and its issue. During all PA functions, managers must be ethical; unethical behavior should be reported through whistle blowing, which we discuss in the next chapter.

Activity/Function	% using	Activity/Function	% using
Political action committee (PAC)	89	Employee volunteer programs	66
Issues management	84	Media relations	64
State government relations	84	Public relations	61
Local government relations	77	Employee communications	59
Community relations	75	Strategic philanthropy	55
Direct corporate contributions	75	Regulatory affairs	43
Business/trade associations	73	Educational relations	34
Public policy group relations	73	International public affairs	32
Grassroots communication	71	Environmental affairs	23
Corporate foundation	71	Stockholder relations	21

■ **Figure 2.1:** Public Affairs Activities and Functions

Source: Adapted from D. C. Richards, "Corporate Public Affairs: Necessary Cost or Value-Added Asset?" *Journal of Public Affairs* 3(1) (2003): 41.

Personal and Professional Applications

4. Select a business you work(ed) for and describe the public affairs activities and functions it performs.

Philip Morris Case Question 3: How does PM interact with its stakeholders in this case?

Although the case is not inclusive of all public affairs activities at PM, it does document the use of the news media, state government interactions (settlement with states), business/trade associations (industry settlement), stockholder relations (investor conference), and legal/regulatory affairs.

The scope and complexity of PA increased to address social activist concerns and significant federal laws in the early 1970s and included issues of discrimination, environmental protection, occupational health and safety, and consumer safety. Today, PA is broader in scope than public relations, but PA continues to include public relations, which is now often referred to as media relations. The use of PA communications is changing with the use of information technology and the Internet.[21]

Just as personnel management evolved to become human resources management, PA evolved from public relations. Thus, public relations executives have changed their title to "public affairs" executive. But whatever the title, PA practitioners formulate strategies to interact with stakeholders.[22]

The use of the term *public affairs* is illustrated in the title of **National Association of Schools of Public Affairs and Administration** (NASPAA) that accredits PA programs. Public affairs is a major focus of the master of public administration (MPA). The **Public Affairs Council (PAC)**, based in Washington, D.C. (www.pac.org), is the leading international association for public affairs professionals. PAC is a nonpartisan, nonpolitical association whose mission is to advance the field of public affairs and to provide members with the training and information resources they need to achieve success while maintaining the highest ethical standards.[23]

> Learning Outcome 2: Differentiate public affairs management from issues management.

Public Affairs Management

Public affairs management is the process of developing corporate public policies and strategies regarding how the business will interact with stakeholders in the business, social, and government environments; it includes issues management, crisis management, and strategic analysis. Corporate public policies are general guidelines to influence how employees will interact with stakeholders. **Ford**'s "Quality is job one" slogan reminds all employees to do quality work regardless of their position. Part of **JC Penney**'s Statement of Business Ethics says it will "not seek an unfair advantage over our competitors," this is also a PA policy.

Why do businesses engage in PA management? Researchers find that PA has many activities and functions that must be managed effectively for the business to be successful. Firms that are more likely to be active in PA management are those that are significantly affected by government. To be more specific, firms highly dependent on government regulation or contracts for economic success, large firms, and those operating in more highly concentrated industries are more politically active.[24]

PA management policies and strategies are part of the overall nonmarket strategy, which, again, must be integrated with market strategies. For a review of nonmarket strategies, which are also called PA strategies, see Figure 1.4 (p. 22). The nonmarket strategies will be discussed in detail in later chapters.

With the increasing complexity of PA, many companies have created specialized departments, with titles such as Public Affairs Department, to manage it. With the emergence of PA departments, it is tempting for line managers to think that they are not responsible for PA. However, this is not the case. Line managers and employee actions are an integral part of PA management. For example, in 2010 when **Apple** came out with the iPhone 4 with its antenna design that caused reception problems, when **J&J** had to recall a half-dozen medicines, when **Facebook** was accused of privacy violations, and even worse when people died because of the **British Petroleum (BP)** Deepwater Horizon disaster,

PA had to respond to the negative press and angry consumers.[25] Thus, all employees need to view PA as part of their day-to-day work, rather than the job of PA professionals.

As stated in our definition of PA management, issues management, crisis management, and strategic analysis are part of PA. We will discuss issues management in this section, crisis management in the next section, and strategic analysis in the last section.

Personal and Professional Applications

5. State some public policies affecting a business you work(ed) for that guide employees in their interactions with stakeholders in the business, social, and government environments.

Learning Outcome 3: Identify the three-phase process of issues management.

Issues Management

Issues management is a public affairs management approach to identifying, monitoring, analyzing, and selecting public issues that may warrant nonmarket strategies. Thus, PA professionals develop and implement issues management. Issues managers may be members of the **Issue Management Council** (www.issuemanagement.org) professional association.

PA and issues management are different while being closely related. PA deals with current issues that need nonmarket strategies, whereas issues management deals with identifying future issues that may need nonmarket strategies—but may not. For example, you would want to know about potential new laws and regulations, so you use issues management. If the government begins to draft new laws or regulations, the issue would become a PA matter that calls for the development of current nonmarket strategies. As long as the government does not implement new regulations, the process of monitoring the issue continues as part of ongoing issues management. So PA nonmarket strategies often come from issues management, but not always. Sometimes the source is a crisis that requires immediate PA nonmarket strategies.

Opportunities and Threats. Issues management is used to anticipate and respond to both threats and opportunities. Business looks for trends that will benefit the company. For example, the aging population trend continues to create a large market for products and health care needed by older people. Threats are discussed next and throughout the book.

The Issues Management Process. The three steps commonly involved in the *issues management process* include: *(1) scanning the environment to identify issues and trends that will affect the business; (2) evaluating the impact issues will have on the firm and ranking issues by priority; and (3) conducting a strategic analysis to develop strategies for dealing with high-priority public affairs issues.* Issues management continues our focus on stakeholder interactions.

1. **Scanning the environment to identify issues and trends that will affect the business**. For example, new legislation or regulation is an issue of concern to business,

such as the financial reform under the Dodd-Frank bill, requiring interaction with stakeholders. Issues develop over time and require that the monitoring process be ongoing. Employees scan publications, such as newspapers, magazines, and specialty publications, and the Internet to develop a list of issues. Several professional associations have publications that discuss issues facing the profession or trade group. Firms also pay scanning fees to experts who provide summaries of publications and offer consultation services. Businesses commonly develop a list of issues and may conduct surveys to determine stakeholder views and public sentiment on those and emerging issues.

2. **Evaluating the impact issues will have on the firm and ranking issues by priority**. With a list of issues compiled, the next step is to determine which ones can benefit or hurt the firm the most. Companies use different systems. For example, **Xerox** used a process of categorizing issues into three classifications: (1) high priority issues that management must deal with; (2) nice-to-know issues that are interesting but not critical or urgent; and (3) questionable events or practices that may not become issues. **PPG Industries** groups issues by their level of importance: Priority A issues must be dealt with, Priority B issues warrant monitoring by line managers, and Priority C issues are monitored only by the PA department.

3. **Conducting a strategic analysis to develop strategies for dealing with high-priority PA issues**. Monitoring the results of strategic action is also part of the analysis. Strategic analysis to develop strategies for dealing with high-priority issues is the heart of issues management, so we discuss strategic analysis as a separate section, after crisis management.

Many firms use issues management software to measure PA efforts in all three steps. **Cymfony, Biz360, VMS**, and **Cision** (formerly **Bacon's Information**) now provide real-time updates on what all aspects of the media are saying about a company, its latest products, and its competitors. Most issues management software is a monthly or annual service, and its price depends on the number of issues or words the firm wants to monitor. The information is delivered in real time to the firm via a software dashboard that resides on the firm's computer desktop.

Some companies use blogs to provide information to the public regarding industry issues.[26] **Google**'s legal counsel and others have blogged about controversies, such as copying books, to state why it is engaging in such practices. Steve Langdon, senior manager of corporate PR, says blogs are a way of quickly providing information about complex topics to the general public. Thus, Google may have been the first company to bring blogs into the realm of issues management.[27] For a review of the issues management process, see Figure 2.2. Note that the issues process is not linear; you can work on more than one phase of the process and/or return to prior phases. The firm continually monitors the issue and makes appropriate changes in all three phases of the process. The business may also deal with multiple issues and phases at the same time.

1. Scanning the environment to identify issues and trends that will affect the business ↔	2. Evaluating the impact issues will have on the firm and ranking issues by priority ↔	3. Conducting a strategic analysis to develop strategies for dealing with high-priority public affairs issues ↔

■ **Figure 2.2:** The Issues Management Process

Personal and Professional Applications

6. Select a business you work(ed) for and discuss its issues management process. Be sure to state any sources it uses/d to gather information on issues.

Issues Management Can Preclude Crisis Management

Of course, not all crises can be planned for and prevented, but many crises can be anticipated through effective issues management programs by identifying and managing risks before they become disasters.[28] Issues managers identify issues that can escalate into a crisis. The better managers deal with issues, the less likely they are to become crises. Effective issues management assists the firm in preventing crises and in planning for crises that may occur. While in recent years **BP** has been in crises, **Exxon** has managed to avoid a crisis.[29] Thus, issues management is a form of precrisis management. But crisis management goes beyond issues management. So let's discuss it separately.

Learning Outcome 4: Define *crisis* and discuss the four stages of crisis management, including the 3 As of crisis communication.

CRISIS MANAGEMENT

Managers need to understand the difference between a problem issue and a crisis. A *crisis is a major unexpected event that has a large negative consequence.* Large negative consequences include injuries, deaths, and large financial costs. Cost is relative to the size of the firm; for example, $1 million would put most small firms out of business, whereas it is a less consequential amount to big businesses like **Toyota**. Recall the crisis in the auto industry and financial crises that led to the federal bailout to prevent **GM** and **Chrysler** and many of the large banks and financial houses from going bankrupt.[30] The crises of current times seem much more extreme than crises of the past.[31] The financial meltdown and other crises prompted some business schools to retool some courses to focus on crisis management.[32] **AIG**, needing a $130 billion government bailout, started offering crisis insurance to businesses in 2011.[33]

ETHICAL DILEMMA 2.1 Can American Airlines Fly Out of Turbulence?

AMR Corporation, the parent company to American Airlines, which has been experiencing financial problems, filed for Chapter 11 bankruptcy protection in February of 2011. Company financials indicated that from 2007 until 2011 revenues went from $22.94 billion to $23.98 billion (its lowest revenue of $19.92 billion occurred in 2009) with net income going into a nose dive in 2008 all the way down to $1.98 billion in 2011.[34]

According to a *New York Times* article the purpose of filing for bankruptcy protection was to "reduce labor costs and shed a heavy debt burden," copying the tactic of other airline companies who had already successfully filed for bankruptcy. AMR's CEO also stated, "Our board decided that it was necessary to take this step now to restore the company's profitability, operating flexibility and financial strength."[35]

Yet a *Forbes* article warned that this bankruptcy filing could lead to less frequency of service to airports and open renegotiations with labor unions, which could harm passengers and employees if not handled in the correct manner.[36] Potential bad press could result in a loss of faith among passengers and employees of AMR, and therefore loss of quality personnel, service, and revenues (profits).

With a depressed economy, rising competition driven by Internet sales, increasing partnerships and alliances between airlines, limited airplane suppliers (Boeing and Airbus), rising oil prices, lack of capital, and now bad press, AMR is clearly flying through stormy weather.[37] Can AMR figure out how to steer its AA into clear skies and avoid further turbulence?

Questions

1. How would an understanding of PA and issues management help AMR better understand the problems they are facing?
2. What steps should AMR take in addressing this issue?
3. Who would be helped or hurt by the board declaring bankruptcy?
4. Given your answer to question 3, if you were on the board, would you have voted for bankruptcy? Why or why not?

We tend to have the mentality that a crisis will not happen to our business because crises tend to have a low probability of occurrence. But crisis can happen in any organization, such as violence (workers or outsiders killing employees and customers—**9/11/01 terrorist attacks** and **Virginia Tech**), accidents (oil spills—**Exxon Valdez** and **BP**), and natural disasters (hurricanes—**Katrina** and **Rita**, floods, fires). One event often causes a crisis in many organizations, and the firms can be far from the initial events.[38]

A crisis can also have long-term negative effects on brands, managers, and company reputations.[39] For example, **BP** (oil spill), **Tiger Woods, Inc**. (affair), and **Toyota** (safety problems) all are working to turn around negative situations.[40] In this section, we discuss a four-stage crisis management process.[41] *The crisis management stages include: (1) developing the crisis team; (2) planning; (3) managing the crisis—communication; and (4) analyzing post crisis.*

1. Developing the Crisis Team

The crisis leader must be supported by a strong team. A crisis management team is usually led by a senior-level executive, often the CEO when the event actually happens.[42] The team has a mix of representatives from all sectors of the organization along with external members, such as a trauma team. The team should work together, not simply divide the tasks, which leads to politics. Members can challenge one another's ideas without resorting to personal attacks, engage in debates without coercion or blame, and unite behind decisions once they are made. Members don't seem to circumvent or undermine each other, instead they work cooperatively, sharing information and encouraging teamwork.

2. Planning—Risk Assessment, Monitoring, and Crisis Prevention

Management at all levels needs to identify and manage risks before they become crises.[43] Good crisis management requires planning.[44] In many events, there are warning signs of the potential crisis. For example, it was known that **BP** had safety problems and the captain of the **Exxon** *Valdez* was repeatedly drunk on the job. People complained about **Toyota** safety problems at least a year before the recalls. Yet, nothing was really done until the oil spills and auto recalls. Most employees who kill people at work start with other acts of violence. Before a crisis some employees warn of the disaster to come. Natural disasters, like floods, are often predicted, giving some time to prepare and evacuate. Risk assessment and planning includes four parts:

- **Risk assessment and ranking**. The crisis team identifies potential events that could happen, determines the organization's necessary level of preparedness, and then makes plans to mitigate future risks.[45] They answer the question, Where are we vulnerable?, by engaging in "what-if" scenario analysis that focuses on creating realistic incidents under each crisis category. How likely is each crisis? **US Airways** and others, for example, recognize the risk of plane crashes.[46]
- **Risk monitoring**. The crisis management team needs the authority to require individuals and departments to keep logs of complaints, warnings, and incidents. It needs to look for increased activity and patterns. Will the event get worse? The crisis team needs to review the events and have a plan to take action when necessary.
- **Risk prevention and damage reduction strategies**. How can the crisis be prevented? What are the warning signs? How can damage be reduced if a crisis occurs? The best-case scenario is to prevent the crisis, followed by limiting the damage of a crisis. Identifying risk prevention and reduction strategies is great, but the plan must be followed up with monitoring, preventing, and limiting actions.
- **The crisis plan**. What is the plan to respond quickly to a crisis? **Exxon Mobil** maintains its own oil spill response teams and equipment stockpiles. It also has supported the establishment of a network of worldwide, industry-supported oil spill response organizations. **US Airways** has a crash playbook and has "dry run" emergency exercises at least three times a year at each airport it serves and has a network of employees who double as "Care Team" members who are dispatched to emergencies at a moment's notice. As a result of good crisis planning and implementing, it has been said that Flight 1549's water landing in the Hudson River in New York may become a model for crisis management.[47]

3. Managing the Crisis—Communication

Proper communication can help to maintain a positive company and brand reputation.[48] Once a crisis happens, the crisis leader and the crisis team must act immediately deal with it. The crisis leader needs to work with the crisis team, not go it alone, which includes putting into motion the crisis plan, adjusted to the situation. The communication plan must be implemented with good public relations,[49] as discussed next.

- **Selecting the spokesperson**. During the actual crisis, the CEO generally is the chief crisis officer,[50] but the CEO doesn't have to be the spokesperson. Companies need to select the right person to be the central voice. Don't throw the CEO in the middle of every story. In the **BP** crisis, former CEO Tony Hayward underplayed the gravity initially, and then he arguably overplayed it because he was on the defensive.[51] The crisis spokesperson should stay engaged, get out and communicate—not hide as Tiger Woods did—and send the message that there is nothing to hide.[52]
- **The crisis spokesperson should follow the "three As" of communicating during a crisis**. Before talking or writing about the crisis, a crisis team needs to plan what a

spokesperson will say; using the 3 As helps. *The 3 As of crisis communication are: Acknowledge the crisis, state the Action to deal with the crisis, and state how the crisis will be Avoided in the future.*

1. **Acknowledge**. Admit to the crisis. Be honest and straightforward. Tell the truth and don't lie or cover for the boss or the organization. But if a company is innocent, go on the offense and don't apologize.[53] **BP** tried to blame at least part of the Gulf oil spill on its partner **Transocean**, the company that owned and ran the vessel that exploded killing 11 men (9 Transocean employees and 2 BP workers) and causing the largest offshore oil spill, but Transocean will not admit even a portion of liability.[54]

2. **Action**. Tell what is being done to contain or repair the crisis damage. **Toyota** recalled more than 8 million vehicles because of several safety problems.[55] Handle those affected with utmost sensitivity; go the extra mile beyond the requirements of the situation. Following the plane crash, "Miracle on the Hudson," **US Airways** was cited as doing so. For example, staffers met the passengers with cash, dry clothes, and prepaid cell phones. Employees escorted each passenger to a new flight or a local NY hotel. They also arranged train tickets and rental cars for those who didn't want to fly.[56]

3. **Avoid**. Establish a plan to avoid a repeat crisis in the future. Although it was slow to acknowledge the safety crisis and take action, **Toyota** is working to regain market share by repairing its image with the help of ads that talk about its Star Safety System and showing that they are changing some processes on new models.

▪ **Communication**. A company today may have only minutes, not hours, to contain a crisis. With the Internet and cable television, the world often knows about a crisis before some managers and the employees. An organization should make itself accessible as quickly as possible. It is generally believed that "within an hour" of becoming aware that a crisis situation may exist, company officials must be prepared to issue an initial statement to the media and other key stakeholder groups, providing facts as they are known, and an indication of when additional details will be made available. However, it is important to balance the desire to say something right away with the need to get the facts. Managers typically speak too soon and have to eat most of what they said.[57] So again, plan the 3 As before speaking or writing about the crisis.

4. Analyzing Post Crisis

Top management should launch an evaluation (preferably conducted by an objective third party) of the organization's effectiveness in managing the crisis, with an assessment of its effectiveness in communicating with key stakeholder groups. The analysis should focus on questions pertaining to how effective the crisis team and the crisis management plan performed, how effectively the organization handled victims and family members, and what worked the least in mitigating the problem. This information is relevant for many reasons, the most important of which are the lessons learned that can help in preventing and minimizing future crises.

The **Institute for Crisis Management** (www.crisisexperts.com) is an excellent source of additional information on this topic. See Figure 2.3 for a review of the four crisis management stages, which, like issues management, is a continuing process.

1. Developing the crisis team
2. Planning—risk assessment, monitoring, and crisis prevention
3. Managing the crisis—communication
4. Analyzing post crisis

■ **Figure 2.3:** The Crisis Management Stages

Personal and Professional Applications

7. Give an example of a business that did a good or poor job of handling a crisis. What did management do right or wrong?

Learning Outcome 5: List and briefly describe the 5 Is of strategic analysis.

ETHICAL DILEMMA 2.2 Susan G. Komen Foundation: Could a Painful Funding "Mastectomy" Have Been Avoided?

The Susan G. Komen for the Cure® is the global leader of the breast cancer movement, having invested more than $1.9 billion since inception in 1982. As the world's largest grassroots network of breast cancer survivors and activists, they are working to save lives, empower people, ensure quality care for all, and energize science to find the cures. They have become the largest source of nonprofit funds dedicated to the fight against breast cancer in the world.[58]

At the end of January 2012 Planned Parenthood announced that its preventive breast cancer funding from the Susan G. Komen foundation had been cut, and women's health advocates were immediately taking to the airwaves to make their dissatisfaction known, decrying the decision as a crass political calculation and urging Komen to reverse the decision. The organization defended its decision as part of an ongoing effort to exact "stronger performance criteria for our grantees," but many Planned Parenthood supporters have accused Komen of caving in to pressure from the political right in what they cast as an ongoing assault on abortion rights. Immediately after the announcement 26 Democratic senators had attached their names to a letter urging Komen to reverse its decision.

Many have pointed to Karen Handel, a new vice president to the Komen foundation, as a possible force behind the decision to cut off grant money to Planned Parenthood. Handel, who ran for governor of Georgia in 2010, describes herself as "staunchly pro-life" and frequently called for an end to abortion during her gubernatorial bid. At least one high-profile Komen staffer, Mollie Williams, resigned in protest over the decision to defund Planned Parenthood.

Regardless of whether the decision was borne out of political motivations, however, its impact has been to dramatically mobilize Planned Parenthood donors. Within 24 hours of the announcement Planned Parenthood had raised more than $400,000 online, mostly from small donors. Additionally, the Fikes Foundation gave Planned Parenthood a $250,000 grant toward starting the Emergency Breast Health Fund in the aftermath of the Komen decision. New York City Mayor Michael Bloomberg announced that he would match up to $250,000 donations from his personal wealth.[59]

1. How might the Komen Foundation have avoided this dilemma surrounding the funding cut before the decision was made?
2. Was the decision to cut Planned Parenthood funding an ethical one given the fact that Planned Parenthood provides other more controversial services besides breast cancer prevention?
3. How should the Komen Foundation handle this public relations crisis? What would you do?

STRATEGIC ANALYSIS: THE 5 IS

Public affairs management is broad in scope and includes issues management and crisis management, and the heart of all three is strategic analysis. In other words, the analysis is used to determine strategies for interacting with stakeholders—PA. Strategic planning is important to businesses,[60] and businesses need to focus on stakeholders when developing strategies.[61]

Integrating market and nonmarket strategies is the primary focus of this entire book, and the text presents nonmarket concepts as integral to stakeholder management. Through a strategic analysis process, individuals develop and use critical thinking skills to analyze business issues and make better decisions in their personal and professional lives.

Researchers have suggested a methodical approach for analyzing stakeholder management. Among the many methods, with some variations, we have developed a detailed process for this text, which your professor may adapt to his or her preference. *The 5 Is strategic analysis stages include: (1) issue identification; (2) interested strategic stakeholders; (3) incentive of stakeholders; (4) information—objectives; and (5) interaction strategies.* A structured framework based on the 5 Is uses a table in case analysis. See the Appendix for a discussion of different case analyses methods and the option of using the Table. In this section, we discuss each of the 5 I stages.

1. Issue Identification

Logically, we need to start our analysis by knowing what the issue is. The sooner the issue is identified (often through issues management), the more time the business has to plan for and deal with it. Some businesses are good at issues management, are proactive, and take nonmarket strategic action to prevent the issue from being brought to the firm. But once the issue affects the business, a PA nonmarket strategy must be developed to deal with the stakeholder issue, even if the strategy is to take no action and monitor the issue. *Issues to business are usually brought to the company by any of its stakeholders because the firm is not meeting expectations and the stakeholder is pressing the firm to take action to meet its special interest.* Thus, PA management is often about solving problems under pressure from stakeholders.[62]

Philip Morris Case Question 4: What are the key issues in this case for PM?

Several of PM's stakeholder groups (consumers, state governments, and the Justice Department) have accused the firm (as well as the industry) of knowingly producing a harmful product and then falsely advertising that product. The situation has been exacerbated by recent public statements by the CEO. The issue for PM is how to minimize the economic damages that may directly (through fines) and indirectly (through depreciated stock prices) affect their stockholders.

Learning Outcome 6: Categorize the issue life-cycle stages with the strategic focus for each stage.

The Nonmarket Issues Life Cycle.

Issues go through a life-cycle, as shown in Figure 2.4. *The issues life cycle includes: (1) identification and formation of the issue and public sentiment; (2) interested stakeholder formation; (3) issue brought to business for voluntary action; (4) legislative and regulation formation; and (5) enforcement and litigation.* The issue may be identified through the news media, and the issue may or may not be brought to business.

Stage 1	Stage 2	Stage 3	Stage 4	Stage 5
ISSUE				
Identification and formation of the issue and public sentiment (possibly news media coverage)	Interested stakeholder formation	Issue brought to business for voluntary action (may be skipped)	Legislative and regulation formation	Enforcement and litigation
STRATEGY				
Informational and *societal* strategies to influence the development of the issue	*Informational* and *societal* strategies, developing coalitions	Varies based on the issue and who brings it	*Political* lobbying to prevent or support change	*Legal*—comply with changes and avoid or bring lawsuits
Issue impact on the business increases with time and stages as managers have less ability to influence the stakeholders involved →				

■ **Figure 2.4:** The Issues Life Cycle and Strategy Focus

Personal and Professional Applications

8. List some business issues and explain the stage of the life cycle each issue is in.

Strategies Change Over the Nonmarket Life Cycle. Note that the following strategies are from Figure 1.4 (p. 22). During the identification and formation of issues and stakeholders, stages 1 and 2, informational and societal strategies focus on affecting the development of the issue including developing coalitions to influence stakeholders for the issue. When the issue is brought to the business, stage 3, strategies vary based on the issue and who brings it to the firm. At the point of legislation and regulation formation, stage 4, political strategies focus on preventing or supporting the changes, primarily through lobbying. Once the law or regulation for the issue has been passed and is enforced, stage 5, the strategic focus is on legal compliance, damage control, and avoiding or bringing lawsuits.

> Philip Morris Case Question 5: What stage of the issues life-cycle model does this case reflect?
>
> This case describes a stage 5 litigation situation in which PM is trying to minimize the damages caused by a series of lawsuits brought by consumers and numerous state governments.

Issue Questions. The two major questions that you must answer during this first step of the analysis are: (1) What is the issue? (2) At what stage of the life cycle is the issue? With this information, you proceed to the second step of the strategic analysis. If you are conducting a case analysis using the Table in the Appendix, this first I analysis goes in column 1.

2. Interested Strategic Stakeholders

Developing stakeholder public policies requires an understanding of stakeholders.[63] A good approach is to first identify the category of stakeholder using Model 1.1. Next, specifically list subgroups by name. For example, which competitors, suppliers, societal interest groups, or government agencies are interested, or have a stake, in the identified issue? If the issue is in life cycle stages 1 or 2, it is not as easy to identify the strategic stakeholders that are critically affected by or that can affect firm performance, as it is in stages 3–5.

Identify Strategic Stakeholders that Are For and Against the Firm. The second part of strategic stakeholder interest is determining which stakeholders can benefit through opportunities the issue presents, and which stakeholders can lose something through the threat of the issue, Will the specific strategic stakeholders be for or against the firm's stance on the issue? For example, if the **Food and Drug Administration (FDA)** wants to make it more difficult for pharmaceutical companies to bring new drugs to the market, several specific societal interest groups and public sentiment may be in favor of the FDA's efforts. However, the industry competitors will be against it, and will likely use the help of industry associations and/or form a coalition to fight new regulations. Business needs to determine which stakeholders it is up against and which stakeholders may support it.

Interest of Strategic Stakeholders Questions. The two questions you must answer are: (1) Who are the specific strategic stakeholders and will they be for or against your firm's stance on the issue?; (2) What do they have to gain or lose by helping or opposing your business? Once you have identified the interested strategic stakeholders, and whether they may help or hurt the business with regard to the issue, the next step is to identify each one's incentive to take action on the issue. If you are doing a case analysis using the Table in the Appendix, this second I analysis goes in column 2. Don't forget to use Model 1.1.

Personal and Professional Applications

9. Select a business issue and list the strategic stakeholders and their interests.

3. Incentive of Stakeholders

Even within the business, society, and government categories, different stakeholders can have different expectations, concerns, and requests for firm action to meet their special interest. Thus, you want to determine stakeholder legitimacy, power, and urgency and the likelihood of their taking action to help or oppose the business on the issue.

Legitimacy. What is the firm's responsibility to the stakeholder, and what is appropriate strategic action based on the issue? Regardless of the stakeholder group's legitimacy, the business's decision is often based on stakeholder power and situational urgency.

Power. If stakeholders do take action against the business, how much pressure can they exert? Can stakeholders really affect the performance of the firm? Or if stakeholders do take action to help the business with an issue, how much can they really contribute? Power is more important than legitimacy, because even if you believe stakeholders' issues are not legitimate, if they can hurt or help the firm, the firm needs to take action.

Urgency. If the issue is legitimate and the stakeholder has power, how quickly does a nonmarket strategy need to be developed and implemented? Figure 2.4 can help you answer this question. Generally, the more advanced the stage is, the more urgent the issue.

Likelihood of Stakeholder Action—Costs vs. Benefits. Although stakeholders may be legitimate and have power, the next question is whether the strategic stakeholders will take action to help or oppose the firm on the issue. One popular method in answering this question is the costs vs. benefits approach, which measures the consequences of issue action. Stakeholders weigh the costs and benefits of becoming active by taking action to help or oppose the firm, which may be a conscious or unconscious decision process. Financial incentives often drive action. Economic benefits can come from gaining something new, keeping what one has, or preventing loss, such as having to incur new costs. These benefits are strong motivators to take action, which means that the greater the benefit, the more likely the stakeholder will become active, and conversely, the greater the cost, the less likely. For large businesses, the benefits and costs can be in the millions of dollars. See Figure 2.5 for a list of stakeholders with their incentive measure of costs vs. benefits and powers. (Note that the stakeholders are presented in Model 1.1, p. 5.)

Potential Action, Consequences, and Preferences. Once you have determined the stakeholders that most likely will take action, the next question is what action they will take. Figure 2.5's last column, Power, lists the actions each stakeholder group might take. These stakeholder strategies will be explained throughout the book. You need to determine the consequences of potential alternative courses of action and the preferences of those stakeholders that are concerned about the issue.

Thus, putting the first three Is together, *strategic stakeholders with incentives can benefit or be hurt by the issue, will be for or against the firm's position on the issue, or may have an incentive (benefit greater than the cost) and will most likely take action to help or oppose the firm on an issue.* Thus, if the cost is greater than the benefit of taking action on an issue, stakeholders do not have an incentive to do so, and nonmarket strategic action may not be needed with these stakeholders.

Stakeholder	Incentive—Measure of Costs vs. Benefits	Power—Strategic Action Stakeholder Might Take
Market Environment		
Stockholders	Sales and profits	Vote for board of directors
	Fair return on investment— dividends	Pressure board and managers
	Increased value of stock	
Managers/ Employees	Compensation (wages and benefits)	Union/collective bargaining
		Work slow down—call in sick
	Job security and opportunities	Strike
	Working conditions	
Customers	Price	Buy from competitors
	Quality	Boycott if products or policies
	Safety	don't meet expectations
Suppliers	Gain, or lose, sales to firm	Provide needed products
	Payment, in full and timely	Refuse to sell to firm
	Relationship, ethical	Slow down delivery
		Sell to competitors
Competitors	May face same issue	Complain to regulators
	Fair competitive practices	File lawsuits
Nonmarket Society Environment		
Societal Interest Group	Monitor firm to ensure compliance with its interest	Picketing
		Organize demonstrations and rallies
		Boycott
		Appeal to press
		Appeal to government
		File law suits
Business Associations	Provide research and information	Provide staff and resource help
		Provide political and legal help
Community and Consumerism	Business creation of value	People are part of other stakeholder group power
	Not hurting environment	
News Media	Inform community of issues	Provide positive news coverage
	Shape public sentiment	Provide negative news coverage
	Shape nonmarket agenda	
Nonmarket Government Environment		
Legislative	Make the laws to help business and society	Make firm practices legal (can do) or illegal (can't do)
Executive	Enforce laws	Tell firm what practices it can and can't perform and make firm comply
	Make and enforce regulations to help business and society	
		Can close down business
Judicial	Interpret the law	Can change laws
	Determine litigation outcome	Decide who wins lawsuits

▪ **Figure 2.5:** Stakeholder Incentives and Powers

This process is relatively easy if the business only has one issue with only one stakeholder. Business situations, however, may involve many issues and are usually more complex due to multiple stakeholders who often have differing interests and conflicting incentives and therefore may make incompatible requests of the firm. Businesses need to know what stakeholders want, what action they might take to pressure the firm to give it to them, and what the consequences are to the firm if it does not meet the stakeholders' requests.

Incentive of Stakeholders Questions. The questions for managers include: Are the stakeholders' interests legitimate? Do the stakeholders have power? Is action urgent? At that point, the ultimate questions become Will the stakeholders take action to help or oppose the business on the issue? and, If so, what action might they take? The business must consequently conduct its own costs vs. benefits analysis to predict which stakeholders will become active and take action on the issue. Another consideration is whether stakeholders will join together to form a coalition to help or hurt the business. Nonmarket strategies must be developed and implemented for the stakeholders that have higher benefit/cost ratios and will more likely take action on the issue. If you are doing a case analysis using the Table in the Appendix, this third I analysis goes in column 3. First, be sure to state what the firm can gain or lose. Secondly, state whether the benefit is greater than the cost (B >C), or if C >B, which means the firm will, or will not, get involved to help or oppose the firm.

Personal and Professional Applications

10. Using the stakeholders from application 9, identify their incentives and power.

---

4. Information—Objectives

The fourth I is information. *Information* is what people know or believe about the issue and the forces affecting the issue's development. To this point, we have used information to determine what the issue is, who the strategic stakeholders are, and what incentives and strategic action the stakeholders are likely to take. The information we are now considering is used to present the business's side of the issue to stakeholders. Before presenting the business's side of the issue, however, you should write objectives.

Objectives. Without an objective, how do you know what you want to accomplish and whether you have achieved it? *Objectives state the end result the business wants to achieve in trying to create value for the stakeholders of the issue.* Writing objectives clarifies what you want to accomplish for the business, and using the writing objectives model helps you write effective objectives to deal successfully with the business issue.

The *writing objectives model* is: *To + action verb + singular, specific, and measurable result to be achieved + target date.* The action verb specifies the end result, such as to "increase" sales, "decrease" cost, or "stop" the strike. Singular means only one end result should be in the objective, or have a new objective for each result you want to achieve. Specific means to state things quantitatively, whenever possible, such as to increase sales by $100,000 and to decrease costs by $50,000. Measurable means that you have a system or process of determining whether you achieved the end result. If your objective for this course is to learn a lot, how do you know if you did? If your objective is to get an A in the course, you'll find out if you met that objective by examining your end-of-semester transcript. The target date tells you at what point you should accomplish the objective. Remember to try to create value for stakeholders when writing objectives.

For example, your course objective would be, "To receive an A in Business, Government, and Society at the end of this Fall 20XX semester." A business objective could be, "To end the strike by midnight July 24, 20XX."In some cases, objectives are ongoing and don't require a date. For example, to keep reject rates to fewer than 2 percent, or to prevent a strike.

Personal and Professional Applications

11. Write at least five personal (i.e., school, diet, health, exercise) and professional (job/career) objectives using the writing objectives model.

12. Select a business issue and write the firm's objective using the writing objectives model.

Information. Now that you have a written objective for an issue, you need information to back it up or help you meet it. Let's discuss how to classify information, the difference between primary and secondary information, what supportive information is, and what information strategies entail, and how to present the business side of the issue.

Classifying Information: Facts, Assumptions, and Sentiments. Information can be classified as facts, assumptions, or sentiments. These classifications are critical for both understanding the issues surrounding a particular business situation (the foundation of a case summary) as well as for providing information that supports a business's nonmarket strategies. Data can be broken down into facts and assumptions and sentiments (feelings derived from facts and assumptions).

Facts. A fact can be proven, whereas an assumption can't. Good PA management is based on facts. Therefore, when analyzing a situation, in order to assert that a piece of information is a fact, you need to examine the source of the information and whether the information can be confirmed from another source. Unfortunately, although facts can be proven, some people will not believe facts due to their biased perception of the information because it doesn't support what they want to hear.

The process starts with examining the source of the information. You first need to determine whether this source is a *strategic stakeholder, a stakeholder, or a disinterested party*. It is usually understood that the more disinterested the party, the more factual the information is from that party, such as an outside source who is an expert on the issue.

Second, once the source of the information has been identified and its level of interest in the business situation determined, its *reputation for veracity and accuracy* must be examined. **The *New York Times* (NYT)** slogan is "all the news that's fit to print," yet even the NYT has come under attack on numerous occasions for being a "liberal" newspaper.[64] Although no source of information is truly objective or always accurate, some sources of information can be considered better than others. An article published in the NYT certainly would be considered far more factual in nature than an article published in ***People*** magazine; both would be deemed more factual than gossip heard at the local barber's shop. As a rule of thumb—always try to determine the relative expertise of the source of information (high, medium, low).

Third, use *data triangulation*—confirming the information presented through a second source of information. The more sources you can locate that present the same data, the more probable the data are factual in nature, especially if the data come from sources with differing interests and agendas. Make sure to determine both the interest and reputation of these sources as well. With all this information gathered about the data sources, you can then make a determination as to whether the information is factual. Figure 2.6 outlines the fact-determination process.

Information Source	Source Interest	Reputation /Expertise	Data Confirmation	Data/Fact Determination
Stakeholders with subgroups 1. Business 2. Society 3. Government	1. Strategic stakeholder 2. Stakeholder 3. Disinterested party	1. High 2. Medium 3. Low	List other sources with interest and expertise ratings	*Guaranteed Fact* Nonmarket sources, disinterested parties, high reputation, multiple sources *Probable Fact* Mixed sources, stakeholder, medium, reputation single or double source *Questionable Fact* Market source, critical stakeholder, low reputation, no confirmation

■ **Figure 2.6:** Determining Whether Information Is Factual in Nature[65]

Assumptions. If information is not a fact, it is an assumption. FreeDictionary.com defines an assumption as "the act of taking for granted . . . something taken for granted or accepted as true without proof; a supposition."[66] If information is evaluated to be at best a questionable fact, as determined using Figure 2.6, then it is an assumption. Firms or stakeholders who act on assumptions as if they were facts tend to create market inefficiencies that negatively impact the stakeholders in a situation—the old adage that when you assume, you make an "ass" out of "u" and "me" can be quite accurate.

Sentiments. Unlike facts and assumptions, sentiments are based solely on the stakeholders' *feelings* about the issue as defined by the facts and the stakeholders' assumptions. Sentiment is the driving force behind stakeholders' actions and interests. The more important the issue is to a broader segment of people, the less likely the business will be able to advance its own interests and ignore stakeholder pressure on that issue.[67]

Ironically negative sentiment (being against something) tends to be a stronger driving force than positive sentiment (being for something), partly because pain avoidance is a stronger lower-level psychological need than pleasure acquisition. Putting it another way, it is human nature to act in opposition to something rather than to support it. (To quote Groucho Marx in the film *A Day at the Races*, "Whatever it is, I'm against it.")

It is essential for business to understand the power inherent in negative sentiment. The business's first priority should be to discern which stakeholders oppose a particular situation and then to develop objectives for dealing with the opposition—in strategic language, deal with threats to the business by taking action, not by inaction, and then build your strategic alliances with supporter stakeholders. Stakeholders that have minimal sentiment toward an issue, on the other hand, will tend to take no position and may be discounted and dropped from a firm's nonmarket strategy.

A Final Word on Classification. As mentioned earlier, business will use information in order to create nonmarket and market strategies so as to ethically create a win-win situation for stakeholders. This information can now be classified into facts, assumptions, and sentiments with the understanding that business will utilize each type of information to implement the strategy and obtain the objectives.

Personal and Professional Applications

13. Select a business issue and classify the information about the issue as facts, assumptions, and sentiments.

Primary and Secondary Information. Information can be primary, you gather data yourself, or secondary, other people gather data and provide information to others. Some view primary data as data gathered for your specific interests.[68] Businesses commonly use primary information from within the firm, such as profits and number of employee accidents. Annual reports and company websites are full of their primary data. Businesses also use secondary information that can be obtained from outside sources directly and through business professional/trade associations, libraries, and over the Internet.

Supportive Information. Good *supportive information contains accurate facts and figures and is stronger when gathered or supported by outside sources.* People trust facts and figures over generalizations. For example, to say that lots of people watch our show isn't supportive. People also trust outside sources of information over inside sources. When a business references outside sources of information, it is supporting its case (e.g., saying, "According to the **Neilsen Ratings**, 100,000 viewers watch our show each week"). Here is an example of how supported information can benefit a business. The late Dr. **Atkins** started his low carbohydrate diet some 30 years ago, with some following. Dr. Atkins consistently claimed it was a healthy diet. However, researchers at **Duke University** conducted a study using facts and figures; the results of the study supported Dr. Atkins' health claims, and the diet became a fad.

Information Strategies. *Three information strategies include outside sources conducting research, getting expert testimony, and getting stakeholder support.* The more detached the business is from the generator of supportive information, the stronger the supportive information.

1. **Outside Source Research Strategy.** The federal, state (and sometimes local) governments, conduct research studies and financially support others to conduct studies, such as the U.S. Census. *Professional and trade associations* also provide information to members, who pay membership fees and sometimes a fee for special reports. Secondary sources often provide generic types of information, such as a review comparing all diets. Consequently, businesses sometimes hire outside specialists to conduct research studies to provide specific information relevant to them, which can be expensive. You can hire outside experts, such as university professors, lawyers, certified public accountants (CPAs), and others to conduct research for your company.

2. **Expert Testimony Strategy.** Businesses also get experts, usually for a fee, to give testimonies. For example, **Merck & Co.** retained well-known doctors to state that its painkiller drug VIOXX does not cause a patient to die. On the other hand, the stakeholder lawyer who took Merck to federal **U.S. District Court in Houston**, accusing that VIOXX did cause a patient to die, videotaped a deposition from Dr. Eric Topol, a top U.S. cardiologist, and Edward Scolnick, a former top Merck scientist, who claimed that VIOXX may lead to heart problems. Thus, you may obtain expert testimony, but you also need to be prepared to counter expert testimony against your business.

3. **Supportive Stakeholder Strategy.** Businesses also use the expertise of supportive stakeholders, usually for free. Consequently, determining who is for and against you on an issue is important. Even stakeholders who are against you on some issue may be supportive on another issue when asked. For example, when **Staples** and **Office Depot** wanted to merge, the CEO of **Office Max** went on record stating that the merger would be good for competition. As discussed, information strategies are critical to PA management.

Personal and Professional Applications
14. Describe the information strategy used by a business to achieve an objective.

The Business Side of the Issue. As you know, every issue has at least two sides. Stakeholders commonly contest an issue because they have different information supporting their side. So another important part of information strategy is to predict the information your strategic stakeholders may use against you, and to be prepared to defend your side of the issue with supportive information. Sometimes, stakeholder information is not accurate, and when the business provides its supportive information (facts), the issue is resolved or the interest demand may change.

A business develops its objectives for the issue in an attempt to create value for stakeholders. However, it is not uncommon for the business to believe its actions are legal, ethical, and appropriate, yet stakeholders don't agree. When contested, you present the business side of the issue by focusing on the information that will support that position. The stakeholder approach to business does not mean that you give a balanced presentation supporting the stakeholder against you. Think of it like a court case or a debate. Your lawyer or your side of the debate presents only your position, while trying to discredit others' information, in an effort to persuade the listeners (judge and jury) that your position has the most merit.

Objective and Information Questions. The questions for managers are: What do we want to accomplish, or what is our objective?, What are the facts, assumptions, and sentiments regarding the issue, interest, and incentives?, and What supportive information should we get to present our side of the issue? When dealing with the government, a key message is that your business creates jobs—that's a story that needs to be told.[69] When analyzing cases, be sure to look for supportive information for and against the business you are analyzing and use it to defend/oppose the firm's side of the issue. If you are doing a case analysis using the Table in the Appendix, this fourth I analysis goes in column 4.

5. Interaction Strategies

The reason for strategic analysis is to formulate and implement strategies, which reflect a stakeholder orientation.[70] Based on your analysis of the issue, the interest and incentives of stakeholders, and on having set objectives, with information supportive of your side of the issue, it's time to develop strategies to deal with the issue—the fifth I. PA managers formulate nonmarket strategies that must be integrated with market strategies to coordinate social issues and business goals. *Developing interaction strategies includes generating alternative strategies to meet the objective, forecasting the market and nonmarket reactions and consequences of each alternative, selecting strategies, and implementing and evaluating strategies.*

Generate Alternative Strategies to Meet the Objective. Here you want to be creative and brainstorm several ways to meet the objective. When brainstorming, the major rule is *not* to evaluate the alternatives as you develop them. Just list any strategy that can be used to meet the objective. For a list of nonmarket strategies that may be used, see Figure 1.4 (on p. 22), which includes information strategies. If you are doing a case analysis using the Table in the Appendix, this fifth I analysis goes in column 5 on the second page.

Forecast the Market and Nonmarket Reactions and the Consequences of Each Alternative. Now you evaluate each alternative to estimate public sentiment, or how the market and the nonmarket stakeholders will react if the business takes the strategic action. A simple method is to classify the reaction as being positive, neutral, or negative (+, =, –); the stakeholders are expected to like the action, not care one way or the other, or not like the action. If the anticipated reaction is not going to be positive, the business will need to deal with the opposition. If you are doing a case analysis using the Table in the Appendix, this fifth I analysis part 2 goes in columns 6 and 7.

Philip Morris Case Question 6: What are the market reaction and consequences of PM's nonmarket strategy of continuing to directly fight lawsuits in the courts and in the news media?

The confrontational approach employed by PM has, at least to the current point in time, deflated the price of the stock. The stock is still considered undervalued and a good buy, yet many investors are hesitant to purchase the stock given the inherent risks associated with continuing court battles and the most recent statements made by the CEO. Only time will tell whether mutual funds managers and individual investors will shake off their hesitancy about this stock or whether the analysts' prediction of a rosier future comes to pass.

Select Strategies. After generating and analyzing each alternative, the next thing to do is select the most feasible alternative or combination of alternatives that will meet the business objective for the issue. When selecting alternatives, it is important to make sure that the alternatives are legal and, in your opinion, ethical; if they are not, don't select them. You also need to consider the power of the stakeholders involved with each strategy. If the stakeholder is powerful, you may need to select some alternative to meet the firm's objective and appease the stakeholder. Strategies should also be consistent with the company's policies, procedures, and rules. Your three select options are: yes, no, or wait. If yes, you go on to develop a strategic plan, and, if no, you don't. Selecting to wait is a contingency plan, with what-if scenarios. For example, wait and see if you get sued, and if so settle. If you are doing a case analysis using the Table in the Appendix, this fifth I analysis part 3 goes in column 8.

Plan, Implement, and Evaluate Strategies. After selecting strategies, you need to develop strategic plans to achieve the objective. Then, you implement the strategies. When determining the time frame of strategy implementation, the more details you can provide in your planning, the better off you are. If you are doing a case analysis using the Table in the Appendix, this fifth I analysis part 4 goes in column 9.

The last part of the strategic analysis is to evaluate the strategy implementation. PA professionals are responsible for evaluating progress in developing and implementing issues management strategies. However, no universal approach to evaluation is available. Most businesses view their issues or environment as unique, calling for their own assessment approach. However, PA managers should base their methods of evaluation on best practices of other firms. Also, evaluation is usually not possible when completing case studies because the focus is on developing "your" strategic plan, not evaluating it after its implementation. However, an evaluation plan should be discussed as part of the implementation plan. If the strategy is successful, the issue should be resolved. If not, you may have to return to prior stages. Strategies also need to change over time, as discussed in the section on the nonmarket issues life cycle.

You may need to redefine the issue, interest, and incentives; change objectives; get more information or change information strategies; reassess market and nonmarket reactions and consequences; select new strategies; or do a better job of implementing strategies. And when you change strategies, you need to assess their success at achieving the objective.

Interaction Strategies Questions. Interaction strategies questions include: (1) What alternatives are there to meet the objective?; (2) What will be the market and nonmarket reaction and consequences of each alternative?; (3) What strategies should we select?; and (4) How do we plan, implement, and evaluate them?

See Figure 2.7 for a review of the 5 Is strategic analysis steps. Note that although the process includes five stages, the analysis is not simply linear; in other words, you may work on multiple stages at the same time and return to any stage at any time.

Where Do We Go From Here? The 5 Is strategic analysis is the model to use when analyzing business issues to determine how to strategically deal with stakeholders. However, the rest of this book provides you with more details on how different issues and various strategic stakeholders require different strategies. The other chapters in the "Business" section of the book (Chapters 3 and 4) focuses on employee and owner stakeholders and how firms can be ethical and socially responsible. The "Society" section of the book (Chapters 5–7) focuses on community, consumerism, news media, and societal interest group stakeholders. The "Government" section of the book (Chapters 8–10) focuses on dealing with the three branches of government. The last section of the book

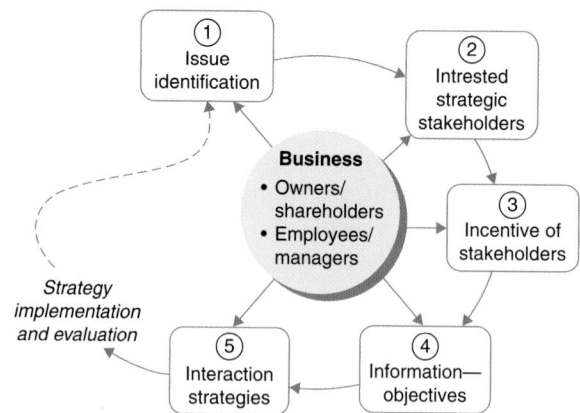

Figure 2.7: The 5 Is Strategic Analysis Steps

(Chapters 11–12) focuses on global stakeholders and technological and natural environmental stakeholders.

Case Studies. The case studies in each chapter give you the opportunity to develop your critical thinking skills and your ability to successfully interact with stakeholders. We recommend reviewing this strategic analysis and applying it when conducting case studies, as directed by your professor, to develop your critical thinking skills. The Appendix includes multiple approaches to case analysis, including the 5 Is Table. You should utilize the 5 Is analysis in your personal life when thinking about business news, and in your professional life as you work and make decisions.

SUMMARY

2

SUMMARY

The chapter summary is organized to answer the learning outcomes for Chapter 2.

1. **Describe stakeholder management and the need to balance stockholder and other stakeholder interests.**
   Stakeholder management is based on attempting to make decisions on specific issues that provide value to strategic stakeholders. Managers have a responsibility to make a profit to give stockholders a return on their investment. However, at the same time they must operate in a legal and ethical manner and not take advantage of other stakeholders. Thus, managers attempt to create a win-win situation for all stakeholders.

2. **Differentiate public affairs management from issues management.**

Public affairs (PA) management is the process of developing corporate public policies and strategies regarding how the business will interact with stakeholders in the business, social, and government environments when dealing with a current issue needing nonmarket strategies; it includes issues management and crisis management. Issues management is a public affairs management approach to identifying, monitoring, analyzing, and selecting public issues that may warrant nonmarket strategies. Thus, PA management is broader in scope and provides general guidelines. It also encompasses issues management, which has a specific three-phase process for dealing with PA issues.

3. **Identify the three-phase process of issues management.**

The three phases of issues management are: (1) scanning the environment to identify issues and trends that will affect the business; (2) evaluating the impact issues will have on the firm and ranking issues by priority; and (3) conducting a strategic analysis to develop strategies for dealing with high-priority public affairs issues.

4. **Define *crisis* and discuss the four stages of crisis management, including the 3 As of crisis communication.**
   A crisis is a major unexpected event that has a large negative consequence.

The four stages of crisis management include:

1. Developing a crisis team with a mix of representatives from all sectors of the organization to deal with the crisis.
2. Conducting a risk assessment to determine potential crises, monitoring events to prevent them from becoming a crisis, and planning how to deal with a crisis if it occurs.
3. Managing the crisis by implementing the plan and communicating to: (a) *acknowledge* or admit to the crisis; (b) state the *action* you are taking to contain or repair the crisis damage; and (c) state how you plan to *avoid* a repeat crisis in the future.
4. Analyzing the organization's effectiveness in managing the crisis, with a focus on doing a better job of preventing and managing future crises.

5. **List and briefly describe the 5 Is strategic analysis.**
   The 5 Is strategic analysis stages include:

1. **Issue identification**. The business identifies issues of stakeholders who want the firm to take some action to meet their special inter-est. The business identifies which stage of the life cycle the issue is in to determine the strategic focus.
2. **Interested strategic stakeholders**. The firm determines which specific strategic stakeholders will be for and against its stance on the issue.
3. **Incentive of stakeholders**. The business determines stakeholder: (a) legitimacy (What responsibility does the firm have to the stakeholder?), (b) power (Can the stakeholder help or hurt firm performance?); (c) urgency (Is quick action needed?); and predicts the (d) likelihood (costs vs. benefits) of their taking action, and (e) what action they will take to help or oppose the business on the issue.
4. **Information—objectives**. The firm states the end result it wants to achieve in trying to create value for the stakeholders of the issue. Information is classified as fact (can be proven), assumption (not factual), or sentiment (feelings about the issue). The firm presents its side of the issue, using information facts and figures to meet its objective through information-gaining strategies—outside sources conducting research, expert testimony, and using information of supportive stakeholders.
5. **Interaction strategies**. Developing interaction strategies involves: (a) generating alternative strategies to meet the objective; (b) forecasting the market and nonmarket reactions and the consequences of each alternative; (c) selecting strategies; and (d) implementing and evaluating strategies.

6. **Categorize the issue life-cycle stages with the strategic focus for each stage.**
   The five stages of the life cycle with their strategy focus are:

1. Identification and formation of the issue and public sentiment. *Informational* and *societal strategies* are used to influence the development of the issue.

2. Interested stakeholder formation. The focus is on *informational* and *societal strategies* including developing coalitions.

3. Issue brought to business for voluntary action. The strategic focus varies based on the *issue and who brings it to the firm.*

4. Legislative and regulation formation. *The political strategic* focus is on preventing or supporting change, primarily through lobbying.

5. Enforcement and litigation. The *legal* strategic focus is on complying with changes and avoiding or bringing lawsuits.

7. **Fill in the blanks with the appropriate key terms (in order of appearance in the chapter):**

_____ *is based on making decisions on specific issues in an ethical manner in ways that provide value to strategic stakeholders.*

_____ are critically affected by a firm's actions, and/or they can affect firm performance.

_____ refers to how business interacts with stakeholders.

_____ is the process of developing corporate public policies and strategies regarding how the business will interact with stakeholders in the business, social, and government environments; it includes issues management, crisis management, and strategic analysis.

_____ is a public affairs management approach to identifying, monitoring, analyzing, and selecting public issues that may warrant nonmarket strategies.

_____ includes: (1) scanning the environment to identify issues and trends that will affect the business; (2) evaluating the impact issues will have on the firm and ranking issues by priority; and (3) conducting a strategic analysis to develop strategies for dealing with high priority public affairs issues.

_____ is a major unexpected event that has a large negative consequence.

_____ include: (1) developing the crisis team; (2) planning; (3) managing the crisis—communication; and (4) analyzing post crisis.

_____ consist of acknowledging the crisis, stating the action to deal with the crisis, and stating how the crisis will be avoided in the future.

_____ stages include: (1) issue identification; (2) interested strategic stakeholders; (3) incentive of stakeholders; (4) information—objectives; and (5) interaction strategies.

_____ are usually brought to the company by any of its stakeholders because the firm is not meeting expectations, and the stakeholder is pressing the firm to take action to meet its special interest.

_____ includes: (1) identification and formation of the issue and public sentiment; (2) interested stakeholder formation; (3) issue brought to business for voluntary action; (4) legislative and regulation formation; and (5) enforcement and litigation.

_____ can benefit or be hurt by the issue, and will be for or against the firm's position on the issue, or may have an incentive (benefit greater than the cost) and will most likely take action to help or oppose the firm on an issue.

_____ state the end result the business wants to achieve in trying to create value for the stakeholders of the issue.

_____ follows the formula: to + action verb + singular, specific, and measurable result to be achieved + target date.

_____ contains accurate facts and figures, and is stronger when gathered, or supported by, outside sources.

_____ include outside sources conducting research, getting expert testimony, and getting stakeholder support.

_____ include generating alternative strategies to meet the objective, forecasting the market and non-market reactions and consequences of each alternative, selecting strategies, and implementing and evaluating strategies.

KEY TERMS (IN ALPHABETICAL ORDER)

3 As of crisis communication (p. 50)
5 Is strategic analysis (p. 52)
crisis (p. 47)
crisis management stages (p. 47)
information strategies (p. 48)
interaction strategies (p. 60)
issues life cycle (p. 53)
issues management (p. 45)
issues management process (p. 45)

issues to business (p. 52)
objectives (p. 57)
public affairs (PA) (p. 43)
public affairs management (p. 44)
stakeholder management (p. 41)
strategic stakeholders (p. 41)
strategic stakeholders with incentives
 supportive information (p. 60)
writing objectives model (p. 57)

REVIEW QUESTIONS

1 In the definition of strategic stakeholders, what do *critical* and *strategic* mean?

2 What is the relationship between issues management and crises management?

3 What is the difference between problems businesses face and a crisis?

4 What is the role of the crisis management team?

5 Why are the 3 As of communication so important to crisis management?

6 Why is it important for a business to know in what stage of the life cycle an issue is?

7 Why is it important for a business to understand the power of stakeholders?

8 Should a business present both the stakeholders' and its own side of the issue?

9 What is the purpose of a strategic analysis?

10 Why should generating and evaluating alternative strategies be done sequentially?

DISCUSSION/CRITICAL THINKING QUESTIONS

Be sure to give a detailed explanation for your answer to each question.

1 Is the stakeholder approach to management appropriate only for big

corporations run by professional managers? After all, professional managers, for the most part, don't take the risk of ownership. Unlike the owners, professional managers get a salary even if the business loses money. If you start your own sole proprietorship business, or already own a business, will you look out for the interest of stakeholders, rather than your own profits?

2 Will the stakeholder approach to management become more or less commonly used in the future?

3 What qualities should public affairs managers possess?

4 How can all managers incorporate public affairs into their job on a daily basis?

5 There are two primary ways to increase profits—increase revenues and decrease costs. Large corporations spend millions on public affairs activities and employees. Doesn't it make sense to dramatically reduce PA spending to increase profits?

6 Issues management is about identifying, monitoring, and analyzing trends and issues that "might" affect business, which is costly. Why not just wait until issues actually do affect the business?

7 Many large corporations spend a lot of time and resources planning to prevent crises, yet they still have crises. So is it really worth having a crises program?

8 The terrorist attack of September 11, 2001, was clearly a major national crisis. Can business, society, and government really be effective in terrorist crises management? Should business focus on terrorist crises management or leave it to the government?

9 Why is it valuable to learn how to conduct a strategic analysis, and who benefits?

APPLICATION EXERCISES 2

APPLICATION EXERCISES

For these two application exercises, try to use a business you work(ed) for or one you would like to work for.

2.1 CRISIS MANAGEMENT

Select a business that has gone through a crisis. Identify the crisis and describe how the business managed the crisis. Be sure to state its 3 As of communicating during a crisis. Could the business have done anything to prevent the crisis? If so, what? How could the business have better handled the crisis?

2.2 CONDUCTING A 5 IS STRATEGIC ANALYSIS

Select a firm that has an "issue to business" as described in the issue iden-tification section. Conduct a complete 5 Is strategic analysis for the issue. Be sure to clearly label each of the 5 Is, including the objective. In essence, you are doing your own selected case study, similar to the case studies at the end of the chapters, without case questions.

Alternative: If your professor is assigning the BSG case analysis table in the Case Analysis approaches, you should study it and follow the analysis format as per the instructor's guidelines.

Before doing a case analysis for this chapter, you may want to read Case Analysis Approaches in the Appendix for ideas on how to conduct a case analysis. Your professor may require a specific case analysis approach.

CASE 2.1

As If Your First Life Wasn't Bad Enough: Suing Your Virtual "Second Life" in Reality

Usually people go into a virtual reality game to get away from their day-to-day problems and to live a different, more care-free lifestyle. Fighting dragons (or each other), going on quests, having virtual dates, this would seem to be the formula for fun in the virtual world. Now, consider the world of Second Life where some residents have taken the game far too seriously and filed real-life lawsuits against one another for actions taken in this virtual world.

Second Life, an online virtual world created by Linden Lab, mimics real life. In this online computer game, users click to accept the Terms of Agreement, create their own avatar (called residents), and then explore the world (known as the grid) to meet other residents, socialize, participate in individual and group activities, and potentially create and trade virtual property and services with one another.[71]

An avatar named Richard Minsky filed a real lawsuit against another avatar in the game as well as two directors at Linden Labs because Keegan (the avatar being sued) opened up an art gallery in Second Life called "SLart," a name that Minsky had originally trademarked in 2008. Minsky felt that his trademark had been violated regardless of the virtual nature of the gallery in question.

Interestingly enough, Minsky's lawyer is someone he met through Second Life and has an avatar himself. Reportedly the lawyer's avatar sent Keegan's avatar a "cease and desist" order and also sent the same orders to the directors of Second Life. In his own defense, Keegan stated, "A Second Life neighbor actually living in Australia did it for me. As a logo I just put SL in capitals followed by art. I may have thought of 'SLart' around the same time as Minsky. But that doesn't matter in U.S. trademark law: who gets there first wins."[72] Since the suit, the sign was officially taken down by Second Life and the trademark was officially given to Minsky in the game's virtual reality as well. This case was considered a bench test of whether real courts can get involved in virtual world disputes.

Second Life has been in other lawsuits as well. The most recent is a class action lawsuit filed by several users accusing Linden Labs of changing the terms of virtual property ownership. Residents claimed they were forced to agree to new terms that eroded their ownership rights to virtual property and goods.[73] They claimed that the promises of ownership were empty and that the company falsely advertised these rights so that they could add new people from around the United States.

Questions:

1. How many critical issues are discussed in this case and what are they?
2. Identify the facts, assumptions, and sentiments (FAS) for each issue of the case.
3. Who are the interested stakeholders for each issue?
4. Choose one issue. What are the stakeholders' incentives?
5. As a director of Linden Labs, you have been asked to testify in court for a lawsuit similar to the ones in the case. Present an argument that can serve as a defense for Second Life.
6. What strategy would you use as director of Linden Labs for accomplishing one of your issue objectives?

CASE 2.2

Pimping a Ride with Management? Labor/Management Sex Scandals at VW

"I was just following orders." That claim, not unlike similar claims of a far more dastardly nature during the post–World War II Nuremberg Trials, emanated from another German's lips 60 years later with regard to accusations that VW asked him to arrange liaisons with prostitutes for prominent union leaders. These were not the words, however, that Dr.-Ing. e. h. Bernd Pischetsrieder, chairman of the board of management of Volkswagen (VW) AG, wanted to hear about his firm.

Klaus-Joachim Gebauer alleged that VW sent a dozen of its top German labor leaders to Brazil for a tour of the company's São Paulo facilities and meetings with local Brazilian union officials. After finishing the official portion of the trip, Gebauer said he and the other men took a bus to Rio de Janeiro and checked into a high-rise hotel on the city's famous Copacabana. Gebauer stated they then picked up prostitutes which he paid for out of his own pocket. He then got VW to reimburse him for the group's expenses for the entire trip. The Rio excursion was the first of dozens of pleasure trips to exotic locations undertaken by VW worker representatives and paid for by the automaker over a nine-year period. The trips caused a criminal investigation of illegally used company funds to pay for top labor leaders to go on junkets involving posh hotels, call girls, and the use of a company plane. Gebauer claimed he was given blanket instructions by his boss to use the trips to garner worker representatives' support for VW management.[74]

VW's initial response to such charges was to attack Gebauer's credibility and fire him for embezzling company funds and seeking kickbacks from potential VW business partners before he blew the whistle on the firm. Gebauer of course denied the charges. In response to these claims VW indicated that "we treat with caution any statements concerning these incidents solely made by a former employee who was dismissed without notice on the grounds of personal enrichment."

After firing Gebauer and another manager for allegedly seeking kickbacks, VW asked the accounting firm KPMG LLP to investigate the abuse of traveling expenses and other expenses at the company. VW then disclosed the auditors' findings, acknowledging it paid about $740,000 to Adriana Barros,[75] an acquaintance of VW's former top labor leader Klaus Volkert, for services that were not appropriate. She was also flown between Brazil and Germany several times using money from VW. The German court charged Barros with "26 counts of being an accessory to breach of trust."[76] The company then acknowledged that "the necessary control systems" for catching improper expenses "were not in place."[77]

Questions:

1. Evaluate VW's actions in handling this crisis by applying the four stages of crisis management to this case situation. What should VW have or have not done in reaction to these allegations?

2. Which stakeholders should Pischetsrieder have contacted when this problem was first uncovered? Why?

3. Firing Gebauer set off a chain of uncontrollable events. What alternatives were available to Pischetsrieder, and why should he and the board have taken them?

4. Assuming that Gebauer was to be fired, apply the 3 As of crisis communication to this situation. Which stakeholders should Pischetsrieder have contacted directly once the decision was made?

5. The union also seems to have some culpability in this situation. How would you handle this crisis from the union's perspective?

INTEGRATIVE CASE (Part 2)

Much Ado about Nothing?

This is a continuation case—please refer back to Chapter 1 and the case entitled "We Have Met the Enemy and the Enemy Is Us!" for further information.

Stephen Hodgetts looked like he had blown a gasket after his colleague, Richard Davis, proposed that they become landlords, or worse slumlords, in order to increase the value of their retirement accounts through real estate investing. Davis knew that although Hodgetts was an overly emotional individual, that there might be more going on than just his knee-jerk reaction to Davis's proposal, especially since Davis had not even been given the opportunity to explain the details of his plan. However, Davis was not going to get the chance to ask Hodgetts about his negative reaction for it was clear that Hodgetts was on a roll. Davis knew from prior experiences working with the Hodgetts that the best thing to do was to sit back and wait for Hodgetts to get it out of his system.

"My dear Richard," continued Hodgetts in his most sarcastic tone, "I could just picture it now. We're at a meeting, or even better, a party, and of course some of our colleagues might be wondering to one another, perhaps even aloud, what are we up to, and no, more specifically, what you've been up to since you seem to be spending most of your time off-campus. They might think, oh that Davis has finally decided to take it easier in his old age and perhaps he is gearing down for his retirement by taking a more leisurely approach to academia. Let's ask him and see what he's been up to."

"They ask you where you've been and what you've been doing with yourself lately, perhaps hoping for a little scandalous gossip they can spread just for the fun of it, when low and behold you tell them outright about our little business venture. They are shocked to find out that their admired associate has not only taken on a business enterprise while remaining a full-time faculty member but that he is in the business of renting homes to people with bad credit ratings, those who probably could not obtain either a mortgage or another rental—that he's become a slumlord! And you are not alone in this fiendish adventure, that Hodgetts is your partner in this devilish crime!"

"Hodgetts, please, do not over dramatize the situation. So what if a few of our so-called esteemed contemporaries are taken somewhat aback by our little business venture? Their reaction will probably be more out of jealousy than actual shock at us being landlords. We're certainly not hurting anyone, unquestionably helping ourselves, and hopefully serving our renters as well. This venture can yield us a very handsome profit while providing a needed service to a portion of our community. What is the crime in that?"

"I'll tell you what the crime will be," fumed Hodgetts. "The moment one of our beloved renters cannot or does not pay the rent what are we going to do? Are we going to evict our poor unfortunate renter, who undoubtedly will have no other place to go but the streets since no one else will rent a home to this person? If we decide not to evict and let the renter stay in the house, then why be in business at all, to lose money?"

"And if we do decide to evict, which we will have to eventually do with a deadbeat renter, could you imagine what would happen if the newspapers ever got hold of the story? You know how the media loves to hate landlords. I can see the local headlines now, 'Scrooge is alive and well and college professors Davis and Hodgetts evict downtrodden family.' And what if the student paper ran this story? What would our students, administration, fellow faculty, friends, and family think of us then? Worse, what if the local television station decided to run this as a human interest story? Or a major paper like the *New York Times* or the *Wall Street Journal* picked up on the story, or a television show like *60 Minutes* thought the situation deserved some air time? What would this publicity do to our business as well as our reputations within the academic and local communities?"

Questions:

1. Which approach, stockholder or stakeholder, do Davis and Hodgetts seem to be taking in this case?

2. What is the critical issue that Hodgetts is worried about as it relates to the business proposed by Davis?

3. How does Hodgetts see this critical issue as becoming a potential crisis?

4. If you were Davis, how would you respond to Hodgetts' fear of a potential crisis?

5. Develop a proactive crisis management plan for dealing with Hodgetts' potential crisis, using the 3 As of communication.

REFERENCES AND NOTES

REFERENCES AND NOTES

2

1 R. F. Hartley, Management Mistakes and Successes, 8th ed. (New York: John Wiley & Sons, 2005).

2 V. O'Connell, "Future of Altria Hangs on Ruling in Tobacco Suit," Wall Street Journal (December 14, 2005): B1.

3 G. Zuckerman, "Altria Soars, Doubters Say: 'D'oh!'" Wall Street Journal (December 16, 2005): C1.

4 W. Civils and P. Lattman "Analysts React to Altria Ruling," Wall Street Journal (December 15, 2005). http://online.wsj.com/article/SB113466843615923619.html?mod=us_business_whats_news.

5 V. O'Connell, "Philip Morris Gets Big Legal Victory," Wall Street Journal (December 16, 2005): A3.

6 L. Salahi, "Philip Morris CEO: Smoking 'Not That Hard' to Quit," ABC News (May 12, 2011). http://abcnews.go.com/Health/Wellness/philip-morris-ceo-smoking-hard-quit/story?id=13589835#.T3lLzGFAu8A.

7 A. Armenakis and J. Wigand, "Stakeholder Actions and Their Impact on the Organizational Cultures of Two Tobacco Companies," Business and Society Review 115(2) (2010): 147–171.

8 M. Van Huijstee, and P. Glasbergen, "NGOs Moving Business: An Analysis of Contrasting Strategies," Business & Society 49(4) (2010): 591–618.

9 R. G. Castro, M. A. Ariño, and M. A. Canela, "Over the Long-Run? Short-Run Impact and Long-Run Consequences of Stakeholder Management," Business & Society 50(3) (2011): 428–455.

10 P. C. Godfrey, N. W. Hatch, and J. M. Hansen, "Toward a General Theory of CSRs: The Roles of Beneficence, Profitability, Insurance, and Industry Heterogeneity," Business & Society 49(2) (2010): 316–344.

11 S. Sorenson, J. E. Mattingly, and F. K. Lee, "Decoding the Signal Effects of Job Candidate Attraction to Corporate Social Practices," Business and Society Review 115(2) (2010): 173–204.

12 H. J. Van Buren III, "Taking (and Sharing Power): How Boards of Directors Can Bring About Greater Fairness for Dependent Stakeholders," Business and Society Review 115 (2010): 205–230.

13 J. P. Walsh, "Taking Stock of Stakeholder Management," Academy of Management Review 30(2) (April 2005): 426–439.

14 J. Wei-Skillern, "The Evolution of Shell's Stakeholder Approach: A Case Study," Business Ethics Quarterly 14(4) (October 2004): 713–729.

15 B. Dyck, K. Walker, F. Starke, and K. Uggerslev, "Addressing Concerns Raised by Critics of Business Schools by Teaching Multiple Approaches to Management," Business and Society Review 116(1) (2011): 1–27.

16 C. H. Amato and L. H. Amato, "Corporate Commitment to Global Quality of Life Issues: Do Slack Resources, Industry Affiliations, and Multinational Headquarters Matter?" Business & Society 50(2) (2011): 388–416.

17 M. D. P. Lee, "Configuration of External Influences: The Combined Effects of Institutions and Stakeholders on Corporate Social Responsibility Strategies," Journal of Business Ethics 102(2) (2011): 281–298.

18 B. Dyck, K. Walker, F. Starke, and K. Uggerslev, "Addressing Concerns Raised by Critics of Business Schools by Teaching Multiple Approaches to Management," Business and Society Review 116(1) (2011): 1–27.

19 C. Walker, "Long-Term Outlook: Corporations in the Dow Jones Sustainability Indexes Reflect on How They Rely on Sustainable Strategies to Boost Performance and Generate Growth for Investors Over Time," Research 28 (May 2005): 80–82.

20 S. Vranica, "Public Relations Learned the Hard Way," Wall Street Journal (December 30, 2010): B6.

21 N. I. Torres, "Dealing with a PR Disaster," Entrepreneur (February 2009): 70.

22 A. Armenakis and J. Wigand, "Stakeholder Actions and Their Impact on the Organizational Cultures of Two Tobacco Companies," Business and Society Review 115(2) (2010): 147–171.

23 The Public Affairs Council, www.pac.org (accessed October 27, 2011).

24 J. P. Bonardi, M. J. Hillman, and G. D. Keim, "The Attractiveness of Political Markets: Implications for Firm Strategy," Academy of Management Review 30(2) (2005): 397–413.

25 S. Vranica, "Public Relations Learned the Hard Way," Wall Street Journal (December 30, 2010): B6.

26 N. I. Torres, "Dealing with a PR Disaster," Entrepreneur (February 2009): 70.

27 "Analysis: The Blogosphere—Google Carves New Path by Blogging to Confront Issues," PR Week (October 10, 2005): 11.

28 G. Colvin, "What Makes a CEO an MPV?" Fortune (June 13, 2011): 27.

29 B. George, "How Do I Keep My Company's Reputation Intact When Our Industry Has Been Tainted by Bad News?" Fortune (March 16, 2009): 30.

30 B. O'Connor, "Donor Profile," Salem Statement (Fall 2011): 8.

31 J. Collins, "How Great Companies Turn Crisis into Opportunity," Fortune (2009): 49–52.

32 A. Lobb, A. Dizik, and J. Porter, "Lessons That Fit the Times," Wall Street Journal (August 20, 2009): B5.

33 E. Holm, "Got a Crisis? Tap AIG," Wall Street Journal (October 12, 2011): C1.

34 http://subscriber.hoovers.com.cwplib.proxy.liu.edu/H/company360/financialSummary.html?companyId=10021000000000.

35 M. De La Merced, "American Airlines Par-

ent Files for Bankruptcy," New York Times (November 29, 2011). http://dealbook.nytimes.com/2011/11/29/american-airlines-parent-files-for-bankruptcy.

36 A. Bender, "American Airlines' Bankruptcy: Who Loses?" Forbes (November 29, 2011).http://www.forbes.com/sites/andrewbender/2011/11/29/american-airlines-bankruptcy-who-loses/.

37 H. Yousuf, "American Airlines CEO: 'We're Facing a Fuel Crisis,'" CNN Money (April 8, 2011). http://money.cnn.com/2011/04/08/news/economy/American_Airlines_fuel_crisis/index.htm.

38 V. M. Desai, "Mass Media and Massive Failures: Determining Organizational Efforts to Defend Field Legitimacy Following Crises," Academy of Management Journal 54(2) (2011): 263–278.

39 M. Rhee and M. E. Valdez, "Contextual Factors Surrounding Reputation Damage with Potential Implications for Reputation Repair," Academy of Management Journal 34(1) (2009): 146–168.

40 S. Vranica, "Public Relations Learned the Hard Way," Wall Street Journal (December 30, 2010): B6.

41 This section primarily adapted from L. Barton, Crisis in Organizations, 6th ed. (Mason, OH: South-Western/Cengage, 2010).

42 B. George, "How Do I Keep My Company's Reputation Intact When Our Industry Has Been Tainted by Bad News?" Fortune (March 16, 2009): 30.

43 G. Colvin, "What Makes a CEO an MPV?" Fortune (June 13, 2011): 27.

44 C. Wilson, "How Do I Keep My Company's Reputation Intact When Our Industry Has Been Tainted by Bad News?" Fortune (March 16, 2009): 30.

45 M. Rhee and M. E. Valdez, "Contextual Factors Surrounding Reputation Damage with Potential Implications for Reputation Repair," Academy of Management Journal 34(1) (2009): 146–168.

46 D. Foust, "US Airways: After the Miracle on the Hudson," BusinessWeek (March 2, 2009): 31–32.

47 D. Foust, "US Airways: After the Miracle on the Hudson," BusinessWeek (March 2, 2009): 31–32.

48 M. D. Groza, M. R. Pronschinkse, and M. Walker, "Perceived Organizational Motives and Consumer Responses to Proactive and Reactive CSR," Journal of Business Ethics 102(4) (2010): 639–652.

49 S. Vranica, "Public Relations Learned the Hard Way," Wall Street Journal (December 30, 2010): B6.

50 E. Dezenhall, "How Do I Keep My Company's Reputation Intact When Our Industry Has Been Tainted by Bad News?" Fortune (March 16, 2009): 30.

51 M. Penn, "Handle a Crisis," BusinessWeek (September 26–October 2, 2011): 104.

52 N. I. Torres, "Dealing with a PR Disaster," Entrepreneur (February 2009): 70.

53 E. Dezenhall, "How Do I Keep My Company's Reputation Intact When Our Industry Has Been Tainted by Bad News?" Fortune (March 16, 2009): 30.

54 P. M. Barrett, "Success Is Never Having to Say You're Sorry," BusinessWeek (July 4–10, 2011): 52–61.

55 S. Vranica, "Public Relations Learned the Hard Way," Wall Street Journal (December 30, 2010): B6

56 D. Foust, "US Airways: After the Miracle on the Hudson," BusinessWeek (March 2, 2009): 31–32.

57 M. Penn, "Handle a Crisis," BusinessWeek (September 26–October 2, 2011): 104.

58 http://ww5.komen.org/AboutUs/AboutUs.html (accessed March 27, 2012).

59 http://www.cbsnews.com/8301-503544_162-57370867-503544/backlash-grows-over-susan-g-komen-planned-parenthood-flap/ (accessed March 27, 2012).

60 C. H. Amato and L. H. Amato, "Corporate Commitment to Global Quality of Life Issues: Do Slack Resources, Industry Affiliations, and Multinational Headquarters Matter?" Business & Society 50(2) (2011): 388–416.

61 M. D. P. Lee, "Configuration of External Influences: The Combined Effects of Institutions and Stakeholders on Corporate Social Responsibility Strategies," Journal of Business Ethics 102(2) (2011): 281–298.

62 M. D. P. Lee, "Configuration of External Influences: The Combined Effects of Institutions and Stakeholders on Corporate Social Responsibility Strategies," Journal of Business Ethics 102(2) (2011): 281–298.

63 M. Rhee and M. E. Valdez, "Contextual Factors Surrounding Reputation Damage with Potential Implications for Reputation Repair," Academy of Management Journal 34(1) (2009): 146–168.

64 http://www.fair.org/index.php (accessed November 11, 2011).

65 Adapted from H. Sherman, "A Model of Communication Processing," in E. Bewayo, J. Cross, B. Kaplan, C. Rodrigues, and H. Sherman (eds.), Selected Readings in Management Process & Organizational Behavior, 2nd ed. (Boston: Ginn Press, 1985).

66 http://www.thefreedictionary.com/assumption (accessed November 11, 2011).

67 M. D. P. Lee, "Configuration of External Influences: The Combined Effects of Institutions and Stakeholders on Corporate Social Responsibility Strategies," Journal of Business Ethics 102(2) (2011): 281–298.

68 Suggestion made by reviewer Professor William Matthews, William Patterson University, (July 24, 2012).

69 N. Easton and T. Demos, "The Business Guide to Congress," Fortune (May 11, 2009): 72–75.

70 A. Armenakis and J. Wigand, "Stakeholder Actions and Their Impact on the Organizational Cultures of Two Tobacco Companies," Business and Society Review 115(2) (2010): 147–171.

71 http://en.wikipedia.org/wiki/Second_Life.

72 U. Khan, "Second Life Lawsuit to Test How Much Jurisdiction Courts Have Over Virtual World." The Telegraph (November 25, 2008). http://www.telegraph.co.uk/technology/3517319/Second-Life-lawsuit-to-test-how-much-jurisdiction-courts-have-over-virtual-world.html.

73 C. McCarthy, "Class Action Lawsuit Targets Second Life," CNET (May 3, 2010). http://news.cnet.com/8301-13577_3-20004004-36.html.

74 S. Power and M. Karnitschnig, "VW's Woes Mount Amid Claims of Sex Junkets for Union Chiefs," Wall Street Journal (November 17, 2005): A1.

75 B. Schmitt. "Volkswagen Sex Scandal, Revisited," The Truth About Cars (March 16, 2012). http://www.thetruthaboutcars.com/2012/03/volkswagen-sex-scandal-revisited/.

76 Associated Press, "Ex-lover of Key Figure in VW Scandal Faces Trial," CBS News (March 15, 2012). http://www.cbsnews.com/8301-505245_162-57397923/ex-lover-of-key-figure-in-vw-scandal-faces-trial/

77 Ibid.

Chapter 3

EMPLOYEES, STOCKHOLDERS, AND CORPORATE GOVERNANCE

Learning Outcomes

In this chapter, you will find out the answers to these key questions:

■ What is the employer–employee relationship like, how does it differ in unionized firms, and what rights do employees have?
■ What rights do stockholders have and how are corporations governed?

After studying this chapter, you should be able to:

1. Analyze old and new employment relationship differences
2. Compare and contrast employment contracts in union and nonunion organizations
3. List and briefly describe six employee rights, in addition to organizing and collective bargaining
4. Compare and contrast mediators, arbitrators, and ombuds
5. Define corporate stakeholders and describe their primary power
6. Explain how the government helps to protect stockholders
7. Differentiate between inside and outside members of the board of directors and the potential problem of insiders
8. Define the following key terms (in order of appearance in the chapter):

employment relationship	employee rights	corporate charter
labor union	employment-at-will	stockholders
collective bargaining	due process	boards of directors
mediator	ombuds	insider trading
arbitrator	privacy rights	Sarbanes-Oxley Act
	whistleblowing	shareholder resolutions
		corporate governance
		inside directors
		stock option

■ Chapter Outline

What's This Chapter About?

The first two chapters focused on the external environment stakeholders. This chapter focuses on the internal environmental stakeholders: employees, stockholder/owners, and managers.

We begin with a section describing employer–employee relations, followed by a section discussing unionized employees, with the third section describing the rights of all employees.

In the fourth section you will learn about how and why professional managers run the company for the stockholders. The fifth section presents the role of the board of directors and how it governs the corporation. The board is responsible for guarding the stockholders' interests while setting policies that affect employees and managers.

Our last section discusses the strategies presented in Chapter 1, Figure 1.4 (p. 22), describing which strategies are generally used to deal with employee and stockholder issues.

Putting it all together, owners, employees/managers, and stockholders are strategic stakeholders. Business can't exist without owners and employees. Management's role is to formulate and implement strategies to achieve the firm's mission and objectives, and they do so through the corporate governance structure.

CASE

North Fork Bancorp: Getting Rich by Selling the Bank (and Selling Out the Employees)

North Fork Bancorporation, Inc., a regional bank holding company, started on the North Fork of eastern Long Island, was acquired by Capital One Financial Corporation, which operates as the holding company for North Fork Bank.[1] Prior to its acquisition, North Fork had more than doubled its total assets, expanding its operation to include the New York metropolitan area and becoming one of the 20 largest banking organizations in the United States.[2] John Kanas, then president of North Fork Bancorp, and the board of directors had a difficult decision to make when approached by Capital One to sell the bank. Should they sell to Capital One, which would net their stockholders a 20+ percent increase in the value of their stock, or should they forgo this sale and continue to follow their strategic plan? Kanas believed the acquisition by Capital One would result in layoffs at North Fork, largely amongst the ranks of the bank's 1,300 back-office staff. "Not all are going to get eliminated," he said.[3]

This decision seemed clouded by CEO Kanas and other executives' personal financial gain. "The top three executives at North Fork Bancorp . . . reaped at least $288 million . . . including roughly $185 million for CEO John Kanas."

"The relative size of the North Fork payouts raised eyebrows among critics of high executive pay. 'It's the highest golden parachute I've ever seen,' said Paul Hodgson, a senior research associate at the **Corporate Library**, an independent corporate-governance research organization. The North Fork payments 'appear to me at a level that would create an incentive for management to go looking for a change of control to trigger that payment.'"

Kanas defended the payouts, saying he was monetizing a life's work at a company. "I know how the story looks, and it's an egregious amount of money but it's not like I flew in here on a private jet three years ago and prettied up the company and then booted it out of here." Raymond A. Nielsen, former chairman of North Fork's compensation committee, declined to address the specifics of the payouts. "My sole comment would be I consider it to be a fair and appropriate package."[4] One can't help but wonder whether the 1,300 back-office employees who lost their jobs would agree with Nielsen's assessment of the situation.

The following questions are related to the North Fork Bancorp case. Answers can be found within the chapter.

1. How is the decision to sell North Fork affected by the employment relationship?
2. What market and nonmarket stakeholders are affected by this decision?
3. How might this decision be determined based on the old and new approaches to the employment relationship?
4. How does employment-at-will affect North Fork's decision in terms of the firm's sale?
5. How does North Fork's board justify this "golden parachute" from a stockholder's perspective?

EMPLOYER–EMPLOYEE RELATIONS

Considering the fact that most adults spend most of their daytime hours at work, it's not surprising that businesses and their employees give considerable attention to employee stakeholder status, treatment, satisfaction, and rights. In this section, we discuss the employer–employee relationship and how it affects other stakeholders, and the new employment contract.

The Employment Relationship

The primary employer–employee (employment) relationship is one of mutual benefit. Employees provide labor for the business, and employers compensate them for their work. Businesses can't operate without employees to make and deliver their goods and provide their services. Behind every business issue ultimately lies a human issue.[5] It's people who improve performance and wealth creation.[6] Thus, the employment relationship must be managed effectively so that both parties benefit, because people provide organizations with a sustained competitive advantage.[7]

Why People Work. People commonly work to meet at least three needs: (1) to obtain wages and often benefits—such as health care and retirement savings; (2) to meet social needs of friendship; and (3) to gain a sense of self-worth.[8] Generally, employees who have these three needs met—who have job satisfaction—are more productive than those who don't.[9]

Rights and Duties. With the employer–employee relationship come rights and duties for both. A *right* means that people are entitled to be treated in a certain way, whereas a *duty* is an obligation or responsibility to do something. Some duties are legal or contractual, while others are social or ethical. For example, employers are obligated to provide some measure of job security, a safe and healthy workplace, equal opportunity for all, and to pay at least the legal minimum wage. Employees have duties to come to work on time and to provide a full day's work, not to use business resources for personal use, and not to hurt others or harm or steal business resources.

> North Fork Case Question 1: How is the decision to sell North Fork affected by the employment relationship?
>
> The employment relationship is one of mutual benefit, one in which both parties (as well as other stakeholders) benefit. The members of the board had to seriously consider any decision, regardless of its benefit to the stockholders, that negatively affects the employment of 1,300 workers. These employees would not only lose their wages and benefits, they would also lose the social interaction at work and possibly their sense of self-worth. The board has an obligation to provide these employees with some measure of job security and therefore needed to carefully consider the consequences of its actions.

We will provide more detail of these rights and duties in the next two sections.

> **Personal and Professional Applications**
>
> 1. What needs do/did you meet at work?
> 2. What rights and duties do/did you have at work?

How the Employer–Employee Relationship Affects Other Stakeholders

The Market Environment. The employer–employee relationship is critical because it affects the performance of the business.[10] The relationship also affects the firm's stakeholder suppliers and customers, and poor relations often benefit the business's competitors. For example, the **National Football League (NFL)** 100 day lockout over how to split $9 billion in annual revenues, of more than 100 days, didn't only affect the owners and players. A typical NFL season generates some $12 billion in sales for enterprises outside the league.[11] During strikes and lockouts when thousands of workers are not getting their normal paychecks, think about the multiplier effects on all the firms these workers are customers of and the negative effects on their families and society.

The Nonmarket Environment. The employer–employee relationship also affects society and the government. For example, when people are not working and making their usual wages, they usually donate less money to nonprofits and they pay less in taxes. Government–employee relations can also affect business performance. For example, during a peak tourism and shopping time, the **New York Transit** workers went on an unauthorized strike and 7 million weekday passengers had to find other ways to get to the city to work and shop.[12] The actions of the transit workers, also affected the employee–employer relationship in the private sector, because people had difficulty getting to their jobs on time, and some people could not go shopping. As you can see, employer–employee relations shape and are shaped by numerous societal, political, and legal public policy issues.

North Fork Case Question 2: What market and nonmarket stakeholders are affected by this decision?

Market stakeholders, such as suppliers and customers, could be affected if Capital One decided not to continue to use North Fork's suppliers or if Capital One imposed banking policies and operations that negatively affected North Fork's current customers (e.g., disallow free checking). Local businesses near North Fork's corporate office that relied on the spending of back-office staff members (e.g., restaurants, gas stations) may also be negatively affected. Nonmarket stakeholders, such as the government and societal interest groups, could be affected through a drop in the local, county, and state taxes paid by North Fork and its dismissed employees as well as a drop in corporate and personal donations to local not-for-profit organizations.

Personal and Professional Applications

3. Give a specific example of how you and other stakeholders have been affected by the employer–employee relationship.

Learning Outcome 1: Analyze old and new employment relationship differences.

The New Employment Relationship

*The **employment relationship** entails employer and employee expectations, rights, and duties.* Note that our definition means that these elements are spelled out in a formal legal contract. If either party's expectations, rights, or duties are not met the relationship can deteriorate or result in issues that need to be resolved.

Why the change in the employment relationship? Influenced by global competition and technology, the employment relationship has changed gradually over the years to its present form. The United States has gone from a system of work characterized by lifetime employment at a single employer to a patchwork system characterized by low security and high volatility. One of the trends is to hire fewer full-time workers and rely more on temporary help and part-time workers.[13] See Figure 3.1 for a comparison of the old and new employment relationships.

Old Employment Relationship	*New Employment Relationship*
Getting a job and being trained to do the work, with continual company training to update your skills	Getting the job based on current skills and experience, and being responsible for updating your own skills
Job security, believing the firm will take care of you professionally	Job at risk, knowing layoffs are always a possibility and that you are responsible for your career future
Good opportunities for advancement within the firm	Fewer opportunities for advancement within firm, with more opportunities elsewhere
Long-term employment, with one employer and career	Short-term employment and contract workers, with multiple jobs and careers
Loyalty to and identification with employer	Loyalty to self and identification with profession
Steady pay increases with good benefits, especially retirement benefits or pension	Pay based on performance with fewer benefits
Management versus labor adversarial relations	Management and labor collaborative relations

■ **Figure 3.1:** From the Old to the New Employment Relationship

North Fork Case Question 3: How might this decision be determined based on the old and new approaches to the employment relationship?

Under the old employment relationship, most workers anticipated a long-term employment with an understanding that job security, advancement, and steady pay and benefits were the operating norm. Although the relationship with labor was adversarial, the expectation was that management would take care of the workers and make sure that they would not be negatively affected by any major changes in the firm's operation. Therefore, under the old employment relationship, one would expect North Fork Bank to have negotiated with Capital One over the firing of the 1,300 back-office staff members (perhaps make this part of the takeover deal), possibly sacrificing some of the benefits accrued to its top three executives in order to ensure the future employment of these workers.

Under the new employment relationship, however, employees understand the short-term nature of their employment (employment at risk) and look ahead to leaving the firm as a means of furthering their careers. Although management and the employees are more cooperative in their interactions, employees have little to no expectation that their needs would be considered over the needs of the stockholders. Therefore, under the new employment relationship, it is easier to understand North Fork Bank's acceptance of Capital One's offer and chalk up the loss of 1,300 jobs as the by-product (and perhaps a deal-making cost-cutting measure) of wealth creation for the stockholders.

Personal and Professional Applications

4. What are your current and future employment expectations?

5. Are your career expectations more in line with the old or new employment relationship? How will you deal with job insecurity?

Learning Outcome 2: Compare and contrast employment contracts in union and non-union organizations.

MANAGEMENT AND UNION RELATIONS

We continue our employee stakeholder discussion by focusing on understanding unionized employment. The management and union relationship is commonly called *labor relations*. One of the employee rights (we will discuss several others in the next section) in the United States, and most other countries, is the right to organize and bargain collectively through unionization. *Labor unions are societal interest groups that represent their members' special interests with employers through collective bargaining.* Rarely does collective bargaining take place in nonunion firms, so workers must individually negotiate their own employment relationship. Companies with unions tend to have a formal, written employment contract covering all unionized employees, whereas nonunion firms don't.

Why study unions? Employer–employee relations are different in unionized and nonunionized firms, and the majority of firms don't have unions. However, all firms tend to face the same employee issues and are subject to the same labor laws. So an understanding of labor relations can also be valuable for those working in nonunion firms, and it can aid in keeping the firm from becoming unionized.[14]

Personal and Professional Applications

6. Do you or anyone you know belong to a labor union?

The State of the Union Movement

Unions in the United States are on the decline. In the 1950s, 34 percent of workers where union members. Union membership began to decline in 1953 until the 1990s, when it leveled off. In 1996 membership dropped again, to 14.5 percent and by 2004 it represented only 12.5 percent of the U.S. workforce. Today, some report that about 1 in 10 workers belongs to a union.[15] A larger percentage of government workers belong to unions than private sector employees.[16]

Part of the membership has shifted from blue-collar workers to include more white-collar, service, and professional workers, including engineers, judges, and doctors. In fact, the largest professional union (with 3.2 million members) is the **National Education Association** (NEA).[17] The **AFL-CIO (American Federation of Labor-Congress of Industrial Organization)** is the umbrella federation for U.S. unions, with 57 unions representing more than 12 million workers from every walk of life.[18] For a list of its 57 members, visit its website (www.aflcio.org). The **International Brotherhood of Teamsters (Teamsters)** with 1.4 million members[19] and the **United Food and Commercial Workers International Union (UFCW)** with 1.3 million members[20] are also large labor unions that quit the AFL-CIO in 2005. One other large union is the **Service Employees International Union (SEIU)** with 2.1 million members.[21]

Despite these problems and the fact that union bosses sometimes squabble among themselves, unions are not giving up and they are planning to reinvent themselves so that they can deal with problems of factory job losses, outsourcing, and the growth of the service sector.[22] However, with the U.S. competitive and financial problems of the heavily unionized auto industry and the airline industry, resulting in thousands of lost jobs and cuts in wages and benefits, only time will tell if unions can stop their declining membership.

Labor Legislation

Figure 3.2 provides information about some of the major labor legislation that has affected employment contracts over the years.

The Norris-LaGuardia Act (1932)	*The act made the yellow dog contract illegal.* Until 1932, employers could require employees to sign a yellow dog contract, which stated that as a condition of employment the employee would not join a union or engage in union activities. If the employee did, he or she was legally fired.
The Wagner Act (also known as the National Labor Relations Act, 1935) and the NLRB	*The act gave employees the right to unionize without fear of prosecution, and it listed unfair practices of employers.* Section 7 states: "Employees shall have the right to self-organize, to form, join or assist labor organizations, to bargain collectively through representatives of their own choosing, and to engage in concerted activities for the purpose of collective bargaining or other mutual aid and protection." The Wagner Act also established the National Labor Relations Board (NLRB). The purpose of the NLRB is to enforce the provisions of the Wagner Act and to conduct elections to determine whether employees will unionize and who will be their representative in collective bargaining.
The Fair Standards Act (1938)	*The act established minimum wages.* As of January 1, 2012, the federal minimum rate was $7.25, but the state minimums can be higher, such as in Oregon and Washington.
The Taft-Hartley Act (1947)	Through the Wagner Act, union membership grew as did union power. In fact, unions became so powerful that the Taft-Hartley Act *was passed to offset some of the imbalance of power between labor and management.* It amended the Wagner Act to include a list of unfair practices by unions.
The Landrum-Griffen Act (also known as the Labor Management Reporting and Disclosure Act, 1959)	*The act was passed to protect union members from corrupt or discriminatory union activities, as it required regulation of internal union affairs.* Unions are still having some problems. For example, Teamster President Ron Carey was investigated for fundraising abuses in his reelection campaign.
The Worker Adjustment and Retraining Notification Act (WARN) of 1988	*WARN requires employers with a 100 or more employees to give 60 days advanced notice of plant closings or mass layoffs of their employees.*

■ **Figure 3.2:** Labor Legislation

The Union-Organizing Process and the NLRB

An illustration of the five stages that typically occur in forming a union is provided in Figure 3.3. Note that the **NLRB (National Labor Relations Board)** generally gets involved with the election and certification stages. Democrats are more pro union and want to make it easier for unions to recruit new members.[23] In January 2012, President Obama appointed three new pro union members to the five-member NLR Board during the Senate recess to circumvent Senate confirmation.[24] The NLRB voted to streamline some procedures in the election process, not the steps themselves, making it easier to unionize. These changes went into affect April 30, 2012.[25] For details of the changes, and for more information on the NLRB, visit its website (www.nlrb.gov).

As unions try to organize employees, managers are fighting to stop the process as early as possible. One tactic the nonunionized Japanese automakers are using at plants in the

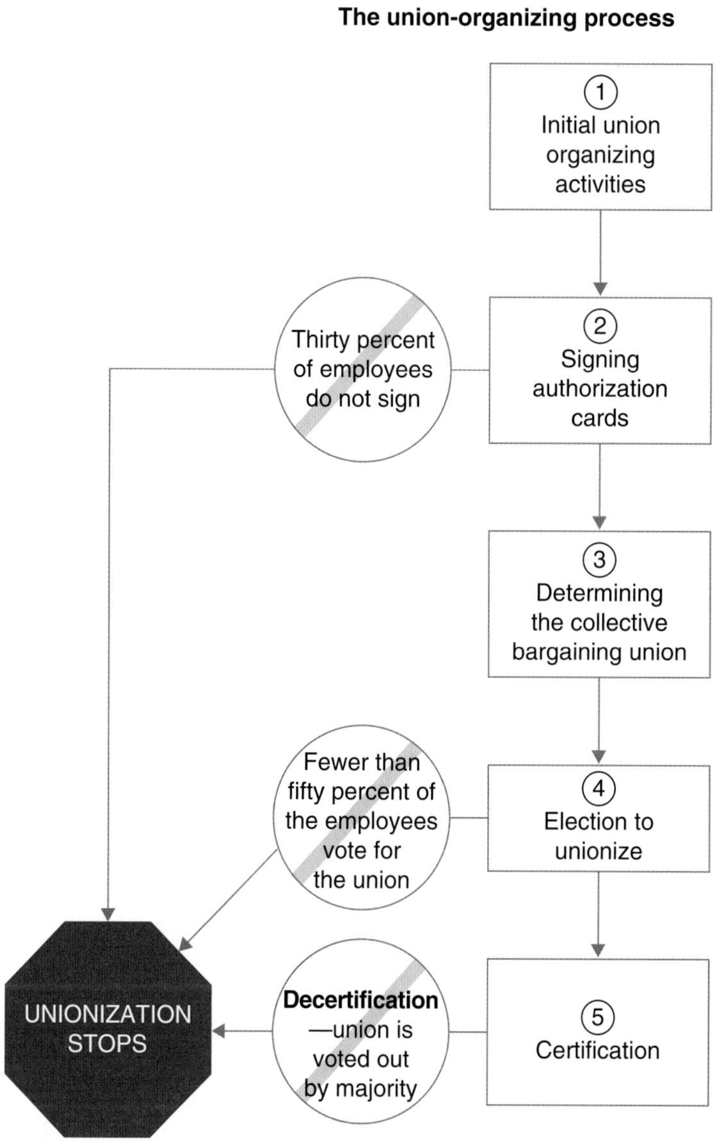

The union-organizing process

■ **Figure 3.3:** Union Organizing

United States to prevent unionization is to give wages similar to what the unionized U.S. autoworkers receive, but with fewer benefits, so that employees don't see the need to unionize. Other businesses, however, take a more adversarial approach to unions. **Walmart** is known to aggressively oppose efforts to unionize its workers with great success. It has even been accused of closing a store to prevent having a union.

Personal and Professional Applications

7. Are you more pro management or labor? Why?

Collective Bargaining and Government Help

Collective Bargaining. *Collective bargaining is the negotiation process resulting in a contract that covers employment conditions.* Employment conditions commonly include wages and benefits, hours (including overtime), and working conditions; but a contract can include any issue that both sides agree to. Today, job security is a major bargaining issue.[26] Employers are not legally required to agree to the demands of unions, but management must bargain in good faith.

When contract negotiations are not going well, unions and management sometimes make threats of work stoppages. Unions may threaten to strike unless their demands are met. In 2001, 45,000 **Verizon** workers went on strike.[27] Management can threaten a lockout (refusing to let employees work, by locking the facility so employees cannot enter, until their demands are met). For example, the **NFL**[28] and the **National Basketball Association (NBA)**[29] both locked their players out in 2011. As deadlines approach, both sides tend to be more willing to compromise to avoid a strike or lockout.

To avoid a strike or lockout, collective bargainers sometimes agree to call in neutral third parties from the **Federal Mediation and Conciliation Service (FMCS)**. The FMCS was established through the Taft-Hartley Act. *A mediator is a neutral party who helps management and labor settle their disagreements.* However, the mediators only make suggestions, which can be ignored. For example, during the dispute between the **United Steelworkers Union** and **Cooper Tire & Rubber**, a mediator was called in, but failed to get the two sides to come to an agreement.[30]

In cases where management and labor are not willing to compromise but do not want to call a strike or lockout, they may call in an arbitrator and agree to abide by his or her decision. *An arbitrator is a neutral party who makes a binding decision for management and labor.* The arbitrator's decision must be followed. Arbitration can be risky. For example, **Exxon Mobil** agreed to arbitration against Venezuelan president Hugo Chavez's nationalization of assets, seeking $7 billion, but was only awarded $908 million.[31] An arbitrator is more commonly used to settle grievances than to deal with impasses in collective bargaining. The FMCS has been credited with helping resolve strikes.

Going to the Government for Help. In addition to FMCS services, both managers and unions can use political strategies to influence labor legislation. They can also appeal to regulators and even to the president, to help them gain what they want, as well as going to the courts for interpretations of laws—even all the way to the **U.S. Supreme Court**. For example, the **Teamsters** union filed a lawsuit against the Obama administration seeking to block the government's plan to allow Mexican trucks back into the United States,[32] and the **NBA Players Association** filed an antitrust lawsuit against the **NBA** alleging the owners ended collective bargaining with an ultimatum.[33]

Nonunion Benefits of Contracts. Although collective bargaining tends to increase the wages and benefits of its union members, nonunion members may also benefit. For example, when blue-collar union shop workers get raises the nonunion white-collar office workers typically get raises too. Furthermore, competing companies that don't have unions might have to raise their wages, although not as high as union wages, in order to recruit new employees and retain good workers, so they don't leave for unionized companies.

Management Resistance to Labor

As presented in Figure 2.5 (p. 56), employees do have power against management, and vice versa, and a strike by unionized employees is the union's most powerful strategic action to get what it wants during negotiations. However, managers don't always give in to union demands, and they even fight back with lockouts and other methods, as **Fiat** did when it threatened to close a plant if workers wouldn't take wage and benefit concessions.[34] **NBA** Commissioner David Stern gave the **NBA Players Association** a take-it-or-leave-it offer saying, "The negotiations are over. You either take it, or you suffer the consequences," which led to the dissolution of the players' union.[35] **Hostess Brands**, and other companies, went into bankruptcy protection largely to gain leverage to reject or modify its 372 labor union contracts with its 19,000 employees.[36] With $1 billion in assets and $1 billion in debt, Hostess needs to reduce its cost to survive and be more competitive.[37]

The Need for Management–Union Collaboration

To compete successfully in the global economy, management and labor need to collaborate and compete with their business competitors, rather than fight amongst themselves. As illustrated in this section, many businesses still have a way to go to develop true collaborative employment contracts. Unfortunately, the clash between management and labor may be moving toward a more combative tone as companies look to lock in wage cuts negotiated during the last recession and workers seek to recoup what they ceded.[38] But will management and labor learn this lesson and collaborate? Only time will tell. Let's move on to other employee rights.

> Learning Outcome 3: List and briefly describe six employee rights, in addition to organizing and collective bargaining.

EMPLOYEE RIGHTS

We continue our discussion of employee stakeholders with a discussion about worker rights. You probably realize that employers really have more rights and the power to tell employees what they can and can't say and do on the job. However, management power is somewhat offset by employee rights through the employment contract. *Employee rights provide workers with desired outcomes and protection from undesired outcomes.* These rights are based on ethical and legal employer expectations, agreements and contracts, and laws and regulations—Figure 3.2 above lists some of the major labor laws. In this section, we discuss six more employee rights: job security, due process, safety, health, privacy, and freedom of speech and whistleblowing.

Job Security and Due Process

Employment-At-Will. The legal common-law basis for the employment relationship goes back to the 1800s. *The employment-at-will doctrine holds that the employment relationship is voluntary and that employees can be fired or quit for any or no reason.* In the early days, employment was at the sole discretion of the employer. If employees complained and wanted to unionize, management just fired them. However, over the years employees have gained more job security through employment and discrimination laws, as well as through union contracts. For example, the **United Auto Workers** (UAW) contract includes job security provisions.[39]

If you are not protected by a union contract or by one of the employment or discrimination laws, your employer is free to let you go for any reason. Some years back, **Ford Motor Company** V.P. Lee Iacocca was fired by Henry Ford II. The reason given was "I don't like you." Overall, the new employment relationship is based less on job security than the old, but there is some job security.[40]

North Fork Case Question 4: How does employment-at-will affect North Fork's decision in terms of the firm's sale?

The employees in question are back-office employees who do not appear to be unionized. Therefore, employment-at-will allows North Fork, or any future employer, to fire these employees for any reason because employment-at-will holds that the employment relationship is voluntary.

Today, it is common for ex-employees to take the firm to court to get back their jobs through *employee lawsuits.* The courts often expect the company to give a good reason for letting employees go and to let employees go during the probation period, rather than after. Courts in 11 states also require the employer to give unsatisfactory employees every "reasonable opportunity" to improve their performance before being fired.

Learning Outcome 4: Compare and contrast mediators, arbitrators, and ombuds.

Due Process. Courts also expect firms to have systems of disciplinary measures or grievance procedures, which are often part of due process. *Due process is the right to be treated fairly and to receive an impartial review of a complaint.* Managers are also expected to be ethical as a complaint goes through due process. If you can't resolve an issue with your manager, the most common procedure is to follow the chain of command by going to your boss's boss up to the top manager. Many firms also use an open-door policy where anyone can go to a top-level manager if they believe they were not treated fairly. For performance problems, many firms follow a four-step due process procedure. The first step is a verbal warning, followed by a written warning, leading to some disciplinary actions, and ultimately firing.

Some firms use ombuds, taken from the Swedish word *ombudsman*, to provide neutral third-party help. *An ombuds investigates complaints and helps to settle them fairly.* Recall that mediators and arbitrators help settle disputes. Grievance committees are also used to hear complaints, somewhat like a court. The grievance committee can be made up of peers, managers, or a mix of both.

Personal and Professional Applications

8. What level of job security do/did you have at work?

9. Explain the due process system where you work(ed).

Safety and Health

The terrorist attacks of 9/11 and continued warnings of potential terrorist attacks have increased attention to safety issues. Regardless of terrorism, many jobs and occupations are inherently hazardous, such as construction, underground and sea tunneling, drilling, and mining. You most likely heard of the **BP** Gulf explosion. A more contemporary category of job-related injuries includes repetitive motion disorders, such as wrist pain experienced by supermarket checkers, meat cutters, and keyboard operators.

According to the **U.S. Department of Labor**, more than 5 million workers, or 6 percent of employees in private industry are injured or become ill while on the job. Employees and customers have the right to a reasonably safe and healthy workplace,[41] employers have the duty to provide one, and the government provides the necessary guidelines to achieve it through the **Occupational Safety and Health Administration (OSHA)**. The *state right-to-know laws* give employees and the public the right to access information concerning hazards and workplace chemicals, and to make sure people understand what the information means in practical terms.

OSHA. The Occupational Safety and Health Administration Act of 1970 established OSHA and gave it the ability to enforce safety and health standards through the executive branch's cabinet-level **Department of Labor**. OSHA's mission, found at its website www.osha.gov, is to assure safe and healthful working conditions for working men and women by setting and enforcing standards and by providing training, outreach, education, and assistance.[42] Employers who are found to be in violation of OSHA standards can be fined, shut down, and even jailed. Under OSHA, the number of workplace deaths has been cut in half and the incidence of illnesses is much reduced. OSHA officials recently said they are taking stronger steps, including steeper fines, to reduce injuries and illness in the workplace.[43]

Health Care. The cost of health care and health insurance has increased at a much faster pace than inflation. To be competitive in the global marketplace, several U.S. companies have cut health care spending, leaving employees to pay more of the cost, and even to lose coverage. The **Patient Protection and Affordable Care Act (PPACA)**, informally referred to as **Obamacare**, is a *U.S. federal statute* signed into law by *President Barack Obama* in March 2010. The law was challenged and was taken all the way to the Supreme Court in 2012, which heavily focused on the legality of requiring people to buy health insurance or be fined. The Supreme Court upheld most of the law, including requiring the purchase of insurance. Only time will tell whether Obamacare will help improve medical care and reduce costs.

Workplace Violence. Incivility (being disrespectful or outright rude) is on the rise, and it leads to violence.[44] Workplace violence is also on the increase, and it can happen anywhere. One million workers are assaulted each year and more than 1,000 workers are killed each year. The best approach is to stop incivility before it becomes violent.[45]

> **Personal and Professional Applications**
>
> 10. How safe and healthy is/was your workplace?
>
> 11. Does/did your employer provide health care benefits, and, if so, have they changed over the years?
>
> 12. Have you seen workplace incivility and violence?

Privacy

No clear legal definition of privacy or invasion of privacy is available. However, most people get upset when they believe their privacy has been violated. For our purposes, *privacy rights protect employees' personal lives from unwarranted intrusion by employers.* Many employees believe that their religious and political views, their health condition, their credit rating, and what they do and say off the job are private matters that are none of the employers' business.

Employers believe they have privacy rights as well, such as protecting sensitive company information. Disgruntled employees could sell confidential information to competitors, or give customer records to a new employer. Some employer policies initiated to protect the firm's interests, may be seen by employees as an infringement on their privacy. For example, an employer can monitor the employees' computer files to determine whether they are doing the work they are being paid to do. It is not uncommon in today's workplace for employees to use the Internet for personal business while being on the clock.

The tricky part about privacy rights is knowing at what point business interests outweigh employee rights to privacy. What is ethical and legal, and what is unethical and illegal? Unfortunately, the courts sometimes have to make the judgment call. We will discuss some privacy issues here and revisit the topic when we discuss technology in Chapter 12.

Monitoring Employees. The old system of personal monitoring gave way to cameras and listening devices, which have largely been replaced with computerized technology to record, store, and monitor employees' activities. Yes, employee monitoring is legal. *The Electronic Communications Privacy Act of 1986* essentially protects individual rights to privacy, but it allows employers to monitor job-related communication. In fact, most large businesses do in fact use some form of electronic monitoring of their employees. Thus, in general, employees have the right to personal off-the-job privacy, but not to business-related privacy.

Employers have the technology to know when employees are using the phone and who they are talking to; machines can record how many calls employees make per hour, how long each call is, and the number of minutes per hour the employee is actually working by talking on the phone. Calls can be recorded and listened to for quality control.

Software has been developed that allows employers to know when employees are using their computers and the Internet, and what they are doing online. They can even read employee computer files and e-mails, even deleted files. Employers can monitor employee whereabouts with cell phones and global positioning systems (GPS). Trucking companies, messenger services, and so on can know where their drivers are, how much time is spent during a stop, how many stops they make, and the total driving time per day. Employers can even monitor bathroom hygiene. "Hygiene Guard" is a system that ensures that employees follow proper hygiene. After a visit to a bathroom, if an employee doesn't wash properly, sensors on the soap dispenser and faucets make the employee's badge flash and it puts a black mark in the file of the employee in the main computer.

ETHICAL DILEMMA 3.1 When Workers Sue the Union: Unions and Privacy Rights

When a union organizer showed up unexpectedly at Elizabeth Pichler's Bethlehem, Pennsylvania, home on a cold Saturday afternoon, she shut the front door on him. "It annoyed me that anybody could go and get information about me and come to my house," says Pichler, a 64-year-old receptionist at uniform company **Cintas Corporation.** A handful of co-workers at the company's Emmaus, Pennsylvania, plant were also annoyed about visits to their homes and complained to their managers. They eventually learned that the union had traced their home addresses from license plates in the company parking lot. That made them angry enough to meet with lawyers provided by the company and then file a suit in alleging their privacy rights had been violated . . . under the little-known Driver's Privacy Protection Act of 1994, which prohibits the disclosure and use of personal information obtained through motor vehicle records.

Officials at **Unite Here** maintain that organizers didn't break the law. Unions traditionally canvassed door to door as a way to sell their message to workers, but most often rely on workers to pass along home addresses of co-workers, say labor experts. A victory for the plaintiffs in this case could cast a shadow over such recruiting methods even if home addresses are obtained by other means. The lawsuit will have a "very chilling effect" on workers' willingness to support the organizing drive at Cintas, says Marick F. Masters, a professor of business administration at the University of Pittsburgh. Meanwhile, a large financial penalty could seriously restrict the union's other organizing activities.

Not all employees agree with the lawsuit. According to Eleuteria Mazon, "There are a couple of workers on the company side, and they are going to do whatever the company wants. In my plant there are no people against the union. There are a lot of people who are afraid to support the union because of the retaliation that the company may have against them."

Pamela Lowe, a spokeswoman for Cintas, said the company respects the rights of its employees to choose union representation. She also denied that the lawsuit was intended to intimidate workers. "This is a lawsuit brought by our employees to vindicate their privacy rights," she said. "Many employees came to us to complain about the union coming to their home and in some instances frightening their families."

Some labor experts say the lawsuit brought by workers against the union should be credited to the company as well, arguing it would not have gotten off the ground without support from Cintas and that the lawsuit raises the bar on aggressive countertactics used by companies. The lawsuit was "devilishly clever on the part of the company, no question about it," says Canoni of **Nixon Peabody**. "I mean, how many people knew about this law?"[46]

Questions

1. What rights of the employees, the firm, and the union are in conflict in this case?
2. Do you believe that the union acted ethically in this case by tracing employees' names and addresses by their license plates?
3. Do you believe that Cintas acted ethically in providing support for this employee lawsuit against the union?
4. What would you do in this situation if you were an employee? Would you support your fellow employees' lawsuit, the union, and/or the firm?

Employee Substance and Honesty Tests. The use and effect of *alcohol and drugs* (substances) on the job cost business billions per year. Employees under the influence of a substance, taken outside of or on the job, are less productive than those who are not, have a lower quality of work, are late and miss more days of work, have more accidents that hurt themselves and others, and are more likely to steal from their employers. Thus, employers are giving *employees substance tests* in the form of preemployment screening, random testing of employees, and testing when there is suspicion of an employee being under the influence of illegal substances.

The Drug-Free Workplace Act of 1988 supported drug testing. The *Americans with Disabilities (ADA) Act of 1990* does provide some protection for substance abusers to rehabilitate, because substance abuse may be considered a disability. For example, former substance abusers can't be denied a job, but an employer can refuse to hire them if they don't pass a drug test. People with acquired immune deficiency syndrome (AIDS) are also given protection under the ADA. For example, people fired because their AIDS or HIV tests were positive had to be given back their jobs, and some have received punitive damages as well.

Employee theft also costs business billions each year, so some businesses are giving *honesty tests* in hopes of not hiring people who are likely to steal. Today's honesty test is not a polygraph (lie detector) test (these tests were outlawed with the *Employee Polygraph Protection Act of 1988)*; it is a paper-and-pencil test that is designed to identify undesirable qualities in the test taker. However, the accuracy of the test has been questioned.

Personal and Professional Applications

13. Has your right to privacy been violated at work?

14. How are/were you monitored on the job?

15. What types of tests have been given where you work(ed)?

Freedom of Speech and Whistleblowing

Freedom of speech is the right to speak out against the government or others without fear of retaliation. Freedom of speech is a right given to Americans by the U.S. Constitution, but it does not explicitly protect freedom of speech in the workplace. Employers are concerned that if employees speak against the firm, it could result in losses for the business. Clearly, an employer doesn't want to pay its employees to hurt it. On the other hand, people say that if the company is doing something unethical or illegal, employees should speak out—"blow the whistle" internally or externally. *Whistleblowing occurs when employees report employer wrongdoing to high-level company managers, the media, or the government.*

Whistleblower Protection. The *Sarbanes-Oxley Act of 2002 (SOA* is discussed in more detail on p. 95) makes it illegal for employers to retaliate in any way against whistleblowers who report information that could have a material impact on the value of a company's stock price. Retaliating managers can receive criminal felony penalties of up to 10 years. The Labor Department is responsible for investigating any complaints of a whistleblower who worked for a publicly held firm and who was harassed, demoted, or terminated. **OSHA** hears whistleblower cases,[47] and so does the **Security and Exchange Commission (SEC).**[48] Employees sometimes even benefit through punitive damages against the employer in court. For example, Henry Boisvert and James Burton took their case to federal court and were awarded more than $300 million in damage awards. Their whistleblowing has been credited with saving countless lives. Burton also wrote a successful book about the experience, *The Pentagon Wars*, which became an HBO movie.

Employees who have not blown the whistle have even been criticized for not doing so by the government. For example, in the 2006 **Fannie Mae** trial, the report named specific executives who missed chances to blow the whistle on questionable practices.[49]

When Should You Blow the Whistle and How? The tricky part about freedom of speech is knowing what business action should be spoken out against. While most illegal actions are clear, ethical or unethical action is not always clear, as is illustrated in the Ethical Dilemmas. Some generally accepted guidelines for blowing the whistle include the seriousness of the action. Is (or will) the firm seriously and considerably harm the public? If yes, the first step is to report the action to your immediate supervisor. If nothing happens, stay internal and go to higher-level managers. Again, if nothing happens, go to outside sources (news media and/or government). Two major exceptions to going outside the firm are when you strongly fear serious retaliation at work and possible harm to you or your family. Sometimes the news media will run a story without listing you as the source of information.

For more information on employee rights and whistleblowing visit the websites for **Workplace Fairness** (www.workplacefairness.org), **National Workrights Institute** (www.workrights.org), **Electronic Privacy Information Center** jointly with **Privacy International** (www.privacy.org), and **National Whistleblowers Center** (www.whistleblowers.org).

ETHICAL DILEMMA 3.2 Rats Sinking the Ship: Whistleblowing and the Cargo Shipping Industry

Over the past 10 years, a U.S. Department of Justice (JOD) Environment and Natural Resources Division's Vessel Pollution Program triggered more than $200 million in fines and 17 years in prison for ship officers and executives. Four corporations that own and operate a Panamanian cargo vessel were fined $1 million last July and banned from doing business in the United States for five years for deliberately dumping waste overboard and trying to hide their crimes.[50]

What is JOD's number one source of information against illegal dumpers? Whistleblowers! Whistleblowers help by giving inspectors scrawled notes or cell phone photos capturing illegal dumping and homemade diversion pipes hidden on board.[51] What is the whistle blowers' motivation? High cash rewards! Under the Act to Prevent Pollution from Ships, those providing information leading to conviction may reap up to half of the criminal fines collected; many rewards reaching six figures.[52]

Case in point. Recently an employee (Salvador Lopez) of the Maltese cargo ship *Aquarosa* managed by Efploia Shipping reported that "the ship had been illegally dumping oily water and sludge overboard, and he had proof: hundreds of photographs stored on his phone."[53] Lopez's whistleblowing did not only impact Efploia Shipping but also impacted two other companies. These firms pleaded guilty in January 2012 to obstruction of justice and other charges and agreed to pay $1.2 million each in penalties and fines. Lopez's pay ticket for his efforts? He is eligible to receive a reward of up to $925,000.

Using whistleblowers is not without its critics. It is purported that some whistleblowers decide they want to make real money and don't report violations to the owner;

instead they go directly to the authorities. JOD is well aware that corporations do not like these protections and reward laws because their own employees are turning them in. Yet the problem remains; how else would JOD know of these violations?[54]

Questions

1. What might be the positive and negative consequences associated with researching and perhaps uncovering these illegal business practices?
2. What are the pros and cons of Lopez's cooperation with the higher authorities from an employee's perspective?
3. Would it be ethical for Lopez to cooperate with these higher authorities and under what circumstances?
4. If you were offered a reward such as the one mentioned but at the risk of being called a "rat" would you still do it?

Personal and Professional Applications

16. Have you witnessed any employer wrongdoing? If yes, what was it?

17. Have you or anyone you know blown the whistle? If yes, did the employer retaliate, and if so, how?

STOCKHOLDERS

We now change our focus to stockholders. The owners of a business are strategic stakeholders because they provide the firm with funds to operate and grow. In a corporation, the legal owners are stockholders. Without stockholders (also called shareholders), the U.S. economy would not have as many businesses, and they would not be as large as they are today. In this section we discuss stockholders and the separation of power, stockholder rights and protection, and shareholder activism.

Learning Outcome 5: Define the corporate stakeholders and describe their primary power.

Stockholders and the Separation of Power

Capital, Stock, and the Stock Market. The corporation only receives money from the original buyers of the stock at its initial public offering (IPO), minus the fees and commissions to financial experts for their services. When investors buy and sell existing stock through the stock market, the company not only doesn't make or get any money, it has the record-keeping expense of tracking who owns each share of stock. Thus, it's the financial institutions and stockbrokers who make money from the stock market, while investors either make or lose money. The stock market is a bit like legalized gambling—the house (financial institutions and brokers) always wins because it gets a commission regardless of profit or loss.

Classification of Stockholders. The two major classifications of stockholders are individual and institutional. *Individual stockholders* buy stock directly from the company, usually through a stockbroker. More than half of U.S. adults own stock. *Institutional investors* buy stock on behalf of their clients or members, including mutual funds (e.g., **Fidelity Magellan**), pensions (e.g., **California Public Employees Retirement System [CalPERS]),** and endowment funds (most likely your college or university has one). The individuals buying stock in institutional stockholders' mutual funds, often for retirement, infuse these funds with trillions of dollars. Institutional investors own millions of shares of stock versus hundreds owned by the typical individual stockholder, giving the institutional investors more power than individual investors. For more information on investing and institutional investing, visit **Investor Responsibility Research Center** (www.irrc.org) and **Council of Institutional Investors** (www. cii.org).

Stockholder Objectives. The primary reason individuals and institutions buy stocks is to make money, but they often have other reasons as well. Shareholders buy stocks believing they will receive a greater return on their investment than if they invested their money in an alternative investment, such as a certificate of deposit or bonds. Although stock prices are sometimes volatile, historically, stocks have provided greater returns than government bonds, bank certificates of deposits, and money markets. Stockholders make money in two ways, both of which are taxed. First, through *capital appreciation*, once shares are purchased, the higher their price rises, the more profitable the investment. Second, through *dividends* a business shares its profits with stockholders. However, due to market fluctuations, stockholders have no guarantee that they will make a profit or how much, so they can lose money.

Separation of Power. With the shift from owners managing the day-to-day operations to managers performing those tasks came the separation of power. U.S. corporations have four major power stakeholders (see Figure 3.4 for an illustration), but several other countries have different structures. Although not a stakeholder, overarching the power players of the corporation is the charter. *A corporate charter is granted by the*

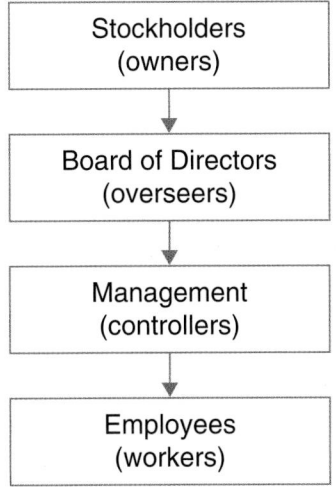

■ **Figure 3.4:** Corporate Power Stakeholders

state giving the firm the right to operate under basic terms of its existence and govern-ance. Generally, businesses are for-profit corporations and societal interest groups have nonprofit charters, and they are commonly referred to as nongovernmental organiza-tions or NGOs.

*The **stockholders** are the legal owners of the corporation.* Their primary power is to vote for the corporate board of directors at the annual meeting, or by *proxy* (absentee bal-lot). Each share of stock counts as one vote, so the more shares that an entity owns the greater its power to select directors.

*The **board of directors** provides strategic direction and governance and oversees the managers of the corporation.* The board is accountable to the stockholders. Its job is to represent the stockholders and look out for their interests. The board's primary power is to select, advise, supervise, and evaluate the top managers; it also has the power to fire top managers. Boards do fire CEOs, including **HP's** Mark Hurd and Carol Bartz of **Yahoo!**[55] The board is responsible for ensuring governance mechanisms are used properly.[56] We will talk more about boards in the corporate governance section.

Managers (and specifically CEOs) plan, organize, lead, and control firm resources to achieve corporate goals. Their primary power is to control the day-to-day operations of the firm. They are responsible for safe-guarding the interests of the stockholders, while also balancing the owner's interests and rights with those of the other stakeholders. How-ever, hiring professional managers creates the risk that executives will put their own self-interests above those of stockholders and other stakeholders, which is known as *agency theory* problems.[57]

Although the managers are not shown at the top of the chart, they have the most power because they control operations. A major focus of this book is the manager's responsibility to balance the interests of stockholders and other stakeholders through integrating market and nonmarket strategies to achieve the mission and objectives of the corporation. To this end, you are continually placed in the role of top management in the cases and other applications of this book. Even if you never become a top man-ager, you should realize the issues managers have to deal with and the decisions they have to make.

The *employees* do the work to provide the corporation's products and other functions. Their primary power includes collective bargaining and striking. Managers are also employees, and both can also be stockholders in publicly held firms. We have already talked about the power of employees and will continue to do so in other chapters. We will be discussing how the stockholders and the board have power over the managers in detail throughout the rest of this chapter.

Personal and Professional Applications

18. Do you own any stocks?

19. Do you work, or did you work, for a corporation? Describe the power of its corpo-rate stakeholders.

Stockholder Rights and Protection

Figure 3.5 provides a list of stockholder rights. Although stockholders have the right to vote for the directors of the board, they have little input into who runs for membership on the board because the board itself nominates the candidates with the input of the top manager. However, shareholder activists can have power.

- ■ To share in the profits through dividend payments, when and if declared by the board of directors
- ■ To sell their shares of stock
- ■ To vote on:
  - ● Board of director members
  - ● Major mergers and acquisitions
  - ● Bylaw and charter changes
  - ● Stockholder proposals
- ■ To know about the affairs of the corporation through information transparency and disclosure
- ■ To receive an annual report with financial performance and condition
- ■ To take the corporation and its officers to court through stockholder lawsuits

■ **Figure 3.5:** Stockholder Rights

Learning Outcome 6: Explain how the government helps to protect stockholders.

The SEC. The primary government agency protector of publicly traded stockholder rights is the **Security and Exchange Commission (SEC)** of the executive branch of the **Department of Justice**. There is a clear relationship between government regulation and corporate governance. The SEC's mission is to protect stockholders' rights by regulating the stock market to ensure it is run fairly and that investment information is fully disclosed. The SEC continues to work to improve the information available to allow investors to make sound stock selections. The SEC works to give shareholders more boardroom clout, including making it easier for shareholders to nominate directors on corporate ballots.[58]

Corporations have an obligation to provide company information of interest to its shareholders and potential investors, which is referred to as *full disclosure* or *transparency*. Disclosures should include information that may affect investment decisions to buy or sell stock. Regular and frequent disclosures may include the nature and activities of the firm, financial matters, strategies and policies, and problems in opportunities facing the firm in the short and long term. The SEC also regulates the illegal practice of insider trading. *Insider trading occurs when a person uses confidential information before it becomes public knowledge to buy or sell the company stock.* You may visit the SEC website (www.sec.gov) to obtain information on corporate filings and corporate governance.

Sarbanes-Oxley Act of 2002 and the SEC. Congressional legislators pass laws to protect stockholders, and they are working to give shareholders more say on executive pay packages.[59] To address the corporate scandals of the early 2000s, Sarbanes-Oxley Act (SOA) of 2002 gave the SEC more power to protect stockholders.[60] *The Sarbanes-Oxley Act reformed corporate governance.* It was characterized as "the most far reaching reforms of American business practices since the time of Franklin D. Roosevelt." The act mandated a number of reforms to improve corporate responsibility, enhance financial disclosures, and combat corporate and accounting fraud, and it created the **Public Company Accounting Oversight Board** (PCAOB) to oversee the activities of the auditing profession. Thus, public affairs managers now operate under new governance.[61] The full text of the act is available at: http://www.sec.gov/about/laws/soa2002.pdf. See Figure 3.6 for a summary of the bill's provisions reforming corporate governance. Proponents of SOA have evidence that it is improving corporate governance, but critics contend that it is too time-consuming and costly to meet the regulations, calling it a curse for small corporations. Corporate governance will be discussed in the next section.

> **Personal and Professional Applications**
>
> 20. Which stockholder rights have you received or exercised (Figure 3.5)?

The Judiciary. Shareholders are also taking businesses to court for interpretation of the laws and determination as to whether their rights have been violated (e.g., recovery of stock price losses). **Time Warner** agreed to pay $3 billion to settle a class action lawsuit fraud claim by shareholders who lost money after the company's merger with **America**

Stockholders

■ Requires shareholders' vote to approve stock option plans

Managers

■ Requires full disclosure of complex financial transactions and changes in firm financial conditions "in plain English"
■ Requires executives to disclose stock sales within two days
■ Requires CEOs and CFOs to give written certification of the truth of corporate financial statements, with the possible penalty of jail for 20 years and $5 million in fines for falsification
■ Requires executives to pay back any bonuses or profits from stocks received based on financial reports that had to be changed at a later date
■ Prohibits the firm from giving personal loans to managers
■ Prohibits executives from making stock transactions when employee pension blackouts prohibit employee stock transactions

Boards of Directors

■ Requires the majority of board members to be outside directors, not employees
■ Requires at least one financial expert be a member of the corporate audit committee
■ Requires the audit committee to approve the selection of auditors, auditor consulting contracts, and 401(k) plans

Outside Auditors

■ Requires the establishment of an independent board to oversee the audit of public corporations
■ Prohibits accounting firms from providing auditing and other services that would create conflicts of interest, thereby limiting consulting work
■ Requires the rotation of the lead outside auditor firm every five years

---

■ **Figure 3.6:** Sarbanes-Oxley Act of 2002: Reforming Corporate Governance

Online (AOL). Unfortunately, the stockholders of **WorldCom** recovered very little of their $4 billion loss because the company went bankrupt and their stock became virtually worthless.

Shareholder Activism

Shareholder activism is on the rise. Some stockholders, especially institutional investors, don't merely rely on the board of directors to look out for their interests; they are becoming activists and pressing managers to meet their demands.[62] One type of shareholder activist is the social activist who tries to change and improve company policies that the activist disagrees with, such as polluting. (We will discuss social interest group activists in detail in Chapter 7.) Another type of shareholder activist is those who want the company to change to improve its return on the shareholders' stock investment. Next we focus on shareholder activists.

Shareholder Resolutions. One of the major ways shareholder activists communicate their concerns to management is through filing a shareholder resolution to get managers to take specific action. *Shareholder resolutions place a suggested action on the proxy statement to be voted on by all stockholders.* For example, **Wendy's**, **KFC**, **Taco Bell**, and **Pizza Hut** received requests to make all their restaurants smoke-free. To file a resolution, a stockholder or shareholder group must obtain a predetermined number of stakeholder signatures to require management to place the resolution on the proxy statement, which is difficult for the average individual investor. So resolutions are more commonly made by institutional investors and by society interest groups. Most resolutions don't pass, but they usually get national publicity for the societal interest group, which helps the group promote its special interest. The AFL-CIO unions have Executive Paywatch that keeps records on executive pay and tries to take money from the CEOs to give to the workers.[63]

Annual Meetings. At annual meetings, shareholder activists are pressuring firms to require that directors are elected by a majority vote to make it easier to get rid of ineffective directors and to help rein in executive pay. **Pfizer**, **Intel**, and **Motorola** have all agreed to majority vote.

Activist stockholders are also showing up at corporate annual meetings to pressure management to explain their decisions and actions. Managers have been asked to explain and defend their high executive compensation, golden parachutes, generous stock options, hostile takeover attempts, plant closings, and stance on environmental issues.

> **Personal and Professional Applications**
>
> 21. What stockholder activism was taken against a business you own stock in or know about?

CORPORATE GOVERNANCE

We now focus on how business is run by its employed managers, with governance established by the board of directors. Just as the government establishes and enforces policies for the nation, the corporation establishes policies as an internal form of governance.[64] *Corporate governance is the legal system of checks and balances defining the power of stockholders, boards of directors, and managers.*

Today's executives understand the importance of effective corporate governance. The U.S. governance of corporations is regulated primarily by the requirements contained in state corporate statutes, giving boards and managers broad discretion in the normal running of business operations through the state corporate charter. However, various state charters give more or less power to managers and stockholders. For example, Delaware tends to be more pro-management and California is more pro-stockholder. Thus, despite its small size, Delaware is the state in which most large firms are incorporated. In this section, we discuss the board of directors and director and executive compensation.

> Learning Outcome 7: Differentiate between inside and outside members of the board of directors and the potential problem of insiders.

The Board of Directors

The word *governance* comes from the Greek word for 'steering'. The board members have a fiduciary responsibility—a trust relationship to act in the best interest of the stockholders. The board of directors is legally responsible for steering the firm by helping to establish and enforce governance control through setting corporate objectives, developing strategies and policies, and selecting top managers to achieve these objectives and strategies.[65] The head of the board is commonly called the chairman of the board, and sometimes chairperson. Most females on the *Fortune* 50 Most Powerful Women do elect to use the title chairman, including Irene Rosenfeld—**Kraft Foods**, Indra Nooyi—**PepsiCo**, and Ellen Kullman—**Dupont.**[66]

Composition. Board composition varies depending on who can best serve the interests of the corporation and its stockholders. Larger corporations tend to have more board members (averaging 11) than smaller firms. The composition includes inside and outside directors.[67] *Inside directors are employees or have other ties to the company.* In many companies, the CEO is also the chairperson of the board, and other employees may be members of the board. The potential problem of inside director employees is that the CEO may hold too much influence as the boss. Employee/directors may feel pressure to agree with whatever decisions the executive wants from the board. Other ties include being a family member, like board members at **Ford** and **Walmart**, and doing business with the firm, including suppliers and customers.

Outside directors are not employees and have no ties to the firm; as independent and impartial outsiders, these directors provide a method of balancing power and a system of checks and balances to help prevent corruption. A potential problem of outside directors is that they are often friends of or otherwise connected to the CEO and may just agree with whatever the executive wants. Outside directors commonly include executives of other firms, retired executives, major stockholders, bankers, former government officials, academics, and representatives of the local community. Board members are predominantly professional white males. Based on the importance of the business–government relations, research has shown advantages to having former government officials as outside directors, and their numbers have grown in recent years.[68]

Committees. Boards typically perform their work in committees throughout the year and during board meetings four or five times per year for a one-day session. Large public corporations tend to have at least five committees. The *executive committee* works closely with the top managers on current important business matters. The *audit committee* has only outside directors who review the financial reports, select the outside accounting auditors, and oversee the internal financial functions. The *compensation committee* evaluates executive performance and recommends terms and conditions of employment, including setting pay and benefits and approving raises. The *public issues* or *public policy committee* helps executives deal with public affairs management (discussed in detail in Chapter 2). The *nominating committee* recruits people to run for election to the board at the annual meeting and to nominate candidates for the top management positions. Some corporations also have a governance committee to review controls and board performance, and some have a *social responsibility committee* to evaluate the firm's social performance. In some companies, the public issues and social responsibility committees perform both functions. We will discuss corporate social responsibility (CSR) in detail in the next chapter.

Personal and Professional Applications

22. Describe the composition of the board of directors where you work(ed).

Director and Executive Compensation

Director Compensation. Outside directors of large public corporations are usually well paid. Director compensation may include retainer fees, meeting fees, grants of stock, stock options, pensions, and all types of expense account perks. The average outside director at larger U.S. public firms works 173 hours per year (3½ hours per week for 50 weeks),[69] and the compensation is more than $150,000 with yearly increases exceeding 10 percent per year.[70] Not bad for a part-time job. On the other hand, the job does have important responsibilities and potential personal liability. Directors can face lawsuits. Although courts rarely hold directors personally responsible and financially liable, they can still be sued and are not guaranteed of "winning." Setting executive compensation is an important function of the board. Boards are being criticized for their pay and for approving lavish CEO compensation. Ken Lay, founder of **Enron**, made about $220 million, and Gary Winnick, founder of **Global Crossing**, received more than $500 million prior to their firms' bankruptcies, while many stockholders lost most or all of their investments.[71] Based on stockholder activist complaints about overpaying CEOs, and during the recession in 2008, some boards cut CEO compensation, but the general trend is bigger increases.[72]

Executive Compensation. *Compensation* refers to the total cost of the employee; executives commonly receive a salary, benefits, bonuses, stock options, and many perks. U.S. executives are by far the highest paid in the world. Executive compensation is based on multiple factors. Firm size and performance affect compensation, as does the power of the executive to influence pay.[73] Some CEOs are also chair of the board and have the power to select directors and to handpick the members of the compensation committee (those who set their pay). Most directors are executives of other companies, and some are friends of the CEO, which is sometimes referred to as the *good old boy network* and contributes to the lack of diversity in top management and on boards of directors.

According to the AFL-CIO Executive PayWatch database, CEOs of the largest companies received an average total compensation of $11.4 million last year. CEO compensation has skyrocketed over the years compared to workers. Back in 1980, CEO pay equaled 42 times the average pay of blue collar workers, but by 2010 it grew to 343 times the pay of workers.[74]

Much of this compensation comes from stock options. *A stock option gives the holder the right to buy a set number of company shares at a fixed price for a specified period.* If the price of the stock goes above the set stock price during the specified time, the option holder can buy and then sell the stock and make a quick profit with no risk of loss. In the wake of corporate scandals at firms, such as **Apple** misdating options, some firms, including **Microsoft**, have stopped giving stock options.

Most executives also get benefits that include exceptional retirement packages and extensive perks, including homes, cars, use of corporate jets for personal travel, and taxes paid. It is common for the CEO's total compensation to include less salary than the cost of the other parts of the compensation package. Total package figures are estimated because firms tend to have hidden compensation. **GE**'s CEO, Jeffrey Immelt, received up to $14.6 million in shares and an unknown perk package to exceed his $15 million salary in 2005.[75]

Some executives get golden parachutes. The *golden parachute* is a special compensation contract that pays top executives in the event the firm is merged or acquired by another business. The objective of the golden parachute is to put the stockholder's interest ahead of the executive's because in many cases the top executives lose their jobs after the takeover. Thus, they would not have to worry about getting paid while looking for another job. It is also used to get rid of them for other reasons.

On the positive side, executive management skill and performance does have an impact on the success of the firm, and poor performers have been fired.[76] CEOs deserve a piece of the pie they help create. Top executives should be paid well; after all, if it weren't for some effective CEOs, such as the late Steve Jobs at **Apple**, companies would not be making the millions of dollars of profits they make each year. The major debate is over what is ethically fair compensation. For more information on corporate governance, visit the **Corporate Library** website (www.thecorporatelibrary.com).

North Fork Case Question 5: How does North Fork's board justify this "golden parachute" from a stockholder's perspective?

Agency theory indicates that the best way to serve the stockholders is to directly tie the personal interests of managers, in this case the CEO, to stockholder interests. "Golden parachutes" are compensation packages that pay top executives in the event the firm is merged or acquired by another business and therein makes up for the CEO's potential job loss (and related compensation). The board can easily justify this payout by noting that stockholders would obtain a 20 percent increase in the value of their stock through this buyout; a buyout that may not have occurred if CEO Kanas were not rewarded for his efforts in making North Fork the twentieth largest bank in the United States.

Personal and Professional Applications

23. Are the top executives where you work ethically and fairly compensated for their performance?

BUSINESS NONMARKET AND MARKET STRATEGIES AND ETHICS

As presented in Model 1.1 and Figure 1.4 (pp. 5 and 22), businesses have a variety of nonmarket strategies they can use through the 5 Is strategic analysis (Chapter 2). Managers are integrating the nonmarket strategies presented here with their market strategies because they know this integration benefits firm performance. The primary nonmarket strategy that top managers use in handling corporate stakeholders is coalition building with the board of directors to get them to support their strategies, knowing that stockholders usually don't have much power and that they, the managers, have great control over employees. Next we discuss how the strategies are used with employees and owners.

Information Strategies

Information strategies are critically important to good employer–employee relations. Managers must know and understand employee and owner interests by listening to them and by trying to meet their needs fairly, but within reason. Corporate governance must be ethical and clear to all stakeholders.[77] The board of directors and each of its members must know their role, duties, and responsibilities. Managers can also get their points of interest across to employees by using facts and figures, clearly stating their assumptions, and by trying to gain positive employee and public sentiment. Managers can have outside sources, experts, and other stakeholders support the accuracy and legitimacy of management's side.

Societal Strategies

Being socially responsible, gaining positive public sentiment, and having good media relations can help relations with employees and owners. However, management needs to be ethical with employees and owners and to meet both parties' conflicting interests, by giving fair compensation to employees and fair returns to owners. The perception of being too generous to one at the expense of the other can cause problems. Sometimes owners and management team members must devise strategies to deal with activists—be they social activists, employee activists, government activists, or stockholder activists. Below we discuss two types of activists: union and stockholder.

Dealing with Union Activists. Unions are societal interest groups, and management can use the *ignoring, opposing, negotiating,* or *working with them* strategies. In the case of unionization, many businesses choose to fight it with these strategies: mandatory employee meetings to present management's side, one-on-one supervisor meetings with employees, using management consultants to stop unionization, distributing antiunion leaflets, mailing antiunion letters, and using antiunion videos. All of these approaches are based on good information strategies.

Businesses are also fighting strikes and using the replacement worker strategy. One area of great concern for unions has been the recent business practice of subcontracting work, especially overseas to less-developed countries (e.g., India and China). Firms can also use business societal interest groups and coalitions to deal with unions. When there is a union, managers must be ethical and bargain in good faith, and the new employment contract calls for the strategy of working together with employees and owners.[78]

Dealing with Stockholder Activists. Strategies for dealing with stockholder activists tend to vary with the power of ownership (number and percentage of shares owned). The smaller the ownership, the more the firm can ignore and oppose it. However, the larger the ownership, the more managers must negotiate and work with it.

Sometimes stockholder activists attempt a takeover of the firm—called a *hostile takeover*—against the other shareholders' wishes, typically by buying enough stock to take control of the corporation. To prevent the hostile takeover, managers use the poison pill strategy. A *poison pill* dilutes activist holdings to make a hostile takeover prohibitively expensive. For example, **Yahoo!** offered shareholders the right to buy one unit of a share of preferred stock for $250 if a person or group acquired at least 15 percent of Yahoo! stock.

Political and Legal Strategies

The major legal strategy businesses currently use in regard to employee rights is to operate in ways to avoid lawsuits. Effective firms also treat employees ethically and fairly through their human resource policies that promote diversity.[79] Successful businesses offer family-friendly workplaces with flexible benefits, flextime work hours, compressed workweeks, and telecommuting from home to help employees balance work and family life. They also cooperate with employees who seek the benefits of the Family and Medical Leave Act.

Effective Human Resource Policies for Employee Rights. Although there is a new employment relationship, many employers try to treat employees fairly, working with unsatisfactory employees to improve performance, and have justifiable reasons for letting employees go. Many large firms offer *employee assistance programs (EAPs)* to provide counseling and other help to employees (for problems involving substance abuse, marriage and the family, gambling, finance and the law, psychological and emotional issues, and stress) so that they can be more effective in both their personal and professional lives. Many employers have formal due process systems that they follow, and they act in good faith to resolve complaints. Managers document their hiring, evaluation, and promotion of employees in case they have to support their decisions in court.

Numerous employers use a political strategy and work with OSHA to set reasonable safety and health standards. They meet or exceed OSHA standards, they inform employees of any potential safety and health problems related to their jobs, and they properly train employees to avoid problems. Workplace incivility and violence are not tolerated, violence prevention strategies are implemented, and corrective action is taken.

Employers that do monitor employees on the job can do so ethically by obtaining the informed consent of employees and applicants before acquiring information about them. Managers inform employees how they are monitored, and they don't abuse the information and protect it from unauthorized sources. Expected behavior is made clear to employees, and managers make sure punishment is fair and violators have access to due process. Personal privacy off the job that is not job related is respected. Only reliable and valid substance abuse, honesty, and other tests are given to employees.

Most managers lead by example and perform in ethical and legal ways so that employees don't have to blow the whistle. However, to ensure good behavior, their strategy is to work with employees through systems for blowing the whistle internally. Managers take all complaints seriously and investigate them immediately with impartial independent groups. The guilty are disciplined, corrective action is taken to quickly change any wrongdoing, and preventive measures are implemented to prevent further wrongdoing. The whistleblower is told of the company action taken, or why no action is being taken, and retaliation against the employee is prohibited.

Effective Corporate Governance Strategies. An important key to successful corporate governance is for managers to be ethical and open and honest with full disclosure, taking a stakeholder approach to governance.[80] Corporations take rating companies' **(GovernanceMetrics, Corporate Library,** and **Institutional Shareholder Services)** assessments of their governance performance and use them to improve their procedures. When **Citigroup** used these assessments, its ratings went from poor to good.

Some effective corporate governance strategies include giving executives an ethical and fair compensation based on performance, and disclosing their salary, benefits, bonuses, stock options, taxes paid for the CEO, and all perks to the public;[81] separating the CEO and the chairman of the board positions to maintain a balance of power and holding board meetings without the CEO to prevent undue influence over board members; limiting the number of inside directors and the power of the CEO to nominate candidates to the board; selecting independent outside directors who are not afraid to challenge management, rather than simply go along with the CEO;[82] nominating multiple candidates for each director position to give stockholders viable choices; promoting diversity by nominating and electing more women and minorities, including stakeholder representatives who are employees, customers, or part of the community; and seeking evaluations of the performance of the board of directors as a group, and also of individual members, by an outsider to ensure that the board is doing a good job and to get ideas for improvements. Implementing these strategies will help break up the good old boy network.

SUMMARY

The chapter summary is organized to answer the learning outcomes for Chapter 3.

1. **Analyze old and new employment relationship differences.**

   Under the old employment relationship, job seekers were expected to be hired and trained for the job, whereas in the new relationship employees are expected to have the skills and experience to get the job. The old relationship provided job security, steady pay increases with good benefits, opportunities for advancement, and long-term employment; whereas the new relationship doesn't, and employees are responsible for their own career future, which is likely to entail having multiple jobs. The old relationship called for loyalty to and identification with the employer, whereas the new one expects loyalty to self and identification with the profession. The old manager–employee relationship was more adversarial, whereas the new one is more collaborative.

2. **Compare and contrast employment contracts in union and nonunion organizations.**

   All employer–employee relations include employment contacts. Nonunion employment contracts are negotiated on an individual basis; they are

   usually implicit, informal, and not written. Union employment contracts are developed through collective bargaining and affect all union members; they are usually explicit, formal, and written legal contracts. Thus, employer and employee relations are different in both environments.

3. **List and briefly describe six employee rights, in addition to organizing and collective bargaining.**

   Employees have the right to reasonable job security; employers generally need a reason to let employees go. Employees have the right to due process, to be treated fairly, and to receive an impartial review of a complaint. Employees have the right to a safe and healthy workplace. Employees have the right to personal off-the-job privacy, but not to business-related privacy at work. Employees also have the right to freedom of speech and to blow the whistle for wrongdoing at work without penalty.

4. **Compare and contrast mediators, arbitrators, and ombuds.**

   Mediators, arbitrators, and ombuds are similar in that they are all neutral third parties who help to resolve employer–employee disputes. However, mediators and arbitrators are used primarily during employment negotiating to help settle disagreements and to make a binding decision for them. Ombuds are primarily used to investigate and help settle employee complaints between employers and employees fairly.

5. **Define the corporate stakeholders and describe their primary power.**
The *stockholders* are the legal owners of the corporation. Their primary power is to select the corporate board of directors. The *board of directors* provides strategic direction and governance and oversees the managers of the corporation. The board's primary power is to select, advise, supervise, and evaluate the top managers. *Managers* plan, organize, lead, and control a firm's resources to achieve corporate goals. Their primary power is in their day-to-day control of operations. *Employees* do the work to provide the products and other functions. The employees' primary power includes collective bargaining and striking.

6. **Explain how the government helps to protect stockholders.**
The legislature passes laws to protect stockholders, such as the Sarbanes-Oxley Act that reformed corporate governance. The Department of Justice's primary government agency that protects stockholder rights is the Security and Exchange Commission (SEC). The SEC's mission is to protect stockholders' rights by regulating the stock market to make sure it is run fairly and that investment information is fully disclosed. Stockholders can use the judicial branch of the government to interpret the law and determine whether stockholder rights have been violated.

7. **Differentiate between inside and outside members of the board of directors and the potential problem of insiders.**
Inside directors are employees or people who have other ties to the company, such as being a family member or friend or doing business with the firm, including suppliers and customers. Outside directors are not employees and have no ties to the firm, so they are independent. The potential problem of inside directors is that they are often obligated to the CEO and may agree with whatever the executive wants.

8. **Fill in the blank with the appropriate key term (in order of appearance in the chapter):**
_____ is the employer and employee expectations, rights, and duties.
_____ are societal interest groups that represent their members' special interests with employers through collective bargaining.
_____ is the negotiation process resulting in a contract that covers employment conditions.
_____ is a neutral party who helps management and labor settle their disagreements.
_____ is a neutral party who makes a binding decision for management and labor.
_____ provide workers with desired outcomes and protection from undesired outcomes.
_____ doctrine holds that the employment relationship is voluntary and that employees can be fired or quit for any, or no, reason.
_____ is the right to be treated fairly and to receive an impartial review of a complaint.
_____ investigates complaints and helps to settle them fairly.
_____ protect employees' personal life from unwarranted intrusion by employers.
_____ occurs when employees report employer wrongdoing to high-level company managers, the media, or the government.
_____ is granted by the state giving the firm the right to operate under

established basic terms for its exist-ence and governance.

_____ are the legal owners of a corporation.

_____ provide strategic direc-tion and governance and oversee the managers of the corporation.

_____ occurs when a person uses confidential information before it becomes public knowledge to buy or sell the company stock.

_____ reformed corporate gov-ernance.

_____ place a suggested action on the proxy statement to be voted on by all stockholders.

_____ is the legal system of checks and balances defining the power of stockholders, boards of directors, and managers.

_____ are employees or have other ties to the company.

_____ gives the holder the right to buy a set number of company shares at a fixed price for a specified period.

KEY TERMS (IN ALPHABETICAL ORDER)

KEY TERMS

3

arbitrators (p. 84)
boards of directors (p. 93)
collective bargaining (p. 84)
corporate charter (p. 93)
corporate governance (p. 97)
due process (p. 86)
employee rights (p. 85)
employment-at-will (p. 86)
employment relationship (p. 80)
inside directors (p. 98)

insider trading (p. 95)
labor unions (p. 81)
mediator (p. 84)
ombuds (p. 86)
privacy rights (p. 88)
Sarbanes-Oxley Act (p. 95)
shareholder resolutions (p. 97)
stockholders (p. 93)
stock option (p. 100)
whistleblowing (p. 90)

REVIEW QUESTIONS

REVIEW QUESTIONS

3

1 What are the three reasons why people work?

2 What is the difference between a right and a duty?

3 What is the term commonly used for the management–union relationship?

4 What are the steps in the union-organizing process?

5 What branch of government over-sees OSHA?

6 What types of questionable employee tests are employers giv-ing employees today?

7 Do whistleblowers have any gov-ernment protection?

8 What are the classifications of stockholders?

9 What are the two primary stock-holder rights?

10 Is it necessary for all three branches of the government to protect stockholders?

11 When should you blow the whistle and how, and are there exceptions to the process?

12 What are the functions of the com-mon committee of the board of directors? List and describe each.

13 What is the primary legal strat-egy managers are using with employees?

DISCUSSION/CRITICAL THINKING QUESTIONS

Be sure to give a detailed explanation for your answer to each question.

1 Do you believe labor unions will make a comeback?

2 Should the government shift to be more pro-business or pro-labor?

3 Should managers fight unionization?

4 What can management and labor do to have a more collaborative relationship?

5 Will management–labor relations shift in a more collaborative direction, or will the adversarial relationship prevail?

6 Is the employment-at-will doctrine fair?

7 Does job security exist today?

8 Do employees have too many or too few rights?

9 Have employers gone too far with electronic monitoring of employees?

10 Is it worth blowing the whistle on your employer? Would you?

11 Is insider trading all that bad?

12 Are top corporate executives paid too much?

13 Is the criticism of boards of directors justified or overly dramatized?

14 How can corporate governance be improved?

APPLICATION EXERCISES

For these two application exercises, try to use a business you work(ed) for or one you would like to work for.

3.1 DEALING WITH AN EMPLOYEE ISSUE

Select a business that experienced an employee issue, such as being accused of violating an employee's right. Describe how the managers dealt with the issue. Which strategies did they use? What would you do differently if you were the top manager dealing with the issue?

3.2 DEALING WITH A STOCKHOLDER ISSUE

Select a business that experienced a stockholder issue, such as being accused of violating a stockholder right by a shareholder activist. Describe how the managers dealt with the issue. Which strategies did they use? What would you do differently if you were the top manager dealing with the issue?

CASE 3.1

Faculty "Striking" Out on Their Own at Long Island University

Long Island University (LIU) is a New York–based multicampus institution of higher learning and one of the largest and most comprehensive not-for-profit private universities in the United States. LIU offers 590 undergraduate, graduate, and doctoral degree programs and certificates, and educates more 24,000 credit-seeking and continuing education students in Brooklyn, Brookville (Post), Brentwood, Riverhead, Rockland, and Westchester.[83] LIU's total revenue in 2011–2012 was $452 million, of which 91 percent came from student's tuition, 8 percent from dorm rentals, food, and other living amenities, and only 0.9 percent from fundraising.[84] For the past several years LIU has consistently raised student tuition approximately 5 percent annually (in concert with faculty salary increases) yet has had difficulty maintaining a break-even status.

In September of 2011 the unionized faculty at its two main campuses (Brooklyn and Brookville) passed a strike vote when the university offered faculty a five-year contract with pay freezes citing the need to cut operating costs. The two campus unions rebutted indicating that faculty salaries accounted for only 15 percent of LIU's total operating budget and that continuing the tuition increase of 5 percent seemed egregious and ill-advised.

Negotiations continued with "the university's insist[ing] on a multiyear pay freeze, followed by raises that would depend in part on the level of tuition income from students."[85] The unions insisted that the university detach raises from student enrollment and that student tuition increases be more in line with proposed faculty raises. Negotiations broke down as both campuses' unions held strikes the first day of class affecting about 14,000 students.

At the start of week two of the strike LIU and the unions reached a tentative agreement. "The new contract provided no raise in the first year, followed by a 1 percent base pay increase in year two, a 1.5 percent increase in year three, and a 2 percent

increase in the remaining two years of the five-year deal. In each of the last four years of the agreement, faculty could also receive lump-sum payments of between 0.5 percent and 2 percent of salary if tuition revenue rises by 3 percent or more."[86] The faculties at both campuses were unhappy with this new agreement because of the tuition revenue provisions and student tuition rates but felt that additional time out of the classroom would negatively affect their students' learning. Tuition increases for students were still at 5 percent with the board projecting a $2 million dollar surplus (less than 0.5 percent of the total budget) based upon projected cost savings.

Questions

1. What are the rights of the union employees in this situation? What are LIU's rights and obligations?

2. How does the new employment relationship described in the text provide insight into LIU administration's thinking?

3. What are the interests of each internal and external stakeholder that are directly affected by the strike?

4. Assume that no agreement could be reached between LIU and the unions, what other options are available to settle the strike?

5. What is your reaction to the final settlement between LIU and the unions? In your opinion, who "won" and who "lost"?

CASE 3.2

Hacking the Hacker: James Murdoch and BSkyB

BSkyB, which is short for British Sky Broadcasting Group, is a British satellite broadcasting company that also offers broadband and telephone services. The company's headquarters are in London and they service customers primarily in England and Ireland. American mass media company News Corporation owns about

39 percent of BSkyB.[87] James Murdoch who served as BSkyB's chairman is the son of News Corporation's founder, Rupert Murdoch.

Why did James Murdoch step down and resign as the chairman of BSkyB? A phone hacking scandal involving voicemails of British royal officials pointed a finger at the Murdoch family's British newspaper group.[88] It was reported that "for months, independent shareholder groups have been calling for his resignation from both the BSkyB board and the board of the News Corporation."[89] Finally in April 2012 James Murdoch announced his resignation as chairman of BSkyB; however, he stayed on the board of directors and was succeeded by the former deputy chairperson Nicholas Ferguson. Murdoch issued the following letter to investors and his colleagues.

Colleagues,

As you know, my actions as a Director of BSkyB have been governed at all times by what is in the best interests of the Company, its customers and its shareholders. I have been privileged to serve first as Chief Executive and then as Chairman of this outstanding company and I am proud of what we have achieved over this period. We have invested to create choice for many millions of customers, grown our contribution to life in the U.K., and significantly increased returns for shareholders.

I have now decided that this is the right time for me to step aside as Chairman and, with the support of the Board and shareholders, continue to serve the Company as a Non-Executive Director. As attention continues to be paid to past events at News International, I am determined that the interests of BSkyB should not be undermined by matters outside the scope of this Company.

I have been transparent in my evidence and have behaved ethically at all times. However, there continues to be extensive and voluminous commentary around these matters. I am aware that my role as Chairman could become a lightning rod for BSkyB and I believe that my resignation will help to ensure that there is no false conflation with events at a separate organization.

BSkyB is a great success story and its positive contribution to British broadcasting and to the country more broadly should not be questioned. With a strong Board and outstanding management team, I am confident that the Company will achieve even more in the future. I look forward to making a continued contribution in my role as a Non-Executive Director.

JRM[90]

Questions

1. Describe how this case addresses the issue of stockholder activism and corporate governance.
2. What is the role of the chair of the board of directors and how does it apply to this case?
3. How do privacy rights and freedom of speech apply in this case?
4. If you were an employee of BSkyB and knew employees were hacking into voicemails of British royal officials, would you have blown the whistle? Why or why not?
5. What actions would you now take if you were BSkyB to minimize the bad press related to this incident?

INTEGRATIVE CASE (Part 3)

DHR Construction, LLC: When a Business Partner Behaves Badly[91]

INTEGRATIVE CASE

3

This is a continuation case—please refer back to Chapters 1 and 2 for further information.

Stephen Hodgetts read the e-mail over and over again and still could hardly believe what he had read. He had just returned from vacation, well rested and refreshed, and this e-mail had dampened his high enthusiasm. It took time to absorb such bad news and for Hodgetts to get over his incredulity. Yet, in the end, Hodgetts accepted the truth; a deep, dark, terrible truth that would not go away. R. J. Davis, his business partner's daughter, had confirmed in an e-mail his worst fears about their new business partner, David Russ. Many thoughts were running through his mind simultaneously, yet each screamed to be heard. How could he and his partner Richard Davis have been so blind, so trusting? How could they have taken on a partner, David Russ, who was such a heinous individual? How could Richard not heed the advice of his wife, Adrienne? What was now going to happen to their new business? Yet the one thought that continued to recur was a quote from Sir Arthur Conan Doyle's beloved character, Sherlock Holmes. "But there are always some lunatics about. It would be a dull world without them."

The Birth of DHR Construction, LLC

Richard Davis had done enough preliminary research on the real estate market in their area to convince Hodgetts that there was money to be made in becoming what Hodgetts half jokingly called "slumlords." In the interim, Davis was approached by one of his graduates, David Russ, who was designing their basements, about cutting out the middle man in terms of the rental business by building their own homes. Russ would act as the contractor—he knew all of the subcontractors who were needed in order to construct new homes and felt confident in his ability to manage the process. Davis had known Russ to be an affable and capable student and vouched for his character.

DHR was quickly incorporated and developed a simple business model. David Russ was made a 25 percent owner of the LLC and would act as the architect and head of operations of construction. His job was to work with the subcontractors to ensure that their work met schedule and building code requirements and to make sure that subcontractors' bills coincided with the work provided. Davis became the principal owner of the firm with both he and Hodgetts owning an equal percentage of the remaining shares. Davis handled the back-office functions of the business while Hodgetts acted as creditor and bankrolled the company's up-front expenses.

Ground was quickly broken. Davis's wife, Adrienne, even got into the operation of DHR, organizing meetings and coordinating communications between the office and the construction site. While on the surface everything seemed to be going fine, an undercurrent of discontent was running through the ranks of DHR's subcontractors, especially Alan and Wilma, their main work team and one of their tenants. They complained bitterly to Adrienne that Russ was both crude and rude in his dealings with them and with the other subcontractors and that Russ had threatened to fire them if they protested his actions to Richard Davis. Other subcontractors were complaining to both Richard and Adrienne that they'd be called into a project by Russ either too early, when the work was incomplete (and therefore they could not do their own work), or too late (they'd have to work around someone else's work).

Adrienne decided to intervene and have a chat with David Russ and to give him a chance to reflect on the feedback that she was getting. She told Hodgetts in an e-mail that "my lunch with David went well. We brainstormed bringing his wife into the business as a PR representative. Meaning, she would schedule the subs, bake cookies for them, and visit the job site to listen to concerns. That would take pressure off David and make him a better manager. There are still rough edges on him, but he enjoyed our time together. I'll do it again."

When the Mice Are Away

It was only a few weeks later that Richard Davis and his wife planned a two-week trip to Europe, after Davis's summer term was over. Hodgetts had plans of his own that also would take him away. R. J., the Davises' daughter, was left to manage the firm. Both Davis and Hodgetts signed proxies giving R. J. formal authority to act on their behalf. R. J. was slightly older than David Russ, had worked as a paralegal, and was the administrative assistant to the chief financial officer of the local hospital.

When Hodgetts came back from his vacation he found the following e-mail:

Just thought you should be aware of some things that are going on. After spending a week at the helm of the business, I became aware of some issues that were going on within the company. I know for a fact that the situation with David is getting worse by the day. I had lunch with Wilma on Thursday, during which she reluctantly provided some rather distressing information about his behavior on the site. After our lunch, I phoned David's wife and left a message asking to have lunch with her the next day to get her perception of how things were going with scheduling and the progress on the houses. (I mentioned nothing of my meeting with Wilma.) Somehow, however, this all got back to David. The fact that I was speaking to others caused him to become quite agitated. He proceeded to threaten Alan and Wilma (in front of his own wife) saying that no one was to speak to anyone but him and that he would report any information necessary to either myself or my parents.

I was not aware of this particular incident as it was happening, but I did quickly become aware that something had happened because Wilma called me a few hours after our lunch and in a very shaky, scared voice begged me to forget everything she had told me. Instinctively, I knew David had gotten to her. I've had enough experience in life to tell me when someone has been threatened.

I fought off my immediate impulse to find David and bluntly tell him that I will speak to whomever I damn well please and that he had no right to address one of our dearest subs in that fashion. But as he seems to feed off of confrontation, I decided to stay calm and quiet. I received calls from David almost daily telling me things were OK, but when I checked in with other people, that's not what I'm told. They are not happy—no matter what they tell David to his face, what I hear behind the scenes is not pleasant.

This is not a healthy arrangement. I have tried to remain as neutral as possible. I have always tried to keep a polite, professional attitude around him. Please understand, I do not enjoy making these statements. I wish to see everything work out for the best. But, try as I did over this past week to make everything better, I fear that I did not do enough to keep it from getting worse.

The houses are wonderful, but the company is strained. My suggestions are: (1) move David to a subcontractor role where he does not have the possibility of asserting false authority; (2) Richard (dad) must be on site more frequently to observe the progress and interactions firsthand (everyone has said that things are better when he's around, so therefore it only makes sense that he make his presence a more common sight); and (3) we need to assert again and again the rules, job descriptions, and ideals of this company. There must be no doubt who we are and what we are here for.

Thank you for allowing me to rant in my report in such a lengthy fashion. I do feel these issues must be brought to light and acted on.

Sincerely,

R. J.

Questions

1. Assume for this case that subcontractors have similar rights as employees. Describe the key issues in this case related to employer–employee relationships. What, if any, employee rights are being infringed on?

2. DHR Construction, LLC is a limited liability corporation with private stockholders. What are David Russ's responsibilities to the major shareholders (Richard Davis and Stephen Hodgetts) and their designated representative (R. J.)?

3. Several people "blew the whistle" on David Russ. Who were they and do you think they were justified in doing so? What did each of them risk?

4. Are David Russ's actions justifiable under either the old or new employment relationship? Why or why not?

5. Evaluate R. J.'s suggestions for dealing with the problem posed by David Russ's treatment of the subcontractors. Do you agree or disagree with them? Are there additional alternatives that Davis and Hodgetts should consider?

REFERENCES AND NOTES

1 http://investing.businessweek.com/research/stocks/private/snapshot.asp?privcapId=292492 (accessed May 15, 2012).

2 http://www.northforkbank.com/About/about.asp (accessed March 14, 2006).

3 J. Drucker and J. Bandler, "North Fork Executives to Receive $288 Million for Capital One Deal," *Wall Street Journal* (*March 14, 2006): A1.*

4 Ibid.

5 K. Sloan, and J. H. Gavin, "Human Resource Management: Meeting the Ethical Obligations of the Function" *Business and Society Review* 115(1) (2010): 57–74.

6 C. Caldwell, "Duties Owed to Organizational Citizens—Ethical Insights for Today's Leader," *Journal of Business Ethics* 102(3) (2011): 343–356.

7 X. Qui, "Does Investing in Employees Affect Firm Debt Levels?" *Academy of Management Perspectives* 25(3) (2011): 76–78.

8 D. Cooper and S. M. B. Thatcher, "Identification in Organizations: The Role of Self-Concept Orientations and Identification Motives," *Academy of Management Perspectives* 23(1) (2009): 76–77.

9 N. Bozionelos, "What Accounts for Job Satisfaction Differences Across Countries?" *Academy of Management Perspectives* 24(1) (2010): 82–84.

10 C. Caldwell, "Duties Owed to Organizational Citizens – Ethical Insights for Today's Leader," *Journal of Business Ethics* 102(3) (2011): 343–356.

11 K. Weise, "Hut, Hut, Strike!" *BusinessWeek* (June 27–July 3, 2011): 24.

12 K. Maher, E. Byron, and A. Frangos, "Benefits Fight Belts New York," *Wall Street Journal* (December 21, 2005): B2.

13 V. Smith and E. B. Neuwirth, "Temporary

Help and the Making of a New Employment Practice," *Academy of Management Perspectives* 23(1) (2009): 56–72.

14 M. Newkirk and F. Bass, "Does Right-to-Work Actually Work?" *BusinessWeek* (October 24–30, 2011): 32.

15 "News Broadcast," National Public Radio (January 20, 2012).

16 "News Broadcast," National Public Radio (October 10, 2011).

17 National Education Association, www.nea.org (accessed March 16, 2012).

18 AFL-CIO, www.aflcio.org (accessed March 16, 2012).

19 International Brotherhood of Teamsters, www.teamsters.org (accessed March 16, 2012).

20 United Food and Commercial Workers International Union (UFCW), www.ufcw.org (accessed March 16, 2012).

21 Service Employees International Union (SEIU), www.seiu.org (accessed March 16, 2012).

22 M. Orey and J. Sasseen, "No Solidarity for Labor," *BusinessWeek* (June 15, 2009): 28–29.

23 S. Armour, "Beyond the Reach of Republicans?" *BusinessWeek* (Winter 2011): 57–58.

24 M. Trottman, "Labor Board Swears in Three New Members," *Wall Street Journal* (January 10, 2012): A3.

25 National Labor Relations Board, www.nlrb.gov (accessed March 16, 2012).

26 M. Dolan, "For UAW, Jobs Trump Pay," *Wall Street Journal* (July 25, 2011): B1.

27 G. Bensinger, "Unions Walk Out at Verizon," *Wall Street Journal* (August 8, 2011): B1.

28 M. Futterman and L.A.E. Schuker, "NFL and Players Agree on New Deal," *Wall Street Journal* (July 26, 2011): A1.

29 K. Clark, "NBA's Owners Win Big," *Wall Street Journal* (November 28, 2011): B3.

30 J. Bennett, "Old-School Labor Brawl Erupts at Ohio Tire Plant," *Wall Street Journal* (December 8, 2011): B1.

31 K. Vyas and A. Gonalez, "Panel Deals a Setback to Exxon in Venezuela," *Wall Street Journal* (January 3, 2012): B5.

32 M. Trottman, "Union Sues Over Truck Pact," *Wall Street Journal* (September 2–3, 2011): A2.

33 K. Clark, "NBA Players File Antitrust Lawsuit," *Wall Street Journal* (November 16, 2011): B3.

34 "Fiat Threatens to Say Arrivederci, Italia,"

BusinessWeek (October 31–November 6, 2011): 30–31.

35 B. Hunter, "Hard Choices," *BusinessWeek* (November 28–December 4, 2011): 116.

36 J. Jargon and M. Spector, "Hostess Tries to Lengthen Shelf Life," *Wall Street Journal* (January 11, 2012): B1.

37 K. Weise, "Hostess Brands," *BusinessWeek* (January 16–22, 2012): 23.

38 G. Bensinger, "Unions Walk Out at Verizon," *Wall Street Journal* (August 8, 2011): B1.

39 M. Dolan, "For UAW, Jobs Trump Pay," *Wall Street Journal* (July 25, 2011): B1.

40 V. Smith and E. B. Neuwirth, "Temporary Help and the Making of a New Employment Practice," *Academy of Management Perspectives* 23(1) (2009): 56–72.

41 S. Carey and J. Nicas, "United Feeling Merger Pains," *Wall Street Journal* (September 27, 2011): B1.

42 OSHA, www.osha.gov (accessed March 19, 2012).

43 S. Armour, "Beyond the Reach of Republicans?" *BusinessWeek* (Winter 2011): 57–58.

44 B. J. Tepper, S. E. Moss, and M. K. Duffy, "Predictors of Abusive Supervision: Supervisor Perceptions of Deep-Level Dissimilarity, Relationship Conflict, and Subordinate Performance," *Academy of Management Journal* 54(2) (2011): 279–294.

45 S. Shellenbarger, "How to Keep Your Cool in Angry Times," *Wall Street Journal* (September 22, 2010): D3.

46. 46 K. Maher, "In Novel Tactic, Cintas Workers Sue Union," *Wall Street Journal* (December 27, 2005): A13.

47 OSHA, www.osha.gov (accessed March 19, 2012).

48 SEC, www.sec.gov (accessed March 19, 2012).

49 J. R. Hagerty, "Some Current Fannie Managers Missed Signals, Report Suggests," *Wall Street Journal* (March 1, 2006): A2.

50 R. Greene, "Illegal Ocean Dumping Persists Despite JD Crackdown" (April 4, 2012), http://www.iwatchnews.org/2012/03/30/8558/illegal-ocean-dumping-persists-despite-JD-crackdown (accessed May 2, 2012).

51 Ibid.

52 Ibid.

53 T. Emery, "With Tips From Whistle-Blowers, More Hands on Deck in Pollution Cases," *New York Times* (February 13, 2012), http://www.nytimes.com/2012/02/13/us/whis-

tle-blowers-help-us-fight-ocean-dumping. html?_r=1&ref=whistleblowers#.

54 R. Greene, "Illegal Ocean Dumping Persists Ddespite JD Crackdown" (April 4, 2012),. http://www.iwatchnews. org/2012/03/30/8558/illegal-ocean-dumping-persists-despite-JD-crackdown (accessed May 2, 2012).

55 C. Buckley, "A Celebration of the Ax," *BusinessWeek* (October 3–9, 2011): 109–110.

56 P. Puranam and B. S. Vanneste, "Trust and Governance: Untangling a Tangled Web," *Academy of Management Review* 34(1) (2009): 11–31.

57 J. He and H. C. Wang, "Innovative Knowledge Assets and Economic Performance: The Asymmetric Roles of Incentives and Monitoring," *Academy of Management Journal* 52(5) (2009): 919–938.

58 K. Scannell, "Policy Makers Work to Give Shareholder More Boardroom Clout," *Wall Street Journal* (March 26, 2009): B4.

59 K. Scannell, "Policy Makers Work to Give Shareholder More Boardroom Clout," *Wall Street Journal* (March 26, 2009): B4.

60 N. M. Pless, T. Maak, and G. K. Stahl, "Developing Responsible Global Leaders Through International Service Learning Programs: The Ulysses Experience," *Academy of Management Learning & Education* 10(2) (2011): 237–260.

61 R. H. Lester, A. Hillman, A. Zardkoohi, and A. A. Cannella, "Former Government Officials as Outside Directors: The Role of Human and Social Capital," *Academy of Management Journal* 51(5) (2008): 999–1013.

62 J. P. Walsh, "CEO Compensation and the Responsibilities of the Business Scholar to Society," *Academy of Management Prospectus* 22(2) (2008): 26–33.

63 AFL-CIO, www.aflcio.org (click Corporate Watch then Executive Paywatch) (accessed March 19, 2012).

64 M. L. Barnett and A. A. King, "Good Fences Make Good Neighbors: A Longitudinal Analysis of an Industry Self-Regulatory Institution," *Academy of Management Journal* 51(6) (2008): 1150–1170.

65 R. Makadok and R. Coff, "Both Market and Hierarchy: An Incentive-System Theory of Hybrid Governance Forms," *Academy of Management Review* 34(2) (2009): 297–319.

66 B. Kowitt and R. Arora, "The 50 Most Powerful Women," *Fortune* (October 17, 2011): 125–133.

67 R. H. Lester, A. Hillman, A. Zardkoohi, and A. A. Cannella, "Former Government Officials as Outside Directors: The Role of Human and Social Capital," *Academy of Management Journal* 51(5) (2008): 999–1013.

68 Ibid.

69 Staff, "The Fading Appeal of the Boardroom," *The Economist* (February 10, 2001): 67.

70 Pearl Meyer & Partners survey, www.pearl-meyers.com (accessed March 9, 2006).

71 "Special Report: Corporate America's Woes, Continued—Enron: One Year On" *The Economist* (November 30, 2002).

72 A. J. Wowak, D. C. Hambrick, and A. D. Henderson, "Do CEOs Encounter Within-Tenure Settling UP? A Multiperiod Perspective on Executive Pay and Dismissal," *Academy of Management Journal* 54(4) (2011): 719–739.

73 Ibid.

74 AFL-CIO, www.paywatch.org (accessed March 21, 2012).

75 K. Kranhold, "GE Chief Gets $15 Million in Pay and up to $14.6 Million in Shares," *Wall Street Journal* (March 3–4, 2006): A1.

76 A. J. Wowak, D. C. Hambrick, and A. D. Henderson, "Do CEOs Encounter Within-Tenure Settling UP? A Multiperiod Perspective on Executive Pay and Dismissal," *Academy of Management Journal* 54(4) (2011): 719–739.

77 N. M. Pless, T. Maak, and G. K. Stahl, "Developing Responsible Global Leaders Through International Service Learning Programs: The Ulysses Experience," *Academy of Management Learning & Education* 10(2) (2011): 237–260.

78 C. Caldwell, "Duties Owed to Organizational Citizens—Ethical Insights for Today's Leader," *Journal of Business Ethics* 102(3) (2011): 343–356.

79 K. Sloan, and J. H. Gavin, "Human Resource Management: Meeting the Ethical Obligations of the Function. Business and Society Review," *Business and Society Review* 115(1) (2010): 57–74.

80 N. M. Pless, T. Maak, and G. K. Stahl, "Developing Responsible Global Leaders Through International Service Learning Programs: The Ulysses Experience," *Academy of Management Learning & Education* 10(2) (2011): 237–260.

81 A. J. Wowak, D. C. Hambrick, and A. D.

Henderson, "Do CEOs Encounter Within-Tenure Settling UP? A Multiperiod Perspective on Executive Pay and Dismissal," *Academy of Management Journal* 54(4) (2011): 719–739.

82 R. H. Lester, A. Hillman, A. Zardkoohi, and A. A. Cannella, "Former Government Officials as Outside Directors: The Role of Human and Social Capital," *Academy of Management Journal* 51(5) (2008): 999–1013.

83 http://www.liu.edu/About.aspx (accessed May 15, 2012).

84 Long Island University Faculty Federation flyer.

85 R. Perez-Pena. "Deal May Be Near in LIU Strike," *New York Times* (September 9, 2011). http://www.nytimes.com/2011/09/10/nyregion/liu-faculty-strike-may-be-near-end.html.

86 P. Hogness, and A. Paul. "Faculty Strike Wins 'Imperfect Victory' at LIU," *PSC CUNY* (September 2011). http://www.psc-cuny.org/clarion/september-2011/faculty-strike-wins-imperfect-victory-liu.

87 D. Sabbagh. "James Murdoch Resigns as News International Chairman," *Guardian* (February 29, 2012), http://www.guardian.co.uk/media/2012/feb/29/james-murdoch-resigns-news-international-chairman.

88 http://www.cbsnews.com/8301-505245_162-57434601/developments-in-british-phone-hacking-scandal (accessed May 15, 2012).

89 J. Burns. "James Murdoch Steps Down from British Broadcaster," *New York Times* (April 3, 2012), http://www.nytimes.com/2012/04/04/world/europe/james-murdoch-steps-down-from-british-broadcaster.html?_r=1&hp.

90 Bloomberg News, "Full Text: James Murdoch's Resignation Letter to BSkyB Board," *Financial Post* Tech Desk (April 3, 2012), http://business.financialpost.com/2012/04/03/james-murdochs-resignation-letter-to-bskyb-board.

91 Adapted from H. Sherman and D. J. Rowley, "DHR Construction, LLC: Parts A & B," *New England Journal of Entrepreneurship* 7(2) (Fall 2004): 33–44.

Chapter 4

CORPORATE SOCIAL RESPONSIBILITY, CITIZENSHIP, AND DIVERSITY

Learning Outcomes

In this chapter, you will find out the answers to these key questions:

- At what level of social responsibility and citizenship should a business operate?
- Should business value diversity?

After studying this chapter, you should be able to:

1. Compare and contrast corporate social responsibility, citizenship, and social performance
2. List the reasons for and against corporate social responsibility
3. Characterize the three levels of corporate social responsibility
4. Describe the five stages of corporate citizenship
5. Compare the motivation and activity for corporate social responsibility (CSR) and corporate social performance (CSP) and the social audit
6. Describe the Equal Employment Opportunity Commission (EEOC)
7. Define the following key terms (in order of appearance in the chapter)

corporate social responsibility (CSR)	ethical CSR	diversity
corporate citizenship	benevolent CSR	protected groups
corporate reputation	corporate social performance (CSP)	harassment
levels of CSR	social audit	sexual harassment
legal CSR	triple bottom line	cause-related marketing

▪ Chapter Outline

What's This Chapter About?

In the last two chapters, we focused on the business side of the interrelationship among business, society, and government (see Figure 1.4, p. 22). We now explore this chapter's unifying question, "Who should address social problems and promote the general welfare of society?" This last chapter of the business part of the book (Chapters 2–4) bridges the gap between business and society.

Top-level managers must decide how socially responsible they and their employees will be, what type of corporate citizen they want to be, if they will report their CSR performance, and to what degree the firm will promote diversity. The firm also needs to develop and implement integrated CSR and diversity strategies.

CASE

Stonyfield Farm: Sustaining More Than Just Profits!

Stonyfield Farm was "founded as a project to help revitalize the struggling New England dairy industry and support family farms. Chairman/Founder Samuel Kaymen, one of the country's early authorities on organic and biodynamic agriculture, and President/CEO Gary Hirshberg, an environmental activist, windmill maker, author, and noted entrepreneur,[1] "wanted to teach people that food came from the earth and that sustainable agriculture is a food system with a future."[2] According to Kaymen and Hirshberg they "began with a few Jersey cows (the ones that make the sweetest milk) and a great-tasting yogurt recipe . . . we're still committed to producing the best-tasting, healthiest yogurts possible, and doing some good in the world while we're at it."[3] "We're committed to healthy food, for healthy people and a healthy planet."[4]

Now a subsidiary of Groupe Danone, "Stonyfield Farm is banking on choosy moms to spend a few cents more to save the planet—or at least buy its natural yogurts and ice cream. . . . Already strong nationally, the company purchased its California-based competitor **Brown Cow West** in 2003 to strengthen its presence in the western U.S. Stonyfield is maintaining the Brown Cow brand of yogurt products sold mostly through natural food stores. . . . Stonyfield's products are now mingling in main-stream America, distributed nationwide through supermarket chains, natural food stores, and wholesale clubs."[5]

Environmental responsibility

"The company recycles most of its manufacturing solid waste; invests in green packaging research and carbon offsets to neutralize its manufacturing plant's contribution to global warming; uses its lids and packaging to promote environmental causes . . . and has converted 90% of its products to organic certification. . . . [They] also collect recyclable cups and turn them into useful products. There's even a toothbrush and razor made from yogurt cups! . . . Wanting to offer its pickier customers a more earth-friendly product, Stonyfield in 2010 began packaging its yogurts in cups made from a corn-based, biodegradable plastic called polylactic acid (or PLA). So far, the company has converted its Stonyfield, YoBaby, YoToddler, YoKids, Be-Healthy, B-Well, Probiotic, and O'Soy multipacks to the new packaging."[6]

Health and nutrition

"Stonyfield Farm is a leader in product innovation and functional yogurts in the U.S. The company's products contain six different live, active cultures, more than any other leading brand. Stonyfield Farm is the only U.S. yogurt that contains *Lactobacillus reuteri*, a probiotic that is clinically proven to boost immunity and enhance digestive health. Stonyfield Farm products also contain inulin, a natural dietary fiber and a prebiotic that has been clinically shown to increase calcium absorption up to 20%. Stonyfield Farm uses only milk from farmers who pledge not to use rBGH, a growth hormone used in U.S. dairy farming but banned in Europe."[7]

Social responsibility

"Profits for the Planet (PFP) puts Stonyfield's guiding principle of corporate social responsibility into action. Each year, 10% of the company's profits are given to efforts that help protect and restore the environment. By directing financial support to those programs that affect positive and meaningful change, PFP embodies the spirit of the company's environmental and educational missions." "Stonyfield . . . was America's first manufacturer to offset 100 percent of its CO_2 emissions from its facility energy use; and installed the fifth largest solar array in New England to help power its production plant—all efforts to reduce global warming." Furthermore, they have "devised a web-based Healthy Vending Machine Makeover Guide [for school cafeterias] that includes a downloadable product list of organic and natural snacks." They also sponsored the "*Stonyfield Farm Strong Women* Summits [which] brought together women committed to getting involved . . . women who wanted to make a difference in their lives, work, and communities."

For its efforts on behalf of the community and the environment, Stonyfield has received numerous awards, including the Clean Air Excellence and Green Power Leadership from the Environmental Protection Agency; *BusinessWeek's* "America's Most Promising Social Entrepreneur" award in 2009; *Consumer Reports'* "Best Companies to Buy From"; and, in 2008, *Working Mother* magazine's "Best Green Companies For America's Children."[8]

In summary, Stonyfield Farm's products taste great and are all natural. Their operations are good for the environment, good for consumers, good for stockholders, good for the economy, good for the local community, and even good for the cows whose milk they utilize. Is this too good to be true or a role model for corporate America?

The following questions are related to the Stonyfield Farm case. Answers can be found within the chapter.

1. How is Stonyfield Farm demonstrating its corporate responsibility?
2. What arguments for social responsibility support Stonyfield's mission of being committed to healthy food, healthy people, and a healthy planet? What are some arguments against the mission?
3. What level of corporate responsibility is Stonyfield operating at?
4. Can Stonyfield's actions be labeled as enlightened self-interest?
5. What stage of corporate citizenship does Stonyfield Farm appear to be in?

CORPORATE SOCIAL RESPONSIBILITY AND CITIZENSHIP

In this section, we define corporate social responsibility (CSR) and citizenship, discuss reasons for and against CSR, present three levels of CSR, and explain corporate responsiveness and social performance (CSP).

> Learning Outcome 1: Compare and contrast corporate social responsibility, citizenship, and social performance.

Concepts of Social Responsibility and Citizenship

Recall from Chapter 1, the role of business is to create value for stakeholders. Business has a responsibility to all its stakeholders.[9] Businesses should try to meet society's expectations so they don't contribute to social problems. For example, managers are responsible for making a profit for the business owners, but at the same time, they also have a responsibility to benefit society by offering customers safe products, to not hurt community environments, and to obey laws and regulations.[10] Society counts on business for jobs, economic growth, products to improve lives, and taxes to pay for government expenses.[11]

The CSR concept means "to pledge back," creating a commitment to give back to all societal stakeholders. The motivation for CSR is based on moral values to do the right thing. A number of alternative definitions are used for corporate social responsibilities.[12] For our purposes, *corporate social responsibility (CSR) is the conscious effort to operate in a manner that balances stakeholder interests.*

The four areas of responsibility include: economic (to make goods and services for a profit), legal (to operate in accordance with the laws), ethical (to treat all stakeholders fairly and morally), and philanthropic (to voluntarily help societal stakeholder, such as donation to nonprofits). These four responsibilities form a pyramid with societal expectations as follows. Economic and legal responsibilities are required of business, ethical is expected, and philanthropic is desired of business by society.[13] So based on the pyramid, companies should be putting profitability first, because profits make it possible to be socially responsible to all stakeholders.[14] Organizations that help business with CSR include **Business for Social Responsibility (BSR)** (www.bsr.org) and **Corporate Social Responsibility (CSR) Europe** (www.csreurope.org). Visit their websites for details on the services they provide.

Stonyfield Farm Case Question 1: How is Stonyfield Farm demonstrating its corporate responsibility?

Stonyfield Farm is consciously trying to operate in a manner that balances its stakeholder's interests by producing organic and healthy products in an environmentally sensitive manner (recycling and humane animal treatment) while becoming involved in the community, funding environmental education, and continuing to grow the firm. In the process iFsitet has acquired a West Coast competitor and has been acquired by Groupe Danone.

The CSR concept has been incorporated into the broader term *corporate citizenship*. Corporate citizenship is a popular topic today,[15] with *The Journal of Corporate Citizenship* devoted to the topic. *Corporate citizenship includes social responsibility, responsiveness, and performance.* Here we will briefly describe these three concepts within corporate citizenship; more details are provided throughout this chapter.

■ *Social responsibility* includes business obligations and accountability to society. What is the responsibility of business? According to billionaire Richard Branson, "Every single businessperson has the responsibility for taking care of the people and planet."[16] Do you agree?

■ *Responsiveness* includes business actions in society. Is it socially responsible? Responsiveness often occurs when a societal interest group brings an issue to the business. Businesses need to respond with a stakeholder-driven approach,[17] because it is important to meet the needs of multiple stakeholders.[18]

■ *Performance* is the results and outcomes of business responsiveness; how does business measure and evaluate its social responsibility? More businesses are making CSR reports a part of their annual report.[19]

Personal and Professional Applications

1. Is the company you work(ed) for more focused on CSR or corporate citizenship?

Learning Outcome 2: List the reasons for and against corporate social responsibility.

Arguments for Corporate Social Responsibility

People debate about the ideal set of corporate citizen characteristics.[20] The question, what obligations do corporations have to be socially responsible, prompts dramatically different answers from different people.[21] For a list of the arguments for and against CSR, see Figure 4.1.

Arguments for CSR	Arguments against CSR
1. Being socially responsible promotes business long-term self-interest.	1. The sole responsibility of business is to maximize profits while obeying the law.
2. CSR improves business value and reputation—public sentiment.	2. The cost of social responsibility is passed on to stakeholders.
3. Society expects business to be socially responsible.	3. Competitors who are less socially responsible may gain a cost advantage.
4. Business is responsible for correcting the social problems it causes.	4. A business involved in social issues can lose its focus on operating as effectively as possible.
5. CSR discourages government regulation.	5. Dealing with social problems is the job of the government, not business.

▬ **Figure 4.1:** Arguments for and against Corporate Social Responsibility

1. Being Socially Responsible Promotes Business Long-Term Self-Interest. Research supports that corporate financial performance (profit) is related to social performance.[22] A business can do well by doing good, such as **McDonald's** offering healthier food choices.[23] This view that CSR pays is supported by the **Business Roundtable (BRT),** an association of chief executive officers of leading U.S. companies with more than 14 million employees. BRT companies give nearly $9 billion a year in combined charitable contributions.[24] For more information on BRT, visit its website (businessroundtable.org). **Dow Jones** created Sustainability Indexes to provide investors with information on the long-term future potential of corporate profitability, and two of the criteria are CSR and stakeholder management.[25]

2. CSR Improves Business Value and Reputation—Public Sentiment. *A corporate reputation affects the business's relationship with stakeholders.* A firm's reputation is one of the most important ways businesses can compete.[26] Starbucks CEO and chairman, Howard Schultz, says that corporate reputation is a means to success, not a by-product of it. CSR is the best adverting.[27] Nonmarket stakeholder societal interest groups, the news media, and the government tend to go easier on firms with good reputations. **Rating Research** measures and rates corporations by reputation and disseminates the ratings.[28]

Public sentiment is very important because the government tends to go after firms that make society angry, Big corporations become big targets if they don't have a good reputation. **Walmart** is the world's largest public company based on sales,[29] and it's one of the world's biggest targets. Walmart has a reputation for low prices, but is consistently under attack by societal interest groups, gets bad press, and is investigated by the government.

Personal and Professional Applications

2. As a consumer, how does a company's reputation influence your purchasing?

3. As a job candidate, did/does company reputation influence your application and selection?

3. Society Expects Business to Be Socially Responsible. In our enlightened day and age, CSR is a given.[30] Over the years, multiple public opinion polls revealed that people expect business to be socially responsible, even at the sacrifice of profits. Taxpayers don't want to pay for businesses' lack of CSR through negative externalities, such as pollution. Society limits the old approach to "business as usual."[31] Recall that if business does not meet the expectations of society, societal interest groups will pressure business to do so and they will also pressure the government to force business to be socially responsible (chapter 2).[32]

4. Business Is Responsible for Correcting the Social Problems It Causes. People are concerned about corporate irresponsibility.[33] If a business pollutes a river over time or spills oil, it should clean it. Only business can deal with some social issues like fair and truthful advertising, manufacturing safe products, and providing a good workplace environment. When a business does not meet its responsibilities, the government has the authority to make the business correct the related problem, and the business may be fined or even closed.

5. CSR Discourages Government Regulation. CSR results in businesses regulating themselves. Self-regulation means less government regulation, which in turn does not burden business with the associated cost of complying with government regulations.[34] The less socially responsible executives and business are, the more the government needs to make laws and regulate them.[35] As discussed in the last chapter, some businesses were not socially responsible in fully disclosing corporate activities. Therefore, Congress passed the Sarbanes-Oxley Act to reform corporate governance.[36] Compliance with the new regulations restricts business freedom, takes time and money to complete government reports, and has been called the curse of small companies.[37] With true CSR the act would not have been needed or passed.

Arguments Against Corporate Social Responsibility

Five major reasons why business should not be more socially responsible are:

1. **The sole responsibility of business is to maximize profits while obeying the law.** This view was popularized by Nobel laureate Milton Friedman.[38] CSR is nothing more than "rational" profit maximization, known as economic rents.[39] In doing so, the firm is being socially responsible by rewarding owners while giving society products and jobs.[40] It is not fair to the owners to spend corporate money on social issues rather than provide profits to the owners.[41] Actually, "when companies do well by doing good, the driving force is the pursuit of profit, not a commitment to social welfare. More often, profit and social welfare are at odds, and executives can't be expected to heed the call for CSR at the expense of stockholder."[42]
2. **The cost of social responsibility is passed on to stakeholders.** In addition to owners getting lower profits, the government gets less money in taxes, and employees may be paid less. The cost is passed on to society as consumers pay a higher price for products and higher taxes.
3. **Competitors who are less socially responsible may gain a cost advantage.** If multiple firms are polluting at the legal limit, and one firm wants to be socially responsible and is the only one to install new equipment that pollutes less, its costs will likely be higher. Thus, it will have to charge customers more or make lower profits than competitors.

4. **A business involved in social issues can lose its focus on operating as effectively as possible.** If a firm has a plant that is not efficient and does not provide a good return on the investment, but it keeps it open to help the community, in essence it is hurting itself and other stakeholders through the lack of efficiency and profits. Indirectly, it also helps competitors who are focused on efficiency take its customers. Seeking CSR may be a distraction from more effective initiatives to solve social problems.[43] If society hinders innovation and growth, the impact can be quite negative over the long term.[44]

5. **Dealing with social problems is the job of the government, not business.** Modern business solves one, and only one, societal problem through the creation of wealth by creating goods and services and jobs through profit maximization. Business generally lacks the skill to solve social problems. The solution is often government laws and regulations. A prime example is pollution. You can't expect businesses to be socially responsible and stop polluting; it requires government regulation with the power to set and enforce standards. But government regulation isn't perfect, and it can even reduce public welfare because of its cost or inefficiency.[45]

Stonyfield Farm Case Question 2: What arguments for social responsibility support Stonyfield's mission of being committed to healthy food, healthy people, and a healthy planet? What are some arguments against the mission?

Rationale for Social Responsible Behavior	Stonyfield Farm's Mission
1. Being socially responsible promotes a business's long-term self-interest.	1. Hoover noted that Stonyfield Farm is banking on choosy moms spending a few cents more to save the planet.
2. CSR improves business value and reputation—public sentiment.	2. The firm's unique mission and quality product has led to the firm acquiring numerous accolades while continuing to expand the firm's operation.
3. Society expects business to be socially responsible.	3. "Healthy" is a cornerstone in their mission statement and their products. Public sentiment and government regulators would tend to turn negative toward unhealthy industries (e.g., alcohol, tobacco, fast foods).
4. Business is responsible for correcting the social problems it causes.	4. Stonyfield Farm is proactive in implementing recycling and educating the public on the need to eat healthy food and cherish the environment.
5. CSR discourages government regulation.	5. Food production is already regulated by the government, yet Stonyfield's proactive recycling discourages government regulation in this area.

Rationale against Social Responsible Behavior	Stonyfield Farm's Mission
1. The sole responsibility of business is to maximize profits while obeying the law.	1. Stonyfield donates 10 percent of its profits to environmental causes—this is not maximization of profits.
2. The cost of social responsibility is passed on to stakeholders.	2. Stonyfield products cost "moms a few cents more to save the planet." Rather than save the planet, why isn't it saving these moms money?

3. Competitors who are less socially responsible may gain a cost advantage.
4. A business involved in social issues can lose its focus on operating as effectively as possible.

5. Dealing with social problems is the job of the government, not business.

3. Stonyfield is a premium product and sells at a higher price than the store's own brand.
4. Stonyfield's stock was acquired by Groupe Danone, which now controls the operation of the firm. Stonyfield might not have been acquired if it was more focused on protecting the firm from corporate takeovers.
5. Stonyfield's founders are not trained in public management and should leave the formulation, implementation, and evaluation of environmental, social, and economic policy to elected officials and government regulators who represent the interests of citizens.

Personal and Professional Applications

4. Is your sentiment more for or against CSR?

5. Which argument(s) for or against CSR best represents top management's view where you work(ed)?

Learning Outcome 3: Characterize the three levels of corporate social responsibility.

Levels of Corporate Social Responsibility

Clearly, in today's society, the question is not whether business should be socially responsible, the question is at what level of CSR should the business operate? Businesses do vary greatly in their social responsibility activities, based on the overall level of CSR at which they decide to operate.[46] Managers can choose to operate the business at one of three levels of CSR. *The levels of corporate social responsibility (CSR) are legal, ethical, or benevolent.* However, a firm can be between levels or be on different levels for different issues. See Figure 4.2 for an illustration of the three levels.

1. Legal CSR. *Legal CSR focuses on maximizing profits while obeying the law.* It also focuses on increasing sales and cutting costs to maximize returns to stockholders. In dealings with market stakeholders these firms meet all of their legal responsibilities, such as fulfilling contract obligations and providing legally safe products while honoring guarantees and warranties. They do what it takes to beat the competition legally. In

3. Benevolent CSR. Focus on profitability and helping society through philanthropy.
2. Ethical CSR. Focus on profitability and going beyond the law to do what is right, just, and fair.
1. Legal CSR. Focus on maximizing profits while obeying the law.

■ **Figure 4.2:** Levels of Corporate Social Responsibility

dealing with nonmarket stakeholders (society and government) they obey all the laws and regulations, such as not polluting more than the legal limits and meeting all OSHA standards. Some firms have been criticized for their behavior at this legal level. **Philip Morris** (PM), and others, sells cigarettes that are not illegal, but some question the ethics of the business.

2. **Ethical CSR**. *Ethical CSR focuses on profitability and doing what is right, just, and fair.* Providing ethical leadership and avoiding questionable practices mean doing more than is required in dealing with market stakeholders, such as treating employees' right and paying them fair wages, providing safer products, not squeezing suppliers, and competing to win business ethically. These companies meet reasonable societal expectations and exceed government laws and regulations to be just and fair to stakeholders. Many companies, including **Costco** and **Dick's Sporting Goods**, have return policies that allow customers to get refunds or exchanges without good reason, exceeding legal requirements.

3. **Benevolent CSR**. *Benevolent CSR focuses on profitability and helping society through philanthropy.* This highest level of CSR is also called "good corporate citizenship." Benevolent firms are *philanthropic*, giving gifts of money, or other resources, to charitable causes. Employees are expected, encouraged, and rewarded for being active volunteers in the community, often during company time. Benevolent firms sometimes team up with NGOs that advance social welfare (**Red Cross** and college), leading to improvements in CSR.[47] These partnerships are increasing.[48] The **United Way** is actively seeking partnerships with companies to innovate CSR; it even ran an advertisement in *BusinessWeek*.[49]

In addition to giving corporate money, many rich entrepreneurs set up foundations and give their own money (e.g., **Carnegie Foundation, Ford Foundation,** and **Bill & Melinda Gates Foundation**). Billionaire Bill Gates (cofounder of **Microsoft**), pledged to give away 95 percent of the Gates' wealth, only giving a fraction—a mere few million—to his three children. Warren Buffet teamed up with the Gates giving billions to the foundation. So far the foundation has given away more than $26 billion.[50]

Stonyfield Farm Case Question 3: What level of corporate responsibility is Stonyfield operating at?

Benevolent CSR focuses on profitability and helping society. This highest level of CSR is also called "good corporate citizenship." Stonyfield, with its focus on healthy food, healthy people, and a healthy environment, is operating at this level by donating 10 percent of its profits to environmental causes, developing healthy food guides for vending machines, and sponsoring developmental seminars for women.

An Overall Approach to CSR. Let's be clear on the difference between an overall and a situational approach to CSR. Top corporate managers decide on the firm's overall commitment, or level, of CSR. The board of directors and managers often make corporate policies to guide employee actions in dealing with stakeholders, and some have CSR mission statements. Some companies even have separate departments and executive titles for CSR.

A Situational Approach to CSR. Although firms have an overall guiding commitment to CSR, the level of CSR can and does vary based on individual issues. CSR has been called *enlightened self-interest* because firms will be motivated to engage in CSR activities when the benefits outweigh the costs as there is a link between single stakeholder-related issues and CSR and financial performance.[51] However, determining the appropriate level of CSR to meet the business's and stakeholders' self-interests is not quick and easy. Each issue requires analysis, risk–reward considerations, and how the stakeholder relations affect the overall health of the corporation.[52]

Stonyfield Farm Question 4: Can Stonyfield's actions be labeled as enlightened self-interest?

Enlightened self-interest is defined as firms engaging in CSR activities when the benefits outweigh the costs. It is difficult in any situation to discern an individual's or a group's motivation (and therefore the true motivation behind the firm's drive for social responsibility). However, it is clear from the case that Stonyfield has been quite successful in acting as a socially responsible firm (the benefits seem to outweigh the costs) and has served the interests of the stockholders.

Personal and Professional Applications

6. Overall, what level of CSR does/did your firm operate on?

7. Give at least two examples of issues for which your firm takes a different level of CSR.

Corporate Social Performance

Corporate social performance (CSP) is the assessment of the firm's corporate social responsibility and responsiveness. Recall that we defined corporate citizenship as having three parts. We have already discussed CSR and responsiveness with some examples. Having CSR and responsiveness action plans is a good idea, but measuring how well the firm actually performed socially is important as well.[53] Firms need to understand their social roles and the impacts of their corporations.[54] So now we expand corporate citizenship to add corporate social performance (CSP) to assess what corporations accomplish, or the outcomes of CSR and responsiveness over time. The **Council on Economic Priorities (CEP)**, a corporate watchdog societal interest group, reports periodically on the CSR of large businesses. We will expand our discussion of CSP later in this chapter.

CORPORATE CITIZENSHIP

As discussed so far, corporate citizenship includes CSR, responsiveness, and performance. We can think of companies as "citizens" in the countries in which they do business. In this section, we expand our discussion of corporate citizenship by presenting the stages of corporate citizenship, explaining global corporate citizenship, and giving examples of business interest in corporate citizenship.

Stages of Corporate Citizenship

Researchers develop theoretical frameworks to explain relationships regarding CSR and corporate citizenship.[55] To this end, Philip Mirvis and Bradley Googins, developed

"Stages of Corporate Citizenship," which is published by the **Boston College Center for Corporate Citizenship**.[56] Here we adapt the model to focus on the five stages with only the citizenship content, as presented in Figure 4.3. Let's discuss each stage.

Learning Outcome 4: Describe the five stages of corporate citizenship.

Stage 1 Elementary. This stage is essentially the same as the first level of CSR—legal. The focus is on profits and in pursuing this aim the firm creates products, jobs, and pays taxes while obeying the law. Companies at this stage are not interested in solving social issues.

Stage 2 Engaged. Companies engage in CSR to be benevolent.[57] Top managers are not just thinking about how to make money.[58] The firm gives away money and other resources to help society through philanthropy. For example, **Walmart** pledged to cut 20 million metric tons of greenhouse gas emissions from its supply chain.[59]

				Stage 5 **Transform** Change the game (Unilever)
			Stage 4 **Integrated** Partnerships, triple bottom line (AT&T)	
		Stage 3 **Innovative** Stakeholder management (Baxter and ABB)		
	Stage 2 **Engaged** Philanthropy, social issues (Chiquita and Nestlé)			
Stage 1 **Elementary** Profit (GE)				

▪ **Figure 4.3:** Stages of Corporate Citizenship

Stage 3 Innovative. At this stage, companies are active in stakeholder management by seeking to help society. Firms actively listen to stakeholders and try to meet their needs, within reason. Companies set up a structure to support these efforts and report their CSP. For example, **Pfizer** pharmaceutical company created a department of corporate citizenship. Pfizer also reports its social performance as part of its annual report.[60]

Stage 4 Integrated. Companies may enter ongoing partnerships with stakeholders.[61] For example, **U.S. Bank, Microsoft, AT&T**, and **GE**, just to list a few, have partnered with the **United Way**.[62] Integrated companies may adopt triple bottom-line measures, which we will explain later.

Stage 5 Transform. Transformers tend to have extensive partnerships with individuals and organizations across businesses, industries, and national borders to address broad social problems and to reach underserved markets, often in less-developed nations. For example, **Marks & Spencer**, a retailer, decided to "change the game" by going eco-friendly and drastically cut the firm's energy use, eliminate waste sent to landfills, acquire raw materials from sustainable sources, and enhance the lifestyle of its suppliers, employees, and customers.

Multilevel. A company can be at more than one stage at once, because it can progress faster in some areas than in others. Each business evolves in a way that reflects the challenges it faces with its unique set of stakeholders on different issues. A firm can also fall back in stage level, which is primarily related to profitability. When profits decrease, or turn to losses, CSR is often a common area to cut back. Again, profits have to come first to be able to be at a high stage of corporate citizenship.[63]

Personal and Professional Applications

8. Overall, what stage of corporate citizenship does/did your firm operate on? Give examples of how the firm operates at that stage.

Stonyfield Farm Question 5: What stage of corporate citizenship does Stonyfield Farm appear to be in?

Stonyfield is a "Stage 5: Transform" citizen given its visionary leadership and commitment to healthy food for healthy people and a healthy planet. The firm was founded to help revitalize the struggling New England dairy industry and support family farms and continues to support those groups (i.e., women) who wish to make a difference in their communities.

Global Corporate Citizenship

As business becomes more global, global corporate citizenship becomes more important. Global markets challenge multinational corporations (MNC) to harmonize CSR and citizenship across a broad spectrum of stakeholders with different corporate responsibilities.[64] An American MNC can't just be a good corporate citizen of the United States; it needs to be a good global corporate citizen. It needs to make a positive difference in the world through CSR and citizenship.[65] However, what is expected of corporate citizens in terms of time, money, and effort in citizenship activities does vary across national and cultural borders. For example, European countries tend to have higher citizenship expectations as part of their culture with more government requirements, whereas in the United States corporate citizenship is more voluntary. However, less-developed Asian and other countries tend to have lower expectations and CSR requirements. But even Asian countries exhibit a variety of expectations and requirements.

Therefore, each MNC needs to carefully tailor its CSR activities to meet the expectations and legal requirements of each country in which it does business. The choice of a configuration of citizenship activities is often referred to as a *citizenship profile* that fits the culture in which the company does business. For MNCs like Coca-Cola selling beverages in more than 200 countries,[66] being a good global corporate citizen with multiple citizen profiles is a complex endeavor. Proper communication of CSR and citizenship activities is important.[67] We will discuss global business in more detail in Chapter 11.

Benefits of Corporate Citizenship

We have already listed advantages of CSR, which are also benefits. Additional benefits and awards that enhance the benefits include the following:

❖ **Enhanced reputation:** A survey found that 93 percent of businesspeople think a company's reputation is very important.[68] Voluntary CSR and citizenship activities enhance a firm's competitiveness and reputation.[69]

❖ **Customer loyalty:** CSR and citizenship activities have emerged as an effective way for firms to create favorable attitudes among consumers.[70] Favorable attitudes can lead to greater customer loyalty and increased sales, whereas a bad reputation can lead to lost customers.

❖ **Better employee relations:** Firms that engage in active CSR and citizenship activities tend to have more satisfied and productive employees. Perceived citizenship had a positive impact on the extent to which participants defined CSR as a personal work role responsibility.[71] A good reputation also leads to attracting good job candidates.[72]

❖ **Awards:** *Corporate Responsibility* journal (formerly *Business Ethics*) publishes its list of Annual Business Corporate Citizenship Awards. The U.S. **Chamber of Commerce** bestows Corporate Citizenship Awards. *Fortune* magazine ranks the Most and Least Admired Companies. The **Conference Board** honors companies with the Ron Brown Award for Corporate Leadership.

> Learning Outcome 5: Compare the motivation and activity for corporate social responsibility (CSR) and corporate social performance (CSP) and the social audit.

CORPORATE SOCIAL PERFORMANCE

CSP activities involve going beyond legal requirements to engage in philanthropy, or CSP at the third level of CSR—benevolent. For example, **Salesforce.com** gives away 1 percent of its time, product, and equity to charity.[73] In this section, we discuss CSP audits, global social audit standards, and the stakeholder triple-bottom-line approach to CSP.

Corporate Social Performance Audits

Although the Security and Exchange Commission (**SEC**) requires corporate financial reporting, it does not require that social or environmental reporting be included in the annual report. However, a trend is growing toward more corporations assessing their commitments to CSR and reporting the results (social audit) of their CSP in their annual reports.[74]. *A social audit assesses the corporation's impact on society.* The audit measures CSR and responsiveness as CSP. The actual cost of CSR programs is difficult to determine, and CSP reports rarely outline their costs, which are difficult to measure.[75] Many corporations just list their CSR initiatives and formal CSP programs. **Atlantic Richfield, Bank of America, Chase Manhattan Bank, Exxon**, and **Philip Morris** were among the first to report social audits.

Global Social Audit Standards

Three major organizations set the global standards that help to unify social audits worldwide. The **Global Reporting Initiative** (www.globalreporting.org) provides a corporate reporting framework unique to each industry—essentially the international standard for corporate reporting on environmental, social, and economic performance. **International Organization for Standardization (ISO)**—*ISO 26000 Social Responsibility* (www.iso. org) provides guidelines for CSR. **AccountAbility's** *AA1000* Stakeholder Engagement Standard (AA1000SES) (www.accountability.org) are principles-based standards to help organizations become more accountable, responsible, and sustainable. All three promote financial and social benefits. (See the publications of these societal interest groups for the details of their standards.)

Stakeholder Triple Bottom Line

CSP is an important concept, but it still lacks strong theoretical foundations and validity.[76] Although benefits to citizenship activities are apparent, no clear generic or universal business case confirms that it does in fact lead to higher levels of financial performance, or that CSP causes it.[77] However, people are seeking a definition of wealth that expands beyond profits. Thus, some corporations replaced the simple stockholder bottom-line reporting of profitability with triple-bottom-line reporting. *The triple bottom line is a stakeholder approach to assessing financial, social, and environmental performance. Financial* performance includes the traditional creation of wealth measured by the balance sheet and income statement; the *social* bottom line includes CSR and CSP; and *environmental* performance includes initiatives to protect and conserve the natural environment. **Rolltronics** measures its triple bottom line and calls it both good citizenship and good business practice.[78]

Socially Responsible Investing

Many people invest their money in socially responsible companies because they want to make money, feel good, and make a difference. Social responsibility investing (SRI) funds have trillions in pension funds, mutual funds, and municipal and private portfolios. For example, **Women's Equity** funds buy from companies that advance the status of women in the workplace. The **Timothy Plan** avoids companies whose practices are considered contrary to Judeo-Christian principles, and the **Amata** funds invest according to Islamic principles. **TIAA-CREF** and others give individual investors several options, including a social choice fund. For more information visit **US SIF: The Forum for Sustainable and Responsible Investment** (www.ussif.org) and **Social Funds** (www. socialfunds.com). Both sites provide information for SRI funds and make comparisons for socially responsible individual investors.

ETHICAL DILEMMA 4.1 A Diamond in the Rough or Just Being Rough? De Beers in Botswana

De Beers S.A. is the holding company of the De Beers mining interests around the world. It oversees **De Beers Consolidated Mines** (DBCM, South Africa) and **The Diamond Trading Company** (DTC, UK). It also controls the De Beers diamond mining interests, including 50 percent stakes in Debswana (with the government of Botswana) and Namdeb (with the government of Namibia), as well as mining interests in Canada, the Congo, and India. At peak levels De Beers produces about 50 million carats annually, mostly from its Debswana operations, the world's highest producing mine. De Beers is owned by South African resources giant **Anglo American** (45 percent), the Oppenheimer family (40percent), and the Botswana government (15 percent).[79]

One report claims De Beers' diamond mining operations in Botswana do not create benefits for communities in the areas where it works. The report, compiled by the Bench Marks Foundation, has undertaken extensive research into corporate social responsibility in Southern Africa and focuses on the activities of Debswana.

The foundation is an agency of churches set up to serve churches and to monitor corporate conduct. The Bench Marks Foundation report said the jointly owned De Beers–Botswana mining firm was a "marriage," creating the perception of a dominant relationship that exists "at the expense of communities, human rights, the environment and sustainable local economic development," according *to Business Day*.

The foundation said that unless Botswana acts to assert its independence and its responsibility to its citizens as a whole, and not just De Beers, then its corporate social responsibility actions will continue to be ineffective.

De Beers has responded with a 22-page response in which it says that the report "neither reflects our experience in Botswana nor the findings of numerous reputable independent studies by academics and bodies ranging from the UN Development Programme to the World Bank."

De Beers said Botswana has used its diamond wealth to drive sustainable development for both individual communities and at the national level. However, the foundation pointed out that unemployment in Botswana remains high at 24–40 percent. Debswana accounts for 70–80 percent of Botswana's export earnings, and contributes 30–40 percent of the country's gross domestic product and about 40 percent of annual government revenues.[80]

Questions

1. What levels of corporate social responsibility (CSR) best describes De Beers S.A.'s operation according to the Bench Marks Foundation report? Do you agree with their findings?
2. Provide several reasons why you think De Beers S.A. operates at the level of corporate social responsibility (CSR) you described in question 1.
3. Examine Figure 4.3. What stage of corporate citizenship best describes De Beers S.A.? Why?
4. Is De Beers S.A. a good global corporate citizen? Why or why not?
5. De Beers S.A. is a highly profitable, well-established business in the diamond industry. Given what you have read would you invest in this firm? Why or why not?

Personal and Professional Applications

9. Describe the corporate social performance reporting where you work(ed).

10. Do you, or would you, invest based on corporate social performance?

DIVERSITY

An important part of being a good corporate citizen is embracing diversity and giving everyone equal employment opportunity, because it is good for society and business. So diversity is an important area of CSR and CSP. In this section, we define diversity and discuss why it is important, how it relates to equal opportunity for all, and how minorities and women are progressing in management and professional jobs.

What Is Diversity and Is It Really Important?

When we talk about diversity, we are referring to characteristics of individuals that shape their identities and their experiences in the workplace. *Diversity refers to the degree of differences among members of a group or an organization.* People are diverse in many ways. The Equal Employment Opportunity Commission (EEOC) is responsible for enforcing federal laws that make it illegal to discriminate against protected groups from workplace discrimination. *Protected groups include race, color, religion, sex (including pregnancy), national origin, age (40 or older), disability, and genetic information.*[81] Although these groups are protected from discrimination, every employee must meet the performance expectations of his or her job. Thus, an employer can't fire employees because of their race, gender, or religion, but they can for poor performance on the job. We must deal with all people in an ethical socially responsible manner.

If you are wondering whether diversity is really all that important, the answer is yes. Homogeneity is not predominant in the widely diverse global village workplace. Of the 7 billion people in the world,[82] less than 5 percent live in the United States, whereas more than a billion people live in China (1.34) and in India (1.2). Together they make up about 36 percent of the world population.[83] Clearly, U.S. business has to compete globally to maintain and increase sales, which is why businesses are integrating global awareness into everyday actions.[84] The likelihood is great that you will work for a foreign company based in the United States, spend some time working in another country, work with employees or customers from or in other countries, compete against foreign companies, or encounter diversity as a customer.

The world Caucasian population is actually declining as more people die than are born each year. While the population of the United States continues to grow, with about 311.6 million people,[85] it is rapidly diversifying,[86] the Caucasian population is not growing; its current ratio is one birth for every death.[87] The world population growth is coming from non-Caucasians, and in the United States more than half the growth is from Hispanics, which now make up the largest minority group.[88] Today, in 10 states white children are the minorities, and in 23 states minorities now make up more than 40 percent of the child population.[89] One in 12 children (8%) born in America is the child of illegal immigrants, making those children U.S. citizens.[90] By 2040 less than one-half of the total U.S. population will be Caucasian.[91] The diversification of the United States is clearly affecting us as individuals as well as business, society, and government. It isn't surprising that CEOs of *Fortune* 500 companies have said that diversity is critically important.

To discriminate against a qualified person because of a perceived difference that does not affect job performance is counterproductive to business success. Even if a good-sized business tried to be prejudicial and discriminatory (e.g., by hiring and promoting only white males), it would not get the talent or customers it needs to succeed in the long run. Besides, discrimination is against the law.

Personal and Professional Applications

11. Describe the diversity of people you have encountered as either a customer or an employee.

Equal Employment Opportunity for All

Diversity is a strategic business imperative, making a policy of inclusion essential. Businesses today are working to provide equal employment opportunity for all.

Employment Laws and Executive Orders. See Figure 4.4 for a description of several important employment laws and executive orders.

Law or Executive Order	Description
Equal Employment Opportunity	
Title VII of the Civil Rights Act of 1964	Prohibited discrimination in all areas of the employment relationship (hiring, compensating, promoting, discharging, and other aspects) based on race, religion, color, sex, or national origin. It also made racial and sexual harassment illegal.
Civil Rights Acts of 1972, 1991	Civil Rights Amendments provided possible compensation and punitive damages for discrimination.
Equal Employment Opportunity Act of 1972	Gave greater power to the Equal Employment Opportunity Commission (EEOC) to combat discrimination.
Executive Order 11246 of 1965— Affirmative Action	Mandated affirmative action for all federal contractors and subcontractors to accelerate the movement of minorities into the workforce. Companies doing business with the government were given preferential treatment if they had set employment percentages and quotas for minorities.
Age Discrimination in Employment Act of 1967	Prohibited age discrimination against people older than 40 and restricted mandatory retirement.
Rehabilitation Act of 1973	Prohibited discrimination based on physical or mental disability.
Americans with Disabilities Act of 1990 (ADA)	Strengthened the Rehab Act to require employers to provide "reasonable

	accommodations" to allow disabled employees to work and to provide access to facilities (ramps, elevators, rest rooms). ADA also required transportation systems and communication systems to facilitate access for the disabled.
Compensation (salary and benefits)	
Equal Pay Act of 1963	Required that men and women be paid the same for substantially equal work.
Pregnancy Discrimination Act of 1978	Prohibited discrimination against women because of pregnancy and childbirth. Prior to the act, employers could exclude health coverage to pay the cost of prenatal care and childbirth.
Family and Medical Leave Act of 1993	Required employers (with 50 or more employees) to provide up to 12 weeks unpaid leave for family (childbirth, adoption, eldercare) or medical reasons.

▪ **Figure 4.4:** Employment Laws and Executive Orders

Learning Outcome 6: Describe the Equal Employment Opportunity Commission (EEOC).

Equal Employment Opportunity Commission (EEOC). Several federal agencies enforce certain aspects of the discrimination laws and executive orders. However, as indicated in its title, the EEOC was created in 1964 as the major federal agency to administer and enforce job discrimination laws to provide equal employment opportunity for all.

The EEOC receives and investigates employment complaints and charges of discrimination. When it believes that unlawful discrimination has occurred, the EEOC attempts to arbitrate with the business and person or group discriminated against to agree on a settlement. When arbitration does not work, the EEOC may file a lawsuit in the federal district court against the employer. Common complaints and charges come in the areas of not being hired, being paid less, not being promoted, being discharged, and so forth. In recent years, the most discrimination complaints filed with the EEOC, in order of frequency, have been race, sex, age, disability, national origin, and religion.

Personal and Professional Applications

12. How have you been discriminated against in your personal life?

13. Have you and/or has anyone you know been discriminated against at work?

Harassment and the EEOC. The EEOC also concerns itself with harassment, which is a form of discrimination. *Harassment* is to persistently annoy, attack, or bother someone. *Workplace **harassment** includes slurs, derogatory comments, or other verbal or physical abuse and creates an intimidating, hostile, or offensive work environment or interferes with an employee's work performance.* Anyone can be illegally harassed. Remember it's being socially responsible to provide equal opportunity for all, not just protected groups. People are sometimes harassed because of their race, age, religion, ability, or the way they look, dress, talk, and so forth.

Sexual harassment occurs when any employee experiences unwelcome sexual advances or when on-the-job conditions are hostile or threatening in a sexual way. Physical and verbal advances are illegal, when submission to or rejection of sex explicitly or implicitly affects an employee's job. Suggestive touching, and sexual innuendoes are also harassment and are illegal from the time they first occur. However, for many other incidents, such as telling a sexual joke or asking for a date, the first offense is not considered harassment unless the behavior continues, is unwelcome, and is repeated after explicit requests to stop. Sexual harassment can also be caused by general behaviors that are blatantly and offensively sexual or intimidating to employees. For example, the courts have ruled that publicly hanging nude pictures of males and females creates a hostile environment.

Most sexual harassment is conducted by men against women, but some women do harass men. The law states that gay and lesbian homosexual harassment at work is also illegal. Sexual harassment can be between any two or more employees, an agent, or a nonemployee. In addition, the person filing the complaint does not necessarily have to be the object of the harasser. For example, a nurse complained about a doctor who repeatedly groped other nurses in her presence.

Do not be afraid to blow the whistle for blatant sexual offenses or if anyone does or says anything about your race, religion, ability, and so forth. Tell the person to stop or you will report him or her for harassment; then report it if the person does it again. To eliminate discrimination and harassment, we all need to be ethical with each other, and we all need to work together to prevent and stop abusive behavior. We need to stick up for each other, not ignore unethical behavior. If others fear blowing the whistle, you may want to report the offense for them. For more information on whistleblowing, see Chapter 3.

The EEOC has 47 field offices across the United States, and it operates a toll-free number (1-800-USA-EEOC) around the clock to provide information on employee rights. You can also get updated information about employment discrimination and litigation, enforcement statistics, technical assistance programs, and how to file a charge of discrimination. Learn more about the **EEOC** by visiting its website (www.eeoc.gov).

Personal and Professional Applications

14. Have you or has anyone you know been racially or sexually harassed at work?

15. What are your views on dating coworkers? Have you, or will you, date coworkers in the future?

ETHICAL DILEMMA 4.2 Guarding More Than Just Coins at the U.S. Mint in Denver

Security, as one might expect, is tight at the **U.S. Mint** in Denver. This government agency produces 32 million coins a day and is protected against intrusion. Yet David Lebryk, acting director of the U.S. Mint who oversees the Denver operation, was dealing with a different type of intrusion; male employees intruding upon female employees' right to a hostile-free work environment.

Lebryk had just received a memo from the highest-ranking woman at the Denver Mint stating that "there have been memos and talk about creating a model workplace environment, but no real action"[92] although Lebryk had recently gone on record as stating that the U.S. Mint is "committed to a model workplace free from discrimination, harassment and favoritism and has instituted programs to achieve this, including training for all employees to prevent harassment or bias and quarterly assessments of work-force attitudes."[93] The letter further noted that some women said that discrimination and sexist comments still occurred and that when they tried to file a complaint with the EEO officer they were told that it would be just their word against their supervisor's. Innuendos in the letter indicated that if no action was taken to resolve this problem that it was quite likely that the women would file a class action lawsuit against the Mint with the Federal EEOC.

Lebryk knew that rumors indicated there were "stashes of sex magazines. A secret attic room where male employees could hide out to peruse them . . . [that] new female employees faced crudely suggestive comments about their appearance. A manager often addressed one woman as a 'fat bitch.'"[94] Numerous complaints had come across Lebryk's desk from the Mint's EEO officer. For example, a 61-year-old female employee said that when she returned from a short bereavement leave following her husband's death, a supervisor propositioned her. In another incident a male coworker offered to pay a young female employee for sex, showing her the balance in his checkbook. She said her supervisor refused to take any action. A third woman had been physically assaulted by her male supervisor. All told, allegations from 71 women, more than half the Mint's female staff, had been made. In every situation, managers denied the charges; an investigation conducted by the EEO officer found no wrong doing, and no disciplinary action was taken.

Questions

1. Were allegations of sexual harassment and a hostile work environment in the memo from the highest-ranking woman at the Denver Mint justified? If so, on what specific grounds?
2. If you were Lebryk, how would you respond to the memo?
3. Based upon this memo, what actions, if any, would you take relative to these rumors of sexual harassment and threats of class action lawsuits?
4. If Lebryk took no action based upon this memo and these rumors, would the highest-ranking female at the Mint be justified in whistleblowing (e.g., talking to the media, filing a complaint with the EEOC)?
5. If you were one of the women who felt she was being sexually harassed, what actions would you take? Why?
6. If you were a male employee at the Mint and knew about the harassment, would you blow the whistle, knowing it might not only mean your job but your career?

Affirmative Action. In general, business is not against the rationale of affirmative action or helping a diversity of people. However, business does not like government mandate. Affirmative action programs require firms doing business with the federal government to take steps to hire and promote people from groups previously discriminated against, with government approval. Businesses with $50,000 or more in annual federal government contracts must submit an affirmative action plan. Local and state government contracts given to business must provide opportunities for women- and minority-owned firms. Progress toward goals is monitored, but the objective is to achieve diversity through good faith efforts, more so than by simply meeting strict goals. Under the EEOC, it is up to the employee to take the initiative to file a discrimination complaint, which puts the employee in a vulnerable position at work. Thus, the EEOC gives employees whistleblower protection. College and university admissions also have affirmative action programs, some of which have been challenged in court for reverse discrimination. But in 2003, the Supreme Court ruled that race can be a factor in admission to law school.

Over the past 40 years, the meaning of affirmative action has changed. Today, *affirmative action* tends to refer to some degree of definite preference in determining access to positions from which a specific individual was formerly excluded. The current business practice commonly used is not to select less-qualified people, but rather qualifications being equal, the minority or female applicant is given preferential opportunity.

With complaints about affirmative action and cases of reverse discrimination, the future of required affirmative action program regulation is uncertain. For several years, the government has not been pressing affirmative action, but many firms continue to have affirmative action programs. For example, **General Electric, AT&T**, and **IBM** said they will continue affirmative action goals and timetables even if they are not required to by law. Why? Because minority groups have buying power and the skills business need that can affect company performance. The bottom line is that diversity and giving equal opportunity for all is good for society and business.

Personal and Professional Applications
16. Have you or anyone you know been helped or hurt by affirmative action?

How Minorities and Women Are Progressing in Management and Professional Jobs

The EEOC *minority* guidelines identify Hispanics, Asians, African Americans, Native Americans, and Alaskan natives as minorities protected under the law. Women are not considered a minority, and in some workplaces they are the majority. But women do have protection against discrimination as a protected group based on sex. Today, many large firms are voluntarily being ethical and socially responsible through implementing diversity programs to actively recruit, train, and promote minorities and women, as well as other diverse groups. So how are they doing?

Minorities. Minorities are making slow progress into management and professional-level jobs. However, their progress has not been rapid enough to make a significant change in the distribution of those jobs. Some Asians, African Americans, and Hispanics are going to college and doing well, but many tend to be concentrated in the lower-wage service-sector jobs. Clearly their level of education is a factor keeping them out of professional and management jobs. Thus, affirmative action can help. Clearly, we need to do a better job of educating all students and making more of an effort to help them advance.

Women. Today, more women are graduating from college than men, and women hold 51 percent of management and professional jobs,[95] but at each stage of advancement, men are at least twice as likely as women to be promoted.[96] Although it is important to have women on executive teams,[97] women face barriers in trying to climb the corporate ladder, particularly in a male-dominated industry.[98] Women only hold about 7 percent of the senior executive jobs (chairman, CEO/president, and senior VP) in big businesses.[99] The barriers to upward mobility in organizations are commonly called the *glass ceiling*, referring to the invisibility of these barriers.[100] The barriers can be insurmountable, especially for working mothers.[101] The United States has a federal *Glass Ceiling Commission* to help eliminate the problems, but it hasn't made much progress in recent years.[102] Only 18 *Fortune* 500 companies (3.6 percent) had a woman CEO in 2012.[103] Gender differences in salary still exist as well, especially for female executives.[104]

A major problem is that inadequate career development has kept women (and minorities) from reaching the top rungs of the corporate ladder, and corporate America needs to do a better job coaching and mentoring them.[105] Many women are frustrated with their lack of advancement, and more women are starting their own businesses. One in every 11 women in the United States is an owner or co-owner of a business. Women have ownership in nearly 9 million businesses (40 percent of all businesses).[106]

Industries and Advancement. Some industries have been more receptive than others to advancing women and minorities. For example, consumer products, financial services, retail, publishing, media, health care, and education tend to have more women and minorities. Greater advancement in jobs is associated with the government (public schools, the post office, and governmental agencies). Do women and minorities progress to higher levels because of better enforcement of laws or because of good voluntary corporate citizenship efforts?

BUSINESS NONMARKET AND MARKET STRATEGIES

As discussed in this chapter, businesses today realize the need to be good corporate citizens engaged in CSR.[107] Therefore, they are developing CSR strategies as part of their overall corporate strategy.[108] The bar for strategic CSR is higher today than ever.[109] Businesses have a variety of nonmarket strategies (see Figure 1.4, p. 22), they can use through the 5 Is strategic analysis (discussed in Chapter 2). Managers are integrating nonmarket strategies presented here with their market strategies because they know integration benefits firm performance. Let's discuss how the strategies relate to CSR, citizenship, CSP, and diversity.

Information Strategies

Clearly, to benefit from CSR, responsiveness, and citizenship activities, CSP must be effectively communicated.[110] Successful firms are reporting triple-bottom-line results that include facts and figures. They are implementing global standards, using outside sources, such as the **Dow Jones** Sustainability Indexes, getting expert testimony, and gaining stakeholder support.

Firms are gaining positive community public sentiment for being socially responsible with diversity programs through their own information strategies and through good relations with the news media that garners positive publicity.[111] *Fortune* magazine publishes a yearly list of the "50 Best Companies for Minorities," and *Working Mother* magazine and others have similar lists geared toward their readership; companies are working hard to get on these lists, and to stay on. Businesses are creating programs to help balance work and family life and improve the overall quality of life.[112]

Societal Strategies

Managers are rethinking the practice of business strategy in view of a range of social issues.[113] One such important issue is diversity. Failure to understand the importance of diversity undermines the management of diversity.[114] Managing diversity is not about tolerating differences, it is about understanding how important diversity is to the success of the organization. Having a diverse workforce no doubt helps a company's image, and can also impact the bottom line by reducing employee turnover, boosting innovation, and attracting new business. To this end, some large corporations are adding chief diversity officers (CDO) to the executive team. Their primary job is to create an environment where women and minorities can flourish.[115] Thus, *managing diversity* is about developing societal strategies that provide true equal employment opportunities for *all* —meeting the work–life needs of all employees.

Cause-Related Marketing. *Cause-related marketing links a corporation or brand to a social issue to benefit the business and societal interest groups.* Some businesses are building coalitions with societal interest groups and giving them donations.[116] For example, **Avon Products** sells primarily to women. To help its brand image, Avon took up the cause of fighting breast cancer. "In 2012, Avon celebrates 20 years of the Avon Breast Cancer Crusade. The company is the leading corporate supporter globally of the breast cancer cause, having raised and donated more than $740 million to fund life-saving breast cancer research and access to quality care."[117]

Business can strategically plan citizenship activities in the long term, but they can't always predict what pressures will come from societal interest groups, and what action they will request. Therefore, the strategy for dealing with societal interest group activists varies based on the issue and the responsibility the firm has to its other stakeholders.

Political and Legal Strategies

As the title of this chapter indicates, the focus is on society more than government. The primary strategy of businesses is to operate in a way to avoid lawsuits. This approach is the lowest level of CSR, and it is implied in the ethical and benevolent levels.

A well-governed competitive business environment with effective rules and regulations encourages efficiencies that move us away from some of the cultural traps of the past—racism, sexism, nepotism, and other types of discrimination. Most businesses are ethical, legally and socially responsible, and value diversity. Some have strategies that foster environments where women and minorities are actively recruited and promoted, and performing acts of corporate citizenship is part of how employees conduct their day-to-day work.[118]

SUMMARY

The chapter summary is organized to answer the learning outcomes for Chapter 4.

1. **Compare and contrast corporate social responsibility, citizenship, and social performance.**

   Corporate social responsibility (CSR), citizenship, and corporate social performance (CSP) all refer to how business operates in society. However, corporate citizenship includes CSR, responsiveness, and CSP. CSR is the conscious effort to operate in a manner that balances stakeholder interests, whereas CSP is the assessment of the firm's CSR and responsiveness. Thus, citizenship is broader in scope and includes CSR (how the firm acts and its activities), and it evaluates the results of its responsiveness performance (CSP).

2. **List the arguments for and against corporate social responsibility.**

   The arguments for CSR: (1) being socially responsible promotes business long-term self-interest; (2) CSR improves business value and reputation—public sentiment; (3) society expects business to be socially responsible; (4) business is responsible for correcting the social problems it causes; (5) CSR discourages government regulation.

   The arguments against CSR: (1) the sole responsibility of business is to maximize profits while obeying the law; (2) the cost of social responsibility is passed on to stakeholders; (3) competitors who are less socially responsible may gain a cost advantage; (4) a business involved in social issues can lose its focus on operating as effectively as possible; (5) dealing with social problems is the job of the government, not business.

3. **Characterize the three levels of corporate social responsibility.**

   The levels of corporate social responsibility are legal, ethical, and benevolent.

Legal CSR focuses on maximizing profits while obeying the law. Ethical CSR focuses on profitability and doing what is right, just, and fair. Benevolent CSR focuses on profitability and helping society through philanthropy.

4. **Describe the five stages of corporate citizenship.**

   Stage 1 Elementary: the focus is on profits. *Stage 2 Engage:* the firm gives away money and other resources to help society through philanthropy, and it may also help with social issues, such as the sustainability of the environment. *Stage 3 Innovative:* companies are active in stakeholder management by seeking to help society and tend to set up a structure to support its efforts and report its corporate social performance. *Stage 4 Integrated:* companies build more coherent initiatives, such as entering ongoing partnerships with stakeholders, and may adopt triple-bottom-line measures. *Stage 5 Transform:* companies tend to have extensive partnerships with individuals and organizations across businesses, industries, and national borders to address broad social problems and to reach underserved markets, often in less-developed nations. *Multilevel:* companies can be at more than one stage at once by progressing faster in some areas than in others.

5. **Compare the motivation and activity for corporate social responsibility (CSR) and corporate social performance (CSP) and the social audit.**

   The motivation for CSR comes from a moral obligation and implies corporate social performance (CSP). However, CSP can be motivated by being moral, by social pressure, by managerial perquisites, or by benefits of corporate citizenship. CSP activities involve going beyond legal requirements to engage in philanthropy, or CSP is at the third level of CSR—benevolent. The social audit measures CSR and responsiveness to report company CSP. The trend toward including social audits as part of the annual report is growing, and global organizations are working to standardize the audits worldwide.

6. **Describe the Equal Employment Opportunity Commission (EEOC).**

   The EEOC is the major federal agency that administers and enforces job discrimination laws to create equal employment opportunities. The five-member commission makes EEO policies and approves all litigation. The EEOC receives and investigates employment complaints and charges of discrimination, including harassment—racial, sexual, and others. In cases of discrimination, the staff mediates between the employers and the people who have been discriminated against. When mediation does not work, the EEOC may file a lawsuit in the federal district court against the employer.

7. **Fill in the blank with the appropriate key terms (in order of appearance in the chapter):**

   _____ is the conscious effort to operate in a manner that balances stakeholder interests.

   _____ includes social responsibility, responsiveness, and performance.

   _____ affects the business's relationship with stakeholders.

   _____ are legal, ethical, and benevolent.

   _____ focuses on maximizing profits while obeying the law.

   _____ focuses on profitability and doing what is right, just, and fair.

   _____ focuses on profitability and helping society through philanthropy.

   _____ is the assessment of the firm's corporate social responsibility and responsiveness.

   _____ assesses the corporation's impact on society.

   _____ is a stakeholder approach to assessing financial, social, and environmental performance.

   _____ refers to the degree of differences among members of a group or an organization.

   _____ include race, color, religion, sex (including pregnancy), national origin, age (40 or older), disability or genetic information.

   _____ includes slurs, derogatory comments, or other verbal or physical abuse, and creates an intimidating, hostile, or offensive work environment, or interferes with an employee's work performance.

   _____ occurs when any employee experiences unwelcome sexual advances or when on-the-job conditions are hostile or threatening in a sexual way.

   _____ links a corporation or brand to a social issue to benefit business and societal interest groups.

KEY TERMS (IN ALPHABETICAL ORDER)

benevolent CSR (p. 124)
cause-related marketing (p. 138)
corporate citizenship (p. 119)
corporate reputation (p. 120)
corporate social performance (CSP)
   (p. 125)
corporate social responsibility (CSR)
   (p. 118)
diversity (p. 131)

ethical CSR (p. 124)
harassment (p. 134)
legal CSR (p. 123)
levels of CSR (p. 123)
protected groups (p. 131)
sexual harassment (p. 134)
social audit (p. 129)
triple bottom line (p. 129)

REVIEW QUESTIONS

1 How is CSR related to corporate citizenship?

2 What are the levels of CSR?

3 What is the difference between the overall and situational approach to CSR?

4 Why should a firm take the time and expense to conduct a social performance audit?

5 What are the parts of the triple bottom line?

6 Are women EEOC minorities?

7 What industries have more women in higher levels of management?

DISCUSSION/CRITICAL THINKING QUESTIONS

Be sure to give a detailed explanation for your answer to each question.

1 Do you really believe that the cost of CSR outweighs the benefits to stockholders?

2 Who should be responsible for solving social problems?

3 Should business focus just on efficiency and profits?

4 Should social audits be standardized globally? Or should all firms report only what they believe is relevant to their situation?

5 Which method of managing ethics is the most important?

6 Is promoting diversity really important?

7 Should minorities and women be given special treatment through affirmative action? Does special treatment create reverse discrimination problems? If so, how should affirmative action be resolved?

8 Should the government press for affirmative action, or get rid of it?

9 Should affirmative action be allowed in college admissions? If yes, who should get what types of preferential treatment?

10 How do you assess the progress of minorities and women in management and professional jobs?

11 Should anything be done to help the progression of minorities and women in management and professional jobs? If so, what? Will doing so create reverse discrimination problems? If so, how should the problem be resolved?

APPLICATION EXERCISES

4.1 CORPORATE SOCIAL RESPONSIBILITY AND ETHICS

Select a large public corporation. Go to its website and find its report on its CSR. It may be included in the annual report. Report your findings.

4.2 CORPORATE DIVERSITY PROGRAM

Select a large public corporation. Go to its website and find information about its diversity program, which may include affirmative action. Report your findings.

4.3 EEOC

Visit the EEOC website (www.eeoc.gov) and report how to file a complaint.

CASES

4

CASE 4.1

Kraft Foods Inc.: Kids Love It, So How Could It Be Bad for Them?

What do Chips Ahoy!, Cool Whip, Cheese Whiz, Jell-O, Kool-Aid, Lunchables, Miracle Whip, Oreo cookies, Oscar Mayer hot dogs and bologna, and Velveeta cheese all have in common?[119] They're all Kraft Foods products that kids love to eat but contain limited nutritional value. Worse, many have accused Kraft of targeting kids' TV programming with their lovable, munchable cartoon characters and have characterized the firm's commercials as "kidsploitation."

"If "someone's in the kitchen with Dinah," it's Kraft Foods. The #1 U.S. food company, #2 worldwide after Nestlé, makes and markets a slew of food products[120] with revenues of $49 billion dollars in 2010 with net profits of $4.1 billion.[121] Kraft "recognizes that our business success is only sustainable if it maintains and strengthens the economic, social, and environmental foundation on which it is built. At Kraft, we are committed to responsible business conduct and we constantly strive to stay in touch with society's changing expectations of us to determine where we can make a meaningful difference. We focus our efforts in seven areas: Agricultural Supply Base, Contributions and Communities, Environment, Governance/Compliance and Integrity, Nutrition, Health and Wellness, People, and Quality and Food Safety. . . . Kraft is committed to making a difference in the communities where we live and work . . . contributing more than $84 million in food and financial support to non-profit organizations throughout the world. Worldwide, we have two main focus areas—healthy lifestyles and hunger relief. Our community and philanthropic giving also covers many other facets of community life, including sustainability, arts, and disaster relief programs."[122]

"Our responsibilities go beyond our commitments to shareholders. They include every aspect of who we are—the quality of the products we make and how we market them; how we treat our employees, consumers, suppliers and business partners; our financial performance; the impact of our business on society and on the environment; our donations of food and funds to address hunger and other important needs around the world; and our compliance with all laws and regulations. Responsibility is, at its heart, about how we conduct our business day-to-day. While the term 'corporate responsibility' may be new to some, operating with high standards of ethical business conduct has been part of Kraft for a very long time."[123]

Yet with all of these positive statements about social responsibility, Kraft has come under attack by critics who claim that their products have led to a massive increase in child obesity and is strongly correlated to their increase in advertising expenditures ($1.2 billion in 2002[124] to $2.3 billion in 2010).[125] Critics have been most vocal about the use of cartoon characters, Clifford the Big Red Dog and Scooby Doo, to advertise "sugary" and "starchy" cookie and cereal products.

Kraft's response to critics has been less than satisfying, at least from the critics' perspective. "Society can respond [to the obesity issue] in a simplistic, counter-productive, punitive way if it wishes, and if it does that, we do have a lot at stake," said Michael Mudd, senior vice president of corporate affairs. Roger Deromedi, co-chief executive, added, "What people eat is ultimately a matter of personal choice, but we can help make it an educated choice. And helping them get more active is every bit as important as helping them eat better. By providing people with products and information they can use to improve their eating and activity behaviors, we can do our part to help arrest the rise in obesity."[126]

Kraft shocked the industry when it announced in January 2006 that it quit advertising certain products to kids under 12. "Our practices have become the model for how and what many other companies advertise to children. We were a founding member of the International Food & Beverage Alliance, and, along with other members, made a global commitment to the World Health Organization to advertise only products that meet specific nutrition criteria to children under age 12 and to monitor our efforts. We've made similar pledges in Australia, Brazil, Canada, India, Mexico, Russia, South Africa, Turkey, U.S. and all EU countries. Implementing pledges at the national level encourages local companies to follow our lead and to improve the types of products *they* advertise to children as well."[127]

Yet, all good intentions aside, Kraft still advertises on TV shows that young children under 12 may see, as long as more than 50 percent of the audience is over 12. They also continue to advertise in certain magazines that kids read and on websites. The company still holds contests for children as young as seven, such as the chance to be one of "The Cheesiest Kids in America," and get their picture on a box of macaroni and cheese. Critics say Kraft has too much discretion in deciding what's healthy and what isn't and call for more stringent government regulation of advertising these products to children. They note the company still reaches young children through cartoon characters on its packaging.[128]

Questions:

1. Identify Kraft Foods Inc.'s definition of its social responsibility using its own description. At what level of corporate responsibility is it?

2. What are the inherent values being espoused by Kraft Foods in its description of social responsibility? Are these values apparent in later statements defending the firm's products relative to the issue of obesity?

3. Which policies or actions of Kraft Foods might be characterized as enlightened self-interest? Why?

4. How does Kraft justify its advertising and sales of these products to children?

5. What actions would you take if you were the CEO of Kraft in response to the critics?

CASE 4.2

J. Christopher Capital: Getting the Straight Talk about Reverse Sexual Discrimination

Talk about a strange turn of fate—a gay man contends that he was fired because he objected to his boss's biased hiring: The boss, he alleged, had a bias against hiring straight people.[129] Jamie Ardigo sued J. Christopher Burch CEO of J. Christopher Capital for $1 million dollars alleging sex discrimination and wrongful termination. Ardigo, who had been hired as HR director, contended that he was fired when he sought to change what he claimed was Burch's and the company's discriminatory practices.

Less than four weeks into the job Ardigo was seated in a meeting where Burch announced that he hired only gay men because they were productive, and because he trusted them. Burch said the same thing, Ardigo asserted, later in meetings with the executive management team, where he'd blatantly stated that he only liked to hire gay men and beautiful women.

Burch's lawyer refuted Ardigo's story stating that "the company has reviewed the allegations and denies any wrongdoing. It denies there was discrimination or retaliation." Ardigo, says Cousin, was fired for "a performance-related issue."[130]

Ardigo found this troubling on two levels: As a gay man, he personally was offended. As an HR professional keenly aware of the need to maintain a nondiscriminatory atmosphere in the workplace; he knew that both the attitude expressed and any hiring that bore it out was contrary to federal and New York City law.

Ardigo, for his part, says he was fired because he called management's attention to instances of discriminatory and inappropriate behavior, including one in which a female employee, when being introduced for the first time to Ardigo, said to the person making the introduction, "Oh, are you going to introduce me to another gay guy?!" In another alleged instance, a male employee insinuated that a female employee had a vibrating dildo in her purse. When Ardigo reported this last incident to management and sought to have the male employee reprimanded, his says his report was ignored and no reprimand was given.

Instead, he says, pressure was brought to bear on him: His supervisor began pressing him to reveal information about himself. "He stated that he needed to trust me, and in order to do that he needed to know more about me." This made Ardigo uncomfortable: "Knowing the culture of the organization, hearing about their hiring only gay men, I felt there was an expectation that I had to reveal that information in order to be successful at work."

As an HR professional, he found this pressure "highly inappropriate." Regarding his job performance, his legal complaint says that not only was his work highly regarded within the company, but that general manager Jennifer Grillo publicly acknowledged the fact. The complaint also said that Ardigo, rather than being a disruptive employee, had been thanked several times for his productive support.[131] Burch's attorney retorted that the defendant denies the allegations of discrimination and retaliation set forth in the complaint and is prepared to mount a vigorous defense.[132]

Questions:

1. What level of social responsibility does J. Christopher Capital seem to be operating at?

2. Using the U.S. definition of sexual harassment, can the complainant's claim against J. Christopher Capital include sexual harassment?

3. Ardigio brought a civil lawsuit against Christopher Burch and J. Christopher Capital. What other options were available to him in order to rectify the matter?

4. Given Ardigo's description of the treatment he received at J. Christopher Capital, do you believe he was being discriminated against because of his sexual orientation? Explain.

5. Assume that you are J. Christopher Burch, CEO of J. Christopher Capital. What actions might you have taken before the lawsuit regarding Ardigo's dismissal in order to protect the firm's interests?

INTEGRATIVE CASE
4

INTEGRATIVE CASE (Part 4)

Landlords: Figures Don't Lie, But Do Liars Figure?

This is a continuation case—please refer back to Chapters 1–3 for further information.

Davis and Hodgetts were discussing the progress of their business ventures and came to an awful conclusion—the patio homes they were constructing were tapping into their cash flow and they needed a way in which to raise cash for the future growth of their business. "I think there is a way to pull money out of each of our rental homes quite quickly and recoup a good portion of our initial investment," said Davis. "Here is the plan. All of our rental homes have unfinished basements. Some of these homes have been framed for basements, others have not. Having looked at the framing, we could easily put in two additional bedrooms and one full bath. This would convert our 3-bedroom, 2-bath homes into 5-bedroom, 3-bath homes and add another 800–1000 square feet of living space to a 1,300–1,400-square-foot home. The values of these homes, according to my real estate broker, would rise about $30,000. We would need to invest $15,000 per home, using our own work crews, to finish the basements."

Hodgetts was in distress. "Let me see if I'm following you correctly and review our current situation," quipped Hodgetts. "We originally planned to invest a total of $100,000 into our little rental venture to the tune of $10,000 per home, for a total of 10 homes. So far, even with our own building firm, we have invested about $30,000 per home or $180,000 excluding, I might add, our investment in the building firm. At this rate, we will need another $120,000 to pay for our next four homes. Our plan, no, I should say your plan, was off by 200 percent. I can live with that, plans are not perfect." Hodgetts paused for dramatic effect, an action not unnoticed by Davis.

"But now," Hodgetts roared, "but now, your brilliant idea is that we finish off the basements, which really means spending more money. I've heard of spending money to make money, but this sounds insane!"

The Plot Thickens

Davis's reaction to Hodgetts's comments, hilarity, quite unsettled Hodgetts yet allowed him some time to cool down and think. Davis controlled his laughter after a few minutes and resorted to using a famous quote from Oscar Levant, "'There's a fine line between genius and insanity, and I have erased this line.' To paraphrase our good friend Oscar Wilde, you, my dear Hodgetts, are wonderfully tolerant. You forgive everything except genius. Now if you would be so kind as to let me finish,

perhaps I can respond to all of your objections."

"First off, remember that it costs us about $15,000 to finish off a basement. You can see that we would clear $15,000 per house if we refinanced these homes after completing the basements. Secondly, when we finish those basements, renters would be charged at an extra $100–$200 per month. I have spoken to several of our renters and they are quite excited about the possibility of getting a lot more house for a little more rent. They are also thrilled that when they go to purchase their home that they would be purchasing a fully finished house."

Hodgetts was calmer but unconvinced. "OK, so we get a little more rent money. Assuming $200 a month for 36 months, that is $7,200. It still does not pay for the basement renovation nor does it immediately put a lot of cash back in our hands. We still have to lay out 15 Gs! Again, where does this money come from?"

"You're right as always," answered Davis. "But let me finish the rest of my analysis. To make the math easy and to match my earlier example, let's assume that our $175,000 home with a finished basement is now assessed at $200,000. Now this home will be worth $210,000 at the end of the first year's lease, $ 220,500 at the end of the second year, and $231,525 at the end of the third year. The home at $175,000 would be worth only $ 202,584 in the third year, a difference of nearly $30,000. So, this $15,000 investment would yield a little over $7,000 in rental fees and $30,000 in increased home value. That's more than doubling our money in a three-year time period! More importantly, we would have pulled an additional $25,000 out of the house through refinancing in the first year—again, assuming a very conservative real estate assessment."

Sherlock or Shylock?

"This is all well and good," Hodgetts sarcastically commented. "But this scheme of yours is dependent on the good graces of our tenants. Would they really allow us to finish their basements, increasing the value and therein the selling price of their homes?"

"But my dear Hodgetts," retorted Davis, again taking on the demeanor of his favorite fictional character, Sherlock Holmes, "it is elementary. There is nothing more deceptive than an obvious fact. You forget that these are our homes, our property, and we can do with them as we like. I agree that we would prefer the cooperation of our tenants, as well as their additional rent, and we would even desire both their good graces and their aspiration to purchase the home in the long run, but business is business and we have to do what is best for our company and ourselves. To quote Mr. Sherlock Holmes, 'What you do in this world is a matter of no consequence. The question is, what can you make people believe that you have done?' I believe we can make a very persuasive argument, buttressed with perhaps some economic incentives, to assist our current tenants in making the right decision. The new tenants, on the other hand, will have to understand that this is just part of the rental agreement."

Hodgetts, who despised the idea of being a landlord in the first place, went along with Davis's original idea for the business because he felt that assisting low-income families in buying their first homes had a strong social value. A landlord who was benevolent was a rare commodity indeed! But now he could not believe his own ears. His face turned white as if he had just seen the Ghost of Christmas Yet to Come. A phrase or two of one of Shakespeare's most famous quotes stumbled softly, barely audible, through his cracked and barely opened lips. "For if you prick them do they not bleed? If you tickle them do they not laugh? If you poison them do they not die? And if you wrong them, shall they not revenge? For is it not enough to speak but to speak true?"

Questions

1. Hodgetts originally went into this business venture because he thought that he and his partner would be more socially responsible than typical landlords (see Part 1 in Chapter 1). Provide rationales for and against being socially responsible that would support Hodgetts's and Davis's positions.

2. At what level of corporate social responsibility is Davis proposing that the firm operate? How does it compare to Hodgetts' position?

3. What stage of corporate citizenship is being exhibited by Davis and Hodgetts?

4. How is Davis justifying his behavior to Hodgetts?

5. If you were Hodgetts, how might you sway Davis to your position?

REFERENCES AND NOTES

REFERENCES AND NOTES

4

1 http://www.stonyfield.com/AboutUs/BarnsEyeView.cfm (accessed April 4, 2006).

2 http://www.stonyfield.com/AboutUs/CompanyProfile.cfm (accessed April 4, 2006).

3 http://www.stonyfield.com/AboutUs/CompanyProfile.cfm (accessed April 4, 2006)

4 http://www.stonyfield.com/AboutUs/ (accessed April 4, 2006).

5 http://subscriber.hoovers.com/H/company360/fulldescription.html?companyI d=103880000000000 (accessed May 17, 2012).

6 http://www.stonyfield.com/healthy-planet/our-roadmap-green-business/environmental-milestones (accessed May 17, 2012).

7 http://www.stonyfield.com/AboutUs/StonyfieldDanone.cfm (accessed April 4, 2006).

8 http://www.stonyfield.com/about-us/our-story-nutshell/full-story (accessed May 17, 2012).

9 H. J. Van Buren III, "Taking (and Sharing Power): How Boards of Directors Can Bring About Greater Fairness for Dependent Stakeholders," *Business and Society Review* 115 (2010): 205–230.

10 M. Rosenwald, "Branson's Advice: Be Like Me," *BusinessWeek* (December 18–25, 2011): 90–91.

11 J. & S. Welch, "Giving in an Unforgiving Time," *BusinessWeek* (June 1, 2009): 80.

12 P. C. Godfrey, N. W. Hatch, and J. M. Hansen, "Toward a General Theory of CSRs: The Roles of Beneficence, Profitability, Insurance, and Industry Heterogeneity," *Business & Society* 49(2) (2010): 316–344.

13 B. Carroll and A. K. Buchholtz, *Business & Society,* 8th ed. (Mason, OH: Cengage, 2012).

14 J. & S. Welch, "Giving in an Unforgiving Time," *BusinessWeek* (June 1, 2009): 80.

15 W. R. Evans and W. D. Davis, "An Examination of Perceived Corporate Citizenship, Job Applicant Attraction, and CSR Work Role Definition," *Business & Society 50* (3) (2011): 456–480.

16 M. Rosenwald, "Branson's Advice: Be Like Me," *BusinessWeek* (December 18–25, 2011): 90–91.

17 P. C. Godfrey, N. W. Hatch, and J. M. Hansen, "Toward a General Theory of CSRs: The Roles of Beneficence, Profitability, Insurance, and Industry Heterogeneity," *Business & Society* 49(2) (2010): 316–344.

18 B. Dyck, K. Walker, F. Starke, and K. Uggerslev, "Addressing Concerns Raised by Critics of Business Schools by Teaching Multiple Approaches to Management," *Business and Society Review* 116(1) (2011): 1–27.

19 V. Pompe and M. Korthals, "Ethical Room for Maneuver: Playground for the Food Business." *Business and Society Review* 115(3) (2010): 367–391.

20 M. Glazebrook, "The Social Construction of Corporate Citizenship," *Journal of Corporate Citizenship* (Spring 2005), pp. 53–68.

21 Staff, "Corporate Social Responsibility: Good Citizenship or Investor Rip-off?" *Wall Street Journal* (January 9, 2006): R6.

22 R. N. Mefford, "The Economic Value of a Sustainable Supply Chain." *Business and Society Review* 116(1) (2011): 109–143.

23 D. Karnani, "The Case Against Corporate Social Responsibility," *Wall Street Journal* (August 23, 2010): R1, R4.

24 Business Roundtable, http://business-roundtable.org (accessed April 2, 2012).

25 C. Walker, "Long-Term Outlook; Corporations in the Dow Jones Sustainability Indexes Reflect on How They Rely on Sustainable Strategies to Boost Performance and Generate Growth for Investors Over Time," *Research* 28 (5 May, 2005): 80–82.

26 M. Rhee and M. E. Valdez, "Contextual Factors Surrounding Reputation Damage with Potential Implications for Reputation Repair," *Academy of Management Journal* 34(1) (2009): 146–168.

27 C. Hymowitz, " Big Companies Become Big Targets Unless They Guard Image Carefully," *Wall Street Journal* (December 12, 2005): B1.

28 The Rating Research, http://ratings-research.com/ (accessed April 2, 2012).

29 Walmart, www.walmart.com (accessed April 2, 2012).

30 J. & S. Welch, "Giving in an Unforgiving Time," *BusinessWeek* (June 1, 2009): 80.

31 T. Hahn, A. Kolk, and M. Winn, "A New Future for Business? Rethinking Management Theory and Business Strategy," *Business & Society* 49(3) (2010): 385–401.

32 T. M. Devinney, "Is the Socially Responsible Corporation a Myth? The Good, the Bad, and the Ugly of Corporate Social Responsibility," *Academy of Management Perspectives* 23(2) (2009): 44–56.

33 C. L. Pearce and C. C. Manz, "Leadership Centrality and Corporate Social Ir-Responsibility (CSIR): The Potential Ameliorating Effects of Self and Shared Leadership on CSIR," *Journal of Business Ethics* 102(4) (2010): 563–579.

34 D. Karnani, "The Case Against Corporate Social Responsibility," *Wall Street Journal* (August 23, 2010): R1, R4.

35 S. Boivie, D. Lange, M. L. McDonald, and J. D. Westphal, "Me or We: The Effects of CEO Organizational Identification on Ageny Costs," *Academy of Management Journal 54* (3) (2011): 509–527.

36 P. Cowen and J. J. Marcel, "Damaged Goods: Board Decisions to Dismiss Reputationally Compromised Directors," *Academy of Management Journal 54* (3) (2011): 551–576.

37 N. L. Wolkoff, "Sarbanes-Oxley Is a Curse

for Small-Cap Companies," *Wall Street Journal* (August 15, 2005): A13.

38 D. Ashlstrom, "Innovation and Growth: How Business Contributes to Society," *Academy of Management Perspectives 24* (3) (2010): 11–24.

39 T. M. Devinney, "Is the Socially Responsible Corporation a Myth? The Good, the Bad, and the Ugly of Corporate Social Responsibility," *Academy of Management Perspectives* 23(2) (2009): 44–56.

40 D. Karnani, "The Case Against Corporate Social Responsibility," *Wall Street Journal* (August 23, 2010): R1, R4.

41 Ibid.

42 D. Karnani, "The Case Against Corporate Social Responsibility," *Wall Street Journal* (August 23, 2010): R4.

43 D. Karnani, "The Case Against Corporate Social Responsibility," *Wall Street Journal* (August 23, 2010): R1, R4.

44 D. Ashlstrom, "Innovation and Growth: How Business Contributes to Society," *Academy of Management Perspectives 24* (3) (2010): 11–24.

45 D. Karnani, "The Case Against Corporate Social Responsibility," *Wall Street Journal* (August 23, 2010): R1, R4.

46 Staff, "Corporate Social Responsibility: Good Citizenship or Investor Rip-off?" *Wall Street Journal* (January 9, 2006): R6.

47 M. Van Huijstee, and P. Glasbergen, "NGOs Moving Business: An Analysis of Contrasting Strategies," *Business & Society* 49(4) (2010): 591–618.

48 D. Baur and G. Palazzo, "The Moral Legitimacy of NGOs as Partners of Corporations," *Business Ethics Quarterly* 21(4) (2011).

49 *Business Week,* www.businessweek.com/adsections: S2–S7 (accessed April 2, 2012).

50 Bill & Melinda Gates Foundation, www.gatesfoundation.org (accessed April 2, 2012).

51 P. Schreck, "Reviewing the Business Case for Corporate Social Responsibility: New Evidence and Analysis," *Journal of Business Ethics* 103(2) (2011): 167–188.

52 J. & S. Welch, "Giving in an Unforgiving Time," *Business Week* (June 1, 2009): 80.

53 P. Schreck, "Reviewing the Business Case for Corporate Social Responsibility: New Evidence and Analysis." *Journal of Business Ethics* 103(2) (2011): 167–188.

54 J. P. Gond, and A. Crane, "Corporate Social Performance Disoriented: Saving the Lost Paradigm?" *Business & Society* 49(4) (2010): 677–703.

55 Ibid.

56 P. H. Mirvis and B. K. Googins, "Stages of Corporate Citizenship: A Developmental Framework," Center for Corporate Citizenship at Boston College Monograph (Chestnut Hill, MA: Boston College, 2006): 3–5.

57 M. Orlitzky, D. S. Siegel, and D. A. Waldman, "Strategic Corporate Social Responsibility and Environmental Sustainability," *Business & Society* 50(1) (2011): 6–27.

58 T. Keene, "Tom Talks with John Taft," *BusinessWeek* (March 12–18, 2012): 18.

59 M. Rosenwald, "Branson's Advice: Be Like Me," *BusinessWeek* (December 18–25, 2011): 90–91.

60 Pfizer, www.pfizer.com (accessed April 4, 2012).

61 D. Baur and G. Palazzo, "The Moral Legitimacy of NGOs as Partners of Corporations," *Business Ethics Quarterly* 21(4) (2011): 541–557.

62 www.liveunited.org/gcl (accessed April 2, 2012).

63 J. & S. Welch, "Giving in an Unforgiving Time," *BusinessWeek* (June 1, 2009): 80.

64 C. H. Amato and L. H. Amato, "Corporate Commitment to Global Quality of Life Issues: Do Slack Resources, Industry Affiliations, and Multinational Headquarters Matter?" *Business & Society* 50(2) (2011): 388–416.

65 P. A. Heslin, "Social Entrepreneurship," *Academy of Management Learning & Education 10* (1) (2011): 164–166.

66 Coca-Cola, www.cocacola.com (accessed April 4, 2012).

67 M. D. Groza, M. R. Pronschinkse, and M. Walker, "Perceived Organizational Motives and Consumer Responses to Proactive and Reactive CSR," *Journal of Business Ethics* 102(4) (2010): 639–652.

68 "Porter Positioning," *Entrepreneur* (January 2009): 22.

69 M. Orlitzky, D. S. Siegel, and D. A. Waldman, "Strategic Corporate Social Responsibility and Environmental Sustainability," *Business & Society* 50(1) (2011): 6–27.

70 M. D. Groza, M. R. Pronschinkse, and M. Walker, "Perceived Organizational Motives and Consumer Responses to Proactive and Reactive CSR," *Journal of Business Ethics* 102(4) (2010): 639–652.

71 W. R. Evans and W. D. Davis, "An Examination of Perceived Corporate Citizenship, Job Applicant Attraction, and CSR Work Role Definition," *Business & Society 50* (3) (2011): 456–480.

72 S. Sorenson, J. E. Mattingly, and F. K. Lee, "Decoding the Signal Effects of Job Candidate Attraction to Corporate Social Practices," *Business and Society Review* 115(2) (2010): 173–204,

73 M. Rosenwald, "Branson's Advice: Be Like Me," *BusinessWeek* (December 18–25, 2011): 90–91.

74 C. H. Amato and L. H. Amato, "Corporate Commitment to Global Quality of Life Issues: Do Slack Resources, Industry Affiliations, and Multinational Headquarters Matter?" *Business & Society* 50(2) (2011): 388–416.

75 D. P. Baron, *Business and Its Environment*, 6th ed. (Upper Saddle, NJ: Prentice Hall, 2010).

76 J. P. Gond, and A. Crane, "Corporate Social Performance Disoriented: Saving the Lost Paradigm?" *Business & Society* 49(4) (2010): 677–703.

77 P. Schreck, "Reviewing the Business Case for Corporate Social Responsibility: New Evidence and Analysis," *Journal of Business Ethics* 103(2) (2011): 167–188.

78 T. Lawrence and J. Weber, *Business and Society* (New York: McGraw-Hill, 2011).

79 http://subscriber.hoovers.com/H/company360/fulldescription.html?companyId=55922000000000 (accessed May 17, 2012).

80 http://www.antwerpfacetsonline.be/nc/articles/single/article/corporate-social-responsibility-report-slams-de-beers-botswana-operations/ (accessed May 17, 2012).

81 www.eeoc.gov (accessed September 24, 2012).

82 United Nations data, *Wall Street Journal* (November 1, 2011): A1.

83 CIA, www.cia.gov (accessed February 27, 2012).

84 M. J. Chen and D. Miller, "West Meets East: Toward an Ambicultural Approach to Management," *Academy of Management Perspectives* 24(4) (2010): 17–24.

85 Census, *Wall Street Journal* (December 22, 2011): A1.

86 National Public Radio, "News Broadcast," on WFCR (March 30, 2011).

87 C. Dougherty, "U.S. Nears Racial Milestone," *Wall Street Journal* (June 11, 2010): A3.

88 M. Jordan, "Births Fuel Hispanic Gains," based on Census Data, *Wall Street Journal* (July 15, 2011): A3.

89 C. Dougherty, "New Faces of Childhood," based on Census Data, *Wall Street Journal* (April 6, 2011): A3.

90 M. Jordan, "Illegals Estimated to Account for 1 in 12 U.S. Births," *Wall Street Journal* (August 12, 2010): A1–A2.

91 S. Reddy, "Latinos Fuel Growth in Decade," based on Census Data, *Wall Street Journal* (March 25, 2011): A2.

92 L. P. Cohen, "A Federal Mint Is Hostile Workplace, Women Tell EEOC," *Wall Street Journal* (March 22, 2006), p. A1.

93 Ibid.

94 Ibid.

95 G. N. Powell and J. H. Greenhaus, "Sex, Gender, and the Work-to-Family Interface: Exploring Negative and Positive Interdependencies," *Academy of Management Journal* 53(3) (2010): 513–534.

96 R. Blumenstein, "A Blueprint for Change," *Wall Street Journal* (April 11, 2011): R1.

97 D. Lee, "The High Cost of the Gender Gap," *Wall Street Journal* (November 21, 2011): R14–R15.

98 R. Ren, "Executive Compensation: Is There a Gender Gap?" *Academy of Management Perspectives* 24(4) (2010): 93–95.

99 J. M. Hoobler, S. J. Wayne, and G. Lemmon, "Bosses' Perceptions of Family-Work Conflict and Women's Promotability: Glass Ceiling Effects," *Academy of Management Journal* 52(3) (2009): 939–957.

100 H. R. Bowles and F. Flynn, "Gender and Persistence in Negotiation: A Dyadic Perspective," *Academy of Management Journal* 53(4) (2010): 769–787.

101 J. S. Lublin, "Coaching Urged for Women," *Wall Street Journal* (April 4, 2011): B8.

102 R. Blumenstein, "A Blueprint for Change," *Wall Street Journal* (April 11, 2011): R1.

103 http://www.huffingtonpost.com/2012/05/07/fortune-500-female-ceos_n_1495734.html (accessed September 24, 2012).

104 U.S. Census, www.census.gov (accessed March 2, 2012).

105 J. S. Lublin, "Coaching Urged for Women," *Wall Street Journal* (April 4, 2011): B8.

106 P. S. Davis, E. Babakus, P. D. Englis, and

T. Pett, "The Influence of CEO Gender on Market Orientation and Performance in Service Small and Medium-Sized Businesses," *Journal of Small Business Management* 48(4) (2010): 475–496.

107 M. Orlitzky, D. S. Siegel, and D. A. Waldman, "Strategic Corporate Social Responsibility and Environmental Sustainability," *Business & Society* 50(1) (2011): 6–27.

108 M. D. P. Lee, "Configuration of External Influences: The Combined Effects of Institutions and Stakeholders on Corporate Social Responsibility Strategies," *Journal of Business Ethics* 102(2) (2011): 281–298.

109 J. & S. Welch, "Giving in an Unforgiving Time," *BusinessWeek* (June 1, 2009): 80.

110 M. D. Groza, M. R. Pronschinkse, and M. Walker, "Perceived Organizational Motives and Consumer Responses to Proactive and Reactive CSR," *Journal of Business Ethics* 102(4) (2010): 639–652.

111 M. Rhee and M. E. Valdez, "Contextual Factors Surrounding Reputation Damage with Potential Implications for Reputation Repair," *Academy of Management Journal* 34(1) (2009): 146–168.

112 C. H. Amato and L. H. Amato, "Corporate Commitment to Global Quality of Life Issues: Do Slack Resources, Industry Affiliations, and Multinational Headquarters Matter?" *Business & Society* 50(2) (2011): 388–416.

113 T. Hahn, A. Kolk, and M. Winn, "A New Future for Business? Rethinking Management Theory and Business Strategy," *Business & Society* 49(3) (2010): 385–401.

114 P. Chattopadhyay, C. Finn, and N. M. Ashkanasy, "Affective Responses to Professional Dissimilarity: A Matter of Status," *Academy of Management Journal* 53(4) (2010): 808–826.

115 L. Kwoh, "Firms Hail New Chiefs (of Diversity)," *Wall Street Journal* (January 5, 2012): B10.

116 M. Van Huijstee, and P. Glasbergen, "NGOs Moving Business: An Analysis of Contrasting Strategies," *Business & Society* 49(4) (2010): 591–618.

117 Avon, http://www.avoncompany.com/corporatecitizenship/breastcancer.html (accessed April 16, 2012).

118 M. Rhee and M. E. Valdez, "Contextual Factors Surrounding Reputation Damage with Potential Implications for Reputation Repair," *Academy of Management Journal* 34(1) (2009): 146–168.

119 http://www.kraftfoodscompany.com/Brands/largest-brands/brands-W/Pages/index.aspx?letter=w (accessed May 23, 2012).

120 http://subscriber.hoovers.com/H/company360/fulldescription.html?companyId=103392000000000 (accessed May 23, 2012).

121 http://www.kraftfoodscompany.com/SiteCollectionDocuments/pdf/Kraft-Foods_10K_20110228.pdf (accessed May 23, 2012).

122 Ibid.

123 Ibid.

124 S. Ellison, "Why Kraft Decided to Ban Some Food Ads to Children," *Wall Street Journal*, (October 31, 2005): A1.

125 http://www.kraftfoodscompany.com/SiteCollectionDocuments/pdf/Kraft-Foods_10K_20110228.pdf (accessed May 23, 2012).

126 http://icmr.icfai.org/catalogue/Business%20Ethics/BECG025.htm (accessed April 5, 2006).

127 http://www.kraftfoodscompany.com/SiteCollectionDocuments/pdf/kraftfoods_deliciousworld.pdf (accessed May 23, 2012).

128 1 S. Ellison, "Why Kraft Decided to Ban Some Food Ads to Children," *Wall Street Journal*, (October 31, 2005): A1.

129 http://abcnews.go.com/Business/gay-man-sues-boss-pro-gay-bias/story?id=16314667 (accessed May 23, 2012).

130 Ibid.

131 Ibid.

132 http://www.nypost.com/p/pagesix/fired_for_not_being_gay_fvkOXdza-2UhloHY3sj8h6M (accessed May 23, 2012).

Part 3

SOCIETY

BUSINESS ETHICS

Learning Outcomes

In this chapter, you will find out the answers to these key questions:

- How do I know what is ethical and unethical?
- What guides are available to help me make ethical decisions?

After studying this chapter, you should be able to:

1. Compare and contrast ethics, business ethics, and managerial ethics
2. Characterize the three levels of moral development
3. Identify reasons why people use unethical behavior and how they justify it
4. List general guides to ethical decision making
5. Compare and contrast virtues, deontological, and utilitarianism guides to ethical decision making
6. Describe the 3-way ethics test
7. Explain how the 5 Is strategic analysis includes the stakeholder approach and ethics
8. Define the following key terms (in order of appearance in the chapter):

universal ethics	justifying unethical behavior	generalization test
relativism ethics	ethical decision guides	utilitarianism ethics
levels of moral development	virtues ethics	utilitarian test
business ethics	virtues ethics test	ethics helpline
ethical dilemma	deontological ethics	ethics audit
ethical rationalization		

■ Chapter Outline

Business Ethics Foundations
   Ethical Concepts
   Moral Development
   Business Ethics and Ethical Dilemmas
   Business Ethics and Managerial Ethics
   Business Ethics Myths

Why People Use Unethical Behavior
   Personal Gain, Self-Interest, and Conflict of Interest
   External Pressure and Cross-Cultural Inconsistency
   How Personality Traits, Attitudes, and the Situation Affect Ethical Behavior
   Ethical Rationalization and How People Justify Unethical Behavior

Guides to Ethical Decisions and Behavior
   General Guides to Ethical Decisions
   Virtues Ethics Guide
   Deontological Ethics Guide
   Utilitarianism Ethics Guide

Using Multiple Ethical Guides
   Why Use Multiple Ethics Guides?
   The 3-Way Ethics Test

Managerial Ethics
   Codes of Ethics
   Managing Ethics

Business Nonmarket and Market Strategies and Ethics
   The Stakeholder 5 Is Strategic Approach Includes Ethics
   Integrating Nonmarket and Market Strategies

What's This Chapter About?

In Part 1, Chapter 1, we discussed the interrelationship of business, society, and government and introduced ethics. In Part 2, Chapters 2–4 we focused on the business side. Here we start Part 3, Chapters 5–7, with a focus on society.

   Chapter 5 begins by presenting ethical foundations. We then move on to understanding why people use unethical behavior. This understanding will help make us aware of the temptations and pressures we will face to use unethical behavior.

   Our third section provides you with guides to help make better ethical decisions, followed by a section on the need to maximize the use of those ethical guides.

   The following section includes methods managers can use to help ensure that employees do make ethical decisions. As usual, we end by explaining how the chapter material can be applied in developing integrated nonmarket and market strategies.

CASE

Take the Money and Run: Disclosing Moral Bankruptcy at Goldman Sachs

Since its founding in 1885, Goldman Sachs (GS) has grown to be one of the world's largest and most important investment banks, employing more than 34,000 people worldwide. GS's commitment to its clients, teamwork, integrity, professional excellence, and entrepreneurial spirit and commitment to its clients was the core of its business, which is embodied in its 14 business principles.[1]

On March 14, 2012, Greg Smith, an executive at GS, delivered a public resignation in the *New York Times*.[2] After working at the firm for 12 years, Smith decided to leave and to also tell the public of GS's destructive and toxic environment. Smith commented that the firm deviated from its 14 core principles that were defined by John Whitehead, former co-chair.[3] He stated that the interests of the client were being sidelined given the way the firm operated and thought about making money. He exclaimed that the firm had ethically veered far from the place when he joined as a summer intern.[4] Smith explained that GS back then wasn't just about making money, and he was sad to say that when he looked around, he saw virtually no trace of the culture that made him love working for this firm for those many years. "Smith said he no longer had the pride or the belief."[5]

In support of Smith's contentions, Carl Levin, chairman of the U.S. Senate panel, declared that the executives at GS behaved recklessly regarding customers' investments.[6] Levin stated that senior sales managers at GS disclosed that "Timber Wolf was a sh_tty deal"[7] for clients and also discovered that GS committed fraud in a CDO deal called Abacus.[8] A CDO is a synthetic collateralized debt obligation, meaning that if the mortgage industry held up, the holder—in this case Goldman—would make steady streams of payments to investors, but in the event it collapsed, the holder would be compensated. GS committed fraud by allowing these securities to be chosen by a client who believed that the deal would fail, which it did. Goldman's client, John Paul netted $1 billion after the failing of these securities. Goldman also created another CDO called "Hudson Mezzanine Funding," which imploded within two years. Goldman reaped a huge reward.[9]

Greg Smith said the firm changed the way it thought about leadership. Leadership used to be about ideas, setting an example, and doing the right thing. "Today, if you make enough money for the firm (and are not currently an ax murderer) you will be promoted into a position of influence."[10] He further stated that it made him ill to hear how callously people talk about ripping off their clients. He questioned the humility and integrity of the managers. He elaborated that employees frequently initiated lucrative and complicated products to clients even if they were not the ones most directly aligned with the client's goals.[11] He hoped this would be a wake-up call to the board of directors to make the client the focal point of GS's business again. He suggested weeding out the morally bankrupt people in order to get the culture right again, so people want to work at GS for the right reasons.[12]

Greg Smith belongs to a generation that put loyalty to values above loyalty to company. To many young professionals, his op-ed resignation from GS may well forecast a new era in ethics on Wall Street and in other workplaces.

The following questions are related to the Take the Money and Run case. Answers can be found within the chapter.

1. Did GS executives exercise universal ethics?
2. Explain at what level of ethical behavior Greg Smith seemed to be operating at.
3. Explain how the application of business ethics by GS's managers would have helped GS maintain its historically positive reputation.
4. How might the myths of ethics help explain the change in GS managers' behaviors?

5. Why might managers at GS have succumbed to unethical behavior?
6. Apply the general guidelines for ethical behavior to the GS case. What are the results?
7. How did Greg Smith handle this ethical dilemma?
8. Did the managers at GS pass the 3-way ethics test?

BUSINESS ETHICS FOUNDATIONS

Corporate social responsibility and ethics are interrelated; CSR is provided by ethics or it is part of CSR. Recall that being ethical is the second level of CSR. In this section, we discuss ethical concepts, moral development, business ethics and ethical dilemmas, business ethics and managerial ethics, and business ethics myths.

Learning Outcome 1: Compare and contrast ethics, business ethics, and managerial ethics.

Ethical Concepts

Let's begin by reviewing ethical terms discussed in Chapter 1 and expand our understanding of the important topic of business ethics.

Ethics. *Ethics is the moral standard (or principles) of right and wrong (or moral and immoral), and fairness that influences behavior—what we do and say or our actions.* We can use the terms *ethics* and *morals* interchangeably. Can demanding moral perfection promote positive social change?[13] Essentially, "society" determines right and wrong behavior and most people behave accordingly. Thus, ethics provides rules of behavior without requiring government laws because we abide voluntarily by the ethical principles that underlie the laws. The police deal with the relatively few people who don't have ethics and break the law.

Ethics requires making moral judgments based on a suitable set of moral principles.[14] Ethics allows us to judge whether our behavior is appropriate to guide us in relating to others ethically and how we expect others to relate to us. Plus, societal moral standards influence our judgments of business behavior that affect a company's reputation.[15]

Whether you are comfortable with ethics or not, all people and organizations have a certain moral standard that guides our behavior. Each of us practices ethics every day in the decisions we make as we interact with people. We have a duty to be ethical, and we can improve our ethical decision making in our personal and professional lives.[16] That is what this chapter is all about.

Honesty. Honesty tends to be a universally accepted measure of ethical behavior.[17] *Honesty* indicates a tendency not to lie, cheat, or steal. We should be honest,[18] because honesty is ethical and dishonesty is unethical behavior.

Personal and Professional Applications

1. Assess the level of honesty and integrity of high-level managers, your boss, and the employees in an organization you work(ed) for.

Values. *Values* are important desired behaviors, and values and ethics are different. Values help shape morals or what is considered ethical and unethical. Values vary among people,[19] or the perception of what is ethical varies.[20] For example some people believe telling the truth is important while others think nothing of lying. Values outside of business are ineffective as a check on the undesirable effects of business on society.[21] So individual values tend to be personal rather than universal, and a business can't let all its employees operate according to their own individual values.

Universal vs. Relativism Ethics. Some scholars say that moral standards are universal, but others do not agree.[22] *Universal ethics is impartial, it applies to everyone, and morals should take precedence over self-interest.* For example, everyone is expected to be honest. It is also called the generalization test because if I justify my action as ethical, so should you.

On the other side, *relativism ethics contends that morals can change based on time, the circumstances of the situation, and personal opinion.* For example, in some circumstances, lying can be considered ethical. Relativists tend to say you can't be too rigid and must consider the situation, whereas universalists tend to say you can't pick and choose actions and justify unethical behavior to meet your own self-interest. We will discuss the differences in greater detail throughout this chapter with an emphasis on universal ethics.

> **Take the Money and Run Question 1: Did GS executives exercise universal ethics?**
>
> Universal ethics requires everyone to be impartial and honest while relativism ethics contends that morals can change based on time, the circumstances of the situation, and personal opinion. Greg Smith contends GS behaved recklessly regarding customers' investments in that it placed firm profitability above the customers' return on investment. If Smith is correct, then one could argue that GS executives are exercising a relativist ethical approach.

> **Personal and Professional Applications**
>
> 2. Does management where you work(ed) have a universal or relativism approach to ethics?

> Learning Outcome 2: Characterize the three levels of moral development.

Moral Development

A factor affecting ethical behavior is *moral development*, which refers to understanding right from wrong and choosing to do the right thing. It is based on moral judgment.[23] *The three levels of moral development are preconventional, conventional, and postconventional.* Our ability to make ethical choices is related to our level of moral development, as discussed in Figure 5.1 based on the work of Lawrence Kohlberg.[24]

Preconventional Level (Self-Centered). At the first level, preconventional, Kohlberg identified two stages: (1) *Punishment avoidance*; and (2) *Reward seeking.* Self-centered behavior often leads to unethical behavior,[25] which in turn has negative consequences for other stakeholders.[26]

Level	Description of Motivation, Behavior, and Leadership	Examples
3. Postconventional *(Principle-Centered)*	Behavior is motivated by universal ethics principles of right and wrong, regardless of the expectations of the leader or group and the possible negative consequences of the behavior. The common leadership style is participative; it is leadership that is committed to serving others and a higher cause while empowering followers to reach this level.	"I don't lie to customers because lying is wrong."
2. Conventional *(Social-Centered)*	Behavior is motivated by the desire to live up to others' expectations, to copy the behavior of the leaders or of those in one's group. Peer pressure is used to enforce group norms. It is common for lower-level managers to use a leadership style similar to the higher-level managers.	"I lie to customers because the other sales reps do it too."
1. Preconventional *(Self-Centered)*	Behavior is motivated by relativism ethics of self-interest (get rewards and avoid punishment). The common leadership style is autocratic toward others while using one's position for personal advantage.	"I lie to customers to sell more products and get higher commission checks."

▪ **Figure 5.1:** Levels of Moral Development

Conventional Level (Social-Centered). Ethical reasoning at the conventional level falls into one of two stages: (3) *Social group norms*. Managers develop ethical norms.[27] (4) *Society norms*. One chooses behavior based on the moral expectations of the group or society at large. You respond to peer pressure and conform to the group or societal norms.

Postconventional Level (Principle-Centered). The postconventional level, also includes two stages: (5) *Fairness ethics*. One chooses behavior based on seeking to be fair and balance the concerns of stakeholders with conflicting needs for the common good.[28] One may challenge societal norms as being unfair.[29]

(6) *Universal ethics*. It is based on strong moral identity.[30] One makes an effort to define moral principles regardless of the leader's or the group's ethics. It takes moral courage.[31] For example, *Martin Luther King Jr.* broke what he considered unjust laws and spent time in jail seeking universal dignity and justice for all people.

Which Level Are You On? Note that most people don't always behave at the same level of moral development, or we can slide up and down depending on the situation. Only about 20 percent of people are estimated to reach the postconventional level and consistently behave with true universal ethics, as opposed to going between levels, using relativism ethics, putting self-interest first, or giving in to peer pressure. How do you handle peer pressure? Overall, at what level of moral development are you? What can you do to further develop your moral level and consistently behave at that level?

Take the Money and Run Question 2: Explain what level of ethical behavior Greg Smith seemed to be operating at.

Greg Smith exercised postconventional ethics in that his behavior seems to be motivated by fairness as well as universal ethical principles of right and wrong, regardless of the expectations of the leader or group and possible negative consequences of the behavior. He voiced his concerns that GS managers were not seeking the best interest of their clients by placing the profitability of the firm above those of the client. They seemed to be operating at the preconventional level of reward seeking and behavior based on personal needs and gains rather than concern for others, leaving stakeholders with negative consequences as in the Abacus and Hudson Mezzanine funding deals. GS managers committed fraud because they were only concerned with their own and the firm's gains and not with the needs of the stakeholders.

Personal and Professional Applications

3. At what level of moral development do you usually behave?

4. Give an organizational example of behavior at each of the three levels of moral development, preferably where you work(ed).

Business Ethics and Ethical Dilemmas

Business ethics is the application of ethics to issues that arise in business. You will face ethical challenges throughout your career.[32] Facing ethical situations is not easy. An ethical awareness helps,[33] and understanding the circumstances is important when making decisions that are ethical.[34] *An ethical dilemma occurs when a decision must be made in the midst of conflicting interests; there is no simple right and wrong answer.* There can be multiple ethical alternatives to choose from. This situation is common in business when you have your own self-interest, coworker interest, the interest of the company, and other stakeholders to consider. So understanding the circumstances is important when making ethical decisions.[35] All of the chapters present you with ethical dilemmas.

Personal and Professional Applications

5. Describe an ethical dilemma you face(d) at work.

Business ethics usually goes beyond legal required behavior. Ethics has been called the interface between business and government.[36] To provide effective guidance for business decisions, moral standards must be stable over time.[37] So ethics should be based on universal ethical moral standards. We must give reasons for our behavior, so justifying our behavior is the heart of business ethics. Thus, business ethics is the discipline of using a systematic process of making decisions using moral judgment based on reason and analysis.[38] However, no single theory, test, or method of making ethical decisions is universally agreed upon. Also, using different theories can result in different decisions, so using multiple theories is encouraged. We present guidelines to help you make ethical decisions later in the chapter.

Business Ethics and Managerial Ethics

As we distinguished between ethics and business ethics, we also distinguish between personal, professional, and managerial ethics. Although the basic principles of ethics always apply, we focus on business ethics as individuals at work in professional positions because business ethics is based on the judgments made by individuals and their behavior.[39] Businesses seek employees who are ethical.[40]

Keep in mind that you are a stakeholder of others; your behavior also affects someone else who has a stake in you using ethical behavior. Unethical behavior at work by you can have negative consequences to you, your coworkers and the company, your industry and profession, as well as society and government. Bernie **Madoff** hurt all these stakeholders through his Ponzi scam.

Managerial Ethics. Managerial ethics also differs from business ethics because managers are not only responsible for their individual behavior at work; they have ethical responsibilities because of their position.[41] Mangers are responsible for developing moral standard policies and procedures to guide employee behavior and for ensuring that their employees behave ethically.[42] Managers face more stakeholders with conflicting interests than employees, and the higher in the organization you go the greater the number of stakeholders. Later in this chapter, we will discuss managerial ethics again with the focus on how managers can help ensure that employees make ethical decisions.

Moral Management. *Moral management* includes moral, immoral, and amoral managers. *Moral managers* strive to consistently behave at the postconventional level (they are principle-centered). When moral managers judge a behavior to be ethically right or unethically wrong, they will or will not engage in the behavior. Unfortunately, some people ignore morals when making decisions.[43] *Immoral managers* knowingly engage in unethical behavior to benefit themselves and their firms in some way. A third category is amoral managers. *Amoral managers* do not believe ethics applies to business or they just don't think about ethics when they make decisions and act on them. Our focus is on developing moral managers who consider ethics when making decisions. We will discuss reasons for unethical behavior in the next section and managing ethics in the last section of this chapter.

Personal and Professional Applications

6. Identify your boss as a moral, immoral, or amoral manager, and describe why.

Take the Money and Run Question 3: Explain how the application of business ethics by GS's managers would have helped GS maintain its historical positive reputation.

Business ethics is defined as the application of ethics to issues that develop in business. Ethics serves as the interface between business, society, and government. In order to be effective in business ethics, moral standards must be present. Managers are the ones responsible for developing moral standard policies and procedures to guide employee behavior, and for ensuring that their employees behave ethically. Managers deal with stakeholders with conflicting interests. If GS managers had displayed moral judgments they would not have made the unethical and illegal decision to defraud clients for their and their firm's gain. These managers therefore did not maintain GS's' positive reputation because they did not act responsibly as individuals and subverted the ethical responsibilities of their positions.

Business Ethics Myths

A variety of myths tend to block us from taking the study of business ethics as seriously as we should.[44]

■ **Myth 1. Ethics is just a matter of opinion**. Try to remember this the next time someone uses unethical behavior with you, such as lying, cheating, or stealing from you. Do you really believe if someone treats you unethically and their opinion is the behavior is ethical that you will not be upset? Do you really think the offender's opinion is as good as your opinion?

■ **Myth 2. There is no point in studying ethics because we all know what is right; it's just a matter of doing what is ethical.** Do you really believe that we all agree on what is right and wrong and that ethics is really all that simple? If so, why do we consistently disagree and read or hear in the news media about some unethical business practice? For a recent example, the CEO of **Best Buy** resigned under investigation of unethical personal conduct.[45] With multiple stakeholders with different conflicting needs, doing what is ethical is not as simple as it might appear.

■ **Myth 3. Business ethics is simple; just follow a guide such as "don't do anything you wouldn't want to appear on the front page of the newspaper."** Then why do we keep seeing ethics scandals on the front page? If you had to have major layoffs or a plant closing, which research shows, damages lives and communities, would you really want the story on the front page? Unfortunately, it may have been the only ethical choice in a difficult situation. We are not saying ethical guidelines don't help, and we do provide some later in this chapter, but it's not simple, by any means. As an example, the *Wall Street Journal Europe* publisher had to quit after an ethics inquiry.[46]

■ **Myth 4. You can't teach and learn business ethics.** If this statement were true, why would major accrediting agencies, such as the Association to Advance Collegiate Schools of Business (AACSB), require ethics? Why does the majority of business schools offer an ethics course and/or integrate ethics throughout their curriculum? An important lesson learned from **Enron** is that "students need to learn the subtlety of how unethical behavior can take hold of you."[47]

■ **Myth 5. We learn ethics as kids and really can't change our behavior to be more ethical as adults.** Research supports that as we develop the capacity to think through our actions, our behavior tends to become more ethical. Our ethical ability can grow throughout our lives. We can change and develop our ability to make ethical decisions.[48] That is what this chapter is all about. Do you really believe that if you make a conscious effort to implement the ethical theories and guidelines that you can't improve? The approach we take in this chapter is that you can improve.

Take the Money and Run Question 4: How might the myths of ethics help explain the change in GS managers' behaviors?

Myths tend to block us from fully taking the study of business ethics seriously but may also block us from acting ethically as well. Many people take a relativist standpoint that ethics is just a matter of opinion (Myth 1) and that right and wrong is defined by the specifics of a situation. This myth might help us understand the underlying thinking behind GS managers' actions to maximize company profits at the expense of customer return on investment; other managers were being rewarded (promoted) for unethical behavior, therefore unethical behavior must be the "right thing" to do. Greg Smith, on the other hand, saw the fallacy in this myth (perspective) because he had a much deeper understanding of GS's historical values and did not compromise his own values.

WHY PEOPLE USE UNETHICAL BEHAVIOR

In this section, we focus on answering the question "why do good people do bad things?" Major reasons include personal gain, self-interest, and conflict of interest; external pressure and cross-cultural inconsistency; how personality traits and attitudes, and the situation affect ethical behavior; and rationalization and how people justify unethical behavior.

> Learning Outcome 3: Identify reasons why people use unethical behavior and how they justify it.

Personal Gain, Self-Interest, and Conflict of Interest

Whenever people interact with others, they always have in mind the often-unasked questions: "What's in it for me?" and possibly "What's in it for my company?" Personal gain for self-interest is not counter to ethics as long as you take a stakeholders' approach and also look out for the interest of others. The problem of unethical behavior occurs when people are only "looking out for number one," when they get *greedy* and seek personal gain at the expense of others by exploitation of stakeholders.[49] So don't let greed motivate your decisions.[50]

Incentive systems can be so tempting that they lead some people to put self-interest first at the expense of others. In the subprime mortgage crises, mortgage brokers and lending officers' failure in their moral duty was partly to blame for the resulting harmful consequences.[51] For example, to get their commission, some told potential home buyers to lie about their income so they could qualify for a loan they couldn't afford. This dishonesty resulted in thousands of people losing their homes.

On the flip side of personal gain, but closely related, is to avoid loss. For example, to avoid a lawsuit, when a **Union Pacific** train collided with a truck an eyewitness suggested that warning lights at the crossing had activated too late. Before the crossing signal box could be impartially inspected, however, a Union Pacific engineer replaced potentially defective parts, so during the inspection, the signal was working properly.[52] People also use unethical behavior, such as lying, for nonmonetary gain to preserve their self-image and/or to protect others.[53]

Conflict of interest occurs when an individual's self-interest conflicts with behaving in the best interest of another when obligated to do so. For example, if you hire a friend or relative who is not qualified for the job, or if you purchase things for your company at a higher price because you get favors or gifts from the supplier.

External Pressure and Cross-Cultural Inconsistency

Penalties for not performing to a certain level can pressure people to act unethically, such as missing sales quotas. Wall Street analysts project the financial performance of major corporations, and if profits are lower than expected, the stock price tends to fall. Thus, some executives have "cooked the books," such as **Enron**, initially thinking, it's no big deal, we will make it up next period and no one will know the difference. They gradually get sucked into increasingly unethical behavior and larger amounts and/or worse behavior to cover up for prior unethical behavior—one lie leads to others. Unfortunately, stockholders lose, and executives end up in jail.

Some people also engage in unethical behavior due to *peer pressure* to fit in, or to avoid some type of harassment or even physical harm. Others will buckle under pressure from *managers* who ask them to engage in unethical behavior, sometimes out of fear of losing their jobs. You should be aware of these pressures and be ready to deal with them.[54]

Global differences in perceptions of what constitutes ethical business practices can also be a factor.[55] Emerging markets are critical to global growth,[56] but corruption is their biggest problem (including China, India, and Russia).[57] Thus, the global economy constitutes a morally complex environment.[58] Paying bribes is illegal in many countries, and the *U.S. Foreign Corrupt Practices Act* prohibits companies that operate in the United States from bribing foreign governments to get business.[59]

But giving bribes is the expected way of doing business in some countries, which can create ethical dilemmas. For example, an American businessperson wanted to have a phone installed in the foreign office. When the person refused to pay a bribe, the installer left. The businessperson complained to the phone company and was told that for a fee (bribe) the matter would be investigated. The **Justice Department** is cracking down on bribes.[60] What would you do? It is plain to see that international ethical dilemmas present a challenge in developing responsible global leaders.[61]

Personal and Professional Applications

7. Give one or more examples of when someone used unethical behavior for personal gain, self-interest, conflict of interest, external pressure, and/or cross-cultural inconsistency.

How Personality Traits, Attitudes, and the Situation Affect Ethical Behavior

You may know that some people have a higher level of ethics than others based on their personality and attitude toward ethics. Our personality and attitude lead to our level of moral development, or lack thereof. Some people are frequent liars, others are not, and the circumstances do make a difference.[62] Think about the people you associate with. Do you find differences based on their personality, attitudes, or circumstances?

Another important factor affecting ethical behavior is the situation.[63] As discussed, *incentive systems* create tempting situations. Highly competitive and unsupervised situations increase the odds of unethical behavior. Unethical behavior occurs more often when no formal ethics policy or code of ethics is in place and when unethical behavior is not punished. Unethical behavior is especially prevalent when it is rewarded. People are also less likely to report unethical behavior (blow the whistle) when they perceive the violation as not being serious and when they are friends of the offender.

Situational characteristics also affect the degree to which we are willing to be influenced by others' unethical behavior.[64] A person–situation interaction is central to supervisor role modeling.[65] Unfortunately, unethical behavior by managers is sometimes copied by employees.[66]

Take the Money and Run Question 5: Why might managers at GS have succumbed to unethical behavior?

Several factors were potentially involved in why GS managers may have succumbed to unethical behavior: personal gain (promotion), being in a position of conflict of interest (if a financial instrument loses money for the client GS is rewarded), external peer pressure (changing leadership), as well as personal traits, attitudes toward ethics, and situational factors (others acting unethically).

Ethical Rationalization and How People Justify Unethical Behavior

As we think through our ethical dilemmas, we tend to come up with rationalizations for the behavior we choose. Our motives lead to our behavior.[67] *Ethical rationalization is the process of determining motives, reasons, explanations, and justifications that lead to particular decisions and behavior when faced with ethical dilemmas.* If we are caught in behavior that is ethically questionable, management tends to ask us why we did it. If we have a good rationalization that justifies the behavior that management agrees with, we tend to stay out of trouble. The problem is that it is common to simply justify our behavior using relativism ethics that don't provide universal ethics rationalizations.

Most people understand the implications of right and wrong behavior and have a conscience. So why do good people do bad things? When most people do something unethical, it is not due to some type of character flaw or being born a bad person. However, current research suggests that a chemical messenger called oxytocin may account for differences in levels of honesty, and that the level of oxytocin can be increased.[68] But the general consensus for unethical behavior is usually motivated by personal gain or other reasons discussed, and the fact that it may be unethical is often not necessarily recognized by the person.

Only about 1 percent of people will never be dishonest, and 1 percent will always be dishonest, so the rest of us are in the 98 percent who are occasionally dishonest, but just a little because we all want to view ourselves in a positive manner. We want the benefits of dishonesty, but we also want to view ourselves as honest.[69] Therefore, when we do use unethical behavior, we justify the behavior to protect our self-concept and avoid having a guilty conscience or feelings of remorse. *Justifying unethical behavior is the process of convincing oneself that a decision is rational and ethical, when in fact it really serves self-interest or provides an easy way out of the ethical dilemma.* Let's discuss nine thinking processes used to justify unethical behavior.

1. **Relativism ethics.** Recall our definition of relativism ethics. Although we do need to make decisions on issues in specific situations, we must be careful not to simply make excuses for our unethical behavior. All of the following justifications tend to be based on ethical relativism. In the next section, we present guidelines to help you avoid simply using your own opinions to make unethical decisions.

2. **Moral justification.** It is the process of reinterpreting immoral behavior in terms of a higher purpose. People state that they have behaved unethically (lied about a competitor to hurt its reputation, fixed prices, stolen confidential information, etc.) for the good of their organization/employees.

    People at the postconventional level of moral development, including *Martin Luther King Jr.*, may seek a higher purpose for the good of society. However, people at the preconventional and conventional levels of moral development more commonly use the following justifications.

3. **Conventional justification.** It is the process of thinking that the behavior is *acceptable* because everyone else does it. Some people do resist peer pressure and do behave

at the postconventional level. Even if many people are being dishonest (e.g., stealing from the company), does it make the behavior right? Do you want people to be dishonest with you?

4. **Displacement of responsibility.** It is the process of blaming one's unethical behavior on others (e.g., I was only following orders, my boss told me to inflate the figures, etc.). In a survey, 53 percent of employees said they would be willing to misrepresent financial information if asked to by a supervisor.[70]

5. **Diffusion of responsibility.** It is the process of the group using the unethical behavior with no one person being held responsible (e.g., I knew the committee decision was wrong, but I didn't say anything). This kind of rationalization is referred to as *groupthink*, which can lead to unethical decisions.

6. **Advantageous comparison.** It is the process of comparing the degree of your unethical behavior against others' behavior (e.g., I only call in sick when I'm not sick a few times a year; Tom and Ellen do it all the time; we pollute less than our competitors do).

7. **Disregard or distortion of consequences.** It is the process of minimizing the harm caused by the unethical behavior (e.g., if I inflate the figures, no one will be hurt and I will not get caught. And if I do, I'll just get a slap on the wrist anyway). Was this thinking the case at **Enron** and **Madoff**?

8. **Attribution of blame.** It is the process of claiming the unethical behavior was caused by someone else's behavior (e.g., it's not my fault. It's my coworker's fault that I repeatedly hit him. He called me/did xxx, so I had to hit him).

9. **Euphemistic labeling.** It is the process of using "cosmetic" words to make the behavior sound acceptable (e.g., "terrorist group" sounds bad but "freedom fighter" sounds justifiable. "Misleading" or "covering up" sounds better than "lying").

ETHICAL DILEMMA 5.1 RadioShack: To Tell the Truth, the Whole Truth, and Nothing But the Truth

Daniel Feehan, RadioShack's executive chairman of the board, pondered the future of the firm as he reflected on how the firm overcame a troublesome past. "RadioShack's improved financial performance [in 2012] suggests it could be turning a corner after a decade of bleeding sales to rivals Best Buy, Wal-Mart, and others. Under the leadership of CEO Julian Day, a turnaround specialist with experience at Safeway and Kmart who joined the company in 2006, RadioShack undertook a major rebranding effort to update its dated image. . . . The improvements sparked rumors that private-equity firms and Best Buy were circling RadioShack, but as yet no offers have been made."[71] Was getting Julian Day as CEO an accident or fate?

Feehan remembered that the then-CEO, David Edmondson, was hired back in 1993 after writing to the board and suggesting marketing ideas for the company.[72] By year end 2005, Radio Shack stock had plummeted 62 percent to 36 cents a share, from 81 cents a share during the same quarter the previous year[73] with net income for the year dropping nearly 21 percent.[74] The firm clearly was in trouble and needed to be reenergized, which should have been enough motivation to replace any CEO, including Edmondson.

However in early 2006 Roberts, the board chairman at the time, received further ammunition when he got an urgent phone call from Mark C. Hill, general counsel and senior vice president for the firm. A possible problem with Edmondson's academic credentials had emerged. Edmondson, who was also awaiting trial on his third driving while intoxicated (DWI) charge in 17 years, had misstated his educational credentials on his job application form by claiming to possess a bachelor of science degree, while in fact he had only obtained a ThG diploma (a three-year degree in theology) at best. None of this new information had yet been confirmed by Hill, although it was noted that a background check had been conducted when Edmondson applied for the job and no problems were uncovered at that time.

Clearly, if this information were to surface it would have devastating effects on the firm and its already depressed stock price, especially in light of the company's recent announced plans to close as many as 700 stores and take a large writedown. The choices seemed simple enough—blow the whistle on its own president and suffer the repercussions, downplay the news and try to spin it in the media as a misunderstanding, or bury the information and hope for the best (although prepare for the worst). All of these choices would most likely lead to disastrous consequences.

Questions

1. What issues of morality and business ethics does this case raise?
2. What are RadioShack's ethical obligations in this situation?
3. Is RadioShack in any way responsible for this crisis?
4. If RadioShack was doing well financially, rather than poorly, would Edmondson's fudging his credentials really be an issue?
5. If you were Roberts, what would you have done?
6. Assuming that further investigation indicated Edmondson did lie about his educational background, what actions should the board take in terms of this information?

Personal and Professional Applications

9. Give one or more examples of how people have justified their unethical behavior.

10. Select justifications you have used, and the one you use most often.

Section Summary. Because research indicates that an awareness of unethical behavior can help to prepare individuals to deal with it, we presented several reasons that prompt unethical behavior. Through conscious effort, you can decrease your focus on personal gain and self-interest, and have less need to rationalize your unethical behavior by using universal ethics. For a review of this section, see Figure 5.2. The next two sections focus on using ethical theories and guides to help you make individual ethical decisions.

GUIDES TO ETHICAL DECISIONS AND BEHAVIOR

Every day in your personal and professional lives, you face situations in which you can make ethical or unethical decisions. It is helpful to have guidance in making ethical choices.[75] *Ethical decision guides provide a structured method for analyzing ethical dilemmas to aid in making ethical choices.* When we are honest and trust others, they are generally more trustworthy in dealing with us.[76] No single best agreed-upon way provides

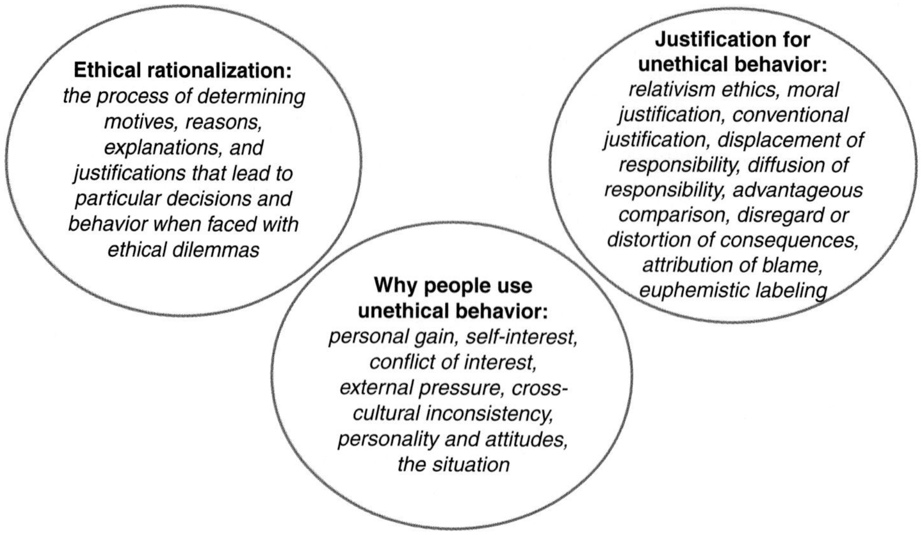

Figure 5.2: Ethical Rationalizations and Unethical Behavior

a guide for making ethical decisions. However, in this section we begin by presenting 10 general guides to ethical behavior followed by 3 more complex approaches. Keep in mind that the ethical decisions guides are not isolated; we recommend using multiple guides at the same time, which we will discuss after you learn the 13 guides.

Learning Outcome 4: List general guides to ethical decision making.

General Guides to Ethical Decisions

The following 10 simple guidelines can help you to make sound ethical choices.

Golden Rule. You most likely know the Golden Rule from the Bible (but it does not require specific religious belief or faith), "Do unto others as you want them to do unto you," or "Don't do anything to anyone that you would not want them to do to you." So before you act, ask yourself, would I want someone to do this to me? If yes, it may be ethical.

Moral Level. We need to make moral judgments.[77] Ask yourself, "What moral level is my decision and behavior coming from?" "Am I only looking out for my own self-interest (preconventional)?" "Am I just following others' expectations without regard for what is really right or wrong (conventional)?" "Am I really doing the right thing (postconventional)?"

Rights. Considering human rights is another guide to making ethical decisions. A right means a person, group, or organization is entitled to something or to be treated in a certain way. The people we interact with, such as friends, coworkers, and customers have the right to be treated with respect, whether we like them or not. A company has the right to set policies and rules that we should follow. Ask yourself, am I meeting or denying the rights of others through my behavior?

Justice. We should attempt to treat all stakeholders fairly or justly. Consider several types of justice: *distributive justice* refers to the distribution of benefits and burdens. But a fair distribution is not necessarily an equal distribution: are the benefits and burdens distributed equitably? *Compensatory justice* compensates people for past injustices, such as in the case of *affirmative action. Procedural justice* (or ethical due process) is a fair decision-making procedure, practice, or agreement. A common ethical question to ask yourself is, "Is the behavior fair and just?"

Common Sense. Ask yourself, "Does the decision and behavior really make sense?" "What are the consequences?" We will discuss consequences in greater detail later with utilitarianism ethics.

Advice. When in doubt, ask people you respect, such as higher-level mangers, for their advice on what action you should take. If you are reluctant to ask others, or only seek out people you know will agree with you, the action may not be ethical.

Comfort. If you are comfortable with a decision and behavior, it may be ethical. However, if you are uncomfortable with the action, it may not be ethical and you shouldn't do it; seek advice. At **Cummings Engine Company** employees are told: "If . . . you are uncomfortable with a particular action . . . then *don't do it*."

Disclosure. Ask yourself, "Am I proud to tell my family, friends, and colleagues my decision and behavior?" "How would I feel if the action was publicly disclosed in the news media?" If you keep rationalizing and justifying your action and you don't want others to know about it, it may not be ethical.

4-Way Test. Rotary International developed a 4-way test to guide your thoughts and behavior in business transactions. The four questions are: (1) Is it the truth? (2) Is it fair to all concerned? (3) Will it build goodwill and better friendships? (4) Will it be beneficial to all concerned? If you can answer yes to all four questions, the action may be ethical.

5-Question Test. Sears, Roebuck and Co. developed the five "Guidelines for Making Ethical Decisions": (1) Is it legal? (2) Is it within Sears' shared beliefs and policies? (3) Is it right/fair/appropriate? (4) Would I want everyone to know it? (5) How will I feel about myself? If you can answer affirmatively to all five questions, the action may be ethical.

Take the Money and Run Question 6: Apply the general guidelines for ethical behavior to the GS case. What are the results?

Based on the 10 simple guidelines that can help in making sound ethical choices:

1. Golden Rule: managers did not treat their clients like they would want themselves treated.
2. Moral level: preconventional.
3. Rights: Client rights were violated when fraud was committed by GS employees.

4. Justice: Clients were not treated fairly (as equals) nor compensated properly.
5. Common sense: Managers described their own actions as "ripping off" clients.
6. Advice: Greg Smith noted that leadership was promoting successful employees regardless of how they achieved that success; employees would have received tainted advice.
7. Comfort: Greg Smith clearly was uncomfortable with the environment at GS. The question is, were other managers just as uncomfortable even if they went along with GS's new unethical culture?
8. Disclosure: Senior managers disclosed their opinions only when questioned by a U.S. Senate panel investigation.
9. 4-way test: Fraud is not the truth, is not fair to all, does not build goodwill, and does not benefit all.
10. 5-question test: Is not legal, doesn't fit Greg Smith's description of GS's original values, it is not fair, would not want fully disclosed, and certainly made Greg Smith feel uncomfortable.

Using the guidelines clearly demonstrates the unethical nature of GS's actions in the case.

Personal and Professional Applications

11. Do you use, or have you used, any of these general ethical guides?

12. Which one or two ethical guides do you believe could best help you make sound ethical decisions in your personal life and at work?

Learning Outcome 5: Compare and contrast virtues, deontological, and utilitarianism guides to ethical decision making.

Virtues Ethics Guide

Plato and Aristotle are credited with developing the first ethics theory, which is commonly called *virtues ethics* today. Virtues ethics focuses on personal character: What type of person do I want to be? The focus is not on rules for correct behavior, or the reasons or consequences of the behavior, which are our next two guides. *Virtues ethics refers to having personal character traits as the basis for ethical dilemma decisions.* The decision choice is ours, but we must behave according to those virtues, and we must be consistent with our choices. Virtue has various dimensions that we discuss below.

Character. Moral character is important in ethics.[78] Virtue is about *character*—the personal traits and qualities that define who we are and why we behave the way we do. *Good character traits* include caring, respect, fairness, trustworthiness, loyalty, promise/commitment keeping, and integrity. These virtues are habits that enable us to live according to reasons. *Strength of character* is the courage that enables one to behave according to personal convictions or moral standards.

Integrity. Integrity is also an important part of virtues. Integrity is about being honest with one's self and being honest with others. Integrity is so important that many organizations give integrity tests as part of the selection of new employees. People of low character traits are not hired to avoid potential dishonest behavior.

Relationships. Character is the key to developing and sustaining relationships. Good relationships are based on good character virtues, and character is essential for organizational success. Think about it. Would you like to work with people you can't trust, lie to you, and manipulate you? To have friends, we need to have good character traits. However, we do have to be careful that our friendships don't lead us into using unethical behavior.[79] The next two guides to ethics also consider how our behavior will affect our relationships.

Ethical Dilemmas. Unfortunately, virtue can be somewhat vague because people can have different perceptions of what virtues are important and virtues can conflict based on the situation. For example, in accounting, assumption and estimates are often needed, and it can be tempting to use numbers to get the results one wants. Also, one can have a commitment to family that conflicts with a commitment at work.

Questions to Ask Yourself. When facing an ethical dilemma, consider these questions:

1. What character traits does the organization value? Will the behavior of my decision be consistent with the values of the firm?
2. Who do I want to be?
3. What type of person will I be defined as and become if I choose a certain behavior?
4. How will the behavior affect my relationships?

For questions 2–4, do you want to choose to lie and become known as a liar who can't be trusted? Lying will hurt most relationships. It can take years to develop trust, but only one lie to make you viewed as untrustworthy.

The Virtues Ethics Test. The test pulls together the above qualities of virtue. To pass the *virtues ethics test, the behavior must be honest, be based on good character traits, and maintain one's integrity and relationships.*

Take the Money and Run Question 7: How did Greg Smith handle this ethical dilemma?

Greg Smith handled this ethical dilemma by taking stock of his values, integrity, and character. He saw that the firm somehow deviated from what he stood for. He didn't see his behavior and decisions as consistent with what the firm seemed to value. Therefore he questioned whether GS was still the company he wanted to work for.

Personal and Professional Applications

13. Identify good character traits (or lack thereof) of your present or past boss, and explain how these traits help (or hurt) your relationship, your job performance, and those of your coworkers.

Deontological Ethics Guide

Virtues ethics focus on personal character, whereas deontological ethics focuses on the behavior (actions or means) we use to achieve our goals. This guide examines the behavior we use and attempts to determine whether a given action is ethical irrespective of the consequences it creates. Thus, we shouldn't manipulate people as a means to an end. *Deontological ethics refers to using standards of conduct to determine right and wrong behavior when making ethical decisions.*

Right and Wrong Behavior. *Deontological* comes from the Greek root "deon," meaning that which is binding or obligatory; it means that standards of human decency govern right and wrong (or ethical and unethical) behavior. Moral standards of right and wrong are found in nearly every religious tradition, such as the Ten Commandments from Judeo-Christians, Hadith from Islam, the five precepts of Buddhism, and morally exemplary actions based on Hindu. The Golden Rule is also expressed in various ways in most religions and in laws globally. Our general guides of rights and justice tend to fit into deontological ethics.

From Deontology to Standards of Conduct. Communities often develop the standards of conduct that determine what is ethical and unethical based on a religion.[80] Groups of people also develop their own norms[81] (informally accepted standards of conduct) and enforce them through peer pressure (e.g., covering for each other's unethical behavior by punching time cards for each other).[82] Every firm has an ethics culture. An ethical climate index is sometimes used to measure how ethical a work culture is.[83]

Personal and Professional Applications

14. Identify one or more norms from a group of coworkers and how the norms are enforced through peer pressure.

Companies and market economies couldn't function without standards of conduct that are stable over time.[84] The standards focus on the common good.[85] Imagine competing for business with firms that fix prices, falsely advertise, or pay bribes to get customers. Companies and industries develop codes of conduct, and the government develops laws and regulations to guide our behavior. We discuss codes later in this chapter and government in Chapters 8–10.

Generalization. Deontology essentially states that we "all" have a moral obligation to follow the standards of conduct—universal ethics. A reason lies behind every action you take. The reason for your behavior therefore is the rationalization for the action. If the reason rationalizes the action for you, then it has to for everyone. So everyone who has the same reason for their behavior would act in the same way. Also, when the reasons for an action are inconsistent (you stole because you were hungry then because you wanted the item and wouldn't get caught), they fail the test of generalization.

To use a generalization, you need to identify the reasons for your behavior as ethical or unethical. The reasons must be necessary and sufficient. A reason must be necessary because if it didn't apply, you wouldn't do the action. For example, you would steal the item if you really wanted it and you believed you could get away with it. If either reason is missing, you will not steal. Every time you want an item and can get away with stealing it, you will. If not, there must be other reasons for the action of stealing. The scope of the justification is too narrow when unnecessary reasons are cited and too broad when some necessary reasons are left out.

Ethical Dilemmas. Unfortunately, imposed obligations sometimes conflict with ethics in a broader sense. *Fiduciary* literally means loyalty, and *fiduciary duty* is interpreted as an obligation to be loyal to stockholders by advancing their financial interests. So ethical dilemmas occur more frequently as a result of facing two or more compelling moral actions, than of simply choosing between right and wrong behavior. Also, recall that business ethics varies globally. For example, an executive faces an ethical dilemma when he or she must make a decision to lay off workers at home and ship jobs overseas, outsource production to sweat shops, or what level of pollution is acceptable in comparison to a legal limit in the quest to make more profits. Deontological ethics has been criticized because of the difficulty in developing a universal set of moral principles.[86]

Questions to Ask Yourself? When facing an ethical dilemma, consider these questions:

1. Does the behavior in the situation violate a standard of conduct or law?
2. Can I rationalize the action as ethical and consistent based on the standards of conduct of the firm, industry, and society, or am I just justifying my unethical behavior?
3. If people find out about my behavior, could it lead to action against me and/or my firm (e.g., lawsuits)?

The Generalization Test. To pass the *generalization test, the reasons for the action must be consistent, and everyone in the same situation with the same reasons will use the same behavior.* The generalization test determines whether your reasons for, say, stealing something would apply if all others with the same reasons would steal. But everyone wouldn't steal. So it fails the generalization test. Thus, knowing and using the standard of conduct helps us to rationalize our behavior as ethical and pass the generalization test.

Personal and Professional Applications

15. Give an example of when someone at work acted in a way that failed the generalization test. Be sure to give the assumed reasons and explain why the action failed the test.

Utilitarianism Ethics Guide

Deontological Ethics vs. Teleological Ethics. Let's begin by contrasting deontological ethics with teleological ethics. As discussed, deontological ethics focuses on developing universal standards of conduct. Teleological ethics, on the other hand, focuses on the rightness of an action in terms of the good its consequences produce. Utilitarianism is a major principle in teleological ethics, which we discuss here. *Utilitarianism ethics refers to making ethical decisions based on the consequences of the behavior.*

We need to consider the consequences of our actions.[87] Unlike virtues and deontological ethics, utilitarianism ethics, also called *consequentialism*, focuses on the end result or consequences, often called *utility*, of our behavior. So the moral worth of our actions is determined by the consequences they will tend to generate without assuming that the behavior is inherently ethical. If the consequences are good, the decision is good.

Does the End Justify the Means? Our behavior tends to have a means and an end. Virtues and deontological ethics tend to focus more on the means and utilitarianism focuses more on the end result of our behavior. So at some point we reach the end for our behavior that justifies the means we use to achieve the purpose. In our personal and professional lives, as well as managers, we set objectives (ends) and develop plans of actions (means) to achieve them. Thus, the end purpose of the behavior we set should be morally defensible in order for the ends to justify the means.

Cost–Benefit Analysis. Utilitarianism ethics is also referred to as *cost–benefit analysis* because utilitarianism attempts to provide the overall amount of good that can be produced by the decisions and behavior. The analysis tends to include financial/economic, social, and human costs and benefits. You attempt to maximize the net sum of utility across all stakeholders. So a loss to some stakeholders is outweighed by a greater utility gain for others. You identify the alternative actions in the given ethical dilemma, determine the set of consequences for all stakeholders in each alternative, and weigh the costs and benefits of each, and make the decision based on the behavior that provides the greatest good.

Ethical Dilemmas. Concerns with using utilitarianism in a given ethical dilemma are the difficulty in knowing the actual consequences to all stakeholders, what to count as costs and benefits, and in accurately measuring the costs and benefits. Financial analysis (sales, profits) tend to be easier, but social and human costs can be very hard to estimate—how much is a good corporate reputation worth, what is the cost of a life, and what is the financial benefit of good employee morale? Without accurate measures, it can be difficult to determine whether a behavior is ethical. Management or the majority of stakeholders may also override the rights of and be unjust to the minority stakeholders in the situation, and one may ignore behavior that is the means to achieving a desired end, which results in self-interest utility. It is also difficult to develop a set of good rules for utilitarianism decision making.

Questions to Ask Yourself. When facing an ethical dilemma, consider these questions:

1. What is the purpose or objective to be accomplished?
2. What are the likely consequences and the cost–benefit of each alternative action to meet the objective?
3. Do the ends justify the means?
4. How can we work together to benefit relevant stakeholders in the long run?

The Utilitarian Test. Unfortunately, the ultimate ends of stakeholders are not universally shared as stakeholders often have conflicting interests.[88] When multiple stakeholders with conflicting interests are involved, cost–benefit analysis can be helpful in making complex decisions, such as closing a plant. For example, some benefits include improving profitability and stockholder value, versus the cost of layoffs, the toll on employees and their families, reduced economic activity in the local community, and so on. So to pass the *utilitarian test, one specific action leads to more favorable consequences than any alternative decision.*

For a review of the 13 ethics guides, see Figure 5.3.

Personal and Professional Applications

16. Give an example of when using the utilitarian test would be a valuable ethics guide.

USING MULTIPLE ETHICS GUIDES

In this section we explain the need to use multiple ethics guides and how to use the 3-way ethics test.

Why Use Multiple Ethics Guides?

Our decisions and behavior are based on a means[89] (deontological ethics) to achieve an end result[90] (utilitarianism ethics), and on our personal character (virtues ethics).[91] Therefore, for our actions to be rationalized as ethical, we must use all three major ethical guides because each used alone has limitations and can lead to unethical behavior.

Avoid Justifying Unethical Behavior. Of course we have to look out for ourselves, but we also have to be careful not to let self-interest or pressures override our sound ethical rationalization by justifying our unethical behavior. We need to have moral sensitivity.[92] If you have to convince yourself your action is rationally ethical, when in fact you are really serving your own self-interest or providing an easy way out of the ethical dilemma, it is probably not ethical. So using multiple ethics guides helps us avoid justifying our unethical behavior and helps us make truly ethical decisions.

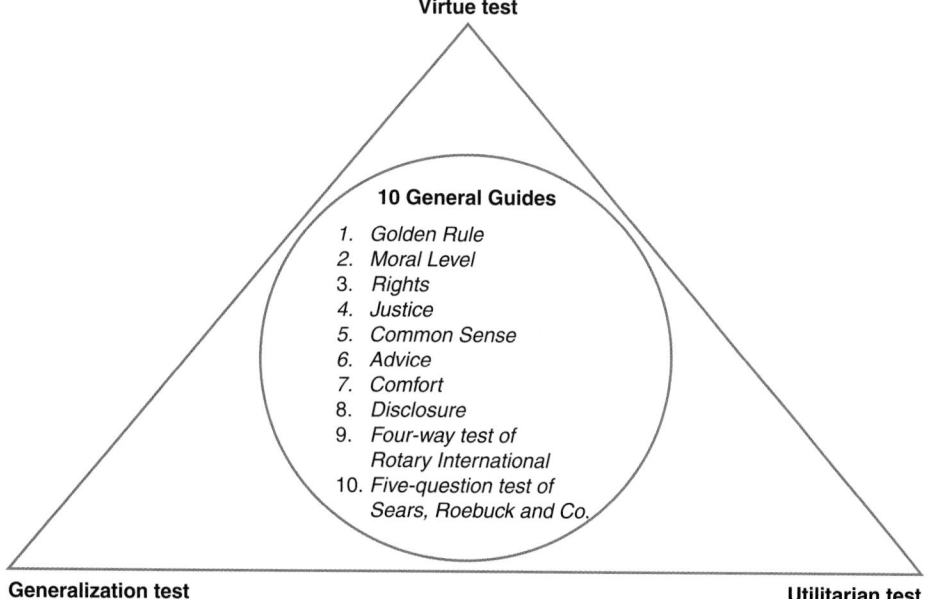

Figure 5.3: The 13 Guides to Ethical Decision Making and Behavior

Combining the Ethical Guides. In Figure 5.3, the 13 guides to ethical behavior are shown together. The general guides are useful but rather simple and incomplete when dealing with complex ethical dilemmas in business. In fact, most of them are also implicitly included within the three more complex guides, which is why they are placed in the center. The virtues, deontological/generalization, and utilitarianism ethics guides and test are more complex, each with its strengths and weaknesses Combined, the ethical guides provide the 3-way ethics test with the 10 general guides included. Putting the ethical guides together is consistent with *stakeholder management* and looking out for stakeholders' interests.

Learning Outcome 6: Describe the 3-way ethics test.

The 3-Way Ethics Test

In order to ensure your decision is ethical, it should pass the 3-way ethics test, which means it has to pass each of the three tests to be truly considered ethical. Here we give an example ethical dilemma and put it to the 3-way test. See Figure 5.4 for an illustration of the 3-way test.

Realize that by using the 3-way ethics test you are identifying key issues and answering important questions to provide a sound rationalization that can be used to defend your decision. However, ethical dilemmas rarely come with a single right answer that everyone will agree on. Some people will say a decision is ethical and others will not.

The ethical dilemma. A common dilemma is being asked to omit relevant information. Here we apply it to a financial advisor, but it can be applied to other types of jobs. You are a financial advisor and your boss asks you to prepare a report for clients. During your one-on-one meeting, the manager asks you to exclude certain past performance numbers for one of your mutual fund products that hasn't been doing well. Past performance influences future client investments and profits based on commissions. The boss is not asking you to change any numbers, which is unethical, but rather to exclude data about the one poor performing product. No law requires companies to show all product performance records. Should you exclude the data or tell your boss you can't do it?[93]

VirtuesTest. To past the test, the behavior must be honest, be based on good character traits, and maintain one's integrity and relationships. Although omitting information is

---

The 3-way ethics test is used to determine whether an action is ethical. The test has three parts taking into account situational factors:

■ To pass the *virtues test*, the behavior must be honest, be based on good character traits, and maintain one's integrity and relationships.

■ To pass the *generalization test*, the reasons for the action must be consistent, and everyone in the same situation with the same reasons will use the same behavior.

■ To pass the *utilitarian test*, one specific action will lead to more favorable consequences than any alternative decision.

To be ethical, the behavior must pass all three tests.

■ **Figure 5.4:** The 3-Way Ethics Test

not always deceptive, in this case your boss is asking you to be dishonest by misleading clients into believing something that you know is not true. This deception is the objective in omitting the product data. Omitting numbers to mislead clients violates good character traits and integrity and is contrary to the mission of your financial advising profession. Your job is to give good advice to help clients make the right investments, but deception is the opposite.

Relationships with clients can be hurt if they find out that you omitted data that would inform their investment decisions. On the other hand, not omitting the data could hurt your relationship with your boss. Virtues ethics requires you to be honest, unless another more important virtue is at stake. For example, if you have heavy financial debt and family obligations and fear losing your job and not being able to get another job, the virtues test is not so easy. If this were the case, you need to do a balancing act and decide whether financial and family obligations are more important than your personal integrity. Be careful not to *justify unethical behavior*. Without the conflicting virtues, however, omitting the data is not ethical and fails the virtues test.

Generalization Test.
To pass the generalization test, the reasons for the action must be consistent, and everyone in the same situation with the same reasons will use the same behavior. The reason, or rationalization, for the behavior of omitting the data is important to the analysis. Dishonesty simply to benefit yourself is not generalizable. As stated, the reason or objective in this situation is to deceive clients. However, another objective of yours may be to benefit your career by obeying your boss. Again, it fails the generalization test because to please your boss you must deceive clients, and not everyone will simply obey the boss in this situation.

If I don't do it, someone else will. This argument is a common one. In most cases, we don't really know that someone else will do it, and if you refuse, maybe the boss would realize the behavior is unethical and not ask anyone else to do it. It doesn't pass the generalization test because not everyone would do it, which makes the argument a poor one even if it is a common one.

Would you be obligated to obey the boss if threatened with some serious consequences if you don't obey? No, because if "all" employees used unethical behavior simply to avoid a perceived vague threat of negative career consequences, then bosses would take advantage of this tendency and unethical behavior would be the norm. Although some employees are willing to be unethical under serious threat, managers rarely issue such threats. Recall whistleblower protection discussed in Chapter 3. Most managers will avoid threats that can result in civil and criminal legal consequences for them and the company.

Utilitarian Test.
To pass the utilitarian test, a specific action will lead to more favorable consequences than any alternative decision. From your boss's perception, the end result of getting more clients is justified by omitting the data as the means to the end. To your boss, dishonesty results in positive consequences for the company and the benefits outweigh the costs, and so it passes the utilitarian test for him.

You are facing three major alternatives: try to change the situation; obey the boss and omit the data; or tell your boss you will not do it. A good place to start is by trying to avoid having to choose between dishonesty and defying your boss. Talking to the boss about the omission and maybe offering some type of a compromise, such as including the data with an honest explanation for the performance not being truly representative is worth a try. A compromise could maximize utility and avoid unethical behavior. Let's assume this approach doesn't work and you have the remaining two options:

1. Obey the boss and omit the data. Clients who make unwise investment choices based on the data will experience a cost. The benefit to you and the company comes in the form of potentially adding more clients and profits. The potential cost to you and the company is that your clients find out you omitted data and change financial advisors and companies. The action could also hurt your reputation and integrity. You may please your boss and have career benefits, or you may obey your boss but have unpleasant career consequences.

2. Defy your boss and don't omit the data. You may experience a cost to your career progress and damage to your relationship with your boss. If you were to lose your job, it would be a cost to your family who relies on your financial help. On the benefit side, your boss may forget about it and not notice the included data or may even respect you for your honesty and courage.

For the boss, as stated, the omission of data passes the utilitarian test. Does the end justify the means to you? For you it may be difficult to say without trying to change the situation first, which would likely change your cost–benefit analysis for the other two options. The test is therefore inconclusive and thus passes the utilitarian test.

The Decision and the Price of Being Ethical. Based on the 3-way test, omitting the data failed the virtues and generalization tests (without conflicting virtues) and passes the utilitarian test. Therefore, it fails the 3-way test, and omitting data is considered unethical. But again, complex ethical dilemmas do not lend themselves to clear-cut outcomes for each test and the combined 3-way test, at least not with a single solution that everyone will agree on.

You may be thinking, "How high a price should I pay to be ethical? What is the limit? Should I risk losing my job?" The boss will not likely threaten you and fire you for not omitting the numbers, but your relationship will be affected and it could have negative consequences in you being given extra work, the worst assignments, lower performance reviews and raises, and no promotions. As you know, relationships at work affect your job satisfaction. If coworkers are also using unethical behavior, you could face peer pressure to conform to the unethical behavior and ostracism by being isolated and excluded from friendly relationships.

So the 3-way ethics test helps you determine whether an action is ethical, but the decision to use ethical behavior often takes courage because you may pay a price to be ethical. It is difficult to be objective and not just look out for our own interests.[94] It is often easy and convenient to simply justify our unethical behavior, rather than use the 3-way test. It takes moral courage to make ethical choices when faced with temptations or pressures.[95]

In many, but not all, situations people maintain their integrity and are satisfied with their job. Others decide to change jobs within the firm, and others leave the company for another position where they find a better fit with the ethics culture. Many people who make the decision to be ethical, at a price, are happy they did so, especially in the long run.

Applying the Ethics Guides. The question isn't will the ethics guides help me make better ethical decisions, research indicates that they do. The question is, do I want to improve my ability to make ethical choices, and will I actually use the guides when faced with ethical dilemmas? The 3-way test (including the 10 general guides) is an effective diagnostic tool that can be used when facing ethical dilemmas, but it is also used with other modes of business analysis in the functional areas of finance/account, operations, marketing, human resources, and others.

Take the Money and Run Question 8: Did the managers at GS pass the 3-way ethics test?

No, GS managers did not pass the 3-way ethics test. In order for someone to pass the test they have to pass on all levels. They failed the virtues test because it requires honesty, good character traits, and integrity and fosters relationships. The managers omitted information on the Abacus deal from some of their clients, which caused financial losses for them, while Goldman gained tremendously. They failed the generalization test because the reason for omitting information to some clients was not to aid them but to defraud them. They passed the utilitarian test because omitting pertinent information may have led more clients to GS, thus justifying the omission.

Personal and Professional Applications

17. Will you consciously use the 3-way ethics test in your personal and professional lives?

MANAGERIAL ETHICS

As noted early in this chapter, managers are responsible for the ethical behavior of employees. So in this section we consider the need for managers to develop codes of ethics and other methods in managing ethics to help ensure that they and their employees are ethical.

Codes of Ethics

To guide employee decision making and behavior, today most professional associations in the functional areas of business have codes of ethics, also called *codes of conduct* and *ethics policies* that indicate behavior professionals should and should not use. The following professional associations have their codes of ethics/conduct available on their websites: **American Institute of Certified Public Accountants (AICPA**, www.aicpa.org), **Chartered Financial Analysts (CFA**, www.cfa.org), **American Marketing Association (AMA**, www.ama.org), **Academy of Management (AoM**, www.aom.org), and the **Association for Computing Machinery (ACM**, www.acom.org). Upon examining the codes, you will realize some of the ethical dilemmas faced in the various professions.

Also, most large corporations have developed written codes of ethics. Codes of ethics provide a fourteenth guide to ethical behavior, but codes are tailored to the specific organization. So we list the areas commonly covered and provide an example. For more example codes of ethics, visit the websites of major corporations.

Conduct. Common areas covered in ethics codes include theft and use of assets, giving and accepting gifts/kickbacks, avoiding conflict of interest, security of proprietary information, avoiding discrimination and sexual harassment, and protecting the environment. **J.C. Penney** was ahead of its time with its code developed back in 1913, which is still used today. See Figure 5.5 for a code of conduct developed by **General Electric**. This code was taken from *The Spirit & The Letter*, a 64-page booklet on ethics, which is just an introduction to *GE Compliance Policies* (www.ge.com).[96]

■ Obey the applicable laws and regulations governing our business conduct worldwide.	■ Foster an atmosphere in which fair employment practices extend to every member of the diverse community.
■ Be honest, fair, and trustworthy in all your activities and relationships.	■ Strive to create a safe workplace to protect the environment.
■ Avoid all conflict of interest between work and personal affairs.	■ Through leadership at all levels, sustain a culture where ethical conduct is recognized, valued, and exemplified by all employees.

■ **Figure 5.5:** General Electric's Code of Conduct

Source: Reprinted with permission of General Electric Company. www.ge.com/file/usa/citizenship/pdf/english.pdf

ETHICAL DILEMMA 5.2 Mr. President You're Fired: Hacking Hewlett-Packard's Code of Conduct and Walking Away a Millionaire!

Hewlett-Packard (HP) is a multinational information technology company with headquarters in Palo Alto, California. It develops and manufactures computer-related hardware and software such as personal computers, servers, storage devices, printers, laptops, and networking equipment and it also provides different types of professional services (e.g., business process outsourcing, application development and management, consulting, and systems integration).[97] The company markets to consumers, businesses, governments, and schools worldwide. About two-thirds of its sales come from outside the United States.[98]

HP has an easy-to-understand code of conduct: "they suggest that employees pose themselves a simple test to decide whether an action is appropriate: 'Before I make a decision, I consider how it would look in a news story.' Mark Hurd [now former CEO of Hewlett Packard] who was fired as the computer giant's chief executive, would appear to have failed that test. . . . The HP board asked for Mr. Hurd's resignation in large part because of the conflict between his actions and the code of conduct, [a code] which he publicly championed in 2006."[99]

What was Hurd's crime? Originally Hurd was accused by a female marketing contractor of sexual harassment. HP determined that Hurd didn't violate HP's sexual harassment policy, but other irregularities were uncovered. A specific part of the code states that "any use of HP assets, resources, or equipment, including the company's computers and information systems, must be solely for HP business purposes and must be consistent with all HP policies and guidelines."[100] An investigation found that Hurd submitted inaccurate expense reports that the company said concealed his relationship with the female contract employee who alleged the sexual harassment.[101] "About $20,000 in expenses were at issue, and the 53-year-old Hurd agreed to pay back the money, according to another person familiar with the matter. 'Sadly, Mark's conduct undermined the standards we expect of our employees, not to mention the standards to which the CEO must be held, and the board decision was unanimous,' said Marc Andreessen, an HP director."

"Corporate governance experts were split on whether HP's board acted properly in forcing Hurd's resignation. Corporate expense offenses can be regarded as relatively minor and can typically be settled if an executive pays back the amount, some experts said. Joseph Grundfest, a professor at Stanford University's Law School and former member of the Securities and Exchange Commission, said HP directors also could have considered a private or public reprimand and financial penalties. 'When all this comes out you'll have directors of other companies saying we would have dealt with it differently,' he said. Indeed, Charles Elson, head of the Weinberg Center for Corporate Governance at the University of Delaware's business school, praised HP directors for forcing out Hurd rather than accepting his offer to repay the disputed expense money."[102]

So what is the downside for Hurd for his code-breaking actions? "Typically employees terminated for offenses under the code of conduct weren't given any severance. Hurd, by contrast, negotiated an exit package that may be worth more than $35 million, including a cash payment of $12.2 million. . . . Even with his sizable exit package, Mr. Hurd is paying a price for the expense-account scandal, some management specialists said. 'Losing his job and reputation is quite substantial for one of the best-performing CEOs in corporate America,' said Bruce Kogut, a professor of leadership and ethics at Columbia University's business school."[103]

Questions

1. Could Hurd's personal relationship with the marketing contractor be considered a conflict of interest?
2. Why would certain firms and experts consider expense offenses as relatively minor?
3. Would you have accepted Hurd's offer to pay back the disputed expense amount without penalty?
4. Hurd was fired and received a substantial exit package; was he dealt with fairly?
5. Do you think Hewlett-Packard's enforcement of its code of conduct with the former CEO serves as an effective deterrent to future unethical behavior?

Personal and Professional Applications

18. Briefly describe the ethics code where you work(ed) and/or at your college.

Warning Signs of Unethical Behavior. In codes of conduct, some companies have developed warning signs of unethical behavior. Common phrases often preclude unethical behavior. The warning signs in Figure 5.6 were developed by **Lockheed Martin** and appears in its 44-page *Setting the Standard: Code of Ethics and Business Conduct* titled "Warning Signs—You're on Thin Ethics Ice When You Hear" (www.lockheedmartin. com), which gives the list of phrases to all employees, telling them that when they hear one, they are coming up on an ethical problem.[104] So if you hear any of the phrases, chances are the user is justifying unethical behavior that shouldn't be done.

"It doesn't matter how it gets done as long as it gets done."	"Well, maybe just this once."
"We didn't have this conversation."	"Everyone does it."
"No one will ever know."	"This will destroy the competition"
"It sounds too good to be true."	"What's in it for me?"
"Shred that document."	"It's okay if I don't gain personally."
"I deserve it."	"No one will get hurt."
"We can hide it."	"This is a non-meeting."
"It's all for a good cause."	

■ **Figure 5.6:** Lockheed Martin Warning Signs of Unethical Behavior

Source: Courtesy Lockheed Martin Corporation.

Personal and Professional Applications

19. Which warning signs of unethical behavior have you used or heard in your personal life, at school, and work?

Managing Ethics

Managing ethics provides a form of self-regulation that can lead to less government regulation. Here we present eight methods for managing ethics.

1. **Consult the U.S. Sentencing Guidelines and Sarbanes-Oxley Act (SOA)**. The **U.S. Sentencing Commission** developed guidelines that businesses can follow to help avoid criminal conduct and to be given shorter sentences for wrongdoing. The guidelines are: (1) establish standards and procedures to reduce criminal conduct; (2) appoint high-level offers responsible for compliance; (3) screen out risky employees/criminals; (4) communicate standards to employees; (5) monitor and set up an anonymous helpline; (6) enforce standards and discipline violators; and (7) assess areas of violation and risk, and continuously improve the ethics system. Refer back to Chapter 3 for a review of how mangers need to implement the SOA law and its regulations.

2. **Establish top-management commitment with board-of-director oversight.** The moral tone of the business is set by top management. The corrupt organization is a top-down phenomenon focusing on benefiting the organization.[105] Evidence that employees at all levels tend to copy the behavior of the top managers, sometimes called "monkey see, monkey do," is supported by research.[106] Executives must be committed to running an ethical business, and they must lead by example through ethical decision making and behavior. Therefore, supervisors at all levels must be role models.[107] Like the top managers, the board of directors needs to lead by example, and the independent board members should oversee ethics programs to ensure that all employees, including top managers, comply with ethics standards.

3. **Have realistic objectives**. Although people are sometimes dishonest purely for their own benefit, as discussed, competitive and social pressures often give rise to unethical behavior. Managers need to set realistic performance objectives so that they don't tempt and pressure lower-level managers and employees to meet the objectives through unethical behavior. The penalties for not meeting objectives should also be reasonable so that employees don't feel pressured to act unethically to meet the objective. So make it safe to tell the truth.[108]

4. **Appoint ethics and compliance officers.** An ethics and compliance officer should be appointed to oversee the ethics methods discussed here. Their job is to ensure that the company complies with the law, such as SOA, and ethics code as they build a culture of ethics that leads the company to become an ethical organization.[109] The officer should report to top management and have direct access to the board of directors. To support each other and improve their performance, ethics officers founded their own business societal interest group—now called the **Ethics and Compliance Officers Association** (ECOA). For more information, visit www.theecoa.org.

5. **Institute ethics codes, communication, and training.** As previously discussed, ethics codes provide guidelines for ethical conduct. Having codes and reminding employees of the codes has a significant effect on how they view their own behavior.[110] So the codes need to be communicated to employees, followed by training on how to understand and apply the codes. For example, **Boeing** trains employees using

its "Questions of Integrity: The Boeing Ethics Challenge." The program includes 54 ethical dilemmas. All its employees are required to have at least one hour of ethics training every year, and managers get at least 5 hours.[111] One form of training is the ethics helpline, something that employees need to know about and how to use.

6. **Set up an ethics helpline**. As stated, when in doubt, get advice. One place to get advice is the ethics helpline. *The ethics helpline is a system through which anonymous callers can get advice on ethical issues and whistleblowing.* **Raytheon** uses its helpline as an early warning system for the development of ethics training programs for its supervisors.

7. **Discipline violators.** When the whistle is blown and employees and leaders get caught violating ethical standards, disciplinary action must be taken to deter others from violating the standards.[112] Jail terms are increasing.[113] When **MassMutual Financial Group's** board of directors fired its CEO, Robert O'Connell, and its top female executive, Susan Alfano, for having an affair and padding his supplemental retirement account with tens of millions of dollars, buying a Florida condominium from the company at a discount price, and misusing corporate aircraft, it sent a strong message to all employees. Claire O'Connell blew the whistle on her husband.[114]

8. **Conduct ethics audits**. *The ethics audit focuses on reporting ethics violations, actions taken, and methods of continuously improving the ethics system.* The ethics audit is the responsibility of the ethics and compliance officer, with the input of the board of directors. **Northrop** reported that 5 percent of its 32,000 employees have used its helpline. **NYNEX** reports thousands of calls per year, most of which request ethical information; about 10 percent are whistleblowing on alleged wrongdoing with many cases found to be without merit.

Personal and Professional Applications

20. Which ethical management methods are used where you work(ed)?

21. How can managers where you work(ed) do a good job of managing ethics?

Business Ethics Resources. For more information on business ethics, visit these websites: **Ethics Resource Center** (www.ethics.org), **Institute for Global Ethics** (www.globalethics.org), the **Society for Business Ethics** *Business Ethics Quarterly* journal (www.societyforbusinessethics.org), *Business Ethics* magazine (www.business-ethics.com), **Health Ethics Trust** (www.healthethicstrust.com), and in the UK, **Institute for Business Ethics** (www.ibe.org.uk). Some of these websites have links to other sources.

BUSINESS NONMARKET AND MARKET STRATEGIES AND ETHICS

As in other chapters, our last section focuses on integrating nonmarket and market strategies.

Learning Outcome 7: Explain how the 5 Is strategic analysis includes the stakeholder approach and ethics.

The Stakeholder 5 Is Strategic Approach Includes Ethics

Some managers need to rethink business strategy in view of a range of social and ethical challenges we face today.[115] Managers can't be morally disengaged in the decision-making process.[116] Managers should follow the 5 Is strategic analysis, which includes the stakeholder approach to management and ethics (balancing owner and other stakeholder interests while focusing on being profitable). The 5 Is (see Chapter 2 and Appendix) are: (1) identifying the issue; (2) determining interested strategic stakeholders; (3) determining the incentive of the stakeholders; (4) developing information for the business side of the issue and setting an objective for the issue; and (5) developing an interaction strategy. The interaction strategy includes four parts: (1) developing alternative strategies to deal with the issue; (2) determining the market and (3) nonmarket consequences of the alternative strategies—costs vs. benefits; and (4) determining whether the action is legal and ethical. Thus, any strategy that is not ethical is not selected.

Integrating Nonmarket and Market Strategies

Ethics guides, especially codes of ethics, are used when selecting and implementing strategic action because they help to eliminate action that is unacceptable on moral grounds, just as the law rules out activities that are illegal. When selecting strategies, ethics provides the basis for evaluating moral claims and assessing responsibilities. Because all employees are expected to act ethically, the codes of ethics must be written so that everyone can easily read and understand what to do, and not do.

The Need to Consider Moral Determinants of Nonmarket Strategic Action. Although *nonmarket* strategic action is often motivated by the firm's self-interest, on many issues it needs to be motivated by moral concerns when dealing with issues in society and government. Thus, ethics provides a basis for anticipating nonmarket actions motivated by moral concerns. Activist interest groups and politicians use moral language to frame their issues to advance their interest by mobilizing those sympathetic to their causes, and set social and political agendas. For example, when the Obama administration mandated that all organizations must pay for birth control, sterilization, and the abortion pill, many religious organizations claimed it was an attack on religious freedom. Thus, management needs to understand moral determinants of nonmarket behavior and assess the implications for the progress of issues through their "issues life cycle and strategy focus" (Figure 2.4, p. 53) in order to meet the challenge of the issue and use the appropriate strategy to deal with it (Figure 1.4, p. 22).

> **Step 1**. Assess the range of moral concerns that individuals, organizations, and the government may have about an issue. Because self-interest and moral concerns are not the same, people who are not directly affected by an issue must be considered because they will likely hear about the issue from activist groups and/or the media, as was the case in the preceding Obama administration example.
>
> **Step 2.** Determine how the nonmarket members will evaluate the company's strategic action concerning the issue. What is the range of moral concerns that may arise from the strategic action? You need to view the issue from the nonmarket perception, so putting yourself in their situation and talking to these people can help. Because people use different moral evaluations, you should use multiple guides to ethics. The code of ethics and 3-way test are valuable tools.
>
> **Step 3.** Conduct a cost–benefit analysis to assess how likely it is that the strategic action will result in media coverage or publicity that will cause negative public senti-

ment and action against the firm. The impact increases with the number of people who will take action on the issue against the firm in some way; their resources in terms of time, energy, and financial resources; and how well organized they are (society interest groups, such as unions). What strategies they are likely to use against the firm, and what nonmarket strategic responses you will use to deal with them are additional concerns.[117]

Step 4. Select the integrated strategy.

Integrating Nonmarket and Market Strategies. An important reason for conducting the cost–benefit analysis is to think in broader terms of consequences to strategic stakeholders. Managers must attempt to balance owner and stakeholder interests while focusing on profitability. Unfortunately, the balance is not always achieved. For example, **Citigroup** and other financial companies focused on the market and sales commissions and profits extensively, and failed to anticipate the morally motivated nonmarket action directed against their subprime lending practices that resulted in many owners losing their homes, which contributed significantly to economic problems and the recession in 2008. In addition, the federal government had to step in and bail out financial firms. These firms failed to effectively determine the consequences of the alternative strategies through cost–benefit analysis, which is an important part of the 5 Is analysis. The moral courage of authentic leaders is critical when faced with temptations and pressures to justify unethical behavior.[118] You can use the 5 Is analysis when completing the chapter ethical dilemmas and cases to improve your skills in developing rational integrated nonmarket and market strategies.

SUMMARY

The chapter summary is organized to answer the learning outcomes for Chapter 5.

1. **Compare and contrast ethics, business ethics, and managerial ethics.**
   Ethics is the moral standard (or principles) of right and wrong (or moral and immoral) and fairness that influences behavior. *Business ethics* is the application of ethics to issues that arise in business. *Managerial ethics* differs from business ethics because managers are not only responsible for their individual behavior at work; they are also responsible for developing moral standard policies and procedures to guide employee behavior, and for ensuring that their employees behave ethically.

2. **Characterize the three levels of moral development.**
   The higher the level of moral development, the more ethical is the behavior.

(1) *Preconventional* (self-centered): At the lowest level of moral development, behavior is motivated by self-interest—avoiding punishment and seeking rewards. (2) *Conventional* (social-centered): At the second level, individuals are motivated by meeting social group and societal expectations to fit in, and therefore they copy others' behavior. (3) *Postconventional* (ethics-centered): At the highest level, behavior is motivated by the desire to do the right thing, even at the risk of alienating the group.

3. **Identify reasons why people use unethical behavior and how they justify it.**
   People use unethical behavior for personal gain and self-interest, because of conflict of interest, external pressure, cross-cultural inconsistency, personality traits and attitudes toward ethics,

and situational factors. People rationalize their unethical behavior and convince themselves that their reasons are justified. Four of the justifications include using relativism ethics (based on the circumstances of the situation: "my personal opinion says the behavior is ethical"), moral justification ("I did it for the good of my company"), conventional justification ("everyone else does it"), and displacement of responsibility ("I was only following orders").

4. **List general guides to ethical decision making.**
    Ten general guides are critical to ethical decision making. Follow the *Golden Rule* and treat others as you want to be treated; act from the postconventional *moral level;* consider the *rights* of others; be fair by seeking *justice;* use *common sense*; seek *advice*; don't do things that violate your *comfort* or that will embarrass you through *disclosure*; use the *4-way test of Rotary International*; and apply the *5-question test of Sears, Roebuck and Co.*

5. **Compare and contrast virtues, deontological, and utilitarianism guides to ethical decision making.**
    All three are guides to aid in making ethical decisions, however their focus is different. Virtues ethics focuses on having personal character traits as the bases for ethical decisions; deontological ethics focuses on using standards of conduct for determining right and wrong behavior; and utilitarianism ethics focuses on making ethical decisions based on the consequences of the behavior. Thus, virtues and deontological ethics focus more on the means to an end, while utilitarianism ethics focuses more on the end result of the decision and behavior.

6. **Describe the 3-way ethics test.**
    The 3-way ethics test is used to determine whether an action is ethical. The test has three parts, and to be ethical the behavior must pass all three—virtues, generalization, and utilitarian—tests. To pass the virtues test, the behavior must be honest, be based on good character traits, and maintain one's integrity and relationships. To pass the generalization test, the reasons for the action must be consistent, and everyone in the same situation with the same reasons will use the same behavior. To pass the utilitarian test, one specific action leads to more favorable consequences than any alternative decision.

7. **Explain how the 5 Is strategic analysis includes the stakeholder approach and ethics.**
    When making decisions on how to deal with issues, identify the issues, the interested stakeholders, and stakeholder incentives. Then devise objectives to deal with stakeholder issues. Generate and evaluate alternative strategies. Assess each alternative for the consequences to strategic stakeholders using a cost–benefit analysis in both the market and nonmarket environments. Each alternative strategy must pass the test of being legal and ethical to be selected and implemented.

8. **Fill in the blank with the appropriate key term (in order of appearance in the chapter):**
    _____ is impartial, it applies to everyone, and morals should take precedence over self-interest.
    _____ contends that morals can change based on time, the circumstances of the situation, and personal opinion.
    _____ are preconventional, conventional, and postconventional.
    _____ is the application of ethics to issues that arise in business.
    _____ occurs when a decision must be made in the midst of conflicting interests; there is no simple right and wrong answer
    _____ is the process of determining motives, reasons, explanation, and justifications that lead to particu-

lar decisions and behavior when faced with ethical dilemmas.

_____ is the process of convincing oneself that a decision is rational and ethical, when in fact it really serves self-interest or provides an easy way out of the ethical dilemma.

_____ provide a structured method for analyzing ethical dilemmas to aid in making ethical choices.

_____ refers to having personal character traits as the basis for ethical decisions.

_____ the behavior must be honest, be based on good character traits, and maintain one's integrity and relationships.

_____ refers to using standards of conduct to determine right and wrong behavior when making ethical decisions.

_____, the reasons for the action must be consistent, and everyone in the same situation with the same reasons will use the same behavior.

_____ refers to making ethical decisions based on the consequences of the behavior.

_____, one specific action leads to more favorable consequences than any alternative decision.

_____ is a system through which anonymous callers can get advice on ethical issues and whistleblowing.

_____ focuses on reporting ethics violations, actions taken, and methods of continuously improving the ethics system.

KEY TERMS (IN ALPHABETICAL ORDER)

KEY TERMS

5

business ethics (p. 158)
deontological ethics (p. 170)
ethical decision guides (p. 165)
ethical dilemma (p. 158)
ethical rationalization (p. 163)
ethics audit (p. 181)
ethics helpline (p. 181)
generalization test (p. 171)

justifying unethical behavior (p. 163)
levels of moral development (p. 156)
relativism ethics (p. 156)
utilitarianism ethics (p. 171)
utilitarian test (p. 173)
universal ethics (p. 156)
virtues ethics (p. 168)
virtues ethics test (p. 169)

REVIEW QUESTIONS

REVIEW QUESTIONS

5

1 Who determines moral standards of behavior?

2 What does honesty include?

3 What are the three levels of moral development?

4 How do you know when you face an ethical dilemma?

5 What are the three types of moral management?

6 Is self-interest unethical, and what is the difference between self-interest and conflict of interest?

7 What are some of the sources of external pressure to use unethical behavior?

8 What is the Golden Rule?

9 What is and isn't the focus of virtues ethics?

10 What is a fiduciary duty?

11 Which ethics guide focuses on means and which one focuses on ends?

12 Why should we use multiple ethics guides?

13 What are the three parts, or test, within the 3-way ethics test?

14 What is a code of ethics?

15 Why is it important for top management to be committed to high ethical standards?

DISCUSSION/CRITICAL THINKING QUESTIONS

Be sure to give a detailed explanation for your answer to each question.

1 Who should set the moral standards of ethical behavior?

2 What are some of your values?

3 Do you agree with universal or relativism ethics?

4 At which level of moral development would you place most of your associates?

5 Which business ethics myth to do agree and disagree with the most? Why?

6 Which is the most common reason for people to use unethical behavior in your opinion?

7 Which justification for their unethical behavior do you believe is most commonly used by people?

8 The Golden Rule is simple, so why doesn't everyone follow it?

9 What percentage of people do you believe actually consider others' rights in making ethical decisions?

10 What good character traits do you most value in your relationships?

11 Identify some of the behaviors society considers right and wrong.

12 Identify some areas in which it is difficult to measure cost and benefits.

13 Is the 3-way test too complex to use when faced with ethical dilemmas on the job? Why or why not?

14 Major corporations have codes of ethics to guide employee decision making, but many acts of unethical behavior still occur. Do codes of ethics work?

15 Does it really help to have a list of "Warning signs of unethical behavior"? Why or why not?

16 Would you like to be an ethics and compliance officer? Why or why not?

APPLICATION EXERCISES

5.1 ETHICS GUIDES

Is the 3-way test too complex to use when faced with ethical dilemmas? If so, what ethical guide will you actually use to help you make ethical decisions? You can select from the 13 guides and/or develop your own guide to ethical decision making.

5.2 USING THE 3-WAY TEST

Select an ethical dilemma you face(d). Describe it and give it the 3-way test. Stu-dents in groups (or as a class or online) may present their ethical dilemmas and have the others give it the 3-way test and discuss options for handling these ethical dilemmas.

5.3 ETHICAL BEHAVIOR

For this exercise, complete the following self-assessment.

Self-Assessment Exercise: How Ethical Is Your Behavior

For this exercise, you will be using the same set of statements twice. The first time you respond to them, focus on your own behavior and the frequency with which it occurs. On the line before the question number, place the appropriate ranking (1, 2, 3, or 4) that represents how often this behavior does or would apply to you. These numbers will allow you to determine your level of ethics. You can be honest without fear of having to tell others your score in class. *Sharing ethics scores is not part of the exercise.*

Frequently			Never

1 2 3 4

The second time you read the statements, focus on other people in an organization that you work(ed) for. Place an "O" on the line after the number if you observed someone doing the behavior. Also place an "R" on the line if you reported (blew the whistle on) this behavior within the organization or externally.

O—observed R—reported

As you read the statements, state how often you engaged in the behavior in the past, if you "do the behavior now," or if you "would engage in the behavior if you had the chance."

1–4 O/R

College

_____ 1. _____ Cheating on homework assignments.
_____ 2. _____ Cheating on exams.
_____ 3._____ Passing in papers as your own that were completed by someone else.

Job

_____ 4. _____ Lying to others to get what you want or stay out of trouble.
_____ 5. _____ Coming to work late, leaving work early, taking long breaks/lunches, and getting paid for it.
_____ 6. _____ Socializing, goofing off, or doing personal work rather than doing the work that should be done and getting paid for it.
_____ 7. _____ Calling in sick to get a day off, when not sick.
_____ 8. ___ Using the organization's phone, computer, Internet, copier, mail, car, etc. for personal use.
_____ 9. ___ Taking home company tools/equipment without permission for personal use and returning it.
_____ 10. ___ Taking home organizational supplies or merchandise and keeping it.
_____ 11. ___ Giving company supplies or merchandise to friends or allowing them to take them without saying anything.
_____ 12. ___ Putting in for reimbursement for meals, travel, and other expenses that were not actually incurred.
_____ 13. ___ Taking spouse/friends out to eat or on business trips and charging it to the organization's expense account.

____ 14. ___ Accepting gifts from customers/suppliers in exchange for giving them business.

____ 15. ___ Cheating on your taxes.

____ 16. ___ Misleading a customer to make a sale, such as promising delivery dates that the company cannot meet.

____ 17. ___ Misleading competitors to get information for use against them, such as saying/pretending to be a customer/supplier.

____ 18. ___ Planting information or making it up so you look good or gain support.

____ 19. ___ Selling more of the product than the customer needs to get the sales commission.

____ 20. ___ Spreading false rumors about coworkers or competitors to make you look better for advancement or to make more sales.

____ 21. ___ Lying for your boss when asked/told to do so.

____ 22. ___ Deleting information that makes you look bad or changing information to look better than actual results—false information.

____ 23. ___ Being pressured, or pressuring others, to sign off on documents that contain false information.

____ 24. ___ Being pressured, or pressuring others, to sign off on documents you haven't read, knowing they may contain information or decisions that might be considered inappropriate.

Use a scale of yes (4) and no (1) on the line before the number 25 and skip O or R.

____ 25. ___ If you were to give this assessment to a person you work with whom you do not get along with very well, would he agree with your answers?

Other Unethical Behavior:

Add other unethical behaviors you observed. Identify whether you reported the behavior using R.

26. ___ _____

27. ___ _____

28. ___ _____

Note: This self-assessment is not meant to be a precise measure of your ethical behavior. It is designed to stimulate your thinking about ethics, your behavior, and others' behaviors from an ethical perspective. This exercise is not looking for a particular score as "correct"; however, each of these actions is considered unethical behavior in most organizations. Another ethical issue of this exercise is your honesty when rating the frequencies of your behavior. How honest were you?

Scoring: To determine your ethics score, add up the numbers from the first set of responses. Your total will be between 25 and 100. Place the number here ____ and refer to the continuum shown below. The higher your score, the more ethical is your behavior; the lower your score, the less ethical is your behavior.

Unethical 25   30   40   50   60   70   80   90   100 Ethical

Questions

1. Who is harmed and who benefits from the unethical behaviors in items 1–3?
2. For items 4–24, select the three (circle their numbers) you consider the most unethical. Who is harmed by and who benefits from these unethical behaviors?
3. If you observed unethical behavior but didn't report it, why didn't you report the behavior? If you did blow the whistle, what motivated you to do so? What was the result?
4. As a manager, it is your responsibility to uphold ethical behavior. If you know employees are doing any of the unethical behaviors above, will you take action to enforce compliance with ethical standards?
5. What can you do to prevent unethical behavior?
6. As part of the class discussion, share any of the other unethical behaviors you observed and listed.

In-Class Exercise

You may be given the opportunity to discuss the self-assessment and questions in class in small groups or as an entire class. If you do discuss the exercise, you are *not* required to state or talk about your score.

CASE 5.1

Does the Fox in the Hen House Make Apple Rotten to Its Core? Suppliers and Child Laborers

CASES

5

Apple, Inc. is a U.S. multinational company that designs and sells electronics, personal computers, and computer software. It is known as a cutting-edge company because it changed the landscape of computers, portable music devices, cell phones, and mobile computing. Some of the most popular items that Apple creates include the iPod, iPhone, and iPad.[119] Former CEO Steve Jobs has been credited with the design of these radical innovations and currently Timothy Cook is running the company as the new CEO after Jobs stepped down shortly before his death in 2011.

Apple may get an unofficial A grade when it comes to stock price, but they can only manage a D grade when it comes to ethical behavior. . . . According to EIRIS (a global provider of independent research into the environmental, social, governance (ESG) and ethical performance of companies), Apple's poor grade stems from its links to suppliers in countries with human rights and labor issues.[120] Yet Apple's code of conduct for suppliers is clear about working conditions and child labor. "Child labor is strictly prohibited. Suppliers shall not employ children. The minimum age for employment or work shall be 15 years of age, the minimum age for employment in that country, or the age for completing compulsory education in that country, whichever is higher."[121]

The *New York Times* discovered that FoxConn factories, which manufacture Apple computers, smartphones, and tablets, operate under horrible working conditions. The accusations against this Chinese supplier include employment of children who are forced to work long hours in unsafe conditions.[122] This factory also produces products for companies such as Amazon, Dell, Hewlett-Packard, Motorola, Nintendo, Nokia, Samsung, and Sony.

Apple CEO Tim Cook stated that "Apple takes working conditions very, very seriously. . . . We care about every worker. . . . No one in our industry is doing more to improve working conditions than Apple."[123] From the products sold in 2011, approximately 70 million iPhones, 30 million iPads, and 59 million other Apple products are manufactured overseas.[124] Even though Apple's profits have been increasing, the question is whether Apple can afford from a social responsibility perspective to keep FoxConn as a supplier. Several petitions have been launched to encourage worker protection for those producing Apple products. This response comes from the general public in an attempt to force moral responsibility on Apple and Cook.[125]

Cook has not been idle in addressing these issues. "'I want to give credit to Tim Cook for this,' said Dara O'Rourke, associate professor of environmental and labor policy at the University of California, Berkeley. 'He's admitting they've got problems.' . . . This year [2012], Apple also became the first technology company to join the Fair Labor Association, and it invited the nonprofit global monitoring group to conduct inspections of its suppliers' factories in China and elsewhere. . . . The group published the results of its first inspections of Apple's supply chain, citing numerous violations of Chinese labor laws and regulations at Foxconn factories, including instances where workers exceeded the 60-hour workweek that is the association's standard. . . . In a statement, Apple said, 'Our team has been working for years to educate workers, improve conditions and make Apple's supply chain a model for the

industry, which is why we asked the F.L.A. to conduct these audits.'"[126]

"Some labor rights advocates, though, said they were not yet convinced that [the] report about conditions in Foxconn factories would lead to meaningful improvements for workers, saying that earlier promises of progress by Apple and its partners had not been fulfilled. 'It looks like a pattern I've observed before,' said Jeff Ballinger, a global labor activist and researcher. 'It's a report to get you over and hopefully things will die down. It's not very convincing.'"[127]

Questions

1. Identify Apple's definition of its moral development. At what level of moral development is it operating?
2. What might be some reasons that Apple has not enforced its own supplier code of conduct?
3. How might utilitarianism apply to this case?
4. Apply the 3-way ethics test to this case and describe your results.
5. What actions must Apple now take to manage the ethics of its suppliers given its supplier code of ethics?

CASE 5.2

Ethically Delicious or Morally Distasteful? An Interview with Ben Cohen, Cofounder of Ben & Jerry's

"Ben & Jerry's corporate culture runs deep. Co-founders Ben Cohen and Jerry Greenfield created the company in 1978 in a renovated gas station in Burlington, Vermont. As the merry prankster of the food industry, Ben & Jerry's is known for pulling off playful PR events and taking stands on social and environmental issues—its products are packed in unbleached cardboard containers and the company boasts a three-part social, product, and economic mission. Today, Ben & Jerry's works to maintain its culture and image even under Unilever's umbrella."[128]

"Ice cream mogul Jerry Greenfield . . . says it's possible for companies to integrate their values into their business and still make money. . . . He sat down with *The Oregonian* to talk about socially minded business. (The interview has been edited for length and clarity.)

You're here to advocate for socially and environmentally aware business. How do you make the case?
Businesses can lead with their values and make money, too. You don't have to simply be purely profit-driven. You can

integrate social and environmental concerns into a business, be a caring business, be a generous business and still do very well financially. It's counter to the conventional thinking about business. The conventional thinking is you need concentrate solely on making money and not stand for anything.

Is that a tougher message to deliver as the economy takes a toll on profit margins?
I don't think it really changes anything. It was actually a tougher message when we started out. In the 80s, when we formalized the mission of the company, I think there was a lot more skepticism and sometimes outright animosity. Now it's much more accepted, and in some cases it's demanded by customers. On the one hand, it does add another factor to consider. It may seem like it's more complex. On the other hand, it's very motivating to our employees and very motivating to our customers to have a business thinking about those things. So I think it's also very beneficial.

What will you tell these business leaders to do with their companies?
Businesses typically look at issues like price, quality, and time of delivery. They don't often think about social and environmental impact because they're focused on their financial bottom line. Look at your business and the activities that you undertake. Then, start to think about not just your economic concerns, but about social and environmental impacts that businesses have. I don't think its big business that's taking the lead in innovating for social concerns or environmental concerns. They are following market forces for that. It may be smaller entrepreneurial companies that are leading the way.

But are bigger businesses changing, too?
I do think businesses respond better. Recycling, packaging, business are changing all of those things because that's what consumers want. I'm going to back up for a second. It's not that businesses need to do this. There's many different ways for businesses to operate. Businesses should only do this if they want to, if they feel like it's a part of who they are and how they want to be. If you want to be a business that just tries to make as much money as you can, who am I to tell you not to do that? I will say that business is an incredibly powerful force in society. It's probably the most powerful force in this society, and it can use its power to either try to make the world a better place or say as a business our job is simply to maximize profit. Well, I would say you're not really going to have a very sustainable world if the most powerful force in society is going to think only about itself.[129]

Yet Ben and Jerry's have had their run in with controversy. The company raised eyebrows in 2006 after releasing a flavor of ice cream called "Black and Tan." It had named the flavor after the alcoholic drink made by mixing stout with pale ale.[130] Later the Center for Science in the Public Interest, a consumer-advocacy group, urged Ben & Jerry's to stop labeling their ice cream as "all natural" due to the company's use of corn syrup, alkalized cocoa, and other chemically modified ingredients. In September 2010, the company agreed to stop labeling their ice cream and frozen yogurt as "all natural."[131]

In 2011, Ben & Jerry's released a flavor named Schweddy Balls, in homage to the Saturday Night Live skit of the same name. The American Family Association protested, saying that the name was too explicit for grocery store shelves.[132] In 2012, Ben & Jerry's created a vanilla-flavored frozen yogurt named "Taste the Lin-Sanity" in honor of Asian-American basketball player Jeremy Lin. It contained lychee honey swirls and fortune cookie pieces, but, after an initial backlash, Ben & Jerry's replaced the fortune cookies with waffle cookies. The company, however, said the primary reason was because the fortune cookies got soggy. It later apologized to anyone offended by their Lin-Sanity flavor.[133]

Questions

1. All three levels of moral development are directly or indirectly referred to in this case. Describe each level and some facts in the case related to that level.
2. What type of moral manager does Jerry Greenfield appear to be? Why?
3. How do Jerry Greenfield's comments highlight the concept of self-interest?
4. How might the fact that Ben and Jerry are now part of the large conglomerate Unilever affect their ability to advance social concerns?
5. Is Ben and Jerry's following its own moral standards given the controversy at the end of the case?

INTEGRATIVE CASE (Part 5)

Advertising and DHR Construction, LLC: We Built It, Nobody Came, Now What?

This is a continuation case—please refer back to Chapters 1–4 for further information.

As Richard Davis drove back home from DHR Construction, LLC's work site, he reflected upon the negative changes in the home construction industry. The Federal Reserve's last Beige Book Report stated that new construction homes sales were down all around the country, spurred by greater consumer debt and poor credit scores, a negative savings rate, increased home inventories, and lower demand. These factors did not bode well for the home construction side of the business, which had seen sales drop from two homes per month to one. In fact, several customers actually had to back out of deals once their homes were built given their inability to obtain a mortgage and Davis and Hodgetts were stuck with inventory they had not planned on. After careful consideration, Richard decided that he should sit down with Stephen and his wife Adrienne and figure out their next move.

At the dinner table that night Adrienne quickly pointed out that all of the sales of homes had resulted from word-of-mouth referrals and from colleagues, friends, business associates, and former renters. No other marketing channels (developer advertising, real estate brokers) had any success. "It is clear then," commented Davis, "that we need to develop our own advertising campaign in order to offset the downturn in the business. We need to increase the flow of perspective buyers through our sites, and we really need to move our existing inventory." "But we know nothing about advertising," responded Hodgetts, "except from our own experiences in buying homes when we first started our rental business." "Exactly," responded Adrienne. "Which is why I have invited an advertising specialist to join us for dessert . . . in fact I think that is Jane at the door now."

The front door bell rings and Adrienne greets Jane Finalbargo, a local media specialist who worked with local small businesses to develop a media campaign. She started by describing the purpose of advertising. "Advertising is an effective and relatively low-cost way of informing customers about new and improved products and services—in your case your quality homes. Ads will increase traffic through your homes, the key to making a sale. Increased sales in the long run will actually lower your marginal costs and allow you to discount your homes and as you know lower prices means even more sales. Besides, the choice to advertise is a constitutional right under the First Amendment to the Constitution!"

Adrienne asked what might be some of the downsides to advertising. Jane noted that some businesses thought advertising was an inefficient tool to inform consumers and wasted capital by increasing the cost of the product without adding functionality. The ads simply provided superfluous information and increased business costs that had to be passed onto the consumer without providing net benefits to them.

Jane then outlined the different forms of media (newspapers, magazines, special fliers, bill board advertisements, radio, television, Internet ads and pop-ups, etc . . .) as well as the related cost factors. Richard and Stephen were quite surprised to learn that television advertising, especially through cable channels such as Lifetime, Discovery, and the Arts and Entertainment Network, were fairly inexpensive and could be quite successful at reaching specific target audiences. They decided that a 30-second TV spot to be run on several cable channels targeting upper-middle-income individuals ages 35–65 was the way to go. The real question was then what the commercial should focus on.

After a few minutes of discussion it was clear that the group was hopelessly divided on what the theme of the commercial should be. Adrienne and Stephen Hodgetts wanted a commercial that focused on the facts about the firm and the type of homes they built; one that included numerous shots of their existing homes (interiors and exteriors), a narration by Richard Davis, with cameos of Richard, Adrienne, Stephen, and their subcontractors busily working on "building that special home just for you." The theme of the commercial would be on the personalized service and attention that each home and customer would receive from a small professional firm.

Jane and Richard Davis, on the other hand, thought that the way to go was to have a more glamorous campaign that would be based upon the same slogan and theme but would include the use of professional models to showcase the homes (Richard liked the idea of having a voluptuous model in the commercial), a professional narrator, with comparisons made to competitors' "inferior" homes. Jane thought that showing a "loving couple" in the house, perhaps newlyweds, enjoying their first night at home in their luxurious master bathroom, together in the Jacuzzi, would really drive the message home. She also suggested TV ads with Internet pop-ups that would be tied to websites dealing with home mortgages, real estate brokers, and the Chamber of Commerce Web page that would discuss how a quality home was sure to be part of a fun-filled lifestyle.

The group clearly had reached an impasse. Stephen and Adrienne were appalled by what they perceived as blatant exploitive commercialism inherent in Richard and Jane's proposed advertisements while Richard and Jane felt that Stephen and Adrienne's advertisements would be ineffective and not grab the attention of the viewers. Richard knew that the firm could not sit on its hands and expect business to walk through the door. How was the situation to be resolved?

Questions

1. Given what you have read in the case, what is the purpose of advertising and how does it apply to this case?
2. Describe Stephen and Adrienne's position on the purpose and role of advertising. How is it different from Jane and Richard's position?
3. What underlying ethical issues are raised by this case in terms of the use of advertising?
4. Whose advertising approach might you deem unethical and why?
5. Which form of television advertising do you think would be the most effective? Why?
6. How should Richard and Stephen resolve this impasse? What type of television commercial do you think they should run?

REFERENCES AND
NOTES

5

REFERENCES AND NOTES

1 http://www.fundinguniverse.com/company-histories/the-goldman-sachs-group-inc-history/ (accessed June 19, 2012).

2 http://www.nytimes.com/2012/03/14/opinion/why-i-am-leaving-goldman-sachs.html?pagewanted=all (accessed June 19, 2012).

3 http://www.goldmansachs.com/who-we-are/business-standards/business-principles/index.html.

4 http://www.nytimes.com/2012/03/14/opinion/why-i-am-leaving-goldman-sachs.html?pagewanted=all (accessed June 19, 2012).

5 Ibid; http://articles.nydailynews.com/2010-04-27/news/27062815_1_goldman-sachs-goldman-traders-john-paulson.

6 "American Greed, Goldman Sachs, Power and Peril," CNBBC (May5, 2012).

7 Ibid.

8 Ibid.

9 http://ftalphaville.ft.com/blog/2010/06/10/256636/a-hudson-cdo-primer/.

10 http://www.nytimes.com/2012/03/14/opinion/why-i-am-leaving-goldman-sachs.html?pagewanted=all; http://www.rollingstone.com/politics/news/the-great-american-bubble-machine-20100405.

11 Ibid.

12 Ibid.

13 E. Spurgin, "Can Businesses Be Too Good? Applying Susan Wolf's 'Moral Saints' to Businesses," *Business and Society Review* 116(3) (2011): 355–373.

14 J. Smith and W. Dubbink, "Understanding the Role of Moral Principles in Business Ethics: A Kantian Perspective," *Business Ethics Quarterly* 21(2) (2011): 205–231.

15 M. Rhee and M. E. Valdez, "Contextual Factors Surrounding Reputation Damage with Potential Implications for Reputation Repair," *Academy of Management Journal* 34(1) (2009): 146–168.

16 C. Caldwell, "Duties Owed to Organizational Citizens—Ethical Insights for Today's Leader," *Journal of Business Ethics* 102(3) (2011): 343–356.

17 B. Macnab, R. Worthley, and S. Jenner, "Regional Cultural Differences and Ethical Perspectives within the United States: Avoiding Pseudo-emic Ethics Research," *Business and Society Review*, 115(1)

(2010): 27–55.

18 J. Shambora, "Eileen Fisher's Timeless Vision," *Fortune* (September 26, 2011): 49–52.

19 V. Pompe and M. Korthals, "Ethical Room for Maneuver: Playground for the Food Business," *Business and Society Review*, 115(3) (2010): 367–391.

20 B. Macnab, R. Worthley, and S. Jenner, "Regional Cultural Differences and Ethical Perspectives within the United States: Avoiding Pseudo-emic Ethics Research," *Business and Society Review* 115(1) (2010): 27–55.

21 D. Bay, K. McKeage, and J. McKeage, "An Historical Perspective on the Interplay of Christian Thought and Business Ethics," *Business & Society* 49(4) (2010): 652–676.

22 P. Ruiz-Palomino and R. Martinez-Cañas, "Supervisor Role Modeling, Ethics-Related Organizational Policies, and Employee Ethical Intention: The Moderating Impact of Moral Ideology," *Journal of Business Ethics* 102(4) (2010): 653–668.

23 A. Arnaud, "Conceptualizing and Measuring Ethical Work Climate: Development and Validation of the Ethical Climate Index," *Business & Society* 49(2) (2010): 345–358.

24 L. Kohlberg, *The Philosophy of Moral Development* (New York: Harper & Row, 1981).

25 G. Beenen and J. Pinto, "Resisting Organizational-Level Corruption: An Interview with Sherron Walkins," *Academy of Learning & Education* 8(2) (2009): 275–289.

26 J. Gilbert, "Moral Duties in Business and Their Societal Impacts: The Case of the Subprime Lending Mess," *Business and Society Review* 116(1) (2011): 87–107.

27 R. G. Castro, M. A. Ariño, and M. A. Canela, "Over the Long-Run? Short-Run Impact and Long-Run Consequences of Stakeholder Management," *Business & Society* 50(3) (2011): 428–455.

28 D. Baur and G. Palazzo, "The Moral Legitimacy of NGOs as Partners of Corporations," *Business Ethics Quarterly* 21(4) (2011): 579–604.

29 E. Spurgin, "Can Businesses Be Too Good? Applying Susan Wolf's 'Moral

Saints' to Businesses," *Business and Society Review* 116 (3) (2011): 355–373.

30 M. J. O'Fallon and K. D. Butterfield, "Moral Differentiation: Exploring Boundaries of the 'Monkey See, Monkey Do' Perspective," *Journal of Business Ethics* 102(3) (2011): 379–399.

31 S. T. Hannah, B. J. Avolio, and F. O. Walumwa, "Relationships between Authentic Leadership, Moral Courage, and Ethical and Pro-Social Behaviors," *Business Ethics Quarterly* 21(4) (2011): 555–578.

32 T. Hahn, A. Kolk, and M. Winn, "A New Future for Business? Rethinking Management Theory and Business Strategy," *Business & Society* 49(3) (2010): 385–401.

33 Y. Luo, "Strategic Responses to Perceived Corruption in an Emerging Market: Lessons from MNEs Investing in China," *Business & Society* 50(2) (2011): 350–387.

34 L. F. Ackert, B. K. Church, X. Kuang, and L. Qi, "Lying—An Experimental Investigation of the Role of Situational Factors," *Business Ethics Quarterly* 21(4) (2011): 605–632.

35 L. F. Ackert, B. K. Church, X. Kuang, and L. Qi, "Lying—An Experimental Investigation of the Role of Situational Factors," *Business Ethics Quarterly* 21(4) (2011): 605–632.

36 A. Lobb, A. Dizik, and J. Porter, "Lessons that Fit the Times," *Wall Street Journal* (August 20, 2009): B5.

37 D. Bay, K. McKeage, and J. McKeage, "An Historical Perspective on the Interplay of Christian Thought and Business Ethics," *Business & Society* 49(4) (2010): 652–676.

38 A. Armenakis and J. Wigand, "Stakeholder Actions and Their Impact on the Organizational Cultures of Two Tobacco Companies," *Business and Society Review* 115(2) (2010): 147–171.

39 K. Sloan and J. H. Gavin, "Human Resource Management: Meeting the Ethical Obligations of the Function," *Business and Society Review* 115(1) (2010): 57–74.

40 S. T. Hannah, B. J. Avolio, and F. O. Walumwa, "Relationships between Authentic Leadership, Moral Courage, and Ethical and Pro-Social Behaviors," *Business Ethics Quarterly* 21(4) (2011): 555–578.

41 J. Gilbert, "Moral Duties in Business and Their Societal Impacts: The Case of the Subprime Lending Mess," *Business and Society Review* 116(1) (2011): 87–107.

42 K. Sloan, and J. H. Gavin, "Human Resource Management: Meeting the Ethical Obligations of the Function," *Business and Society Review* 115(1) (2010): 57–74.

43 A. Armenakis and J. Wigand, "Stakeholder Actions and Their Impact on the Organizational Cultures of Two Tobacco Companies," *Business and Society Review* 115(2) (2010): 147–171.

44 Myths adapted from J. Hooker, *Business Ethics as Rational Choice* (Boston: Prentice Hall, 2011).

45 M. Bustillo, "Best Buy CEO Quits in Probe," *Wall Street Journal* (April 11, 2012): B1.

46 P. Sonne and B. Orwall, "WSJE Publisher Quits After Ethics Inquiry," *Wall Street Journal* (October 12, 2011): B2.

47 G. Beenen and J. Pinto, "Resisting Organizational-Level Corruption: An Interview with Sherron Walkins," *Academy of Learning & Education* 8(2) (2009): 275–289.

48 J. Hooker, *Business Ethics as Rational Choice* (Boston: Prentice Hall, 2011).

49 H. J. Van Buren III, "Taking (and Sharing Power): How Boards of Directors Can Bring About Greater Fairness for Dependent Stakeholders," *Business and Society Review* 115 (2010): 205–230.

50 A. Lobb, A. Dizik, and J. Porter, "Lessons that Fit the Times," *Wall Street Journal* (August 20, 2009): B5.

51 J. Gilbert, "Moral Duties in Business and Their Societal Impacts: The Case of the Subprime Lending Mess," *Business and Society Review* 116(1) (2011): 87–107.

52 V. M. Desai, "Mass Media and Massive Failures: Determining Organizational Efforts to Defend Field Legitimacy Following Crises," *Academy of Management Journal* 54(2) (2011): 263–278.

53 L. F. Ackert, B. K. Church, X. Kuang, and L. Qi, "Lying—An Experimental Investigation of the Role of Situational Factors," *Business Ethics Quarterly* 21(4) (2011): 605–632.

54 S. T. Hannah, B. J. Avolio, and F. O. Walumwa, "Relationships between Authentic Leadership, Moral Courage, and Ethical and Pro-Social Behaviors," *Business Ethics Quarterly* 21(4) (2011): 555–578.

55 B. Macnab, R. Worthley, and S. Jenner, "Regional Cultural Differences and

Ethical Perspectives within the United States: Avoiding Pseudo-emic Ethics Research," *Business and Society Review* 115(1) (2010): 27–55.

56 Y. Luo, "Strategic Responses to Perceived Corruption in an Emerging Market: Lessons from MNEs Investing in China," *Business & Society* 50(2) (2011): 350–387.

57 G. Colvin, "The Biggest Problem for Developing Economies: Corruption," *Fortune* (May 2, 2011): 48.

58 S. T. Hannah, B. J. Avolio, and F. O. Walumwa, "Relationships between Authentic Leadership, Moral Courage, and Ethical and Pro-Social Behaviors," *Business Ethics Quarterly* 21(4) (2011): 555–578.

59 E. Dwoskin and D. Voreacos, "The U.S. Goes After Bribery, On a Budget," *BusinessWeek* (January 23–29, 2012): 31–32.

60 D. Searcey, "U.S. Cracks Down on Corporate Bribes," *Wall Street Journal* (May 26, 2009): A1, A4.

61 N. M. Pless, T. Maak, and G. K. Stahl, "Developing Responsible Global Leaders Through International Service Learning Programs: The Ulysses Experience," *Academy of Management Learning & Education* 10(2) (2011): 237–260.

62 L. F. Ackert, B. K. Church, X. Kuang, and L. Qi, "Lying—An Experimental Investigation of the Role of Situational Factors." *Business Ethics Quarterly* 21(4) (2011): 605–632.

63 V. Pompe and M. Korthals, "Ethical Room for Maneuver: Playground for the Food Business." *Business and Society Review*, 115(3) (2010): 367–391.

64 M. J. O'Fallon and K. D. Butterfield, "Moral Differentiation: Exploring Boundaries of the 'Monkey See, Monkey Do' Perspective," *Journal of Business Ethics* 102(3) (2011): 379–399.

65 P. Ruiz-Palomino and R. Martinez-Cañas, "Supervisor Role Modeling, Ethics-Related Organizational Policies, and Employee Ethical Intention: The Moderating Impact of Moral Ideology," *Journal of Business Ethics* 102(4) (2010): 653–668.

66 M. E. Brown and M. S. Mitchell, "Ethical and Unethical Leadership: Exploring New Avenues for Future Research," *Business Ethics Quarterly* 20(4) (2010): 583–616.

67 A. Arnaud, "Conceptualizing and Measuring Ethical Work Climate: Development and Validation of the Ethical Climate Index," *Business & Society* 49(2) (2010): 345–358.

68 P. J. Zak, "The Trust Molecule," *Wall Street Journal* (April 28–29, 2012): C1–C2.

69 D. Ariely, "Why We Lie," *Wall Street Journal* (May 26–27, 2012): C1–C2.

70 J. Kurlantzick, "Liar, Liar: A Culture of Lying Is Infecting American Business. Can You Help Stop the Epidemic?" *Entrepreneur* (October 2003): 68–71.

71 http://subscriber.hoovers.com/H/company360/fulldescription.html?companyId=11441000000000 (accessed June 19, 2012).

72 G. McWilliams "RadioShack CEO Agrees to Resign," *Wall Street Journal (February 21, 2006): A3.*

73 Ibid.

74 http://premium.hoovers.com/subscribe/co/fin/factsheet.xhtml?ID=11441 (accessed April 4, 2006).

75 D. Bay, K. McKeage, and J. McKeage, "An Historical Perspective on the Interplay of Christian Thought and Business Ethics," *Business & Society* 49(4) (2010): 652–676.

76 P. J. Zak, "The Trust Molecule," *Wall Street Journal* (April 28–29, 2012): C1–C2.

77 A. Arnaud, "Conceptualizing and Measuring Ethical Work Climate: Development and Validation of the Ethical Climate Index," *Business & Society* 49(2) (2010): 345–358.

78 Ibid.

79 J. Smith and W. Dubbink, "Understanding the Role of Moral Principles in Business Ethics: A Kantian Perspective," *Business Ethics Quarterly* 21(2) (2011): 205–231.

80 D. Bay, K. McKeage, and J. McKeage, "An Historical Perspective on the Interplay of Christian Thought and Business Ethics," *Business & Society* 49(4) (2010): 652–676.

81 R. G. Castro, M. A. Ariño, and M. A. Canela, "Over the Long-Run? Short-Run Impact and Long-Run Consequences of Stakeholder Management," *Business & Society* 50(3) (2011): 428–455.

82 A. Armenakis and J. Wigand, "Stakeholder Actions and Their Impact on the Organizational Cultures of Two Tobacco Companies," *Business and Society Review* 115(2) (2010): 147–171.

83 A. Arnaud, "Conceptualizing and Measuring Ethical Work Climate: Development

and Validation of the Ethical Climate Index," *Business & Society* 49(2) (2010): 345–358.

84 D. Bay, K. McKeage, and J. McKeage, "An Historical Perspective on the Interplay of Christian Thought and Business Ethics," *Business & Society* 49(4) (2010): 652–676.

85 D. Baur and G. Palazzo, "The Moral Legitimacy of NGOs as Partners of Corporations," *Business Ethics Quarterly* 21(4) (2011): 579–604.

86 J. Smith and W. Dubbink, "Understanding the Role of Moral Principles in Business Ethics: A Kantian Perspective," *Business Ethics Quarterly* 21(2) (2011): 205–231.

87 J. Gilbert, "Moral Duties in Business and Their Societal Impacts: The Case of the Subprime Lending Mess," *Business and Society Review* 116(1) (2011): 87–107.

88 R. G. Castro, M. A. Ariño, and M. A. Canela, "Over the Long-Run? Short-Run Impact and Long-Run Consequences of Stakeholder Management," *Business & Society* 50(3) (2011): 428–455.

89 L. F. Ackert, B. K. Church, X. Kuang, and L. Qi, "Lying—An Experimental Investigation of the Role of Situational Factors," *Business Ethics Quarterly* 21(4) (2011): 605–632.

90 R. G. Castro, M. A. Ariño, and M. A. Canela, "Over the Long-Run? Short-Run Impact and Long-Run Consequences of Stakeholder Management," *Business & Society* 50(3) (2011): 428–455.

91 A. Arnaud, "Conceptualizing and Measuring Ethical Work Climate: Development and Validation of the Ethical Climate Index," *Business & Society* 49(2) (2010): 345–358.

92 Ibid.

93 This ethical dilemma and testing is based on J. Hooker, *Business Ethics as Rational Choice* (Boston: Prentice Hall, 2011).

94 J. Smith and W. Dubbink, "Understanding the Role of Moral Principles in Business Ethics: A Kantian Perspective," *Business Ethics Quarterly* 21(2) (2011): 205–231.

95 S. T. Hannah, B. J. Avolio, and F. O. Walumwa, "Relationships between Authentic Leadership, Moral Courage, and Ethical and Pro-Social Behaviors," *Business Ethics Quarterly* 21(4) (2011): 555–578.

96 GE, *Integrity: The Spirit & the Letter of Our Commitment*, www.ge.com/files/usa/ citizenship/pdf/english.pdf (accessed May 11, 2012).

97 http://subscriber.hoovers.com.cwplib. proxy.liu.edu/H/company360/fulldescription.html?companyId=10723000000000 (accessed June 20, 2012).

98 Ibid.

99 http://online.wsj.com/article/SB10001424 05274870426800457541780083288 5086. html (accessed June 20, 2012).

100 Hewlett Packard Code of Conduct, https:// h20168.www2.hp.com/classC/spweb-docs/code-of-conduct%20ctw%20tlr%20r ev9.pdf (accessed June 20, 2012).

101 J. Pepitone, "4 HP Directors Step Down," CNN Money (January 20, 2011), http:// money.cnn.com/2011/01/20/technology/HP_board_of_directors/index.htm (accessed June 20, 2012).

102 http://online.wsj.com/article/SB10001424 05274870426800457541780083288 5086. html (accessed June 20, 2012).

103 Ibid.

104 Lockheed Martin, *Setting the Standard*, http://www.lockheedmartin.com/content/ dam/lockheed/data/corporate/documents/ setting-the-standard.pdf (accessed May 11, 2012).

105 G. Beenen and J. Pinto, "Resisting Organizational-Level Corruption: An Interview with Sherron Walkins," *Academy of Learning & Education* 8(2) (2009): 275–289.

106 M. J. O'Fallon and K. D. Butterfield, "Moral Differentiation: Exploring Boundaries of the 'Monkey See, Monkey Do' Perspective," *Journal of Business Ethics* 102(3) (2011): 379–399.

107 P. Ruiz-Palomino and R. Martinez-Cañas, "Supervisor Role Modeling, Ethics-Related Organizational Policies, and Employee Ethical Intention: The Moderating Impact of Moral Ideology," *Journal of Business Ethics* 102(4) (2010): 653–668.

108 J. Shambora, "Eileen Fisher's Timeless Vision," *Fortune* (September 26, 2011): 49–52.

109 K. Sloan, and J. H. Gavin, "Human Resource Management: Meeting the Ethical Obligations of the Function," *Business and Society Review* 115(1) (2010): 57–74.

110 D. Ariely, "Why We Lie," *Wall Street Journal* (May 26–27, 2012): C1–C2.

111 Boeing, www.boeing.com (accessed May 14, 2012).

112 M. E. Brown and M. S. Mitchell, "Ethical

and Unethical Leadership: Exploring New Avenues for Future Research," *Business Ethics Quarterly* 20(4) (2010): 583–616.

113 C. Bray and R. Barry, "Long Jail Terms on Rise," *Wall Street Journal* (October 13, 2011): C1.

114 J. Bandler and J. S. Lublin, "Inside Mass-Mutual Scandal, An Angry Wife Sparked Probes," *Wall Street Journal*, (August 19, 2005): A1.

115 T. Hahn, A. Kolk, and M. Winn, "A New Future for Business? Rethinking Management Theory and Business Strategy," *Business & Society* 49(3) (2010): 385–401.

116 A. Armenakis and J. Wigand, "Stakeholder Actions and Their Impact on the Organizational Cultures of Two Tobacco Companies," *Business and Society Review* 115(2) (2010): 147–171.

117 Y. Luo, "Strategic Responses to Perceived Corruption in an Emerging Market: Lessons from MNEs Investing in China," *Business & Society* 50(2) (2011): 350–387.

118 S. T. Hannah, B. J. Avolio, and F. O. Walumwa, "Relationships between Authentic Leadership, Moral Courage, and Ethical and Pro-Social Behaviors," *Business Ethics Quarterly* 21(4) (2011): 555–578.

119 http://subscriber.hoovers.com.cwplib. proxy.liu.edu/H/company360/fulldescription.html?companyId=12644000000000.

120 http://edition.cnn.com/2012/05/02/business/eco-business-sustainability-grade/ index.html (accessed June 20, 2012).

121 http://images.apple.com/supplierresponsibility/pdf/Apple_Supplier_Code_of_Conduct.pdf (accessed June 20, 2012).

122 Moore, Malcolm. "Apple 'attacking problems' at its factories in China," *Telegraph* (January 27, 2012), http://www.telegraph. co.uk/technology/apple/9043924/Apple-attacking-problems-at-its-factories-in-China.html.

123 R. Nutting, "Apple's Chinese Labor Problem," *Wall Street Journal* (February 29, 2012), http://online.wsj.com/article/SB10001424052970204880404577225060951572728.html.

124 C. Duhigg, "How the U.S. Lost Out on iPhone Work," *New York Times* (January 21, 2012), http://www.nytimes.com/2012/01/22/business/apple-america-and-a-squeezed-middle-class.html?_r=1&pagewanted=all.

125 "Apple Petitioners Tell Firm to Protect Chinese Workers," BBC News, (February 1, 2012), http://www.bbc.co.uk/news/technology-16832106.

126 http://www.nytimes.com/2012/04/02/ technology/apple-presses-its-suppliers-to-improve-conditions.html?pagewanted=all (accessed July 2, 2012).

127 Ibid.

128 http://subscriber.hoovers.com/H/company360/fulldescription.html?companyId=12763000000000 (accessed July 5, 2012).

129 http://www.oregonlive.com/business/ index.ssf/2011/11/ben_jerrys_co-founder_jerry_gr.html (accessed July 5, 2012).

130 O. Bowcott, "Ben & Jerry's New Flavour Leaves Bad Taste," *Guardian* (UK) (April 19, 2006).

131 http://www.npr.org/blogs/health/2010/09/ 27/130158014/ben-jerry-s-takes-all-natural-claims-off-ice-cream-labels (accessed July 5, 2012).

132 http://www.ibtimes.com/articles/217779/20110921/shweddy-balls-ben-and-jerrys-ben-jerry-s.htm (accessed July 5, 2012).

133 http://espn.go.com/new-york/nba/story/_/ id/7617213/ben-jerry-apologizes-lin-sanity-flavor (accessed July 5, 2012).

Chapter 6

COMMUNITY, CONSUMERISM, AND THE MEDIA

Learning Outcomes

In this chapter, you will find out the answers to these key questions:

■ How does a business become a good corporate citizen of the local community?
■ How should a business treat its customers and consumers and deal with consumerism and the media?

After studying this chapter, you should be able to:

1. Define community and briefly explain the business–community interrelationship
2. Discuss community relations and community involvement programs
3. Explain differences between customers, consumers, and consumerism
4. Characterize each of the five consumer rights
5. State what the federal consumer protection regulatory agency acronyms CFPB, CPSC, FTC, FDA, NHTSA, and SEC stand for, and discuss their regulatory responsibilities
6. Compare and contrast various types of warranties
7. Describe what makes a story newsworthy, including its coverage and treatment
8. Define the following key terms (in order of appearance in the chapter):

community	consumers	implied warranty
community relations	consumerism	product liability litigation
community involvement	consumer rights	strict liability
community involvement programs	product liability	newsworthy stories
collaborative partnerships	warranty	advocacy advertisements
customers	express warranty	

▪ Chapter Outline

What's This Chapter About?

The first two separate but related concepts we discuss in this chapter are community and consumerism. Consumers use the firm's products, and they live in communities. The community is where the firm conducts business, and we discuss the interrelationship between business and the community and how firms are socially responsible in helping the local community.

Business must respect consumer rights and obey government laws and regulations set and enforced by a variety of agencies. Companies must offer warranties that their products will meet reasonable consumer expectations; if they do not offer warranties, they may face lawsuits.

The media are themselves businesses. Media have a special role in society by providing information, shaping attitudes and values—public sentiment, and developing nonmarket issue agendas. Media are the major providers of news information about issues. As with prior chapters, we end with a discussion about strategies that businesses use to deal with issues discussed in the chapter—community and consumers and the media in nonmarket strategies.

CASE

TASER International, Inc.: The "Shocking" Facts

"Tom Smith, President of TASER International . . . was happily reflecting on his successful trip to Europe where he presented his products to a national police force. . . . Worldwide, more than 16,000 law enforcement agencies in more than

40 countries have purchased TASER brand products for testing or deployment. Now that the company was more established in this market, perhaps it was time to reconsider the consumer market. 'Should we try to enter the consumer market? If so—how?'"[1]

The answer came to him like a jolt of electricity: "TASER C2, a compact device that provides the same NMI effectiveness as the market-leading TASER X26 law enforcement version. Private citizens who buy the C2 for their own personal defense must undergo identification verification before the device is activated"[2]

What then is a TASER? "The TASER has been classified as a less-lethal or non-lethal weapon, specifically, an electric-shock weapon [as compared to a projectile weapon] . . . it allow[s] the user to fire two probes from a replaceable cartridge up to a distance of 21 feet . . . [delivering] 50,000 volts of electrical pulses along the wires and into the body of the target through up to two inches of clothing. These electrical signals completely over[ride] the central nervous system and directly [control] the skeletal muscles, causing an uncontrollable contraction of the muscles. This 'lock up' effect physically debilitates even an aggressive target, regardless of pain tolerance or mental focus."[3]

Who could object to a non-lethal weapon that protects the average citizen, no less a law enforcement officer, while not inflicting deadly force on the perpetrator? "Amnesty International acknowledges the importance of developing non-lethal or 'less than lethal' force options to decrease the risk of death or injury inherent in the use of firearms or other impact weapons such as batons. However, the use of stun technology in law enforcement [and especially by the general public] raises a number of concerns for the protection of human rights. Portable and easy to use, with the capacity to inflict severe pain at the push of a button without leaving substantial marks, electro-shock weapons are particularly open to abuse by unscrupulous officials, as the organization has documented in numerous cases around the world. Although U.S. law enforcement agencies stress that training and in-built product safeguards (such as chips which can record the time and date of each TASER firing) minimize the potential for abuse, Amnesty International believes that these safeguards do not go far enough."[4]

Substitute products for TASERs are currently available to the public as well as to law enforcement. "There is a wide array of less-lethal options, especially in the consumer market, including chemical sprays (pepper spray and tear gas), stun guns, and batons. These products [do] not normally cause death or serious injury."[5]

"There have been disturbing reports of inappropriate or abusive use of TASERs in various U.S. jurisdictions, sometimes involving repeated cycles of electro-shocks. . . . They have been used against unruly schoolchildren; unarmed mentally disturbed or intoxicated individuals; suspects fleeing minor crime scenes and people who argue with police or fail to comply immediately with a command. Cases include the stunning of a 15-year-old schoolgirl in Florida, following a dispute on a bus, and a 13-year-old girl in Arizona, who threw a book in a public library. In many such instances, the use of electro-shock weapons appears to have violated international standards prohibiting torture or other cruel, inhumane, or degrading treatment as well as standards set out under the United Nations (UN) Code of Conduct for Law Enforcement Officials and the Basic Principles on the Use of Force and Firearms by Law Enforcement Officials.

"Amnesty International is further concerned by the growing number of fatalities involving police TASERs. Since 2001, more than 70 people are reported to have died in the United States and Canada after being struck by M26 or X26 TASERs, with the numbers rising each year. While coroners have tended to attribute such deaths to other factors (such as drug intoxication), some medical experts question whether the TASER shocks may exacerbate a risk of heart failure in cases where persons are agitated, under the influence of drugs, or have underlying health problems such as heart disease. In at least five recent cases, coroners have found the TASER directly contributed to the death, along with other factors such as drug abuse and heart disease. . . . Amnesty International is reiterating its call on federal, state, and local authorities and law enforcement agencies to suspend all transfers and use of electro-shock weapons, pending an urgent rigorous, independent, and impartial inquiry into their use and effects."[6]

"The company also continues to be challenged by the considerable debate surrounding its TASER devices' impact on public health (specifically the device's effect on the human heart) and public safety (especially as it relates to alleged excessive force by police). Despite the fact that TASER devices are designed to be non-lethal weapons, more than 50 lawsuits name TASER International as a defendant in cases in which a plaintiff alleges either wrongful death or personal injury in situations where a TASER device was used by law enforcement officers in an arrest or a training exercise. Meanwhile, the company reports that more than 120 lawsuits against it have already been dismissed or have been found in favor of TASER International."[7]

Assuming that the reports of public health and safety are even partially true, coupled with the continued lawsuits, why would Tom Smith, president of TASER, produce TASERs for distribution to the public, a public with less training and experience in handling potentially violent situations?

The following questions are related to the TASER case. Answers can be found within the chapter.

1. How might the community play a role in TASER International's operation?
2. Why would community relations and civic engagement be critical for a company like TASER?
3. In developing TASER's community outreach program, what might CEO Tom Smith need to keep in mind?
4. TASER now sells its products directly to the public. What consumer rights might be applicable given TASER's products and services?
5. Looking at Figure 6.3, Federal Consumer Protection Agencies and Their Major Regulatory Responsibility, which agencies might regulate TASER Technology?
6. What issues of product liability must TASER be aware of?
7. What is the media's responsibility in reporting on TASER technology and products relative to law enforcement personnel and public safety?
8. TASER International has certainly had its share of press coverage. If you were a reporter, how would you determine the newsworthiness of Amnesty International's claims against TASER products?

COMMUNITY

Community involvement is part of CSR that operates at the ethical and benevolent levels of CSR; company actions in the community must be ethical (Chapters 4 and 5). In this section, we discuss the business–community interrelationship, community relations, and community involvement programs.

Learning Outcome 1: Define community and briefly explain the business–community interrelationship.

Business–Community Interrelationship

Stakeholders in the community are affected by business.[8] *Community is the local area in which businesses operate and affect stakeholders.* Community is the city and state where the business resides. Large corporations with multiple business units have a community for each unit. Multinational corporations (MNC) have communities all over the world. Community traditionally referred to geographical location, but today it is used in a broader context that includes cyber communities on the Internet. With the technological advances of communication and transportation, the term *global community* is also used today.[9]

Interrelationship. Regardless of a business's size and location, the business–community relationship is interrelated or interdependent.[10] Business and community need to work together for the common good.[11] Businesses need community support with infrastructure (gas and electric power, phones, water and sewer), transportation systems (roads, railways, airports, and harbors), public safety (police and fire departments), health care (medical personnel and hospitals), employees, usually customers, and other support. The community needs business for economic development, products, jobs and training, taxes to help pay for community services, help with some social problems, among other things.[12] In order to attract and retain quality people in our communities, we need good education, a safe environment, and activities for our youth. Thus, business and community must work together to improve the quality of community life where we live and work.

Community Power. Communities do have power over business with local laws and regulations that are heavily influenced and developed by community members who try to balance the power between community consumers and producers.[13] Communities sometimes deny a company the license to operate because they fear the firm will create too much traffic, pollute, decrease property values, hurt small local businesses, or engage in activities that are viewed as offensive or inappropriate (pornography). **Walmart** has had to fight to locate stores in many communities, and it has sometimes lost. Although a business may be licensed to operate, the local government can make it difficult and costly for the business by changing laws and regulations (including taxes). Having a good corporate reputation for being socially responsible does help with community relations.[14] In other words, being a good community corporate citizen pays.

TASER Case Question 1: How might the community play a role in TASER International's operation?

The community has the right, through local laws and regulations, to deny the use of TASERs in their locality.

TASER is an international firm that has communities all over the world. In order for TASER to be successful with its business products, it must work closely with the community in order to ensure that the community accepts TASERs as a suitable alternative for personal defense, not only for the community's law enforcement officials but for its private citizens as well.

Eminent Domain. Eminent domain, the government's ability to take private property for government use, has been around for many years. In 2006 it was extended to include giving the government the power to take private land to sell it for business use. For example, a local government could decide that it wants a **Lowe's** or other business in town, and it can buy business property as well as homes and sell them (perhaps to new businesses) based on what the government deems to be the public good.[15]

Personal and Professional Applications

1. Identify some of the major businesses in your community and how they help and harm the community.

2. Describe the business–community interrelationship where you work(ed).

3. How do you feel about the government's ability to buy your house or your neighborhood and turn it into a business or mall?

Layoffs and Plant Closings. Although most companies want to be socially responsible and employ community members, sometimes a business can't compete and must make the financial decision to lay off employees and even close plants in the community. When large numbers of people lose their jobs, the local economy can be severely damaged. The *Worker Adjustment and Retraining Notification Act (WARN)* protects communities by requiring employers to provide notification 60 calendar days in advance of plant closings and mass layoffs.[16]

CSR. CSR is often community based.[17] In the case of layoffs, many firms take steps to be socially responsible by helping workers move to jobs at other facilities, by assisting them in finding new jobs, by providing training to get other jobs, and by giving workers severance pay to help meet their financial obligations until they can find new jobs.

In addition to CSR for specific issues, such as layoffs and plant closings, a business must also decide on its overall level of CSR.[18] CSR and corporate citizenship are broad in scope and include community relations. How much, and what types of support will the business provide to the community?[19] Some of the possibilities are discussed below.[19]

Learning Outcome 2: Discuss community relations and community involvement programs.

Community Relations and Department

Community relations is the organized involvement of business with local society and government. Companies regard their involvement in the community as a key business strategy and a linchpin in their corporate citizenship. According to the **Center for Corporate Citizenship**, attention given to community public relations is increasing.[20] For example, the statement by Eli Lilly and Company about its commitment to community relations is provided in Figure 6.1.

At Lilly, we're committed to being a leader in corporate responsibility, which includes being an active participant in the communities we serve. We have a robust history of community involvement and believe we can make an impact that extends far beyond the medicines we make. Many of our donations—including those provided through the Eli Lilly and Company Foundation—focus on improving access to medicines and quality health care for millions of people around the globe.[21]

■ **Figure 6.1:** Eli Lilly and Company and Its Corporate Social Responsibility to Community.

© Copyright Eli Lilly and Company. All Rights Reserved. Used with Permission.

Role of Community Relations. As part of public affairs management (Chapter 2), many firms create specialized community relations departments. Community relations, an expansion of *public relations,* focuses more on media relations and entails relationships with a wide variety of stakeholders. Community relations take place even if a separate department does not exist to deal with them. The role of the *community relations department* is to interact with community citizens and the news media, to develop community involvement programs, and to work with local governments. Common areas of relations include education, economic development, health care, environmental issues, transportation, housing, job training, child care, and unemployment. Let's describe community involvement programs.

Civic Engagement: Community Involvement Programs

The word *civic* pertains to cities and communities. Civic engagement by business is commonly called community involvement. *Community involvement is business participation in changing and improving communities.* Recall (Chapter 2) that *stakeholder management* is based on attempting to make decisions on specific issues that provide value to strategic stakeholders. In many ways, the community is a stakeholder, and through community involvement, the business uses the stakeholder approach to provide value to the community, which can create a win-win situation for both the business and the community.[22] Community involvement can contribute to business success.[23] Getting media coverage for community involvement can help the company's reputation,[24] and it can lead to consumers responding through buying products.[25] The community relations manager oversees three primary community involvement programs. *Community involvement programs include volunteers, philanthropic giving of resources and cash, and collaborative partnerships.*

Volunteer Programs. Businesses encourage—and reward—their employees to do volunteer work for nonprofit organizations in the community, including societal interest groups. **Miller Brewing** holds a "day of caring" in which the entire company gives up its time for community projects in Milwaukee. **Kraft** employees who give 50 hours of service to a charity get a $1,000 donation for the charity from the company.

Philanthropic Resource (In-Kind) Giving. Businesses give and lend their resources, including products and services, to help the community, a practice that is referred to as *in-kind* contributions. **Baystate Medical Center** provides low-cost and free health care to the needy. **LensCrafters** provides some free vision care to the needy. Many companies donate their old equipment as they replace it to nonprofits or NGOs. **Smith & Wesson** let the city recreation department use the land next to its plant for soccer fields and a large free parking area.

Philanthropic Cash Giving. Companies give money to charitable organizations. **Friendly's Ice Cream** gave several million dollars to the local colleges and health care facilities. Your college may have received corporate cash gifts. **General Mills** spent $2.5 million, plus gave employee time and expertise, to revitalize a neighborhood near its headquarters in Minneapolis.

The **Foundation Center** is a nonprofit leading source of information about philanthropy worldwide. Through data, analysis, and training, it connects people who want to change the world to the resources they need to succeed. The Center maintains the most comprehensive database on U.S. and, increasingly, global grant makers and their grants.[26] (For more information, visit http://foundationcenter.org.)

Collaborative Partnerships. *Collaborative partnerships are voluntary relationships among business, society groups, and/or government for community improvement.* Partnerships between business and NGOs are increasing.[27] Popular areas of collaboration include business with education, health and human services, civic and community groups, and culture and arts organizations. Some companies adopt a school and provide it with cash, equipment, and volunteers to work in the schools. Business also helps societal interest groups and government administrators develop their managerial skills through training. **IBM** has the *Smarter Cities Challenge* grants valued at $50 million. The program deploys teams of top IBM experts to work with 100 cities around the world addressing key urban problems.[28]

Business in the Community is a UK business-led charity focused on promoting responsible business practice. It asks members to work together to transform communities by tackling issues where business can make a real difference. It has more than 850 company members and a further 10,700 companies engaged in its campaigns globally.[29] For more information visit http://www.bitc.org.uk. Other websites to visit include the **Committee Encouraging Corporate Philanthropy** (www.corporate-philanthropy.org) and the **National Committee for Responsive Philanthropy** (www.ncrp.org).

Personal and Professional Applications

4. What types of volunteer work have you done?

5. Does a company you work(ed) for have a community relations department, and what community involvement programs does it have?

TASER Case Question 2: Why would community relations and civic engagement be critical for a company like TASER?

Community relations is the organized involvement of a business with local society and government, while civic engagement is the business's participation in changing and improving communities. Because TASER's products have been developed to support community protection (its police officers enforcing the law; citizens' self-protection) it is critical that TASER develops collaborative partnerships (voluntary relationships among business, society groups, and/or government for community improvement) with key stakeholders including local community associations (e.g., neighborhood watch groups), police benevolent associations, and government agencies (e.g., police force) to informally educate these stakeholders as to the benefits of their products while working on related civic projects.

Managing Community Involvement

With increased stakeholder pressure, managers are being more responsive to community involvement. See Figure 6.2 for an adapted list of standards developed by the **Center for Corporate Citizenship** at **Boston College** (BC). The Standards of Excellence are the framework for managing a company's corporate community involvement.[30] For more information on corporate citizenship, visit the BC website (www.bcccc.net) and the **Conference Board** (www.conference-board.org).

1. **Leadership.** Top managers demonstrate support, commitment, and participation in community involvement programs.
2. **Issues Management.** Managers engage in issues management (Chapter 2) to identify and monitor issues important to company operations and corporate reputation.
3. **Relationship Building.** Managers build and maintain trust relationships with the community as part of the company's operations and strategy.
4. **Strategy.** Managers develop and implement a strategic plan for community involvement on issues of mutual benefit to the business and the community.
5. **Accountability.** Managers at all levels have specific roles and responsibilities for community involvement.
6. **Infrastructure.** Managers incorporate systems and policies for supporting, communicating, and instigating community involvement.
7. **Measurement.** Managers monitor and evaluate community involvement programs and their effect on the firm and the community.

■ **Figure 6.2:** Standards of Excellence in Corporate Community Involvement

TASER Case Question 3: In developing TASER's community outreach program, what might CEO Tom Smith need to keep in mind?

CEO Tom Smith must be cognizant of the Standards of Excellence in Corporate Community Involvement (Leadership, Issues Management, Relationship Building, Strategy, Accountability, Infrastructure, and Measurement) as well the four steps to community involvement (know the community, know the company resources, select and monitor projects). In using these standards and steps, he might conclude that the firm's need to go beyond its immediate stakeholders as mentioned in case question 2 might be met by becoming involved in non-security-related organizations and civic projects (e.g., Toys for Tots) and by reaching out to organizations serving the global community including Amnesty International.

> **Personal and Professional Applications**
>
> 6. Assess how well a company where you work(ed) manages community involvement. How could it improve?

CONSUMERISM

In this section, we discuss the consumer movement and advocacy, and five consumer rights.

> Learning Outcome 3: Explain differences between customers, consumers, and consumerism.

The Consumer Movement and Advocacy

Consumers are important,[31] because they use businesses' products (goods and services).[32] Therefore, businesses try to create favorable attitudes among consumers.[33] Before we get into consumerism, let's be clear on the difference between customers and consumers.

Customers and/or Consumers. *Customers buy products from business. Consumers use business products.* Many businesses sell their products to customers, who in turn sell them to consumers. For example, **GM** sells its **Chevrolets** to dealerships who sell them to their customers. So GM dealers are its customers and the drivers and passengers are GM consumers. **GM dealerships** have customers who buy the cars, who are usually also consumers.

You can be both a customer and consumer or either of the two. For example, one family member may be the customer and the entire family and friends may consume the product—cars, houses, their furnishings, and food. People who buy gifts are customers, and receivers of gifts are not customers, only consumers. Are you a customer or consumer on **Facebook**? You don't have to pay to be on Facebook, so you are not a customer, you are a consumer.

> **Personal and Professional Applications**
>
> 7. Give a few examples of how you are a customer but not a consumer and a consumer without being the customer.

Consumerism. *Consumerism is the organized collective efforts to safeguard all consumers by promoting their rights and power.* Everyone is a consumer. So the concept *consumerism* is broader in scope than consumer, therefore, consumerism is a society issue in the nonmarket environment, whereas customers are part of the market environment. Societal interest group advocates are watchdogs helping to protect consumers by pressuring business to be ethical and socially responsible, and they pressure the government to force business to do so. The government makes and enforces laws and regulations to protect consumers.

The Consumer Movement. Consumers have always wanted to be treated fairly and honestly; unfortunately, over the years some businesses have intentionally (**R. J. Reynolds** and **Philip Morris** were accused of knowing cigarettes are unhealthy) or unintentionally (**Dow Corning Company** unintentionally manufactured and sold breast implants that leaked) sold hazardous products, or have not given consumers proper information. Consumerism became more sophisticated, through what is called the *consumer movement*, as consumer rights and power grew to gain government consumer protection. The goal of the consumer movement is to counterbalance the power of business.[34]

Consumer Advocacy. Probably the best-known consumer advocate is Ralph Nader. Nader and his associates founded **Public Citizen** (www.citizen.org) to protect health, safety, and democracy. There are several hundred consumer advocacy groups, and one organization—the **Consumer Federation of America (CFA)** (www.consumerfed.org)—brings about 300 nonprofits together enabling CFA to speak for virtually all consumers.

On the business side, the **Better Business Bureau** (BBB, www.bbb.org) helps business self-regulate and screen out unethical companies and those that are not socially responsible. If you are unsure whether a business is legitimate, you can call the local bureau and ask about it. If the firm is a member, the BBB can provide information about it; if not, BBB may be able to give you some feedback in regard to any complaints about the business.

Consumer Union, a nonprofit, conducts extensive testing on selected consumer products and publishes the results, with ratings on brand-name products, in *Consumer Reports* magazine, also online at www.consumerreports.org.

> Learning Outcome 4: Characterize each of the five consumer rights.

Consumer Rights

Consumer rights essentially came from President John F. Kennedy. Kennedy listed four rights called the consumer's *Magna Carta*, or simply consumer rights. The idea behind consumer rights is to guarantee these rights so consumers feel more confident in dealing with big business. *Consumer rights include safety, information, choice, voice, and privacy* (note that the right to privacy was not in the *Magna Carta*).

1. **The right to safety.** Protection against products that are hazardous to your health and life. The government punishes companies that sell products that hurt people. **Merck** was brought to court and paid damages for selling VIOXX, a drug that led to the death of consumers.
2. **The right to be informed.** Protection against products marketed through fraudulent, deceitful, or grossly misleading information, advertising, labeling, or other practices. Consumers expect business to be honest. The right to accurate information is based on the temptation of business to promote its products in the best light possible in order to sell more products. For example, **General Mills** was required by the FDA to stop claiming that *Cheerios* is clinically proven to help lower cholesterol.[35]
3. **The right to choose.** Assurance of a variety of products at competitive prices, wherever feasible. When competition is not feasible, such as with utilities, monopolies will be regulated by the government to ensure satisfactory quality and service at fair prices. (We will discuss regulation and antitrust in Chapters 8–10.) Using the Internet and smartphones, consumers can easily compare products and prices instantly.

4. **The right to be heard**. Assurance that consumer interests will receive full and sympathetic consideration in the formulation and implementation of government policies, laws, and regulations. It is the right of consumers to have fair and expeditious treatment in the administration of cases brought to agencies and the courts against businesses. (We will discuss regulation and litigation in Chapters 8–10.)

5. **The right to privacy**. Protection from misuse of personal information. Laws recently passed address privacy in educational records, medical information and records, and identity theft. More than 40 million credit card numbers, including those issued by **MasterCard, Visa, American Express,** and **Discover**, were stolen from **CardSystems**, one of the companies that processes merchant requests for credit card authorizations.[36] With the growth of the Internet, the right to privacy will continue to be a hot social issue. (We will discuss technology and privacy in Chapter 12.)

TASER Case Question 4: TASER now sells its products directly to the public. What consumer rights might be applicable given TASER's products and services?

The consumer has the right to safety, information, choice, voice, and privacy as it relates to the use of TASER's products and services. For example, TASER's products require that consumers undergo an identification check in order to purchase the product, and therefore their privacy becomes an issue. Clearly a product of this nature will have a myriad of safety issues (use, training, and storage) about which consumers need to know. In addition, consumers should be aware of associated legal liabilities that may arise with the discharge of the TASER (criminal as well as civil liabilities).

ETHICAL DILEMMA 6.1 JPMorgan Chase & Co.: Jacking Up More than Just the Interest?

The largest U.S. bank holding company with more than $2 trillion in assets, JPMorgan Chase has more than 5,500 branches in a couple dozen states (and counting) and is also among the nation's top mortgage lenders and credit card issuers (it holds some $132 billion in credit card loans). Active in some 60 countries, it also boasts formidable investment banking and asset management operations. Led by CEO Jamie Dimon, JPMorgan Chase closed a couple of very high profile deals as the economic crisis claimed numerous victims. It acquired Bear Stearns, one of Wall Street's top investment banks, and the operations of Washington Mutual (WaMu), the largest bank to fail in U.S. history. (Both deals closed in 2008.) Dimon is often regarded as being one of the best bank CEOs in the business.

Its strategy for growth includes expanding across all of its business lines, from entering new markets and opening new bank branches to increasing its lending activities. However, lower interest income and investment banking fees led to a dip in revenues. Overall, revenues slipped by some 5 percent in 2011, but the company's net income grew, largely due to a reduction in the provision for credit losses (as a result of improving delinquency trends).[37]

How has JPMorgan Chase dealt with this slower growth? One method has been to ratchet up interest rates for late payments or defaults, without formally notifying its credit cardholders even if such a policy appears in the fine print of its cardholder agreement. AARP (American Association for Retired Persons) claimed that the bank violated the Truth in Lending Act by increasing interest rates retroactively to the start of a payment cycle following a cardholder's default and failing to specify in its cardholder agreement when rates would go up and by how much. What's at stake? More than two-thirds of older Americans who have filed for bankruptcy cite credit cards as the reason, according to a study by John Potlow, a professor of law at the University of Michigan.[38] Older individuals are relying more and more on credit cards to defray financial obligations that previously were paid by other means. As the recession continues, credit card usage among older people remains brisk. According to data compiled by AARP, within the 50-plus population, 76 percent have at least one credit card. AARP supports improving the rights of consumers by curtailing unfair increases in interest rates, prohibiting exorbitant and unnecessary fees, reallocating payments so that higher rate balances are paid off first, eliminating double cycle billing, and banning universal default on existing balances.[39]

Questions

1. What consumer rights are impacted by JPMorgan Chase's decision to raise interest rates without prior notification to their credit card holders?
2. What is AARP's role in protecting the rights of older credit cardholders (those in the 50-plus population)?
3. Assuming that JPMorgan Chase had the legal right to raise these rates without prior notification, if you were CEO Jamie Dimon would you do so? Why or why not?
4. What actions would you take as AARP to protect the rights of older credit card users?
5. AARP represents older Americans. Would it make more sense for them to broaden their advocacy efforts to include all credit cardholders? Why or why not?

Personal and Professional Applications

8. Give examples of violations of your consumer rights by businesses.

CONSUMER LAWS AND REGULATIONS

Congress passes the laws that affect consumers, regulators enforce the laws, and the courts interpret the laws and the outcomes of litigation by determining whether consumer rights have been violated. (We will discuss how laws are passed, as well as regulation and litigation in Chapters 8–10.) The job of the government is to protect its people, and everyone is a consumer, so clearly consumer protection is an important issue to the government. Consumer laws and regulations are made and enforced at the local, state, and federal levels.

Every state and local government has extensive consumer protection laws. State government has the power to investigate illegal practices like price fixing and set insurance rates (Massachusetts auto insurance). A local government can prohibit a business from operating in its city to protect consumers.

Learning Outcome 5: State what the federal consumer protection regulatory agency acronyms CFPB, CPSC, FTC, FDA NHTSA, and SEC stand for, and discuss their regulatory responsibilities.

Major Consumer Protection Agencies

With regard to the federal government, Congress has given the responsibility and power to enforce its laws to protect consumers to executive branch agencies. More than 50 federal agencies and bureaus protect consumers in some way. Below, we present the responsibilities of six major agencies. Note that the Consumer Financial Protection Bureau (CFPB) was established in 2010 as a result of the financial crisis of 2008–2009, and it is similar to the Consumer Product Safety Commission (CPSC) with a focus on financial services. Consumers can file complaints with these agencies online. More information is available at each agency's website.

Agency	Regulatory Responsibility
Consumer Financial Protection Bureau (CFPB) www.consumerfinance.gov	Enforces laws protecting consumers of financial products, such as mortgages, home equity loans, payday loans, bank accounts, credit reporting, credit cards, leasing, truth in lending, and savings.
Consumer Product Safety Commission (CPSC) www.cpsc.gov	Protects the public by setting safety standards to avoid unreasonable risks of injury or death from thousands of consumer products, especially products that pose fire, electrical, chemical, or mechanical hazards or can injure children. It has the power to recall and require repair of faulty products.
Federal Trade Commission (FTC) www.ftc.gov	Prevents business practices that are anticompetitive or deceptive or unfair to consumers. It maintains free and fair competition and protects consumers from unfair or misleading practices. It is responsible for enforcing antitrust laws, which we will discuss in Chapter 10.
Food and Drug Administration (FDA) www.fda.gov	Responsible for protecting the public health by assuring the safety, effectiveness, and security of human and veterinary drugs, vaccines and other biological products, medical devices, our nation's food supply, cosmetics, dietary supplements, and products that give off radiation. In addition to setting safety standards, it has the power to recall products.
National Highway Traffic Safety Administration (NHTSA) www.nhtsa.gov	Works to achieve the highest standards of excellence in motor vehicle and highway safety. It works daily to help prevent crashes and their attendant costs, both human and financial. Regulates virtually all features of the automobile industry, sets fuel economy standards, and can recall products.
Securities and Exchange Commission (SEC) www.sec.gov	Protects investors; maintains fair, orderly, and efficient markets; and facilitates capital formation. It is responsible for regulating publicly traded companies and the stock market. It has the *Electronic Data Gathering, Analysis, and Retrieval* system (EDGAR) database (www.sec.gov/edgar.shtml) of disclosure documents that public companies are required to file with the commission.

■ **Figure 6.3:** Major Federal Consumer Protection Agencies and Their Regulatory Responsibility

TASER Case Question 5: Looking at Figure 6.3, which agencies might regulate TASER Technology?

Of the six agencies listed in Figure 6.3—the CFPB and the FDA may regulate TASER in some fashion. For example, the CPSC would ensure that TASER's products are safe to use and that they meet industry standards, while the FTC would ensure that TASER is not restraining trade or employing deceptive business practices. As a publicly traded firm, TASER is regulated by the SEC, which ensures that truthful information about the firm is readily available to the public.

Personal and Professional Applications

9. How do the CFPB, CPSC, FTC, FDA, NHTSA, and SEC regulations affect you personally and a business you work(ed) for?

SaferProducts.gov is the Publicly Available Consumer Product Safety Information Database of the CPSC. Through SaferProducts.gov, consumers can submit reports of harm (Reports) involving consumer products. Manufacturers and private labelers identified in Reports will receive a copy of any Reports, and have the opportunity to comment on them. Completed Reports and manufacturers' comments are published online at www. SaferProducts.gov for anyone to search.

Personal and Professional Applications

10. Choose three of these other agencies and describe how they affect you personally and a business where you work(ed)?

PRODUCT LIABILITY

Product liability is a major consumer issue because of the number of products that have caused illness, injury, and death.[40] *Product liability is the firm's legal responsibility for its actions and products, especially costs or damages.* Although product liability cases are handled in local, state, and federal courts, in this section, we again focus on the federal level. We discuss warranties, product liability litigation, strict and absolute liability, the cost of product liability and reform.

Learning Outcome 6: Compare and contrast various types of warranties.

Warranties

Have you ever bought a product that did not work or did not work properly? In this situation, warranties and guarantees come into play. *A warranty is a contract in which the seller guarantees the integrity of the product, and the buyer is entitled to compensation for any consequent harm and defective goods.* The manufacturer or seller can be held liable for a breach of either an express warranty or an implied warranty, and a warranty can be full or limited.

Express Warranties. *An express warranty is an explicit claim made by the producer to the consumer.* The expressed claim may be given orally through advertising or through claims made by salespeople. Written warranties may express that the product will perform in a specified way, provide a description of the product, or display a picture that shows a model of the product. An express warranty is commonly a formal certificate that comes with the product, and that the consumer returns to the manufacturer to validate the warranty.

Businesses have tried to limit their liability through explicit warnings and warranties. For example, before you can ride a horse at the **Ridin-Hy Ranch** in New York, you have to sign a waiver indicating that you understand the danger involved. However, if the saddle is defective and falls off the horse while you are riding the horse, throwing you to the ground and injuring you, the ranch and/or saddle manufacturer is liable for your damages. The courts have restricted business from limiting its liability by expanding the warranty to the implied warranty.

Implied Warranties. *An implied warranty is an unwritten guarantee that the product is adequate to meet reasonable expectations for intended purposes.* What are the "reasonable, prudent person's" expectations of product performance? For example, let's say you buy a blouse at **Macy**'s and you are informed that the blouse is sold as is—no returns or exchanges. When you get home and look more closely at the blouse, you notice it has a hole in it. Even though Macy's stated the blouse could not be returned or exchanged, Macy's is still liable to give you compensation of an exchange or refund because the "hole" constitutes something beyond a reasonable expectation. Now let's discuss what happens when the warranty is not met and when you are harmed by a product.

Full vs. Limited Warranty. The Magnuson-Moss Warranty Act of 1975 helped to clarify a variety of misunderstandings about warranties, particularly if they are full or limited. A *full warranty* must express unconditional assurance that the product will be replaced or repaired within a reasonable time and without charge. A *limited warranty* conditionally excludes certain parts of the product or particular types of defects from coverage. A statement such as "complete satisfaction" without any fine print would be considered to be a full warranty. Most businesses offer a limited warranty. The express warranty certificate should state whether it is limited and what the conditions are.

Extended Warranty. You can also get an *extended warranty* that lengthens the warranty period offered at an additional cost. Extended warranties can be express or implied and full or limited based on the warranty agreement. Extended warranties tend to be profitable for the salesperson and store, so you may be asked to buy them. However, consumer advocates tend to advise against buying most extended warranties because the cost–benefit often is not worth it. Also, if you buy an extended warranty on everything you buy, in most cases you pay a lot more than you gain in the long run.

Shipping Charges. Who pays service shipping charges and fees? We use the term *service* to include repairs, exchanges, and returns of defective products. With online shopping, which entails shipping merchandise to the buyer, an increasingly important question is who should pay shipping charges when a defective product must be sent to the factory/ retailer for service/return. Shipping information can be stated in the warranty. A common business practice is not to discuss return shipping charges when the order is placed but to pay them when asked to do so. For example, let's say you need to send a product back. The sales or customer representative gives you the information on where to send it, without discussing shipping costs. However, if you ask if the company will pay for shipping, the rep will often then tell you how to get the company to pay, possibly by including a copy of the shipping bill for reimbursement or by giving you a prepaid shipping label.

On a related note, if you are charged a financial (bank or credit card) fee, such as for a late payment, if you call and request the fee be taken off, giving a viable reason, the firm may do so. It pays to ask. **L.L.Bean** offers one of the best warranties; as shown in Figure 6.4. Note that it does not *say* that it will pay for the shipping back to Maine, but it does pay.

Personal and Professional Applications

11. Give an example of a product that you bought that did not meet the express warranty and one that did not meet your implicit expectations. Were they full or limited warranties?

12. Give an example of a breach of warranty where you work(ed). State whether it was an express or implied and full or limited warranty.

Product Liability Litigation

Today, we live in a litigious society; consumers readily take businesses to court for liability issues, and the damage awards are large.[41] A *tort* is a private wrong committed by one person against another person or his or her property. Thus, an injury to a consumer caused by a defective product is one type of tort. *Product liability litigation is the process of a consumer filing a lawsuit against a firm seeking compensation for harm resulting from defective products or business actions.* We use the term *harm* to include illness, injury, loss, damage, and death. In the lawsuit, the consumer suing the business is usually represented by a lawyer and is called the *plaintiff*, and the business being sued is the *defendant*. Compensation does not have to be cash; it could be a new product (exchange) or a refund, but plaintiffs often seek cash for damages caused by physical and mental harm.

A product can be *defective* for many reasons, including simply being the wrong size. The term "defective" is open to interpretation in court. Is the product really faulty or not functioning properly for its "intended" use? Even experts who testify disagree, leaving the interpretation to the judge and jury to determine whether the plaintiff or defendant is right.

Negligence. Torts are based on either an intentional or a negligent act that causes harm. *Negligence* is an unintentional failure to act as a reasonable prudent person exercising ordinary care. Intentional harm is rarely claimed in product liability lawsuits; plaintiffs more often accuse the business of negligence. Like "defective," "negligence" is open to

---

GUARANTEED TO LAST[SM]

Our products are guaranteed to give 100% satisfaction in every way. Return anything purchased from us at any time if it proves otherwise. We do not want you to have anything from L.L.Bean that is not completely satisfactory.

■ **Figure 6.4:** L.L. Bean Warranty

Source: L.L. Bean 2012; reprinted with permission.

interpretation by the judge and jury who must determine what a "reasonable, prudent person" would do in the specific circumstances of the case.

Types of Litigation. Most product liability is between one consumer and one business, but there are also class action suits. A *class action lawsuit* joins plaintiffs into a group to litigate a case against a business, agreeing to one common judgment. Plaintiffs in a class action suit are able to handle the high cost of litigation if they lose the case because the monetary loss to each individual is small. The total is split amongst all plaintiffs. The asbestos (**Johns Manville Co.**), tobacco (**R. J. Reynolds/Philip Morris**), and breast implants (**Dow Chemical**) class action lawsuits each had tens of thousands of individual plaintiffs. **Merck**'s VIOXX strategy was to try each case separately, rather than in one class action lawsuit.

Settlements. Most lawsuits don't make it to court. Because the legal costs are expensive, in many lawsuits the business settles out of court by compensating the plaintiff, especially if the business thinks it will lose the case in court. Many businesses anticipate that the cost of fighting the lawsuit will outweigh the benefits of winning, so they frequently pay off the consumer, even if they are confident they could win the trial. However, **Walmart** is an exception to this rule; its policy is to go to court.

Strict and Absolute Liability

Strict Liability. *Strict liability means that the plaintiff does not have to prove negligence when the activity or product is inherently dangerous.* Strict liability is also referred to as liability without fault. If **Paul Bunyan Wood Company** cuts down a tree and it lands on the house next door, it doesn't matter how reasonable, prudent, and careful the cutter was, the firm is liable to repair the damages to the house.

Absolute Liability. It extends strict liability to the unknown, making chemical and drug research and product development very risky. For example, employees with asbestos illness sued **Johns Manville Co.** for damages. The court ruled that the firm was liable for failure to warn of the product's hazard even though there was no scientific knowledge at the time of manufacture and sale. So a firm is liable even though it utilizes state of the art information and technology available to it at one point in time, having no way of knowing the product might cause a problem later. Many drugs, including **Merck**'s VIOXX pain-relief medicine, are sold with government approval and the belief that they are safe and helping people with health problems, only to be the cause of negative side effects years later.

TASER Case Question 6: What issues of product liability must TASER be aware of?

TASER must understand that the firm has legal responsibility for its actions and products, especially costs or damages. It must understand any express or implied warranties associated with its product and services and designate whether these warranties are limited or full. It should be aware that absolute liability may be associated with its product or service. For example, assuming that its TASERs met or even exceeded CPSC standards, consumers brought litigation against the firm, claiming that TASER's products resulted in injuries to the users as well as perpetrators.

The Cost of Product Liability and Reform

Cost of Product Liability. Clearly, consumers and business, as well as society, are harmed by the consequences and cost of poor business actions and defective products. What greater price is there to pay than with your health and life? Multimillion-dollar lawsuits against business are not uncommon today.

Unfortunately, the cost of litigation is commonly passed on to all customers. The estimated societal cost of litigation is over $200 billion per year, with more than half the cost going to legal fees and expenses.

Product Liability Reform. The nonprofit interest group **Common Good** (www. cgood.org) is devoted to restoring common sense to U.S. law, and it has had great success in collaborating with leading organizations and institutions from around the country to come up with solutions to simplify, streamline, and make the U.S. legal system more effective.[42] Below are arguments for and against product liability reform.

Support for Product Liability Reform. Business societal interest groups, medical associations, local and state governments, and insurance companies call for reform because the current system is ineffective, raises the costs of litigation, and hurts innovation and competitiveness. Some of their arguments are that strict liability is excessively costly and unfair. Liability insurance rates, settlements, and legal fees have increased dramatically over the years, especially for small business. Business questions the fairness of paying consumers and legal fees when the business has not been negligent. Fear of liability sometimes slows research and innovation. Thus, business lobbies for the following specific reforms in the law.

- **Uniform federal liability standards**. Many states have different laws. Businesses have to go through repeated trials on the same charges in many different states, making it difficult and more costly to manage product liability. Going to federal court would hone the process into a single event.
- **Limit punitive damages**. Current damage awards are not based on compensating the victim for actual losses but rather on punishing the producer for wrongdoing.

The woman who spilled hot coffee in her lap at **McDonald's** suffered burns, and many argue that she should be compensated, but was her $2.9 million jury award fair?

▪ **Place the burden of proving liability on consumers—eliminate absolute liability**. Even though the business meets government standards, it is not a good legal defense. In general, when meeting standards without negligence, compensation but not punitive damages should be awarded to the plaintiff. With absolute liability, consumers would have to prove the manufacturer knew or should have known that the product design was defective before production, thereby giving business protection from future harm when meeting government standards and acting in good faith to help consumers.

Defense for the Current System. Society's consumer and citizen groups support the current system believing that business is exaggerating the problems with the current law and litigation system. Reforming the laws would only weaken consumer protection, and powerless small consumers need to be protected from big powerful businesses that don't want to pay for their mistakes. We need the laws to protect consumers, who should be compensated and given punitive damages when they are harmed by business. Ralph Nader believes we need trial lawyers to ensure that wrongdoers are held accountable to the victims and to society. The Nader-founded **Public Citizen** (www.citizen.org) has a litigation group to fight for consumer safety. The **American Association for Justice (AAJ)** (www.justice.org) represents consumer and other attorneys, defends the existing system because it puts needed pressure on business to make products safe, and helps balance the power between consumers and business.[43]

Research provides support for those who want to keep the current system and those who want reform. Laws have led to some safety improvements, but the same laws have also hindered innovation and American competitiveness in the global market. The product liability debate is sure to continue for years to come.

ETHICAL DILEMMA 6.2 Creekstone Farms Premium Beef: Mad Cow Disease or Just Plain Mad?

The **Creekstone Farms** legacy began nearly a decade ago with Louisville, Kentucky, natives John and Carol Stewart, and one simple idea: provide superior quality food products to satisfy the most discerning of palates. Rolling Kentucky pastures proved an ideal environment for raising purebred Black Angus cattle, considered the gold standard for premium beef. "It's just a very high-quality product," said Peter Moretti, executive chef at the Wichita Marriott. "There's a lot of marbling, and that's the main reason it's very tender."[44] In 2004 they made a decision to take their Black Angus Beef program to a new level. To meet the needs of consumers searching for beef raised humanely and without added hormones and antibiotics, Creekstone Farms Natural Black Angus Beef was launched."[45]

 Chief executive John Stewart was a great believer in his product and wanted to conduct tests on his beef that would assure his customers and consumers, especially his foreign customers in Japan, that his beef was of the highest quality and was not infected with mad-cow disease. Stewart noted that the Japanese ban on U.S. beef had cost the industry $1.4 billion and resulted in his firm cutting production and laying off about 150 employees. He informed the **U.S. Department of Agriculture (USDA)** that his firm was going to test every slaughtered animal, and their response, surprisingly enough, was to threaten Creekstone with criminal prosecution if they did the tests. "Testing for mad-cow disease in the U.S. is controlled by the Agriculture Department, which tests about 1% of the 35 million cattle, or about 350,000, that are slaughtered each year. The department is planning to reduce that level of testing."[46]

"We're not in any way saying that U.S. beef isn't safe; we believe it's the safest beef supply in the world, but that's not the issue," Stewart said at a news conference. "We're talking about consumers, and consumers want the product tested." Stewart said he was surprised at the plan to scale back testing. "Given the concerns internationally, I'm not so sure that's the right thing to do."

"Private companies certified by the department make screening tests used to detect mad-cow disease. The department says it has sole authority over the sale and use of the tests. Department officials say they oppose 100 percent testing because it doesn't ensure food safety. The disease is difficult to detect in younger animals, which are the source of most beef. Larger meatpackers worry that insistence from Japanese buyers would force them to do testing and that a suspect result might scare consumers away from eating beef. It would cost about $20 per animal to do the tests, adding about 10 cents per pound to the cost of meat, according to Stewart. Japan tests nearly all its cattle for mad-cow disease. Although individual companies there may want more testing in the United States, Japan's government isn't asking the United States to do the same.[47]

The bottom line for the government is that Creekstone shouldn't be allowed to test beef for mad-cow disease on its own because it could hurt the U.S. cattle industry. "They are creating a false assurance" because the test Creekstone wants to use can't show that meat is completely free of bovine spongiform encephalopathy, or mad-cow disease, according to Justice Department attorney Eric Fleisig-Greene. "The test is not only unnecessary, but it has no value whatsoever."[48] In an astonishing turn of events, Stewart finds himself in the unenviable position of deciding whether he should raise his standards and better serve his customers and consumers by testing every cow for mad-cow disease, therein risking federal prosecution. The government is supposed to protect consumers and increase local employment—who are they protecting by their actions?

Questions

1. How would you categorize the types of warranties are being made by Creekstone Farms about its premium beef?
2. What type of liability is Stewart trying to guard against with the testing of every cow for mad-cow disease, testing that goes beyond the standards set by the Department of Agriculture?
3. Do you believe that Stewart would be acting ethically if he went ahead and tested every cow for mad-cow disease? Why or why not?
4. Do you believe that the USDA would be acting ethically if it prosecuted Creekstone Farms for testing every cow? Who is it protecting through this prosecution?
5. What actions would you take if you were Stewart?

THE MEDIA

The media have an enormously important effect on the relationship between business and society. The media informs and shapes societal attitudes. In this section, we discuss the nature of the media, three roles of the media, and the news media.

Nature of the Media

Media Concepts. The *media* are the combined means of mass communication that influences society. The traditional combination of mass communications includes television, newspapers, and radio. However, over the years of information technology advances, especially the Internet, the media means have been broadened, while printed newspaper sales have declined. The *media industry* includes firms specializing in broadcasting technology, broadcasting content, and service delivery. *Broadcasting technology* includes the sending and receiving of messages/images via transmission equipment, cable lines, wireless devices, and receivers. *Broadcasting content* includes news and entertainment conveyed via TV, movies, newspapers, magazines, music and radio, and the Internet. *Service delivery* includes TV networks, satellite companies, cable and Internet companies, theaters, and video stores. As you know, the Internet is increasingly replacing print media. Americans are spending four to five hours a day consuming video.[49]

Society and Government and the Media. Society is influenced by the media because media are the primary source of information and means for information delivery; it is through the media that most people find out about what is going on in their community, the nation, and the world. The government is also part of society and its employees are influenced by the media. Regulators often first hear about business issues through the media, which in turn affects their behavior on the job. The media are critical to political elections, informing society about the candidates at all levels of government.

The **Federal Communications Commission (FCC)** is an independent U.S. government agency charged with regulating interstate and international communications by radio, television, wire, satellite, and cable.[50] For our purposes, the *Federal Communications Commission (FCC)* regulates the media industry. The FCC regulations include approving mergers and acquisitions of media companies.

Business Ownership of the Media. With a few exceptions that include relatively small, nonprofit organization competitors to media giants, **Public Broadcasting Service (PBS), Public Radio (PR),** and religious media (e.g., **Eternal Word Television Network [EWTN]),** the media are owned by for-profit businesses. However, due to the media's important role in informing society and government about issues, the media plays a critical role in a democracy. Today, a handful of corporations dominate all aspects of mainstream media and influence public sentiment by deciding which issues we will focus on and which will be ignored or be given minimal coverage.

The Media Business. Media companies work to attract readers and viewers because revenue generated by subscriptions and advertising depends on audience size. So the media industry is really in the business of selling subscriptions and ads, and it needs news or entertainment to attract consumers. Business pays for the audience to watch its ads; it doesn't buy news or entertainment, and the larger the audience, the more the ads cost.

Media and Advertising. Businesses use the media to advertise, so businesses are customers of the media. Thus, business and the media are important stakeholders to each other. Based on mergers, in some cases, including **AOL, Time Warner,** and **GE**, the same company makes and sends the ads through its own media.

Personal and Professional Applications

17. What is your primary media source for finding out what is going on in the world?

18. Which primary media source does your present or past employer and/or the producer of the products it sells use to advertise?

Media Roles A democracy needs the media to survive and thrive. The media include both news information and entertainment, and many media companies offer both. Here we focus on three important roles of the media, or how the news influences business, society, and government: (1) to provide information; (2) to shape attitudes and values—public sentiment; and (3) to develop nonmarket issue agendas.

Provide Information. The media are often referred to as "the protector of the public's right to know." An important role of the media is to provide information for those in the market and nonmarket environment so that people know what is going on in the world, primarily so that business, society, and government can make better decisions. Media ads provide information to sell products. News stories provide facts and assumptions. *Businesses* provide the media with information, and they are media sources themselves through their communications, websites, publications, and so forth. Business learns about the economic, financial, political, legal, and social activities that will or currently affect it. Business learns about what its competitors are doing through the media. Thus, business relies on the media for the information it uses to make strategic long- and short-term decisions, and it is an important part of the 5 Is strategic analysis (Chapter 2).

Society and the *government* also learn about what is going on in the market and nonmarket environment through the media. Moreover, societal interest groups and the government are also media sources of information. The government provides an unbelievable amount of free information through hundreds of publications and its hundreds of websites and links for its various government branches. The **U.S. Government Printing Office (GPO)** disseminates official information from all three branches of the federal government. **GPO Access** is a Web service (www.gpoaccess.gov) that provides a one-stop source for information about the executive, legislative, and judicial branches. Individuals, societal interest groups, and government are often the sources of controversial business news—sometimes through whistleblowing. Furthermore, individuals, societal interest groups, and the government use media information to make decisions.

Shape Attitudes and Values—Public Sentiment. The media have a key role in deciding what becomes reality for society.[51] The informational facts and assumptions chosen for coverage by the media shape individual attitudes and values about issues, which result in public sentiment. *Attitudes* are personal views, opinions, and general feelings about an issue; attitudes tend to be on a scale from strong to weak. People often agree with what they hear in the media—good or bad news—about business, so the media influence attitudes. *Public sentiment* is the prevailing attitude among groups about an issue. Clearly, business, society, and government have differing sentiments on a variety of issues.

Media influence goes far beyond its ability to inform, to entertain, and to sell products. The media influence *cultural values*: beliefs, customs, practices, and acceptable social behavior. Values are stronger and harder to change than attitudes, and values influence our attitudes. People with pro-life and pro-choice values have different attitudes about abortion (which is a business), and media coverage often makes changing values difficult in the short term, however, over time values do change, such as views about homosexuality (which was once illegal) and same-sex marriage (now legal in some states).

The media has been criticized by societal interest groups, including **American Academy of Pediatrics (AAP)** (www.aap.org), for having too much violence and sex, and that it should not be viewed by children because it has negative consequences in child behavior.[52]

Personal and Professional Applications

19. Do you believe the media air too much violence and sex, and do children need to be protected from violence and sex in the media?

20. Does your current/past employer, or the producer of the products it sells, promote violence and sex, and if so, is it to children and teens?

Develop Nonmarket Issue Agendas. Business, society (especially societal interest groups), and government use the media to determine which issues they will pursue. When the government hears about inappropriate or unfair business activities, it may take action against the business; other businesses and society interest groups may pressure the business directly and also try to get the government to change the negative business practice (e.g., **Nike** was pressured because its products were being produced overseas in sweatshops). News stories that get a lot of media attention tend to get on the issues agendas of business, societal interest groups, and government.

Unethical acts committed by business become major headlines and news stories that expose business activities to society and government. Through these news stories, the media have the power to influence the government. For example, when corporate scandals were exposed and the financial crisis hit, the congressional *Sarbanes-Oxley Act* and the creation of the **CFPB** gave the government more power to regulate business.

Developing a nonmarket issue agenda is part of public affairs issues management (discussed in Chapter 2). Recall that *issues management* is a public affairs management approach to identifying, monitoring, analyzing, and selecting public issues that warrant nonmarket strategies—its agenda.

TASER Case Question 7: What is the media's responsibility in reporting on TASER technology and products relative to law enforcement personnel and public safety?

The media include both news information and entertainment and three important roles of the media (how the news influences business, society, and government) include: (1) to provide information; (2) to shape attitudes and values—public sentiment; and (3) to develop nonmarket issue agendas. The media clearly has a role in reporting on such a controversial product as a TASER and to make sure that the government, related businesses, law enforcement personnel, consumers, and the general public are aware of the pros and cons of product usage by law enforcement officials as well as the general public.

Personal and Professional Applications

21. How has the media helped to shape your attitude about specific issues, and how has it helped to shape your values?

22. Give an example of a nonmarket issue that became an agenda item for a business.

The News Media

Here we focus on the news media and its responsibility to provide information in an accurate and unbiased manner so that people can formulate their own conclusions about issues, public relations, and news strategies.

Learning Outcome 7: Describe what makes a story newsworthy, including coverage and treatment.

Newsworthy Coverage. There are usually more news stories to report than time or space to present them to society. So reporters and editors need to determine which stories will be covered—that is, which ones are newsworthy. The first criterion of a newsworthy story is *interest*. The more interesting issues are covered and given more air time (TV, radio) and space (print).

The second criterion for selecting coverage is *social significance*. Issues high in significance are more newsworthy of media coverage, and the greater the significance, the greater the coverage. Issues of high significance include health, safety, privacy, environmental protection, human rights, security, and social justice. So the more people interested in the issue, and the more it matters to them, the more newsworthy the story. *Newsworthy stories are interesting and have social significance; they are about people, are immediate or urgent, involve controversy or conflict, and are easy to tell.*

Characteristics of Newsworthy Stories. The following four characteristics contribute to a story being of interest and social significance.

1. **People.** Stories that are about people (vs. places and things), being told by the people involved in the issue (interviews), and stories in some way involving celebrities (about them or a position they take on the issue) are more newsworthy.
2. **Immediate or urgent.** Reporters are always seeking to be the first to tell the story.
3. **Controversy or conflict.** Stories with dispute and disagreement are more newsworthy. Controversial ads have led to many news stories.
4. **Easily told.** Stories that are too complex become boring. Most business issues are complex and not easily told, which is especially problematic when the news is aired (TV and radio) in limited time slots.

Treatment of Newsworthy Stories. Treatment refers to how the news story is presented. There are at least four types, or levels, of treatment of stories: (1) *factual stories* just report what happened or what is going on; (2) *interpretation stories* explain the meaning of the issue; (3) *implication stories* state why the story is important and how it affects society; (4) *advocacy stories* support a position or course of action; they are commonly editorials.

Coverage and Treatment. Media coverage is based more on interest, and treatment level is based more on significance. Thus, the greater the interest, the greater the coverage, and the greater the significance, the higher the level of treatment. In general news reporting, most business issues get low coverage with factual treatment, unless there is a major catastrophe like the BP oil spill in the Gulf. [53]

Personal and Professional Applications

23. Has a business where you work(ed), or a business that makes the products it sells, been in the news?

News Fairness and Balance. The media role of informing the public about business activity issues should be treated fairly with balanced coverage that provides information on all sides of the issue; the public has the right to know the viewpoints of all sides involved to make an informed decision about the issue. So society, government, and business should all have an equal opportunity to present their side of the issue.

Business groups have complained that the news media are not always fair to business when they present information about business activities, that business gets poor news coverage and treatment, that reporters oversimplify stories and don't do a good job of presenting the business side of the issue, and that the media do not provide enough information for society to make rational decisions.

Media Bias. The media in general have been accused of being biased in selecting what issues do and don't get coverage and for taking sides on issues, rather than being impartial and presenting both sides of issues.[54] Many journalists use what is called *point-of-view journalism* and put their biases in their reports.[55] The media tend to air negative stories about business, which may be true but can include some bias that does affect a company's reputation.[56] For example, **Toyota** with its safety recalls and **BP** with its oil spill.[57]

According to the **American Society of Newspaper Editors (ASNE)** (www.asne. org), 61 percent of reporters are liberal versus 9 percent being conservative; 61 percent described themselves as Democrats and only 10 percent as Republicans.[58] Intended or not, judgments can lead to different treatment of stories. The news media have been criticized for being antibusiness—taking the side against business and including only selected facts in their news reports. Journalism is a profession and reporters can feel pressured to get a story (ethical dilemma) and to make it newsworthy to be successful.

Newsworthy? An example of a story that received news coverage was the **Beef Products Inc. (BPI)** "lean finely textured beef." It was: (1) about people's health; (2) it became urgent; (3) it included controversy over the safety of the product; and (4) the story was easy to tell. Media coverage showed bias in calling the product "pink slime," gross, and unsafe. *BusinessWeek* ran a story questioning whether BPI was unfairly targeted by the media. Iowa Governor Terry Branstad sought a congressional investigation of what he called a "smear campaign" against BPI. The media stated that the product includes ammonia hydroxide. What most reporters neglected to say was that lean finely textured beef has been used for more than 30 years with no reported illness and ammonia hydroxide is added for safety, it occurs naturally in beef and other foods, it is FDA approved as safe, and it has long been used in many other products, such as cheese and pudding. The negative media coverage and treatment helped lead to lost customers and sales, resulting in the closing of three of BPI's plants and layoffs for around half its workers (700), and BPI is struggling to avoid going out of business.[59]

Personal and Professional Applications

24. Do you believe the media are biased when it comes to business?

TASER Case Question 8: TASER International has certainly had its share of press coverage. If you were a reporter, how would you determine the newsworthiness of Amnesty International's claims against TASER products?

Amnesty International claims that TASERs have been misused and abused by law enforcement officials, which has resulted in not only injuries but fatalities. They also claim that viable alternatives to the use of this non-lethal weapon are available and that the product is not safe enough to release to the general public. The story seems newsworthy in that it involves people and is urgent, controversial, and easily told. The press however needs to be cautious as to how they treat the story (fact, interpretations, implications, or advocacy) in the hopes of providing a fair and balanced account of the situation.

BUSINESS NONMARKET AND MARKET STRATEGIES AND ETHICS

With the increased power of communities and consumers, managers need to develop strategies to deal with their issues and interests.[60] Managers know the benefits of integrating nonmarket strategies (presented in Figure 1.4 and discussed here) with their market strategies 5 Is analysis (Chapter 2). Let's discuss strategies used with communities and consumers using the media.

INFORMATION AND ADVERTISING STRATEGIES

Information strategies are critically important to good community and consumer relations in the *nonmarket environment*. Managers must know and understand their communities' and consumers' interests by listening to them and by trying to meet their needs fairly, but within reason. Relations and products must be ethical and safe for all stakeholders. Managers can get their points of interest across to the community and consumers by using facts and figures, by clearly stating their assumptions, and by trying to gain public sentiment and a good corporate reputation.[61] Managers can have outside sources, experts, and other stakeholders support the accuracy and legitimacy of management's side of the issues. Businesses are doing a better job of informing the public through honest product *labeling*, good *instructions* on proper use of products, and clear *warnings* of danger. When *recalls* are necessary, businesses are cooperating by contacting customers to inform them of how they will be compensated.

Properly communicating the firm's CSR can lead to increased sales.[62] Business also develops good relations with the media to provide positive news coverage to help corporate reputation and to help ensure fair and balanced news coverage.

In the *market environment*, providing information is what advertising is all about, and business uses the media to help sell its products. Successful firms use ethical *advertising* that is clear—not deceptive, accurately supported by facts and figures, and adequate—not withholding relevant information, to inform consumers about their products. Ethical firms don't use ambiguous ads to mislead consumers, conceal relevant facts, make exaggerated claims, or take advantage of emotions. Ethical ads are backed by good products that provide consumer satisfaction that leads to positive public sentiment and a good corporate reputation.[63]

Advertising is a commonly used market strategy, but it is expensive. A 30-second ad for the 2013 Super Bowl will cost $3.8 million, so **GM** (the third-largest buyer of media ads) will not spend this much.[64] After losing market share to **Coca-Cola**, **Pepsi** increased its marketing budget to $600 million.[65]

Public Relations and News Media Strategies

People tend to believe what they hear and see in the media, and thus the media affects public sentiment toward business with regard to specific issues. Thus, the media can affect a firm's corporate reputation. Most large businesses have a public relations (PR) department to deal with the news media. (Refer to Chapter 2 for a review of public relations.)

PR media specialists keep in regular contact with reporters and develop professional relationships with them. Business–media relationships are used by the PR department as an ongoing strategy to help maintain fairness and balance in media coverage of the firm. The media relationship is important for getting positive publicity for the business and to clearly explain to the media the business's point of view on any issue that could result in negative news.

Media Relations Guidelines. PR media specialists contact the media themselves; they also train the managers who speak to the media, preparing them for news interviews by reporters. Businesses should follow these seven guidelines when dealing with the media issues.

1. **Reality.** Assume that everything you say is "on the record"; don't expect to see a copy of the story before it goes public, and expect to be misquoted and taken out of context. Your summary points can help clarify information (see #5 below).
2. **Truth.** Tell the truth in plain English and admit mistakes. Once you get caught in a lie, things get much worse (e.g., **Enron**).
3. **Audience.** The information should be tailored to the audience. Information about issues going only to the business press can contain more technical jargon and be more technical in nature than those going to a general audience.
4. **Society-benefits strategy.** Use information strategies (Chapter 2), focusing on how the firm is or will be helping society stakeholders. The general public doesn't care about what's in it for the business and profits. Provide facts and figures, use outside sources, and get expert and other stakeholder support statements to back up your side of the issue.
5. **Summary points.** Begin with a summary of key points to the business side of the issue. Discuss details of how the business side helps society stakeholders. Don't hesitate to repeat key answers. End with the summary of key points.
6. **Elaborate.** Don't simply answer questions; add positive statements about the issue to your remarks.
7. **Crisis.** Follow the crisis management plan. The crisis leader (or spokesperson) should follow the "three As" of crisis communication: *acknowledge* the crisis, state the *action* to deal with the crisis, and state how the crisis will be *avoided* in the future. (See Chapter 2 for crisis management details.)

Advocacy Advertising as a Media Strategy. *Advocacy advertisements are used to present the business side of a controversial social or political issue.* They are also called issue advertising. Rather than inform and persuade consumers to buy its products, business wants to inform and persuade society and the government that it is doing a good job or being socially responsible and ethical; this ad strategy promotes the maintenance of a good corporate reputation and positive public sentiment. The ads can be in any medium. **Mobil** pioneered the use of advocacy ads focusing on issues of gasoline price controls and environmental regulations when the ads were largely unknown, and it is still running ads with **Exxon**. When the media reported safety issues with acetaminophen, the medicine in **Tylenol**, the company ran full-page advocacy ads to help ensure consumers knew it was a safe product when used as directed.[66]

Societal Community Strategies

Companies need strategies in view of social issues and challenges.[67] Community strategies can give the firm a competitive advantage and lead to success even for small businesses.[68] Public relations with local community stakeholders are important to business success. Managing community involvement and implementing a stakeholder approach are important parts of business success, as they are measures in the Dow Jones *Sustainability Indexes*. Many successful corporations are dealing with the community by using a stakeholder approach in working with them, often through community involvement programs that meet the **Standards of Excellence in Corporate Community Involvement** and are headed by a *community relations department* manager who follows the four steps to effectively manage community relations. Companies can have good community relations programs by providing volunteers, implementing philanthropic programs, and forming collaborative partnerships. Businesses are gaining community public sentiment for being ethical and socially responsible. The media help improve corporate reputations by publicizing community involvement programs. Cause-related marketing is also used at the community level.

   Whole Foods Markets, a natural food retailer, is a good example of managing community relations effectively. It believes that its business is intimately tied to the neighborhoods and larger community that it serves and in which it operates. Whole Foods donates about five times the average of all U.S. companies, giving food and 5 percent of its after-tax profits to nonprofit organizations. It also supports its Whole Planet Foundation, which focuses on community development.[69]

Societal Consumer Strategies

Customer Relations Management (CRM). Customers are so important to business that the late management guru Peter Drucker said that only one definition of the purpose of business is valid: to create a customer.[70] A prerequisite to business success is to ethically provide products that consumers want, at the price, place, and time they want to buy products, and doing so is being socially responsible. Consumers are aware of their rights, and they actively comparison shop in stores and online. Therefore, companies know that repeat customers and referrals to buy the companies' products are critical to their success. In the 1990s, researchers found that a small increase in customer retention rates leads to dramatic profit increases.[71] Today, a major business focus is on CRM. Thus, the formulation and implementation of a consumer-oriented stakeholder management strategy is critical to business success, and quality is important to CRM.

The Consumer Affairs Department. The department's primary responsibility is handling consumer inquires for product information and resolving complaints. Often hotlines are used for customer questions and complaints. For example, **Frito-Lay** has a toll-free number (1-800-352-4477) that consumers can call with questions and comments.[72] The consumer affairs department is also responsible for handling consumer complaints and working on product recalls. It is quick to take action to resolve complaints when the local retailer is not doing a good job. Businesses also have extensive product information on their websites, and consumers can use the "contact us" feature to ask questions and lodge complaints.

Total Quality Management (TQM). An important part of CRM is offering quality products. With *TQM* all business functions are blended into a holistic integrated philosophy built around the concepts of quality, teamwork, productivity, and customer understanding and satisfaction. Regardless of the term the company uses, the focus is on customer satisfaction through continuous improvement.

Six Sigma Quality. Six Sigma is a TQM development. The Six Sigma level of operations relates to having only 3.4 defects per million. **Motorola** started Six Sigma, **Allied Signal** experimented with it, and **GE** perfected it. For more information on Six Sigma go to (www.6-sigma.com).

American Society for Quality (ASQ). **ASQ** (www.asq.org) is a global community of people passionate about quality, who use the tools, their ideas, and experience to make our world work better.[73]

International Organization for Standards (ISO) and Quality. **ISO** (www.iso.org) sets global quality standards and certifies companies that meet its standards. Most major corporations are members of ISO and require their suppliers to meet ISO quality standards.

Ethics and Codes of Conduct. Members of ASQ and ISO are expected to live according to their codes of ethics. In addition, many companies' codes of conduct go beyond the requirements of ASQ and ISO. Some industries develop their own voluntary codes of conduct stating how they will treat their customers, partly to forestall even stricter government regulation.

Political and Legal Strategies

Successful companies go beyond simply operating in a way to avoid lawsuits by working with government to develop fair laws and regulations to protect consumers and help the media (including advertisers).[74] Businesses are also developing cooperative partnerships with government to improve their efficiency. Firms lobby politicians to change and avoid new consumer protection and media regulations, sometimes by using grassroots campaigns or by giving donations. Business works with its societal interest groups and builds coalitions to influence community and consumer laws and regulations. Managers give testimony at hearings to present the business side of the issue. Businesses sometimes sue other businesses over consumer products, such as for patent infringement.

SUMMARY

The chapter summary is organized to answer the eight learning outcomes for Chapter 6.

1. **Define community and briefly explain the business–community interrelationship.**

   Community is the local area in which business operates and affects stakeholders. The business–community relationship is interrelated. Business needs community support with infrastructure, transportation systems, public safety, health care, employees, customers, and other support. The community needs business for economic development, products, jobs and training, taxes to help pay for community services, and help with some social problems, among other reasons. This interrelationship enhances the quality of community life where we live and work.

2. **Discuss community relations and community involvement programs.**

   Community relations are the organized involvement of business with local society and government. Community relations are often managed by a community relations department. Community involvement is business participation in changing and improving communities. There are three primary types of community involvement programs: (1) volunteer programs encourage and reward employees for doing work for community nonprofit organizations, sometimes during paid work hours; (2) philanthropic programs give resources of products, services, and cash funds to the community; (3) collaborative partnership programs are voluntary relationships among business, social interest groups, and/or government to solve a social problem.

3. **Explain differences between customers, consumers, and consumerism.**

   Customers buy products from the busi-

ness, and *consumers* use the products. Many businesses sell their products to customers, who in turn sell them to consumers. Interactions between the company and its customers and the consumers of its products are business issues within the market environment. *Consumerism* is the organized collective efforts to safeguard all consumers by promoting their rights and power. Everyone is a consumer, so consumerism is broader in scope than consumer, and consumerism is a society issue in the nonmarket environment.

4. **Characterize each of the five consumer rights.**

   Consumers have five rights. The right to *safety* protects consumers against products that are hazardous to their health and life. The right to be *informed* protects consumers against the marketing of products through fraudulent, deceitful, or grossly misleading information, advertising, labeling, or other practices. The right to *choice* assures consumers of choosing from among a variety of products at competitive prices, wherever feasible. The right to be *heard* assures that consumer interests will receive full and sympathetic consideration in the formulation of government policies, laws, and regulation. The right to *privacy* protects consumers from misuse of personal information.

5. **State what the federal consumer protection regulatory agency acronyms CFPB, CPSC, FTC, FDA, NHTSA, and SEC stand for, and discuss their regulatory responsibilities**.

   The Consumer Financial Protection Bureau *(CFPB)* regulates financial products. The Consumer Product Safety Commission (*CPSC*) protects the public against unreasonable risks of injury associated with consumer products, through setting and enforcing safety standards. The Federal Trade Commission (*FTC*) regulates practices that are anticompetitive or deceptive or unfair to consumers. The Food and Drug Administration (*FDA*) regulates the safety of human and veterinary foods, drugs, vaccines, cosmetics, and medical and radiation devices. The National Highway Traffic Safety Administration (*NHTSA*) regulates standards of excellence in motor vehicle and highway safety. The Securities and Exchange Commission (*SEC*) protects investors; maintains fair, orderly, and efficient markets; and facilitates capital formation.

6. **Compare and contrast various types of warranties.**

Warranties are contracts in which the seller guarantees the nature of the product and the buyer is entitled to compensation for any consequent harm. However, variations in warranties include express versus implied and full versus limited warranties. An *express warranty* is an explicit claim made by the producer to the consumer, whereas an *implied warranty* is an unwritten guarantee that the product is adequate to meet reasonable expectations for intended purposes. A *full warranty* must express unconditional assurance that the product will be replaced or repaired within a reasonable time and without charge, whereas a *limited warranty* conditionally excludes certain parts of the product or particular types of defects from coverage.

7. **Describe what makes a story newsworthy, including its coverage and treatment.**

Newsworthy stories are of interest to the audience and have social significance. Newsworthy stories: (1) are generally about people; (2) are about immediate or urgent issues; (3) include controversy or conflict; and (4) are easily told. Media coverage, the stories that make the news, is determined according to the level of interest. Thus, the greater the interest, the greater the coverage, and the greater the significance, the higher the level of treatment. Treatment levels are based on providing more or fewer facts, offering interpretation, highlighting the implications, and stating advocacy.

8. **Fill in the blank with the appropriate key term.**

_____ is the local area in which businesses operate and affect stakeholders.

_____ is the organized involvement of business with local society and government.

_____ is business participation in changing and improving communities.

_____ include volunteers, philanthropic giving of resources and cash, and collaborative partnerships.

_____ are voluntary relationships among business, society groups, and/or government for community improvement.

_____ buy products from business.

_____ use business products.

_____ is the organized collective efforts to safeguard all consumers by promoting their rights and power.

_____ include safety, information, choice, voice, and privacy.

_____ is the firm's legal responsibility for its actions and products, especially costs or damages.

_____ is a contract in which the seller guarantees the integrity of the product, and the buyer is entitled to compensation for any consequent harm and defective goods.

_____ is an explicit claim made by the producer to the consumer.

_____ is an unwritten guarantee that the product is adequate to meet reasonable expectations for intended purposes.

_____ is the process of a consumer filing a lawsuit against a firm seeking compensation for harm resulting from defective products or business actions.

_____ means that the plaintiff does not have to prove negligence when the activity or product is inherently dangerous.

_____ are interesting and have social significance; they are about people, are immediate or urgent, involve controversy or conflict, and are easy to tell.

_____ are used to present the business side of a controversial social or political issue.

KEY TERMS (IN ALPHABETICAL ORDER)

KEY TERMS

6

advocacy advertisements (p. 227)
collaborative partnerships (p. 206)
community (p. 203)
community involvement (p. 205)
community involvement programs
  (p. 205)
community relations (p. 205)
consumerism (p. 208)
consumer rights (p. 209)

consumers (p. 208)
customers (p. 208)
express warranty (p. 214)
implied warranty (p. 214)
newsworthy stories (p. 223)
product liability (p. 213)
product liability litigation (p. 215)
strict liability (p. 216)
warranty (p. 213)

REVIEW QUESTIONS

REVIEW QUESTIONS

6

You may have to do an online search to get the answers for questions 3, 5, 7, and 9.

1 What is the role of the community relations department?

2 What are the seven Standards of **Excellence in Corporate Community Involvement?**

3 What are Norton Company's four steps to manage community involvement?

4 Why is it important to differentiate customers, consumers, and consumerism and their environment?

5 What does the phrase *caveat emptor* mean?

6 What are the five consumer rights?

7 What is the difference between federal, state, and local regulatory powers over consumer laws and regulations, and which one takes precedence?

8 Who or what is EDGAR?

9 What do the federal consumer protection regulatory agency acronyms USDA, DHS, TSA, DOT, EPA, FDIC, PBGC, NTSB, and EEOC stand for?

10 Why don't more businesses offer full warranties?

11 Who really pays the shipping costs of getting the product to the consumer and for returns to the company?

12 What is product liability litigation?

13 Which government agency primarily regulates the media?

14 Who owns the media?

15 Which media industry firms specialize in broadcasting technology, broadcasting content, and service delivery?

16 What is the business–media advertising relationship?

17 Is the role of the media really all that important in the global economy?

18 What is GPO Access?

19 What is CRM, and is it really all that important?

20 What is the primary responsibility of a consumer affairs department?

21 What is TQM, and is it really all that important?

22 What is Six Sigma, and is it really all that important?

23 What is ASQ, and what does it do?

24 What is ISO, and is it really all that important?

DISCUSSION/
CRITICAL THINKING
QUESTIONS

6

DISCUSSION/CRITICAL THINKING QUESTIONS

Be sure to give a detailed explanation for your answer to each question.

1 Do businesses do more good or more harm to communities?

2 How much and what kind of power does your local community have over business?

3 Should business spend owner profits on community involvement programs? If yes, how much and how should the amount spent be determined?

4 Should consumer movement pressure on business be increased or decreased?

5 Do consumers really have rights, and do they have too much or too little power over business?

6 Does the government have too many or too few consumer regulations?

7 Are there too many government agencies responsible for consumer regulations? Should the authority system be changed? If yes, how and why?

8 Does business offer good product liability?

9 Are the high damage awards for product liability justified? Should awards be increased or decreased?

10 Is the overall cost of product liability too high?

11 Overall, are you a defender of the current product liability system or a supporter of reform?

12 Do you disagree or agree with each of the following:

   i. having uniform federal liability standards

   ii. limiting punitive damages

   iii. placing the burden of proving liability on consumers

   iv. eliminating absolute liability?

13 Are the media really ethical and socially responsible?

14 What are the chances of the government stopping all advertising?

15 Do ads really persuade you to buy products you would not have bought if you hadn't seen the ad?

16 If business really should be ethical in advertising, giving clear, accurate, and adequate information to consumers, why is there advertising abuse?

17 Does it pay to employ ethical ads to sell products?

18 Does business really care about its relationship with customers?

19 Does business really care about the quality of its products?

20 Was the hot coffee issue that went to court handled well by McDonald's?

APPLICATION EXERCISES

6.1 COMMUNITY AND CONSUMER RELATIONS

Select a business, preferably one where you work(ed) or would like to work. Do some research (call or visit its website, or use other sources) and report on its position regarding community relations, consumer relations, and/or product liability.

6.2 EDGAR SEARCH

Select a large public corporation. Go to the SEC website for an EDGAR search (www.sec.gov/edgar.shtml). Report the financial condition of the company.

6.3 VISIT SAFERPRODUCTS.GOV

Visit the website and click "Search (Recalls & Reports)." Then do your own search on any product or select a category from the menu. Read it and state whether it is a recall or report and give the date (number for a report) and its name and a brief description. Comment on your findings.

6.4 CONSUMER ADVOCATE.

Select one of the consumer advocate groups discussed in this chapter, or another one you are interested in learning more about. Visit its website and report your findings.

CASE 6.1

Walt Disney and the FCC: The Lion that Squeaked or the Mouse that Roared?

The Walt Disney Company is the world's largest media conglomerate, with assets encompassing movies, television, publishing, and theme parks. Its Disney/ABC Television Group includes the ABC television network and 10 broadcast stations, as well as a portfolio of cable networks including ABC Family, Disney Channel, and ESPN (80-percent-owned). Walt Disney Studios produces films through imprints Walt Disney Pictures, Disney Animation, and Pixar, and its Marvel Entertainment is a top comic book publisher and film producer. In addition, Walt Disney Parks and Resorts operates the company's popular theme parks including Walt Disney World and Disneyland.

Like other media conglomerates, the company depends on its wide array of entertainment offerings across its film, television, and theme parks divisions to generate revenue; it also earns money by distributing its content through multiple channels.

A substantial part of Disney's business also comes from ancillary products, mostly aimed at children, created from its trove of characters and other intellectual property. Its consumer products division—which includes the Disney Store retail chain (with about 200 stores in North America, 100 stores in Europe, and 45 stores in Japan) and Disney Publishing Worldwide—makes products such as straight-to-video movies, spin-off books, and licensed apparel.[75]

In December 2011 the FCC proposed "to relax the ban on cross-ownership (newspaper with other mass media like television) in the top 20 markets, essentially codifying waivers granted companies like Tribune and News Corp. that own TV–newspaper combinations in the top markets."[76] This would also allow firms like ABC/Walt Disney to enter the newsprint market. Comments filed by the National Association of Broadcasters and the Newspaper Association of America (NAA) claimed the FCC rules were all but killing news-papers and hamstringing TV stations from competing in a fragmented media market-place. "Technology and market forces have moved light-years ahead of this outdated rule," said Caroline Little, NAA president and CEO. "Consumers have more choices among media voices than ever. It makes absolutely no sense to keep a rule on the books that has shackled newspapers and broadcasters since 1975." Little added, "In these times of challenge for the news industry, it is irrational and unwise to keep a rule that suppresses investment in news-paper companies."[77]

Consumer groups said that the FCC's rules won't accomplish what broadcaster and newspaper owners claim. "Increasing cross-ownership will not help the newspa-per industry; it will only push it further into debt while also harming the production of quality local news. There is simply no credible evidence showing that relaxing the newspaper–broadcast cross-ownership rule will benefit the public. In fact, it's quite the opposite. The majority of research—including the FCC's own study—shows that TV–newspaper consolidation results in less news in local markets, as well as fewer independent producers of local news," said Corie Wright, senior policy counsel for Free Press.[78]

Disney's response to this ownership controversy? Disney has surprisingly stayed out of this debate on media ownership by not filing comments with the FCC's review of its rules per congressional and court mandates. Instead Disney has flaunted their neutrality on the issue and in reply com-ments gave the FCC advice by noting "that the FCC would be better served to broaden its inquiry to consider the full panoply of challenges facing broadcasters, ways to give incentives for ownership of over-the-air broadcast stations, and whether some elements of the overall regulatory regime have become outdated."[79]

Questions:

1. What is the role of the FCC as it relates to this case?
2. Why would the FCC originally rule that newspaper firms could not merge or be owned by other mass media com-panies like Disney?
3. Why would the FCC change its posi-tion on media ownership?
4. Why are consumer groups opposing this loosening of the regulations?
5. From a public relations perspective, why would Disney take the position they are taking on this issue?
6. If you were the CEO of Disney, what might be other nonmarket responses to this issue you would consider?

CASE 6.2

The Federal Aviation Administration: Shooting Down a Low-Flying Industry through Government Regulation?

The U.S. airline industry includes about 600 companies with a combined annual revenue of about $175 billion. Major companies include American (owned by AMR), Delta, and United Continental, as well as the air operations of express delivery companies such as FedEx and UPS. The industry is highly concentrated: the 10 largest companies account for more than 75 percent of industry revenue.[80]

What are some of the issues for this indus-try that drive down profitability?

1. Profitability Depends on Business, Consumer Travel—Both business and tourist travel are reduced when the economy slows. Global aviation traffic rises and falls at twice the pace of economic output, so a change in the economy doubles the impact for

airlines. Because of the relatively high fixed-costs of airplanes, airport facilities, and labor, airlines can't easily adjust to reduced passenger traffic.

2. Fuel Costs Can Vary Highly—Aviation fuel accounts for 20 to 30 percent of industry operating costs, relatively more for airlines with low labor costs. Fuel costs can change rapidly, making it difficult for airlines to adjust ticket prices. Some airlines use futures contracts to protect against cost increases. Newer planes have better fuel consumption.

3. Capital-Intensive Industry—Airplanes are expensive to acquire and maintain. Most new airplanes typically cost between $50 and $250 million (with seating capacity ranging from for 110 to 400 passengers). Newer planes are usually more fuel-efficient, but the high prices deter many airlines from buying them.

4. Industry Widely Regulated—The FAA (Federal Aviation Administration),, DOT (Department of Transportation), and TSA (Transportation Security Administration) impose various fees on the industry, and can interfere with airline operations. To expand operations, airlines need to get route permission from DOT and gates from local airports.

5. Airlines Depend on Skilled Employees—Airlines can't fly without FAA-certified pilots and mechanics, whose training takes years. The unions that represent these employees at most airlines have an exceptionally important voice in labor issues.[81]

The industry has seen 10 major U.S. airlines declare bankruptcy while others have merged in order to reduce competition and obtain economies of scale. It is worth noting the only major U.S. airline that has been able to grow and produce profits on a steady basis is **Southwest Airlines**. Fare wars continue with the advent of discount carriers, especially Southwest Airlines and Jet Blue, who have proven to be large hurdles the larger carriers have not yet been able to compete against successfully.[82]

"In some respects the global airline industry has come back [from 9/11] stronger than ever. Traffic is up, plane occupancy is at an all-time high, overcapacity issues have been addressed, and world economies are on the upswing. So why is the industry still in trouble? In short, fuel prices and brutal price competition. North America has been the region in which it is hardest to make a buck. In fact, it is the hard-hit value of a buck on international markets that has been a big part of the problem. While pricing competition is tough all over, it is particularly tough in North America as U.S. travelers prowl the Internet for low fares, and the U.S. government passes the cost of increased airport security on to the airlines."[83]

It is not surprising then that Giovanni Bisignani, director general and CEO of the International Air Carrier Association (IACA), a professional association representing the major airlines, reacted vehemently when he read in the *Wall Street Journal* that the FAA was proposing new regulations about airplane vehicle maintenance and inspection that was, from his perspective, going to cost the industry a small fortune. An excerpt from the article follows:

In the midst of these troubling times, the FAA is continuing to follow their mission by focusing on increasing the quality of plane inspections. Marion Clifton Blakey, Administrator of the FAA, has proposed "new inspection and maintenance standards that could result in faster retirement of some aircraft and cost airlines an additional $325 million over 20 years. . . . The proposal questions widely held industry views that commercial jets routinely can fly for 25 years or more as long as incipient cracks are monitored. Instead, it calls for enhanced inspection programs, covering those planes intended to be operated past predetermined retirement limits based on total number of flights.

The proposed package is largely designed to anticipate potential structural problems before the first signs occur, and to create a system that places more responsibility on airlines and plane makers to demonstrate the continued safety of aircraft. The agency said changes are necessary "to heighten the awareness of the threat" from the most serious types of age-related metal fatigue, adding that current safeguards are inadequate. Thousands of existing and future jetliners could be affected by the proposal.[84]

An Overview of the FAA

The FAA is responsible for the safety of civil aviation. It's major roles include regulating civil aviation to promote safety; encouraging and developing civil aeronautics, including new aviation technology; developing and operating a system of air traffic control and navigation for both civil and military aircraft; researching and developing the National Airspace System and civil aeronautics; developing and carrying out programs to control aircraft noise and other environmental effects of civil aviation; and regulating U.S. commercial space transportation.[85] The FAA regulates all aspects of air transportation from the licensing of pilots, aircrafts, and airlines to providing up-to-minute information on air status and delays and accident reports. Its mission "is to provide the safest, most efficient aerospace system in the world [and its] . . . vision is to improve the safety and efficiency of aviation, while being responsive to customers and accountable to the public."[86] Marion Clifton Blakey, administrator of the FAA, is proud of FAA's values, which include safety, quality, integrity, and the strength of their employees.

Questions

1. What consumer rights are being protected by the FAA? Against what type of liabilities?
2. Given those rights and liabilities, and the current industry circumstances, how might the FAA proposal to increase the quality of plane inspections impact those rights?
3. What quality standards and quality systems might airlines consider utilizing in response to this FAA proposal?
4. Given the current problems in the airline industry, what actions could the FAA take to safeguard the industry?
5. If you were the CEO of any major airline, how would you react to the proposal?
6. What actions, if any, should be taken by Bisignani and the IACA in response to the proposal?

INTEGRATIVE CASE

6

INTEGRATIVE CASE (Part 6)

Community Outreach or Community Marketing: Does Charity Begin and End at Home?

This is a continuation case—please refer back to Chapters 1–5 for further information.

Richard Davis and Stephen Hodgetts, academics and co-owners of a small home rental agency and two small construction companies, were sitting around the dinner table with Richard's wife Adrienne, discussing possible ways in which the firm could get involved in their local community. Adrienne was actively involved in a local church, having in past years worked on fund-raising events and weekend socials, and felt it was time that the firm make a concerted organized effort to be a good community citizen.

"I understand that you've both been caught up in your own projects and trying to get the businesses off the ground," started Adrienne, "but it is now time for you two to spend some time thinking about community-minded activities that each or you, and the business, could get involved with. You both have much to offer the community—your time, your energy, your creativity, and your resources. It's time that you give back to the community from which you're making a living."

"Wait a minute," jumped in Hodgetts. "We're both extremely busy individuals. Richard is still a full-time academic at the university, which means that besides his work for the firm, which is quite extensive, he teaches four courses each semester, advises students, is involved in several campus committees, and still is involved with several professional associations. He has no free time!"

"That's right," chimed in Richard Davis, coming to Hodgetts' support. "And Hodgetts has the onerous task of the same academic responsibilities as well as carrying the full brunt of our research, writing, and publishing. Just because we're in business doesn't mean that we have abandoned our continuing search for knowledge!"

"Yes!" seconded Hodgetts. "Also, do not forget that I am also the editor of a new online journal and quite actively involved in the organization of several academic conferences. We're very committed to our work, so when are Richard and I supposed to have time to get involved with community projects?"

"Excuses, excuses. You're starting to sound like your students!" pronounced Adrienne. She knew that her latest quip would hit them very hard since both Richard and Stephen always complained that their students would rather complain about working than do the work. She had trapped them in their own game!

Richard and Stephen took very hard looks at each other, looked at Adrienne, and then looked to each other for direction. They knew that there was no way of getting out of the trap that Adrienne set, it was just a matter of how bad the consequences were going to be for getting caught! However, maybe there was a way to weasel their way out! "Adrienne," Richard spoke rather softly. "You're assuming that Stephen and I are not contributing to the local community given our involvement in our businesses. But how is that possible? As two budding entrepreneurs we have hired local subcontractors, created jobs, purchased building supplies, supported local businesses, supplied housing, provided shelter, paid for government services through licensing fees, and paid more than our fair share of taxes (real estate, sales, and corporate). And don't forget that our rental operation is based on helping those with little to no credit build up their credit and gather the money to make a down payment so that they can eventually buy their own home. What more could the community expect from us?"

Hodgetts saw where Richard's line of reasoning was going and jumped on the bandwagon. "Exactly! Any time that Richard and I would take away from the business volunteering for charity events would be time that we could spend in the business becoming more efficient, passing the savings onto the consumer, or becoming more effective, growing our business, hiring employees, and paying more taxes. If you want us to contribute to the community, why can't we just write a check to a local charity and be done with it? Especially a charity that deals with addressing housing issues, issues that we care about."

"You mean issues that you profit from!" retorted Adrienne. "You're both missing the point. Charitable contributions are tax deductible; you are in essence getting paid by the government to donate to charities. Secondly, unless you donate the money anonymously to a charity, the name of the firm gets some publicity associated with the donation as well as being a promotional tool for future advertisements. Haven't both of you seen the commercial by a nonprofit organization talking about tobacco companies spending millions of dollars promoting their donation of $125,000 to feed the poor. That's disgusting! You should contribute your time and energy to the community because it is the right thing to do, not because you're getting some return on 'your investment'"!

Questions

1. What are the three distinct ways in which Richard Davis and Stephen Hodgetts can be involved in their community? Given these methods, which method is Adrienne Davis advocating and why?

2. What seems to be Richard's and Stephen's perspectives on community outreach and community involvement? Do you agree with their perspectives? Why or why not?

3. If you were Richard and Stephen, how would you respond to Adrienne's last comment that they should not profit from their community service?

4. What steps or actions would Richard and Stephen need to take in order to properly manage their level of community involvement?

5. Assuming that Richard and Stephen were to volunteer their time, what types of projects or organizations could they work with that would help them publicize their business?

REFERENCES AND NOTES

REFERENCES AND NOTES

6

1 S. K. Williams, J. S. Anderson, J. Dustman, and S. D. Rogers, "TASER International, Inc.—Grappling with Growth" *The CASE Journal* 2(2) (Spring, 2006): 24.

2 http://subscriber.hoovers.com/H/company360/fulldescription.html?company Id=105070000000000 (accessed June 5, 2012).

3 S. K. Williams, J. S. Anderson, J. Dustman, and S. D. Rogers, "TASER International, Inc.—Grappling with Growth" *The CASE Journal* 2(2) (Spring, 2006): 24.

4 Amnesty International, "UNITED STATES OF AMERICA: Excessive and lethal force? Amnesty International's concerns about deaths and ill-treatment involving police use of TASERs," *AMR* 51(34) (November 2004): 3.

5 S. K. Williams, J. S. Anderson, J. Dustman, and S. D. Rogers, "TASER International, Inc.—Grappling with Growth" *The CASE Journal* 2(2) (Spring, 2006): 28.

6 Amnesty International, "UNITED STATES OF AMERICA: Excessive and lethal force? Amnesty International's concerns about deaths and ill-treatment involving police use of TASERs," *AMR* 51(34) (November 2004): 3–4.

7 http://subscriber.hoovers.com/H/company360/fulldescription.html?company Id=105070000000000 (accessed June 5, 2012).

8 A. Armenakis and J. Wigand, "Stakeholder Actions and Their Impact on the Organizational Cultures of Two Tobacco Companies." *Business and Society Review* 115(2) (2010): 147–171.

9 A. Nadim and R.N. Lussier, "Small Business, Community Relations and Sustainability: New Approaches to Success," *Journal of Small Business Strategy* 21(2) (2012): 79–95.

10 Ibid.

11 D. Baur and G. Palazzo, "The Moral Legitimacy of NGOs as Partners of Corporations," *Business Ethics Quarterly* 21(4) (2011): 579–604.

12 T. Hahn, A. Kolk, and M. Winn, "A New Future for Business? Rethinking Management Theory and Business Strategy." *Business & Society* 49(3) (2010): 385–401.

13 R.J. Adams, "Prescription Drug Labeling and 'Over-Warning': The Disturbing Case of Diana Levine and Wyeth Pharmaceutical," *Business and Society Review*, 115 (2010): 231–248.

14 M. Rhee and M. E. Valdez, "Contextual Factors Surrounding Reputation Damage with Potential Implications for Reputation Repair," *Academy of Management Journal* 34(1) (2009): 146–168.

15 R. Leung, "Eminent Domain: Being Abused?" *60 Minutes* (February 11, 2009), http://www.cbsnews.com/stories/2003/09/26/60minutes/main575343.shtml (accessed May 15, 2012).

16 "Plant Closings and Mass Layoffs Worker Adjustment and Retraining Notification Act (WARN) (29 USC §2101 et seq. 20 CFR 639)" *U.S. Department of Labor.* http://www.dol.gov/asp/programs/guide/layoffs.htm (accessed May 15, 2012).

17 P. A. Heslin, "Social Entrepreneurship," *Academy of Management Learning & Education* 10(1) (2011): 164–166.

18 P. Schreck, "Reviewing the Business Case for Corporate Social Responsibility: New Evidence and Analysis," *Journal of Business Ethics* 103(2) (2011): 167–188.

19 P. H. Mirvis and B. K. Googins, "Stages of Corporate Citizenship: A Developmental Framework," Center for Corporate Citizenship at Boston College Monograph (Chestnut Hill, MA: Boston College, 2006): 3–5.

20 K. Witter, *Community Involvement Index 2003* (Boston: Center for Corporate Citizenship at Boston College, 2003).

21 Eli Lilly and Company. *Communities,* http://www.lilly.com/Responsibility/communities/Pages/communities.aspx (accessed May 15, 2012).

22 P. A. Heslin, "Social Entrepreneurship," *Academy of Management Learning & Education* 10(1) (2011): 164–166.

23 A. Nadim and R. N. Lussier, "Small Business, Community Relations and Sustainability: New Approaches to Success," *Journal of Small Business Strategy* 21(2) (2012): 79–95.

24 M. Rhee and M. E. Valdez, "Contextual Factors Surrounding Reputation Damage with Potential Implications for Reputation Repair," *Academy of Management Journal* 34(1) (2009): 146–168.

25 M. D. Groza, M. R. Pronschinkse, and M. Walker, "Perceived Organizational Motives and Consumer Responses to Proactive and Reactive CSR," *Journal of Business Ethics* 102(4) (2010): 639–652.

26 Foundation Center, http://foundationcenter.org (accessed May 15, 2012).

27 D. Baur and G. Palazzo, "The Moral Legitimacy of NGOs as Partners of Corporations," *Business Ethics Quarterly* 21(4) (2011): 579–604.

28 IBM, http://smartercitieschallenge.org/2012_winners.html (accessed May 15, 2012).

29 Business in the Community, www.bitc.org.uk (accessed May 15, 2012).

30 Center for Corporate Citizenship, *Standards of Excellence in Corporate Community Involvement* (Boston College), www.bc.edu/corporatecitizenship (accessed May 15, 2012).

31 A. Armenakis and J. Wigand, "Stakeholder Actions and Their Impact on the Organizational Cultures of Two Tobacco Companies," *Business and Society Review* 115(2) (2010): 147–171.

32 R. J. Adams, "Prescription Drug Labeling and 'Over-Warning': The Disturbing Case of Diana Levine and Wyeth Pharmaceutical," *Business and Society Review* 115 (2010): 231–248.

33 M. D. Groza, M. R. Pronschinkse, and M. Walker, "Perceived Organizational Motives and Consumer Responses to Proactive and Reactive CSR," *Journal of Business Ethics* 102(4) (2010): 639–652.

34 R. J. Adams, "Prescription Drug Labeling and 'Over-Warning': The Disturbing Case of Diana Levine and Wyeth Pharmaceutical," *Business and Society Review* 115 (2010): 231–248.

35 J. C. Dooren, "Cheerios' Heath Claims Break Rules, FDA Says," *Wall Street Journal* (May 13, 2009): B1.

36 Staff, "Take Care of Your Cards!" *Employee Services Newsletter,* www.theEAP.com (accessed May 15, 2012).

37 http://subscriber.hoovers.com/H/company360/fulldescription.html?companyId=10322000000000 (accessed June 6, 2012).

38 http://www.aarp.org/politics-society/government-elections/info-12-2010/mcCoy_chase_cons.html (accessed June 6, 2012).

39 Ibid.

40 R. J. Adams, "Prescription Drug Labeling and 'Over-Warning': The Disturbing Case of Diana Levine and Wyeth Pharmaceutical," *Business and Society Review* 115 (2010): 231–248.

41 Ibid.

42 www.cgood.org (accessed May 17, 2012).

43 R. J. Adams, "Prescription Drug Labeling and 'Over-Warning': The Disturbing Case of Diana Levine and Wyeth

Pharmaceutical," *Business and Society Review* 115 (2010): 231–248.

44 http://www.creekstonefarms.com/images/content/files/Creekstone_Eagle_JAN2_2011.pdf (accessed June 6, 2012).

45 http://www.creekstonefarmspremiumbeef.com/about.html (accessed April 18, 2006).

46 "Kansas Meatpacker Sues U.S. Over Bar of Mad-Cow Tests," *Associated Press* (March 23, 2006).

47 Ibid.

48 http://www.bloomberg.com/apps/news?pid=newsarchive&sid=a798RwAI5fyg&refer=japan (accessed June 6, 2012).

49 C. Rose, "Interview with Hulu CEO Jason Kilar," *BusinessWeek* (March 5–11, 2012): 48.

50 FCC, www.fcc.gov (accessed May 17, 2012).

51 Suggested by an anonymous reviewer.

52 "Policy on Media and Children," www.aap.org (accessed June 15, 2012).

53 Suggested by an anonymous reviewer.

54 Suggested by an anonymous reviewer.

55 T. James, "Skewed News: Can You Recognize It?" *AFA Journal* (April, 2011): 16–17.

56 M. Rhee and M. E. Valdez, "Contextual Factors Surrounding Reputation Damage with Potential Implications for Reputation Repair," *Academy of Management Journal* 34(1) (2009): 146–168.

57 S. Vranica, "Public Relations Learned the Hard Way," *Wall Street Journal* (December 30, 2010): B6.

58 ASNE. Chapter "Characteristics of the Respondents," www.asne.org (accessed April 28, 2006).

59 B. Gruley and E. Campbell, "Slimmed: Was a Food Innovator Unfairly Targeted?" *BusinessWeek* (April 16–22, 2012): 18–20.

60 R. Van der Merwe, L. F. Pitt, and R. Abratt, "Stakeholders Strength" PR Survival Strategies in the Internet Age," *Public Relations Quarterly* 50 (Spring 2005): 39–49.

61 M. Rhee and M. E. Valdez, "Contextual Factors Surrounding Reputation Damage with Potential Implications for Reputation Repair," *Academy of Management Journal* 34(1) (2009): 146–168.

62 M. D. Groza, M. R. Pronschinkse, and M. Walker, "Perceived Organizational Motives and Consumer Responses to Proactive and Reactive CSR," *Journal of Business Ethics* 102(4) (2010): 639–652.

63 M. Rhee and M. E. Valdez, "Contextual Factors Surrounding Reputation Damage with Potential Implications for Reputation Repair," *Academy of Management Journal* 34(1) (2009): 146–168.

64 S. Terlep and S. Vranica, "GM to Forgo Pricey Super Bowl Ads," *Wall Street Journal* (May 19–20, 2012): B1.

65 G. Chon, "Activist Moves into PepsiCo," *Wall Street Journal* (May 16, 2012): B1.

66 TYLENOL ad, *Wall Street Journal* (July 3–5, 2009): A14.

67 T. Hahn, A. Kolk, and M. Winn, "A New Future for Business? Rethinking Management Theory and Business Strategy," *Business & Society* 49(3) (2010): 385–401.

68 A. Nadim and R. N. Lussier, "Small Business, Community Relations and Sustainability: New Approaches to Success," *Journal of Small Business Strategy* 21(2) (2012): 79–95.

69 Whole Foods, www.wholefoodsmarket.com (accessed May 18, 2012).

70 P. F. Drucker, *Management: Task, Responsibilities, Practices* (New York: Harper & Row, 1973): 61.

71 F. F. Reichheld, *The Loyalty Effect* (Cambridge, MA: Harvard Business School Press, 1996).

72 Information taken from Frito-Lay Lay's packaging (May 18, 2012).

73 Vision taken from the ASQ, www.asq.org (accessed April 14, 2006).

74 J. Sasseen and K. Epstein, "A Backlash Against Obama's Budget," *BusinessWeek* (March 16, 2009): 16–22.

75 http://subscriber.hoovers.com/H/company360/history.html?companyId=11603000000000 (accessed June 6, 2012).

76 http://www.adweek.com/news/fcc/broadcasters-newspapers-call-media-ownership-rules-outdated-138766 (accessed June 6, 2012).

77 Ibid.

78 Ibid.

79 http://www.broadcastingcable.com/article/483387-Disney_s_Ownership_No_Comment_Still_Suggests_Some_Regs_May_Be_Outdated.php?rssid=20065 (accessed June 6, 2012).

80 http://subscriber.hoovers.com/H/industry360/description.html?industryId=1600 (accessed June 6, 2012).

81 http://subscriber.hoovers.com/H/industry360/businessChallenges.html?industryId=1600 (accessed June 6, 2012).

82 C. Brahma, *E-Business: Strategic Thinking*

and Practice (Boston, MA: Houghton-Mifflin Company, 2003).

83 http://premium.hoovers.com/subscribe/ind/overview.xhtml?HICID=1600 (accessed April 19, 2006).

84 A. Pasztor, "FAA Seeks Tighter Aircraft Rules," *The Wall Street Journal* (April 19, 2006): D12.

85 http://www.quantechserv.com/faa.htm (accessed April 19, 2006).

86 http://www.faa.gov/about/mission/ (accessed April 19, 2006).

Chapter 7

STRATEGIES OF SOCIETAL AND BUSINESS INTEREST GROUPS

Learning Outcomes

In this chapter, you will find out the answers to these key questions:

- ■ What are societal and business interest groups, and what is the difference between them?
- ■ What strategies do societal activists and business interest groups use against each other?

After studying this chapter, you should be able to:

1. Describe the objective and roles of societal activists
2. Compare and contrast societal interest groups' and business interest groups' operations and financing
3. Explain the difference between peak and trade groups and their advantages and disadvantages
4. Describe the objectives and roles of business interest groups
5. List and briefly explain seven strategies activists use against business
6. List and briefly explain eight nonmarket strategies business interest groups use against activists
7. Compare and contrast strategies used by activists and businesses against each other
8. Define the following key terms (in order of appearance in the chapter):

societal interest group activists	business interest groups	grassroots efforts
	peak interest groups	boycotts
activists	trade groups	coalitions
Public Citizen	Better Business Bureau (BBB)	grand nonmarket
Consumer Federation of America (CFA)	U.S. Chamber of Commerce	strategies
	Business Roundtable (BRT)	lockouts
Common Cause	National Federation of	
Center for Public Integrity	Independent Business (NFIB)	

■ Chapter Outline

What's This Chapter About?

This chapter focuses on nonprofit societal interest groups. We discuss two major types of interest groups, which are often in opposition, and the strategies they use against each other to further their own cause.

First, we discuss societal interest group activists that pressure business and government to get business to meet their needs. Then we discuss the business interest groups that represent business against societal activists and present the business side of the issue to government to meet its needs.

The next two sections explain strategies activists use against business, followed by strategies businesses use against activists to meet their needs.

As usual, our last section briefly discusses nonmarket and market strategies and ethics from the business perspective.

CASE

AOL and Yahoo! Attack Spam and Get Ambushed by Guerilla Activists

The news had just been released by their public relations departments that AOL/ Yahoo! was going to attack spammers with e-mail fee charges[1] and a backlash was already underway. As reported by the Associated Press, "A variety of interest groups have joined forces to fight a proposed bulk e-mailing fee they claim strikes at the heart of online communication—a level playing field for rich and poor. . . . The alliance protesting the move includes liberal activist group MoveOn, the conservative activist group RightMarch.com, the U.S. Humane Society, labor and environmental groups, and online medical communities."[2]

"The proposal was for a new paid mail service as a way to sidestep spam. The concept is that users purchase packs of 500 virtual stamps at a cost of $5, or one cent per stamp. Proceeds from the sales are then given to a participating charity selected by the user, and each of the e-mail stamps carries the logo of the charity.

Yahoo! is also hoping that the program will cut down on spam, as by adding the unique stamp to each message, it is hoped that the e-mail will breeze through spam filters."[3]

"It was just a simple marketing strategy for raising revenue, providing a better service, and off-setting large operating costs," stated Jonathan Miller, chairman and CEO of AOL, a subsidiary of Time Warner Communications. According to Terry Semel, chairman and CEO of Yahoo! Inc., "All we wanted to do was to charge businesses and other bulk e-mailers a fee to route their e-mail directly to a user's mailbox without first passing through junk mail filters. And what did we get for announcing these brand new services? Trouble, tons of trouble."[4]

What's the big to-do? Opponents of the plan complain that those who pay a fee will have guaranteed e-mail delivery, while those who don't are likely to run into increasing problems with timely delivery—because AOL (and Yahoo!) would naturally spend more time and effort looking after its paying customers. Mark Harris, vice president of SophosLabs, claimed that Yahoo!'s theory is sound up to a point, that while pay-per-e-mail would make it uneconomical for spammers, it would have the same effect on thousands of legitimate companies as well. "Legitimate e-mail marketing, newsletters, subscriptions to groups, even our own notifications about new malware campaigns would very quickly become too expensive and either the cost would have to be passed on or e-mail would stop being used. If you had to pay for a letter to be delivered at your home, and you couldn't see what it was till you paid, the postal service never would have taken off."[5]

And trouble was not the word for it—AOL and Yahoo! had raised a hornet's nest. Eli Pariser, executive director of MoveOn.org Civic Action, said, "The creativity and ingenuity that have driven the Internet have always relied on an open platform where the haves and have-nots get treated equally. This e-mail tax system is a big step toward dismantling that system." Gilles Frydman of the Association of Cancer Online Resources said bulk e-mail charges will cause problems for organizations like his. "We cannot pay for the service, we don't have the money. We have been doing this for 11 years based on the standards of Internet communication. Those standards do not include paying for service. This one company is trying to transform unilaterally how the Internet works." "We're a grassroots organization," said William Green, president of RightMarch.com. "We're not funded by big donors. If we're sending two to three million e-mails a week, paying a penny per e-mail will price us out."[6]

The following questions are related to the AOL/Yahoo! case. Answers can be found within the chapter.

1. What was the role(s) of the activists relative to AOL and Yahoo!'s announcement of a fee-based e-mail service?
2. What other activist groups mentioned in previous chapters might also support the protestors' position?
3. Of the four activist groups listed in Figure 7.1, which organization would be the most likely not to support the protestors' position?
4. If AOL and Yahoo! wanted to form a trade interest group to counter the activists, which would be more appropriate: a peak interest group or a trade group?
5. If AOL and Yahoo! formed a trade group, what roles would this interest group implement relative to the activists' actions?
6. Which business interest group in Figure 7.2 would be the most likely to support AOL and Yahoo!'s position?
7. What activist strategies may be used to combat AOL and Yahoo!'s proposed e-mail policy?
8. What nonmarketing strategies are available to AOL and Yahoo! for dealing with the activist groups?

SOCIETAL INTEREST GROUP ACTIVISTS

Recall that we defined *society* as including interest groups and the communities affected by business, with *interest groups* defined as nonprofit organizations that promote a cause (Chapter 1). Recall that nonprofits are also known as nongovernmental organizations (NGOs). NGOs play an important role in the business, society, and government interface.[7] Unions are NGOs, thus they are societal interest groups, as are business associations and trade groups. When we discussed societal interest groups in prior chapters, we included both those representing society and business. In this chapter, we define and clearly differentiate them as we expand our coverage. In this section, we discuss societal interest group activists, their objectives and roles, and examples of activists.

Activists

Activist Concepts. In Chapter 2, we discussed how *issues about business* are usually brought to the company by any of its stakeholders because the firm is not meeting expectations, and the stakeholder is pressing the firm to take action to meet its special interest.[8] Societal interest group activists represent their stakeholders and commonly bring issues to business.[9] Thus, *societal interest group activists are advocates of nonprofit organizations that aggressively pursue social issues with business and government to promote their interests.* Many interest groups focus on a single issue as they press business and government to meet their special interests. Some activists use the term *institute* in their name (e.g., **National Workrights Institute,** http://workrights.us). Activists pressure government because businesses will not address some issues unless government intervenes.[10]

Activist groups go beyond the nonprofit organization societal interest group. *Activists include societal interest groups, their members, and anyone interested in their causes.* We just use the term "activist" rather than societal interest group. The activist group encourages its members and anyone interested in its cause to become individual activists who also pressure business and government into supporting their special interest.[11] Due to activist pressure from more than 550 health professionals and NGOs, and fear of more government regulations, **McDonald's** decreased the size of its *Happy Meal* fries and added apple slices.[12] Unfortunately, some extreme activists have used unethical and illegal methods to pressure business. Societal activists also join together in coalitions to form a united activist group supporting the same issue against business while pressuring government to take a stance against business.[13]

Activists are also referred to as *advocates* because they provide support, speak, intercede, and act on their stakeholders' behalf as they plead their case to business, society, and government. Activists are sometimes referred to as *watchdogs* because they protect their stakeholders' interests, and some even refer to this job in their name (e.g., **CEO Pay-Watch**, www.aflcio.org/Corporate-Watch/CEO-Pay-and-the-99, and **Corporate Watch**, www.corpwatch.org).

Operations and Financing. Societal activists are NGOs, so most of them seek revenues to pay their expenses through membership (**Sierra Club**, www.sierraclub.org, and **AARP**, www.aarp.org) and donations (**PETA**, www.peta.org) from supporters, who are sometimes called sponsors. Some businesses donate to activist groups that are pressuring them (**Anheuser-Busch** donates to **MADD**, www.madd.org). In addition to membership and donations, some interest groups get funding from the government or sell services (sometime based on income) to raise money (**Planned Parenthood**, www.plannedparenthood.org, for sexual and reproductive health including abortions**)**. Some interest groups also sell products, such as books and videos (**Focus on the Family**, www.focusonthefamily.com**)** related to their missions, to raise money. Commonly used methods of combining some of these other revenue sources are fund-raising events and activities, such as walk-a-thons and dinners.

Personal and Professional Applications

1. Are you a member of or have you donated to or bought anything from a societal activist?

Learning Outcome 1: Describe the objective and roles of societal activists.

The Objectives and Roles of Activists

The *objective* of an activist is to pressure business and government to take action that they would not have taken on their own to meet the special interests of the activist. Desired business action is to change its activities, policies, and procedures. For example, **Nike** and other companies would not have required their contract manufacturers producing their products in other countries to improve their sweatshop conditions without activist pressure. Activists perform three roles:

1. **Provide information about business activities.** Societal interest group activists provide information about business activities to business, society, and government. Activist watchdogs keep a close eye on business and inform it and others of its activities, with the objective of bringing about business changes. Activists provide facts and figures supporting their side of the issue against business activities. Activists

communicate regularly and frequently (letters, newsletters, phone calls, e-mails, and websites with information) with their members and others interested in their causes to inform them of business activities. Activists try to get the media to run stories about business activities to inform society of issues and to gain public sentiment for their side of the issues. Activists also have direct communication with the government to gain support against business.

2. **Develop nonmarket agenda issues for business**. Note the overlap with the role of the media in providing information (Chapter 6) and developing nonmarket agenda issues. Activists are advocates for society, they tend to protect society from business abusive practices. Business hears about issues through the media and by activists pressuring it to change. Even though many businesses use a stakeholder approach to management (Chapter 2), business tends to see things from its own perspective.[14] Thus, activists help business to understand their stakeholders' point of view, and the importance of the issue to them. Activist pressure requires business to address issues and develop strategies for dealing with them. Refer to Chapter 2 for a discussion of *issues management*—a public affairs management approach to identifying, monitoring, analyzing, and selecting public issues that warrant nonmarket strategies.

3. **Set voluntary standards and influence laws and regulations**. Societal interest groups work with business to set voluntary standards and with the government to influence the development of laws and regulations. Activists work with business and government to get business to meet their special interests, which usually are to benefit society, such as through safer products, healthier workplaces, and cleaner environments in which to work and live. Activists sometimes take businesses and government to court when they don't work with activists to make the changes activists want.

AOL and Yahoo! Case Question 1: What was the role(s) of the activists relative to AOL and Yahoo!'s announcement of a fee-based e-mail service?

The three roles that any activist group can implement are: (1) to provide information about business activities; (2) to develop nonmarket agenda issues for business; and (3) to set voluntary standards and to influence laws and regulations. Although the obvious role that these activist groups were taking relative to the announcement was to establish an issue agenda for business (keeping the use of the Internet free to all users), they were simultaneously informing the public, setting voluntary standards, and indirectly trying to influence laws and regulations.

Personal and Professional Applications

2. How do you and society benefit from societal activists? Give specific examples.

3. Have you taken any activist action against a business?

Societal Interest Group Examples

Big businesses are big targets for activists unless they guard their corporate reputation carefully, and **Walmart,** as the world's largest public company, is one of activists' biggest targets. So businesses are more apt to give in to activist pressure when they believe it will promote a positive external corporate image.[15] We have already listed and discussed many societal interest groups. Review Chapters 1–6 for examples, including MADD, CEO Pay Watch, and the Red Cross.

AOL and Yahoo! Case Question 2: What other activist groups mentioned in previous chapters might also support the protestors' position?

Figure 7.1 lists all of the activist groups mentioned in previous chapters. The most likely groups to support this protest might include any group that is highly dependent on the use of e-mails to solicit support for its cause. The groups currently supporting this protest include public rights, labor and environmental groups, and online medical communities, including groups like the Consumer Union, Consumer Federation of America, and Public Citizen (consumer activist groups); Teamsters, United Auto Workers, National Teachers Association (NTA), AFL-CIO, Service Employees International Union, United Food and Commercial Workers, Aircraft Mechanics Fraternal Association, Professional Flight Attendants Association, and Airline Pilots Association (labor activist and union groups); and Rainforest Action Network, Group of the South Fork, Greenpeace, and the Sierra Club (environmental groups).

The *Encyclopedia of Associations* by **Dialog** (www.dialog.com) is a comprehensive source of detailed information that lists more than 151,000 nonprofit membership organizations worldwide. Its family of publications includes the *National Organizations of the United States*, which covers U.S. associations of national scope; *International Organizations*, which covers multinational, binational, and non-U.S. national associations; and *Regional, State, and Local Organizations of the United States*, which covers U.S. associations with interstate, state, intrastate, city, or local scope or membership. It provides addresses and descriptions of professional societies, trade associations, labor unions, cultural and religious organizations, fan clubs, and other groups of all types.[16] For more information, visit its website.

Let's discuss four associations in greater detail here; see Figure 7.1 for a list of activists and what they do. Visit their websites for more information.

ETHICAL DILEMMA 7.1 Going into a "Song and Dance" or Harpooning the Whaling Industry? Greenpeace versus Sea Shepherds

In February 2011, in the midst of Japan's widely criticized research whale hunt, the Japanese Agriculture Minister Michihiko Kano called the whaling fleet home months ahead of plan and hundreds short of its kill quota. The reason given for the abrupt end to the whaling season was harassment by an NGO called the Sea Shepherd Conservation Society (Sea Shepherds). For years, the Japanese fleet had taken pride in its ability to outrun environmental activists, and Japan had refused to put an end to its research whaling operations in the face of resolutions from the International Whaling Commission (IWC) and repeated cessation requests. Ultimately, it was confrontation instigated by a renegade group, rather than any international resolution or NGO pressure, that brought an abrupt end to Japan's controversial whaling practices.

In the Southern Ocean, two types of environmental campaigns have targeted the whaling industry. One approach, employed by Greenpeace, utilizes consumer boycotts and protests to encourage divestment from the industry. The other approach, taken by the Sea Shepherds, uses a fleet of ships to directly intervene in and obstruct whaling operations in the Southern Ocean.

Greenpeace's approach exemplifies protest activism, which consists of publicly organized, undoubtedly legal activities meant to put indirect pressure on the governmental or private entities that are purportedly violating international law. This law-promoting or perhaps law-prescribing function aspires to shift public policy and community expectations. Breaking the law is not recommended. The Sea Shepherds' approach, in contrast, exemplifies interventionist activism, a model that involves either borderline or blatantly illegal tactics to confront violators directly. Interventionist action generally includes law invocation and direct application of force to implement existing laws and policies.[17]

Anthony L. I. Moffa in Yale's *Journal of International Law* concluded that "the abrupt end of the Japanese whaling season demonstrates that environmental NGOs now have the ability to compel compliance with international commitments through unilateral action . . . that despite serious drawbacks, there are certain circumstances under which NGOs should adopt more interventionist activism to enforce international environmental law."[18]

Questions

1. What are the roles of Sea Shepherds and Greenpeace as activist groups in this case? Do these roles overlap?
2. How does the existence of multiple activist groups complement, complicate, and/or produce potential conflict in this matter for the activists? For the Japanese Whaling industry? For the International Whaling Commission?
3. What might be some ethical dilemmas facing an activist group such as Sea Shepherds given their illegal terrorist-like activities?
4. Given Greenpeace's ineffectiveness using legal protest activism, what ethical dilemmas might they face in using confrontational tactics with a similar problem?
5. How would you have tried to get the Japanese Agriculture Ministry to cease whaling operations? Protest or intervention activism?

Public Citizen	a consumer advocate to the government
Consumer Federation of America (CFA)	a consumer advocate, source of information and education, and service activist group
Common Cause	a public advocate for the public interest in the political process, holding elected leaders accountable
Center for Public Integrity	a nonadvocacy institute that provides investigative journalism on issues of public concern

■ **Figure 7.1:** Societal Interest Groups and Their Functions

Public Citizen (PC). *Public Citizen is a consumer advocate to the government.* Public Citizen serves as the people's voice in the nation's capital. To be more specific, PC (www.publiccitizen.org) is a national nonprofit consumer advocacy organization with more than 80,000 members that represents consumer interests to Congress, the executive branch, and the courts. Its overarching goal is to ensure that all citizens are represented in the halls of power. PC fights for openness and democratic accountability in government; for the right of consumers to seek redress in the courts; for clean, safe, and sustainable energy sources; for social and economic justice in trade policies; for strong health, safety, and environmental protections; and for safe, effective, and affordable prescription drugs and health care. PC has five policy groups: Congress Watch division, the Energy Program, Global Trade Watch, the Health Research Group, and Litigation Group.[19]

Consumer Federation of America (CFA). *The Consumer Federation of America is a consumer advocate, source of information and education, and service activist group.* CFA (www.consumerfed.org), as an association of nonprofit consumer organizations, advances the consumer interest through research, advocacy, education, and service. In more detail, CFA provides consumers a well-reasoned and articulate voice in decisions that affect their lives. CFA's professional staff gathers facts, analyzes issues, and disseminates information to the public, policy makers, and the rest of the consumer movement. CFA brings some 300 nonprofits together to represent millions of people, enabling CFA to speak for virtually all American consumers.[20]

Common Cause. *Common Cause is an advocate for the public interest in the political process, holding elected leaders accountable.* Common Cause (www.commoncause.org) is a nonpartisan, grassroots organization dedicated to restoring the core values of American democracy, reinventing an open, honest, and accountable government that serves the public interest, and empowering ordinary people to make their voices heard in the political process. With about 435,000 members, it represents everyone against special interests and for government of, by, and for the people.[21]

Center for Public Integrity. The *Center for Public Integrity is a nonadvocacy institute that provides investigative journalism on issues of public concern.* The Center for Public Integrity (www.publicintegrity.org) is one of America's oldest and largest nonpartisan, nonprofit investigative news organizations. Its mission is to reveal abuses of power, corruption, and dereliction of duty by powerful public and private institutions in order to motivate them to operate with honesty, integrity, accountability, and to put the public interest first. *iWatch News* is the Center's online publication dedicated to investigative and accountability reporting. It provides original and exclusive daily stories as well as in-depth investigations and commentary.[22]

AOL and Yahoo! Case Question 3: Of the four activist groups listed in Figure 7.1, which organization would be the most likely not to support the protestors' position?

Three of the four activist groups discussed (Public Citizen, Consumer Federation of America, and Common Cause) are advocacy groups whose purpose is to support consumer interests by advocating to the government, businesses, and elected officials. Only the Center for Public Integrity is a nonadvocacy interest group that provides investigative journalism on issues of public concern and would therefore solely report the issue rather than take a position and advocate on behalf of consumers.

> **Personal and Professional Applications**
>
> 4. Has a business where you work(ed), or the producers of products it sells, been pressured by activists?

BUSINESS INTEREST GROUPS

Business interest groups are part of the society nonmarket environment. Business interest groups are not part of the business market environment because they are nonprofit organizations representing business interests for societal issues. (See Model 1.1, p. 5, for an illustration.) However, because we are distinguishing them from interest groups that often advocate against business, we refer to them here as business interest groups. In this section, we discuss business interest groups and their objectives and roles and give some business association and trade group examples.

> Learning Outcome 2: Compare and contrast societal interest groups' and business interest groups' operations and financing.

Business Associations and Trade Groups

Business interest groups are nonprofit organizations comprised of groups of firms joined together to advocate their interest on issues. Business interest groups are commonly called *associations*, *organizations*, and *groups*. There are two major types of business interest groups: peak associations and trade groups.

> Learning Outcome 3: Explain the difference between peak and trade groups and their advantages and disadvantages.

Peak and Trade Groups. *Peak interest groups represent businesses from several industries on a broad range of general business interest issues.* Peaks are also called *umbrella organizations*. Peak associations include the **Chamber of Commerce**, the **Better Business Bureau**, the **Business Roundtable**, and the **National Federation of Independent Business**. We describe these four associations later in this section.

Trade groups represent businesses on a narrower range of industry- or business-specific interest issues. Trade groups include the **National Automobile Dealers Association** (**NADA**, www.nada.org), **National Association of Home Builders** (**NAHB**, www.nahb.org), **National Association of Realtors** (**NAR**, www.realtor.org), and **American Petroleum Institute** (**API**, ww.api.org). See Figure 7.2 and identify which are peak and which are trade associations.

Peaks groups are fewer in number compared to trade groups. Peaks have the advantage of representing large numbers of companies and industries with large resources, but a disadvantage is that their members have different interests that sometimes conflict, making unified advocacy difficult at times. More than 6,000 trade associations represent companies from virtually every industry and line of business. Trade groups have the advantage of more unity of interest, but the disadvantage of smaller size and fewer resources.

Here is an example of the power and influence that trade associations can have over government laws and regulations. For years, the **NADA** has kept the government from dramatically increasing fuel efficiency (miles per gallon) of autos stating it would increase cost and hurt sales, and jobs.[23] The **rental-car industry** did a good job of preventing or minimizing tax increases on rentals. However, the trade group was dissolved, leaving the rental car industry without an advocate to the government. Later the same year rental-car taxes increased to the point of almost doubling the cost of renting an economy car in some locations.[24]

Dual Membership. To gain the advantages and minimize the disadvantages of peak and trade groups, many businesses belong to both types of organizations and often more than one peak and trade group. Most large businesses also do their own advocating.

Operations and Financing. Like societal interest groups, business interest groups have members that provide the interest group with revenues, but its members are mainly businesses whereas societal members are usually individuals. Unlike societal interest groups, business interest groups generally do not solicit donations or do fund-raising for their own use, nor do they generally get government funding. Business interest groups also tend to provide many more services to their members, some for a fee, than societal interest groups. Therefore, they raise more revenue than societal interest groups through membership products and services by selling services and some goods.

AOL and Yahoo! Case Question 4: If AOL and Yahoo! wanted to form a trade group to counter the activists, which would be more appropriate: a peak interest group or a trade group?

Peak interest groups represent businesses from several industries on a broad range of general business interest issues, while trade groups represent businesses on a narrower range of industry- or business-specific interest issues. Since the activist groups are focusing on a specific business interest, charging for higher level e-mail service, a trade group would be the more appropriate interest group to use to counter the activist groups.

Personal and Professional Applications

5. What are the business interest groups that represent your current and/or future profession or trade?
6. Are you, or do you plan to be, a member of any professional or trade associations?
7. Is a business where you work(ed) a member of any business interest groups? Identify it as a peak or trade association.

Learning Outcome 4: Describe the objectives and the roles of business interest groups.

The Objectives and Roles of Business Interest Groups

For-profit businesses interact with nonprofit business interest groups, and many are members of both.[25] Business interest groups serve a variety of market and nonmarket functions.

The *objectives* of business interest groups are to advocate to society and government and to provide services to their members. In so doing, they perform four roles.

1. **Provide information.** Business interest groups provide information to business, society, and government. One of their functions is to collect market and industry statistics, much of which is made public and available on their websites. Some information is available only to members. Business interest groups also monitor potential and current legislative activity, regulatory rule making, and administrative actions for their members to keep them informed of issues that can affect business operations and profits. So, like societal activists, business interest groups also help to set the business-issues agenda through the information provided to their members.

2. **Advocate the business side of the issue.** Business interest groups regularly present the business side of the issue to other business, society, and government organizations. Business interest groups often advocate in response to being pressured by societal activists for changes in their business practices. Collective action of businesses being represented by interest groups reduces the costs of lobbying and grassroots efforts.

   Here is an example of a business interest group pressuring businesses. The **Recording Industry Association of America (RIAA,** www.riaa.org**)** is against file sharing, claiming it violates copyright laws and deprives artists of royalties due to the decrease in record sales. The RIAA sent cease-and-desist letters to several file-sharing companies, including **BearShare**, **LimeWire**, and **WinMX**, asking them to stop activities that allowed users to download copyrighted music.[26]

3. **Provide member services.** In addition to information and advocacy, most business interest groups also provide a variety of services to their members, sometimes at extra cost.

4. **Set voluntary standards and influence laws and regulations.** Business interest groups often set a variety of voluntary standards for their members, including codes of ethics and conduct. Trade associations often develop technical standards for their industry, such as establishing uniform sizing for certain products. They also work with societal interest groups to set voluntary standards.[27] Like societal activists, they work with the government to influence the development of laws and regulations that meet their interests, often in opposition of activist groups.[28]

AOL and Yahoo! Case Question 5: If AOL and Yahoo! formed a trade group, what roles would this interest group implement relative to the activists' actions?

Trade groups, like their societal counterparts, provide information, advocate for business's side of the issue, provide member services, and set voluntary standards to influence laws and regulations. The trade group would enact all of these roles and decide, with its members, what nonmarket strategies it would employ in order to deal with the activist groups.

Personal and Professional Applications

8. How do you and society benefit from business interest groups? Give specific examples.

9. Have you been involved in any activist action for a business?

Business Interest Group Examples

We have already listed and discussed many business interest groups. Review Chapters 1–6 for examples including NAR, Society for Business Ethics, and ISO.

Of the thousands of business interest groups, let's discuss four peak organizations in more detail here; see Figure 7.2 for a list of interest groups and what they do. Visit their websites for more information.

Better Business Bureau (BBB). *The Better Business Bureau (BBB) is a neutral third-party interest group that helps consumers and businesses maintain an ethical marketplace.* The BBB vision is an ethical marketplace where buyers and sellers can trust each other (www.bbb.org). BBB's mission is to be the leader in advancing marketplace trust by: creating a community of trustworthy businesses, setting standards for marketplace trust, encouraging and supporting best practices, celebrating marketplace role models, and denouncing substandard marketplace behavior. The BBB system in the United States extends across the nation with local BBBs. Business accreditation is voluntary and the firm must meet the BBB standards, agree to follow the highest principles of business ethics and voluntary self-regulation, and have a proven record of marketplace honesty and integrity.[29] It has around 385,000 accredited businesses.[30]

The BBB is somewhat between a societal interest group and business interest group because it is a neutral third party. Its website has a business and consumer section, and one for charities and donors. It tells consumers about businesses and charities (reviews) and whether they have received complaints about the firm. The BBB is stepping up its online effort as more consumers are now turning to review sites like **Yelp** and **Angie's List**.[31]

U.S. Chamber of Commerce. *The U.S. Chamber of Commerce is the largest business advocate to government and society.* It is the world's largest business organization, representing the interest of more than 3 million businesses of all sizes, sectors, and regions (www.uschamber.org). It includes hundreds of associations, thousands of local chambers, and is international. Its core mission is to fight for business and free enterprise before Congress, the White House, regulatory agencies, the courts, the court of public opinion, and governments around the world.[32] The local Chambers are also needed to make business's case to Congress.[33]

Business Roundtable (BRT). The *Business Roundtable is an association of chief executive officers of leading U.S. corporations that serves as a business advocate to gov-*

Better Business Bureau (BBB)	a neutral third-party interest group that helps consumers and businesses maintain an ethical marketplace
U.S. Chamber of Commerce	the largest business advocate to government and society
Business Roundtable	an association of chief executive officers of leading U.S. corporations that serves as a business advocate to government
National Federation of Independent Business (NFIB)	a small and independent business advocate to government that serves as a key resource to its members

■ **Figure 7.2:** Peak Business Interest Groups and Their Functions *ernment.* BRT (www.brt.org) consists of U.S. corporations with more than $6 trillion in annual revenues and a workforce of more than 14 million employees. Through uniting and amplifying the diverse business perspectives and voices of America's top CEOs, BRT innovates and advocates to help expand economic opportunity for all Americans. It uses direct personal participation of its CEO members, who present government with reasoned alternatives and positive policy suggestions. BRT identifies issues early, employs careful research, and understands the problems faced by government as well as business. Roundtable CEOs are surveyed to report their views on the business environment, and BRT publishes the *CEO Economic Outlook* quarterly.[34]

National Federation of Independent Business (NFIB). The *National Federation of Independent Business (NFIB) is a small and independent business advocate to government that serves as a key resource to its members.* The NFIB (www.nfib.org) is the leading advocacy organization representing small and independent businesses in Washington, DC, and all 50 state capitals. NFIB members are a diverse group consisting of high-tech manufacturers, retailers, farmers, professional service providers, and many more. The NFIB sets its public policy positions by regularly polling its members and acting on their advice by carrying a unified message to Congress and the state legislatures on behalf of small business owners.

The NFIB is a key business resource; it gives its members power in the marketplace. By pooling the purchasing power of its members, it gives them access to many business products at discounts. It also provides timely information designed to help small businesses succeed.[35]

AOL and Yahoo! Case Question 6: Which business interest group in Figure 7.2, Peak Business Interest Groups and Their Functions, would be the most likely to support AOL and Yahoo!'s position?

The business interest groups in Figure 7.2 are all peak interest groups and, therefore, are generally unlikely to represent the interests of online Internet service providers like AOL/Yahoo! Of the four listed, however, the Better Business Bureau, a neutral third-party interest group that helps consumers and businesses maintain an ethical marketplace, would certainly have an interest in the issue, given the fact that consumer interest groups perceive that their interests are at stake. Ironically, the NFIB, which advocates on behalf of small and independent businesses, may join the societal interest groups if they perceive smaller firms as experiencing a competitive disadvantage through higher e-mail costs.

ETHICAL DILEMMA 7.2 Coca-Cola, and PepsiCo: Losing the Fizz over the American Legislative Exchange Council

Two of America's best-known companies, Coca-Cola and PepsiCo, have dropped their memberships in the American Legislative Exchange Council, a low-profile conservative organization behind the national proliferation of "stand your ground" gun laws.[36]

"The American Legislative Exchange Council works to advance the fundamental principles of free-market enterprise, limited government, and federalism at the state level through a nonpartisan public-private partnership of America's state legislators, members of the private sector and the general public."[37] ALEC promotes business-friendly legislation in state capitals and drafts model bills for state legislatures to adopt. They range from little-noticed pro-business bills to more controversial measures, including voter-identification laws and stand your ground laws based on the Florida statute. About two-dozen states now have such laws. Florida's stand your ground law has been cited in the slaying of Trayvon Martin, an unarmed teen who was shot and killed by neighborhood watch volunteer George Zimmerman.

"We have a long-standing policy of not taking positions on issues that don't have a direct bearing on our company or on our industry," said Coca-Cola spokeswoman Diana Garza Ciarlante, after the soft drink giant dropped its membership in ALEC. Coca-Cola's announcement came hours after a civil rights group, ColorOfChange. org, launched an online drive calling on Coca-Cola to stop underwriting the ALEC agenda on voter ID laws in several states. PepsiCo, another soft drink giant, belonged to ALEC for 10 years. A company vice president told ColorOfChange that it wouldn't renew for 2012. An ALEC spokeswoman said the company told them it pulled out for budgetary reasons.

Progressive groups and shareholder activists want to drive a wedge between ALEC and its corporate members. "There was no real downside because there was no public accountability. There was no transparency," said Doug Clopp, deputy director of programs with Common Cause. "Everything up until now had been done behind closed doors, and these memberships were not known to the American people." Common Cause, a nonprofit citizens lobbying group, is also part of the campaign calling on corporate members to end their partnership with ALEC.[38]

Questions

1. As a business-focused institute, what services does ALEC provide the business community and its customers?
2. How does the departure of firms like Coca-Cola and PepsiCo from ALEC highlight ALEC's need to reexamine some of their nonpartisan activities and/or redefine their mission?
3. Why would social interest groups like ColorOfChange and Common Cause challenge ALEC's activist agenda by criticizing its business members?
4. If you were ALEC, what nonmarketing strategies would you employ to address social and shareholder activist groups' actions in terms of your organization and its corporate members?

Personal and Professional Applications

10. Is a business where you work(ed) a member of any of the four peak business interest groups discussed? How much are the dues, and what benefits does(did) it get through its membership?

ACTIVIST STRATEGIES AGAINST BUSINESS

Now that we understand the difference between societal activist groups and business interest groups, let's discuss the strategies activists use against business to pressure it to meet their needs. Throughout the first six chapters, we focused on how business develops strategies to deal with stakeholder issues. Here we change the focus to the strategies that activists use against business. In this section, we discuss activists' assessment of likely business strategies and seven common activist strategies against business: grassroots efforts; demonstrations, including picketing and rallies; boycotts; news media relations and advocacy advertising; building coalitions; appeals to government; and litigation.

Activists' Assessment of Likely Business Strategies

Activists are effective at developing and implementing strategies that pressure business to change.[39] For example, **Coca-Cola, Pepsi,** and other soft drink manufacturers were pressured from consumer advocates and parents and agreed to halt sales of sugared sodas in some schools and limit the size and caloric content of other beverages they sell in schools. The agreement goes beyond the voluntarily restrictions adopted earlier by the **American Beverage Association (ABA,** www.ameribev.org), the industry's interest group.[40] Activist shareholder **Relational Investors** is pressuring **PepsiCo** to separate its **Frito-Lay** unit from the rest of the company.[41]

As business develops nonmarket strategies, so do activists. Figure 2.5 presented a list of strategies used by societal interest groups against business. However, before activists select their strategies against a business, they consider how the business will react to each strategy to determine which strategy will most likely get the best results. They also use a combination of strategies.[42] **Common Cause** employs a number of strategies, both internally as well as in coalition with partners and other stakeholders, including grassroots and media relations strategies.[43] Next we explain seven activist strategies that are shown in Figure 7.3.

> Learning Outcome 5: List and briefly explain seven strategies activists use against business.

Grassroots Efforts

Grassroots efforts involve getting stakeholder support to pressure organizations to meet activists' special interests. Both activists and businesses use grassroots strategies against each other, but the stockholders and special interest groups are commonly in opposition. Grassroots strategies show the support of the people whom the societal interest group represents. The common approach is to have the societal interest group contact the business, and often the government as well, directly and to ask its members and supporters of the issue to contact the business and government directly to pressure for change. The larger the grassroots efforts, the more pressure there is on the government to investigate and on the business to voluntarily change its practices. Several unions, including **AFL-CIO** and the **Teamsters**, used a grassroots strategy by asking their members and others to contact

---

Grassroots Efforts
Demonstrations: Picketing and Rallies
Boycotts
News Media Relations and Advocacy Advertising
Building Coalitions
Appeal to Government
Litigation

■ **Figure 7.3:** Activist Strategies Against Business

their congressional representatives and encourage them to pass the Employee Free Choice Act (EFCA) that would make it easier to establish unions in businesses.[44]

Activist grassroots efforts mobilize members and supporters to contact business and government in one or more of the following ways:

1. **Visits**. One of the most powerful methods, but also the most difficult to accomplish, is to get supporters to visit the business or government to ask it to meet activists' special interest on the issue.

2. **Calls**. Activists ask supporters to call the business or government to protest the business activity.

3. **Letters**. Activists ask supporters to write personalized letters to the business or government.

4. **Preprinted letters and postcards**. Activists send them to their supporters asking them to mail the letters or postcards to the business or government. Preprinting makes it easier for supporters.

5. **Grass-tops**. Activists try to get prominent citizens (such as celebrities) to pressure the business or government and to attract more supporters.

6. **Internet, e-mails, and cyber advocacy**. The Internet has changed the way activists communicate with members and supporters.[45] Prior to the Internet, activists primarily had to call or mail supporters during grassroots campaigns. Today, the Internet and *computerized phone banks* have increased the speed of contacting supporters while reducing cost, making communication much more effective. Activists can quickly and cheaply ask millions of people to contact business and government. Activists are using typed e-mails that supporters can simply and quickly send at no cost. Thus, grassroots support has increased via e-mail. Some supporters who would not visit, call, or write are willing to quickly click and send e-mails. Activists also have professional websites that provide up-to-the-minute news on their latest activities.

Personal and Professional Applications

11. Have you participated in a grassroots effort against a business?

12. Has a business where you work(ed), or a company whose products it sells, had a grassroots strategy used against it?

Demonstrations: Picketing and Rallies

When societal interest group unions go on strike, they picket the business asking people not to be customers of the firm. Activist groups also put on rallies and picket. For example, pro-choice activists of the **National Organization of Women (NOW,** www.now. org) picketed **Domino's Pizza** outlets, claiming the company opposed abortion rights because its founding owner Thomas Monaghan gave a personal (not business) contribution to the **Committee to End Tax-Funded Abortions,** even though Dominos had no company policy on abortion.[46] Demonstrations can drive customers away and hurt a corporate image, whether the firm did something wrong or not.

Personal and Professional Applications

13. Have you participated in a demonstration against a business?

14. Has a business where you work(ed), or a company whose products it sells, been demonstrated against?

Boycotts

Boycotts are activist requests that society not do business with a firm. Boycotts can be in combination with other strategies. For example, **NOW** activists also called for a boycott against Dominos. **Ford Motor Co**. was asked by 44 pro-family groups to stop taking sides on social issues and stop supporting homosexual groups. After Ford refused to do so, the 44 activist groups called for a boycott against Ford.[47] The **National Rifle Association (NRA)** boycotted **Conoco-Phillips** for fighting an Oklahoma law preventing a firm from firing an employee for keeping a gun in the car at work.[48] Businesses sometimes give in to boycotts, seeking to further their own self-interest.

Personal and Professional Applications

15. Have you participated in a boycott against a business?

16. Has a business where you work(ed), or a company whose products it sells, been boycotted?

News Media Relations and Advocacy Advertising

Activists are good at developing media relations and getting stories against business in the news; they even get professional PR help. Both activists and business use the media against each other, but the media's side of the issue is commonly in opposition to business (Chapter 6). Activists use information strategies (outside sources, experts, and stakeholder support) to tell their side of the issue. Activists know what makes a story newsworthy (Chapter 6) and which news reporters will help in telling their story. The broader the news coverage and the more public sentiment activists can get against business, the greater the odds are that business will change to meet activists' special interests. The **AFL-CIO** *Executive PayWatch* sends reports to the press and posts them on its website to help pressure business into reevaluating such high compensation, and the information is also reported in academic journals.[49]

Like business, social activists also use advocacy advertising to tell their side of the issue. The **Humane Society** (www.humanesociety.org) ran TV ads to crack down on farmers raising livestock in cramped quarters, and has won new state regulations.[50] The **Sierra Club** (www.sierraclub.org) and other environmental groups took out advertisements against the judicial appointment of Judge Samuel Alito in hopes of gaining public sentiment against his appointment to the **U.S. Supreme Court**.[51]

Personal and Professional Applications

17. Have you participated in a media or advertising strategy against a business?

18. Has a business where you work(ed), or a company whose products it sells, had negative media coverage?

Building Coalitions

For any given societal issue, multiple interest groups will sometimes work together in a coalition.[52] *Coalitions include diverse organizations and interest groups working together temporarily for a common interest.* Both activists and businesses use coalitions against each other. The organizations can be business, nonprofit, and government, and the interest groups can be societal or business. In opposition to Judge Alito's appointment, more than a half-dozen environmental groups cooperated, voicing their concerns.[53] Coalitions allow the members to share resources and to coordinate their efforts for increased effectiveness at attaining the common goal.

Businesses also work in coalitions with nonprofits and activists.[54] For example, the **United Egg Producers** (www.unitedegg.org) partnered with their prior enemy the **Humane Society** in order to improve conditions for raising chickens.[55] **Gibson Guitar** uses scarce woods and teamed up with **Greenpeace** and other environmentalist groups to show it is serious about preserving forests.[56] Also, the **National Center for Missing and Exploited Children (NCMEC,** www.ncmec.org) lists featured partners in its efforts to prevent abductions and abuse (including **AOL, Old Navy, Microsoft, Sprint,** and **Walmart).**[57]

Personal and Professional Applications

19. Have you participated in a coalition strategy against a business?

20. Has a business where you work(ed), or a company whose products it sells, had a coalition strategy used against it? If yes, who was in the coalition?

Appeals to Government

Activists also put direct pressure on government to take action against business. The government action against business can be to investigate business wrongdoing or to change laws and regulations to force business to change. Recall that Chapter 6 discussed consumer rights, including the right to be heard. Consumers have assurance that consumer interests will receive full and sympathetic consideration in the formulation and implementation of government policies, laws, and regulations. Consumers have the right to fair and expeditious treatment in the administration of cases brought to agencies and the courts against businesses. Activists also lobby government to influence laws and regulations. We will discuss lobbying in detail in the government chapters.

Constant pressure by tobacco-control advocates called for the government to restrict tobacco use.[58] **American Family Association (AFA,** www.afa.net) contacted the **U.S. Department of Justice (DOJ,** www.justice.gov) and asked it to investigate **Movie Gallery** for violation of federal obscenity statutes. Recall that if the government finds a business in violation of any laws and regulations, it has the power to require the business to change its practices, to fine it, or even to close it.

Personal and Professional Applications

21. Have you complained to the government against a business?

22. Has a business where you work(ed), or a company whose products it sells, had to respond to government inquiries as a result of activist pressures?

Litigation

Activists also have the right to take a business to court. The **Air Line Pilots Association** (www.alpa.org) sued **United Continental Holdings** over inadequate safety issues that failed to meet passengers' expectations.[59] The **NBA Players Association** filed a suit against the **National Basketball Association (NBA)** for failing to collectively bargain in good faith.[60] **Public Citizen** has a *Litigation Group* that specializes in bringing lawsuits against businesses; other activists also have litigation groups and outside lawyers. Recall that most lawsuits are settled out of court. Just the threat of litigation often leads businesses to settle, which activists like to call victory over business. Shareholder activist groups got the following businesses to change corporate governance through settlements: **Enterasys Networks**, **Hanover Compressor**, **HCA**, **Homestore**, and **Sprint**.[61]

AOL and Yahoo! Case Question 7: What activist strategies may be used to combat AOL and Yahoo!'s proposed e-mail policy?

The choice and timing of activist strategies are closely tied into what actions AOL and Yahoo! take in order to accommodate the demands of these activist groups. If they are accommodating and want to work with activist groups, little additional action would be required. If AOL and Yahoo! decide to oppose these activist groups and reject developing voluntary standards, then the activist groups may use strategies to convince legislatures to create laws and regulations dealing with Internet access and service pricing.

Personal and Professional Applications

23. Have you participated in a class action or other lawsuit against a business?

24. Has a business where you work(ed), or a company whose products it sells, had a lawsuit filed against it?

Learning Outcome 6: List and briefly explain eight nonmarket strategies businesses use against activists.

Learning Outcome 7: Compare and contrast strategies used by activists and businesses against each other.

BUSINESS STRATEGIES AGAINST ACTIVISTS

Recall that Figure 1.4 (p. 22) lists nonmarket strategies businesses use to deal with issues. Here we expand on the list and explain the strategies. In this section, we discuss the 5 Is Strategic Analysis and eight strategies used in the last step of analysis: gaining community public sentiment for being socially responsible, grand nonmarket strategy, lockouts, grassroots efforts, news media relations and advocacy advertising, building coalitions, appeal to government, and litigation.

5 Is Strategic Analysis

Business has to deal with NGOs.[62] Businesses should take a stakeholder management approach to strategy formulation and implementation.[63] When selecting strategies to deal with activists, businesses must consider their self-interests while creating value for stakeholders by balancing their self-interests. Let's discuss how business selects strategies to deal with issues or how business selects nonmarket strategies as part of the 5 Is Strategic Analysis (Chapter 2).

1. **Issue identification**. In most cases, the issue is brought to the business by activists, so the first step is to determine the stage of the life cycle (Figure 2.4, p. 53) the issue is in and which activist strategy, or combination, is being used against the business. Issues are commonly brought to business in the early stages of the issue life cycle, so business often has a chance to influence or even stop the issue from progressing through the life cycle. How much public sentiment will there be against the business side of the issue? Great public sentiment often accelerates the issue through the life cycle.

2. **Interested strategic stakeholders**. Who are the activists? Is there one societal interest group or a coalition? What is the likelihood of other activists joining against the business? Does the activist have a newsworthy story the news media will cover to influence public sentiment against the business? Which stakeholders are with and against the firm on the issue? Unfortunately, the interests of activists and the interests of the business often are in direct conflict because changing to meet activist interests tends to cost the firm financial and/or other resources.

3. **Incentive of stakeholders**. What is the objective of the stakeholders? Have the activists stated clearly what action they want the business to take to satisfy their interest? If the business does take the requested action, will the activist stop pressuring the firm with its strategies, and if the firm doesn't take action will the activist step up its strategies (demonstrations, boycotts)? Is the request (a) legitimate and (b) urgent? If so, business is usually more willing to accommodate activist requests. What (c) power does the activist have? Can the activist hurt the performance of the firm? The more legitimate, urgent, and powerful the activist is, the greater the need to deal with the issue to resolve it. Managers choosing not to ignore the activist group often agree to meet with it to discuss the issue to get information to answer the questions in steps 1–3 of the strategic analysis.

4. **Information—objectives**. Information strategies providing facts are an important part of developing strategies to deal with issues that affect public sentiment. What information strategies (use of facts and figures, outside sources, expert testimony, and stakeholder support) will the firm use to present its side of the issue to the activists, the public, and possibly the media and government? What is the objective of the business in dealing with the activist?

5. **Interaction strategies**. (a) Which alternative nonmarket strategies (discussed next) can be used to deal with the issue? (b) What will be the market and nonmarket reaction and consequences to the strategic action? (c) Which strategy or combination of strategies should be selected to deal with the activist? (d) Implement and evaluate the strategy. Business often meets again with activists to present its side of the issue and to discuss what, if any, action it will take to meet the activists' interests. The strategy may be to negotiate or work with the activists to resolve the issue; ignoring activists does not result in any meetings, and the opposition strategies often do not require a meeting with activists. See Figure 7.4 for a list of strategies.

Gaining Community Public Sentiment for Being Socially Responsible
Grand Nonmarket Strategies
Lockouts
Grassroots Efforts
News Media Relations and Advocacy Advertising
Building Coalitions
Appeal to Government
Litigation

■ **Figure 7.4:** Nonmarket Strategies Businesses Use Against Activists

Gaining Community Public Sentiment for Being Socially Responsible

Of the eight strategies, gaining public sentiment for being socially responsible is a proactive strategy to help prevent activists from taking issues to business or for resolving them in the early stages. Socially responsible businesses (Chapter 4) are effective at *issues management*—identifying, monitoring, analyzing, and selecting public issues that warrant nonmarket strategies (Chapter 2)—and they are less likely to be activist targets. When they are targets of activists, the relations are usually less hostile because the firm strives to create value for all relevant stakeholders. **Whole Foods** and **Starbucks** use this strategy because they believe that corporate reputation is a means to success, not a by-product of it. Starbucks believes that its guiding principles, including "providing a great work environment" and "contributing positively to our community" are the best advertising.[64] Although businesses may try to head off problems proactively, managers need to formulate strategies to react to activists.[65]

> **Personal and Professional Applications**
>
> 25. Has a business where you work(ed), or a producer of the products it sells, used the Gaining Community Public Sentiment for Being Socially Responsible strategy?

Grand Nonmarket Strategies

When a societal interest group, which we call activists, bring an issue to a business, the business has to determine its grand or overall approach to dealing with the activist issue. *Grand nonmarket strategies include donating, ignoring, opposing, negotiating, and working with activists.* It is important to realize that it is not unusual for a business to have different grand strategies based on the specific issue. So a business can be facing multiple issues at the same time and using one or all of the following grand strategies for different issues at the same time.

1. **Donate to activists**. This proactive approach works to develop and maintain relations with activists so that they are less likely to take action against the firm. **Anheuser-Busch** uses this strategy by giving donations to **Mothers Against Drunk Drivers (MADD)**. Donations are not advisable when activists bring an issue to business and the money might be viewed as a bribe to pay off the activists to stop pressuring business.

2. **Ignore activists.** The business has the option of ignoring the activist. For example, don't even respond to any correspondence by activists or their supporters. This strategy often gets the activists angry and creates more hostility toward the business, but it can work with weak activists that have few supporters and fail to gain new supporters and media coverage of the issue.

   Activist author **Eric Schlosser** has criticized the fast-food industry, especially **McDonald's**, by claiming that fast-food companies are responsible for the nation's childhood obesity epidemic and criticizing them for being low-wage employers. However, fast-food companies have refused to discuss any of the issues raised by Schlosser's work or to appear in any public forum with him.[66]

3. **Oppose activists.** For some issues, business believes strongly that it is right and the activists are wrong; usually the firm will have negative consequences if it changes strategy to satisfy the activists. Thus, the firm does not want to change strategy to meet the interests of the activists and prepares to fight. Opposition strategies are also called the *defensive mode* because the firm wants to maintain things as they are. Tobacco companies, **Altria** and **Reynolds American**, face constant pressure and continue to defend their products against activists who would like to stop the sales of tobacco products.[67] **McDonald's** was pressured to drop *Ronald McDonald* and toys from its *Happy Meals*; but it refused and publicly stated: "Ronald isn't going anywhere—nor are the toys."[68]

   Although businesses sometimes decide that they have to fight, firms generally prefer to negotiate with activists in order to avoid the negative publicity and possible damage to their corporate reputation. Firms don't like to create enemies, especially powerful ones with strong media ties and the ability to gain negative news stories that can hurt the firms' performance.

4. **Negotiate with activists.** For issues that activists have a legitimate right to bring up and in areas where they are powerful, businesses are willing to negotiate, usually voluntarily when they fear negative consequences to the firm, such as lost sales, are greater than the cost of compliance. Both the business and the activist get some of what they want and give up something in return. Negotiating is also referred to as the *accommodating mode* because the firm is willing to *co-opt* other groups to its viewpoint and it adapts to the changing environment without a departure from the status quo. Professional activists are more difficult to co-opt, but they can be more practical.[69] The **National Advertising Division (NAD**, www.nadreview.org) includes input from activists in setting voluntary standards for ethics in advertising.

   Under pressure from the anti-childhood-obesity alliance between the **William J. Clinton Foundation** (www.clintonfoundation.org) and the **American Heart Association** (www.heart.org), **Coca-Cola**, **Pepsi**, and others agreed to stop selling sugar soda in some schools, but they negotiated to keep water, unsweetened fruit drinks, and low-fat or nonfat milk products in elementary and middle schools; high schools also sell diet soft drinks and sports drinks (which contain sugar).[70] Thus, the negotiated agreement was primarily to replace the sugar products sold with healthier water and juice. Fighting the change could have resulted in a long and costly battle, and a possible ban on the sale of all Coke and Pepsi products. So negotiating was in the best interest of beverage makers.

5. **Work with activists.** Sometimes it is a good strategy to say, "We want to work with you."[71] In working with activists, the business is more open to meeting the legitimate requests of the activists to help society. This strategy is good when the issue is of minor importance with minimal negative consequences to the business. In working with activists, the business develops positive public sentiment and a reputation for

being socially responsible. Working with activists can also be called the *proactive mode* because the firm is willing to change to benefit itself and its stakeholders or to minimize its losses, which is also in its best interest.

Business generally prefers self-regulation to government regulation. Under pressure from activists and the fear of government regulation, business works with advocates. **McDonald's** was creating a major solid-waste disposal problem and was confronted by **Environmental Defense Fund (EDF**, www.edf.org**).** McDonald's voluntarily worked with EDF and agreed to reduce waste, to recycle, and to change some of its packaging to help solve the problem.[72] Six **cable companies** told a **Senate** committee that they would offer a bundle of family friendly packages even though the cable industry projected lost revenues by bundling any types of programming.[73]

Contingencies are things that may happen. An event, problem, emergency, or expense might arise somewhat unexpectedly, but it needs to be dealt with; therefore, preparations for it require a plan. It is common for business to start at a lower-level strategy for dealing with activists. However, as activists respond to the business strategy, the firm must be flexible and may need to change strategies, such as to stop ignoring the activist and negotiate. After an issue is resolved, the business may begin to donate to the activist.

Recall that strategies should also change as an issue moves through the issue's life cycle (Chapter 2). Another way of thinking about contingency planning is in terms of "if, then" scenarios. For example, if activists get negative media coverage for the issue, then we will stop ignoring them and oppose them with advocacy advertisements.

Personal and Professional Applications

26. Which grand strategy has a business where you work(ed), or a producer of the products it sells, used to deal with activists for a specific issue?

Lockouts

Lockouts occur when the business does not allow employees to come and work, usually only with unionized employees when labor negotiations break down. For example, the **National Football League (NFL)** and the **National Basketball Association (NBA)** both had lockouts in 2011.[74] The NFL locked players out of practice for 136 days until the player representatives for the 32 teams voted to approve a new collective bargaining agreement.[75] The NBA lockout lasted 149 days, delaying the start of the season, and the league cancelled some games.[76] In many industries, it is common to bring in *replacement workers* (called "scabs" by union workers) during a lockout or a strike to keep business operations going, such as at the lockout in the Ohio **Cooper Tire & Rubber** as union picketers jeered at temporary workers who were bused in to do their jobs.[77]

Grassroots Efforts

Like activists, business also may use grassroots efforts. Business often relies on its peak association and trade groups to develop and implement grassroots efforts for it or to coordinate with its own grassroots efforts. However, business usually asks its stakeholders to contact the government in opposition to activists pressuring for new laws and regulations. The business stakeholders are also generally from the market environment and can include stockholder owners, employees, customers and consumers, suppliers, and competitors who will also be affected by a change in business practices required to meet activist interests.

Personal and Professional Applications

27. Has a business where you work(ed), or a company whose products it sells, used grassroots efforts to deal with activists for a specific issue?

News Media Relations and Advocacy Advertising

Like activists, businesses also develop good relations with the news media to get favorable press coverage, and they also use advocacy advertising. The amount of negative press that activists get affects the business's media strategy. Business also uses professional PR practitioners to help develop its media campaign for specific issues. PR consultants are independent and are in a better position to see what is newsworthy within a company.[78]

McDonald's side of the issue against activist Schlosser's work was covered in the news, including an article in the ***Wall Street Journal***. McDonald's publicized the fact that it has brought out healthier choices, including salads, and has shown Ronald McDonald as an ambassador of balanced lifestyles, which includes coverage of him exercising.[79]

Personal and Professional Applications

28. Has a business where you work(ed), or the producers of products it sells, used news media relations and/or advocacy advertising to deal with activists for a specific issue?

Building Coalitions

Like activists, businesses also build coalitions; in fact, coalitions, or partnering with NGOs, have become common practice.[80] On any given issue, multiple businesses and industries, as well as some nonprofits and societal interest groups, have a common interest, and they often join forces to promote their cause through joint action. Business peak associations and trade groups are in and of themselves permanent coalitions that advocate the business side of issues. In addition, peak and trade groups also join together to form coalitions, working together temporarily for a common interest. Individual businesses also build coalitions and work with other groups, sometimes activists, to promote their causes.[81]

A number of federal and state initiatives attempted to restrict global outsourcing, keeping jobs in the United States. Most large corporations realized this issue was a threat to their ability to compete globally. So the **U.S. Chamber of Commerce**, **Business Roundtable**, **National Association of Manufacturers**, other peak and trade industry interest groups, and individual companies joined forces to prevent outsourcing restrictions by forming the formal *Coalition for Economic Growth and American Jobs*, which is a coalition, not a new separate organization.[82]

Personal and Professional Applications

29. Give an example of when you built a coalition to help you get what you wanted.

30. Has a business where you work(ed), or a producer of the products it sells, used coalitions to deal with activists for a specific issue?

Appeals to Government

Like activists, businesses also appeal to the government. But as a strategy against activists, business is usually trying to stop the government from changing the current laws and regulations that will harm it in some way, such as increasing its cost of doing business. So business commonly presents its side of the issue to get government to ignore activists by staying with the status quo. When appealing to the government, it is common to combine this strategy with grassroots efforts and coalitions. When the *Dodd-Frank Wall Street Reform and Consumer Protection Act* of 2009 was being written to address the financial crises by increasing regulation of the financial industry, and after it passed, most financial institutions, including **Wells Fargo** and the **Goldman Sachs Group**, continued to lobby to try to influence the details of the regulations.[83] The Dodd-Frank Law covers 2,300 pages with 400 new regulations.[84]

Businesses also appeal to government by asking for regulation to give them competitive advantage. For example, with big tax preparation companies' suggestion, the Internal Revenue Service **(IRS)** decreed that all tax preparers must register with it, take an exam, and undergo a minimum of 15 hours of continuing education each year. The IRS says it is to protect consumers, but Steve Forbes says it is just another way to put more needless regulations on small independent business while helping large business, and at the same time squeezing more taxes out of small business.[85]

Personal and Professional Applications

31. Has a business where you work(ed), or a producer of the products it sells, appealed to the government in response to dealing with activists for a specific issue?

Litigation

Like activists, businesses also take activists to court. For example, **Cattleman Jim Chilton** filed a defamation lawsuit against the **Center for Biological Diversity** (www.biological-diversity.org), an activist group known for its lawsuits against ranching practices, when it came after him. The jury in the **Arizona Superior Court in Tucson** awarded Chilton $600,000, including $500,000 in punitive damages against the environmental group.[86]

Businesses more often, however, have to defend themselves in court against lawsuits brought against them by activists. Litigation can be very expensive, so it is commonly used as a scare tactic. When push comes to shove, litigation is often the last resort strategy. As discussed, business usually settles out of court.

AOL and Yahoo! Case Question 8: What nonmarketing strategies are available to AOL and Yahoo! to deal with the activist groups?

The nonmarketing strategies available to AOL and Yahoo! are similar to those available to activist groups and include gaining community public sentiment for being socially responsible, grand nonmarket strategies (donating, ignoring, opposing, negotiating, and working with activists), grassroots efforts, news media relations and advocacy advertising, building coalitions, appeal to government, and litigation.

As mentioned in case question 7, the timing and strategies employed by AOL and Yahoo! will depend on the actions of these advocacy groups. These businesses specifically need to determine whether they should be proactive, accommodating, or defensive, based on the apparent strategies of the activist groups and the importance of the issue to the firm's financial performance. Concurrently, AOL and Yahoo! need to develop contingency nonmarket strategies for each possible activist strategy.

For example, if the only actions of activist groups are a series of press releases indicating these groups' displeasure with the new e-mail policy, and the industry ignores the press with no evident retaliation, then no additional action needs to be taken. On the other hand, if the activist groups file charges against both firms (either civil or criminal), then the firms are forced into a defensive mode and must seek legal recourse.

Personal and Professional Applications

32. Has a business where you work(ed), or a producer of the products it sells, brought a lawsuit against an activist or defended itself against a lawsuit?

BUSINESS NONMARKET AND MARKET STRATEGIES AND ETHICS

This chapter is a bit different in that we have just spent an entire section focusing on nonmarket strategies businesses use against activists. So we will be brief in this section.

Information Strategies

Regardless of the strategy business uses against activists, public relations information strategies (Chapter 6) are critically important to good relations with activists. Managers can get their points of interest across to activists by using facts and figures, clearly stating their assumptions, and trying to gain public sentiment and a good corporate reputation. Managers can have outside sources, experts, and other stakeholders support the accuracy and legitimacy of management's side of the issues.

Societal Strategies

Progressive businesses use a stakeholder approach to management to promote their corporate reputation.[87] They are reenvisioning ethics as they look at opportunities to serve stakeholder interests, not at minimizing their impact, to gain social returns on investment beyond financial profits.[88]

Effective businesses are socially responsible, protect their self-interest, voluntarily self-regulate, and maintain ethical relations with all stakeholders when they develop and implement the eight nonmarket strategies against activists. Managers must know and understand activist interests by listening to them and by trying to meet their legitimate needs fairly but within reason.[89] Employing the opposing grand strategy is appropriate in some situations, but businesses are striving to do a better job of being proactive and negotiating and working with activists.

Political and Legal Strategies

In the next section of the book, Government, we will discuss political and legal strategies in detail, as we did with societal strategies for dealing with activists in this chapter.

SUMMARY

The chapter summary is organized to answer the learning outcomes for Chapter 7.

1. **Describe the objective and roles of activists.**

   The objective of activists is to pressure business and government to take action that they would not have taken on their own to meet activists' special interests. Activists play three roles: (1) provide information about business activities to business, society, and government; (2) develop nonmarket agenda issues for business; and (3) work with business to set voluntary standards and with the government to influence the development of laws and regulations.

2. **Compare and contrast societal interest groups' and business interest groups' operations and financing.**

   Societal and business interest groups are similar in that both are nonprofit organizations representing their members and other stakeholders. However, business interest group members are primarily business firms whereas societal members are individuals. They both get revenues from members. On the other hand, societal interest groups also get revenues from donations, fund-raisers, and government funding whereas business interest groups do not. They both get revenues from selling products. However, business interest groups tend to provide more services to their members than societal interest groups, so they raise more revenue by selling products.

3. **Explain the difference between peak and trade groups and their advantages and disadvantages.**

   Peak, or *umbrella, interest groups* represent businesses from several industries on a broad range of general business interest issues. Peaks are fewer in number and have the advantage of representing large numbers of companies and industries with large resources, but a disadvantage is that the members have different interests, which sometimes conflict, making a unified advocacy difficult. *Trade* groups represent businesses on a narrower range of industry- or business-specific interest issues. There are more trade associations representing companies from virtually every industry and line of business. Trade groups have the advantage of greater unity of interest but have the disadvantage of smaller size and fewer resources.

4. **Describe the objectives and roles of business interest groups.**

   The objectives of business interest groups are to advocate to society and government and to provide services to their members. Business interest groups play four roles: (1) provide information to business, society, and government; (2) advocate the business side of the issue to society and government; (3) provide a variety of services to their members; and (4) set voluntary standards for their members, work with societal interest groups to set standards, and work to influence the development of laws and regulations.

5. **List and briefly explain seven strategies activists use against business.**

   (a) *Grassroots efforts* involve getting stakeholder support to pressure organizations to meet a special interest; activists mobilize grassroots supporters to contact business and government in one or more of the following ways: visits, phone calls, letters, preprinted letters and postcards, grass-tops, and the Internet through e-mail.

(b) Activists also use *demonstrations (picketing and rallies)* to pressure business for change.

(c) Activists use *boycotts* to request that society stop doing business with a firm.

(d) Activists give negative stories to the *news media* about businesses and use *advocacy advertising* to gain public sentiment for their cause against business.

(e) Activists use *coalitions* with diverse organizations and interest groups working together temporarily for a common interest against business.

(f) Activists *appeal to government* to take action against business; the action can be to investigate business wrongdoing or to change laws and regulations.

(g) Activists also have the right to bring *litigation* against business. Activists' strategies against business are commonly combined to increase their effect to pressure business to accommodate their special interests on issues.

6. **List and briefly explain eight non-market strategies businesses use against activists.**

The eight nonmarket strategies businesses use against activists are as follows:

1. *Gaining community public sentiment for being socially responsible* is a proactive strategy to help prevent activists from taking issues to business or for resolving them in the early stages.

2. *Grand nonmarket strategies* include donating, ignoring, oppos-

ing, negotiating, and working with activists; grand strategies are developed for the specific issue and do change.

3. *Lockouts* occur when business does not allow employees to come and work.

4. *Grassroots efforts* involve mobilizing business stakeholders from the market environment, which can include stockholder owners, employees, customers and consumers, suppliers, and competitors who will also be affected by a change in business practices to meet activist interests.

5. *News media relations* are developed to get favorable press coverage, and *advocacy advertising* is used to present the business side of the issue to influence public sentiment and corporate reputation.

6. Businesses *build coalitions* to join forces with other stakeholders to promote their common cause through joint action.

7. Businesses commonly *appeal to government* to stop changes in the current laws and regulation that will harm them in some way.

8. As a threat, and often last resort, business can use costly *litigation*.

7. **Compare and contrast strategies used by activists and businesses against each other.**

Both activists and businesses have strategies they commonly use against each other. Five of the strategies are the same: grassroots efforts, news media relations and advocacy advertising, coalitions, appeals to the government, and litigation. However, activists are usually on the offensive, pressuring business and government for change, and business is on the defensive trying to maintain the status quo. Activists also use demonstrations and boycotts to get businesses to change whereas businesses use lockouts and gaining community public sentiment for being socially responsible as a proactive strategy to help avoid and minimize conflict, and firms develop a grand strategy to react to activist pressure.

8. **Fill in the blank with the appropriate key term (in order of appearance in the chapter)**

_____ are advocates of nonprofit organizations that aggressively pursue social issues with business and government to promote their interests.

_____ include societal interest groups, their members, and anyone interested in their causes.

_____ is a consumer advocate to the government.

_____ is a consumer advocate, source of information and education, and service activist group.

_____ is an advocate for the public interest in the political process, holding elected leaders accountable.

_____ is a nonadvocacy institute that provides investigative journalism on issues of public concern.

_____ are nonprofit organizations comprised of groups of firms joined together to advocate their interest on issues.

_____ represent businesses from several industries on a broad range of general business interest issues.

_____ represent businesses on a narrower range of industry- or business-specific interest issues.

_____ is a neutral third-party interest group that helps consumers and businesses maintain an ethical marketplace.

_____ is the largest business interest group advocate to government and society.

_____ is an association of chief executive officers of leading U.S. corporations that serves as a business advocate to government.

_____ is a small and independent business advocate to government that serves as a key resource to its members.

_____ involve getting stakeholder support to pressure organizations to meet activists' special interests.

_____ are activist requests that society not do business with a firm.

_____ include diverse organizations and interest groups working together temporarily for a common interest.

_____ include donating, ignoring, opposing, negotiating, and working with activists.

_____ occur when the business does not allow employees to come and work.

KEY TERMS (IN ALPHABETICAL ORDER)

activists (p. 245)
Better Business Bureau (BBB) (p. 254)
boycotts (p. 259)
business interest groups (p. 251)
Business Roundtable (p. 254)
center for public integrity (p. 250)
coalitions (p. 259)
common cause (p. 250)
Consumer Federation of America (CFA) (p. 250)

grand nonmarket strategies (p. 263)
grassroots efforts (p. 257)
lockouts (p. 265)
National Federation of Independent Business (NFIB) (p. 255)
peak interest groups(p. 251)
public citizen (p. 249)
societal interest group activists (p. 245)
trade groups (p. 251)
U.S. Chamber of Commerce (p. 254)

REVIEW QUESTIONS

1 Is there a difference between activists and advocates?

2 What is the difference between societal interest group activists and business interest group activists?

3 How do societal interest group activists get revenues?

4 How are the four societal interest groups (Public Citizen, Consumer Federation of America, Common Cause, and Center for Public Integrity) similar and different?

5 What is the difference between business associations and trade groups?

6 Are business interest groups part of the market or nonmarket environment? Why?

7 How are the four business interest groups (Better Business Bureau, U.S. Chamber of Commerce, Business Roundtable, and National Federation of Independent Business) similar and different?

8 Which association is somewhat between a societal interest group and a business interest group?

9 What are the five core services of the Better Business Bureau?

10 What is the largest business interest group?

11 Are grassroots efforts worth all the time and effort?

12 Do demonstrations and boycotts get businesses to change?

13 Do negative news media stories about a business affect public sentiment about the business and its corporate reputation?

14 Does the government really listen to activists' complaints about business, and do coalitions help?

15 Can activists beat big business in court?

16 What does the 5 Is Strategic Analysis have to do with selecting nonmarket strategies to use against activists?

17 How does the gaining public sentiment for being socially responsible strategy differ from the other six business nonmarket strategies?

18 Does business generally select the opposing activist grand strategy? Why or why not?

19 Do grassroots efforts really work for business against activists?

20 When should a business appeal to the government?

21 When should a business litigate?

DISCUSSION/CRITICAL THINKING QUESTIONS

Be sure to give a detailed explanation for your answer to each question.

1 Do activists really help society, or do they just cause problems for business?

2 Are activists successful at providing information about business, developing nonmarket agenda issues, helping set voluntary standards, and influencing laws and regulations?

3 Because business interest groups represent business, should they be allowed to be societal nonprofit organizations?

4 Do business interest groups encourage decreasing competition?

5 Do you agree with the Business Roundtable belief that the basic interests of business closely parallel the interests of the American people?

6 Can you give an example of a news story that presented the activist side of an issue against business, such as a *20/20* story?

7 Can you give an example of a news story that presented the business side of an issue in response to activists?

8 Is it ethical to build coalitions to help you get what you want?

9 Should the government listen to and be influenced by appeals from activist and business interest groups?

10 Would the government do a better job of running the country if it made activist and business interest groups illegal—to get rid of the influence of special interest?

11 Are activists ethical in dealing with business?

12 Is business ethical in dealing with activists?

APPLICATION EXERCISES

7.1 ACTIVIST STRATEGIES

Find a news story about an activist group pressuring a business to change, or use one for a business where you work(ed). Identify the activist and business and the strategies they used against each other.

7.2 ACTIVIST INTEREST GROUP

Select an activist interest group you would like to learn more about. Go to its website and report on what you find out about the group.

3 BUSINESS INTEREST GROUP

Select a business interest group you would like to learn more about, one that is not in the text and is preferably a trade association for the industry you work for or would like to work for. Go to its website and report on what you find out about the interest group.

APPLICATION EXERCISES

7

CASE 7.1

The Sierra Club: Rediscovering the "Roots" of the Organization

CASES

7

Lisa Renstrom, president of the Sierra Club, was stumped. The oldest, largest, and most influential grassroots environmental organization had "failed to stop the Environmental Protection Agency (EPA) from easing up on standards that govern manure-dumping and other processes at massive feedlots where much of the nation's beef and pork are produced. Despite intense lobbying in Washington by the club and other environmental groups, the EPA decided to let the feedlots be more secretive about their operations."[90] Where could she and the club have gone wrong?

"The Sierra Club's members are more than 1.4 million of your friends and neigh-bors, who want a safe and healthy community, smart energy solutions to combat global warming, and an enduring legacy for America's wild places. Since 1892, the Sierra Club has been working to protect communities, wild places, and the planet itself."[91] "The Sierra Club is uniquely qualified to lead this grassroots action to save the Earth. We are America's largest and most effective grassroots environmental organization—an experienced, respected, and committed fellowship of citizen activists. Within our ranks lie the expertise, wisdom, and vitality to find the new directions needed to meet the challenges of the future. We offer proven ability to influence public policy and empower individuals to confront local, national, and global problems. From town halls to our nation's capital to global institutions, Sierra Club activists are scoring enormous victories for the environment through personal action, education, litigation, lobbying, and participation in the political process."[92]

Perhaps the Sierra Club had forgotten what made them successful in the first place: people power. Environmentalists are discovering that green politics, like other politics, is local. In pushing a national agenda, environmental groups have gained little traction. Critics say the locally focused environmentalists are more interested in fund-raising, litigation, and promoting partisan political agendas than in helping people with local problems— charges the green groups deny. They likely believe that local lobbying will create pressure on Washington.[93] But locally, across the country, green groups are joining with traditional adversaries on local issues and making some inroads. . . . The local politicians are proving easier for environmentalists to work with than national politicians, in part because many also oppose some White House environmental policies.[94]

The Sierra Club and President Renstrom are learning from their mistakes. "The Sierra Club teamed with informal groups of farmers, who in this state generally are conservative on political issues, to help get state legislation passed that nullified part of some EPA rule changes. Those reduced public scrutiny over so-called concentrated animal-feeding operations, or 'factory animal farms,' as critics call them. As part of the new EPA regulations, the feedlot operators no longer had to keep a copy of their manure-management plans on file with state agencies for public inspection. Under the rules, the plans would only have to be kept at a plant, and only be made available to state regulators—not the public. . . . Democratic environmentalists and Republican farmers lobbied for the manure-management measure, which sailed to bipartisan approval in the legislature."[95]

But this was certainly no easy row to hoe, according to Laura Krebsbach, a local Sierra Club activist and now the recognized backbone of the organization at the grassroots level. "'When I first started, the reaction I got was, 'Oh, not you tie-dyed, Birkenstock vegetarians,' says Krebsbach, who was raised on a Nebraska farm. . . . [yet she] recalls how quickly a roomful of farmers warmed up to her [when] she spoke of something they agreed on: stopping a plan to build a large hog farm nearby. . . . Armed with information Krebsbach presented that night, the farmers petitioned Thayer County commissioners to reject a facility that could house up to 2,500 hogs. After the commission approved it, Krebsbach helped the farmers start legal proceedings to block it. 'I don't know where we'd be,' says farmer Scott Fangmeier, a life-long Republican, 'if it weren't for Laura.' . . . Helping to lead that effort has been State Rep. Brian Palmer, Michigan's Republican majority whip. 'I find myself in a very strange and unique alliance with the environmental groups on this issue because I believe they are absolutely right.'"[96]

Questions

1. What activist role(s) are discussed in this case? Which role does this case focus on?
2. What is the function of the Sierra Club? How does this function compare with the four other activist groups described in Figure 7.1?
3. What activist strategies against business seem to be employed by the Sierra Club? Which seem to be the most successful? Why?
4. Which activist strategies not being employed by the Sierra Club do you think would also be successful? Why?
5. If you were a large corporate beef or pork producer in Nebraska, what nonmarket strategies might you have employed to combat the Sierra Club's efforts to reverse EPA regulations easing standards that govern manure dumping?

CASE 7.2

Recording Industry Association of America (RIAA) and College Students: Defending the Industry or Biting the Hand that Feeds You?

Going after illegal shareware companies is one thing, but going after music consumers, especially college students who represent the industry's largest and poorest market segment, may seem to be the equivalent of economic genocide. Yet "the Recording Industry Association of America (RIAA), on behalf of its member record companies, has sent a new wave of 401 pre-litigation settlement letters to 12 universities citing individuals for online music theft via peer-to-peer services such as Ares, BitTorrent, Gnutella, Limewire, and Morpheus. . . . The pre-lawsuit letters, sent to individuals at more than 150 schools, are one piece of a multi-faceted industry campaign to encourage fans to enjoy music legally. Despite years of warnings, educational campaigns, and the availability of multiple legal options, online music theft, especially on campuses, remains a major problem for the music community and saps opportunities for investment in new bands."[97]

Recipients of the letter have the opportunity to avoid a potential lawsuit by settling out of court for a reduced fee. "While the minimum fine for each copyrighted recording is $750 under the law, students who contact the RIAA before they file the lawsuit can pay a settlement fine of approximately $3,000, according to an e-mail from attorney Bruce Phillips of Student Legal Services at Virginia Tech."[98]

Formal lawsuits have been filed against 2,465 letter recipients. These individuals either disregarded settlement opportunities or were not given the option to settle early because the university failed to forward the letters.[99] Individuals who have not settled and been brought to court by the RIAA have paid huge fines. For example, a federal jury found Jammie Thomas-Rasset liable for file-sharing, dinging her $1.92 million for infringing 24 songs.[100] Joel Tenenbaum was fined $675,000 for illegally downloading and distributing 30 copyrighted songs.[101]

How does the RIAA justify these harsh actions? "[In support of their policies and tactics, RIAA cites] a survey by Student Monitor found that more than half of college students download music and movies illegally. According to market research firm NPD, college students alone accounted for more than 1.3 billion illegal music downloads in 2006. Additionally, the Institute for Policy Innovation (www.ipi.org) estimated that the global theft of sound recordings cost the U.S. economy $12.5 billion in lost revenue and more than 71,000 jobs and $2 billion in wages to U.S. workers. 'One year into our legal campaign, we've seen an emerging legal marketplace that would have struggled to gain traction were it not for our efforts to clamp down on online music theft,' said Cara Duckworth, Director of Communications, RIAA. 'The exponential growth of illicit peer-to-peer file sharing has stabilized and music lovers know what they can and can't do when getting music online. This has fostered a climate that helps music companies earn a fair return so that they can invest in the next generation of artists and new bands can have a shot at realizing a dream. Unfortunately, too many students continue to ignore the law and get music from illegal services like Limewire that do not invest a penny in nurturing music or compensating the artists, labels, and the thousands of behind-the-scenes workers bringing music to the public. . . . For those who choose to ignore all the content-rich alternatives and get music the wrong way, they run the risk of legal action, potential disciplinary enforcement from a university and crippling both their computer and the university network."[102]

Questions

1. What is the issue that the RIAA is raising with college students, and how does it affect the industry it represents? Which role is RIAA utilizing to protect the industry?

2. What is the business activist strategy the RIAA is using to protect the music industry's interests? What additional strategies could it employ?

3. What options are available to college students and their universities for dealing with the RIAA's activist strategies?

4. If you were a college or university, would you take a proactive, defensive, or accommodating stance with the RIAA? Why?

5. If you received a pre-lawsuit letters from the RIAA how would you respond? Why?

INTEGRATIVE CASE

7

INTEGRATIVE CASE (Part 7)

DHR Construction, LLC and The Home Builders Association: I'm Making You an Offer You Can't Refuse!

This is a continuation case—please refer to Chapters 1–6 for further information.

Richard Davis was in his office going through the mail when he noticed a brochure from the Home Builders Association (HBA), an affiliate of the National Association of Home Builders (NAHB). He perused the brochure for a few minutes, looked at his watch, and noticed that he was running late to his next meeting. Without a second thought, he filed the brochure in his "circular file"—a waste basket that he kept by his desk for junk mail. Little did Richard know how important that little tidbit of information was going to be.

Weeks later, Richard Davis and Stephen Hodgetts were meeting with the president of Benefit Bank to go over new bank lending policies. A year ago, the bank had extended DHR Patio Homes a $2.5 million line of credit so that Davis and Hodgetts could go ahead with the building of custom homes in the Mountain Trails section of the Snowy Mountain Development. The developer of Snowy Mountain, Justin Martin, had brokered the deal between DHR and Benefit Bank in order to facilitate the selling of the lots in Mountain Trails. The deal was touch and go for a while because the bank required a $500,000 deposit (20 percent) as well as the land as collateral for the loan. The deal was finally made, and Davis and Hodgetts began building.

A year had gone by, and Davis and Hodgetts had paid off a good portion of the credit line (about 75 percent). However, Davis noticed that his requests for funds, which he needed from time to time in order to pay his suppliers, were taking longer and longer to be approved by the bank's lending committee and that the documentation needed to justify the fund requests were becoming more and more detailed and, therefore, quite time consuming. Delay in paying his suppliers not only had a negative impact on his relationship with them, and hence the timeliness of their deliveries, it also required that he pay late fees and sometimes even penalties. Davis and Hodgetts requested a meeting with Benefit Bank's president John Virgilson to clarify the situation and explain how the bank's changing policies were negatively affecting their business.

The Meeting

"Listen John," stated Richard, "this is nothing personal, but your bank's new policies and increased due diligence is costing us goodwill, time, and money—none of which I can afford at this time given the slowdown in home sales. We've paid off most of the credit line and should have the rest of it paid off in another six months, even with slow sales, so what is going on?"

"Why nothing," said John quite innocently. "The bank's lending committee has instituted a new set of guidelines for approving credit-line withdrawals over $10,000. You always seem to withdraw far more than that amount at any one time; therefore, your requests must meet the committee's new standards."

Richard looked highly perplexed, and Stephen was fidgeting in his seat. "I don't get this at all," grunted Davis. "This credit line was extended to us for the life of the project, and, at that time, all we needed to do was submit our bills. You now require outside inspectors to verify that the work was done and competitive bidding data on projects—what gives?"

"Again, nothing," politely replied John. "We're just requiring additional documentation for our auditors—they want us to have a third party verify your requests."

"I just don't understand that," jumped in Richard. "We've nearly paid off the loan. Are your trying to lose our business?" The statement hung in the air like a smoke ring, dissipating as the moments ticked on.

"You tell me," curtly responded John. John's comment was most poignant and quickly ended the meeting.

Post-Mortem Meeting and Follow-Up

Richard and Stephen met that night over dinner and discussed the results of the meeting. Both could not believe their ears, that it seemed the bank could not care less if it lost them as a customer. They resolved to move their credit line to another bank, a bank with less stringent requirements for issuing checks against a credit line. Their instincts, however, told them that there was more to this story than they were being told. Richard remembered the brochure that he had thrown away about the HBA and decided to see if they knew something he and Stephen Hodgetts didn't.

HBA president Mark Kessler was happy to take Richard Davis's phone call and discuss the situation with him. "Listen Richard, we're a nonprofit trade organization of home builders and related industry professionals.

The association is dedicated to promoting high ethical standards, education, and leadership for its growing membership of home builders and their subcontractors. Through our active involvement, the goal of the association is to be responsible to our communities and our environment while serving the interests of the home building community. We provide information, services, and resources, thereby enhancing the quality of life within our communities."

"That's a real nice speech," Richard retorted. "But that doesn't tell me what is going on with Benefit Bank. I can't imagine a bank turning away good customers, especially a customer who was paying off his credit line early!"

"Okay, okay," Mark chortled. "I had to get my plug in for the association. We'd really like to have you and your company as a member. Dues are $525 a year and include membership in the state and national association. Our services include powerful advocacy; invaluable news and information; networking; opportunities to market your business; expert advice and counsel; exposure to the latest building products and services; and group discounts on business, health, and liability insurance."

Mark could hear that Richard was getting impatient. "This issue not only affects you but also affects all of our members doing business with Benefit Bank. I'll make you a deal, Richard. You promise to become a member, and in 48 hours or less, I'll guarantee that I can dig up the information about what is going on at Benefit Bank. I assure you that I do not know what is going on at the moment, but I know that I can ferret out the information through my contacts with commercial lenders. Our network is just that good, and our influence even better. In all candor, no one even breathes in this town if it deals with home construction without us knowing about it; ask around and see what your subcontractors and competitors say. We're great in dealing with building inspectors, too; know what I mean? By the way, how has the college been treating you?"

Richard was floored. He had not mentioned his connection to the university to any one of his subcontractors, and Stephen Hodgetts and Davis's wife, Adrienne, rarely went to the building sites. Also, he certainly had not revealed to anyone besides Stephen and Adrienne the problems that DHR was having getting its homes to pass inspection. And what did this guy mean by "being great in dealing with inspectors"? Mark had obviously done his homework and probably knew far more than he was telling. The question Richard debated with himself while on the phone was whether this was the type of organization that he and Stephen should be affiliated with. What was the real cost of membership? And could they now afford not to join? Richard knew he had to reply to Mark's proposition, but

what his answer was going to be was still a mystery.

Questions

1. Describe the problem that Richard was having with Benefit Bank. How would you describe the bank's position?
2. Richard and Stephen decided to transfer their loan to another bank. What nonmarketing strategies might they have employed to influence the bank's new lending policy?
3. Richard contacted the HBA for assistance. Besides providing information, how else might the HBA help Richard with this problem?
4. What is your reaction to the deal that Mark proposed to Richard in terms of exchanging membership in the HBA for information about Benefit Bank? Is this an ethical exchange?
5. What would you say to Mark if you were Richard?

REFERENCES AND NOTES

REFERENCES AND NOTES

7

1 http://www.scmagazineuk.com/yahoo-announces-plans-to-charge-for-email-but-claims-made-that-it-will-damage-legitimate-mass-mailers/article/146723/ (accessed June 11, 2012).
2 Anonymous, "Interest Groups Fight Fees for Bulk Email," *Associated Press* (February 28, 2006).
3 http://www.scmagazineuk.com/yahoo-announces-plans-to-charge-for-email-but-claims-made-that-it-will-damage-legitimate-mass-mailers/article/146723/ (accessed June 11, 2012).
4 Anonymous, "Interest Groups Fight Fees for Bulk Email," *Associated Press* (February 28, 2006).
5 http://www.scmagazineuk.com/yahoo-announces-plans-to-charge-for-email-but-claims-made-that-it-will-damage-legitimate-mass-mailers/article/146723/ (accessed June 11, 2012).
6 Anonymous, "Interest Groups Fight Fees for Bulk Email," *Associated Press* (February 28, 2006).

7 N. M. Dahan, J. Doh, and H. Teegen, "Role of Nongovernmental Organizations in the Business—Government— Society Interface: Special Issue Overview and Introductory Essay," *Business & Society* 49(1) (2010): 20–34.
8. M. D. P. Lee, "Configuration of External Influences: The Combined Effects of Institutions and Stakeholders on Corporate Social Responsibility Strategies," *Journal of Business Ethics* 102(2) (2011): 281–298.
9 M. Van Huijstee and P. Glasbergen, "NGOs Moving Business: An Analysis of Contrasting Strategies," *Business & Society* 49(4) (2010): 591–618.
10 A. Armenakis and J. Wigand, "Stakeholder Actions and Their Impact on the Organizational Cultures of Two Tobacco Companies," *Business and Society Review* 115(2) (2010): 147–171.
11 M. Van Huijstee and P. Glasbergen, "NGOs Moving Business: An Analysis of Contrasting Strategies," *Business & Society* 49(4) (2010): 591–618.

12 J. Jargon, "Under Pressure, McDonald's Adds Apples to Kids Meals," *Wall Street Journal* (July 27, 2011): B1.

13 A. Armenakis and J. Wigand, "Stakeholder Actions and Their Impact on the Organizational Cultures of Two Tobacco Companies." *Business and Society Review* 115(2) (2010): 147–171.

14 A. Armenakis and J. Wigand, "Stakeholder Actions and Their Impact on the Organizational Cultures of Two Tobacco Companies," *Business and Society Review* 115(2) (2010): 147–171.

15 M. Rhee and M. E. Valdez, "Contextual Factors Surrounding Reputation Damage with Potential Implications for Reputation Repair," *Academy of Management Journal* 34(1) (2009): 146–168.

16 Dialog, library.dialog.com/bluesheets/html/bl0114.html (accessed May 21, 2012).

17 http://www.yjil.org/print/volume-37-issue-1/comment-%7Ctwo-competing-models-of-activism-one-goal-a-case-study-of-anti-whaling-campaigns-in-the-southern-ocean (accessed June 11, 2012).

18 Ibid.

19 Public Citizen, www.publiccitizen.org (accessed May 14, 2012).

20 Consumer Federation of America (CFA), www.consumerfed.org (accessed May 21, 2012).

21 Common Cause, www.commoncause.org (accessed May 21, 2012).

22 Center for Public Integrity, www.publicintegrity.org (accessed May 21, 2012).

23 M. Ramsey, "Dealers Fight Mileage Rules," *Wall Street Journal* (January 18, 2012): B3.

24. 27 A. Johnson, "Travelers Hit With Slew of New Taxes on Rental Cars," *Wall Street Journal* (November 11, 2005): D1.

25 M. Van Huijstee and P. Glasbergen, "NGOs Moving Business: An Analysis of Contrasting Strategies," *Business & Society* 49(4) (2010): 591–618.

26 S. McBride, "File-Sharing Firms Are Urged to Protect Music-Industry Rights," *Wall Street Journal* (September 15, 2005): D8.

27 M. Van Huijstee and P. Glasbergen, "NGOs Moving Business: An Analysis of Contrasting Strategies," *Business & Society* 49(4) (2010): 591–618.

28 M. Ramsey, "Dealers Fight Mileage Rules," *Wall Street Journal* (January 18, 2012): B3.

29 Better Business Bureau (BBB), www.bbb.org (accessed May 22, 2012).

30 G. A. Fowler and A. Loten, "Old Watchdog Learns New Web Tricks," *Wall Street Journal* (March 8, 2012): B1.

31 Ibid.

32 U.S. Chamber of Commerce, www.uschamber.org (accessed May 22, 2012).

33 N. Easton and T. Demos, "The Business Guide to Congress," *Fortune* (May 11, 2009): 72–75.

34 Business Roundtable, www.brt.org (accessed May 22, 2012).

35 National Federation of Independent Business, www.nfib.org (accessed May 22, 2012).

36 http://www.npr.org/2012/04/05/150013705/boycotts-hitting-group-behind-stand-your-ground (accessed June 11, 2012).

37 http://www.alec.org/about-alec/ (accessed June 11, 2012).

38 http://www.npr.org/2012/04/05/150013705/boycotts-hitting-group-behind-stand-your-ground (accessed June 11, 2012).

39 W. J. Henisz and B. A. Zelner, "Legitimacy, Interest Group Pressures, and Change in Emergent Institutions: The Case of Foreign Investors and Host Country Governments," *Academy of Management Review* 30(2) (2005): 361–382.

40 B. McKay, "Beverage Firms Yield to Pressure on School Sales," *Wall Street Journal* (May 4, 2006): D6.

41 G. Chon, "Activist Moves Into PepsiCo," *Wall Street Journal* (May 16, 2012): B1.

42 M. Van Huijstee and P. Glasbergen, "NGOs Moving Business: An Analysis of Contrasting Strategies," *Business & Society* 49(4) (2010): 591–618.

43 Common Cause, www.commoncause.org (accessed May 22, 2012).

44 M. Orey and J. Sasseen, "No Solidarity for Labor," *BusinessWeek* (June 15, 2009): 28–29.

45 R. Van der Merwe, L. F. Pitt, and R. Abratt. "Stakeholders Strength: PR Survival Strategies in the Internet Age,." *Public Relations Quarterly* 50 (Spring 2005): 39–49.

46 D. P. Barron, *Business and Its Environment*, 5th ed. (Upper Saddle, NJ: Prentice Hall, 2006).

47 American Family Association, "Ford Asked to Honor Commitment," *AFA Journal* (March 2006): 1.

48 Staff, "The NRA," *Wall Street Journal* (August 2, 2005): A1.

49 J. P. Walsh, "CEO Compensation and the Responsibilities of the Business Scholar to Society," *Academy of Management Prospectus* 22(2) (2008): 26–33.

50 A. Bjerga, "Ending a Housing Crisis for Hens," *BusinessWeek* (February 20–26, 2012): 33

51 J. Cummings, "Green Groups Mobilize Against Alito," *Wall Street Journal* (December 14, 2005): A4.

52 D. Baur and G. Palazzo, "The Moral Legitimacy of NGOs as Partners of Corporations," *Business Ethics Quarterly* 21(4) (2011): 579–604.

53 J. Cummings, "Green Groups Mobilize Against Alito," *Wall Street Journal* (December 14, 2005): A4.

54 D. Baur and G. Palazzo, "The Moral Legitimacy of NGOs as Partners of Corporations," *Business Ethics Quarterly* 21(4) (2011): 579–604.

55 A. Bjerga, "Ending a Housing Crisis for Hens," *BusinessWeek* (February 20–26, 2012): 33.

56 J. Hagerty and K. Maher, "Gibson Guitar Wails on Federal Raid," *Wall Street Journal* (September 1, 2011): B1.

57 National Center for Missing and Exploited Children, www.ncmec.org (accessed May 23, 2012).

58 A. Armenakis and J. Wigand, "Stakeholder Actions and Their Impact on the Organizational Cultures of Two Tobacco Companies," *Business and Society Review* 115(2) (2010): 147–171.

59 S. Carey and J. Nicas, "United Feeling Merger Pains," *Wall Street Journal* (September 27, 2011): B1.

60 K. Clark, "NBA Players File Antitrust Lawsuit," *Wall Street Journal* (November 16, 2011): B3.

61 P. Plitch, "Governance at Gunpoint," *Wall Street Journal* (October 17, 2005): R6.

62 N. M. Dahan, J. Doh, and H. Teegen, "Role of Nongovernmental Organizations in the Business—Government— Society Interface: Special Issue Overview and Introductory Essay," *Business & Society* 49(1) (2010): 20–34.

63 M. D. P. Lee, "Configuration of External Influences: The Combined Effects of Institutions and Stakeholders on Corporate Social Responsibility Strategies," *Journal of Business Ethics* 102(2) (2011): 281–298.

64 Starbucks, www.starbucks.com (accessed May 23, 2012).

65 R. Van der Merwe, L. F. Pitt, and R. Abratt. "Stakeholders Strength: PR Survival Strategies in the Internet Age," *Public Relations Quarterly* 50 (Spring 2005): 39–49.

66 J. Adamy and R. Gibson, "McDonald's Readies Strategy to Deflect Critic's Next Barrage," *Wall Street Journal* (April 12, 2006): B3.

67 A. Armenakis and J. Wigand, "Stakeholder Actions and Their Impact on the Organizational Cultures of Two Tobacco Companies," *Business and Society Review* 115(2) (2010): 147–171.

68 J. Jargon, "Under Pressure, McDonald's Adds Apples to Kids Meals," *Wall Street Journal* (July 27, 2011): B1.

69 D. P. Barron, *Business and Its Environment*, 6th ed. (Upper Saddle, NJ: Prentice Hall, 2010).

70 B. McKay, "Beverage Firms Yield to Pressure on School Sales," *Wall Street Journal* (May 4, 2006): D6.

71 N. Easton and T. Demos, "The Business Guide to Congress," *Fortune* (May 11, 2009): 72–75.

72 D. P. Barron, *Business and Its Environment*, 6th ed. (Upper Saddle, NJ: Prentice Hall, 2010).

73 A. Schatz and J. Flint, "Under Pressure, Cable Offers Family Packages," *Wall Street Journal* (December 12, 2006): B1.

74 J. Gay, "Scandals, Lockouts and Crazy Comebacks," *Wall Street Journal* (December 27, 2011): D6.

75 M. Futterman and L. Schuker, "NFL and Players Agree on New Deal," *Wall Street Journal* (July 26, 2011): A1.

76 K. Clark, "NBA's Owners Win Big," *Wall Street Journal* (November 28, 2011): B3.

77 J. Bennett, "Old-School Labor Brawl Erupts at Ohio Tire Plant," *Wall Street Journal* (December 8, 2011); B1.

78 P. Roythorne, "Special Report-Public Relations: The Specialist Subject," *Marketing Week* (April 21, 2005): 37.

79 J. Adamy and R. Gibson, "McDonald's Readies Strategy to Deflect Critic's Next Barrage," *Wall Street Journal* (April 12, 2006): B3.

80 D. Baur and G. Palazzo, "The Moral Legitimacy of NGOs as Partners of Corporations," *Business Ethics Quarterly* 21(4) (2011): 579–604.

81 J. P. Bonardi and G. D. Keim, "Corporate Political Strategies for Widely Salient

Issues," *Academy of Management Review* 30(3) (2005): 555–576.

82 A. B. Carroll and A. K. Buchholtz, *Business & Society*, 8th ed. (Mason, OH: South-Western, 2012).

83 N. Easton and T. Demos, "The Business Guide to Congress," *Fortune* (May 11, 2009): 72–75.

84 K. Weise, "It's Your Call: Read All 2,300 Pages of Dodd-Frank. Or Read This," *BusinessWeek* (January 16–22, 2012): 30.

85 S. Forbes, "IRS Illegality," *Forbes* (April 23, 2012): 16.

86 J. Carlton, "Rancher Turns the Table," *Wall Street Journal* (August 19, 2005): B1.

87 M. Van Huijstee and P. Glasbergen, "NGOs Moving Business: An Analysis of Contrasting Strategies," *Business & Society* 49(4) (2010): 591–618.

88 M. D. P. Lee, "Configuration of External Influences: The Combined Effects of Institutions and Stakeholders on Corporate Social Responsibility Strategies:" *Journal of Business Ethics* 102(2) (2011): 281–298.

89 M. Van Huijstee and P. Glasbergen, "NGOs Moving Business: An Analysis of Contrasting Strategies," *Business & Society* 49(4) (2010): 591–618.

90 J. Carlton, "It's Easier Being Green at the Local Level," *Wall Street Journal* (May 17, 2006): A8.

91 http://www.sierraclub.org/welcome (accessed June 11, 2012).

92 http://www.sierraclub.org/policy/downloads/goals.pdf, p. 5 (accessed June 11, 2012).

93 J. Carlton, "It's Easier Being Green at the Local Level," *Wall Street Journal* (May 17, 2006): A8

94 Ibid.

95 Ibid.

96 Ibid.

97 http://www.riaa.com/newsitem.php?id=B0FAEEC1-A56A-0F04-D999-94A807ADAA6E (accessed June 11, 2012).

98 Ibid.

99 Ibid.

100 http://www.wired.com/threatlevel/2009/06/riaa-jury-slaps-2-million-fine-on-jammie-thomas/ (accessed June 11, 2012).

101 http://www.computerworld.com/s/article/9136159/Tenenbaum_hit_with_675_000_fine_for_music_piracy (accessed June 11, 2012).

102 http://www.riaa.com/newsitem.php?id=B0FAEEC1-A56A-0F04-D999-94A807ADAA6E (accessed June 11, 2012).

Part 4

GOVERNMENT

Chapter 8

LAWMAKING AND POLITICAL STRATEGIES

Learning Outcomes

In this chapter, you will find out the answers to these key questions:

- What is the role of government in business?
- How does Congress make the laws?
- What strategies do businesses use to influence lawmaking?

After studying this chapter, you should be able to:

1. Describe the branches of the federal government
2. Discuss how business rules are made and enforced
3. Explain the business–government relationship, public policy, and the types of economic public policies
4. Describe how a bill becomes a law
5. Identify the legislative stage business should focus on to influence lawmaking and who should be the strategic focus
6. Discuss political information strategies and message framing
7. Explain the reasons for political campaign contributions, the role of PACs, and the difference between hard and soft money
8. Describe what lobbyists do, access, and the revolving door
9. Define the following key terms (in order of appearance in the chapter):

supremacy clause	monetary policy	message framing
regulations	taxation policy	political action committees
natural monopoly	trade policy	(PACs)
externalities	Democrats	hard money
rules	Republicans	soft money
public policy	legislative process	prisoners' dilemma
industrial policy	pivotal voters	lobbying
fiscal policy	political information strategies	

■ Chapter Outline

The U.S. Government
   The Role and Branches of the Federal Government
   State and Local Government
   Reasons for Government Regulation of Business
   Business Rules

Business–Government Relations and Public Policy
   Business–Government Relations
   Public Policy
   Types of Public Policy
   Government Nonregulatory Influence on Business

Lawmaking
   Political Parties
   Congress
   The Legislative Process
   Influencing the Legislative Process
   Current Laws Affecting Business

Business Nonmarket and Market Strategies and Ethics
   Levels of Political Involvement
   Information Strategies
   Societal, Political, and Legal Strategies

Political Strategies
   5 Is Strategic Analysis
   Business Interest Groups
   Campaign Contributions and PACs
   Grand Nonmarket Strategies
   Lobbying
   Grassroots Constituency Lobbying
   Coalition Building
   Testimony
   Advisory Panels and Committees

What's This Chapter About?

We began the book with an overview of the business, society, and government interrelationship (Chapter 1, Figure 1.5). We described business (Chapters 2–4) and society (Chapters 5–7) in detail, and now we discuss government (Chapters 8–10).

In this chapter, we start with an overview of the three branches and levels of U.S. government, with a discussion of business regulation. Next, we present the relationship between business and government, including how they influence each other. We proceed with an explanation of how Congress makes laws.

As in prior chapters, we discuss nonmarket and market strategies and ethics, with an explanation of which types of businesses need to be more involved in politics. Because there are several political strategies, we include an additional section to present the strategies business uses to influence the outcomes of the legislative process.

CASE

No Good Deed Goes Unpunished: Former CEO of AIG Sues the Government over AIG Bailout

President Obama's administration thought they were doing AIG and the banking industry a favor when they bailed out AIG for $ 130 billion. They expected flak from all sides, except one, AIG. So what did they learn? After three years of complaints no one likes bailouts. Not even, apparently, the people being bailed out.

In two lawsuits filed against the government and the Federal Reserve, a company controlled by AIG's former CEO Hank Greenberg claims that when the government came to the rescue of the insurance giant, which was facing huge losses in late 2008, it did it illegally. Why so? Greenberg essentially accuses the government of the equivalent of snatching a person's house to build a highway, and then giving the owners a fraction of what the house was actually worth. Greenberg says the government stiffed him and other AIG shareholders [for] at least $25 billion. (That's the minimum, he says, the government should pay out to him and others.) So can it be that the government, which shelled out $130 billion to rescue the soon to go under insurance giant, underpaid?

Here's the oddity of the AIG case. No one disagrees that AIG was in bad financial straits in late 2008, and without the help of the government would have gone under. Not even Greenberg is making that claim . . . even though he has said in the past that AIG was in much better shape than many have said. The question is about how much AIG should have to have paid for that bailout.

According to the lawsuit, AIG had a $130 billion market cap at the beginning of 2008. That figure looks like the government overpaid, not underpaid, for the insurance giant. The government only got an 80 percent ownership stake for its $130 billion, not 100 percent. But of course market cap is not the only measure of a company's worth, and most takeovers (if that's the way you should think about this, and I am not sure you should) do happen at a premium.

Still, Greenberg argues that another reason it's clear the government underpaid is that Citigroup and others got a much better deal. One of the Greenberg lawsuits' claims is that the interest rate AIG was charged – over 14% – on the emergency loans it got from the government was excessive given that the Federal Reserve was charging other banks a much lower rate. . . . [Yet] 14% seems like a pretty good rate for a deeply troubled company at the height of the credit crunch. No one other than the government would have made the same loan. What's more, it's not that Citigroup's deal was at market price. The government had the power to seize all of Citigroup's shares, and probably should have, based on the $45 billion in direct investment and $300 billion in loan guarantees the government had to shell out to save Citigroup. But it made a policy decision not to take over the bank. Still, just because Citigroup or another bank got a too-sweet deal, doesn't mean that AIG got a raw one.

Perhaps the best sign that the government didn't under pay is this – AIG, even three years after the financial crisis, is still worth less than the money the government put into it to save it. The government's remaining $50 billion stake is only worth about $30 billion. . . .

What Greenberg's case clearly shows is that bailouts are messy. And even if the government doesn't end up shelling out any money to Greenberg and his group, the legal battle will cost something. And it's all another reason we should want to have the regulations in place to avoid bailouts in the future. The real injustice of the financial crisis is that it's still not clear that is the case.[1]

The following questions related to the AIG Bailout Case. Answers can be found within the chapter.

1. What government role(s) allowed the government to bailout AIG?
2. What government role(s) might support the position that bailouts should be avoided?

3. What checks and balances are in place to ensure that the bailout was legal?
4. What reason(s) could the government use to support their bailout of AIG?
5. Which types of public policy issues are addressed in this case?
6. Does the bailout of large corporations like AIG fit the Democratic Party's economic and social policies?
7. Greenberg chose to sue the government over the AIG bailout, what other options were available to him?

THE U.S. GOVERNMENT

This section includes an overview of the U.S. government. We discuss the role and branches of the federal government, state and local government, reasons for government regulation of business, and business rules.

Learning Outcome 1: Describe the branches of the federal government.

The Role and Branches of the Federal Government

To better understand what government is and why it is necessary, imagine what life would be like without a government. There would be no nation, no American citizenship with rights and privileges, no flag, and no order in our lives. Can you image life without transportation and communication systems, schools, police, or a military to protect us? Government does matter. It addresses public problems and promotes the general welfare of the nation. Citizenship means loyalty, pride, and respect for our nation and giving something to the government in return (such as taxes). We must give up some of our freedom to abide by laws to ensure everyone has rights and freedom to live happily and in safety.

The Role of Government. The key role of government is to provide an organized system by which we can live as a nation in peace, safety, and prosperity. It helps society and business function effectively.[2] Government plays an important role in economic development. From the business perspective, government has a significant impact on the way business is conducted.[3] Government creates and enforces laws and regulations—rules that business must obey, fostering capitalism and competition. From the societal activist perspective, government protects society from business. It investigates and prosecutes businesses that break the law.[4] So in a sense, government helps keep us safe and works with business to help us prosper legally, while government and societal activists act as guards over business to promote social issues.

AIG Bailout Case Question 1: What government role(s) allowed the government to bailout AIG?

The government bailed out AIG and other banks during the financial crisis in 2008 as part of its role to foster economic development—to protect the country's economic security and thereby protect its citizens' prosperity and well-being. The government's role also includes protecting society from business and therefore the bailout could be seen as the government protecting its citizens from business blunders.

The U.S. Constitution and Branches of Government. On July 4, 1776, the *Continental Congress* voted for independence by passing the *Declaration of Independence*, written by Thomas Jefferson, which said governments should receive their power from the people and announced America's right to declare itself free of British rule. Americans developed a *Constitution*, a written statement, dating back to 1788, outlining the basic principles and laws by which our country is organized and governed, which continues to evolve today. Our Constitution requires every federal and state official to pledge, with an oath, to support and uphold our Constitution. Thus, our government was created based on the Declaration of Independence and the Constitution.

The *U.S. Constitution* was founded on two principles—that all persons are created equal with certain unalienable rights and that governments derive their power from the consent of the people; therefore, the government must serve the people, and people must be protected from the possibility of losing their rights and freedoms. The Constitution created two systems—a central federal government and separate state governments. The dual structure allows different states to create different laws, making conducting national business more complex. However, it also created the supremacy clause to avoid conflicting laws. *The supremacy clause gives federal laws precedence over state laws.* Thus, a state law can't break a federal law.

AIG Bailout Case Question 2: What government role(s) might support the position that bailouts should be avoided?

Government's role is also to foster capitalism and competition by creating and enforcing laws and regulations that ensure an equal and fair playing field. It could be argued that bailouts, regardless of the particular circumstance, provide an unfair advantage to the firm being bailed out. The lawsuit, which charges that the government underpaid for AIG and charged AIG a higher interest rate compared to other banks (Citigroup), is a result of the perception that AIG was treated unfairly, a perception that could have been avoided if there were no bailouts.

There is a need for checks and balances.[5] The Constitution established a system of checks and balances so no one branch would have too much power. (See Figure 8.1 for an illustration of the government branches and responsibilities, separation of power, checks and balances, and government officials.) In this chapter, we describe the legislative branch, and in the next two chapters we discuss the executive and judicial branches of government.

AIG Bailout Case Question 3: What checks and balances are in place to ensure that the bailout was legal?

The article identifies the Obama administration, the Office of the Executive, for being the government branch responsible for AIG's bailout. The Supreme Court could have, through judicial review, claimed the act unconstitutional in that the executive branch was creating law through this action, not enforcing it. Congress could have withheld the funds allocated for the bailout and/or threatened impeachment claiming the President had overstepped his boundaries. None of these actions occurred.

Legislative Branch	Executive Branch	Judicial Branch

Lawmaking	**Law Enforcement**	**Law Interpretation and Determination**
Congress—the Senate and the House of Representatives, and agencies that support Congress. It has the following checks over the executive branch: • May override presidential vetoes with a two-thirds vote • Has the power over the purse strings to actually fund any executive actions • May remove the president through impeachment • Senate approves treaties • Senate approves presidential appointments Has the following checks over the judicial branch: • Creates lower courts • May remove judges through impeachment • Senate approves appointments of judges[6]	*President—cabinet departments* and *regulatory agencies* It has the following checks over the legislative branch: • Veto power • Ability to call special sessions of Congress • Can recommend legislation • Can appeal to the people concerning legislation and more Has the following checks over the judicial branch: • President appoints Supreme Court and other federal judges[7]	*Courts*—Supreme Court, Lower Courts, Special Courts, court support organizations It has the following checks over the executive branch: • Judges, once appointed for life, are free from controls from the executive branch • Courts can judge executive actions to be unconstitutional through the power of judicial review Has the following checks over the legislative branch: • Courts can judge legislative acts to be unconstitutional[8]

■ **Figure 8.1:** Government Branches

Personal and Professional Applications

1. Give examples of how the three federal branches of government have affected you personally.

2. Give examples of how each federal government branch affects your present or past employer.

State and Local Government

Our federalist system of government shares power between the federal and state levels. The federal government has exclusive power over international affairs and national defense. The federal government has jurisdiction over interstate business, whereas state government has power over intrastate business. Education, crime control, housing, taxes, and other matters also fall between the federal and state levels, which can cause tension over the roles and responsibilities of each.

State Government. State government is structured similarly to the federal government, but on a much smaller scale. Every state is different, but each has a constitution and the same three branches. State governments make and enforce business laws for all firms transacting business in their states. State law governs liability standards, insurance and public utility regulation, occupational licensure, some aspects of labor and securities law, incorporation law, and commercial law. States can tax people and businesses and have the primary responsibility for education and the administration of some welfare programs. States have established departments and agencies, such as consumer protection, hazardous waste, drug abuse, and energy conservation.

Governors are the chief executives of their states and oversee the executive branches. They can declare a state of emergency and call in the **National Guard**; they are the commander in chief of the state law enforcement agencies and National Guard; they draft an annual state budget; and like the president, they can (except in North Carolina) veto bills passed by the state legislature. Other executive branch positions include lieutenant governor, in all but eight states, a position similar to that of vice president of the United States. All states have an attorney general, who is the highest legal officer of the state, representing the state in legal matters before the state courts, while interpreting and enforcing state laws. All but two states have secretaries of state. Unlike the federal secretary of state, state secretaries certify election results and maintain official documents and records. State treasurers, or comptrollers, are responsible for collecting and investing state money, overseeing state agency spending, and paying state bills.

Every state has a state legislature that works with its governor to create laws and set public policy. Most of the approximately 7,500 state legislature jobs are part-time low-pay positions with around a quarter of them being held by lawyers who practice law part-time. The number of legislators varies greatly by state. The most common state legislative issues are: education, roads and highways, health and welfare benefits, law enforcement, and conservation efforts. All states have courts that interpret and determine litigation of state matters. States also share power with local and municipal governments. Business taxes, income taxes, sales taxes, gambling and lotteries are common sources of revenue.

Local Government. Local government makes and enforces business laws for all firms transacting business in their counties or cities within the state. Although we focus more on federal, with some state focus, most citizens and small businesses are affected more by their local governments. The most common jurisdiction of local government throughout the United States is *county government* in all but three states. There are 3,066 counties with their own local governments. County governments are unique because they are not incorporated like cities and they have no reserved or constitutional powers. Their primary task is to administer the functions delegated by the state.

Municipalities are cities or towns with local self-government. Most businesses dealing with the public need some type of city government license or permit to conduct business. Almost 80 percent of the U.S. population lives in or near a metropolis (a city with at least 50,000 residents). Some states define cities as any town or municipality, regardless of size, whereas others regard large municipalities as cities and smaller ones as boroughs, towns, or villages. Forms of city government are the mayor–council system, council–manager system, and commission system. An important local government issue is school districts to determine where students should attend school. Business taxes and real estate and excise taxes are common sources of revenue to pay the largest expense, which is usually education.

There are also some *regional governments* that extend beyond city or town borders but are different from county government. Regional government is attractive to city planners and politicians who want to extend borders to combine resources and spend tax dollars more effectively. Regional schools and other facilities are a good example.

USA.gov. For more details on the U.S. government, visit its "Government Made Easy" website, USA.gov (www.usa.gov). It is the official Web portal, making it easy for the public to get U.S. government information and services on the Web. USA.gov's mission is to provide trusted, timely, valuable government information and services when and where you want them.[9] It provides links to other government websites for more details, so it has been called the one-stop shopping for government information.

Personal and Professional Applications

3. Describe your local government and give examples of how your state and local government affect you personally.

4. Give examples of how state and local government affect your present or past employer.

Reasons for Government Regulation of Business

Of all the powers that government exerts on business, regulation is the most pervasive, and often the least understood. Regulation is the governmental process of establishing rules of conduct by which citizens, nonprofit organizations, businesses, and government must behave. For our purposes, *regulations are the business rules of conduct.* There are at least four reasons for government regulation of business:

1. **Natural monopoly.** In some industries, especially utilities, it is more effective to have a natural monopoly. *A natural monopoly occurs when one large business can supply the entire market more efficiently and cheaply than several small firms due to economies of scale.* A natural monopoly has the ability to underprice competitors and drive them out of business or to deter them from entering the market. For example, the electric utility industry required a system of poles and wires to supply local customers. A duplication of the system would be inefficient and often unsightly. Other industries that have some natural monopolies include cable TV, cable Internet services, and railroads.

   The problem with natural monopolies is that these companies have the power to lower output and raise prices. They can charge high prices because there is no competition to provide the incentive to keep costs low. Therefore, the state government commissions regulate natural monopoly prices to keep the monopolies from taking advantage of customers.

2. **Controlling negative externalities**. Many businesses have side effects. For example, the cost of air and water pollution, toxic waste, trash landfills, noise, and odor are not

completely paid for by the business and its customers but rather by the community. Negative externalities are also called market failure and social costs. *Externalities are costs of production borne by society rather than the businesses causing them.* Government is needed to deal with social and environmental ills[10] and to prevent business from doing harm to society.[11]

It is usually costly to reduce negative externalities, so businesses are reluctant to spend the money. A firm will find it problematic to spend money on being socially responsible when competitors do not; this expense causes the firm to have a competitive cost disadvantage. Therefore, government needs to create regulations to protect our community environments, health, and safety by providing a level business playing field so that all businesses pay the cost and so that no firm gets an advantage by avoiding responsibility for the negative externalities it creates.

3. **Inadequate information**. To make good product decisions, customers need clear, accurate, and adequate information, which the marketplace is not always capable of providing. Businesses often don't really want to provide information about the negative aspects of their products, so consumers will not know about product dangers. For example, cigarette manufactures **Altria** and **Reynolds America** and the **Tobacco Institute** would rather people not know about the risks of smoking; and they concealed this fact for years.[12] Government regulates product information conveyed to consumers, so that information about the product, and any risks associated with it, is clear and accurate. This is the justification underlying much of the health, safety, and consumer protection regulation (discussed in Chapter 6). Thus, products are required by law to provide labels about product contents and warnings; furthermore, advertising is regulated.

4. **Achieving social goals**. The government also regulates business to promote the general welfare of and to provide social benefits to special interest groups. For example, business is regulated to protect workers and to provide equal opportunity for all; minorities and women were given special treatment under *Affirmative Action*. The *Americans with Disability Act* requires businesses to make their facilities accessible to people with disabilities, as discussed in Chapters 3 and 4. The terrorist attacks of 9/11/01 changed security regulations for many businesses.

AIG Bailout Case Question 4: What reason(s) could the government use to support their bailout of AIG?

The reasons that government controls business include: deterring natural monopolies, controlling externalities, providing adequate information, and achieving social goals. Government's bailout of AIG, as well as other financial institutions, was in reaction to an external threat to the economy and therein society. It could be argued, however, that the businesses involved in the financial crisis of 2008 should pay the cost for their own bad decision-making so that no firm gets an advantage by avoiding their fiduciary responsibility. A government bailout may not be justifiable if the businesses involved do not bear some of the burden of their responsibility (i.e. higher interest rates, lower buyout price.)

Personal and Professional Applications

5. Give specific reasons why the government should regulate your present or past employer.

Business Rules

All three branches of the government have input into the rules of business (see Figure 8.2 for an illustration). In short, *rules are developed by regulatory agencies to implement laws passed by Congress*. So when we use the term "rules," we mean laws and regulations that govern business behavior. Breaking rules can lead to civil and criminal punishment through the courts.

Congress has created regulatory agencies to develop and enforce rules. As discussed in Chapters 3–6,

- the *Wagner Act* established the **National Labor Relations Board (NLRB),**
- the *Taft-Hartley Act* established the **Federal Mediation and Conciliation Services (FMCS),**
- the **Consumer Product Safety Commission (CPSC)** was established as an independent regulatory agency by Congress through the *Consumer Product Safety Act*, the *Occupational Safety and Health Administration Act* established **OSHA**,
- the *Sarbanes-Oxley Act* created the **Public Company Accounting Oversight Board (PCAOB)**, the *Equal Employment Opportunity Act* established the **EEOC**,
- the *Congressional Food and Drug Act* created the **FDA**, the **SEC** was established by Congress to enforce the *Securities Exchange Act*, and
- the *Communications Act* established the **Federal Communications Commission (FCC).**

Congressional laws provide guidance to the regulators for setting the rules, and the amount of leeway the regulators have varies with individual laws. Congress also oversees the regulators, giving them more power in rule making. We will provide details of the regulatory process in Chapter 9, when we discuss the executive branch regulators. Let's continue discussion of business–government relations to include public policy and then get into the details of Congress and how it passes statutes that become laws and rules.

Legislative Branch	Executive Branch	Judicial Branch

Lawmaking	**Law Enforcement**	**Law Interpretation and Determination**
Congress—passes statute and delegates the responsibility for writing and enforcing the law to regulatory agencies.	*President*—signs statutes into law *Regulatory agencies*—write the rules and enforce them.	*Courts*—determine if rules are constitutional, interpret their meaning and how they are applied, and determine litigation for breaking the rules.

■ **Figure 8.2:** Laws, Regulation, and Enforcement

Personal and Professional Applications

6.   Give examples of business rules that affect you personally.

7.   Give examples of business rules that affect your present or past employer.

BUSINESS–GOVERNMENT RELATIONS AND PUBLIC POLICY

In this section, we discuss business–government relations, public policy, types of public policy, and government nonregulatory influence on business.

Learning Outcome 3: Explain the business–government relationship, public policy, and the types of economic public policies.

Business–Government Relations

Government and business are two of the most powerful institutions in the United States. There are business–government linkages.[13] The relationship between them greatly influences the performance of the economy and the lives of society.[14] Thus, government and business need each other. The role of government is often cast as a choice between the free market and government intervention.[15] However, the United States tries to have a balance. A hotly debated issue today is how much the government should intervene in the operation of private enterprise in our capitalistic system.[16]

The relationship between business and government is complex and continues to change with the different elected officials because the pro- and anti-business sentiment varies with different government officials. The government influences business through regulations, and business influences government regulations, primarily through lobbying,[17] which we will discuss later in this chapter. Governments worldwide are involved with business, and this relationship needs to be managed.[18] So learning the intricacies of government is important to advancing to top level management.[19]

The business–government relationship also varies based on the issue. For some issues in which the government and business have a common interest, such as in competing in the global marketplace, their relationship is often cooperative. Congress pledged to work in partnership with the automakers to develop alternative fuels to decrease U.S. dependence on foreign oil. However, for other issues in which they have conflicting goals, such as achieving social goals, the relationship is often more adversarial.

Recall in Chapter 2 that *public affairs management* is the process of developing corporate public policies and strategies regarding how business will interact with government. Governments at all levels are involved in business decision making, so many large corporations have departments to handle government affairs, while some have offices in Washington and separate units to deal with state and local governments. We will discuss political strategies used by business with government in the last section of this chapter.

Personal and Professional Applications

8.   Explain the business–government relationship of your present or past employer.

Public Policy

At any given time, the government is faced with several issues, so an important part of government is determining which issues to work on. The selected issues become public policy. *Public policy is the action government takes to deal with issues.* Government action commonly includes changing laws and regulations, which can also be done through the courts. Thus, new government regulation of business is public policy, and businesses influence the public policy process with political strategies.[20] We will discuss how they influence public policy in the following sections.

Public Policy Input and Selection. Government hears about issues from its employees, the media, societal and business interest groups, and businesses. The government generally selects issues to become public policy that have strong public sentiment calling for change; the more pressure on government, the greater are the chances of making and changing public policy. Politicians pay attention to public opinion polls that attempt to measure public sentiment on issues, and many conduct their own polls.

Public Policy Goals. In developing public policy, the government needs to set goals for a particular issue. The goals can be broad, such as full employment and equal opportunity for all, or narrow, such as regulation of miles per gallon of automobiles. Goals provide the justification for taking government action.

Public Policy Action. After selecting an issue and setting goals, the next step is to determine the actual action the government will take. The government considers alternatives and the costs and benefits, and, as in all public policy, some people benefit and some are harmed. For example, the Sarbanes-Oxley Act helped to protect investors, but it also placed a large burden on small businesses.

Public Policy Effect. After implementing public policy, government assesses the effect the action has on society. Public policy action always has some unintended consequences lawmakers didn't foresee.[21] Are the goals of the public policy being met? If there are complaints about the public policy, government can change the policy. For example, the Civil Rights Act of 1972 was changed in 1991.

Industrial Policy. One type of public policy directly related to business is industrial policy. *Industrial policy is government action directing resources to the development of specific industries.* Most industries have specific regulations based on their unique operations. The government also helps industries in time of need. For example, when the **GM** and **Chrysler Corporation** and many firms in the financial industry were faced with bankruptcy, the government bailed them out. After the *World Trade Center* attack on 9/11/2001, the **airline industry** was crippled. Congress passed a bailout program of $15 billion, with $5 billion in immediate cash assistance and $10 billion in loan guarantees. The government also protects natural monopolies and some industries against foreign competition to make them more competitive by placing tariffs and quotas on certain foreign imports. Changes in public policy also result in shifts in the types of activities businesses pursue.[22]

Types of Public Policy

There are two major types of public policy: economic and social.

1. ***Economic policy***. Government economic policies play an important role in economic development.[23] Economic policy focuses on national prosperity. There are two primary types of economic policy used by the government: fiscal and monetary policy.

   a. *Fiscal policy includes government taxing and spending to support and/or stimulate the economy.* Areas of federal government spending include the military for defense, international relations, and all types of public works projects, such as transportation systems (airports and roads). Local government spending includes the salaries of teachers, police officers, and firefighters, as well as public works employees. The **president** proposes the national federal budget, which must be approved by **Congress**. See Figure 8.3 for the Federal Budget.[24] For more details and updates, visit budget.house.gov.

   b. *Monetary policy includes the supply, demand, and value of the U.S. currency.* The supply of money affects interest rates and demand for loans. The value of the dollar affects society and business both at home and abroad because the value affects buying power, the stability and value of savings, and our confidence in investing to provide needed capital to business. The **Federal Reserve (Fed)** (www.federalreserve.gov) sets the nation's monetary policy to promote the objectives of maximum employment, stable prices, and moderate long-term interest rates.[25] It raises and lowers the interest rate (the discount rate) it charges to loan money to private banks to influence the size of our national money supply and the value of the dollar. Secondary economic policies include industrial policy as already discussed, taxation policy, and trade policy. *Taxation policy raises and lowers taxes on individuals and businesses to encourage or discourage spending.* Taxes pay the government's bills. One issue that unites business is its opposition to increasing taxes that President Obama proposed,[26] and the uncertainty in taxes, and other policies, results in business waiting to see what will happen before taking strategic action.[27] We'll discuss taxes in the next chapter. *Trade policy encourages or discourages international trade with specific countries.* We'll discuss trade policy in Chapter 11.

2. ***Social policy***. Social policy focuses on the well-being of citizens to solve social problems. The government has been portrayed as the friend of the downtrodden.[28] The U.S. government has rapidly increased its spending on social services, especially for health- and education-related programs. Are you getting any kind of government support for your college education? In the next chapter, you will learn about the different cabinet departments that run the social services.

	2012—Actual	**2013—Projected**	**2014—Projected**
Revenues	$1,866,454,000,000.	$2,127,981,000,000.	$2,324,503,000,000.
Budget Outlays— expenses	$2,947,916,000,000.	$2,915,241,000,000.	$2,902,944,000,000.
Deficit (over spending)	($1,081,462,000,000.)	($787,260,000,000.)	($578,441,000,000.)
Debt help by public	$11,418,000,000,000.	$12,216,000,000,000.	$12,797,000,000,000.

▨ **Figure 8.3:** Federal Government Budget

Source: H. CON. RES. 34.

The **National Center for Policy Analysis** (**NCPA**, www.ncpa.org) is a nonprofit non-partisan public policy research organization that develops and promotes private free market alternatives to government regulation and control, solving problems by relying on the strength of the competitive entrepreneurial private sector.[29] The **Heritage Foundation** (www.heritage.org) is a research and educational institution—a think tank—whose mission is to formulate and promote conservative public policies based on the principles of free enterprise, limited government, individual freedom, traditional American values, and a strong national defense. NCPA and Heritage research is given to government officials to aid in making public policy decisions.[30]

AIG Bailout Case Question 5: Which types of public policy issues are addressed in this case?

The differing types of public policies include industrial, fiscal, monetary, trade, taxation, and social. In this case the government is directing resources to the development of a specific industry and therefore the bailout is part of the government's industrial policy. The bailout includes government spending taxpayer funds to support and/or stimulate the economy and therefore the bailout is part of its fiscal policy as well.

ETHICAL DILEMMA 8.1 State Legislators, the Supreme Court and Business: Becoming "Alienated" by State Anti-Immigrant Laws

They line up at 7–11s all around the country looking for work, but nowhere is the migrant worker population, some illegal immigrants, so prevalent as at the 7–11 in Southampton, New York. Southampton is part of the Hamptons, a well-to-do community on the east end of Long Island, New York, where the average price of a home is over $2 million and where a strong underground economy has emerged to service the needs of the local community. The local community, once a fairly homogenous population save for the presence of the Shinnecock Indians, has become quite heterogeneous and includes a large Hispanic population, which now has its own grocery stores, restaurants, and religious institutions.

Fifty or more migrant workers line up every weekday at the corner of Noyac Road and Route 39 for the opportunity to earn an average of $10 an hour, working at construction sites and for home repair businesses, lawn care services, pool maintenance services, restaurants, and odds and ends "pick-up" work. And employers in their work trucks willingly cruise the area looking for eager helpers since historically there were none available before the migrants came, willing to work for those wages. Yet, hiring illegal immigrants is illegal in this country. Are there illegal immigrants among the local workers? Sure there are, but the unwritten code between employee and employer has been "don't ask, don't tell." Protesters calling themselves the Minutemen line up alongside of the immigrants every Saturday, holding up signs asking the U.S. government to enforce the existing immigration and labor laws.[31]

"[Yet] there has been no significant movement toward federal immigration reform since a bipartisan effort died in 2007, blocked by conservative opposition. But it has been the subject of a fever of legislation at the state level . . . In December 2011, the Supreme Court agreed to decide whether Arizona may impose tough anti-immigration measures. Among them, in a law enacted in 2010 and challenged by the Obama administration, is a requirement that police in Arizona question people they stop about their immigration status. The ramifications of the court's decision for immigration policy; for other states; and possibly for presidential politics are far-reaching.

Federal judges have now struck down portions of state immigration laws in Alabama, Arizona, Georgia, Indiana, Utah, and South Carolina. But not all rulings have favored immigrants' rights groups. In Alabama, a federal judge upheld the majority of the state law."[32]

Employers of low-skilled workers say [that any additional enforcement of immigration laws] would leave them hundreds of thousands of workers short. Even supporters warned that the [new laws] would be difficult to enforce.[33]

"'People have no idea how essential these guys are to the economy,' said the business owner, who explained as he drove that he had just moved his 100-employee business to a warehouse previously used by another company. He asked that his name not be used. He explained that he needed weeks of temporary labor to reorganize rows of industrial shelving that would be used to store the air conditioning products he builds and sells. 'I could have my regular employees do it, but they are somewhat skilled and need to concentrate on building the product,' he said. 'In this business environment, I need to be as competitive as possible . . . So I'll go to the corner [7–11] for a few weeks.'"[34]

Questions

1. What are the government social and economic policy issues that are imbedded in the topic of illegal immigration?
2. How does the immigration issue pit national, state, and local social and economic policies against one another and the business community?
3. What is the ethical dilemma facing employers who hire illegal aliens and the key stakeholders impacted by the passed state legislation?
4. What would you do if you were an employer dependent on illegal immigrants for your labor supply? If you were a homeowner, would you hire a contractor who you suspected hired illegal immigrants?

Personal and Professional Applications

9. Give examples of how specific public policies have personally affected you.
10. Give examples of how specific public policies have affected your present or past employer.

Government Nonregulatory Influence on Business

So far our discussion of government and business relations has focused on regulations that tend not to be thought of as helping business for many of the policy issues. However, the government is a great help to business through the following six influences.

1. **Government pay**. The three levels of U.S. government employ millions of people with good incomes. Virtually all of these government employees buy products from businesses.
2. **Government purchases**. All three levels of government spend a substantial portion of their budget, on business products from pens, to computers, to autos, to aircraft. The government is a major customer to many businesses, especially the **defense industry**.

3. **Transfer payments**. The government provides billions to individuals, often called entitlements, including welfare, medical care, and social security. Most of the transfer payments go to purchasing business products.

4. **Government subsidies**. The government gives businesses money, often called business welfare, especially to agriculture, fishing, nuclear energy, transportation, housing, and mining. On the other hand, government also competes with some businesses, for example the **U.S. Postal Service** competes with **FedEx** and **UPS**.

5. **Government loans and credit**. The government also acts as a bank providing loans to businesses and individuals, as well as other categories of borrowers. Federal lenders include the **Department of Housing and Urban Development (HUD)** (www. hud.gov)**, Export-Import Bank** (www.exim.gov)**, and the **Small Business Administration (SBA)** (www.sba.gov). Some of the loans go to business development and some of the loans are used to purchase business products. The government also guarantees private loans.

6. **Tax incentives**. The federal government gives special tax breaks to businesses to encourage efficiency, such as developing and buying energy-saving equipment, and for being socially responsible, such as by hiring minorities and disabled people. Taxes are important criteria in selecting business locations, so state and local governments often use tax breaks to entice businesses to locate in their communities.

BusinessUSA. Government agencies were asked to think beyond their organizational boundaries in the best interest of serving America's business community, and start thinking and acting more like the businesses they serve. They created **BusinessUSA** (www.business. usa.gov), a centralized one-stop platform to make it easier than ever for businesses to access services to help them grow and hire.[35] For more information and help, visit its website.

Personal and Professional Applications

11. Give examples of how specific government nonregulatory influences affect your present or past employer.

LAWMAKING

In this section, we discuss political parties, Congress, the lawmaking process, and the legislative process, and we present a review of some current laws.

Political Parties

The current U.S. system of government operates based on political parties; without political parties, the government could not operate. So let's cover the basics.

Democrats and Republicans. Andrew Jackson is given credit for starting the *Democratic Party* in the 1820s. The *Republican Party* officially started in 1854 as a movement of people dedicated to stopping slavery (Abraham Lincoln was its first president), and it attracted pro-business members. It is also referred to as the Grand Old Party (GOP).

Other political parties include the Green Party, the Reform Party, the Libertarian Party, and more recently the Tea Party. Although their candidates win very few national and state elections, they do play an important role in the electoral process. Third parties take votes away from the Republicans and Democrats. It is difficult to state exactly how the two parties differ as they sometimes do agree on policies to deal with issues.

Party and Issue Differences. It is difficult to state exactly how the two major parties differ because there is some overlap. Democrats have been known more as the party of wage earners, union members, and minorities. Republicans have been known more as the party of free enterprise, and, generally, members are more highly educated professionals. During elections, candidates often talk about the issues that they want to make public policy. The two parties tend to take a different stance on moral issues (such as pro life vs. pro choice and homosexual marriage) and the role of government.

By its nature, government wants a bigger role, more workers, and a greater scope for intrusions into our lives through laws and regulations. Modern socialists know you can control large parts of the economy through overwhelming regulations. The Obama administration has heavily regulated health care, the financial industry and student loans, telecommunications, and energy.[36] It wants more taxes on income, consumption, property, and wealth.[37] An important philosophical difference when it comes to taxes is who to trust to spend the money: the people or the government. Another difference is how to grow the economy and regulate business: through government or free enterprise. If you believe the government is a better allocator of resources, then you advocate for increasing taxes, more regulations, and bigger government.[38]

Democrats are generally more liberal regarding moral issues and in favor of more government regulation, more spending, and more taxation. They are also more in favor of redistributing income by taking from the rich (taxing individuals and business) to give to the poor. *Republicans are generally more conservative regarding moral issues and in favor of free markets with less government regulation, less spending, and less taxation.* Although Republicans tend to be more pro-business, some Democrats are too. Corporations use public affairs management to attempt to maintain a good relationship with both Democrats and Republicans.

AIG Bailout Case Question 6: Does the bailout of large corporations like AIG fit the Democratic Party's economic and social policies?

The bailout, as noted by the case, is a complicated political issue. Democrats have historically favored more government regulation and more government spending and have tended to support the wage earner and small businesses. The bailout of AIG and other financial institutions fits the Democratic philosophy of government intervention and using government resources for economic development yet at face value seems counter to their "little guy" public policy approach. Republicans on the other hand have historically been pro-business and would therefore seem inclined to support the bailout but they have always opted to support a minimal government, free enterprise system; clearly anti-government intervention and therefore the bailout.

Personal and Professional Applications

12. Discuss your involvement with political parties. Do you vote?

13. Does your employer get involved in political parties and elections?

14. Are the top managers where you work(ed) more likely to be Democrats or Republicans?

Congress

Two Houses. The U.S. Congress is made up of two houses, also called chambers. The lower chamber, the *House of Representatives*, has 435 representatives, based on state population, who are elected every two years; each represents about 600,000 people. All tax bills and monetary bills must originate in the House. The speaker of the House, who is the majority political party leader, is the highest ranking congressional officer.

The upper chamber, the *Senate*, has 100 senators, two from each state, elected every six years. The Senate was originally viewed as advisory to the president, but it does have power over the president. Only the Senate has the power over presidential appointees and control over approval of treaties with foreign nations.

Congressional Power. Below are some of the most important powers of Congress.

- ■ **Create laws**. The most important power given to Congress is to make the laws, with presidential approval. We will explain the process in the next section.
- ■ **Override presidential veto**. If the president elects not to sign a bill into law, Congress can override the veto with a two-thirds vote.
- ■ **Amend Constitution**. Congress can change the Constitution with two-thirds of the states' approval. The first amendment is the freedom of speech, and the first 10 amendments are called the *Bill of Rights*.
- ■ **Senate confirms presidential appointments**. The Senate can stop the appointment of people to key positions (i.e., cabinet members, ambassadors, and the Supreme Court justices).
- ■ **Provide regulatory oversight**. Congress has the power to ensure the laws it passes are being properly administered and enforced. Congress can hold committee and subcommittee hearings, conduct investigations, and subpoena documents to make this determination.
- ■ **Investigate matters of national importance**. Congress investigated gasoline price gouging and excessive profits. Congressional investigations sometimes lead business to institute self-regulation.[39] Recall that a congressional investigation motivated cable companies to make family-friendly packages available to subscribers.
- ■ **Control government organizational structure**. Congress oversees the federal bureaucracy. As stated, Congress establishes regulatory departments and agencies to enforce the laws. It can reorganize (as was done for Homeland Security) and disband departments and agencies. Congress also controls regulatory budgets, so it can increase and decrease agency size and power.
- ■ **Oversee offices**. Congress also oversees the following offices: General Accounting Office, Government Printing Office, Congressional Budget Office, and the Library of Congress.
- ■ **Impeach or remove any civil officer**. Former President Bill Clinton was impeached—charged with a crime, but he was not removed from office.
- ■ Declare war. Although presidents have gotten the U.S. into wars, only Congress can officially declare war.

Personal and Professional Applications

15. Give specific examples of how the power of Congress affects your past or current employer and/or producers of the product it sells.

Learning Outcome 4: Describe how a bill becomes a law.

The Legislative Process

In prior chapters, we discussed several laws; now we will describe how laws are made. *The legislative process includes committee action, floor action, conference action, a vote by both chambers, presidential approval, and, if vetoed, Congress.* A bill can be stopped at any stage, and most bills never become laws. In 2011, 5,929 bills were introduced. Guess how many became law? Just 80 (1.35 percent) made it through the legislative process.[40] See Figure 8.4 for the steps of how a bill becomes a law, which are described here.

1. **Committee action**. Bills are commonly introduced in both houses at the same time or in one chamber and then the other when they get through committee action. Both chambers work separately on the same bill through committee and floor action. Each bill is introduced by a senator or a representative who sends it to his or her clerk to be given a number and title. The house version number begins with H and Senate version number begins with S; both chambers have different numbers. The bill then goes to the proper committee.

   Committees specialize in different issue areas, such as budget or small business, and are made up of small groups of senators or representatives. The committee may decide the bill is unnecessary and *table* it, thus killing it at once. Or it may decide the bill is worthwhile and send it to a *subcommittee* to hold hearings, during which experts and other interested persons present facts and opinions, and to offer amendments. The subcommittee sends the bill with amendments back to the full committee where more hearings and revisions may take place, and a full committee vote is taken. If the vote is favorable, the bill is sent to the floor of the chamber. However, most bills that don't get passed never make it past the committee stage. There was even a 12-member "supercommittee" charged with finding ways to reduce future budget deficits by $1.5 trillion over 10 years.[41]

2. **Floor action**. The House and Senate version of the same bill go to the full chamber for debate, revision, and a vote. If either house does not vote in favor of the bill, it dies. If both chambers pass their bill, it is sent to conference action

3. **Conference action**. To progress, a bill must be in the same wording from both chambers. Thus, a conference committee, with members from both chambers, works out the differences between the two versions and sends the revised bill to both chambers for a vote.

4. **Vote by both chambers**. The House and the Senate vote on the bill. To progress to the president, the majority of both chambers must vote in favor of the bill. Again, bills have another opportunity to die.

---

1. Committee action—developing and voting on the bill in both chambers by smaller groups with expertise
2. Floor action—further bill development and vote by both chambers
3. Conference action—creating one bill for both chambers
4. Vote by both chambers—House and Senate debate and vote
5. President—signs into law or vetoes
6. If vetoed, Congress—can override veto with a two-thirds vote of both chambers

---

■ **Figure 8.4:** How a Bill Becomes a Law

5. **President**. The president can either sign the bill into law or refuse to sign it—vetoing it back to Congress. Presidents tend to sign most, but not all, bills largely due to the fact that they give Congress input on what is needed for the bill to be signed into law.
6. **If vetoed, Congress**. If the president vetoes the bill, it goes back to Congress, which can create the law if two-thirds of both chambers vote to override the president's veto. Overriding vetoes is difficult.

Filibuster. Again, a bill can be stopped at any stage of the process. One tactic used to delay or stop a vote is the *filibuster*. The most common form of filibuster occurs when a senator attempts to delay or entirely prevent a vote on a bill by extending the debate on the measure. The rules permit a senator, or a series of senators, to speak for as long as they wish and on any topic they choose, unless "three-fifths of the Senators duly chosen and sworn" (usually 60 out of 100 senators) brings debate to a close by invoking *cloture* under Senate Rule XXII.[42]

> Learning Outcome 5: Identify the legislative stage business should focus on to influence lawmaking and who should be the strategic focus.

Influencing the Legislative Process

To compete effectively in our market economy, executives need experience in dealing with government.[43] **Fannie Mae** executives really excelled at managing politicians.[44] Fannie Mae and **Freddie Mac** were set up by the government and during the financial crises they were actually mixed entities being part government and business.[45] We have two very short but very important messages that managers need to know; plus two sources that help business influence government.

1. **Focus on the committee stage**. The further along a bill is in the legislative process, the harder it is to influence the bill in becoming law. If business wants to kill a bill or influence its content, it needs to focus on the very first stage—the committee stage. Thus, to influence lawmaking, business must focus on the committee action stage.[46] The CEOs of the big three U.S. automakers—**Chrysler**, **Ford**, and **GM**—have met many times with committees to kill and influence legislation.
2. **Focus on pivotal voters**. Business also needs to focus on the committee's pivotal voters. *Pivotal voters are those most likely to switch the outcome of the vote because they are often undecided and they can be influenced.* Business will not make much headway by trying to convince strong opponents to vote for its side of the issue, and it doesn't take much effort to convince those who are already on its side to vote its way. So managers must focus most of their time and effort on the pivotal committee members because they are the most likely to listen to the business side of the issue and be swayed to cast a vote that supports business' interests.

ALEC. The American Legislative Exchange Council (www.alec.org) works to advance the fundamental principles of free-market enterprise, limited government, and federalism at the state level through a nonpartisan public–private partnership of America's state legislators, members of the private sector, and the general public.[47] Some of its members include **Bayer**, **ExxonMobil**, **Pfizer, Visa**, and **Walmart**. ALEC actually writes model bills with business executives and state legislators serving on bill-writing task forces. Bills are voted on separately by the executives and legislators to approve them. Once model bills are complete, the legislators take them back to their home state and sponsor them into law. It gets about 200 state laws passed each year.[48]

BGOV. Bloomberg Government (www.bgov.com) is a customizable resource for professionals who need to understand the business implications of government actions so they can work quickly, decisively, and effectively.[49] BGOV quantifies the impact of legislative action, regulatory decisions, and policy making on companies, industries, and markets.[50] Thus, executives can use this information to know when to get involved and information to influence government laws and regulations.

Current Laws Affecting Business

In prior chapters, we have discussed several laws affecting business. Now you know how they became laws. So we will just list them in Figure 8.5 by chapter as a review.

Chapter 3

Labor Legislation	The Norris-LaGuardia Act of 1932	The Wagner Act (also known as the National Labor Relations Act, 1935) and the NLRB
The Fair Standards Act of 1938	The Taft-Hartley Act of 1947	The Landrum-Griffen Act (also known as the Labor Management Reporting and Disclosure Act, 1959).
The Worker Adjustment Retraining Notification Act (WARN) of 1988	The Occupational Safety and Health Administration (OSHA) Act	The Electronic Communications Privacy Act of 1986
The Drug-Free Workplace Act of 1988	Americans with Disabilities (ADA) Act of 1990	Employee Polygraph Protection Act of 1988
Freedom of speech—the U.S. Constitution.	The Sarbanes-Oxley Act (SOA) of 2002	

Chapter 4

Employment Laws and Executive Orders	Title VII of the Civil Rights Act of 1964	Civil Rights Acts of 1972, 1991
Equal Employment Opportunity Act of 1972	Executive Order 11246 of 1965—Affirmative Action	Age Discrimination in Employment Act of 1967
Rehabilitation Act of 1973	Americans with Disabilities Act of 1990	Equal Pay Act of 1963
Pregnancy Discrimination Act of 1978	Family and Medical Leave Act of 1993	

Chapter 5

Sarbanes-Oxley Act (SOA) of 2002	U.S. Foreign Corruption Act 1977	

Chapter 6

Magnuson-Moss Warranty Act of 1975	Communications Acts of 1934, 1996	

Chapter 7

Dodd-Frank Wall Street Reform and Consumer Protection Act of 2009

■ **Figure 8.5:** Current Laws Affecting Business

However, recall that the *Wall Street Reform and Consumer Protection Act* has 400 regulations that need to be finalized by 10 different agencies,[51] so it was a work in progress when this book was written. The Act has been called the most sweeping financial law enacted since the Great Depression.[52] Needless to say, business generally wanting less government regulation is against the bill and is working hard to influence the regulations that will affect them. Many businesses will try to find loopholes to get around the new regulations.[53]

A few other new laws that have affected business include the *Credit Card Act of 2009* that provides consumers with more information about their accounts and sets limits on the ways fees can be increased. *The Patient Protection and Affordable Care Act of 2010* extends health insurance to 32 million uninsured people, extends the period adult children can be covered under their parents insurance, and prohibits denial of coverage due to preexisting conditions. Also, known as *Obama Care*, the health law takes a few years to implement and the legality of the law is being challenged in the Supreme Court as this book was being written. So the law may change.

BUSINESS NONMARKET AND MARKET STRATEGIES AND ETHICS

Again, government has a significant impact on how you conduct business,[54] so you have to develop strategies to deal with the government. As presented in Figure 1.4 (p. 22), businesses have a variety of nonmarket strategies they can use through the 5 Is Strategic Analysis (Chapter 2). Departing from our usual strategy discussion, let's begin by discussing the levels of political involvement, which is a starting point in the political strategy process.

Learning Outcome 6: Discuss political information strategies and message framing.

Levels of Political Involvement

Political involvement through the various strategies is both time-consuming and expensive. When the Obama administration increased business regulation, this required business to spend even more time trying to limit the influence of government on business.[55] Today, executives need an understanding of regulatory issues.[56] Therefore, firms need to determine their overall political involvement for specific issues, and business NGOs, **BGOV.com** and **ALEC** can help.[57] Researchers find that firms are most likely to engage in political strategies when the government significantly affects their business, which includes large firms, those highly dependent on government regulation or contracts, and those operating in more highly concentrated industries.[58]

Size. Generally, large corporations have higher levels of political involvement than smaller firms. For example, in the U.S. auto industry, **Ford** and **GM** participate at high levels using all eight political strategies when appropriate. Small businesses tend to get involved through having their business societal interest groups, such as the **NFIB**, represent their interest.

Government Sales. Generally, the larger the percentage of sales to the government is, the more important the political involvement. For example, in the aerospace industry,

Boeing is very politically involved, using all political strategies. Boeing is consistently working to increase government spending on its products.

Government Regulations. Generally, the more a firm is affected by government regulations, the higher the levels of political strategies needed to influence changes in regulations. For example, **Pfizer** with patented drugs uses political strategies to accelerate the **FDA** approval of new drugs, while also working to slow the entry of generic drugs.

Concentrated Industries. Generally, the more highly concentrated the industry is, the greater the political involvement will be. For example, the steel industry is highly specialized, offering a narrow range of products. **U.S. Steel**, **Bethlehem Steel,** and other companies lobbied for and received tariffs on steel imports.

Issue Benefit vs. Cost. In addition to an overall level of political involvement, each firm must decide on its level of involvement for a specific issue. Anticipating changes in business legislation is critical to companies.[59] Recall that **BGOV.com** specializes in quantifying the impact of legislative action.[60] Regardless of company size, when the benefit of getting involved politically is greater than the cost, businesses will use political strategies. Benefits can mean keeping the status quo, rather than losing something, such as by stopping a tax increase.

Likelihood of Success. The odds of stopping legislation or influencing it also affect the level of political strategies. Before engaging in political strategies, business does an assessment of its chances of success.[61] The greater the likelihood of success is, the greater the political involvement will be, and vice versa.

Personal and Professional Applications

16. Discuss the level of political involvement of a past or current employer and/or producers of the product it sells.

Information Strategies

Business needs to influence public policy, and information strategies are a critical part of corporate political strategy success.[62] But business must develop information strategies that are ethically and socially responsible.[63] Therefore, business develops political information strategies and is careful with message framing.

Political Information Strategies. *Political information strategies focus on technical facts and how the business side of the issue will benefit politicians and their constituents.* The information helps government understand the consequences of the different public policy alternatives. When approaching politicians, managers need to realize that politicians' primary concerns are getting reelected and serving their constituent voters, not business operations and profits. So don't be naïve and think that members of Congress really want to hear your business side of the story, especially if you are being attacked and getting negative press.[64] There's a perception that members of Congress won't do what is right because they just want to hold on to their offices.[65] They don't really want to hear that a regulation will mean more work or less profit for the company. They want to know what's in it for them and their constituents.

Large corporations fighting major issues do the research, usually with the help of consultants using outside sources, experts, and stakeholders' support, to come up with realistic facts and figures. This information must be relevant for each pivotal politician to kill or influence bills at the committee stage.

Message Framing. *Message framing refers to the terms used to gain public sentiment for one's side of an issue.* Message framing is an important market strategy and even includes the name of a company and the names of products, to influence sales. But it is also important for nonmarket strategies as well. Think about the message framing terms "pro-life" and "pro-choice." They are not opposites, but each tells a very different story for the same issue.

Jobs. Government officials care about jobs. So the message you need to frame for federal and state Congress and regulators is how an issue will affect jobs. Businesses create jobs. This is the story that needs to be told.[66] Again, use facts and figures ethically to support your side of the issue using outside experts.

ETHICAL DILEMMA 8.2 Caterpillar Inc. and China: Accidentally Stepping on the Caterpillar While Slaying the Sleeping Dragon?

"Caterpillar Chairman and CEO Doug Oberhelman [had just] announced the expansion plans in Xuzhou at an event attended by senior Caterpillar leaders and representatives from the Xuzhou government. 'As we have done around the world for more than 85 years, these investments in China are made with a long-term view toward the market and building out an industry-leading range of products and support services for our growing base of customers in China, . . . our continued investment in China also provides a base of operations in country to support our growing exports from the United States to China. In fact, in the last seven years as we have grown our operations in China, Caterpillar's exports from the United States to China have more than doubled, supporting jobs in the United States and proving the benefits of trade for both countries.'"[67]

"Considered #1 in the world, Caterpillar (Cat) makes construction and mining machinery; diesel and natural gas engines; underground mining equipment; industrial gas turbines; and electrical power generation systems. It operates plants worldwide and sells equipment through some 3,500 offices in more than 180 countries. . . . Caterpillar took a hit in the Great Recession due to the negative impact on the construction industry; however, as recovery got underway in late 2009, the company was able to recover. Caterpillar posted a revenue increase of more than 30% and a profit increase of 202% in 2010 over 2009. The company's decision to bump up production in its machinery business (economic recovery spurred increased machine purchases) paid off with sales increasing 50% over 2009—shipments to Asia/Pacific and Latin America showed record and near-record highs, and North America's appetite increased about 50%."[68]

Caterpillar's growth in China was particularly impressive. "Caterpillar has a long history in China. The company sold its first products there in 1975 and opened an office in Beijing in 1978. Beijing is home to Caterpillar's marketing headquarters for China, and it is also the headquarters for Cat China Financial Leasing. In the 1980s, Caterpillar launched technology transfer agreements with Chinese manufacturers who began building Caterpillar licensed products. . . . Today, Caterpillar operates 13 facilities—both joint venture and wholly owned businesses—which, together with its network of independent Caterpillar dealers, offer customers in China the best-in-class products, services and support that have made it a global leader."[69] "Caterpillar Tianjin in China is investing $300 million to build a manufacturing facility in Tianjin; the plant is scheduled to become operational in 2013."[70]

Picking up the *New York Times*, Mr. Oberhelman was dismayed to read that "the Senate, seizing on the argument that the American jobs crisis is partly China's fault, voted to move forward with tough trade legislation that would impose tariffs on some Chinese goods to punish Beijing for keeping its currency artificially depressed. The bill . . . would require the Treasury Department to determine whether China is manipulating its currency, and then order the Commerce Department to impose retaliatory tariffs on certain Chinese goods.

China intervenes in currency markets to keep the value of its currency artificially low, which makes Chinese goods cheaper in the United States—a practice that lawmakers and some economists say undercuts American businesses and worsens the nation's jobless rate. 'Trade has helped us export our values of a free democratic society,' said Senator Jeff Sessions, Republican of Alabama and one of the bill's co-sponsors, 'but like democracy itself, trade must operate under a set of rules and values.'"[71]

Former CEO Jim Owens best represents Caterpillar's position on U.S. government tariffs. "Personally, I can think of no faster path to a world-wide recession than for the twin engines of the global economy—the United States and China—to turn against one another."[72] The current CEO, Doug Oberhelman, knew that unhampered trade with China, which has the fastest growing economy in the world, was critical to Caterpillar's long-term success, and the U.S. Senate's interference could ruin relations with China. Yet he also knew that there were grave concerns about China's fiscal and monetary policies that already negatively impacted his and other U.S. firms' imports from and exports to China. For China to become a true player in the market economy, it would have to make major changes in the way it regulates its economy, including far better enforcement of intellectual property protections, a continued commitment to fair currency valuation with a meaningful revaluation, and greater reliance on market-based principles.[73] The tariff, or the threat of imposing a tariff, may be the only way to get the Chinese government to make those needed changes.

Questions

1. What factors would determine the level of political involvement of Mr. Oberhelman and Caterpillar relative to the proposed tariff on Chinese goods?
2. What technical information should Mr. Oberhelman provide the Senate relative to the business side of the issue, and how this will benefit politicians and their constituents?
3. What is the ethical dilemma facing Mr. Oberhelman?
4. What would you do if you were Mr. Oberhelman?

Personal and Professional Applications

17. Give a specific example of how a past or current employer and/or a producer of the products it sells, framed a message. Be sure to specify the terms and why it chose them.

Societal, Political, and Legal Strategies

Stakeholders have gained more power over business over time.[74] Yet business should use the stakeholder approach in decision making,[75] while being ethical and socially responsible.[76] **American Airlines** was losing billions and sought bankruptcy so it could plot a solo flight path. But **US Airways** made the strategic decision to acquire larger **American Airlines,** more than twice its size, it used the stakeholder strategy and approached all the relevant stakeholders to build support for its takeover.[77]

With the increase of activists pressuring the government to make business change, corporate executives are spending more time countering activists' pressure on government. Thus, business often needs a grand strategy in dealing with the government for specific issues. Executives and politicians know that it's emotions, not logic, that shape public sentiment about issues and candidates. The extensive impacts of government on business decision making have resulted in executives spending more time developing nonmarket political strategies because business does have some of the power needed to influence public policy. Nonmarket political strategies are as important, and in some cases are more important, than market strategies.[78] Thus, political strategies are an important part of this chapter. Therefore, we will present several political strategies next, in a separate section. Business does use the legal strategies of operating in a way to avoid lawsuits, and business does occasionally, mostly as a last resort, sue the government.

POLITICAL STRATEGIES

In this section, we discuss the 5 Is Strategic Analysis and eight political strategies. See Figure 8.6 for the list of strategies.

5 Is Strategic Analysis

Let's discuss how business selects nonmarket strategies to deal with issues as part of the 5 Is Strategic Analysis (Chapter 2).

1. **Issue identification**. Through issues management, business finds out about potential changes in regulations. Political issues are commonly brought to business in the fourth stage of the issues life cycle—legislative and regulation formation (Figure 2.4, p. 53). So business still has a chance to influence or even stop the issue from becoming law.

2. **Interested strategic stakeholders**. Are there activists pressuring the government for change, or is the change coming from lawmakers? Who are the lawmakers, and how many of them are pressing for business to change—is there a coalition? Which stakeholders are with and which are against the firm on the issue?

3. **Incentive of stakeholders**. What is the objective of each stakeholder? Have the lawmakers clearly stated the action they want the business to take? What power do the lawmakers have to change the regulations, and what are the odds of them changing the regulations? If the business agrees to implement voluntary self-regulation, will the lawmakers stop pursuing regulatory changes?

4. **Information—objective**. Information strategies that provide facts are an important part of developing strategies to deal with issues that affect public sentiment. What political information strategies (discussed above) will the firm use to present its side of the issue to the lawmakers, the public, and possibly the media? What is the objective of the business in dealing with the lawmakers?

5. **Interaction strategy**. Major corporations use PR specialists to develop nonmarket strategies:[79]

(a) Which political strategies (Figure 8.6) can be used to deal with the issue?

(b) What will be the market and nonmarket reactions and consequences to the strategic action?

(c) Which strategy or combination of strategies should be selected to deal with the issue—have a good chance of success?

(d) Implement and evaluate the strategy.

Business Interest Groups

As discussed in Chapter 7, the major responsibilities of both peak and industry business associations are to provide information, to advocate the business side of the issue to government, to provide member services, to set voluntary standards, and to influence laws and regulations. Thus, being a member of a business interest group is an indirect lower level of political involvement. Most large companies combine their use with other political strategies.

> Learning Outcome 7: Explain the reasons for political campaign contributions, the role of PACs, and the difference between hard and soft money.

Campaign Contributions and PACs

Another lower-level political strategy is simply donating money to political campaigns. Businesses can encourage their employees and stockholders to register and vote but may not recommend how they should vote. However, when corporations establish and manage political action committees (PACs) and provide other resources to candidates (such as volunteer workers and staffing get-out-the-vote campaigns), they are using higher-level political strategies. Thus, *electoral strategies* focus on providing important resources to political candidates, which are primarily campaign contributions.

Reasons for Campaign Contributions. There are three primary reasons for campaign contributions:

1. **Affect the outcomes of elections.** The business wants to get a candidate who will represent the business's interests in hopes that the politician can influence laws and regulations in favor of the business. Businesses also tend to give to candidates they expect to win in order to show their support, hopeful of politicians' support in return.

Business Interest Groups
Campaign Contributions and PACs
Grand Nonmarket Strategies
Lobbying
Grassroots Constituency Lobbying
Coalition Building
Testimony
Advisory Panels and Committees

▪ **Figure 8.6:** Political Strategies Used by Business with Government

2. **Obtain access to officeholders**. Politicians are busy, and it is difficult to get to meet with them to present the business side of an issue; therefore, campaign contributions help to open the door to business. Politicians are more likely to meet with those whose names they recognize and those to whom think they have some obligation—at least listen to their side of the issue. Committee and subcommittee chairs are given more money because of their importance in influencing the outcomes of bills.

3. **Influence regulations.** Politicians are somewhat indebted to large donors, and they often represent business interests by helping to influence regulations and to defeat or enact a bill. Politicians who want to get reelected may not want to go against business in fear of losing campaign donations, and worse, in fear that business will work to defeat them.

PACs. PACs are the primary way businesses use financial resources to influence government. *Political action committees (PACs) are company-sponsored methods of obtaining campaign funds from employees and distributing the funds to candidates.* PACs carry the company name, but employee funds given to political campaigns cannot include business money. However, the business does pay the PAC administrative expenses. Other interests also use PACs, including peak and trade groups and societal interest groups, unions. It is common for PACs to give money to both parties' candidates, especially in close elections, to ensure supporting the winning candidate.

Super PACs. Super PACs are officially known as "*independent-expenditure only committees.*" In 2010, the *Supreme Court* and the *Court of Appeals* for the D.C. Circuit ruled that PACs that did not make contributions to candidates, parties, or other PACs could accept unlimited contributions from individuals, unions, and corporations (both for profit and NGOs) for the purpose of making independent expenditures. The new Super PACs may not make contributions to candidate campaigns or parties, but may engage in unlimited political spending independently of the campaigns. Also unlike traditional PACs, they can raise funds from corporations, unions and other groups, and from individuals, without legal limits. Thus, wealthy business people can now give millions of their own money to influence the outcomes of elections.

The Federal Election Commission (FEC). To limit business influence on elections, primarily by limiting campaign spending, Congress passed the *Federal Election Campaign Act of 1975* with multiple amendments and established the FEC (www.fec.gov) to enforce compliance with the federal election law. According to *FEC advisories*, Super PACs are not allowed to coordinate directly with candidates or political parties. This is intended to prevent them from operating campaigns that complement or parallel those of the candidates they support. However, it is legal for candidates and Super PAC managers to discuss campaign strategy and tactics through the media. Super PACs may support particular candidacies. In the 2012 presidential election, super PACs played a major role by spending more than the candidates' election campaigns.

Hard vs. Soft Money. *Hard money is a direct contribution to a candidate's political campaign. Soft money is a contribution to a political party committee for use in party-building activities.* Thus, the funds cannot be used for a specific candidate's political election. Soft money can be used to fund political ads, provided the ad promotes "issues advocacy," such as government spending and taxation. However, soft money cannot be used for "express advocacy," urging "voting for" and "support" or "defeat" of a candidate. Based on the FECA, most PAC contributions are considered soft money.

Elections and NGOs. **The Center for Responsive Politics** is a societal interest group that provides a guide to money in U.S. elections funding at its website (www.opensecrets. org). *Open Secrets* provides information on PACs, how much they give, and who they give to, by party and politician.[80] **Common Cause** (www.commoncause.org) is a watchdog to curb the excessive influence of money on government decisions and elections; to promote fair, honest, and transparent elections.[81]

Electoral Strategies and the Prisoners' Dilemma. *The prisoners' dilemma is a situation in which if one competitor uses a strategy to gain an advantage, the others must follow, even when all lose.* For example, the **airline industry** price war hurt all the carriers who would have been more profitable with higher ticket prices. Related to campaign contributions, many business and societal interest groups would rather not make the donations but do so out of fear of other competing interest groups getting what they want.

Personal and Professional Applications

18. Have you ever contributed to a political campaign with your time or money?

19. Discuss the electoral strategy used by your past or current employer and/or a producer of the products it sells.

Grand Nonmarket Strategies

As with societal strategies, discussed in the last chapter, business has four possible options for dealing with the government.

1. **Ignore**. When business hears about a congressional bill, it can simply ignore it and take no action to influence the bill. Ignoring is often based on the cost–benefit analysis and the likelihood of winning. However, if Congress is doing an investigation, ignoring is not an option.

2. **Oppose**. When business hears about a congressional bill, it can oppose it and use a *majority building strategy* of developing the needed votes to change or defeat the bill. The majority building strategy is also used to enact a bill that business wants passed when negotiating and working with the government. Again, the focus is on the committee action stage of the legislative process with the focus on pivotal voters. **ExxonMobil** and others fought some of the regulations under the *Dodd-Frank Act*.[82]

3.
4. **Negotiate and work with.** Congress sometimes invites business leaders to attend committee meetings to give input into drafting the bill, so business may be able to do some negotiating[83] and work with Congress to influence the bill. For example, **Senator** Reid said that Congress will "work as partners" with the **auto industry** to help resolve U.S. foreign oil dependency and high gas prices by developing alternative fuels.[84]

During congressional investigations, business may have little ability to negotiate, but it can be cooperative and work with Congress to resolve the issue, which sometimes includes paying fines without admitting guilt rather than going to court. At the state and local levels, business has more economic leverage in negotiating with the threat of moving the business if its interests are not met. **FedEx** threatened to cancel the purchase of billions of dollars worth of **Boeing** cargo planes if Congress passed a law that made it easier for unions to organize at its package-delivery company.[85]

Learning Outcome 8: Describe what lobbyists do, access, and the revolving door.

Lobbying

Lobbying is considered the most important political strategy because more time, effort, and resources are devoted to lobbying than to any other political strategy.[86] **Common Cause** calls lobbying a hidden way for business to buy its way into the legislative process.[87] Lobbying has always been an important strategy, but with the Obama administration laws and heavy regulations in several business industries (Obama care, Dodd-Frank financial), lobbying has become critical to business and a boon for lobbyists.[88]

The most profitable investments nowadays are in lobbyists.[89] **Lockheed** doubled its lobbying expenditures to $3.26 million in the first quarter of 2009.[90] **Ford** spent $5.6 million in all of 2010 and **GM** spent nearly $3.6 million in the first quarter of 2011. **Google** spent $5.4 million in the first three quarters of 2011.[91] In 2011, business spent $3.32 billion on lobbyists.[92]

Lobbying Objectives, What Lobbyists Do, and Government Officials. *Lobbying is representing a particular interest to influence political policy on issues.* All types of special interest groups have lobbyists. Many business peak and trade associations, NGOs, and societal interest groups, including unions, have lobbyists. On a low level of political involvement, any company belonging to a business interest group with lobbying uses this strategy. However, on a higher level of involvement, PACs and large businesses also have lobbyists.

The objective of lobbying is to influence government officials to enact or defeat legislation and to influence regulatory outcomes for lobbyists' special interests. Lobbyists meet personally with officials to present the special interest *political information strategy* to influence their thinking and action on public policy issues. Today, the business information to push is jobs.[93] The information often provides facts and figures to counteract other special interest groups' information.

Government officials can include the president, a governor, executive branch officials, members of Congress or state legislatures, their staff, local officials, and committee staff. Regulatory and administrative agencies are also lobbied. As usual, our focus will be on business at the federal level primarily in Congress in this chapter and regulators in the next chapter, which together we call *lawmakers*.

Professional Lobbyists, Access, and the Revolving Door. Many business and societal interest groups and large businesses hire professional consultant lobbyists to represent them full-time in Washington, DC, state capitals, and/or local cities as part of *issues management* (Chapter 2) to keep informed of government activities that could affect business performance. In 2011, there were 12,655 registered lobbyists.[94] Professional lobbyists', referred to as "influence peddlers," most important service is *access to lawmakers* so that business is represented in face-to-face meetings, sometimes over tennis and golf games. Lobbyists can get access to key members of Congress.[95]

Both chambers of Congress give corporate lobbyists access through regularly scheduled meetings. On some issues, legislators work together with lobbyists to draft, amend, enact, or defeat bills; lawmakers even form coalitions with lobbyists. Visit the **Center for Public Integrity** (www.opensecrets.org) for more information on lobbying firms and how much industries and companies spend on lobbying.[96] **Public Citizen** (www.citizen.org) also provides lobbying information.

Businesses also have some of their own employee lobbyists. Some **Fortune 500** CEOs, including **Business Roundtable** members, make personal visits to lawmakers because they often want to indicate concerns of high-level business leaders regarding an issue and because they can make commitments that lobbyists and others can't make.

The *revolving door* refers to people changing jobs between business and government, as some businesspeople run for public office or take regulatory jobs, and lawmakers leave government posts to become consultants and lobbyists for business. Some businesses hire former government officials as political consultants and lobbyists who can help business get through the political bureaucratic red tape and gain access to lawmakers. The number of former government officials serving on corporate boards has increased dramatically in recent decades.[97]

Lobbying Laws and Disclosure. Lobbyists are protected under the right of freedom of speech and the right of citizens to contact government officials. U.S. law does not place any limits on how much money organizations can spend on lobbying. When the **pharmaceutical industry** encountered the issues of prescription drug benefits for Medicare recipients, keeping generic brands off the market, and drug imports from Canada, it lobbied aggressively by hiring 675 lobbyists and spent a record $91.4 million on lobbying activities for these issues.[98]

However, under the *Lobbying Disclosure Act*, there are limits to the value of gifts to lawmakers. Lobbyists can't pay for sports tickets, travel to conferences or events, or job offers, and they can't even take lawmakers to a restaurant. Lobbyists are required to register with the government, to file reports stating earnings (external lobbyists) or organization expenses (internal lobbying), and to identify the issues and legislation that were the focus of lobbying.

Lobbying is Commonly Combined with Other Political Strategies. Lobbying is the central component of most political strategies. However, it works best when combined with other strategies.[99] Large companies with lobbyists are also members of peak and trade business associations, so they combine efforts. Lobbying is commonly combined with *campaign contribution* strategies. However, the donations should be given during the political campaign. Thus, when lobbying, campaign contributions are usually not made because they could be considered bribes. Lobbying is also used as an electoral strategy to help elect or defeat a political candidate. Lobbyists are involved in *grassroots lobbying* and *building coalitions* to provide other stakeholder support for their sides of the issues on public policy.

Lobbying Congress. Professional lobbyists are paid well to develop and help implement comprehensive political strategies, with the primary focus on pivotal voters in the committee stage of the legislative process. Lobbyists can attend committee meetings, but only former members of Congress can attend floor meetings. However, lobbyists hang around to meet members as they pass by in the lobby (where the name comes from) and hallways, which are often crowded.

When lobbying Congress, with its 535 members, it can be difficult to determine who the important pivotal voters are. Priorities must be set and meetings set up quickly when there is limited time in the committee stages of legislation. In order to get quick access, lobbyists maintain ongoing communications with committee members of Congress, especially chairs, dealing with their issues.

Personal and Professional Applications

20. Discuss lobbying used by your past or current employer and/or by a producer of the products it sells.

Grassroots Constituency Lobbying

Grassroots strategies are based on the connection between constituents and their government representatives. Constituency building can enable business to improve public sentiment toward its side on issues.[100] When using a grassroots strategy, business often relies on its peak and trade groups to develop and implement grassroots strategies for it, such as the **U.S. Chamber of Commerce** (www.chamber.org).[101] Businesses also use business NGOs in coordination with its own grassroots efforts, often led by lobbyists. Business asks its stakeholders to contact committee members and/or their own Congress person (or other government official) to let Congress members know that their constituency supports the business side of the issue.[102]

The grassroots business stakeholders are from the market environment and can include stockholder owners, employees, customers and consumers, suppliers, franchisees, distributors, and competitors who will also be affected by a change in business practices. The more constituents there are to contact Congress (visits, calls, faxes, letters, preprinted letters and postcards, grass-tops, and Internet e-mails), the greater will be the chances that business interests will be met.

Management must assess the likelihood of the participation of stakeholders in grassroots lobbying. The greater the benefit to the stakeholders, the more likely they are to contact the government representative. Grassroots strategies can be time-consuming and expensive, so management must determine if the benefits of grassroots will outweigh the costs and which stakeholders to mobilize. **Chrysler** asked its dealers to contact key members of the auto task force urging them to approve more aid for the auto maker.[103]

Coalition Building

Companies compete in industries, but when it comes to new government regulation and taxes, they tend to work together to keep the status quo.[104] Media companies (e.g., **Atlantic** and **Columbia** records) often build coalitions with artists' organizations (e.g., **Recording Industry Association of America**) to fight copyright abuses, even though they oppose each other on other issues.[105] Peak and trade groups are coalitions of businesses with similar interests joining in collective political action. "PACs travel in packs"; working together to provide increased pressure on government to meet business interest creates bargaining power.[106] Combining campaign contributions, lobbyists, grassroots lobbying, and coalitions tends to make a powerful political strategy.

When building coalitions, there is always the possibility of facing the free-rider problem. *Free-riders* benefit from coalition action without contributing. The **U.S. Chamber of Commerce** is the largest lobbyist, which influences government to meet business' interests. However, nonmembers often gain the same benefits as members, as happens in some union situations.

> **Personal and Professional Applications**
>
> 21. Give an example of a time when you were involved in a group project with a free-rider.
>
> 22. Discuss political coalitions used by your past or current employer and/or a producer of the products it sells.

Testimony

Business testifies before congressional committees, regulatory agencies, administrative agencies, and courts. Some of the reasons for hearings include: to identify and understand issues, to gather information, to draft or amend a bill, to make public policy decisions, to shape regulation and how it is implemented, and to contribute to precedent-making cases in court. Testimony is an important political information strategy because it can be used to bolster other information to subsequently affect public policy decisions and because it creates a record that may serve as a basis for judicial review if the business wants to challenge a new law in court. Here we discuss testimony in congressional hearings; in Chapter 9, regulatory testimony; and in Chapter 10, court testimony.

Public Congressional hearings are held for a variety of reasons, and businesses may be invited to speak, to ask questions, or to be given information. When business practices are being questioned by Congress, you are on the hot seat. The best strategy is to be dull, stick with the script, and avoid making the news. It's about having a conciliatory tone and saying you want to work with the government to improve business practices.[107]

Testimony is often backed by a firm, interest group, or coalition study, including facts and figures, outside source research, and expert and stakeholder support. Business often lobbies Congress on the issue before it comes to a hearing, so it doesn't always present new information. The real objective of some hearings is to generate publicity and to mobilize public sentiment support for a particular position, which can be against business. Members of Congress also ask zingers. *Zingers* are questions whose only possible answer supports the questioner's side of the issue. For example, **Boeing** was asked, "Are we not subsidizing the competition of our own foreign carriers?"[108]

> **Personal and Professional Applications**
>
> 23. Have you ever given testimony?
>
> 24. Has your past or current employer and/or a producer of the products it sells, given testimony?

Advisory Panels and Committees

The key role of advisors is to provide expertise to the government on issues of current importance. The U.S. government often needs information about the scientific and economic consequences of proposed alternative action to make better public policy decisions. Therefore, it makes use of an estimated 1,050 advisory panels and committees.[109] Thus, giving advice is an excellent way to influence government.[110] While expert testimony is given to all three branches of the government, advisory panels and committees are primarily used by regulatory agencies of the executive branch. Therefore, we will discuss this strategy in the next chapter.

AIG Bailout Case Question 7: Greenberg chose to sue the government over the AIG bailout, what other options were available to him?

Businesses have the following political options in which to influence government policies and activities: business interest groups, campaign contributions and PACs, grand nonmarket strategies, lobbying, grassroots constituency lobbying, coalition building, testimony and advisory panels and committees. More specifically the business could chose to ignore, work with, or oppose government actions. The case notes that the value of the government's investment in AIG has gone down significantly in value and therefore suing the government nearly four years after the bailout over the bailout price would seem to be a strategy that would garner few supporters besides those who were also hurt by the bailout (other stockholders). However, the question of timing would seem to be critical here. Political options four years after an action (post Stage 5) has already been taken that could reverse the decision may be minimal. Secondly, the underlying question is what political actions were taken by Greenberg as CEO of AIG to influence the decision makers while the issue was in its infancy (Stage 1)?

SUMMARY

The chapter summary is organized to answer the learning outcomes for Chapter 8.

1. **Describe the branches of the federal government.**

   The three branches of government are the legislative, executive, and judicial. The legislative branch, which makes the laws, includes Congress: the Senate and the House of Representative. The executive branch includes the president and cabinet department regulatory agencies that enforce the laws. The judicial branch includes the courts that determine the constitutionality of laws, interpret their meaning, and conduct trials.

2. **Discuss how business rules are made and enforced**

   All three branches of the government have input into the rules of business. *Congress* passes statutes that the president signs into law. Congress delegates the responsibility of writing the rules to *regulatory agencies* with the power to enforce the rules. The *courts* can determine if rules are constitutional, interpret rule meanings as they are applied to business, hold trials to determine guilt for violating the rules, and punish guilty parties for breaking the rules.

3. **Explain the business–government relationship, public policy, and the types of economic public policies.**

   The relationship between business and government is complex and continues to change with different elected officials. The business–government relationship also varies based on the issue. For some issues in which the government and business have common interest, their relationship is often cooperative, whereas for other issues in which they have conflicting goals, the relationship is often more adversarial. Public policy is the action government takes to deal with issues. Economic policy focuses on national prosperity. Primary economic policies include: fiscal policy of taxing and spending to support and/or stimulate the economy and monetary policy of the supply, demand, and value of the U.S. currency. Secondary economic policies include: industrial policy directing resources to the development of specific industries, taxation policy raising and lowering taxes on individuals and businesses to encourage or discourage spending, and trade policy encouraging or discouraging international trade with specific countries.

4. **Describe how a bill becomes a law.**

The common legislative process is as follows. *Committee action* is the development of a bill by committees and subcommittees that specialize in issue areas. If the committee votes in favor of the bill, it progresses to the floor; however, most bills never make it through committee action. *Floor action* entails the House and Senate versions of the same bill going to the full chamber for debate, revisions, and a vote; if both chambers pass their bill, it is sent to conference. *Conference action* is a committee with members from both chambers that works out the differences between the two versions and sends one bill to both chambers for a vote. The *vote by both chambers* requires a majority of both chambers to progress to the president. The *president* can either sign the bill into law or refuse to sign it—vetoing it back to Congress. *If vetoed, Congress* can create the law if two-thirds of both chambers vote to override the president's veto.

5. **Identify the legislative stage business should focus on to influence lawmaking and who should be the strategic focus.**

To influence laws being made, business should focus on the committee action stage because the further along in the legislative process a bill is, the harder it is to influence the bill. Business needs to focus primarily on the pivotal voting members of the committee because they are undecided on how they will vote; therefore, they are the most likely to listen to the business side of the issue and meet its special interest through the bill or to kill bills business is against.

6. **Discuss political information strategies and message framing.**

Politicians' primary concern is getting reelected and serving their constituent voters. Therefore, political information strategies focus on how the business side of the issue will benefit politicians and their constituents. Businesses give information containing facts and figures using outside sources, experts, and stakeholders' support to inform the politician of the consequences of future public policy. Message framing is important to a business because the terms it uses to tell its side of an issue influence public sentiment for or against the firm.

7. **Explain the reasons for political campaign contributions, the role of PACs, and the difference between hard and soft money.**

The three reasons for political campaign contributions are to affect outcomes of elections, to obtain access to officeholders, and to influence regulations. Political action committees (PACs) are company-sponsored methods of obtaining campaign funds from employees and distributing the funds to candidates. Hard money is a direct contribution to a candidate's political campaign. Soft money is a contribution to a political party committee for use in party-building activities. Thus, hard money can be given directly to a political campaign whereas soft money cannot.

8. **Describe what lobbyists do, access, and the revolving door.**

Lobbyists meet personally with government officials to present the special interest political information strategy to influence officials' thinking and action on public policy issues. Access refers to the ability to lobby government officials. To gain access, many businesses hire professional lobbyists. The revolving door refers to people changing jobs between business and government as some business people run for public office or take regulatory jobs and some lawmakers become consultants and lobbyists for business.

9. **Fill in the blank with the appropriate key term (in order of appearance in the chapter).**

_____ gives federal laws precedence over state laws.

_____ are the business rules of conduct.

_____ occurs when one large business can supply the entire market more efficiently and cheaply than several small firms due to economies of scale.

_____ are costs of production borne by society rather than the business causing them.

_____ are developed by regulatory agencies to implement laws passed by Congress.

_____ is the action government takes to deal with issues.

_____ is government action directing resources to the development of specific industries.

_____ includes government taxing and spending to support and/or stimulate the economy.

_____ includes the supply, demand, and value of the U.S. currency.

_____ raises and lowers taxes on individuals and businesses to encourage or discourage spending.

_____ encourages or discourages international trade with specific countries.

_____ are generally more liberal regarding moral issues and are in favor of more government regulation, more spending, and more taxation.

_____ are generally more conservative regarding moral issues and are in favor of free markets with less government regulation, less spending, and less taxation.

_____ includes committee action, floor action, conference action, vote by both chambers, the president, and, if vetoed, Congress.

_____ are those most likely to switch the outcome of the vote, because they are often undecided and can be influenced.

_____ focus on technical facts and how the business side of the issue will benefit politicians and their constituents.

_____ refers to the terms used to gain public sentiment for one's side of an issue.

_____ are company-sponsored methods of obtaining campaign funds from employees and distributing the funds to candidates.

_____ is a direct contribution to a candidate's political campaign.

_____ is a contribution to a political party committee for use in party-building activities.

_____ is a situation in which if one competitor uses a strategy to gain an advantage, the others must follow, even when all lose.

_____ is representing a particular interest to influence political policy on issues.

KEY TERMS (IN ALPHABETICAL ORDER)

Democrats (p. 300)
externalities (p. 292)
fiscal policy (p. 296)
hard money (p. 311)
industrial policy (p. 295)
legislative process (p. 302)
lobbying (p. 313)
message framing (p. 307)
monetary policy (p. 296)
natural monopoly (p. 291)
pivotal voters (p. 303)

political action committees (PACs) (p. 311)
political information strategies (p. 306)
prisoners' dilemma (p. 312)
public policy (p. 295)
regulations (p. 291)
Republicans (p. 300)
rules (p. 293)
soft money (p. 311)
supremacy clause (p. 288)
taxation policy (p. 296)
trade policy (p. 296)

REVIEW QUESTIONS

1 What is the key role of government?

2 How does the supremacy clause help government and business?

3 There is much duplication between the federal and state government, so wouldn't it be more effective to eliminate state governments? Is there anything preventing the elimination of state government?

4 What is the difference between a municipality and a metropolis?

5 What are the reasons for government regulation of business?

6 Wal-Mart has the ability to underprice competitors and drive them out of business or to deter them from entering the market. So is Walmart a natural monopoly?

7 What are the steps in the public policy process?

8 What are the two major types of public policy?

9 What are the six government non-regulatory influences on business?

10 How do Democrats and Republicans differ on issues of morality and the role of government?

11 What are the key functions political parties perform?

12 What are the three most important powers of Congress?

13 What is message framing, and is it really important?

14 How are grassroots constituencies and coalition strategies similar and different?

15 How are testimonies in hearings similar to and different from advisory panels and committees?

DISCUSSION/CRITICAL THINKING QUESTIONS

Be sure to give a detailed explanation for your answer to all discussion questions.

1 Is the government too large?

2 Do we really need three branches of government?

3 Do we really need three levels of government?

4 Can the government control negative externalities?

5 Do consumers really have inadequate information?

6 Should business have to pay for social goals?

7 Which political party is the best?

8 Is it important to vote in political elections?

9 Passing a law through Congress is rather complicated; should the legislative process be simplified?

10 Do you believe that politicians don't really care about business?

11 Should PACs be outlawed to prevent special interest groups from influencing politicians?

12 Should lobbying be made illegal to prevent special interest groups from getting what they want?

13 Should the revolving door be closed to stop people from changing jobs between business and government to reduce special interest groups getting what they want?

APPLICATION EXERCISES

8.1 STATE GOVERNMENT

Visit the website of your state—the name of your state .gov. The site may have a link for business. Browse the site and report on at least three things you learned that you did not already know about your state government.

8.2 THOMAS

Visit THOMAS at the Library of Congress (www.congress.gov). In the "Legislation in Current Congress" search area, select "Browse Bills by Sponsor," find your "Representative" in the House, and click "GO." Report on the bills your rep. is currently working on.

8.3 POLITICAL PARTIES

Select one of the major political parties and visit its national committee website (www.gop.com or www.democrats.org). Browse the site and report on at least three things you learned that you did not already know about the political party.

8.4 LOBBYISTS

Go to the **Center for Responsive Politics** website (www.opensecrets.org) and click the "Lobbying" link. Do a search by name, industry, or issues you are interested in learning more about. Report on your findings.

CASE 8.1

Will the Republican House's ABM Destroy NLRB's Missile Aimed at Boeing's Charleston Plant or Will the Democratic Senate Abort Its Liftoff?

"The world's largest aerospace company, Boeing is the #2 maker of large commercial jets (behind rival Airbus) and the #2 defense contractor behind Lockheed Martin. Boeing's business units include Commercial Airplanes and Boeing Defense, Space & Security. Representing more than half of the company's revenue stream, Boeing's Commercial Airplanes segment designs and manufactures commercial jet aircraft for passengers and cargo. . . . Boeing plans to increase production of the 737 to 38 planes a month and of the 777 to 8 a month in 2013 . . . [and] has launched a second assembly line for 787 production in South Carolina."[111]

The National Labor Relations Board which prohibits companies from relocating a factory when workers go on strike filed "a complaint against Boeing last April, accusing the company of building an assembly plant in North Charleston, S.C., as a form of retaliation against unionized employees in Washington State who have engaged in five strikes since 1977, including a 58-day-walkout in 2008. . . . Republicans have repeatedly criticized the board's acting general counsel for filing a complaint against Boeing . . . [and] asserted that the N.L.R.B.'s move was causing some foreign companies to think twice about opening operations in the United States . . . [and] that the board was overreaching its authority and should not be dictating where companies can locate their operations."[112]

While the case was pending before an administrative law judge the House of Representatives decided to take the matter into their own hands by approving "a Republican-backed bill that would prohibit the National Labor Relations Board from trying to block Boeing from operating a new $750 million aircraft assembly line in South Carolina. The largely party-line vote was 238 to 186. Under the bill, an unusual effort to curb a federal agency's actions in a pending case, the labor board would be barred from seeking to have an employer shut, transfer or relocate employment or operations 'under any circumstances.'

The bill, called the 'Protecting Jobs from Government Interference Act,' is expected to face a battle in the Democratic-controlled Senate. . . . Democrats and union leaders [have] condemned the legislation, arguing that it undercut an independent federal agency and favored Boeing, a potent lobbying force and prominent political donor. . . . Representative Rush Holt, a New Jersey Democrat, said the bill 'would be devastating to workers across this country. It makes it easier to shift jobs overseas. It eliminates the only remedy to force companies to bring back work from overseas. This outsourcing [of the] Bill of Rights is not only bad for the interests of workers, it's bad for the economy at large.' . . . More than 250 professors signed a letter criticizing the legislation as 'unprecedented interference with a pending legal proceeding for the benefit of a particular employer.' They said the legislation would severely diminish the board's power to move against employers that illegally retaliate against unionization efforts or protests over working conditions by moving their operations elsewhere. . . .

Republicans argue that the bill would still let the labor board pursue many other remedies, among them back pay, although the opening of the assembly line in South Carolina has not caused any layoffs of Boeing workers in Washington State. . . . Jay Timmons, president of the National Association of Manufacturers, applauded the House vote. 'The N.L.R.B.'s actions are having a chilling impact on job creation and causing a great deal of uncertainty for manufacturers throughout the country.

Today's vote is just one step in the process of reining in this rogue agency.'. . .

The labor board's acting general counsel, Lafe Solomon, said that his decision to file a complaint against Boeing 'was based on a careful investigation and a review of the facts under longstanding federal labor law. The decision had absolutely nothing to do with political considerations, and there were no consultations with the White House. Regrettably, some have chosen to insert politics into what should be a straightforward legal procedure. These continuing political attacks are baseless and unprecedented.' The general counsel is independent from the full labor board and prosecutes cases asserting unfair labor practices. To prove that Boeing's move was retaliatory, Mr. Solomon pointed to statements by top Boeing officials saying their unhappiness over past strikes motivated them to build the South Carolina plant. But Boeing officials say South Carolina's low production costs were the reason behind the move."[113]

Questions

1. How does this case illustrate the government checks and balance system?
2. What government role(s) would support the House's and the NLRB's position on Boeing's Charleston plant?
3. Which types of public policy issues are addressed in this case?
4. How does this case highlight the differences in the United States' two major political parties' especially concerning business?
5. Given Figure 8.4, how could the opponents to the House bill block its passage?
6. What specific actions can and should Boeing take to influence the passage of the House bill into law?

CASE 8.2

Another Bailout, Another Bad Deal? The Proposed Government Bailout for Unions' Pension Plans

If we can bail out bad business decisions made by the U.S. financial industry why not bad decisions made by union benefits plans—what is good for the goose should be good for the gander!

On October 3, 2008 "the Senate passed the $700 billion bank bailout bill to buy mortgage-backed securities that were in danger of defaulting. By doing so they took these debts off the books of the banks, hedge funds and pension funds that held them. . . . The Senate got this past the House [who defeated an earlier version of the bill] by attaching it to a bill that was already under consideration. This side-stepped the House of Representatives, which usually must introduce any funding bills. The Senate's tactic resulted in successful passage of the bill by the House, and President Bush signed it into law. . . . By 2012, banks had repaid [most] of TARP funds, leaving only $120 billion still outstanding."[114]

So now that the government has recovered a portion of the bank loans "Senator Bob Casey has one more deal for you. If the Pennsylvania Democrat gets his way, U.S. taxpayers will also pick up the astonishing tab for poorly managed union pension plans. . . . In 2006 Congress passed the Pension Protection Act to prod companies and unions to shape up their pension plans, whether by lowering benefits, increasing contributions from employers and workers, or even raising retirement ages. The fact [is] that many unions and companies have refused to use these tools [and want to] make their mistake the obligation of U.S. taxpayers.

Mr. Casey is gathering support for his curiously named 'Create Jobs and Save Benefits Act,' a bailout for union-run retirement plans. Similar to House legislation from North Dakota Democrat Earl Pomeroy and Ohio Republican Patrick Tiberi, the bill would transfer tens of billions of dollars worth of retiree liabilities to the Pension Benefit Guaranty Corporation

(PBGC), i.e., to taxpayers.

At issue are multi-employer pension plans, in which companies across an industry pay into a single pension pool. The plans are predominately run by unions and for years have distinguished themselves by poor management. The Labor Department in 2008 listed 230 multi-employer plans that were either endangered (less than 80% funded), or critical (less than 65% funded), or that had applied to government for funding relief. By 2009 that number had soared to 640. . . .

Unions love multi-employer plans because they let workers keep their retirement benefits even if they switch jobs to another participating company. This encourages lifelong union membership. . . . When a company in an industry goes out of business, meanwhile, the remaining firms are still on the hook for all costs of the multi-employer plan. . . . Mr. Casey's bill would cordon off 'orphaned' pensions—those for which an employer has stopped contributing or withdrawn from a multi-employer fund—and put them into a separate account. Surviving companies would pay benefits to these orphans for five years, after which they'd get kicked to the PBGC, which would shoulder the benefits until the last retiree or beneficiary dies. The remaining multi-employer plan would be back in the black, free to start the negative-feedback loop of underpayments and overpromises again.

[Ironically the bailout seems to be] . . . a raw deal for union pensioners who worked a lifetime in expectation of certain benefits. The PBGC's current maximum payment to any plan participant is $12,800 a year. Mr. Casey's bill raises that to $21,000 year, still only a fraction of existing pension promises. Not that the PBGC has the cash to pay more. The agency's deficit was $21 billion . . . and it is expected to rise to an estimated $34 billion by 2019. Mr. Casey is claiming his multi-employer-bailout scheme will cost a mere $8 billion, but Moody's estimated that multi-employer plans were $165 billion underfunded. The tab is likely to be much higher given the moral hazard Mr. Casey would create. As Hudson Institute economist Diana Furchtgott-Roth notes, the bill creates 'a vicious circle. Once PGBC took over some plans, other employers would want to declare bankruptcy, unload plans on the PGBC, and reorganize under another name. The incentives to do this would be enormous.'"[115]

Questions

1. What seems to be the reason for Congress to pass legislation bailing out union-managed pension plans?

2. Under what authority does Congress have the right to bailout the private sector and related unions?

3. What are the implications for this proposed legislation and bailouts in general for other corporations?

4. How does message framing explain why companies and unions may lobby Congress on this issue?

5. How does this case challenge or support the checks and balance system of government?

6. Assuming that nonunionized businesses decided to develop political strategies to combat this proposed legislation, what specific strategies would you propose?

INTEGRATIVE CASE
8

INTEGRATIVE CASE 8.3

DHR Construction, LLC and the Town Council: We Have Met the Enemy and the Enemy Is Us!

This is a continuation case—please refer to Chapters 1–7 for further information.

It was supposed to be a day like any other day for Richard Davis, managing partner of DHR Construction, LLC, a firm that specialized in custom home construction. Richard was going through his usual morning ritual, checking the fax machine and telephones (including cell phones) for messages, reading through his e-mails, and reviewing his "bills to be paid," "bills to write," and "money to collect" piles. All seemed to be in order even after he checked in with his foreman at the construction site, so Richard could then concentrate his efforts on the more important, less day-to-day activities of strategic planning. As Richard sat down by his keyboard and fired up his business planning software package, the phone rang. That's all he needed—interruptions! Praying it was not a complaining customer, he gently answered the phone to find out that on the other end of the line was his partner, Stephen Hodgetts.

"Richard, you won't believe this," stated Hodgetts in a rushed and harried voice. "I just heard from Mark Kessler, president of the Home Building Association (HBA), that the town council has called an emergency session to discuss what they have characterized as the town's increasing "urban sprawl." No one knows exactly what the town council has in mind, but Mark is calling all of the builders in the HBA to make sure that we have a good turnout at the meeting. I'm heading over to the town hall as we speak and would ask that you meet me there asap."

Fifteen minutes later, Richard walked into a packed town hall with a standing-room-only crowd comprised predominately of builders, reporters, and local politicians. The media were in full force, with the local radio and TV networks clearly displaying their microphones and portable TV cameras. Richard spotted Hodgetts squashed in the far corner of the meeting hall and joined him and Mark Kessler.

"So what's the deal?" Richard barked over the noise of the crowd.

"The HBA runs this town in that the majority of the members of the council, including the mayor, have received campaign donations from the HBA as well as from our bigger individual members, yet even we just don't know," responded Mark. "The mayor, the city council members, and even the town clerk have been absolutely silent. None of my contacts within city hall or even the mayor's office has an inkling as to what this is all about except that it has to do with building within the town. If I do not know what is going on, I can tell you that that is a very bad sign because nothing ever gets done in this town without me knowing about it first!"

Mark's last comment sent shivers up the spine of both Richard Davis and Stephen Hodgetts. Since they had joined the HBA, their relationship with the local government, specifically the government building inspectors, had vastly improved. Mark had become a valuable resource for this fledgling little business and seemed to have taken a liking to these academics-turned-builders. He was a well-connected powerful ally who had gotten Richard and Stephen easy access to local politicians and local government administrators in the building department. He would even joke with Richard and Stephen that, if they ever got tired of playing builder, there was always a place for them in the HBA. If Mark admitted that something was afoot, then clearly trouble was brewing.

A gavel had to be pounded several times in order for the mayor to call the emergency meeting to order. "The town council has asked that I make a statement to the press and then immediately take questions from the audience," began the mayor. "As you all know, in the last 10 years, our town has grown from a sleepy little rural community, predominantly made up of farms, small homes, and shops, to a large bedroom community featuring corporate offices, shopping malls, and upscale homes. Over the years, this council has tried, in conjunction with our planning and zoning board, to control the growth so that town services could keep up with the ever increasing town population. To our dismay, we have failed—failed miserably—to do so."

A murmur ran through the crowd with the mayor's last statement. Rarely does a politician admit failure, and worse, in a very public forum. "As you all know," continued the mayor, "our town has grown in physical size as we have built more and more homes, malls, and offices. With the influx of new community members, we have seen an increase in traffic, housing costs, crime, and taxes and a flight out of our town of the friends and neighbors—the lower middle class and the poor—who cannot afford to live here anymore. Some may call this progress; the town council and I would differ. We believe that the very character of our community, a community where many of us are born, live out our lives, and die, is under attack. Without pointing any fingers, many of you in this room know who the culprits are who have transformed our once great community into just another series of strip malls, Anywhere, USA."

Hodgetts and Davis looked at one another to confirm the very bad feeling in their gut while Mark Kessler was on his cell phone, presumably telling the party on the other end what was being said at the meeting. The mayor took a deep breath and continued his statement. "Well, today, the town council and I have taken measures to take back our town and get it under our control. In an emergency session that we just held, the town council voted unanimously to institute a one-year moratorium on building within town limits. Current building projects that have already been issued building permits will be allowed to continue, yet no new permits will be issued for the next six months. During that time period, we will hire an engineering firm to study the town's layout and growth and then have them recommend new building and zoning codes that would allow us to better control the quality of life in our town. We, of course, reserve the option to continue the moratorium if additional time is needed in order to allow for public input and enactment of new legislation."

A boom came forth from the crowd once the mayor finished his statement. The builders protested vehemently against the moratorium while members of the local community applauded the town council's brave actions. It took 10 minutes to finally restore order to the meeting and to then have the mayor handle questions from the audience. After taking questions from reporters and posing for snapshots, the mayor finally took questions from the audience.

"Many of you know me. I have lived in this town for many years, and I love this town," began Richard Davis. "Mr. Mayor, I congratulate you and the town council for bringing the problem of uncontrolled town growth to the forefront as a policy issue. We, the builders who live and work in this community, only want what is best for the town and are willing to cooperate with you and the town council in any way that you see fit. However, let me point out that your moratorium will cost this town dearly in jobs and lost tax dollars. I would estimate that we probably have six to nine months worth of building projects approved so that the effects of the moratorium will not be felt immediately. When these projects come to an end, though, there will be no new construction. Builders like me will then have to fire our employees, many of whom live in the town, and let go of our subcontractors, again, most located within the town's limits. Maybe these people can swing their mortgage and tax payments for three to six months; maybe they can't. Some won't be able to and will have to move out of town, leaving a glut of homes on the market and reducing property values.

Furthermore, many of us builders buy our supplies from local distributors. They, too, will have to let some of their personnel go since we represent a sizable portion of their business. And what about the local banks and finance companies? They'll lose out twice: once when we builders no longer borrow money for land acquisitions and construction loans and a second time when homeowners or commercial businesses no longer finance their mortgages. More fired personnel. Finally, in order to obtain a certificate of occupancy (CO), the builder pays the town a 5 percent fee based on the assessed value of the home or building. Since the average home in this area runs around $300,000, the town will lose $15,000 a home; commercial buildings, of course, have a much higher average assessed value. Do the math, Mayor, and see what your total revenue loss is just on the COs of home construction. This loss will have to be made up in higher real estate taxes."

The crowd was buzzing with excitement and apprehension, and clearly Richard had stirred the pot. "Mr. Mayor," Richard continued, "you may think that you have saved the town with this moratorium. Let me tell you that you have not. In fact, you may very well have signed its death warrant by increasing unemployment and taxes while reducing property values. The path to hell is paved with good intentions, Mr. Mayor, and I believe that you are well intended. But please, before this path is cemented over, reconsider this measure. You may be cementing more than just the moratorium." Mark Kessler winked at Stephen Hodgetts, patted Richard Davis on the back, and knew that he had just had his coming out party for the future leader of the HBA.

Questions

1. In general, what are the reasons for local government regulation of home and commercial construction in communities?

2. What political strategies does the HBA use to influence local politicians? What other options are available?

3. How did the town frame its message in order to support the moratorium? How did Richard Davis try to reframe that message?

4. What alternative nonmarket strategies could the town council have employed to obtain support for its objective of limiting town growth?

5. Assuming the town council does not repeal the moratorium, what nonmarket strategies should the HBA and DHR Construction, LLC employ to deal with it?

REFERENCES AND NOTES

1 http://business.time.com/2011/11/22/was-the-governmentbailout-of–aig-illegal (accessed June 12, 2012).

2 N.M. Dahan, J. Doh, and H. Teegen, "Role of Nongovernmental Organizations in the Business—Government— Society Interface: Special Issue Overview and Introductory Essay," *Business & Society* 49(1) (2010): 20–34.

3 R.H. Lester, A. Hillman, A. Zardkoohi, and A.A. Cannella, "Former Government Officials as Outside Directors: The Role of Human and Social Capital," *Academy of Management Journal* 51(5) (2008): 999–1013.

4 J. Carreyrou, "Home–Health Firms Blasted," *Wall Street Journal* (October 3, 2011): B1.

5 C.L. Pearce and C.C. Manz, "Leadership Centrality and Corporate Social Ir-Responsibility (CSIR): The Potential Ameliorating Effects of Self and Shared Leadership on CSIR," *Journal of Business Ethics* 102(4) (2010): 563–579.

6 http://americanhistory.about.com/od/usconstitution/a/checks_balances.htm (accessed June 13, 2012).

7 Ibid.

8 Ibid.

9 www.usa.gov (accessed May 24, 2012).

10 T. Tracy, "First Fracking Rules Unveiled," *Wall Street Journal* (April 19, 2012): A3.

11 M. Eckblad, "Pilgrim's Pride Tried to Manipulate Prices of Chicken, U.S. Judge Rules," *Wall Street Journal* (October 4, 2011): B2.

12 A. Armenakis and J. Wigand, "Stakeholder Actions and Their Impact on the Organizational Cultures of Two Tobacco Companies," *Business and Society Review* 115(2) (2010): 147–171.

13 R.H. Lester, A. Hillman, A. Zardkoohi, and A.A. Cannella, "Former Government Officials as Outside Directors: The Role of Human and Social Capital," *Academy of Management Journal* 51(5) (2008): 999–1013.

14 C. Marquis and Z. Huang, "The Contingent Nature of Public Policy and the Growth of U.S. Commercial Banking," *Academy of Management Journal* 52(6) (2009): 1222–1246.

15 S. Forbes, "Election Armageddon," *Forbes* (May 7, 2012): 11–12.

16 Ibid.

17 R.H. Lester, A. Hillman, A. Zardkoohi, and A.A. Cannella, "Former Government Officials as Outside Directors: The Role of Human and Social Capital," *Academy of Management Journal* 51(5) (2008): 999–1013.

18 P. O'Connell and J. McGregor, "Managing Through the Economic Storm," *BusinessWeek* (June 29, 2009): 46–48.

19 G. Colvin, "What Makes a CEO and MPV?"*Fortune* (June 13, 2011): 27.

20 R.H. Lester, A. Hillman, A. Zardkoohi, and A.A. Cannella, "Former Government Officials as Outside Directors: The Role of Human and Social Capital," *Academy of Management Journal* 51(5) (2008): 999–1013.

21 J. Zweig, "Pay Collars Won't Hold Back Wall Street's Big Dogs," *Wall Street Journal* (February 7–8, 2009): B1.

22 C. Marquis and Z. Huang, "The Contingent Nature of Public Policy and the Growth of U.S. Commercial Banking," *Academy of Management Journal* 52(6) (2009): 1222–1246.

23 I.P. Mahmood and C. Rufin, "Government's Dilemma: The Role of Government in Imitation and Innovation," *Academy of Management Review* 30(2) (2005): 338–360.

24 Budget link, http://www.gpo.gov/fdsys/pkg/BILLS-112hconres34eh/pdf/BILLS-112hconres34eh.pdf (accessed May 24, 2012).

25 www.fideralreserve.gov (accessed May 28, 2012).

26 J. Sasseen and K. Epstein, "A Backlash Against Obama's Budget," *BusinessWeek* (March 16, 2009): 16–22.

27 S. Cutler, "Fixing America: A CEO's Master Plan," *Fortune* (March 19, 2012): 21.

28 S. Forbes, "Election Armageddon," *Forbes* (May 7, 2012): 11–12.

29 www.ncpa.org (accessed May 24, 2012).

30 www.heritage.org (accessed May 28, 2012).

31 http://www.27east.com/news/article.cfm/Southampton-Village-Surrounding-Areas/423278/Counter-Protest–By-Immigrant-Laborers-Held-At-Southampton-7-Eleven (accessedJune 14, 2012).

32 http://topics.nytimes.com/top/reference/timestopics/subjects/i/immigration-and-emigration/index.html (accessed June 14, 2012).

33 J. Kronholz and S. Lueck, "Immigration Bill Passes Senate, Still Faces Chasm Immigration," *Wall Street Journal (May 26, 2006), A2.*

34 http://www.newsday.com/news/local/longisland/ny-ff5,0,7145841.story (accessedMay 30, 2006).

35 www.business.usa.gov (accessed May 28, 2012).

36 S. Forbes, "Tele-Socialism," *Forbes* (June 4, 20212): 14.

37 D. Malpass, "Pushing Back: A Government-Centered Society," *Forbes* (May 21, 2012): 32.

38 S. Forbes, "Taxes, Trade, Social Security and More–George Bush Speaks Outs," *Forbes* (May 21, 2012): 15–18.

39 M.L. Barnett and A.A. King, "Good Fences Make Good Neighbors: A Longitudinal Analysis of an Industry Self–Regulatory Institution," *Academy of Management Journal* 51(6) (2008): 1150–1170.

40 J. Tozzi and L. Litvan, "I Rise to Introduce a Bill That I Have Carefully Crafted to Fail," *BusinessWeek* (February 13–19, 2012): 36.

41 R. Robin and B. Roth, "Lobbyists Set Their Sights on the Supercommittee," *BusinessWeek* (August 15–28, 2011): 25–26.

42 "Precedence of motions (Rule XXII)," *Rules of the Senate.* United States Senate, http://rules.senate.gov/public/index.cfm?p=RuleXXII (accessed May 25, 2012).

43 P. O'Connell and J. McGregor, "Managing Through the Economic Storm," *BusinessWeek* (June 29, 2009): 46–48.

44 D. Bennett, "Business Bestseller Tom Rath," *BusinessWeek* (August 11, 2011): 89–90.

45 S. Forbes, "Taxes, Trade, Social Security and More–George Bush Speaks Outs," *Forbes* (May 21, 2012): 15–18.

46 D.P. Barron, *Business and Its Environment*, 6th ed. (Upper Saddle, NJ: Prentice–Hall, 2010).

47 www.alec.org (accessed May 25, 2012).

48 A. Fitzgerald, "How a Bill Really Becomes a Law," *BusinessWeek* (August 1–7, 2011): 30.

49 www.bgov.com (accessed May 25, 2012).

50 "What is BGOV? *BusinessWeek* (Spring 2011): B1.

51 K. Weise, "It's Your Call: Read All 2,300 Pages of Dodd-Frank. Or Read This," *BusinessWeek* (January 16–22, 2012): 30.

52 S. Coll, "ExxonMobil vs. Dodd-Frank," *BusinessWeek* (May 14–20, 2012): 8–9.

53 J. Zweig, "Pay Collars Won't Hold Back Wall Street's Big Dogs," *Wall Street Journal* (February 7–8, 2009): B1.

54 R.H. Lester, A. Hillman, A. Zardkoohi, and A.A. Cannella, "Former Government Officials as Outside Directors: The Role of Human and Social Capital," *Academy of Management Journal* 51(5) (2008): 999–1013.

55 D. Malpass, "Pushing Back: A Government-Centered Society," *Forbes* (May 21, 2012): 32.

56 P. O'Connell and J. McGregor, "Managing Through the Economic Storm," *BusinessWeek* (June 29, 2009): 46–48.

57 www.alec.org (accessed May 25, 2012); www.bgov.com (accessed May 25, 2012).

58 J.P. Bonardi, M.J. Hillman, and G.D. Keim, "The Attractiveness of Political Markets: Implications for Firm Strategy," *Academy of Management Review* 30(2) (2005): 397–413.

59 S. Holt, "Building Law-Abiding Businesses," *Suffolk Business Magazine* (Fall 2011): 38–39.

60 What is BGOV? *BusinessWeek* (Spring 2011): B1.

61 J.M. Stevens, H.K. Steensman, D.A. Harrison, and P.I. Cochran, "Symbolic or Substantive Document? The Influence of the Ethics Codes on Financial Executive Decisions," *Strategic Management Journal* (26 February 2005): 181–195.

62 J.P. Bonardi and G.D. Keim, "Corporate Political Strategies for Widely Salient Issues," *Academy of Management Review* 30(3) (2005): 555–556.

63 D. Doane, "Beyond Corporate Social Responsibility: Minnows, Mammoths and Markets," *Futures* (March–April 2005): 215–230.

64 N. Easton and T. Demos, "The Business Guide to Congress," *Fortune* (May 11, 2009): 72–75.

65 S. Forbes, "Taxes, Trade, Social Security and More–George Bush Speaks Outs," *Forbes* (May 21, 2012): 15–18.

66 N. Easton and T. Demos, "The Business Guide to Congress," *Fortune* (May 11, 2009): 72–75.

67 http://www.caterpillar.com/cda/layout?x=7&m=393518&id=3418240 (accessed June 14, 2012).

68 http://subscriber.hoovers.com/H/company360/fulldescription.html?companyId=10304000000000 (accessed June 14, 2012).

69 http://www.cat.com/cda/components/fullArticleNoNav?ids=322444&languageId=7 (accessed May 31, 2006).

70 http://subscriber.hoovers.com/H/company360/fulldescription.html?companyId=10304000000000 (accessed June 14, 2012).

71 http://www.nytimes.com/2011/10/04/business/global/us-senate-backs-tough-china-trade-moves.html (accessed June 14, 2012).

72 J. Dean, "U.S. Senators Offer Hope to China on Tariffs," *Wall Street Journal* (March 24, 2006), A4.

73 http://www.cat.com/cda/components/fullArticleNoNav?ids=322444&languageId=7 (accessed May 31, 2006).

74 R. Van der Merwe, L.F. Pitt, and R. Abratt. "Stakeholder Strength: PR Survival Strategies in the Internet Age," *Public Relations Quarterly* 50 (Spring 2005), 39–49.

75 A. Armenakis and J. Wigand, "Stakeholder Actions and Their Impact on the Organizational Cultures of Two Tobacco Companies." *Business and Society Review* 115(2) (2010): 147–171.

76 P. Schreck, "Reviewing the Business Case for Corporate Social Responsibility: New Evidence and Analysis." *Journal of Business Ethics* 103(2) (2011): 167–188.

77 M. Schlangenstein and J. McCracken, "Outmaneuvered," *BusinessWeek* (May 14–20, 2012)" 25–26.

78 D.P. Barron, *Business and Its Environment*, 6th ed. (Upper Saddle, NJ: Prentice-Hall, 2010).

79 R. Van der Merwe, L.F. Pitt, and R. Abratt. "Stakeholder Strength: PR Survival Strategies in the Internet Age," *Public Relations Quarterly* 50 (Spring 2005): 39–49.

80 www.opensecrets.org (accessed May 29, 2012).

81 www.commoncause.org (accessed May 29, 2012).

82 S. Coll, "ExxonMobil vs. Dodd–Frank," *BusinessWeek* (May 14–20, 2012): 8–9.

83 W.J. Henisz, "Legitimacy, Interest Group Pressures, and Change in Emergent Institutions: The Case of Foreign Investors and Host Country Governments," *Academy of Management Review* 30(2) (2005): 361–382.

84 L. Meckler, "Auto Makers Support Alternative–Fuel Measures," *Wall Street Journal* (October 10, 2005): A7.

85 A. Roth, "FedEx Threatens to Cancel Jet Orders," *Wall Street Journal* (March 25, 2009): B1.

86 D.P. Barron, *Business and Its Environment*, 6th ed. (Upper Saddle, NJ: Prentice-Hall, 2010).

87 A. Fitzgerald, "How a Bill Really Becomes a Law," *BusinessWeek* (August 1–7, 2011): 30.

88 S. Coll, "ExxonMobil vs. Dodd-Frank," *BusinessWeek* (May 14–20, 2012): 8–9.

89 D. Malpass, "Pushing Back: A Government-Centered Society," *Forbes* (May 21, 2012): 32.

90 A. Cole, "Lockheed Doubles Lobbying Outlays," *Wall Street Journal* (May 12, 2009): B3.

91 R. Levine, "Google's Spending Tentacles of Influence," *BusinessWeek* (October 31–November 6, 2011): 43–44.

92 www.opensecrets.org/lobby/index.php (accessed May 29, 2012).

93 N. Easton and T. Demos, "The Business Guide to Congress," *Fortune* (May 11, 2009): 72–75.

94 www.opensecrets.org/lobby/index.php (accessed May 29, 2012).

95 J. Sasseen and K. Epstein, "A Backlash Against Obama's Budget," *BusinessWeek* (March 16, 2009): 16–22.

96 www.opensecrets.org/lobby/index.php (accessed May 29, 2012).

97 R.H. Lester, A. Hillman, A. Zardkoohi, and A.A. Cannella, "Former Government Officials as Outside Directors: The Role of Human and Social Capital," *Academy of Management Journal* 51(5) (2008): 999–1013.

98 Staff, "Drug Industry Sees Increase in Lobbying," *Wall Street Journal* (June 24, 2003): A4.

99 D.P. Barron, *Business and Its Environment*, 6th ed. (Upper Saddle, NJ: Prentice–Hall, 2010).

100 J.P. Bonardi and G.D. Keim, "Corporate Political Strategies for Widely Salient Issues," *Academy of Management Review* 30(3) (2005): 555–576.

101 M. Orey and J. Sasseen, "No Solidarity for Labor," *BusinessWeek* (June 15, 2009): 28–29.

102 N. Easton and T. Demos, "The Business Guide to Congress," *Fortune* (May 11, 2009): 72–75.

103 N.E. Boudette, "Chrysler Loan Drive Seeks Dealers' Help," *Wall Street Journal* (March 21–22, 2009): B5.

104 J. Sasseen and K. Epstein, "A Backlash Against Obama's Budget," *BusinessWeek* (March 16, 2009): 16–22.

105 R. Levine, "Google's Spending Tentacles of Influence," *BusinessWeek* (October 31–November 6, 2011): 43–44.

106 W.J. Henisz, "Legitimacy, Interest Group Pressures, and Change in Emergent Institutions: The Case of Foreign Investors and Host Country Governments," *Academy of Management Review* 30(2) (2005): 361–382.

107 N. Easton and T. Demos, "The Business Guide to Congress," *Fortune* (May 11, 2009): 72–75.

108 D.P. Barron, *Business and Its Environment*, 6th ed. (Upper Saddle, NJ: Prentice–Hall, 2010).

109 Ibid.

110 R.H. Lester, A. Hillman, A. Zardkoohi, and A.A. Cannella, "Former Government Officials as Outside Directors: The Role of Human and Social Capital," *Academy of Management Journal* 51(5) (2008): 999–1013.

111 http://subscriber.hoovers.com/H/company360/fulldescription.html?companyId=10221000000000 (accessed June 14, 2012).

112 http://www.nytimes.com/2011/09/16/business/house-approves-bill-restricting-nlrb.html (accessed June 14, 2012).

113 Ibid.

114 http://useconomy.about.com/od/criticalssues/a/govt_bailout.htm (accessed June 18, 2012).

115 http://online.wsj.com/article/SB10001424052702303491304575188263180553530.html#articleTabs%3Darticle (accessed June 18, 2012).

Chapter 9

LAW ENFORCING AND REGULATORY STRATEGIES

Learning Outcomes

In this chapter, you will find out the answers to these key questions:

▪ How is the executive branch of government organized with regulatory agencies?
▪ How are business rules made by government?

After studying this chapter, you should be able to:

1. List the organizational structure of the federal executive branch of government and the three primary powers of the president
2. Explain the relationship between regulatory impact analysis, the *Federal Register*, and Regulations.gov
3. Describe the rule-making process
4. Compare and contrast cross-subsidization, cost-of-service regulation, privatization, and deregulation
5. Discuss the differences in the use of campaign contributions, lobbying, grassroots lobbying, and testimony strategies used by businesses to influence Congress versus influencing regulatory agencies
6. Identify the role of advisors and the reasons why businesses serve on advisory panels and committees
7. Define the following key terms (in order of appearance in the chapter)

Executive Office	Administrative	cross-subsidization
cabinet	Procedures Act (APA)	cost-of-service regulation
executive departments	procedural due process	privatization
independent agencies	substantive due process	deregulation
regulatory impact analysis (RIA)		
Federal Register		
Regulations.gov		

▪ Chapter Outline

What's This Chapter About?

In the last chapter, we briefly discussed the three branches of government, followed by details of the legislative branch. In this chapter, we focus on understanding the executive branch of government and the strategies businesses use to influence how they are regulated.

We begin by discussing the organizational structure and responsibilities of the executive branch of the federal government. Next, we give an overview of how the *rules* are developed by regulatory agencies to implement laws passed by Congress, and how the government decides when regulation is needed. We progress by giving the step-by-step process used to make the rules, which business can challenge, and then discuss some of the regulatory agencies responsible for enforcing the rules.

Our fourth section discusses how business wants regulations to be reformed, the trend toward the privatization of government functions, and the deregulation of business. As usual, we discuss nonmarket and market strategies and ethics. We include an additional section to present the many strategies business uses to influence the outcomes of regulations.

CASE

The Man of Steel: More Powerful than a Locomotive, Able to Bend Steel in His Bare Hands, It's . . . ?

Being surrounded by a myriad of reporters who hang on his each and every word, the man that many businesses consider the most powerful and influential person in the world has hundreds of economists analyzing his speeches, not only line by line but word for word. They are looking for clues, hints, and perhaps subtle nuances that might reveal his next move, a move that might shake the very foundation of the financial community, bring the stock markets of the world to a trading halt, or create the reverse—a trading frenzy—and, in so doing, change the world economy as we know it. Yet this "superman" is not, as many would suspect, the president of the United States; is not elected by the people, for the people; and in fact, is not a politician at all. In not running for office, he is unaffected by terms of office and lobbyists trying to earn his good graces with campaign contributions. He is not confronted by opponents trying to besmirch his name and his reputation and does not have to make promises he can't keep to appease a demanding public or his contributors. He is the benevolent guiding light of economic reason, the caretaker of the U.S. economy, and a presidential appointee with "powers beyond those of a normal man." Who is this "man of steel . . . the protector of the American way?" Why, of course, the chairman of the Federal Reserve, Ben S. Bernanke.

"The Federal Reserve System is a quasi-governmental, decentralized central bank. It is composed of a central Board of Governors in Washington, D.C., twelve regional Federal Reserve Banks located in major cities throughout the nation, numerous member banks and other entities. . . . The Federal Reserve System was created via the Federal Reserve Act of 1913 which 'established a new central bank designed to add both flexibility and strength to the nation's financial system.' . . . The main tasks of the Federal Reserve are to supervise and regulate banks, implement monetary policy by open market operations, setting the discount rate, and setting the reserve ratio, maintain a strong payments system, control the amount of currency that is made and destroyed on a day-to-day basis (in conjunction with the Mint and Bureau of Engraving and Printing). Other tasks include economic research, economic education, [and] community outreach."[1]

"Fed board members are appointed by the US President and confirmed by the Senate for one-time 14-year terms, staggered at two-year intervals to prevent political stacking. The seven governors comprise the majority of the 12-person Federal Open Market Committee, which determines monetary policy. The five remaining members are reserve bank presidents who rotate in one-year terms, with New York always holding a place. Although the Fed enjoys significant political and financial freedom (it even operates at a profit), the chairman is required to testify before Congress twice a year. National member banks must own stock in their Federal Reserve Bank, though it is optional for state-chartered banks."[2] The chairperson and the board members may be removed from office by the president if they are unable to perform their duties and functions.

So why is the Federal Reserve (and therefore the chair) so important to business? The Federal Reserve affects the money supply, the available capital that flows into and out of the marketplace. The Federal Reserve has two powerful tools at its disposal in which to do this—bank reserves and setting lending rates. "Here's how it works. The Federal Reserve requires commercial banks and other financial institutions to hold as reserves a fraction of the deposits they accept. Banks hold these reserves either as cash in their vaults or as deposits at Federal Reserve banks."[3] The more reserve that a bank is required to hold, the less that the bank can lend to commercial institutions, and the less that commercial institutions can borrow to grow their businesses. "In the

United States [however] the Federal Reserve rarely alters the reserve requirement."[4] Beginning October 2008, the Federal Reserve banks pay *interest on required reserve balances and excess balances*. As of 2012 the required reserve ratio in the United States was 10 percent on transaction deposits (component of money supply "M1") of over $71 million, and zero on time deposits and all other deposits.[5]

The Federal Reserve prefers to impact money flow through lending rates. "By setting the discount rate [the base rate at which its member banks may borrow] and the federal funds rate [the rate at which banks borrow from each other], the Fed influences the pace of lending and, many believe, the pace of the economy itself. The discount rate has fluctuated dramatically over the past decade: from 6% in 2000 to .75% in 2002, then slowly creeping back to 6.25% by 2006, then quickly dropping to .5% by 2008[6] and ticking back up to .75% by 2012."[7]

How do these shifts affect individual businesses? The cost that banks pay to borrow money from the Federal Reserve and each other must be passed on to its customers, those businesses and consumers that borrow money from the banks. The banks' most favored customers pay what is called the prime lending rate, which usually is calculated by adding three percentage points to the Federal Funds rate (i.e., 0.75% + 3% = 3.75%). The higher the federal fund rate (FFR), the higher the cost of capital to the banks and therefore the higher the cost of capital to businesses. In the preceding example, a preferred business would have to make at least a 3.75 percent profit on borrowed money in order to break even, which is much lower than the firm would have had to earn in the year 2000 (6% discount + 3% for federal funds = 9%). The higher the interest rate, the higher the profit margins have to be in order for a firm that borrows money to break even. Imagine that in 1979 the FFR was 19 percent,[8] requiring most favored customers to pay 22 percent interest! As you can imagine, higher interest rates slow down the economy; lower rates accelerate it.

Higher interest rates also make it more difficult for firms to raise capital through their corporate stocks and bonds. Investors in June of 2003 found that they couldn't even earn 1 percent interest in their risk-free bank money market accounts, making riskier investments in corporate bonds and stocks very appealing. As of July 2012, risk-free money-market accounts were earning less than 1 percent,[9] having a positive impact on the sale of both corporate bonds and stocks.

No one raises their children telling them that they should grow up to be the chairperson of the Federal Reserve. Given the power of that office and the long-term tenure of the position, maybe they should!

The following questions are related to the Man of Steel case. Answers can be found within the chapter.

1. Why do you think the Federal Reserve chairperson is not a member of the president's cabinet?
2. What part of the executive branch of government is the Federal Reserve?
3. What authority does the president have over the Federal Reserve?
4. What are the regulatory functions of the Federal Reserve?
5. Why might the Federal Reserve prefer to alter U.S. monetary policy through the discount rate rather than through bank reserves?
6. What actions by the Federal Reserve might be published in the *Federal Register* and at Regulations.gov?
7. What, if any, congressional oversight is there of the Federal Reserve?
8. What might be the impact of deregulating bank reserve ratios?
9. What might be some reasonable nonmarket strategies that businesses could employ with the Federal Reserve?

THE EXECUTIVE BRANCH OF GOVERNMENT

Learning Outcome 1: List the organizational structure of the federal executive branch of government and the three primary powers of the president.

In this section, we discuss the organization of five parts of the executive branch of the government. The president is the head of the executive branch, which includes many departments and agencies. See Figure 9.1 for a simple organization chart. Each of these five areas is discussed in greater detail in this section.[10]

- Executive Office of the President
- Executive Departments
- Independent Agencies and Government Corporations
- Boards, Commissions, and Committees
- Quasi-Official Agencies

■ **Figure 9.1:** The Executive Branch Organization

Executive Office of the President

The Executive Office of the president is made up of White House offices and agencies. These offices, such as National Security and the Office of Management and Budget, help develop and implement the policies and programs of the president. (See Figure 9.2 for a list of offices.)

Executive Departments

The Cabinet. The tradition of the cabinet dates back to the beginnings of the presidency itself. One of the principal purposes of the cabinet (drawn from Article II, Section 2 of the Constitution) is to advise the president on any subject relating to the duties of their respective offices. *The cabinet includes the heads of the 15 executive departments.*

- Council of Economic Advisers
- Council on Environmental Quality
- Executive Residence
- National Security Staff
- Office of Administration
- Office of Management and Budget
- Office of National Drug Control Policy
- Office of Science and Technology Policy
- Office of the United States Trade Representative
- Office of the Vice President
- White House Office: many other entities exist within the White House Office

■ **Figure 9.2:** Executive Office of the President

The Man of Steel Case Question 1: Why do you think the Federal Reserve chairperson is not a member of the president's cabinet?

The Federal Reserve was established as a quasi-governmental decentralized central bank with the notion of being an independent entity from the president's office. It was established in 1913, over 100 years after the establishment of the president's cabinet, and has been viewed as an independent agency delegated to supervising and regulating banks, implementing monetary policy by open market operations, setting the discount and the reserve ratio, maintaining a strong payments system, and controlling the amount of currency that is made and destroyed on a day-to-day basis. Making the chairperson part of the president's cabinet might negatively impact the ability of the Federal Reserve to act in a nonpartisan apolitical manner.

Executive Departments and Their Agencies. See Figure 9.3 for a list of the 15 executive departments. *Executive departments have their own offices, regulatory agencies, and advisory committees*, which are not shown in Figure 9.3 because there are hundreds of them. For a full list of offices, agencies, bureaus, and other information about each department, visit the **USA.gov** website (www.usa.gov). Click on the links find government agencies, executive branch, executive department, and any of the 15 departments.

Independent Agencies and Government Corporations

Independent agencies include regulators that are not part of and do not report to any of the 15 executive departments. Note that we include government corporations within our regulators definitions. Independent establishments are created by Congress to address

1. Department of Agriculture (USDA): *guaranteeing quality food supply*
2. Department of Commerce (DOC): *supporting the economy*
3. Department of Defense (DOD): *defending U.S. interests within the United States and abroad*
4. Department of Education (ED): *investing in our future by assuring quality instruction*
5. Department of Energy (DOE): *protecting current sources of energy and supporting R&D for future sources*
6. Department of Health and Human Services (HHS): *providing for the social welfare of the citizens*
7. Department of Homeland Security (DHS): *keeping America safe from within*
8. Department of Housing and Urban Development: (HUD) *ensuring housing and caring for inner cities*
9. Department of Justice (DOJ): *providing law enforcement*
10. Department of Labor (DOL): *overseeing worker rights and employer responsibilities*
11. Department of State (DOS): *addressing global challenges and advancing diplomacy*
12. Department of the Interior (DOI): *defending our natural resources*
13. Department of the Treasury: *taking responsibility for U.S. fiscal and monetary policy*
14. Department of Transportation (DOT): *ensuring safe and reliable movement of goods and people*
15. Department of Veterans Affairs (VA): *taking care of those who have served in the armed forces*

■ **Figure 9.3:** Executive Departments

concerns that go beyond the scope of ordinary legislation. Independent agencies are responsible for keeping the government and economy running smoothly, and they too have advisory committees. See Figure 9.4 for a partial list and visit USA.gov (www.usa. gov) for a list of 69 independent agencies and corporations that regulate business. Click on the links find government agencies, Executive Branch, **Independent Agencies and Government Corporations.** Note from Figure 9.4 that we have discussed some of the independents in prior chapters.

Central Intelligence Agency (CIA)	FTC
Commission on Civil Rights	National Railroad Passenger Corporation
CPSC	(AMTRAK)
EEOC	National Science Foundation (NSF)
EPA	NLRB
FCC	Peace Corps
FDIC	SEC
FEC	Small Business Administration (SBA)
Federal Mediation and Conciliation	Social Security Administration (SSA)
Service	United States Postal Service (USPS)

■ **Figure 9.4:** Independent Agencies and Government Corporations

Two Types of Regulatory Agencies. As discussed, the two types of regulatory agencies fall within the executive department or are independent. One way you can sometimes tell them apart is by their titles. Independents often use the term "commission" in their title, but not always, as you can see in Figure 9.4

Personal and Professional Applications

1. Which executive department/agency or independent agency has the most effect on you?

2. Which executive department/agency and/or independent agency has the most effect on your present or past employer and/or a producer of the products it sells?

Boards, Commissions, and Committees

Regulators have boards, commissions, and committees to aid the executive branch in making sound public policy. See Figure 9.5 for a partial list of advisors on business issues and visit USA.gov (www.usa.gov) for a list of all 68 advisors. Click on the links to Branch, Boards, Commissions and Committees, and a separate list of **Federal Advisory Committees (FAC)**. The Federal Advisory Committee Act (FACA) database is used by federal agencies to continuously manage an average of 1,000 advisory committees government-wide. Business uses it to stay abreast of important developments resulting from advisory committee activities.

Chief Financial Officers Council	Federal Accounting Standards Advisory Board (FASB)	Interagency Alternative Dispute Resolution Working Group
Chief Information Officers Council		National Bipartisan Commission on the Future of Medicare
	Federal Financial Institutions Examination Council	Regulatory Information Service Center
		Social Security Advisory Board
		Taxpayer Advocacy Panel

■ **Figure 9.5:** Boards, Commissions, and Committees

Quasi-Official Agencies

Quasi-official agencies are not officially executive agencies but are required by statute to publish certain information on their programs and activities in the *Federal Register* (to be discussed later in this chapter). They include the Federal Reserve System, Legal Services Corporation, Smithsonian Institution, State Justice Institute, and U.S. Institute of Peace.

> The Man of Steel Case Question 2: What part of the executive branch of government is the Federal Reserve?
>
> The Federal Reserve is a quasi-governmental decentralized central bank. The Federal Reserve System was created via the Federal Reserve Act of 1913, which established a new central bank designed to add both flexibility and strength to the nation's financial system.

Powers of the President

The major duties and responsibilities of the president include appointments, legislative and veto power, and international trade agreements, which are the three most important powers. Appointments and veto power have the most direct effect on business in general, with the trade agreements and others having more effect on specific industries and businesses. For more details, see Figure 9.6.

> The Man of Steel Case Question 3: What authority does the president have over the Federal Reserve?
>
> Fed Board members are appointed by the U.S. president and confirmed by the Senate for one-time 14-year terms, staggered at two-year intervals to prevent political stacking. The chairperson and the board members may be removed from office by the president if they are unable to perform their duties and functions.

- As the *chief executive*, the president is in charge of enforcing the laws through the executive branch and personally nominates cabinet members and Supreme Court justices to *appointments* with Senate approval.
- As *legislator in chief*, the president proposes legislation and works closely with congressional leadership. The president can veto congressional bills.
- As the *head of state* and *chief diplomat*, the president has the authority to make and break foreign treaties, to recognize foreign governments, and to enter into executive agreements with other heads of state (*trade agreements*), with some restrictions.
- As *commander-in-chief* of the military the president has the authority to commit troops to battle, but only Congress can officially declare war.
- The *federal government budget* is developed by the president's office, which must be approved by Congress.
- As *comforter in chief,* in times of emergencies, crises, and tragedies (9/11/01 and natural disasters), the president has the power to declare a *state of emergency*, requiring the quick allocation of government resources.

■ **Figure 9.6:** Powers of the President

ETHICAL DILEMMA 9.1 Winning the Battle over Health Care Reform: Presidential Power or Presidential Debacle?

In 2012, U.S. President Obama, who campaigned for reelection, staked much of his political capital on his new health care reform—but at what price? In June 2012, the Supreme Court largely let stand the Affordable Care Act—President Obama's sweeping health care overhaul, in a mixed ruling that Court observers were rushing to analyze. The law, passed by Congress in March 2010, put in motion the creation of a nationwide insurance system that would sharply reduce the number of Americans without coverage, a goal that Democratic presidents had unsuccessfully pursued for 75 years.

The high court's 5-to-4 decision was a striking victory for the president and Congressional Democrats, with a majority, including the conservative chief justice, John G. Roberts Jr., affirming the central legislative pillar of President Obama's term. The court case centered on the so-called individual mandate, a requirement that all Americans obtain health insurance or pay a fine. Republicans challenged it as an unconstitutional expansion of federal power. The Obama administration argued that it was needed to fix basic flaws in the insurance market and that it was crucial to provisions such as the requirement that insurers accept all comers without regard to preexisting health conditions.

The court's decision did significantly restrict one major portion of the law: the expansion of Medicaid, the government health insurance program for low-income and sick people. The ruling gives states some flexibility not to expand their Medicaid programs without paying the same financial penalties that the law called for.

Even with the court's decision, the debate over health care remains far from over, with Republicans vowing to carry on their fight against the law. The presumptive Republican presidential nominee, Mitt Romney, promised to undo it if elected.

Having lost one battle in the Supreme Court, Congressional Republicans continued their attempt to repeal the law, although they acknowledged that such votes were purely symbolic. On July 11, less than two weeks after the Supreme Court decision, the House passed a bill to repeal President Obama's health care law. The bill was approved by a vote of 244 to 185, with five Democrats supporting repeal. It had no chance of approval in the Senate and faced a veto from Obama if it ever got to him. But the House debate exposed the depth of passion over efforts to remake the health care system and suggested that the fight would continue the following year, regardless of who won the November elections for president and Congress.

Republican governors and state legislators also began planning a new approach that could have the effect of undercutting large parts of the law, which relies heavily on state governments for implementation. Leaning on the Supreme Court's ruling, the governors of Texas, Florida, Louisiana, and South Carolina said they would reject the law's proposal to expand Medicaid, and others said they were leaning toward rejecting it. Other critics began planning a challenge to President Obama's interpretation of another important provision, under which the federal government will subsidize health insurance for millions of low- and middle-income people.[11]

President Obama is in for the battle of his presidency over health care and only time will tell whether he picked the right battleground to wage his war against the Republicans and Mitt Romney.

Questions

1. Under what powers and authority can a president of the United States propose new health care standards?
2. What executive departments and agencies might the president consult with in setting up these new health care standards?
3. What is the ethical dilemma facing President Obama relative to his fight on health reform?
4. What would you do if you were President Obama?

Personal and Professional Applications

3. How does the power of the president affect you?

4. How does the power of the president affect your present or past employer and/or a producer of the products it sells?

REGULATORY INFORMATION

Free enterprise works well,[12] but for various reasons, regulations are still necessary and they affect how business operates.[13] *Regulations* are the business rules of conduct, and the *rules* are developed by regulatory agencies to implement laws passed by Congress. In this chapter, we focus on rules. In this section, we discuss federal regulatory agencies, benefits, and costs of regulation, regulatory impact analysis, the *Federal Register*, Reginfo.gov, and Regulations.gov.

Federal Regulatory Agencies

More than a hundred regulatory agencies declare rules, establish policies, and resolve disputes. Each year, federal regulators write thousands of new rules that affect you and business; plus businesses must comply with thousands of state and local regulations as well. Here, we focus on the federal level.

Types of Rules. The many different types of rules have different objectives. Some rules state what a business can and can't do. Some rules set standards and specify how business will meet the standards. Other rules only ask for information, set prices, provide licenses, and give subsidies to business.

> **The Man of Steel Case Question 4: What are the regulatory functions of the Federal Reserve?**
>
> The main tasks of the Federal Reserve are to supervise and regulate banks, implement monetary policy by open market operations, set the discount rate, set the reserve ratio, maintain a strong payments system, and control the amount of currency that is made and destroyed on a day-to-day basis. The Federal Reserve specifically regulates the U.S. economy (and indirectly the world economy) through the monetary supply to businesses by setting the reserve rates at banks and by setting the discount rate at which banks can borrow money from the Federal Reserve.

Benefits and Costs of Regulation

Government's goal is for the regulatory benefits to outweigh the costs to society, so it provides benefits and costs analysis information to ensure new regulations are cost effective.

Benefits. Some costs benefit business and are paid for by taxpayers. For example, some farmers benefit by getting subsidies that increase their income, and the cost of the subsidies is paid out of taxes collected from citizens. We have discussed the regulatory benefits of employees being treated more fairly and having a safer work environment (Chapters 3–4), consumers getting more product information and safer products (Chapter 6), and community improvements (Chapters 2, 4–5). In Chapter 7, we discussed the need for government regulations and how the government benefits business. Although government is frequently very helpful to business, firms don't like to be regulated and complain about regulatory burdens and cost. Business prefers self-regulation.[14] With regulations, typically someone is helped and someone is hurt by them.[15]

Costs. Costs are usually easier to estimate than benefits, especially the cumulative benefits to society. The number of regulations and their costs continue to increase significantly under the Obama administration.[16] *Obama Care* and *Dodd-Frank* financial rules are complex and costly.[17] However, critics are calling for more and better regulation.[18] Two negative effects of regulation include less new product innovation, because firms are more reluctant to risk the high cost of research with the possibility of being sued, and less new investment in plants and equipment, because funds are diverted to pay the cost of regulatory compliance.

Two researchers have estimated the total cost for business to comply with federal regulations to be $843 billion a year,[19] which does not include the cost of more than 140,000 regulatory employees.[20] No measurements of the indirect costs of employment or productivity or the indirect costs to other firms and communities have been taken.[21] So the more than $1 trillion figure underestimates the real total cost of regulation. The cost is also higher for small businesses based on cost per employee.[22] One cost is certain: unintended consequences that aren't considered during the regulation process.[23]

The Man of Steel Case Question 5: Why might the Federal Reserve prefer to alter U.S. monetary policy through the discount rate rather than through bank reserves?

The Federal Reserve may have conducted a cost–benefit analysis that indicated that the least expensive way to modify the money supply is through the market mechanism of discount rates rather than through required reserves. Altering the discount rate requires no additional paperwork (as opposed to changing the reserve rate, which requires banks to change the reserve ratio in all of their calculations and reports) and no additional controls (i.e., audits), unlike the reserve ratio that may require onsite audits to ensure the banks comply with the new reserve requirements.

Personal and Professional Applications

5. Describe some of the benefits and costs of regulation that affect you.

6. Describe some of the benefits and costs of regulation that affect your present or past employer.

Learning Outcome 2: Explain the relationship between regulatory impact analysis, the *Federal Register*, and Regulations.gov.

Regulatory Impact Analysis

Based on executive orders, new major regulatory proposals are made to the **Office of Management and Budget (OMB)** (www.omb.gov) with a three-part regulatory impact analysis (RIA).[24] A "major" rule is predicted to have an annual impact on the economy of $100 million or more. The goal of an RIA is to ensure that the regulation is really needed, that the best alternative method of implementing the rule is used, and that the benefits outweigh the costs. *Regulatory impact analysis (RIA) includes a statement of the need for the proposed regulatory action, an examination of alternative approaches, and an evaluation of the benefits and costs.* The benefits and costs are quantitative and qualitative for each of the main alternatives. The OMB provides details on how the RIA should be prepared. The OMB may require changes in the rule or approve it.

Congress requires that the OMB issue guidelines to agencies to make their RIAs available for public review, and the OMB submits proposed and final rule submissions to the *Federal Register*. For rules that adversely affect business, firms inform government of the costs to the business economy in hopes of stopping such rules.

Federal Register

To inform business and the general public about regulatory proposals and final versions, the federal government developed the *Federal Register* (www.federalregister.gov*), which is published by the Office of the *Federal Register*, **National Archives and Records Administration (NARA)**, of the **Government Printing Office (GPO)**. The GPO works for Congress. *The **Federal Register** is a daily journal publication of rules, proposed rules, notices, and other public regulatory information.* Other information includes executive orders and other presidential documents.[25]

Business needs to anticipate changes in laws and regulations.[26] Some use BGOV to analyze how changes in regulations will affect them.[27] Clearly, businesses need to keep a close eye on the *Federal Register* as an important part of their issues management strategy (Chapter 2) to identify, monitor, analyze, and select public issues that warrant nonmarket strategies.

Regulations.gov and RegInfo.gov

In coordination with the *Federal Register,* the U.S. government provides a regulations website (www.regulations.gov).[28] *Regulations.gov enables users to find, view, and comment on regulations for all federal agencies.* You can use the search options to access federal actions, choosing to search among all regulations or just the regulations that are open for comment. When searching regulations and federal actions, the site indicates agency posts of *Federal Register* documents, supporting materials, and public submissions. So anyone, which includes you, can comment on a proposed regulation to state your side of the issue.

Out of the *Executive Office of the President*, the **Office of Information and Regulatory Affairs—RegInfo.gov** (ww.reginfo.gov) provides information by agencies and the stage at which rules are in the regulatory process.[29] Visit these two websites for more information.

Personal and Professional Applications

7. How can your present or past employer and/or a producer of the products it sells, use the *Federal Register,* Regulations.gov, and/or RegInfo.gov?

RULE MAKING, OVERSEEING, AND ENFORCING

In this section we discuss rule making and congressional oversight of regulators, and we provide some examples of rule enforcement.

Learning Outcome 3: Describe the rule-making process.

Rule Making

In the previous chapter, we discussed how Congress passes bills, the president signs them into law, and the regulators write the rules that provide the ground rules for competition.[30] Rule making is the most important function of most executive and independent regulatory agencies.[31] Under Obama, the regulatory environment will continue to become much more rigorous.[32] It can take several months or years to make new rules.

Administrative Procedures Act (APA). The law-making process was set forth in the APA, which was passed in 1946. *The Administrative Procedures Act (APA) developed the rule-making process that includes providing public notice and allowing comments during agency rule making, prior to agency action.* Although some additions to the APA's procedural requirements have been made, today it still stands as the basic statement of process for developing rules in agencies. With the Internet and **Regulations.gov**, it is easy for business to know about and comment on proposed regulations.

Agencies, however, can adopt their own rule-making process that is consistent with the APA procedures. They can use either an informal or formal process. See Figure 9.7 for a simplified rule-making process that follows the APA for new major regulatory rules, which may or may not be preceded by a congressional bill signed into law by the president. For a more detailed *Informal Rule Making Process*, visit www.reginfo.gov and view the "**Reg Map**."[33] Rules that are not new major regulations do not require RIA and OMB approval. **Boards, commissions, and committees, including business interests, may give input into rule making, and business, with some restrictions, may lobby during the process.** As with congressional bills, business wants to influence regulations early in the process.

The Man of Steel Case Question 6: What actions by the Federal Reserve might be published in the Federal Register and at Regulations.gov?

Any actions of the Federal Reserve might be published in the *Federal Register* if they deal with rules, proposed rules, notices, and other public regulatory information. For example, proposed changes in the way in which banks report their depository holdings relative to the reserve ratio would first be published in the *Federal Register* to allow for public comment. After the comment period, the Fed might revise the reporting requirements and then publish the final version in the *Federal Register*. Regulations.gov enables anyone to find, view, and comment on regulations for the Federal Reserve.

Challenging Rule Legality. As with any law, rules can be challenged for violating the *Constitution*. The APA grants businesses the right to sue for judicial review of new rules for procedural and substantive due process. *Procedural due process allows business to challenge a rule by claiming that the agency did not follow the APA procedures in making the rule.* APA requires that agency actions not be "arbitrary, capricious, and [there is no] abuse of discretion, or otherwise not in accordance with law." To avoid judicial review, agencies are careful to follow procedures and base their decisions on the record, but they don't always win in court. For example, a federal court of appeals ruled that the **FDA** approval of a generic version of the cancer drug **Taxol** was "arbitrary and capricious," stopping the generic drug from being sold.[34]

Congress creates regulatory agencies and writes the authorizing statutes for an agency to develop and enforce laws. Thus, Congress specifies agency authority. *Substantive due process allows business to challenge a rule by claiming that the agency exceeded its scope of the regulatory authority.* Rules must be seen as bearing a relationship to the proper public purpose and be neither arbitrary nor discriminatory for the requirements to satisfy due process.

Rules can also be stopped by higher-level officials in the executive branch. For example, as requested by **Teva Pharmaceutical Industries**, the **FDA** approved allowing young

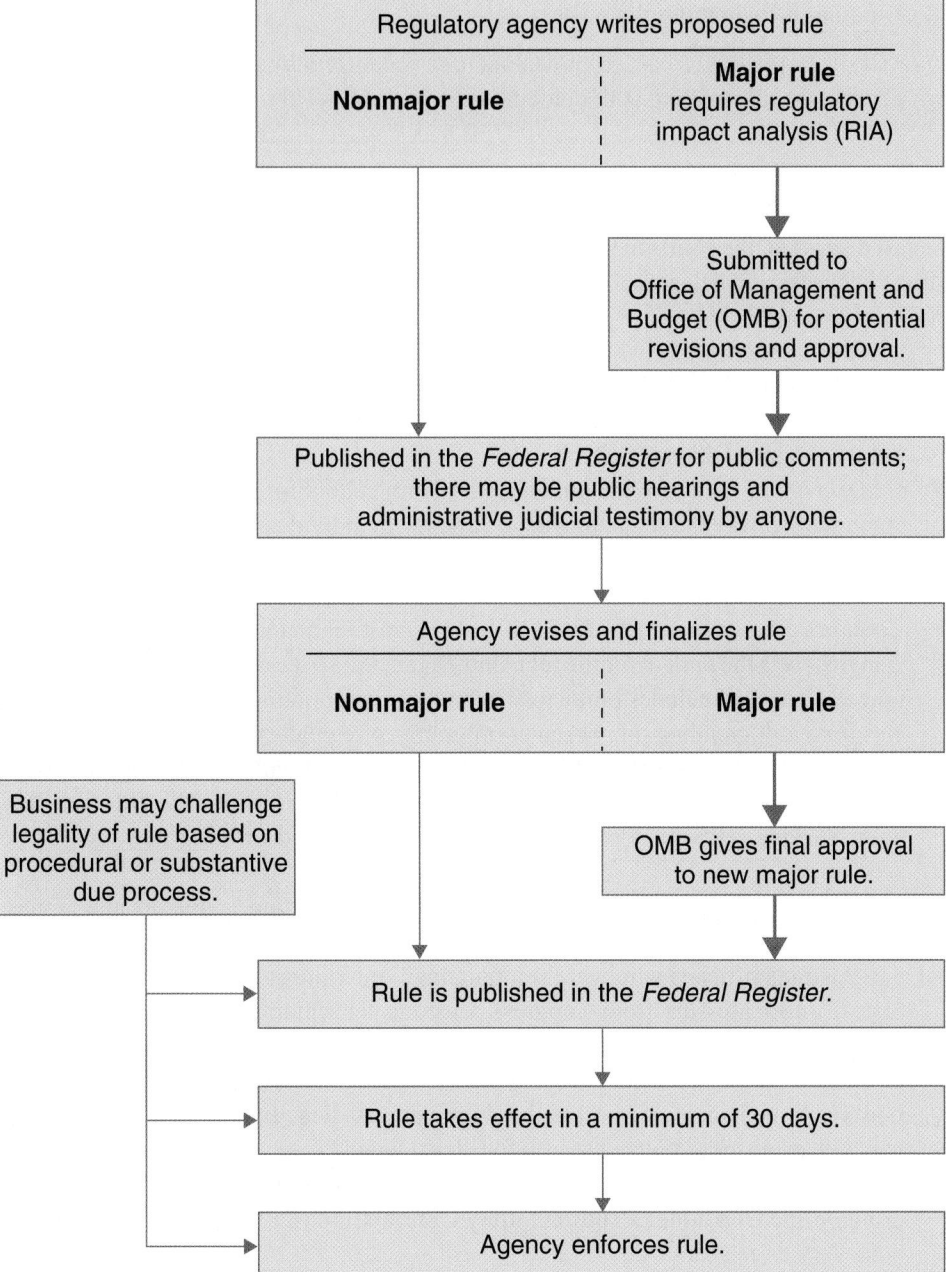

■ **Figure 9.7:** The Rule-Making Process

teens to get the Plan B emergency contraceptive pill without a prescription. However, the **Health & Human Services (HHS**, www.hhs.gov) Secretary overruled the decision, saying the data submitted did not prove it was appropriate for girls to take without a prescription.[35] The FDA is one of several agencies within the HHS executive department.[36]

Business and other special interest groups frequently appeal regulatory decisions. The process frequently involves battles of competing interests, often business against activists and business against business. Heated rivalry can get nasty. But business must be actively involved to influence the rules it has to live with.

> **Personal and Professional Applications**
>
> 8. Has your present or past employer and/or a producer of the products it sells, given input into rule making at the federal, state, or local level of government?

Congressional Oversight of Regulators

As just discussed, the courts have influence over rules through judicial review. As another means of checks and balances, Congress develops the APA and has oversight of regulators in the following ways:

■ Congress oversees the regulators with a *Congressional Oversight Committee*. The *Federal Register* and **FACA** database keep Congress informed of related executive branch programs and agencies.

■ *Congressional laws* provide guidance to the regulators for setting the rules, and the amount of leeway the regulators have varies with individual laws, as some use broad terms, such as "the public interest," while others are very detailed, such as "establishes safety standards for automatic garage door openers."

■ Congress can *revise statutes and block changes* of regulatory agencies.

■ Congress sets the *budget* for the regulatory agencies, so it can expand or contract their power. Congress includes provisions in budget appropriations bills, preventing agencies from any spending on particular programs or regulatory initiatives.

■ *Committees* (the ones that draft the bills) pressure regulators through oversight hearings to discuss regulatory actions they are not happy with. The **Internal Revenue Service (IRS)** was pressured into being nicer and offering more and better services.[37]

■ *Members* of Congress provide pressure by calling or writing regulators and requesting explanations for agency actions; they always respond. Three members wrote to the **Customs** officials who were stopping mail order drugs from entering the United States. Under pressure from Congress, Customs let seniors receive their drugs from Canada.[38] Some members of Congress demanded more details from the **Department of Justice (DOJ**, www.justice.gov) regarding a seizure of ebony wood at **Gibson Guitar.** Armed agents suspected the shipment was illegally imported from India; so why did agents need guns to search for illegal wood?[39]

■ Under some statutes, agencies must be *reauthorized* by Congress to continue. For example, the **Consumer Product Safety Commission (CPSC)** requires reauthorization every three years.

> The Man of Steel Case Question 7: What, if any, congressional oversight is there of the Federal Reserve?
>
> Federal Reserve Board members are approved by the Senate, and the chairman is required to testify before Congress twice a year.

Rule Enforcement

Here we present a sample of guidelines and rule making, product review and approval, and rule enforcement that have been in the news recently.

Recall from Chapter 6 that the new **Consumer Financial Protection Bureau (CFPB**, www.consumerfinance.gov), and nine other agencies had to write the details of 400 new regulations in 2011–2012.[40] Its related agency, the **Consumer Product Safety Commission** (**CPSC**, www.cpsc.gov), through Congressional law, prohibited the use of phthalates in toys (substances added to plastics to increase their flexibility, transparency, durability, and longevity) and to have all current inventory taken off store shelves; with only 100 hours (2½ days) notice. The **Retail Industry Leaders Association** (**RILA**, www.rila.org) said the recall of toys would cost hundreds of millions of dollars.[41]

The **Department of Transportation** (**DOT**, www.dot.gov) reached a settlement with **American Eagle** to pay a $650,000 fine and $250,000 to passengers for violating the tarmac rule by 18 minutes over the 3-hour limit on domestic flights.[42] The DOT is also recommending to auto makers that drivers' ability to use auto installed Internet interactive devices to go online should only work while the car is stopped. The suggestion is to help prevent a spike in accidents due to the distractions of **Facebook**, **Twitter**, **Google**, and others.[43] Under the DOT, the **National Highway Traffic Safety Administration** (**NHSA**, www.nhsa.gov) investigated the safety of the GM Chevy Volt's battery pack after fires were reported.[44]

Under the Obama administration, the **Environmental Protection Agency** (**EPA**, www.epa.gov) has placed more regulations on the energy industry including power plants, refineries, cement plants, and other big factories.[45] New pollution regulations for power plants drew criticism from the industry, loudly protesting it as being the most extensive intervention into the power market that the EPA has ever attempted to implement. The coal producers put the price tag at $21 billion, saying electricity prices will spike 12 percent, dozens of plants will close, and thousands of workers will lose their jobs. But on the other side, businesses that manufacture pollution-reducing equipment are pleased, saying their sales and jobs will increase.[46]

The **Federal Trade Commission** (**FTC**, www.ftc.gov) imposed a legal settlement with **Google** for privacy violations, and a year later investigated whether Google had violated its pledge not to "misrepresent" its privacy practices to consumers.[47]

The **National Labor Relations Board** (**NLRB**, www.nlrb.gov), under the Obama administration, has sided with unions in several cases involving rules for organizing and representing workers, which many business groups claim as being unfair to business.[48]

The **Securities and Exchange Commission** (**SEC**, www.sec.gov) took a record 735 enforcement actions against business in 2011.[49] The SEC made settlements and fined **Citigroup**, **Goldman Sachs**, and **JPMorgan Chase** over claims they misled investors in financial products linked to risky mortgages. Under pressure from lawmakers and judges, the SEC made a small exception to allowing companies and individuals to settle civil charges and pay fines without admitting or denying guilt.[50] Following elaborate SEC regulations concerning an initial public offering (IPO), **Facebook** in now owned by shareholders.[51] But on a more important note, the SEC is making regulations for "crowd funding" so that small companies can sell their stock online to the public.[52]

ETHICAL DILEMMA 9.2 Congress versus the President: Trying to Regulate the Injustice of the Justice Department

"'Congress now faces a moment of decision between exerting its full authority . . . or accepting a dangerous expansion of executive branch authority.' Thus Darrell Issa, a Republican Congressman from California, made the case for finding Eric Holder, the [U.S.] attorney general, in contempt of Congress. On June 20th [2012] the committee Mr. Issa chairs approved a resolution against Mr. Holder for failing to produce documents it had subpoenaed. On the same day [President] Barack Obama, for the first time in his presidency, cited executive privilege as a justification for withholding the documents. What with an ongoing row about the president's habit of using executive orders to bypass congressional opposition to his policies, Mr. Obama and the Republican leadership in the House of Representatives are on the verge of a constitutional showdown. . . .

The row involving Holder centers on a botched operation to curb gun-running from America to Mexico run by the Bureau of Alcohol, Tobacco, Firearms and Explosives (ATF), a division of the Justice Department. ATF agents allowed 2,000 guns to be smuggled across the border in an attempt to learn who was behind the trade. They soon lost track of the guns; two subsequently showed up at a shoot-out in which a Border Patrol agent was killed.

When Congress originally asked the Justice Department about the operation last year, it first denied that the ATF had permitted any smuggling to proceed before reversing itself ten months later. The department has since provided the committee with 7,600 pages of documents related to the operation, but Mr. Issa, on the lookout for a cover-up, has asked for more. He is especially curious about how and when the department realized it had misled Congress and what discussions led up to its decision to come clean. . . .

[Yet many believe] it is a battle the Republicans will not win. If the full House, as is likely, now votes to hold Mr. Holder in contempt, it will in theory fall to federal prosecutors to bring him into line. But in similar spats in the past, the prosecutors, who after all work for the president, have been inclined to accept the claim that releasing records of the internal deliberations of the executive branch would make it difficult for the president and his advisers to do their jobs."[53]

Questions

1. What is the purpose of congressional oversight of the Justice Department?
2. Under what authority does Republican Congressman Issa have the right to request information from the Justice Department?
3. Under what authority can President Obama withhold information from Congress? Is this ethical?
4. Is it ethical for federal prosecutors to investigate the head of their own Justice Department?
5. Assuming Congress took President Obama and the Justice Department's action to the Supreme Court for clarification of presidential executive privilege, how do you think they should rule? Why?

Personal and Professional Applications

9. How has your present or past employer and/or a producer of the products it sells been affected by regulatory guidelines, rule making, product review and approval, or rule enforcement?

Learning Outcome 4: Compare and contrast cross-subsidization, cost-of-service regulation, privatization, and deregulation.

REFORMING REGULATION, PRIVATIZATION, AND DEREGULATION

In this section, we discuss methods of regulatory reform. Privatization and deregulation are in essence types of regulatory reform to increase efficiencies in government and the market environment. However, they are quite unique, so we discuss them separately.

Reforming Regulation

Although regulators have the public good in mind, estimates of regulatory benefits and costs are typically subject to criticism that the costs place a heavy and growing burden on businesses and the economy, with costs often outweighing the benefits. Regulations have forced some firms to go out of business, such as the EPA regulations leading to coal energy plant closures.[54] With its desire to get out from under the new finance regulations, **MetLife** sold its retail deposit business to **GE**.[55]

Other problems arise in drafting statutes and preparing agency rules: some regulations never achieve their objective, they conflict with other regulations, they are poorly implemented, they impose directives that are better developed by business, and they become outdated with changing times. Thus, the need to reform regulations is ongoing. However, reforming the large federal bureaucracy is extremely difficult and time-consuming, with no guarantee of success. Suggested reforms include the following:

- ▪ **More self-regulation**. As discussed in prior chapters, business and entire industries set some self-regulations, and they prefer to do so.[56]
- ▪ **Eliminating cross-subsidization**. *Cross-subsidization occurs when one group of customers pays less than the cost and others pay more to offset that loss.* The **U.S. Postal Service (USPS**, www.usps.gov) uses other services to cross-subsidize first-class mail. **Verizon** and others must make payments to the **FCC's Universal Service Fund**, which subsidizes phone service for rural and low-income customers.[57]
- ▪ **Eliminating cost-of-service regulation**. *Cost-of-service regulation occurs when prices are regulated based on costs that are passed on to customers, which reduces the incentive to keep costs down.* With government cost-of-service pricing and no competition, companies tend to continue to raise rates. The **cable industry (TV/phone/Internet)** is an example.

> **Personal and Professional Applications**
>
> 10. Explain which methods of reforming regulations would be beneficial to your present or past employer and/or a producer of the products it sells. Be sure to state how the business would benefit.

Privatization

Privatization is government allowing business to perform functions and services for it. The shift can be to allow business to perform part or all of the government's tasks, and it also sells assets to businesses, such as military bases that are no longer in use. Privatization can help eliminate cross-subsidization. It also helps eliminate increasing costs associated with the cost-of-service regulations because competing companies bid to get the privatization contract, and the government can accept the lowest bid.

Government has contracted with business to manage prisons and build roads, and public utilities have been sold to business. Municipal and local governments have contracted out food services, vehicle towing, legal services, street light and repair operations, trash collection and waste disposal, firefighting, snow plowing, and many other services.

The **Reason Foundation (www.reason.org)** advances a free society by developing, applying, and promoting libertarian principles, including individual liberty, free markets, and the rule of law. It produces respected public policy research on a variety of issues and publishes the critically acclaimed monthly *Reason* magazine and the *Annual Privatization Report* with information on privatization efforts. You can visit its website for more information.[58]

Personal and Professional Applications

11. Give specific examples of privatization not listed in the textbook, preferably privatization that affected your present or past employer and/or a producer of the products it sells.

Deregulation

Part of the reason that industries are deregulated is to reform regulation by eliminating cross-subsidization and cost-of-service regulation. *Deregulation is a significant reduction in the regulation of an industry.* Industries are deregulated to improve economic performance.[59] Starting in the 1970s, several industries that were heavily regulated were deregulated. Deregulated industries include commercial airlines, electricity, financial institutions, railroads, shipping, telecommunications, and interstate trucking. However, under the Obama administration the trend has shifted to more government regulation and control.[60] The financial industry is back to heavy regulations.[61] Reasons for deregulation include increasing competition, lowering prices, stimulating innovation, and putting an end to abuses caused by regulation while at the same time increasing economic efficiencies.

The Man of Steel Case Question 8: What might be the impact of deregulating bank reserve ratios?

The Federal Reserve requires commercial banks and other financial institutions to hold as reserves a fraction of the deposits they accept. Banks hold these reserves either as cash in their vaults or as deposits at Federal Reserve banks. The more reserve that a bank is required to hold, the less the bank can lend to commercial institutions, and the less commercial institutions can borrow to grow their businesses. The required reserve ratio in the United States was 10 percent on transaction deposits over $71 million (component of money supply "M1"), and zero on time deposits and all other deposits.

By deregulating bank reserve ratios and allowing banks to determine how much they will hold in reserve, the government increases the uncertainty of the availability of capital to businesses since individual banks may employ differing reserve policies, policies that could change over time based upon individual banks' needs. This ambiguity over the availability of capital may have several negative effects: (1) increase the overall demand for capital to offset the uncertainty (businesses holding a surplus of capital creates slack), therein driving up the cost of capital; (2) allow banks, at any point in time, to carry so low a percentage of capital that immediate demands for capital by depositors may not be met; (3) allow banks to carry too high a percentage of capital so as not to meet the capital demands of businesses (stifle growth); and (4) have huge swings in the availability and cost of capital, making it difficult for businesses to make long-term plans for growth and development.

Personal and Professional Applications

12. Give examples of how deregulation has affected you.

13. Is your present or future career industry regulated or deregulated?

14. Give specific examples of how deregulation has affected your present or past employer and/or a producer of the products it sells.

BUSINESS NONMARKET AND MARKET STRATEGIES AND ETHICS

As presented in Figure 1.4 (p. 22), businesses have a variety of nonmarket strategies they can use through the 5 Is Strategic Analysis (Chapter 2). Managers integrate nonmarket strategies with their market strategies because they know it benefits firm performance. As usual, in this section, we discuss information, societal, political, and legal strategies.

Information Strategies

Information strategies are a critical part of corporate political strategy success,[62] and leading firms develop information strategies that are ethical and socially responsible.[63] Recall our discussion of *political information strategies* and the importance of message framing when dealing with legislators. Although regulators are appointed, not elected, they need business information too. The information should help government understand the consequences of the different public policy alternatives. Again, business should focus on stakeholder benefits, especially jobs, and not waste time telling the regulators what's in it for business.[64]

Large corporations fighting major regulatory issues do the research, usually with the help of consultants using outside sources, experts, and stakeholders' support to come up with realistic facts and figures to influence new rules and to change old rules. Again, as with congressional bills, business wants to influence regulations early in the process. So keeping an eye on the **FederalRegister.gov**, **Regulations.gov**, and **InfoReg.gov** is important.

Societal, Political, and Legal Strategies

Businesses take a stakeholder approach to dealing with societal issues.[65] They try to balance social and financial performance.[66] Business often needs a grand strategy to counter activists in dealing with regulators for specific rules. Business builds coalitions and works at developing good media relations in order to promote positive stories and gain public sentiment for its side of issues. By being ethically and socially responsible, it is more likely to gain public sentiment, and in turn, regulators are less likely to take negative action against them.[67]

Business has some power to influence regulators who make public policy rules. Regulators' extensive impacts on business decision making have resulted in executives spending more time developing nonmarket political strategies[68] because nonmarket political strategies are as important as, and in some cases are more important than, market strategies.[69] Political strategies are an important part of this chapter; therefore, we will present several political strategies next in a separate section. Business also uses legal strategies to avoid lawsuits, and business occasionally challenges rules through due process.

REGULATORY POLITICAL STRATEGIES

In this section, we discuss the 5 Is Strategic Analysis and eight political strategies; see Figure 9.8 for the list of strategies. In reading Figure 9.8, you should realize that it is the same as Figure 8.6. The reason is that the same political strategies are used with both Congress and the executive branch agencies. The major difference is that, with Congress, the focus is on influencing statutes, whereas with regulators, the focus is on influencing rules. So although the same strategies are used, they are used differently. You need to understand the role of regulatory agencies and government[70] and skillfully manage relationships with them.[71] Let's compare and contrast congressional and regulatory approaches using the same political strategies.

Business Interest Groups
Campaign Contributions and PACs
Grand Nonmarket Strategies
Lobbying
Grassroots Constituency Lobbying
Coalition Building
Testimony
Advisory Panels and Committees

▪ **Figure 9.8:** Political Strategies

5 Is Strategic Analysis

Let's discuss how business selects nonmarket strategies, but this time with a focus on rule making as part of the 5 Is Strategic Analysis (Chapter 2).

1. **Issue identification**. Through issues management, business finds out about potential changes in regulations. Rules are in the fourth stage of the issue's life cycle—legislative and regulation formation (Figure 2.4, p. 53). So business still has a chance to influence or even stop the rule.
2. **Interested strategic stakeholders**. Are activists pressuring the regulators for change, or is the change coming from regulators? What agency is proposing the rule change? Which stakeholders are with and which are against the firm on the issue?
3. **Incentive of stakeholders**. What are the odds of the regulators changing the regulations? If the business does take voluntary self-regulation, will stakeholders stop pursuing regulatory changes?[72] If so, business is usually more willing to accommodate requests voluntarily.[73]
4. **Information—objectives**. Again, information strategies are an important part of developing strategies.[74] What political information strategies will the firm use to present its side of the issue to regulators? What is the objective of the business regarding the rule?
5. **Interaction strategies**. Strategy formulation and implementation are critical to nonmarket success. Thus, major corporations use PR specialists to develop nonmarket strategies[75]: (a) Which alternative nonmarket strategies (Figure 1.4) can be used to deal with the issue? (b) What will be the market and nonmarket reaction and consequences to the strategic action? (c) Which strategy or combination of strategies should be selected to deal with the regulators? (d) Implement and evaluate the strategy.

Business Interest Groups

As discussed previously, the major responsibilities of both peak and industry business associations are to provide information, to advocate the business side of the issue to government, to provide member services, to set voluntary standards, and to influence laws and regulations. Thus, NGOs help business,[76] and being a member of a business interest group is indirectly a lower level of regulatory involvement. The **Airlines for America** (**A4A**, www.airlines.org) trade group wrote a letter to the **Export-Import Bank** (www.exim.gov) asking the independent federal agency to stop helping foreign airlines by slashing subsidies to all overseas buyers of **Boeing** jets.[77] (Refer to Chapter 7 for a discussion of business interest groups.) However, most large companies combine their use with other political strategies.

> Learning Outcome 5: Discuss the differences in the use of campaign contributions, lobbying, grassroots lobbying, and testimony strategies used by business to influence Congress versus influencing regulatory agencies.

Campaign Contributions and PACs

Campaign contributions and PACs are indirect strategies to influence regulators because they are appointed, not elected. Business can't give money to regulators because contributions would be illegal bribes. During the presidential campaign between Democratic Obama and Republican Romney, many businesspeople and companies gave financial contributions to Romney because he held Republican views of lower taxes, less regulation of business (as Obama heavily increased them), and smaller government.

Grand Nonmarket Strategies

As with the societal strategies discussed in the last chapter, business has four possible options for dealing with the regulators.

Ignore. When business hears about a proposed new rule or change, it can simply ignore it and take no action to influence the rule. Ignoring is often based on the cost–benefit analysis and the likelihood of winning. However, if a department/agency is doing an investigation, ignoring is not an option.

Oppose. When business hears about a rule, it can oppose it. However, unlike Congress, regulators don't take a vote, but lobbying is usually used to stop the rule. Again, the focus is on early writing and revising rule-making stages of the APA rule-making process. After the rule is approved, business can challenge it.

Negotiate and Work With. The second stage of the rule-making process, as required by the APA, allows public comments on the rule. Public hearings and testimonies provide business the opportunity to work with the agency in forming the rules. Regulators are usually open to business input and meet with managers in drafting and revising rules. So business tends to use the advisory and testimony strategies. At the state and local levels, business has more economic leverage in negotiating by threatening to move the business if its interests are not met.

Lobbying

Under the First Amendment to the Constitution, business has the right to petition government, including regulators. Lobbying is considered the most important political strategy because more time, effort, and resources are devoted to lobbying than to any other political strategy.[78] In carrying out their political strategy, lobbyists meet with government officials to present business's strategy information concerning the issue to influence rules. In addition to members of Congress, government officials can include the president, executive branch officials, a governor, state and local officials, and their staff.

Lobbying Congress and regulators is similar in some situations in which business can't contact regulators outside of public meetings based on *ex parte rules*. Some agencies authorizing statutes require public hearings for certain types of actions, and the agencies are restricted from having contact with interested parties outside the proceedings. As in lobbying Congress, lobbying regulators works best when combined with other strategies.

Lobbying is important, but results are mixed.[79] For example, just before Obama changed the head of the FDA, **ReGen Biologics** successfully lobbied the FDA (www.fda.gov) and overcame repeated rejections by FDA scientists to gain approval of its *Menaflex* device to treat knee injuries.[80] In another example, the **National Crowdfunding Association** (www.nlcfa.org), the **Crowdfunding Professional Association** (**CFPA**, www.crowdfundingprofessional.org), and other NGOs helped get the **SEC** (www.sec.gov) to allow crowdfunding, which will help small businesses go public.[81] **AT&T** spends millions on lobbying and has had a history of success in lobbying the **FCC** (www.fcc.gov), but it lost big time when the FCC refused to allow it to merge with **T-Mobile**.[82]

Grassroots Constituency Lobbying

Business often relies on its peak and trade groups to develop and implement grassroots strategies for it, or in coordination with its own grassroots efforts, often led by lobbyists.[83] Business asks its stakeholders to contact regulators (often through Regulations.gov), letting them know that the stakeholders support the business side on the rule. The grassroots business stakeholders are from the market environment and can include stockholder owners, employees, customers and consumers, suppliers, franchisees, distributors, and competitors who will also be affected by the rule.

When using grassroots lobbying with regulators, business has an option that is not available with Congress. In addition to Regulations.gov, business commonly asks stakeholders to go to the agency's webite and make online comments supporting the business side of the rule during the "public comment stage" of the rule-making process. Management must assess the likelihood of the participation of stakeholders in grassroots lobbying. The greater the benefit to the stakeholders, the more likely they are to contact the government representative. Grassroots strategies are time-consuming and can be expensive, so management must determine whether the benefits of grassroots lobbying will outweigh the costs involved in mobilizing stakeholders.

Coalition Building

Businesses often work with each other to deal with issues. Peak and trade groups are coalitions of businesses with similar interests joining in collective political action.[84] Businesses, often within the same industry, work together by providing increased pressure on government to meet their interests, giving business bargaining power.[85] When building coalitions, however, businesses always face the possibility of the *free-rider* problem.

Testimony

Businesses influence regulatory agencies directly through their participation in hearings and other regulatory proceedings. Business testifies before committees, before regulatory and administrative agencies, and in the courts. The major reason for attending hearings is to shape regulation and how it is implemented. Recall that APA procedures require public comments to proposed rules, which are a form of testimony. Comments can be made online at the agency's website and Regulations.gov. Also, some agencies have formal public hearings and allow testimonies from anyone present.

Information presented can affect regulatory decisions. Therefore, testimony is often backed by a firm, interest group, or coalition study that includes facts and figures, outside source research, and expert and stakeholder support. Businesses often lobby regulators on the rule before it comes to a hearing, so they don't always present new information when they give testimony.

Many regulatory rulings are challenged in court under procedural and substantive due process, so testimony needs to stand up to cross-examination during hearings, and testimony provides a basis for a possible court challenge.

> Learning Outcome 6: Identify the role of advisors and the reasons why businesses serve on advisory panels and committees.

Advisory Panels and Committees

Even though expert testimony is given to all three branches of the government, advisory panels and committees, which we will simply call advisors, are primarily used by regulatory agencies of the executive branch.

Advisory Role. The role of advisory panels and committees is to provide expert information to the government on proposed regulations. Therefore, the federal government makes use of an estimated 1,000 advisory panels and committees.[86]

To be more specific, businesses, scientists, and other professionals help regulators make better-informed regulatory rulings by providing expert information about the economic and scientific consequences of proposed alternative rules. Advisors also assess reactions to proposed alternative rules, so agencies use advisory panels and committees as a means of building support for their proposed rules. Thus, advisors can give the agency enhanced power relative to Congress and other government agencies.

Reasons for Business to Serve on Advisory Panels and Committees. Four major reasons underlie the benefits of serving on such a panel:

1. Public volunteer service helps build a reputation for being socially responsible.
2. Serving alerts business to proposed rules.
3. Serving can lead to placing proposed rules to benefit business on the agency's agenda.
4. Serving provides access to regulators who will listen to input that can influence the agency's decision to benefit business.

Advisory Oversight. Advisory panels and committees are overseen by the **General Services Administration** (**GSA**, www.gsa.gov). The GSA requires a balance of representation on all advisory panels and committees so that no special interest has too much influence over agency rule making.[87] Nevertheless, advisors have been criticized by Congress and the public for serving special interests. **Public Citizen** has raised concerns about advisors having too much influence over regulators.

Advisory Influence. Here is an example. The **FDA** has an advisory panel for suggestions on the safety and efficacy of new drugs. The FDA considered requiring longer psychiatric drug studies. The pharmaceutical industry was against it, and **Merck**, **Pfizer**, and **GlaxoSmithKline** testified against the FDA proposal during hearings. A panel of outside medical experts unanimously voted against the idea, stating that the current rule was better than the proposal. Clearly, these factors influenced the FDA decision.[88] Without the APA-required comment stage and the use of an advisory panel, the FDA may have simply changed the rule, which could have been to the detriment of psychiatric patients.

The Man of Steel Case Question 9: What might be some reasonable nonmarket strategies that businesses could employ with the Federal Reserve?

Because members of the Federal Reserve are appointed by the president for 14-year terms, it would be safe to assume that attempts at campaign contributions and PACs would make little sense in persuading the Federal Reserve members to change their monetary policies. However, other strategies, such as organizing business interest groups, creating coalitions, lobbying Congress and the president, working with the Federal Reserve by providing testimony at hearings, and serving on advisory panels and committees, may be excellent nonmarket approaches to educate the Federal Reserve about the impact of its policies on the economy and U.S. businesses (information strategies), thereby persuading the Federal Reserve to temper its monetary policies. Individual businesses, even those as large as **General Motors**, must understand that the Federal Reserve is not going to change its monetary policies just to suit one corporation; it will be persuaded by arguments that indicate that the proposed policy changes are good for the overall U.S. economy.

Personal and Professional Applications

15. How has your present or past employer, and/or a producer of the products it sells, served as an advisor to the government?

SUMMARY

The chapter summary is organized to answer the learning outcomes for Chapter 9.

1. **List the organizational structure of the federal executive branch of government and the three primary powers of the president.**
   The federal executive branch of government's organizational structure includes the Executive Office of the president; the cabinet; executive departments and their agencies; independent agencies and government corporations; boards, commissions, and committees; and quasi-official agencies. The primary powers of the president are making executive and judicial appointments (with Senate

approval), influencing and vetoing legislation, and making international trade agreements.

2. **Explain the relationship between regulatory impact analysis, the *Federal Register*, and Regulations.gov.**
   New major regulations require a *regulatory impact analysis (RIA),* which includes a statement of the need for the proposed action, an examination of alternative approaches, and an evaluation of the benefits and costs. The RIA ends up in the *Federal Register,* which is a daily journal publication of rules, proposed rules, notices, and other public regulatory information. In coordination with the *Federal Register,* the Regulations.gov website enables users to find, view, and comment on regulations for all federal agencies.

3. **Describe the rule-making process.**
   The rule-making process was set forth in the Administrative Procedures Act (APA) and includes the following steps. (1) The regulatory agency writes the proposed rule. (2) The rule goes to the *Federal Register* for public comments by anyone, and public hearings and administrative judicial testimony may take place. At the same time, the rule goes to the Office of Management and Budget (OMB) for potential revisions and approval. (3) The agency revises and finalizes the rule. (4) The rule is published in the *Federal Register* with OMB final approval. (5) Rules take effect in a minimum of 30 days. (6) Business may challenge the legality of the rule, and it may be stopped. (7) The agency enforces the rule.

4. **Compare and contrast cross-subsidization, cost-of-service regulation, privatization, and deregulation.**
   Cross-subsidization, cost-of-service regulation, privatization, and deregulation are similar in that all of them are a means of reforming regulations to increase efficiencies in government and the market environment. Deregulation is a means of eliminating cross-subsidization and cost-of-service regulation inefficiencies. They are different in that cross-subsidization occurs when one group of customers pays less than the cost and others pay more to offset that loss. Cost-of-service regulation occurs when prices are regulated based on costs that are passed on to customers, which reduces the incentive to keep costs down. Privatization is government allowing business to perform functions and services for it. Deregulation is a significant reduction in the regulation covering an industry.

5. **Discuss the differences in the use of campaign contributions, lobbying, grassroots lobbying, and testimony strategies used by business to influence Congress versus influencing regulatory agencies.**
   Business gives direct *campaign contributions* to members of Congress to help them get elected to support business interests. Conversely, regulators are appointed, so businesses can't give them donations. However, business gives contributions during presidential election campaigns in hopes that, indirectly, the appointed regulators will serve the business interest. *Lobbying* is contacting members of Congress to influence legislation, commonly by using a professional lobbyist, and campaign contributions help gain access to politicians. Lobbying regulators is similar except that there are some situations in which businesses can't contact regulators outside of public meetings. *Grassroots lobbying* is having stakeholders contact Congress and regulators; with regulations, businesses commonly ask stakeholders to make online comments supporting businesses' side of the specific rule during the "public comment stage" of the rule-making process, using Regulations.gov (www.regulations.gov). *Testimony* is not always an available option with Congress; it is not required during the legislative process.

However, APA regulatory procedures require public comment about proposed rules, which are a form of testimony.

6. **Identify the role of advisors and the reasons why businesses serve on advisory panels and committees.**
Businesses, scientists, and other professional advisors help regulators make better-informed regulatory rulings by providing expert information about the economic and scientific consequences of proposed alternative rules. Four major reasons business leaders serve on advisory panels and committees include the following: (1) public volunteer service helps build a reputation for being socially responsible; (2) serving alerts business to proposed rules; (3) serving can lead to placing proposed rules to benefit business on the agency's agenda; and (4) serving provides access to regulators who will listen to input that can influence the agency's decision to benefit business.

7. **Fill in the blank with the appropriate key term (in order of appearance in the chapter).**
_____ of the president is made up of White House offices and agencies.
_____ includes the heads of the 15 executive departments.
_____ have their own offices, regulatory agencies, and advisory committees.
_____ include regulators that are not part of and do not report to any of the 15 executive departments.

_____ includes a statement of the need for the proposed regulatory action, an examination of alternative approaches, and an evaluation of the benefits and costs.
_____ is a daily journal publication of rules, proposed rules, notices, and other public regulatory information.
_____ enables users to find, view, and comment on regulations for all federal agencies.
_____ developed the rule-making process that includes providing public notice and allowing comments during agency rule making, prior to agency action.
_____ allows business to challenge a rule by claiming that the agency did not follow the APA procedures in making the rule.
_____ allows business to challenge a rule by claiming that the agency exceeded its scope of regulatory authority.
_____ occurs when one group of customers pays less than the cost and others pay more to offset that loss.
_____ occurs when prices are regulated based on costs that are passed on to customers, which reduces the incentive to keep costs down.
_____ is government allowing business to perform functions and services for it.
_____ is a significant reduction in the regulation of an industry.

KEY TERMS (IN ALPHABETICAL ORDER)

REVIEW QUESTIONS

1 Why does the president need a cabinet?

2 What are the international relations powers of the president?

3 What is the difference between a law and an executive order?

4 What are quasi-official agencies?

5 What are the five characteristics of federal agencies?

6 Why does the government require cost–benefit analyses for proposed regulations?

7 Which executive office oversees new major regulatory proposals, and what does it require?

8 Where can you get the *Federal Register*?

9 What was the objective of the Administrative Procedures Act (APA)?

10 What are the two challenges to the legality of rules?

11 How does Congress oversee regulatory agencies?

12 What are seven ways government can reform regulation?

13 Why are society strategies included in this chapter on regulations?

14 Why can't businesses make campaign contributions to regulators?

15 Which branch of government makes the greatest use of advisory panels and committees?

16 Who has oversight of advisory panels and committees?

DISCUSSION/CRITICAL THINKING QUESTIONS

Be sure to give a detailed explanation for your answer to each question.

1 Should the executive branch of government be reorganized? If so, how?

2 Does the president of the United States have too much or too little power?

3 Do you mind paying higher prices to cross-subsidize others so that they can pay less?

4 Do you believe having cost-of-service regulation leads to higher prices?

5 Should the government be more or less active in enforcing regulations?

6 Do you believe business is more productive than government? Why or why not, and what makes one more productive?

7 What would you like to see privatized as a potential business opportunity?

8 Would you prefer to work in a regulated or deregulated business? Why?

9 Are you for or against deregulation?

10 Are political information strategies more important for dealing with congressional bills or for dealing with regulatory rules?

APPLICATION EXERCISES

9.1 EXECUTIVE BRANCH OF GOVERNMENT

Visit www.usa.gov. Click "Explore Topics" and select one to research. Report on at least three things you didn't know before your research.

9.2 THE *FEDERAL REGISTER*

Visit the online *Federal Register* (www.federalregister.gov). Click "Current Issue" and select one. Report on something of interest to you.

9.3 REGULATIONS.GOV

Visit Regulations.gov (www.regulations.gov) and make a comment on a current rule that is open for comment. Report your comment for class purposes.

9.4 RULE ENFORCEMENT

Find a news story about an agency enforcing a rule that affects business. Report on the enforcement.

9.5 ADVISORY PANELS AND COMMITTEES

Visit the website of a federal agency and do a search for advisory committees. You may go to the agency directly, or for a selection, use USA.gov (www.usa.gov) and select one. Identify the agency and report on the advisory panels and committees it uses.

CASE 9.1

Baseball, Hot Dogs, Apple Pie and Chevrolet—Do They Go Together in the Good 'Ole USA?[89]

Daniel F. Akerson, chairman and CEO of GM, thought GM had really turned the economic corner, yet little did he suspect that he and his company were to be sideswiped by the 2012 Republican presidential candidate. Throughout its financial woes, GM has received billions of dollars in loans from the Canadian and U.S. governments, negotiated concessions with labor unions, and jettisoned brands. The auto giant went through a six-week bankruptcy protection in 2009; it issued an initial public offering and returned to the stock market in 2010. The [U.S.] government owned more than 60 percent of GM when it emerged from Chapter 11 in mid-2009.

"[Yet] responding to a wave of willing investors, GM's stock opened at the top of the price range set by the car maker.

The IPO kept on pace during its first day and took in approximately $15.8 billion, excluding the sale of preferred shares and an overallotment option. It was the second-largest IPO in U.S. history. The Treasury Department now [in 2012] owns about 32%. The remainder is held by a group of minority interests, including the Canadian federal government and a United Auto Workers retiree health care trust. . . . Retaking its spot as the world's largest car maker from Toyota and driving into a market share of about 12% worldwide and 19% in the United States, GM enjoyed a net income of $9.2 billion and a jump of about 11% in total net sales and revenue in 2011. As of year-end 2011 GM's liquidity (cash and marketable securities) was $31.6 billion."[90]

"Given GM's comeback through direct and continued government support and intervention, who, including CEO Akerson, would have predicted that 'the government's bailout of General Motors [would have] become a hot political issue in the run-up to the 2012 presidential election. Presumptive Republican presidential candidate Mitt Romney, who opposed federal loans to GM and Chrysler, said he'd sell the Treasury's 26 percent stake in GM quickly if he wins the election. 'There is no reason for the government to continue to hold (GM shares)' . . . the only reason the government is holding on to its GM shares is to avoid an embarrassing news story about another loss. But last month an assistant Treasury secretary told *The Detroit News* there was no timetable for selling the GM stock because the administration had to 'balance maximizing recovery for the taxpayers with the speed of exit.' Treasury has never planned to remain in the auto business, but . . . the government would lose about $16 billion if it sold its shares now."[91]

"Taxpayers pumped $49.5 billion into GM to save the company and hundreds of thousands of jobs around the time Romney wrote a 2008 op-ed piece for *The New York Times* titled 'Let Detroit Go Bankrupt.' In fairness to Romney, his title of his guest editorial was 'The Way Forward for the Auto Industry.' A *Times* editor changed the headline but the piece itself was not changed. 'My own view is that the auto companies needed to go through bankruptcy before government help . . . and frankly, that's finally what the president did. He finally took them through bankruptcy.'"[92]

"Facing one of the worst economic meltdowns in U.S. history, with capital credit markets contracting and some financial institutions on the verge of collapse, the government provided financing to help GM and Chrysler. The [Republican] Bush administration wrote the first checks. Chrysler has since repaid its government loans and is now posting record sales, making Romney's recent bid to take credit for the industry's rebound a pretty hard sell.

'The last time Governor Romney weighed in on the future of the auto industry, it was to suggest we let Detroit go bankrupt, a betrayal no Michigander is likely to forget,' Obama campaign spokesman Matt McGrath told *The Detroit News*. 'As someone who was dead wrong about the industry's present, Mitt Romney is the last person who should be offering advice about its future.' Romney accused Democrats of 'distorting' his position.

'If they needed help coming out of bankruptcy and government support, that was fine, but I was not in favor of the government writing billions of dollars in checks prior to them going into bankruptcy,' Romney said .

Romney also said he wants to end federal loans and guarantees to help private companies develop alternative energy. 'The government is now picking winners and losers—or in the case of this president—it's picking losers, and private sector does a much better job,' Romney said in a *Detroit News* interview.

"'The reality is that Solyndra [a bankrupt solar panel maker in California] received [$535 million] funding through a Department of Energy program created [by Congress] under the [Republican] Bush Administration—a program that has supported tens of thousands of jobs across the country and is moving forward with investments in innovative projects like the first nuclear plant built in the U.S. in decades and the world's largest wind farm,' an Obama campaign spokeswoman told the *News*."[93]

Questions:

1. What is the role of the U.S. Treasury Department as a regulatory agency?
2. Assuming that the Treasury's bailout and purchase of GM and Chrysler stock would constitute a major rule, what types of analysis would the Department have to conduct to justify these actions?

3. What are the steps that this proposed action must have had to go through in order to be considered a rule?
4. What legal challenges might those who opposed the bailout, such as Mitt Romney, have taken?
5. If you were GM CEO Akerson, what nonmarket strategies might you take

to in light of Mitt Romney's perceived opposition to continued government support of GM?

6. If you were presidential candidate Mitt Romney, what nonmarket strategies might you take to support your opposition to the continued "bailout" of GM?

CASE 9.2

Rydex and the SEC: Death by Bureaucracy!

Carl G. Verboncoeur, CEO of Rydex Investments, was proud of his firm and its performance to date for his investors. "Rydex Investments is a leader in developing specialized investments that are essential components of a modern portfolio. Through continuous innovation, Rydex anticipates the evolving needs of investors. Rydex is committed to helping investors and investment advisors maximize the value of our investing tools and strategies and to providing an outstanding level of customer service in our industry. One of the nation's fastest growing fund families, Rydex offers more than 51 mutual funds, as well as Rydex S&P Equal Weighted ETF and Rydex Russell Top 50 ETF. Our products include: Funds benchmarked to well-known indices, Sector funds, Inverse (or short) funds that move opposite the market, two leveraged international funds, [and] Rydex S&P Equal Weighted ETF and Rydex Russell Top 50 ETF."[94]

ETFs (exchange-traded funds) are one of the hottest investment tools to emerge in recent years (which essentially are mutual funds that trade on exchanges like shares of stock) and have blossomed recently, thanks to their low fees and tax advantages. "ETFs in the United States have grown to account for approximately $1 trillion in assets, or approximately 10 percent of the long-term U.S. open-end investment company industry, with U.S.-domiciled ETFs making up approximately two-thirds of global

offerings. As ETFs gained in popularity, ETPs expanded from ETFs tracking equity indexes into the development of a variety of ETPs, including those based on fixed-income instruments, commodities, currencies, and foreign securities. This product development also has generated increasingly complex structures, such as leveraged, inverse, and inverse leveraged ETFs. Because of the growth and development in such ETFs and ETPs, the [Security and Exchange] Commission has been actively following, and continues to engage in the analysis of, these products."[95]

"All ETFs have special qualities that may require closer scrutiny than typical mutual funds. Because investors can buy them on an exchange, for instance, they don't always get a prospectus. That means they can miss out on one of the basic tools for learning about an investment's risks, though some product information is delivered to investors. The SEC requires traditional mutual funds to provide investors a prospectus. And while typical mutual funds are priced once a day, at the end of stock trading, the price of shares in ETFs fluctuate all day long, since shares are traded on an exchange. That means the price can differ from the underlying value of its holdings, unlike other mutual funds. An unwary investor could buy the fund at a price above its true value—just one of the different risks of ETFs."[96]

CEO Verboncoeur knew a great investment instrument when he saw one, and he was staking his and his company's reputation and future on six new ETFs, including ones tracking the Swedish krona, Mexican peso, and Australian dollar.[97] The only problem was a big one—ETFs had to be approved by the Securities and Exchange Commission (SEC), and the SEC was in no hurry to approve ETFs.

What's the SEC's problem? "Amid a rush by money-management firms to add offerings, applications for new ETFs . . . are piling up at the Securities and Exchange Commission. . . . 'The sheer number of ETF applications and proposals may be bogging down the system,' says Dan Culloton, an ETF analyst at research firm Morningstar Inc. Still, he says, if the SEC's approval process prevents the launch of too many products at once, 'that's probably beneficial' since it can help prevent investors from piling into me-too offerings or possibly chasing a market fad. The pressure for quicker approvals comes as new ETFs get more esoteric and steer further away from their original goal of simply tracking stock indexes in a cheap and tax-efficient way. Now they track commodities, foreign markets or industry sub-sectors like energy equipment or computer hardware."[98]

"What's behind the backups? For one thing, the SEC's investment-management division, which is key in ETF approval, has been sidetracked by a series of industry crises in recent years. Culture is a factor too. 'The SEC staff often has reluctance when evaluating new products,' says Barry Barbash, a partner at law firm Willkie Farr & Gallagher LLP who formerly headed the SEC's investment-management division. The concern is letting a bad product or service slip through—especially a faddish new product that has a different structure and different regulatory requirements than a typical mutual fund. Though ETFs have been around for more than decade, SEC regulations still treat them as kind of an oddball product that requires special handling. They must go through a complicated, multi-step process. That mattered

less when ETF applications were rarer, but now they're flooding in."[99]

"The SEC has promised to speed things up. The division that plays a big role in approvals 'is conducting a top-to-bottom review' of its ETF process and 'looking for opportunities to make the process routine,' said SEC Chairman Christopher Cox in an interview, calling the changes 'a priority.' Mr. Cox was asked about the issue at a hearing of the House Committee on Financial Services. Despite these concerns, speeding up the process is an SEC priority. A letter from Louisiana Republican Rep. Richard Baker calling for 'expedited review' [or exemption] of ETFs, Mr. Cox wrote that he is 'very keen' to 'make it easier and quicker for staff to complete their reviews.'"[100]

"Yet in March 2010, Commission staff determined to defer consideration of exemptive requests for ETFs. . . . While staff recognized that the use of derivatives is not a new phenomenon, the staff determined that the increasing complexity of derivatives and their growing use by funds made it the right time to reevaluate the Commission's regulatory protections. . . . Although the staff recognizes the competitive impact of the decision to defer the consideration of exemptive relief, the staff is committed to the Commission's mission to protect investors."[101]

CEO Verboncoeur recognized that "the modern market calls for unconventional thinking. It may be important to combine core investment strategies with a more active approach to portfolio management. And [investors] need investment products designed specifically for modern markets."[102] He also knew that timing was everything and that he and his company could not afford to have their new ETFs tied up in SEC red tape because competitor products were starting to hit the market. He reluctantly picked up the phone and called Nick Bonos, senior vice president in charge of legal compliance, to see what options were available to move the approvals of these ETFs along—he was anything but hopeful.

Questions:

1. What are the problems associated with the SEC processing ETF applications in a timely manner?
2. What other activities described in this chapter have the SEC been involved in that may hinder its ability to process ETF applications?
3. What is the potential impact of unreasonably slow approval of ETFs on Rydex Investments, other investment houses, and consumers of investment products?
4. Assuming that Louisiana Republican Rep. Richard Baker persuades the SEC to develop an expedited review process for ETFs, what steps would this new regulation have to go through?
5. What nonmarket strategies can CEO Verboncoeur and Rydex Investments employ to move their ETF applications along and support an expedited review process?

<table>
<tr><td>INTEGRATIVE CASE

9</td></tr>
</table>

INTEGRATIVE CASE (Part 9)

DHR Construction, LLC and the Federal Reserve: The Cards Have Been Dealt Boys—Read 'Em and Weep

This is a continuation case—please refer to Chapters 1–8 for further information.

It was déjà vu all over again, and Richard Davis and Stephen Hodgetts felt powerless to do anything about it. Way back in the summer of 2002, Davis and Hodgetts saw the value of their stock portfolios, more specifically their retirement accounts, drop about 20 percent, the same 20 percent that the Dow Jones average had lost in just three months. It was then and there that they decided to take control of their financial futures, first by going into the home rental business and then by becoming home builders.

Although they encountered numerous obstacles and problems along the way, Davis and Hodgetts had always counted on the strength of the real estate market and the continued high demand for newly constructed homes to pull them through. Now they were not so sure. It was the summer of 2006 and, normally summer was the busiest time of the home-buying season. Kids would be out of school (and therefore families could easily move), and parents and other working adults would have excellent weather and more free time (due to vacations) in which to drive through neighborhoods and look at model homes. In the summer, construction was also the easiest, given both weather conditions and the greater availability of labor, and homes could be at their peak showing condition with landscaping in an excellent well-cared-for state. Yet business was slow and seemed to have dried up overnight.

"I don't get it," stated Hodgetts. "The town never did go through with that building moratorium, thanks to you and your great speech, Richard, and the press on the moratorium seemed to have little impact on home sales at that time. We weathered that storm quite well; in fact, you became a bit of a local hero."

"Hero, schmearo," mumbled Richard Davis in a whimsical, yet satirical manner. "I'd trade my hero status for a good sale any day or night. All I know is that foot traffic through our show homes is down considerably, and so are sales. Even the parade of homes, our trade association marketing campaign that features member home builders, could not generate the type of customer base that we're used to. I think I'll give Mark Kessler, president of the HBA, a call and see what he has to say. He usually knows something we don't know and is quite happy to share it with us."

The Higher Authority

Mark Kessler confirmed Davis's worst fears—sales were down for the entire HBA membership.

"It's bad news all over," started Mark, "and it sounds like it is not going to get better any time soon. I know that John over at Best Homes has already laid off half of his crew due to his slowing business, and George at Superior has actually stopped building out at his section of development over at Tuscany. He's got nearly 40 homes standing, all up for sale, and no takers. Sold only 2 of them. Two out of 42—that's a formula for bankruptcy!"

"What in heaven's name is going on, Mark?" queried Davis. "Are people opting to buy existing homes over new homes? Are people too in debt to afford even a no-money-down deal on a new home?" A silence seemed to spread from the airwaves into both Davis's and Kessler's phones until Mark Kessler finally broke the silence with a faint whisper, as if he were telling a deep, dark secret. "It's the government, Richard; it's the Feds. They've killed the business for us all."

"The Feds? What in the world are you talking about?" shouted Davis. "Has the federal government banned home ownership? Have we become a socialist state? Or have they taken away the tax breaks for mortgages and property taxes? I know that we stopped our local politicians from implementing the moratorium; what have the big political muckety-mucks done in Washington that would affect us here in our little community?"

"No, no," replied Kessler. "You have it all wrong. This is nothing that our elected politicians have done, no sir. They don't have the guts to mess with the National HBA. They're in our back pockets, and we can pull their strings anytime we want; we can even get to the president! Who do you think contributes the most to his reelection campaign? We do! No, this came from a higher authority."

Davis stared incredulously into the phone, a rather silly habit which affirmed his shock and dismay. "What are you saying, Mark, that this has been ordained by a higher power? Outside of our control?"

"In a way," chuckled Mark, "you're right. The group is outside of our control, even the direct control of the president. Blame it on them; blame it on the Federal Reserve!"

Power and Chaos

Mark explained to Davis how the Federal Reserve set monetary policy. Especially how the Federal Reserve tried to control inflation and the flow of capital through raising and lowering interest rates to and between banks.

"OK, Mark, thanks for Money and Banking 101. What I need to know now is how the cost of capital to banks affects the real estate industry."

"That's easy," answered Mark. "Lending institutions like banks and other financial institutions drive the real estate industry in this country because very few individuals have the immediate assets with which to purchase a home. Therefore, they are forced to borrow money, that is, obtain a mortgage in order to have the wherewithal with which to buy a home from you, the builder. These lending institutions are going to charge fees and interest rates that account for the cost of capital that they have to borrow with which to make their loans while factoring in the risk of the loan and their profit margins. It is very simple; the more these institutions are charged for borrowing money, the more they charge their customers. And, if we take this the next step further, the more they charge their customers, the higher the monthly mortgage will be on a particular home."

"That makes sense," responded Davis. "I guess it is then safe to assume that customers will realize that, at a certain interest rate, they can no longer afford to pay the mortgage on a certain priced home and that they would have to settle for a cheaper home. Is that what is happening?"

"Quite possibly," countered Mark, "but that wouldn't account for the slowing down of traffic in all of the homes in our area. Interest rates are quite low now, and people want to buy homes, they just can't afford them because they either lack the large down payment they need or have poor credit ratings. So they are waiting."

"Waiting for what?" Davis quipped back.

"Good question. What I think has happened is that the Federal Reserve raised interest rates a few years back and drove many people with variable mortgages into bankruptcy because they could not pay their higher mortgage rates. Banks then repossessed these homes and resold them as "short sales," much lower than market prices. These sales lowered the value of homes in the market and many homeowners found that they had mortgages larger than the value of their homes. These homeowners either renegotiated their mortgages with the lenders for lower rates or walked away from their homes. In any event, mortgage companies took a shellacking and have yet to recover their losses. These firms have now imposed stringent mortgage qualifying requirements. Simply stated, no mortgage no home sales."

"So what are our options?" Davis quipped.

"Why," laughed Mark, "you can sit idle on your inventory until you'll have to drop the prices of your homes to a point where the consumer would have a mortgage payment they can qualify for. The buyer is also figuring that you also have borrowed money to pay for your land and your speculation homes and that you'll eventually be forced to lower prices. The mortgage companies (and therefore the consumer) have served the ball into your court, Richard, thanks to the Federal Reserve!"

"So what is the National and local HBA going to do about this!" demanded Davis. "You're supposed to protect our interests. If we lower our prices, we lower our revenues and our profits. Lower profits mean fewer future investments and less motivation to build more homes."

"Exactly," replied Kessler. "Some builders will drop out of the market; others will drop their prices to survive. Lower prices reduce inflation—exactly what the Federal Reserve wants. This is all part of the business cycle."

"And what do we do until then?" asked Davis.

"Why," Mark responded, "perhaps you should consult an even higher authority!"

Questions

1. How do the actions of the Federal Reserve in terms of setting overnight and interbank interest rates affect the real estate industry?

2. Assuming that the president was convinced by his Council of Economic Advisers, his National Economic Council, and the secretary of the Treasury that the Federal Reserve's policies were inadvertently negatively impacting the real estate industry and the public, under what authority and actions could he directly and indirectly address this issue?

3. Given the negative implications of setting interest rates for the real estate industry, Hodgetts proposes deregulating the Federal Reserve's ability to set the federal fund and discount rates. Do you agree or disagree? Why?

4. What nonmarket actions can the local and national HBA take to directly and indirectly influence the Federal Reserve?

5. What nonmarket actions can DHR Patio Homes LLC take to directly and indirectly influence the Federal Reserve?

REFERENCES AND NOTES

1 http://en.wikipedia.org/wiki/Federal_Reserve (accessed June 15, 2006).

2 http://premium.hoovers.com/subscribe/co/overview.xhtml?ID=fffrftsccffrshscrf (accessed June 15, 2006).

3 http://www.econlib.org/library/Enc/MoneySupply.html (accessed June 15, 2006).

4 http://en.wikipedia.org/wiki/Reserve_requirement (accessed June 15, 2006).

5 http://www.federalreserve.gov/monetary-policy/reservereq.htm (accessed July 23, 2012).

6 http://www.newyorkfed.org/markets/statistics/dlyrates/fedrate.html (accessed July 23, 2012).

7 http://www.bankrate.com/rates/interest-rates/prime-rate.aspx (accessed July 23, 2012).

8 http://en.wikipedia.org/wiki/Federal_funds_rate (accessed June 15, 2006).

9 http://www.moneymarketaccounts.com/ (accessed July 23, 2012).

10 www.usa.gov (accessed May 29, 2010).

11 http://topics.nytimes.com/top/news/health/diseasesconditionsandhealthtopics/health_insurance_and_managed_care/health_care_reform/index.html (accessed July 23, 2012).

12 S. Forbes, "Election Armageddon," *Forbes* (May 7, 2012): 11–12.

13 C. Marquis and Z. Huang, "The Contingent Nature of Public Policy and the Growth of U.S. Commercial Banking," *Academy of Management Journal* 52(6) (2009): 1222–1246.

14 M. L. Barnett and A. A. King, "Good Fences Make Good Neighbors: A Longitudinal Analysis of an Industry Self-Regulatory Institution," *Academy of Management Journal* 51(6) (2008): 1150–1170.

15 "Who's Afraid of a Little Regulation?" *BusinessWeek* (February 13–19, 2012): 31–33.

16 D. Malpass, "Pushing Back: A Government-Centered Society," *Forbes* (May 21, 2012): 32.

17 K. Weise, "It's Your Call: Read All 2,300 Pages of Dodd-Frank. Or Read This," *BusinessWeek* (January 16–22, 2012): 30.

18 D. Armstrong, "How the New England Journal Missed Warning Signs of VIOXX," *Wall Street Journal* (May 15, 2006): A1.

19 W. M. Crain and T. D. Hopkins, "The Impact of Regulatory Costs on Small Firms," *U.S. Small Business Administration* (Washington, DC: REP No. SBAHQ-00-R-0027).

20 S. Dudley and M. Warren, "Regulatory Response: An Analysis of the Shifting Priorities of the U.S. Budget for Fiscal Years 2002 and 2003," Regulatory Budget Report 24, *The Metcatus Center* (www.mercatus.org).

21 W. M. Crain and T. D. Hopkins, "The Impact of Regulatory Costs on Small Firms," *U.S. Small Business Administration* (Washington, DC: REP No. SBAHQ-00-R-0027).

22 Ibid.

23 J. Zweig, "Pay Collars Won't Hold Back Wall Street's Big Dogs," *Wall Street Journal* (February 7–8, 2009): B1.

24 omb.gov (accessed May 30, 2012).

25 www.federalregister.gov (accessed May 30, 2012).

26 S. Holt, "Building Law-Abiding Businesses," *Suffolk Business Magazine* (Fall 2011): 38–39.

27 "What Is BGOV?" *BusinessWeek* (Spring 2011): B1.

28 www.regulations.gov (accessed May 30, 2012).

29 www.reginfo.gov (accessed May 30, 2012).

30 C. Marquis and Z. Huang, "The Contingent Nature of Public Policy and the Growth of U.S. Commercial Banking," *Academy of Management Journal* 52(6) (2009): 1222–1246.

31 D. P. Barron, *Business and Its Environment,* 6th ed. (Upper Saddle, NJ: Prentice Hall, 2010).

32 P. Grauer, "My Metric," *Fortune* (February 2, 2009): 14.

33 www.reginfo.gov (accessed May 30, 2012).

34 D. P. Barron, *Business and Its Environment,* 6th ed. (Upper Saddle, NJ: Prentice Hall, 2010).

35 J. C. Dooren, "Obama Health Chief Blocks FDA on Morning After Pill," *Wall Street Journal* (December 8, 2011): A1, A2.

36 USA.gov (accessed May 30, 2012).

37 R. G. Matthews, "IRS's Tougher," *Wall Street Journal* (August 1, 2005): A4.

38 "Customs Officials Yielded," *Wall Street Journal* (October 4, 2006): A1.

39 K. Maher, "Raid at Gibson Strikes Sour Note," *Wall Street Journal* (September 21, 2011): B4.

40 K. Weise, "It's Your Call: Read All 2,300 Pages of Dodd-Frank. Or Read This," *BusinessWeek* (January 16–22, 2012): 30.

41 J. Pereira and M. Trottman, "Retailers Urge Rollback on Children's Safety Law," *Wall Street Journal* (February 10, 2009): B3.

42 D. Cameron, "U.S. Levies First Tarmac-Delay Fine," *Wall Street Journal* (November 15, 2011): B2.

43 A. G. Keane, "What's Dumber than Texting and Driving," *BusinessWeek* (May 28–June 3, 2012): 32.

44 S. Terlep, "GM Scrambles to Defend Volt," *Wall Street Journal* (November 29, 2011): B1.

45 R. Smith and T. Aeppel, "EPA's Carbon Proposal Riles Industries," *Wall Street Journal* (December 8, 2009): B1.

46 "Who's Afraid of a Little Regulation," *BusinessWeek* (February 13–19, 2012): 31–33.

47 J. Angwin, "Google in New Privacy Probes," *Wall Street Journal* (March 16, 2012): A1.

48 M. Trottman, "Business Irked as Labor Board Backs Unions," *Wall Street Journal* (August 31, 2011): B1.

49 D. Leonard, "Outmanned, Outgunned, and on a Roll," BusinessWeek.com/adsections pp. 60–66.

50 J. Gallu, "The SEC Stands by a Controversial Phrase," *BusinessWeek* (January 16–22, 2012): 42–43.

51 "The Ultimate Guide to Facebook's IPO," *BusinessWeek* (February 13–19, 2012): 44–47.

52 R. Schmidt, "Lobbyists Wanted: No Experience Required," *BusinessWeek* (May 28–June 3, 2012): 31–32.

53 http://www.economist.com/node/21557325 (accessed July 23, 2012).

54 "Who's Afraid of a Little Regulation," *BusinessWeek* (February 13–19, 2012): 31–33.

55 A. Dowell and L. Scism, "GE Banking on MetLife Deposits," *Wall Street Journal* (December 28, 2011): A1, A2.

56 M. L. Barnett and A. A. King, "Good Fences Make Good Neighbors: A Longitudinal Analysis of an Industry Self-Regulatory Institution," *Academy of Management Journal* 51(6) (2008): 1150–1170.

57 http://transition.fcc.gov/wcb/tapd/universal_service/ (accessed May 31, 2012).

58 Reason Foundation Annual Privatization Report, http://reason.org/news/show/annual-privatization-2011-federal (accessed May 31, 2012); Reason Public Policy Institute, www.privatization.org (accessed June 5, 2006).

59 B. Kim and J. E. Prescott, "Deregulatory Forms, Variations in the Speed of Governance Adaptation, and Firm Performance," *Academy of Management Review*, 30 (April 2, 2005): 414–425.

60 S. Forbes, "Election Armageddon," *Forbes* (May 7, 2012): 11–12.

61 K. Weise, "It's Your Call: Read All 2,300 Pages of Dodd-Frank. Or Read This," *BusinessWeek* (January 16–22, 2012): 30.

62 J. P. Bonardi and G. D. Keim, "Corporate Political Strategies for Widely Salient Issues," *Academy of Management Review* 30(3) (2005): 555–576.

63 W. R. Evans and W. D. Davis, "An Examination of Perceived Corporate Citizenship, Job Applicant Attraction, and CSR Work Role Definition," *Business & Society 50*(3) (2011): 456–480.

64 N. Easton and T. Demos, "The Business Guide to Congress," *Fortune* (May 11, 2009): 72–75.

65 A. Armenakis and J. Wigand, "Stakeholder Actions and Their Impact on the Organizational Cultures of Two Tobacco Companies," *Business and Society Review* 115(2) (2010): 147–171.

66 P. Schreck, "Reviewing the Business Case for Corporate Social Responsibility: New Evidence and Analysis," *Journal of Business Ethics* 103(2) (2011): 167–188.

67 P. Roythorne, "Special Report–Public Relations: The Specialist Subject," *Marketing Week* (April 21, 2005): 37.

68 P. O'Connell and J. McGregor, "Managing Through the Economic Storm," *BusinessWeek* (June 29, 2009): 46–48.

69 D. P. Barron, *Business and Its Environment,* 6th ed. (Upper Saddle, NJ: Prentice Hall, 2010).

70 A. Lobb, A. Dizik, and J. Porter, "Lessons That Fit the Times," *Wall Street Journal* (August 20, 2009): B5.

71 G. Colvin, "What Makes a CEO an MPV?" *Fortune* (June 13, 2011): 27.

72　M. L. Barnett and A. A. King, "Good Fences Make Good Neighbors: A Longitudinal Analysis of an Industry Self-Regulatory Institution," *Academy of Management Journal* 51(6) (2008): 1150–1170.

73　W. J. Henisz, "Legitimacy, Interest Group Pressures, and Change in Emergent Institutions: The Case of Foreign Investors and Host Country Governments," *Academy of Management Review* 30(2) (2005): 361–382.

74　J. P. Bonardi and G. D. Keim, "Corporate Political Strategies for Widely Salient Issues," *Academy of Management Review* 30(3) (2005): 555–576.

75　R. Van der Merwe, L.F. Pitt, and R. Abratt. "Stakeholders Strength: PR Survival Strategies in the Internet Age," *Public Relations Quarterly* 50 (Spring 2005): 39–49.

76　N. M. Dahan, J. Doh, and H. Teegen, "Role of Nongovernmental Organizations in the Business—Government—Society Interface: Special Issue Overview and Introductory Essay," *Business & Society* 49(1) (2010): 20–34.

77　D. Michaels, "U.S. Airlines Fire on Aid to Foreign Carriers," *Wall Street Journal* (November 14, 2011): B4.

78　D. P. Barron, *Business and Its Environment,* 6th ed. (Upper Saddle, NJ: Prentice Hall, 2010).

79　N. Easton and T. Demos, "The Business Guide to Congress," *Fortune* (May 11, 2009): 72–75.

80　A. Mundy, "Political Lobbying Drove FDA Process," *Wall Street Journal* (September 6, 2009): A1.

81　R. Schmidt, "Lobbyists Wanted: No Experience Required," *BusinessWeek* (May 28–June 3, 2012): 31–32.

82　B. Greeley and T. Shields, "Behind AT&T's Epic Lobbying Failure," *BusinessWeek* (December 12–16, 2011): 40–42.

83　N. Easton and T. Demos, "The Business Guide to Congress," *Fortune* (May 11, 2009): 72–75.

84　J. P. Bonardi and G. D. Keim, "Corporate Political Strategies for Widely Salient Issues," *Academy of Management Review* 30(3) (2005): 555–576.

85　W. J. Henisz, "Legitimacy, Interest Group Pressures, and Change in Emergent Institutions: The Case of Foreign Investors and Host Country Governments," *Academy of Management Review* 30(2) (2005): 361–382.

86　General Services Administration, http://www.gsa.gov/portal/content/104514 (accessed June 1, 2012).

87　Ibid.

88　J. C. Dooren, "FDA May Scrap Plan to Require Longer Psychiatric Drug Studies," *Wall Street Journal* (October 26, 2005): D5.

89　http://www.autobytel.com/car-ownership/road-trip/baseball-apple-pie-and-chevrolet-1390/ (accessed July 23, 2012).

90　http://subscriber.hoovers.com/H/company360/fulldescription.html?companyId=10640000000000 (accessed July 23, 2012).

91　http://www.upi.com/Business_News/2012/06/10/Auto-Outlook-GMs-bailout-fuels-automotive-politics/UPI-89611339320600/ (accessed July 23, 2012).

92　Ibid.

93　http://www.upi.com/Business_News/2012/06/10/Auto-Outlook-GMs-bailout-fuels-automotive-politics/UPI-89611339320600/ (accessed July 23, 2012).

94　http://www.rydexfunds.com/WebSite/About_fset.cfm?Channel=1 (accessed June 17, 2006).

95　http://www.sec.gov/news/testimony/2011/ts101911er.htm (accessed July 23, 2012).

96　D. Gullapalli, "Growth of Hot Investment Tool Slowed by Bureaucratic Backlog," *Wall Street Journal* (June 17, 2006): A1.

97　Ibid.

98　Ibid.

99　Ibid.

100　Ibid.

101　http://www.sec.gov/news/testimony/2011/ts101911er.htm (accessed July 23, 2012).

102　http://www.rydexfunds.com/WebSite/About_fset.cfm?Channel=1 (accessed June 17, 2006).

Chapter 10

LAW INTERPRETING, ANTITRUST, AND JUDICIARY STRATEGIES

Learning Outcomes

In this chapter, you will find out the answers to these key questions:

■ What is antitrust?
■ How does the judiciary system work?

After studying this chapter, you should be able to:

1. Compare and contrast four antitrust laws
2. Compare and contrast acquisitions and mergers
3. Describe the different types of mergers
4. Discuss antitrust enforcement and merger investigation guidelines
5. Explain merger investigation guidelines
6. Describe the types of laws, lawsuits, courts, and court functions
7. Define the following key terms (in order of appearance in the chapter):

antitrust laws	acquisition	common law
predatory pricing	merger	judicial review
price-fixing	horizontal mergers	criminal lawsuits
Sherman Act	vertical mergers	civil lawsuits
Clayton Act	conglomerate mergers	public lawsuits
price discrimination	legal precedents	
director interlock	consent decrees	
tying contracts		
Federal Trade Commission Act		
Antitrust Improvement Act		

■ Chapter Outline

Antitrust Laws
    Objectives of Antitrust Laws
    The Sherman Act (1890)
    The Clayton Act (1914)
    Federal Trade Commission Act (1914)
    Antitrust Improvement Act (1976)

Mergers and Antitrust
    Acquisition or Merger?
    Horizontal Mergers
    Vertical Mergers
    Conglomerate Mergers

Antitrust Enforcement
    Department of Justice and Federal Trade Commission
    Merger Investigation Guidelines
    Private Enforcement and State Attorneys General
    Antitrust in Federal Courts

The Judicial Branch
    Judicial Concepts
    Federal Courts
    State and Local Courts

Business Nonmarket and Market Strategies and Ethics
    Information Strategies
    Societal Strategies
    Political Strategies

Judiciary Strategies
    Avoiding Lawsuits
    Filing Lawsuits
    Lawsuits

What's This Chapter About?

In this chapter, we continue our discussion of law enforcement from the last chapter by discussing antitrust. Antitrust law includes statutes and court decisions interpreting those laws, making antitrust legal advice important to business. So we put law enforcing and then law interpreting together in this chapter.

We begin with a discussion of the major antitrust laws, followed by mergers and how they can violate antitrust laws. Our third section describes how the government enforces antitrust laws. We proceed to discuss the judicial system through which cases are tried—law determination. As in prior chapters, we discuss nonmarket and market strategies and ethics, with a final section presenting an in-depth discussion of judiciary strategies that business uses to meet its objectives.

CASE

Microsoft and the European Union (EU): Troubles Ahead, Troubles Behind

Microsoft is a household name, and rightly so. "The world's #1 software company provides a variety of products and services, including its Windows operating systems and Office software suite. The company has expanded into markets, such as video game consoles, interactive television, and Internet access."[1] Yet being so well-known and so aggressive with its Windows software has landed Microsoft in a lot of legal hot water and in the sights of its major competitors and the U.S. government.

"The early 1990s brought monopoly charges from inside and outside the industry. In 1995 antitrust concerns scotched a $1.5 billion acquisition of personal finance software maker **Intuit**. . . . In 1997 **Sun** sued Microsoft for allegedly creating an incompatible version of Java; Microsoft countersued. (The ongoing court battle, settled by Microsoft in 2001 for $20 million, prevented the company from releasing new Java tools or accessing any of Sun's advances). . . . The **U.S. Justice Department,** backed by 18 states, filed antitrust charges in 1998 against the software giant, claiming that it stifled Internet browser competition and limited consumer choice. . . . A federal judge's ruling that Microsoft used its monopoly powers to violate antitrust laws left the prospect of two (smaller) **Microsofts**, a decision the company aggressively appealed. Under the terms of the settlement, Microsoft agreed to uniformly license its Windows operating systems, cease to offer exclusive contracts with manufacturers, and allow competing software to be included with its operating systems. . . . **Netscape Communications** filed suit in 2002 against Microsoft, seeking unspecified damages and injunctions against the company's alleged antitrust actions. . . . Microsoft settled the suit with Netscape in 2003, agreeing to pay **AOL** $750 million as part of a larger settlement that includes AOL licensing Microsoft's Internet Explorer browser and its digital media technology."[2]

With all of the settlements with competitors, the U.S. government essentially stopped pursuing antitrust action against Microsoft; however, its competitors decided to attack Microsoft through another government, one more apt to be sympathetic, the European Union (EU). "U.S.-based rivals have increasingly turned to the EU to aid their cause . . . including **International Business Machines Corp.**, **Oracle Corp.**, **Sun Microsystems Inc.**, **Red Hat Inc.**, **RealNetworks Inc.** and **Adobe Systems Inc.** . . . At heart, the battle is over the same issue as the U.S. antitrust fight: promoting competition in global software markets that Microsoft dominates. Because it produces both Windows, the basic brains of most PCs, and other software that runs seamlessly with Windows, Microsoft has a huge advantage over other software companies, the EU and the rivals say. They want a level playing field. But Microsoft argues the EU wants it to hand its competitors valuable intellectual property."[3]

"The EU investigation began in December 1998, prompted by a complaint from **Sun**. The Santa Clara, California, software maker claimed Microsoft was trying to cripple its business by concealing technical information Sun needed. As a result, Sun said, its office-networking software couldn't communicate easily with other Microsoft networking products or personal computers using Microsoft Windows—the operating system used by the employees of most of its large corporate customers. Sun says that put it at a disadvantage against Microsoft's competing product. . . . Separately, Microsoft paid more than $3 billion to **Sun**, Massachusetts software maker **Novell Inc.,** and **RealNetworks** to drop their related complaints in both Europe and the United States. That removed the company's strongest adversaries from direct involvement in the EU case."[4]

"In 2001, the EU opened a separate investigation into whether Microsoft was illegally hurting makers of music and video-playing software, such as **RealNetworks**, by embedding Microsoft's own Windows Media Player software free of charge in its Windows programs. . . . In March 2004, the EU issued its antitrust ruling, which carried a $613 million fine and ordered Microsoft to do two things to help its rivals compete. First: Stop building a free copy of its media player into Windows, so other makers of media-playing software would have a better chance to compete. Second: Produce an instruction manual to help rivals write Windows-compatible software for knitting together complex office computer networks."[5]

"Microsoft [in 2006 produced] a compliant version of its flagship operating system without Windows Media Player available under the negotiated name Windows XP N. . . . Microsoft also appealed the case, and the EU had a week-long hearing over it. . . . On September 17, 2007, Microsoft lost an appeal against the European Commission's case. The €497 million fine was upheld, as were the requirements regarding server interoperability information and bundling of Media Player. . . . On October 22, 2007, Microsoft announced that it would comply and not appeal the decision. . . . On February 27, 2008, the EU fined Microsoft an additional €899 million (US$1.44 billion) for failure to comply with the March 2004 antitrust decision. . . . On May 9, 2008, Microsoft lodged an appeal in the European Court of First Instance seeking to overturn the €899 million fine, officially stating that it intended to use the action as a "constructive effort to seek clarity from the court."[6]

On June 27, 2012, the General Court upheld the fine . . . [the] commission's decision to fine Microsoft was not challenged by the court, saying the company had blocked fair access to its markets. EU competition commissioner, Joaquín Almunia, has said that such fines may not be effective in preventing anticompetitive behavior and that the commission now preferred to seek settlements that restrict businesses' plans instead. As such, the *New York Times* called the Microsoft decision "a decision that could mark the end of an era in antitrust law in which regulators used big fines to bring technology giants to heel."[7]

A spokesperson for Microsoft said the company was "'disappointed with the court's ruling' and felt the company had 'resolved [the commission's] competition law concerns' in 2009, making the fine unnecessary. [The spokesperson] declined to say whether Microsoft would file an appeal or not. . . . [Many believe] the ruling [is] a vindication of the crackdown on Microsoft. . . . 'The judgment confirms that the imposition of such penalty payments remains an important tool at the commission's disposal.' . . . The commission's actions against Microsoft had allowed 'a range of innovative products that would otherwise not have seen the light of day' to reach the market."[8]

The following questions are related to the Microsoft and EU case. Answers can be found within the chapter.

1. What objectives of the U.S. antitrust laws apply to the EU's antitrust case against Microsoft?
2. Under what antitrust laws would the federal government have pursued an antitrust case against Microsoft?
3. What type of merger or acquisition was Microsoft proposing with Intuit, and why did the government stop it?
4. What would be examples of vertical and conglomerate mergers or acquisitions for Microsoft?
5. Which types of organizations have taken antitrust enforcement action against Microsoft?
6. What type of law and lawsuits were brought against Microsoft?
7. What U.S. court actions have taken place relative to the antitrust suits against Microsoft?
8. What judiciary strategies has Microsoft employed in terms of the antitrust lawsuits?

Learning Outcome 1: Compare and contrast four antitrust laws.

ANTITRUST LAWS

Continuing our law enforcement discussion from the last chapter, antitrust laws date back to the late nineteenth century when big business was growing by means of abusive competitive practices. Pressure from multiple interest groups helps to change laws and contributes support for government to better control large business in order to maintain a competitive capitalistic system. Some organizations are exempt from antitrust laws. Those that are exempt include **unions**, **agricultural cooperatives**, and some business transactions related to national defense. **Insurance companies** are exempt because they are regulated by state, not federal, law. Congress also exempted **Major League Baseball (MLB)**. However, the **Department of Justice** did investigate the **National Collegiate Athletic Association** (**NCAA**, www.ncaa.org) football *Bowl Championship Series* on antitrust grounds questioning why it doesn't have playoffs and requesting information supporting steps it has taken to create a playoff.

In this section, we discuss the objectives of antitrust laws and four key antitrust laws; see Figure 10.1 for a list of them. Although we present four laws that are dated, the regulators continue to update the rules. However, not everyone agrees that government intervention to ensure competition is needed; they believe free market competition will curb antitrust far better than government bureaucrats can.[9] Partly because antitrust and relevant acts are some of the most complex laws in business and legal transactions.

Objectives of Antitrust Laws

The government is the protector of our free-market economy. *Antitrust laws preserve capitalism by protecting competition to benefit consumers.* Thus, government establishes the ground rules of competition.[10] Antitrust policy can be thought of as a control over economic power.[11] Antitrust laws have multiple objectives. Here we briefly discuss three of those objectives.

1. **To protect competition.** Antitrust laws preserve and protect competition by outlawing monopolies and by prohibiting unfair competition and collusion. Competition is the major objective, so we will discuss competition in detail later in this chapter. Antitrust laws also block mergers that would allow a single company to dominate a market, which could result in the elimination of competition, allowing big business to manipulate the supply relative to demand and, therefore, the prices of products.

The Sherman Act (1890)	The Clayton Act (1914)	Federal Trade Commission Act (1914)	Antitrust Improvement Act (1976)
prohibited unreasonable restraints of trade and monopolization	prohibited anticompetitive mergers, price discrimination, director interlock, and tying contracts	prohibited unfair competition and deceptive practices and created the FTC to help enforce antitrust laws	required premerger notification and approval and allowed states to sue business for price fixing

▪ **Figure 10.1:** Antitrust Laws

Under antitrust, free market competition is preserved, but firms are not protected from going out of business, although a government bailout of the financial industry was made with the thought of too big to fail. Through heavy competition, firms go out of business every day. Antitrust keeps its focus on consumers, so every charge of anticompetition is evaluated based on its effect on consumers. Thus, many mergers, although they reduce competition, are allowed because of the consumer benefits, usually through lower prices that can be passed on to consumers due to increasing economies of scale.[12]

2. **To protect consumers**. Antitrust laws protect consumer welfare by prohibiting deceptive and unfair business practices. Government helps protect consumers from being misled and exploited.[13] Recall our discussion of consumer protection and advertising regulation in Chapter 6. We will also be discussing consumer protection throughout this chapter because protecting competition to benefit consumers is the focus of antitrust.

3. **To protect small business from large business**. Antitrust laws protect small business by prohibiting predatory pricing and price discrimination to preserve competition that benefits consumers and to ensure that trade is not restrained.[14] *Predatory pricing is selling products below cost to drive competitors out of business*. Once the competition is gone, the prices go up. When **Walmart** comes to a town, it drives some small firms out of businesses, but it does so with its everyday low prices, not with predatory pricing. Price discrimination is covered in the following discussion of the Clayton Act.

Microsoft and the EU Case Question 1: What objectives of the U.S. antitrust laws apply to the EU's antitrust case against Microsoft?

The three objectives of the antitrust laws are to protect competition, to protect consumers, and to protect small business from large business. Sun claimed that Microsoft was trying to cripple its business by concealing technical information, putting Sun at a disadvantage against Microsoft's competing product (anticompetition). The EU issued its antitrust ruling and ordered Microsoft to do two things to help its rivals compete. First, stop building a free copy of its media player into Windows, so other makers of media-playing software would have a better chance to compete. Second, produce an instruction manual to help rivals write Windows-compatible software for knitting together complex office computer networks. This ruling stopped Microsoft from unfairly competing against smaller businesses by giving away its media player as part of its Windows package and provided consumers viable choices of media players.

The Sherman Act (1890)

Government addresses public problems to promote the general consumer welfare. The Sherman Act was the first and is considered the foundation of antitrust regulation; in fact, it was the basis for one of the antitrust cases against **Microsoft**.[15] Two excerpts from the Sherman Act follow:

Section 1: "Every contract, combination in the form of trust or otherwise, or conspiracy in restraint of trade or commerce . . . is hereby declared to be illegal." For example, *price-fixing is competitors colluding to explicitly or implicitly agree on the price they will charge*. **Pilgrim's Pride** was found guilty of knowingly trying to manipulate the price of chicken and paid $26 million in damages.[16] The **Department**

of Justice (**DOJ**, www.justice.gov) brought a civil antitrust lawsuit alleging that **Apple** and five publishers (**Simon & Schuster**, **Hachette**, **Penguin**, **Macmillan**, and **HarperCollins)** conspired to raise e-book prices in competition with **Amazon**.[17]

Section 2: "Every person who shall monopolize, or attempt to monopolize . . . trade or commerce . . . shall be deemed guilty." Numerous companies have been investigated for having monopolization power, including **Google**,[18] **Intel**,[19] **IBM**,[20] and **Microsoft**.[21] Government investigations commonly come under the request of smaller competitors who claim to be harmed by the firm's antitrust violation.

To put it in concise terms, the *Sherman Act prohibits unreasonable restraints of trade and monopolization*. Because the terms *restraint of trade* and *monopoly* were vague and open to interpretation, demands were made to define the terms. In response, Congress passed the Clayton Act and the Federal Trade Commission Act in the same year.

The Clayton Act (1914)

The Clayton Act defined many anticompetitive practices. Here are four major practices that were made illegal. *The Clayton Act prohibits anticompetitive mergers, price discrimination, director interlock, and tying contracts.*

Mergers through the purchase of shares or assets of competitors are illegal if they lessen competition or create a monopoly. The Obama administration has blocked more mergers than in the past. The government stopped the mergers of **Nasdaq** and **NYSE**, **H&R Block** and **TaxACT**, and **AT&T** and **T-Mobile**.[22] Thus, the Clayton Act strengthens the Sherman Act with regard to monopoly.

Price discrimination is selling products to a customer for less without evidence of a lower cost for serving the customer. The prohibition against price discrimination prevents manufacturers from selling products for less to one business (often big business) than to others (often small business) without proof of lower cost. For example, when **Coke** and **Pepsi** run lower-price soda specials, they must offer the same price to supermarkets as they do to the convenience stores.

Director interlock is having a director serving on the boards of two companies that are in direct competition. For example, **Dell** computer founder Michael Dell can't serve on the board of directors of **Hewlett-Packard (HP)**.

Tying contracts require the buyer to purchase additional products as a condition of the sale. **Mercedes-Benz** requires its car dealers to have a room/store selling products with its logo, which are not usually profitable, and carrying only Mercedes parts. **Microsoft** was accused of tying, also called *bundling*, its Internet Explorer browser with its Windows operating systems, rather than letting the buyer select only the operating system. Was the intent to monopolize the browser market by discouraging PC users from having to buy another browser?

Federal Trade Commission Act (1914)

Section 5(a) 91) states, "Unfair methods of competition in commerce, and unfair or deceptive acts or practices in commerce, are hereby declared unlawful." *The Federal Trade Commission Act prohibits unfair competition and deceptive practices; it created the FTC to help enforce antitrust laws.* **Facebook** agreed to a 20-year privacy settlement with the FTC (www.ftc.gov) that requires the company to ask users for permission before changing the way their personal information is released.[23]

Unfair competition and deceptive practices were not defined in the act. The act was later amended to define some unfair practices, such as *misleading advertising* and *bait-*

and-switch merchandising to get the customer to buy more expensive products when lower-priced products were being advertised but were not available to purchase. **Glaxo-SmithKline** agreed to a settlement of $3 billion for promoting antidepressants *Paxil* and *Wellbutrin* for uses not approved by the **FDA** (www.fda.gov), an illegal practice known as *off-label marketing.*[24]

Antitrust Improvement Act (1976)

The Antitrust Improvement Act requires premerger notification and approval, and it allows states to sue businesses for price-fixing. The relatively new law strengthens the government's ability to enforce the other three antitrust laws in three important ways. First, the law expands the **Department of Justice (DOJ)** antitrust investigative powers.

Large corporations are required to notify the **DOJ** and the **FTC** about merger and acquisition plans so that the DOJ and FTC can study any possible violations of antitrust laws, order any divestitures necessary to allow the proposal, or deny the merger or acquisition before it takes place. As required, **Staples** and **Office Depot** did notify the DOJ and FTC of their intentions and the merger was not allowed.[25]

The attorneys general of all 50 states are authorized to bring lawsuits against businesses that engage in price-fixing and to recover damages for consumers. The **GlaxoSmithKline** settlement started in the Colorado attorney's office then moved to the attorney's office in Massachusetts.[26] They can also appeal laws. For example, all 50 attorneys general opposed the Affordable Care Act, often called ObamaCare due to the regulations and cost to their states.

Microsoft and the EU Case Question 2: Under what antitrust laws would the federal government have pursued an antitrust case against Microsoft?

The following laws pertain to antitrust issues raised in terms of Microsoft's operation:

1. The Sherman Act (1890)—prohibits unreasonable restraints of trade and monopolization. It could be argued that Microsoft restrained free trade by not sharing its technical codes with other software developers and tried to monopolize media players by bundling its player with Windows for no charge.
2. The Clayton Act (1914)—prohibits anticompetitive mergers, price discrimination, director interlock, and tying contracts. Microsoft was accused of tying its Internet Explorer browser with its Windows operating systems, rather than letting the buyer select only the operating system.
3. Federal Trade Commission Act (1914)—prohibits unfair competition and deceptive practices; creates the FTC to help enforce antitrust laws. This act does not seem to apply to this case (i.e., act includes misleading advertising and bait-and-switch merchandising).
4. Antitrust Improvement Act (1976)—requires premerger notification and approval, and it allows states to sue businesses for price-fixing. Microsoft was not allowed to buy Intuit, another software firm.

Personal and Professional Applications

1. How do the antitrust laws protect you, and how do they affect a business you work(ed) for?

MERGERS AND ANTITRUST

Combining companies often leads to bigger businesses with larger market share that can decrease competition and create a monopoly. Therefore, mergers come under antitrust laws and need to be approved by the government.[27] In this section, we discuss the difference between acquisition and merger and three types of mergers with their possible antitrust practices.

> Learning Outcome 2: Compare and contrast acquisitions and mergers.

Acquisition or Merger?

Although similar, mergers and acquisitions (M&As) are usually different financial structures, but many people use the terms interchangeably because the deals don't always fit neatly into one or the other category. Technology changes have led to a wave of M&As.

Acquisitions. Generally, an *acquisition occurs when a larger company buys a smaller company* and acquires its stock. However, smaller companies do acquire larger companies. The acquired company often becomes a division, and the stockholders of the acquired company get new stock in the acquiring company. For example, **Merrill Lynch** acquired **Advest,** and Merrill Lynch stock replaced the Advest stock, which ceased to exist, then **Bank of America** bought Merrill Lynch. **PepsiCo** acquired **Quaker Oats** to expand its **Frito-Lay** snacks and, primarily, to get its **Gatorade** sports drink. So you can't buy stock in Quaker Oats, Frito-Lay, or Gatorade, only PepsiCo.

Mergers. Generally, a *merger occurs when two relatively equal sized companies combine*. The two companies often combine their names. The newly merged company has a few options. It can select one of the two names, combine them, or create a new one. For example, **XM Satellite Radio** and **Sirius Radio** merged to become **SiriusXM Satellite Radio**. **Chase Manhattan Corporation** merged with **J.P. Morgan & Co** to become **JPMorgan Chase. Sprint/Nextel**, **PriceCostco**, and **ExxonMobil** are three more examples. **SBC Communications** acquired smaller **AT&T** and took the AT&T name.[28] The merged company can create a new company stock and issue shares to both groups of stockholders, or it can select one of the two companies' shares to replace the other with the new company name.

Hostile Takeovers. Often both companies are interested in M&As, but just as often, one company is not. *Hostile takeovers* occur when one company does not want to be acquired. The acquirer generally makes an offer to buy the outstanding shares of the company for more than the current stock market price. When enough stockholders sell their shares, the acquirer can gain a majority of votes and take control of the company. Around 55 percent of **CVR Energy's** outstanding shares were tendered to **Carl Icahn** in support of his hostile bid for the petroleum-refining company making him the company's largest shareholder.[29]

Consequences of M&As. One thing is for sure: M&As create even larger big businesses. Through any M&A, some stakeholders benefit and some are hurt. Business claims that being larger is necessary to compete in the global economy. Thus, many large U.S.

companies have entered M&As with both American and foreign companies. Stockholders don't always benefit, and some shareholders are worse off than if the merger or acquisition had never occurred, given the debt that many firms take on in order to implement this strategy. Some employees lose their jobs when duplication is eliminated, particularly white-collar workers, but some do get better jobs within the firm or at another business. Some communities also are hurt when some facilities are no longer needed. On the other hand, M&As have led to economies of scale and lower prices for many consumers. In any case, the number of M&As varies from year to year, but this business strategy is clearly here to stay.

Blurred Lines Between M&As. For example, **HP** repeatedly referred to its merging with **Compaq** computer, giving the impression that the two companies were relatively equal. Yet, although it kept the Compaq brand name, it was really more of an acquisition because HP was much larger and eliminated Compaq stock. **AOL** acquired the much larger **Time Warner**. The company name became **AOL-Time Warner**, and AOL stock was replaced with Time Warner shares. An article discussing an M&A can use both terms. For example, title: "**UPS** Near Deal to *Buy* **TNT Express**," Within the article: "UPS is close to *acquiring* Dutch rival TNT Express." "A *merger* would give UPS a market-leading position in Europe."[30]

Integrating Market and Nonmarket Strategies. For our purposes, when we talk about a merger, it can also be an acquisition. There are three types of mergers (and acquisitions): horizontal, vertical, and conglomerate. M&A decisions, including which type, are market growth strategies to increase sales that need a nonmarket strategy to get the government to approve the new larger company. Without a good nonmarket strategy, the government will not allow the M&A of big business.

Thus, knowing the difference between acquisitions and mergers and using their proper terms can help in developing a nonmarket strategy to get the government to approve the deal. So in summary, an acquisition takes place when one company buys another company and the acquired company shareholders get stock in the acquiring company. So you can't buy or hold stock in the acquired company, only the acquiring company. With a merger, two or more companies become one new company with one new stock.

See Figure 10.2 for an overview of the types of mergers. In the following discussion, we look at each type of merger separately.

Learning Outcome 3: Describe the different types of mergers.

Horizontal Mergers

Horizontal mergers combine two companies in the same industry. Horizontal mergers commonly occur between direct competitors, which eliminates competition. For

Horizontal mergers	Vertical mergers	Conglomerate mergers
combine two companies in the same industry	combine two companies at different stages of the supply chain	combine a company with a firm in an unrelated industry

■ **Figure 10.2:** Types of Mergers

example, two of the largest U.S. oil companies, **Exxon** and **Mobil**, combined to become the world's largest and most profitable oil company. **BayBank** was acquired by **Fleet Bank**, which was acquired by **Bank of America,** which acquired many other banks over the years as well.

Nondirect competitor Horizontal Mergers. Horizontal mergers can also be in the same industry without being direct competitors, a *concentric diversification strategy*.[31] **McDonald's** acquired **Boston Market** and it bought a majority interest in **Chipotle Mexican Grill,** but it later sold both.[32] **PepsiCo** not only sells *Pepsi-Cola* brands, but over the years, it acquired **Frito-Lay** brands, **Tropicana** juice brands, **Quarter**, and **Gatorade** brands.[33]

Potential Antitrust. Horizontal mergers that combine direct competitors usually get a closer examination by the FTC and DOJ than do vertical and conglomerate mergers, especially under the Obama administration.[34] Recall that **AT&T** could not acquire **T-Mobile**.[35] Some industries used to include several competitors, but to compete in a global market, many have merged, reducing the number of competitors. The fewer the competitors, the easier it is to *restrain trade*, *fix prices*, and create a *monopoly* in violation of antitrust law. The business also has more resources to offset losses, making *predatory pricing* easier.

Personal and Professional Applications

2. Who could your current or former employer, and/or a producer of the products it sells, merge with horizontally? How could the employer benefit?

3. Give examples of horizontal mergers. Be sure to specify whether they were actually acquisitions or mergers.

Vertical Mergers

Vertical mergers combine two companies at different stages of the supply chain. The *supply chain* includes firms at various stages of a production process, channel, or distribution. The Obama administration approved, with conditions, the following vertical M&As: **Ticketmaster** and **Live Nation**, **Comcast** and **NBC Universal**, and **Google** and **ITA Software**.[36] The supply chain includes all activities from acquiring the raw materials, to the production and the distribution of a product to the customer and consumer. See Figure 10.3 for a simple supply chain example.

Backward Vertical Mergers. When a company merges with another company, moving away from the customer, it makes a backward vertical merger. For an example based

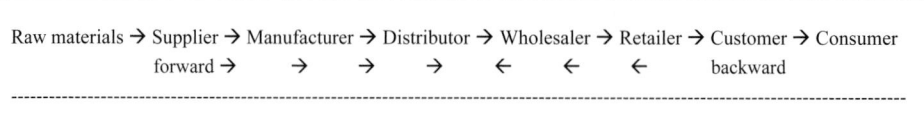

▪ **Figure 10.3:** Supply Chain

on Figure 10.3, **7-Up** is primarily a manufacturer using lots of lemons and limes in its soda. So rather than buy all its lemons and limes, it acquired some groves as sole suppliers of fruit, which can be considered a raw material. Retailer **Sears** acquired some tool manufacturers to make its **Craftsman** tools, rather than simply buy them from manufacturers.

Forward Vertical Mergers. When a company merges with another company, moving toward the customer, it makes a forward vertical merger. As an example based on Figure 10.3, **UPS**, a company in the delivery business, which had focused primarily on package delivery and services, acquired **Mail Boxes, Etc.**, to increase its services by working more directly with consumers. **FedEx** followed suit and acquired **Kinko's** to get closer to retail consumers.

Dell became successful at supply chain management by changing the traditional strategy. Dell does not specialize in manufacturing. It does not make or keep monitors in inventory, and it buys most of its computer components from suppliers through just-in-time inventory. Dell specializes in customizing consumer computers, or it puts together *suppliers'* components to *customer* specifications. It has even eliminated steps in the supply chain by selling directly to the customer, cutting out the retailer; thus, it keeps costs down by minimizing inventory. Dell primarily uses **UPS** to deliver its computers and other products directly to customers who are often also consumers.

Potential Antitrust. The following practices are *not technically illegal*, but they can become illegal when the intent is to restrain trade and create a monopoly. Therefore, these practices are subject to antitrust scrutiny. In the following examples, a producer can be a manufacturer or a franchiser, such as **McDonald's**, and a distributor can be a retail store, such as **Sears**.

■ *Refusal to deal* occurs when a producer refuses to sell to a distributor or retailer.
■ *Exclusive dealing* occurs when a producer grants only one distributor the right to sell its product.
■ *Exclusive territory* occurs when a producer allows only one distributor to sell in an area.
■ *Resale price maintenance* occurs when a producer requires the distributor to sell the product for a minimum price.
■ *Tying contracts* occur when a producer requires the distributor to sell a line of products.

Personal and Professional Applications

4. Point out with whom your current or former employer, and/or a producer of the products it sells, could create a vertical merger. How could the employer benefit?

5. Give examples of vertical mergers. Be sure to specify whether they were backward or forward and whether they were actually acquisitions or mergers.

Conglomerate Mergers

Conglomerate mergers combine a company with a firm in an unrelated industry. Conglomerate mergers are more commonly acquisitions. In a sense, conglomerates tend to be a diversity of companies (called *strategic business units* or *SBUs*)[37] owned by one

company. It is not unusual to hear the name of a product or company and think it is independent when, in fact, it is actually owned by another company. **General Electric (GE)**
is ranked as one of the world's largest[38] and most admired companies.[39] In keeping with
its strategy of being first or second in an industry, GE has acquired and sold hundreds of
businesses in multiple industries. GE has a wide diversity of thousands of products in the
following business units: Appliances, Aviation, Consumer Products, Electrical Distribution, Energy, Finance–Business, Finance–Consumer, Healthcare, Lighting, Oil & Gas,
Rail, Software & Services, and Water.[40]

Tyco International Ltd. is another well-known conglomerate with a global portfolio
of diversified brands. It is composed of three business units: ADT, Fire & Security, and
Flow Control. It provides thousands of products including electronic security solutions
and alarm monitoring, fire-fighting equipment and breathing apparatus, as well as water
transmission and distribution, heat tracing and flow control solutions.[41]

**Microsoft and the EU Case Question 3: What type of merger or acquisition was
Microsoft proposing with Intuit, and why did the government stop it?**

The three types of mergers or acquisitions are; horizontal mergers (combine
two companies in the same industry); vertical mergers (combine two companies at different stages of the supply chain); and conglomerate mergers
(combine a company with a firm in an unrelated industry). Of the three types
of mergers or acquisitions, horizontal mergers are between direct competitors and eliminate competition; therefore, they usually get closer scrutiny by
the FTC and DOJ than do vertical and conglomerate mergers. Microsoft's (the
largest software firm in the world) planned acquisition of personal finance
software maker Intuit was stopped in 1995 due to antitrust concerns, because
this would have been a horizontal integration of two software giants, would
have reduce competition, and lead to potential restraint of trade, price-fixing,
and predatory pricing.

Specialized Conglomerates. Managing a portfolio of diverse companies is more
complex than managing a company with horizontal and vertical mergers. Because it
is difficult being an expert in many industries and because of the pressure of global
business, many conglomerate firms have divested some businesses to focus more on a
core line of business. For example, **PepsiCo** used to own **Pizza Hut**, **KFC**, and **Taco
Bell** restaurants but sold them to **Yum Brands** to concentrate on its core businesses
of beverages and snacks. It later acquired **Quaker Oats**, with its **Gatorade**, in order
to grow by adding products.[42] **Tyco** continues to seek acquisitions but now only seeks
companies that fit within its three lines of business; it divested companies that did not
fit into these lines.[43]

Potential Antitrust. Of the three types of mergers, conglomerates tend to have the
least potential for restraint of trade and monopoly because the lines of business are different. However, typically being large businesses, conglomerate mergers must be evaluated
for antitrust violations and must be approved by the government. The primary scrutiny is
for the elimination of potential competitors.

Microsoft and the EU Case Question 4: What would be examples of vertical and conglomerate mergers or acquisitions for Microsoft?

An example of forward vertical integration for Microsoft (buying a firm that is a purchaser of computer software and selling that software to the consumer) would be if Microsoft were to purchase a company like **Best Buy** (a retailer of computer software) or **Dell** (a manufacturer that sells computers, with Microsoft software installed, directly to consumers). Backward integration would involve purchasing a firm that supplied the resources necessary for creating and duplicating software; for example, **eCentia Inc.** is a personnel agency that supplies computer programmers and experts to the software industry.

Conglomerate diversification, on the other hand, would require that Microsoft purchase a firm in an unrelated industry—that is if Microsoft were to purchase **McDonald's** (a fast-food company) or **ExxonMobil** (an energy company).

ETHICAL DILEMMA 10.1 AT&T and T-Mobile: The Urge to Merge Purged by a Government Surge!

First it was BellSouth, and now T-Mobile: What does AT&T have to do to get approval from the Justice Department for a merger? "The push for a merger [with T-Mobile] was spearheaded by Randall L. Stephenson, AT&T's chairman and chief executive, in his first bold strategic step since taking the reins in 2007. To support the deal, AT&T lined up an assortment of lawmakers, corporate customers, and local partners to promote the benefits of the merger. But that campaign held little sway over government regulators, who were skeptical of arguments that uniting two of the nation's biggest wireless companies would not harm competition.

The Justice Department joined with several state attorneys general in its antitrust lawsuit and hired prominent outside counsel. And the FCC published its staff's 157-page internal report laying out its concerns about the deal. AT&T had prepared for battle with the government, adopting at times an openly hostile stance toward the FCC. And few people thought the Justice Department would be able to fend off AT&T, whose Washington lobbying operation is legendary. Still, the companies said from the beginning that they were willing to consider conditions that might be required to allow the deal to proceed. And the Justice Department had taken criticism for approving other big deals, including Comcast's takeover of NBC Universal. In the case of AT&T, Justice Department officials repeatedly signaled that they would oppose the deal, and finally sued the company in late summer.

"[In 2012] AT&T ended its effort to buy T-Mobile USA, acknowledging that it could not overcome stiff opposition by the Obama administration to form the nation's biggest cellphone service provider. The decision to scrap the $39 billion takeover—which would have been the biggest deal of the year—is a major setback for AT&T, which had pinned its hopes for growth on the acquisition. The company wanted T-Mobile's cellular airwaves, or spectrum, to relieve its congested network and offer faster service for data-hungry devices like the iPhone. And the deal's end leaves T-Mobile, the weakest of the four national operators, with an uncertain future."[44]

"For the Obama administration, the collapse of the deal is confirmation that it has reinvigorated antitrust oversight that it said had become weak under its predecessor. . . . 'People in this town didn't think that the department was willing to take the risk to litigate big, complex cases,' said a senior Justice Department official, who spoke on the condition of anonymity because employees were not authorized to go beyond the department's public statement. 'But this puts down a very firm marker that we are taking antitrust enforcement very seriously. . . .'"[45]

"A merger of the two companies, consumer advocates had said, would have created a duopoly of AT&T and Verizon Wireless with almost three-quarters of the market between them. 'Consumers won today,' Sharis A. Pozen, the Justice Department's acting assistant attorney general for antitrust, said in a statement. 'Had AT&T acquired T-Mobile, consumers in the wireless marketplace would have faced higher prices and reduced innovation.' [However] T-Mobile is probably going to be profoundly damaged by this," Tero Kuittinen, an independent research analyst, said. "They should have done some strategic rethinking instead of chasing this mirage, this dream of a merger. Now they've lost a lot of time."[46]

Questions

1. What antitrust laws regulate the acquisition of T-Mobile by AT&T?
2. What actions did AT&T take to support the merger? Were they ethical?
3. What actions would you have taken if you were CEO Stephenson to support the merger?
4. Would you, like AT&T, have ended your efforts to acquire T-Mobile? Why or why not?
5. Do you believe that this merger would have created a monopoly? Why or why not?
6. What retaliatory actions, if any, should T-Mobile take against AT&T and/or the government?

Personal and Professional Applications

6. Is your current or former employer a conglomerate? If not, it most likely does business in some way, such as buying and/or selling its products, with conglomerates. Identify a conglomerate and identify its product lines.

ANTITRUST ENFORCEMENT

In this section, we discuss antitrust law enforcement. See Figure 10.4 for an overview of federal antitrust enforcement.

Learning Outcome 4: Discuss antitrust enforcement.

The Department of Justice and Federal Trade Commission

The two main antitrust enforcement agencies are the DOJ and FTC; they both have an **Antitrust Division.** They have parallel jurisdictional powers and often work together, but only the FTC can enforce the *Federal Trade Commission Act*, and only the DOJ can bring criminal charges under the antitrust laws. The DOJ can only enforce antitrust laws through suits filed in federal courts whereas the FTC has authority to issue orders without court action. The DOJ stopped **H&R Block** from acquiring **TaxAct**[47] and **AT&T** from acquiring **T-Mobile**[48] through an antitrust lawsuit. The FTC is investigating **Google**'s

Department of Justice (DOJ) Federal Trade Commission (FTC)	Private citizens, NGOs, and companies	State attorneys general	Federal courts
▓ Investigations, settlements, and lawsuits ▓ Guidelines and advice ▓ Prevent or allow mergers	▓ Lawsuits	▓ Investigations ▓ Lawsuits	▓ Litigation determination ▓ Law interpretation ▓ Precedents ▓ Consent decrees

▓ **Figure 10.4:** Antitrust Enforcement

advertising practices, how it handles search queries, and whether it's using its dominant position in Internet search and advertising to restrain competitors and jack up rates.[49]

The DOJ and FTC have an interagency liaison agreement and allocate cases primarily by industry and secondarily by the nature of the complaint. The DOJ has enforcement responsibility for computer software and the FTC for semiconductors, so the DOJ filed the antitrust lawsuit against **Microsoft** and the FTC filed against **Intel**.[50] The Obama antitrust-enforcement team moved aggressively against companies seeking M&As and for using market dominance to raise prices.[51] The FTC even hired a high-profile lawyer to help lead a **Google** investigation.[52] The following discussion covers the functions that the DOJ and FTC perform.

Investigations, Settlements, and Lawsuits. The DOJ and FTC investigate possible violations of antitrust laws. When the DOJ or FTC investigation turns up evidence of antitrust violations, they try to make a settlement, often by imposing a fine: recall the $3 billion settlement with **GlaxoSmithKline**.[53] The FTC got **Reebok** and a unit of **Adidas**, to pay $25 million in customer refunds to settle charges of false advertising, claiming its toning shoe could work better than normal footwear to whip muscles into shape—although Reebok settled, it stands behind its claim.[54] If the company does not agree to settle or comply with the settlement, the agency takes it to court. Like **Microsoft** before it, **Google** is facing a rising tide of discontent about its market dominance and is facing ongoing lawsuits for a variety of antitrust violations.[55]

M&A Notification, Guidelines, and Conditions. Large companies are required by law to file a *Premerger Notification and Report Form* with the DOJ and FTC of proposed mergers; we explain it shortly. They must provide additional information, and companies can be fined for not providing the requested information. The DOJ and FTC investigation of M&As commonly takes several months to complete.

The DOJ and FTC give guidelines and conditions to companies that are planning an M&A. Conditions are given on things that must be done to win the M&A. Legally binding restrictions are placed on the acquirer's ability to use its larger power to unfairly harm competitors, such as the need to divest certain duplicate products of the acquired company that could create a near monopoly **(Pfizer–Pharmacia)**. The M&As of **Ticketmaster** and **Live Nation**, **Comcast** and **NBC Universal**, and **Google** and **ITA Software** were all approved with conditions.[56] The DOJ also monitors compliance with the conditions, such as Google with ITA.[57]

Prevent or Allow Large M&As. Technically, the DOJ and FTC do not approve M&As of large companies; they simply allow them by not stopping them. If the DOJ or FTC don't approve of an M&A, they request a federal court to issue a *preliminary injunction* to stop the merger. With the threat of, or an actual, injunction, most companies drop the merger plans, including **AT&T**.[58] The FTC filed for a preliminary injunction to block the **Staples–Office Depot** merger, even though the companies worked with the FTC by following its guidelines and advice.[59]

Learning Outcome 5: Explain merger investigation guidelines.

Merger Investigation Guidelines

The DOJ and FTC jointly developed "Horizontal Merger Guidelines," which continue to evolve. These guidelines are incorporated in the *Premerger Notification and Report Form* that prospective merging companies must file. Here we discuss four important factors that are considered in investigating mergers (see Figure 10.5).

Market Definition and Concentration. The first thing is to define the market where the merger is to take place because the other factors are also based on the market. Then the impact on concentration, or market share, is assessed. The market is generally defined by specific products and geographic areas affected by an M&A. How the market is defined can make the difference between a merger being allowed or stopped.

In the **Staples–Office Depot** merger, the companies defined the market as "all office supplies sold," which included discounters (**Walmart**, **Kmart**, and **Target),** drug stores (**Walgreens** and **CVS)**, and wholesale clubs (**BJ's** and **PriceCostco)**. Their combined market share was less than 6 percent, clearly not a monopoly. However, the FTC defined the market as "office supplies sold through office superstores." In 42 geographic market areas across the United States, the combined company would have a dominant market share, and in 15 markets, it would have 100 percent concentration.[60] Unfortunately for Staples–Office Depot, the court agreed with the FTC. (The merger also did not meet the other three merger factors.)

Competitive Effects. When two companies, especially large ones, merge, there is elimination of competition and increased concentration. The fewer the competitors, the easier it is to legally increase prices as well as to collude to set prices and engage in other practices deemed anticompetitive under antitrust law. Therefore, antitrust investigations closely examine competitive effects to ensure that adequate competition will continue.

Market definition and concentration	Competitive effects	Entry	Efficiency gains and consumer benefits
What specific products and geographic areas are affected by the merger, and what market share will the merged firm have?	Will adequate competition continue, and will consumer prices increase?	How easy is it for new competitors to enter the market?	How will the merged company be more efficient, and how will it lower prices and increase customer service?

▨ **Figure 10.5:** Investigating Merger Factors

Recall that the FTC and DOJ often require conditions on things the companies must do to maintain competition.

Agency investigation includes determining the possibility that consumer prices will increase due to decreased competition. **Staples** and **Office Depot** were the two largest office superstores, with **OfficeMax** being much smaller. After its seven-month investigation, the FTC concluded that the merger would significantly increase concentration and be anticompetitive. The FTC believed that the merger could result in higher consumer prices without the two competing. The court agreed with the FTC.[61]

Entry. Antitrust investigation includes determining whether other companies can enter the market. It is more difficult to raise prices and to engage in anticompetitive practices when it is easy for a competing business to enter a market. When companies are profitable and it is easy to enter a market, competitors will enter the market and compete for customers' business.[62] The guidelines state that entry must be timely and able to counter potential anticompetitive merger practices. The **AOL–Time Warner** merger conditions met the guidelines by assuring free entry of competition. AOL's market share has dropped significantly over the years as competitors have stolen its customers.

Staples–Office Depot claimed that entry into the office superstore chain market was easy. The FTC disagreed, citing the fact that office superstore chains dropped from 23 down to only 3, and the merger would drop it to only 2.[63] Once again, the court agreed with the FTC.

Efficiency Gains and Consumer Benefits. Merging partners have to specify efficiency gains and consumer benefits. It is common for business to exaggerate the efficiencies, cost savings, and increased service to consumers. Business efficiencies can be verified, but it is usually questionable whether and how much of the savings will be passed on to consumers in lower prices.

The **Staples–Office Depot** "Efficiencies Analysis" claimed that the cost savings would be between $4.9 and $6.5 billion over the first five years and that two-thirds of the cost savings would be passed on to consumers. The FTC questioned the amount and whether the savings claimed would be passed on to consumers in lower prices, and the court again agreed with the FTC. Based on the four factors, especially the market definition, the court issued the preliminary injunction requested by the FTC. Shortly thereafter, the two companies dropped their merger agreement.[64]

Private Enforcement and State Attorneys General

Private Enforcement. The three primary private enforcement groups include private citizens, NGOs, and companies. Most antitrust enforcement actions are initiated by private enforcement, rather than by the DOJ or the FTC.

Citizens. Enforcement commonly happens through lawyers who represent the citizen or company. The lawyers have a professional association—**American Bar Association (ABA)** with an *Antitrust Law Section* (www.americanbar.org/antitrust) that provide Section members with the opportunity to develop.

NGOs. The **NBA Players Association** filed an antitrust lawsuit against the NBA.[65] The DOJ and FTC agencies usually investigate antitrust violations at the request of others.

The **American Antitrust Institute** (**AAI**, www.americanantitrustinstitute.org) has a mission to increase the role of competition, with a particular focus on the effects of anticompetitive practices on consumers.[66] AAI provides information to the DOJ and FTC to aid them in selecting cases to investigate and in enforcing antitrust laws. The AAI gave the DOJ and FTC an extensive white paper detailing why the **AT&T** acquisition of **T-Mobile** should not be allowed, and it takes credit for popularizing opposition to the merger.[67]

Business. **Sprint Nextel** filed a lawsuit challenging the **AT&T** acquisition of **T-Mobile**.[68] (We will provide more business examples in the strategy section.) It's a lot cheaper if the business can get the DOJ to file the lawsuit. **Netscape** helped persuade the DOJ to launch a successful antitrust case against **Microsoft**.[69] **Barnes & Noble** lobbied the DOJ to investigate Microsoft for frivolous patent suits against its *Nook e-reader*.[70]

State Attorneys General. States also have their own antitrust laws, so they can investigate violations. Recall that the **GlaxoSmithKline** investigation started in the attorney's office in Colorado then in Massachusetts before going to the DOJ.[71] The **National Association of Attorneys General** (**NAAG**, www.naag.org) *facilitates interaction among attorneys general as peers to facilitate the enhanced performance of attorneys general and their staffs.* NAAG fosters an environment of cooperative leadership, helping attorneys general respond effectively to emerging state and federal issues, individually and collectively. NAAG often cooperates in DOJ and FTC investigations and lawsuits. The DOJ was joined by 19 state attorneys general in an antitrust lawsuit against **Microsoft**.[72] All 50 state attorneys general sued 18 of the country's largest banks (including **BofA**, **JPMorgan Chase**, and **Goldman Sachs**) for selling toxic mortgage-backed securities.[73]

Antitrust in Federal Courts

Recall that the DOJ takes its cases to federal court, so here we discuss the court's role in antitrust.

Litigation Determination. The courts determine whether companies are innocent or guilty of antitrust violations, fines and damages paid to citizens and companies for their losses, imprisonment, and whether to issue preliminary injunctions. Lawsuits may be tried before a single judge, a panel of judges, or before a jury.

U.S. Court of Appeals. Companies found guilty often try to again prove their innocence by going to a court of appeals. The ultimate appeal is to the *Supreme Court*. **Microsoft** lost its antitrust case and fought the decision by going to the court of appeals. However, the judge did not reverse the guilty verdict. **Staples–Office Depot** decided to drop the merger rather than appeal the preliminary injunction.

Law Interpretation and Precedents. The language of antitrust law is vague, so the courts often have to interpret it. Court opinions and decisions are very important because they create antitrust law through precedents, so the law is continually changing. *Legal precedents require judges to follow decisions of superior or previous courts.* Past decisions of courts are referred to as *common law*. Precedents are used to establish the long-term development of antitrust legal and illegal business practices. When antitrust lawyers prepare and present their case in court, they review prior trials and use the opinions and decisions to support their side of the case. Prior cases are used as an example to justify a similar action, calling for a similar decision. **Enron** former executives, Lay and Skilling were convicted of fraud, and the guilty verdicts fueled the fire of prosecutors chasing other companies.[74]

Consent Decrees. Courts also approve consent decrees. *Consent decrees are agreements reached by the litigants under the sanction of a court.* The *settlements* impose a fine and a change in business practices of some type on the company. They do not involve a judicial determination, and thus do not signify a violation of the law, and do not set a precedent for other cases. The company settles without admitting guilt, often simply because it is cheaper to settle than go to court or because the company is guilty but doesn't want to risk being found guilty in court.

The consent decree can be a one-time action and/or an action for a set time or indefinitely, requiring both parties and the court to end or change it. For example, **AT&T** was split into seven regional operating companies and a residual unit by consent decree. The FTC staff negotiated a consent decree with **Staples** and **Office Depot** in an agreement to allow the merger if they sold 63 stores to **OfficeMax**, but later management overruled its staff with a 3-to-2 vote and stopped the merger.[75] The **SEC** had a consent decree with big banks, but a federal judge ruled that the SEC was too lenient on the fine, calling it "pocket change." But the SEC chief wants to fight the judge stating it is "unwise to have to reject proposed settlements."[76]

Microsoft and the EU Case Question 5: Which types of organizations have taken antitrust enforcement action against Microsoft?

Four types of organizations can take antitrust enforcement action against any firm: (1) two government agencies (Department of Justice (DOJ), and the Federal Trade Commission (FTC); (2) private citizens and companies; (3) state attorneys general; and (4) federal courts. Microsoft has come under scrutiny from all of these organizations, including foreign government agencies.

In 1997, **Sun** sued Microsoft for allegedly creating an incompatible version of Java, while **Netscape Communications** filed suit in 2002 against Microsoft, seeking unspecified damages and injunctions against the company's alleged antitrust actions. The DOJ, backed by 18 states (**state attorneys general**), filed antitrust charges in 1998 against the software giant, claiming that it stifled Internet browser competition and limited consumer choice, while a **federal judge's** ruling in 2000 declared that Microsoft used its monopoly powers to violate antitrust laws. In March 2004, the EU issued an antitrust ruling against Microsoft.

Personal and Professional Applications

7. Have you ever been involved in any antitrust practices?

8. Has your current or former employer, and/or a business it deals with, been involved in antitrust practices? Did the firm get caught and convicted through enforcement?

THE JUDICIAL BRANCH

We now move from law enforcing (executive branch) to law interpreting (judicial branch). The Constitution states that "the judicial Power of the U.S. shall be vested in one supreme

Court, and in such inferior Courts as the Congress may from time to time ordain and establish." Thus, the court system started with the Supreme Court, and Congress later passed laws to create a larger judiciary system. In this section, we discuss judicial concepts, federal courts, and state and local courts.

> Learning Outcome 6: Describe the types of laws, lawsuits, courts, and court functions.

Judicial Concepts

Types of Laws. Before we get into details of the judicial branch of government, let's review the laws that courts interpret, make, and enforce. The three basic types of laws are *legislative, executive,* and *judicial.* As discussed in Chapter 8, the *legislative* branch of government, including Congress, state legislatures, and local government bodies, creates laws. As discussed in Chapter 9, the *executive* branch of government agencies and commissions make the rules of business. As discussed in this chapter, the *judicial* branch of government creates common law. *Common law consists of the precedents from the rulings in courts on cases brought by plaintiffs.* Common law forms the basis for important branches of the law, including contracts that are critical to many business relationships and transactions. Breach of contract can result in litigation.

Judicial Review. *Judicial review is a judge determining whether laws are legal under the Constitution or whether officials have exceeded their authority.* It is the courts' greatest power and serves as a check and balance against the legislative and executive branches because the courts can overrule acts of Congress, the executive branch, and states and their government officials. The power of judicial review does not come from the Constitution but from the Supreme Court landmark case, *Marbury v. Madison.* All judges have the power of judicial review, but higher-level judges can overrule lower-level judges.

The *Supreme Court* ruled on a case against the **EPA** (www.epa.gov) over abuse of its regulatory powers regarding the nation's wetlands.[77] A *district court* judge struck down a rule designed to make it easier for unions to hold organizing elections on the grounds that the **National Labor Relations Board** (**NLRB**, www.nlrb.gov) lacked a quorum when it passed the regulation.[78]

Checks and Balances on the Courts. If the Supreme Court judicial review overrules a statute, *Congress* has the power to amend the *statute* or pass a new one to invalidate it, and the same can happen at the state level. For example, in 1993, Congress passed the *Religious Freedom Restoration Act (RFRA)* to overturn a 1990 Supreme Court ruling that it found too restrictive on religious freedoms. But two years later, the Supreme Court declared the RFRA unconstitutional. On very rare occasions, only four times to date, Congress will take the extraordinary measure of *amending the Constitution* to invalidate a Supreme Court decision. Congress and state legislators rarely use their powers over court decisions. Some complain that judges are overstepping their authority and claim that rather than interpreting the Constitution, judges are simply creating the laws they want. They question why one single judge's opinion can overrule that of the public and their elected representatives.[79]

In addition to making judicial appointments that have some limited impact on the courts, the president and other government officials have *judicial implementation* power, that is, the power to enforce or choose not to enforce judicial decisions. The court can only interpret the law; it must rely on the legislature and executive branch to enforce its judgments and decrees. For example, in 1954, after the Supreme Court ordered desegregation of public schools, the governor of Arkansas used the state's National Guard to block African Americans from entering white schools. Following a riot, President Eisenhower was forced to send federal troops to facilitate desegregation.

Court Functions. The Constitution lists the governing principles to guide the courts, but it doesn't state exactly how to implement them. The courts are responsible for three major functions.

- **Law interpretation**. Again, the laws are vague, so the courts interpret the laws through judicial review. When interpreting the law, judges also apply the law to the situation. It is common for judges to interpret and apply the laws of a case differently.
- **Litigation determination**. Courts determine the outcomes of litigation. Everyone is guaranteed the right to a fair trial with fair punishment for crimes.
- **Protect the individual**. Courts protect the rights of all individuals so that everyone is treated equally under the law. As courts review laws, they consider how to use a law so that it is fair to the people.

Judicial Appointments. Unlike legislative and executive branch officials who are elected, federal judicial officials are appointed with approval of the Senate. The authors of the Constitution wanted the judiciary to be above politics so that they did not have to worry about public opinion and getting reelected. Thus, appointments are long-term, up to a lifetime.

Types of Lawsuits. The three types of lawsuits are criminal, civil, and public. Recall that lawsuits can be individual or class action (Chapter 6), which applies under these classifications. *Criminal lawsuits are cases brought by the government against a person or group for breaking the law.* The government can be the state or federal level, and the government's trial lawyers are usually from the district attorneys' offices. In a criminal case, the government is accusing someone of having broken the law. The objective of a criminal case is to obtain justice through punishment by imprisonment and/or a fine. Recall that former **Enron** executives, Lay and Skilling were convicted of fraud, and sentenced to prison.

Civil lawsuits are cases brought by a plaintiff against a defendant seeking compensation for damages. The plaintiff and defendant are called *parties*. A party can be one person, a group, or a business. As discussed previously, businesses sue other businesses. Compensation is often money, but it can be anything of benefit, such as being able to keep or break a contract, preventing or stopping a business from using its patents, or replacing an asset. Civil suits are a judiciary strategy, so we will give several examples later in this chapter. Some civil suits also involve criminal actions. When they do, both types of suits are tried separately. **Enron** faced civil charges, and later Lay and Skilling were convicted of a criminal offense.

Public lawsuits are cases brought by a plaintiff against the government for failure to act in accordance with its statutory obligations. Businesses can sue the government when it does not do its job. For example, **Sandoz**, a generic unit of **Novartis**, sued the **FDA**, alleging that it violated federal law by failing to either approve or reject Sandoz's application to market *Omnitrope*, a version of human growth hormone. The district court judge ruled in favor of the company against the government, requiring a decision.

Microsoft and the EU Case Question 6: What type of law and lawsuits were brought against Microsoft?

The three basic types of laws are legislative, executive, and judicial; and the three types of lawsuits include criminal, civil, and public. Because antitrust laws were enacted by **Congress**, the **DOJ** investigated Microsoft for antitrust violations under criminal law because criminal lawsuits are cases that are brought by the government against a person or group for breaking the law. On the other hand, **Sun** and **Netscape Communications**, as private firms and plaintiffs, also sued Microsoft for antitrust behavior, but their civil lawsuits were seeking compensation for their business losses and, therefore, were under common law jurisdiction (consists of the precedents from the court ruling in previous cases).

Interestingly, these firms could have filed a public lawsuit against the U.S. government if they believed that the government had failed to act in accordance with statutory obligations of antitrust. They settled with Microsoft in the United States and decided to resubmit their claims through the EU, which took action.

Types of Courts. The many different categories of courts all fall within the jurisdiction of either federal, state, or local systems. Each court is designed to decide certain kinds of cases, and sometimes a court is identified by the type of case it handles—juvenile court and tax court for example. Federal courts involve interpreting the Constitution, and cases are between an individual or business and a state or federal government. Next we discuss federal courts, followed by state and local courts.

Federal Courts

The federal courts essentially include three levels. Cases are commonly tried by the district courts, requests to change the verdict go to the courts of appeals, and some appeals and other cases make it to the Supreme Court. This court structure is discussed here. See Figure 10.6 for its organization chart.[80] To learn more about the federal courts, visit www.uscourts.gov.[81]

The United States Federal Courts

Supreme Court

▪ U.S. Supreme Court

Appellate Courts

▪ U.S. Court of Appeals

 – 12 Regional Circuit Courts of Appeals
 – 1 U.S. Court of Appeals for the Federal Circuit

Trial Courts

▪ U.S. District Courts

 – 94 Judicial District Courts
 – U.S. Bankruptcy Court

▪ U.S. Court of International Trade
▪ U.S. Court of Federal Claims

Federal Courts and Other Entities Outside the Judicial Branch

▪ U.S. Tax Court
▪ Military Courts (trial and appellate)
▪ Court of Veterans Appeals

▪ **Figure 10.6:** The Federal Courts

Trial Courts. The **U.S. District Courts** are the trial courts of the federal court system. The district courts have jurisdiction to hear nearly all categories of federal cases in both *civil* and *criminal* matters. The 94 federal judicial districts provide at least one district in each state, the District of Columbia and Puerto Rico, and the three territories of the United States.

Two special trial courts have nationwide jurisdiction over certain types of cases: the **U.S. Court of International Trade** addresses cases involving international trade and customs issues; the **U.S. Court of Federal Claims** has jurisdiction over most claims for monetary damages against the United States, disputes over federal contracts, unlawful "taking" of private property by the federal government, and a variety of other claims against the United States.[82]

Appellate Courts. If a business loses in trial court, it can go to the next level. The 94 districts are organized into 12 regional circuits, each of which has a **U.S. Court of Appeals**. A court of appeals hears appeals from the district courts located within its circuit, as well as appeals from decisions of federal administrative agencies. Because courts of appeals are not trial courts, they only review questions of law; for example, was the law properly applied to the facts? Not many cases are overturned at this level. But if business loses again, it may try to appeal to the Supreme Court.

In addition, the **U.S. Court of Appeals for the Federal Circuit** has nationwide jurisdiction to hear appeals in specialized cases, such as those involving patent laws and cases decided by the Court of International Trade and the Court of Federal Claims.[83]

The Supreme Court. The U.S. Supreme Court is the highest-level court. At its discretion, and within certain guidelines established by Congress, the Supreme Court each year hears a limited number of the cases it is asked to decide. Those cases may begin in the federal or state courts, and usually involve important questions about the Constitution or federal law.[84] For example, in June 2012, the Supreme Court ruled that most of the Affordable Care Act was constitutional.

The Supreme Court is located in Washington, DC, and it consists of the Chief Justice and eight associate justices. Like all federal judges, they are appointed by the president, with Senate approval. They are appointed for life, but they can be impeached. For more information about the U.S. Supreme Court, visit www.supremecourt.gov.

State and Local Courts

The state court system handles most cases, so most legal decisions are given by the state and its local courts. The state court system structure is similar to the federal system, but it has more courts; about 80 percent of all courts are state courts, including the local courts, with limited jurisdiction. For some lawsuits, the plaintiff can choose between filing a case in a state or a federal court.

Local Courts. Local or minor courts are often considered as part of the state system, at the bottom of the hierarchy. State subjurisdictions include traffic, juvenile, family, city, county, municipal, and magistrate courts to administer state law and local ordinances. They deal with minor cases, such as criminal misdemeanors with sentences of less than one year and *civil lawsuit* disputes involving less than $1,000.

State General Trial Courts. State courts conduct most of the cases, including most business *civil lawsuits*. Each state divides its areas into different judicial regions. In most states, those accused of crimes are entitled to a trial by jury with 12 jury members or a grand jury of 12–23 citizens. However, the judge can throw out the jury verdict if the judge determines that not enough facts were presented for a fair decision to be made.

State Court of Appeals. General trial decisions can be appealed. The judgments in many types of cases are final. However, when questions about the state or federal constitution are raised, the case may be appealed to the state supreme court.

State Supreme Courts. Similar to the U.S. Supreme Court, the state supreme courts are the highest to determine state laws. State supreme courts' law interpretation can't be overruled, even by the U.S. Supreme Court, unless a state law specifically goes against the U.S. Constitution. In such cases, an appeal to the U.S. Supreme Court can be made, but as is the case with other appeals, the U.S. Supreme Court can elect not to hear the case.

> Microsoft and the EU Case Question 7: What U.S. court actions have taken place relative to the antitrust suits against Microsoft?
>
> A federal judge's ruling in 2000 indicated that Microsoft used its monopoly powers to violate antitrust laws. This ruling was aggressively appealed by Microsoft. The initial ruling to split Microsoft into two companies was later struck down, leading to a settlement between the company and the DOJ. With all of the settlements with competitors, the U.S. government essentially stopped pursuing antitrust action against Microsoft.

> **Personal and Professional Applications**
>
> 9. Have you or has someone you know ever been to court? What type of court and case were you part of?
>
> 10. Has your current or former employer, and/or a business it deals with, been the defendant in a court case? What type of court and lawsuit was involved?

BUSINESS NONMARKET AND MARKET STRATEGIES AND ETHICS

As presented in Figure 1.4, businesses have a variety of nonmarket strategies they can use through the 5 Is Strategic Analysis (Chapter 2). It is important to know the rules.[85] The decision to acquire or merge (M&As) with another company is a market strategy that results in changes in corporate structure and control,[86] but it also requires an integrated nonmarket strategy in dealing with the DOJ and FTC to get approval of the M&A. So we need to integrate the two strategies. As usual, in this section we discuss information, societal and political strategies, and the importance of ethics.

Information Strategies

Leading businesses develop information strategies that are ethically and socially responsible. They are ethically responsible in obeying the antitrust laws and maintaining fair competition, and they are socially responsible in their dealings with consumers because they use a stakeholder approach to management.[87] Corporations that are being investigated for antitrust violations or that are settling or are involved in an antitrust lawsuit need a good information strategy.

M&A decisions are based on good information. Companies approaching a potential partner need a good information strategy to convince the other firm to be acquired or to merge. Businesses often get advice and information from consultants, such as investment bankers. Filling out the *Premerger Notification and Report Form* provides needed information.

Large corporations involved in litigation do research, usually with the help of lawyers using outside sources, experts, and stakeholders' support, to come up with realistic facts and figures to influence court outcomes. For example, when **Staples** and **Office Depot** wanted to merge, they got a vice president of **OfficeMax** to make a public statement supporting the merger and agreeing that two competitors would be better than three. Unfortunately for the companies, the **FTC**'s information strategy was more convincing to the judge who stopped the merger.[88]

Societal Strategies

Business often needs a *grand strategy* to counter activists who are trying to prevent an M&A, claiming antitrust violations, and pushing for litigation. Recall that the **AAI** protested the **AT&T** acquisition of **T-Mobile** to the **FTC** by supplying it with information to stop it. AT&T's information and societal strategies were not strong enough to convince the DOJ and FTC to allow the acquisition.[89]

Being socially responsible contributes to sustainability in business, so more companies are seeking effective social and financial performance.[90] Businesses are being ethically and socially responsible in gaining public sentiment on their side so that they are less likely to face antitrust investigations and litigation. Businesses build *coalitions* and work at developing good *media relations* to get positive stories to gain public sentiment for their side of issues.[91]

Political Strategies

When dealing with mergers, businesses may develop **coalition strategies** to get support for the merger discussions with the FTC and/or DOJ. When dealing with mergers and litigation, businesses often get information from *business interest groups*. Typically, companies use an M&A *grand strategy* in working with these agencies to provide requested information and to abide by their conditions. Under antitrust violation subpoena by the **DOJ** and **FTC**, **Google** stated it was happy to cooperate with the investigators.[92]

Campaign Contributions. A primary political strategy used by business is campaign contributions as an indirect way to influence the appointment of judges. When supporting a presidential candidate who is pro-business, the company also supports the appointment of pro-business judges. Again, Republicans are generally more pro-business than Democrats.

President George W. Bush's appointments of U.S. Supreme Court Chief Justice John Roberts and Justice Samuel Alito were supported by many businesses because of the justices' records of siding with positions backed by business leaders.[93] President Obama's appointments of Justices **Sonia Sotomayor and Elena Kagan—who are less pro-business—were opposed by some business leaders**. With the appointment of specific judges, business combines campaign contributions with lobbying.

Lobbying. Business sometimes lobbies the president and staff to influence the selections of judges who will be pro-business. On occasion when a proposed judge has been selected by the president and the Senate is undecided on the appointment, business may lobby senators for or against the candidate judge. Some Democratic senators tried to block the appointments of Justices Roberts and Alito, while some Republicans tried to block Sotomayor and Kagan.

Business also lobbies Congress and regulators to influence antitrust laws and their enforcement. For example, the **FTC** issued complaints against seven national-brand soft drink syrup makers (including **Coca-Cola**, **PepsiCo**, **Seven-Up**, and **Canada Dry**), charging them with exclusive territorial distributorships that were illegal vertical restraints of trade. They decided to fight the FTC by appealing the decision and having the **National Soft Drink Association** (**NSDA**, www.nsda.org) lobby for a bill to permit exclusive territorial arrangements. Despite opposition from the **FTC** and **DOJ**, Congress passed the *Soft Drink Interbrand Competition Act* that protects the producers from antitrust lawsuits, which the president signed into law.

Because they are an important part of this chapter, we will discuss legal strategies next in a separate section.

Personal and Professional Applications

11. Has your current or former employer, and/or a business it deals with, used a political strategy to influence a judicial appointment?

JUDICIARY STRATEGIES

Judiciary strategies are important because 45 percent of U.S. companies spend at least $1 million a year on litigation.[94] The two major legal strategies are avoiding lawsuits and filing lawsuits against others. In this section, we discuss both strategies followed by example lawsuits.

Avoiding Lawsuits

Many successful companies conduct business by obeying the law and going beyond the law by being ethically and socially responsible. Doing so is operating in a way to avoid lawsuits. Unfortunately, many highly regarded companies have been sued even though they were being ethically and socially responsible. For example, consumer products thought to be safe are later revealed to be dangerous, such as asbestos, lead paint, and certain drugs.

Settlements. When a lawsuit is filed against a business, it is unlikely to make it to court because most businesses settle prior to a court appearance.[95] When the business is sued and wants to settle out of court, its *grand strategy* is to *negotiate* with the other party in an effort to resolve the case without litigation. Recall that **GlaxoSmithKline** settled and paid $3 billion.[96]

Defendants. When a business is sued and goes to court, its *grand strategy* is to *oppose* the other party and try to win the case. A legal defense can be expensive. So expensive, especially to a small business, that some firms have been put out of business by a lawsuit.

For example, **Biovail** and **Overstock.com** both sued independent stock research firm **Gradient Analytics**, putting it out of business.[97] **Walmart** is known for not settling, and it has a large team of lawyers who defend it through the court system. After 16 years, **Microsoft** is still defending against **Novell**'s WordPerfect vs. Word antitrust lawsuit.[98] **Google** continues to defend itself against accusations of antitrust violations,[99] and the **tobacco industry** defends itself against health issues.[100]

Legal Charges and Defense. When a business is taken to court for antitrust violations, charges come under two categories. *Per se violations* are always illegal, and the only defense is that the business did not commit the antitrust violation. Price-fixing, minimum resale prices, output restraints, and the allocation of customers among competitors are antitrust per se violations.

As stated, antitrust laws are often vague and need to be interpreted and applied to specific situations. *Rule of reason violations* question the legality of the specific act and the defense is that the business did not commit the act or that it did commit the act but it was not unreasonable to do so. In the **Microsoft** antitrust case that charged anticompetitive conduct, clearly Microsoft was "tying" its software, so its defense was that it was not unreasonable to do so.

Filing Lawsuits

Initiating legal action in federal or state court is a nonmarket strategy. As discussed in the last chapter, the judicial strategy also includes quasi-judicial action against executive regulatory agencies through administrative law. Here we focus on being the plaintiff in litigation.

Reason for Filing Lawsuits. Judicial strategies are commonly used to enforce rights, to obtain damages, and to correct unfair competitive practices. A firm may be seeking more than one of these resolutions. To protect their intellectual property, many businesses aggressively file trademark, patent, and copyright infringement lawsuits. Some patent owners sue multiple businesses at once hoping that they will settle rather than shell out the $1 million or more it would take to fight it out in court.[101]

Cost–Benefit Analysis. Filing a lawsuit is relatively inexpensive. But actually following through and going to court is not taken lightly because the cost of litigation can be millions of dollars in legal fees. For example, the **DOJ** antitrust lawsuit against **AT&T** to break up the Bell system took eight years before it was settled out of court. The legal cost was estimated at $360 million for AT&T and $15 million for the government.[102] Thus, a cost–benefit analysis is conducted by most businesses. In some cases, the benefits can be very large, clearly outweighing the cost. For example, *Novell v. Microsoft* is a $1 billion lawsuit.[103]

Staples and **Office Depot** went to court to fight the preliminary injunction, rather than drop the merger agreement. What made these companies do all this work and spend millions in legal fees? Net income would combine their $74 million and $132 million for a total of $206 million. The number of stores would go from 550 to 1,050. The reason they thought they could win in court was based on the market definition. With less than 6 percent of total office supply sales, they clearly believed that they were not creating a monopoly.[104] If the court agreed with its market definition, they most likely would have won the case, and the benefits would have outweighed the cost.

Damages. One of the benefits of attempting to win a lawsuit is the potential damages awards that may be won. If **Novell** wins, **Microsoft** may have to pay it $1 billion.[105]

Microsoft and the EU Case Question 8: What judiciary strategies has Microsoft employed in terms of the antitrust lawsuits?

Microsoft has used a combination of appeals, settlements, and compliance in dealing with antitrust actions brought against the firm. In 1997, **Sun** sued Microsoft for allegedly creating an incompatible version of Java; Microsoft countersued. The ongoing court battle, settled by Microsoft in 2001 for $20 million, prevented the company from releasing new Java tools or accessing any of Sun's advances. Microsoft aggressively appealed a federal judge's ruling that would have split the firm into two operating companies. It won on appeal, which led to a settlement between the company and the U.S. Justice Department. Microsoft settled the suit with Netscape in 2003, agreeing to pay **AOL** $750 million as part of a larger settlement that includes AOL licensing Microsoft's Internet Explorer browser and its digital media technology.

Microsoft also paid more than $3 billion to **Sun**, Massachusetts software maker **Novell Inc.,** and **RealNetworks** to drop their related complaints in both Europe and the United States, which removed the company's strongest adversaries from direct involvement in the EU case. In response to an EU 2004 ruling, which carried a $613 million fine and ordered Microsoft to stop building a free copy of its media player into Windows and to produce an instruction manual to help rivals write Windows-compatible software for knitting together complex office computer networks, Microsoft appealed the ruling to the EU's court of appeals, which they later lost. A spokesperson for Microsoft said the company was disappointed with the court's ruling and felt the company had "resolved [the commissions'] competition law concerns" in 2009, making the fine unnecessary.

Lawsuits

Here we present some examples of lawsuits that take place each day. You probably can't find an issue of the *Wall Street Journal* that doesn't contain a short or full news story about a business lawsuit. In the following examples, we focus on four types of lawsuits business is commonly involved in: civil cases of consumers and NGOs versus business, criminal and civil cases of government versus business, civil cases of business versus business, and public cases of business versus government.

ETHICAL DILEMMA 10.2 Groupon: Balancing the Books by Discounting More than Just Meals!

"Savvy consumers get their coupon on with Groupon,"[106] but stockholders think that Chairman Eric Lefkofsky has been inflating the books. Groupon "has been hit with [yet] another lawsuit from a shareholder upset with the daily-deals company's recent bookkeeping flubs. The latest complaint . . . accuses the daily-deals site's directors of management failure. Theresa Monturano's 31-page filing . . . claims the company's management failed its responsibilities when it announced late last month that an accounting error would force it to revise its first set of financial results as a public company. (A derivatives lawsuit is filed when a shareholder seeks to prevent or remedy a wrong to the company.) . . . The complaint comes on the heels of another shareholder lawsuit that cited the financial revision as evidence the company misled investors about its financial health. Shareholder Fan Zhang said he paid nearly $62,000 for 3,000 Groupon shares between February 9 to March 6 [2012], only to sell them [later] in March for a loss of more than $9,000."[107]

"'By reason of their positions as officers, directors, and/or fiduciaries of Groupon and because of their ability to control the business and corporate affairs of Groupon, defendants owed Groupon and its shareholders fiduciary obligations of good faith, loyalty, and candor,' the complaint states. 'Defendants intentionally, recklessly, or negligently breached or disregarded their fiduciary duties to protect the rights and interests of Groupon.'"[108]

"The Chicago-based company revealed in a regulatory filing that it had discovered 'material weakness' in internal controls over its financial statement and that its fourth-quarter results were worse than previously stated because of higher refunds to merchants. The revisions increased its net loss for the fourth quarter by $22.6 million and reduced revenue for the quarter by $14.3 million to $492.2 million. In addition to unspecified damages, Monturano's lawsuit seeks the right to nominate at least three candidates for the company's board of directors."[109]

"In addition to the shareholder lawsuits, the company may face increased regulatory scrutiny. After Groupon announced its financial revision, there were reports that the company's accounting procedures had again attracted the attention of the U.S. Securities and Exchange Commission, though the commission has reportedly not yet elected to launch a formal investigation of the company. An SEC review of Groupon's accounting procedures forced the daily-deals provider to revise its IPO filing papers last year after the company reported that it generated $713.4 million in revenue in 2010, while the SEC said that the figure should be $312.9 million."[110]

Questions

1. What legal actions were taken against Groupon and by whom?
2. What judiciary strategies could Groupon have taken to avoid these legal actions?
3. What is the ethical dilemma facing Chair Eric Lefkofsky?
4. What would you do if you were Lefkofsky?

Consumers vs. Business. Consumers can sue as individuals and also be represented by societal activist interest groups and multiple consumers in class action suits. In these civil cases, business is the defendant. A class action discrimination lawsuit filed against **Walmart**. However, the case went all the way to the **U.S. Supreme Court**, which threw out the case stating that the employees didn't have one clear employment practice violation tying all their 1.5 million claims together.[111] The **Air Line Pilots Association (ALPA,** www.alpa.org) sued **United Continental** airlines.[112]

Individuals also need to be careful; bloggers are increasingly getting sued or threatened with legal action for everything from defamation to invasion of privacy to copyright infringements. Blogger Shellee Hale is being sued by a software company over her Web posts. Fashion designer Dawn Simorangkir sued rocker **Courtney Love** for libel accusing her of posting disparaging remarks about her designs on **Twitter** and **MySpace**.[113]

NGOs and businesses can also sue individuals. The **Recording Industry Association of America** (**RIAA**, www.riaa.org) sued several people for downloading file-shared songs in violation of copyright law, primarily as an educational process to make sure people knew it was illegal.[114] **Microsoft** used Melanie Suen, Eric Lam, and Gordon Lam for so-called click fraud—clicking on ads on Microsoft websites for financial gain, primarily as a deterrent to such illegal practices.[115]

Government vs. Business. In these civil case examples, business is the defendant. The **DOJ** filed suit against **Apple** and five e-book publishers for price-fixing.[116] The DOJ filed a complaint against **Johnson & Johnson** alleging it paid kickbacks to **Omnicare**.[117] The **Federal Housing Finance Agency** (**FHFA**, www.fhfa.gov) is suing 18 of the largest U.S. banks for selling $200 billion in toxic mortgage-back securities to **Fannie Mae** and **Freddie Mac**, for which it might get $40 billion in damages: and all 50 state attorneys general are seeking $20 billion to redress alleged foreclosure-related abuses.[118]

Business vs. Business. One party is the plaintiff filing the lawsuit and the other is the defendant who probably was trying to avoid a lawsuit. So we are putting the two legal strategy examples together. Sometimes businesses use a lawsuit as a threat. **Google** was stealing some of **Microsoft**'s employees, so Microsoft filed a lawsuit against Google. Google filed a court document calling the Microsoft lawsuit a scare tactic to keep its employees from leaving.[119]

Nike, who has NFL merchandising rights, sued **Reebok** to stop it from selling **NFL** quarterback Tim Tebow jerseys and T-shirts after he was traded to the **New York Jets**. Reebok had to buy the jerseys back from retail stores as part of the lawsuit settlement.[120] **Apple** sued **Samsung** for alleged patent infringement of its hit iPhone.[121] Then it sued over its iPad, and Samsung filed a countersuit against Apple.[122] **Kodak** had a patent suit against Apple and **RIM**.[123] **Versata Software** won a $345 million patent suit verdict against **SAP**, and **i4i** won $200 million from **Microsoft**.[124] **Sprint Nextel** went to court to stop the **AT&T** acquisition of **T-Mobile**.[125]

Business vs. Government. In these public case examples, business is the plaintiff. Business *public litigation* against government is less common. U.S. tobacco companies, including **Reynolds American**, took the **FDA** to court and got them to stop new larger graphic warning labels on cigarette packs.[126] **Craigslist** went on the offensive and sued the attorney general of South Carolina, after having its executive threatened to be prosecuted for having adult-oriented ads; the suit sought a restraining order to prevent the attorney general from filing criminal charges.[127] Drug makers **Pfizer** and **Eli Lilly** (having settled with fines of $2.3 and $1.4 billion for off-label marketing) are suing regulators to allow them to pitch medicines for uses not listed on the label.[128]

Personal and Professional Applications

12. Has your current or former employer, and/or a business it deals with, been the plaintiff in a court case? What type of court and lawsuit were involved?

SUMMARY

The chapter summary is organized to answer the learning outcomes for Chapter 10.

1. **Compare and contrast four antitrust laws.**

   The various antitrust laws are similar because they have the same objective of preserving capitalism by protecting competition to benefit consumers. The Sherman Act was passed first to prohibit unreasonable restraints of trade and monopolization. However, its terms were vague, so Congress passed the Clayton Act to prohibit anticompetitive mergers, price discrimination, director interlock, and tying contracts. The same year, it passed the Federal Trade Commission Act to prohibit unfair competition and deceptive practices, creating the FTC to help enforce antitrust laws. Years later, the Antitrust Improvement Act strengthened the other antitrust laws by requiring premerger notification and approval, and it allowed states to sue businesses for price-fixing.

2. **Compare and contrast acquisitions and mergers.**

   Acquisitions and mergers are similar in that they both occur when two companies combine. In fact, the lines between the two are blurred, and the terms are commonly used interchangeably. However, they usually have different financial structures. Acquisitions commonly occur when a larger company buys a smaller firm. The acquired company often becomes a division and the stockholders of the acquired company get new stock in the larger acquiring company. Mergers usually occur between two companies that are relatively equal in size. The new merged company has a few options. It can select one of the two names, combine them, or create a new one. The merged company can create new company stock and issue shares to both groups of stockholders, or it can select one of the two companies' shares to replace the other.

3. **Describe the different types of mergers.**

   The three types of mergers are horizontal, vertical, and conglomerate. Horizontal mergers combine two companies in the same industry, which are commonly direct competitors. Vertical mergers combine two companies at different stages of the supply chain between raw materials to delivery to consumers. A merger moving away from the consumer is a backward vertical merger, and moving closer to the customer is a forward vertical merger. Conglomerate mergers combine a company with a firm in an unrelated industry.

4. **Discuss antitrust enforcement.**

   Antitrust laws are enforced in four major ways. The two main antitrust enforcement agencies are the Department of Justice (DOJ) and Federal Trade Commission (FTC). They investigate allegations of antitrust violations, make settlements, and bring lawsuits against business. The DOJ and FTC also provide guidelines and advisory opinions, especially in merger investigations, which they can prevent by filing a preliminary injunction. However, most lawsuits are brought to court through private citizens and companies who believe they were hurt by antitrust practices, seeking compensation for damages. State attorneys general also investigate antitrust violations and file lawsuits against businesses, sometimes in cooperation with the DOJ and FTC. The federal courts determine the outcomes of litigation, interpret the law, set precedents, and approve consent decrees.

5. **Explain merger investigation guidelines.**

Four important factors are considered in investigating mergers. The first step is to define the market where the merger is to take place and then determine the concentration the merged firm will have. Competitive effects are investigated to ensure adequate competition will continue and that consumer prices will not increase. The investigation includes a determination of the ease of entry into the market to maintain competition. Lastly, merging partners have to specify efficiency gains and consumer benefits.

6. **Describe the types of laws, lawsuits, courts, and court functions.**

The three basic types of laws are legislative, executive, and judicial. The legislative law includes those laws enacted by Congress, state legislatures, and local government bodies. The executive branch of government agencies and commissions make the rules of business. The judicial courts create common laws through precedents.

The three types of lawsuits include criminal, civil, and public. Criminal suits are cases brought by the government against a person or group for breaking the law. Civil suits are cases brought by a plaintiff against a defendant seeking compensation for damages. Public lawsuits are cases brought by a plaintiff against the government for failure to act in accordance with its statutory obligations.

Of the three types of courts, federal and state courts have a similar structure with district courts that hear the cases, courts of appeals that hear contested cases, and a supreme court that has final authority over court decisions. The third type, local courts, deals with misdemeanors and minor cases.

The court has three major functions: law interpretation, litigation determination, and individual protection.

It interprets the laws through judicial review to determine whether the laws are legal under the Constitution or whether officials have exceeded their authority. Courts determine the outcomes of litigation. Courts also protect the rights of all individuals so that everyone is treated equally under the law.

7. **Fill in the blank with the appropriate key term (in order of appearance in the chapter).**

_____ preserve capitalism by protecting competition to benefit consumers.

_____ is selling products below cost to drive competitors out of business.

_____ is competitors colluding to explicitly or implicitly agree on the price they will charge.

_____ prohibits unreasonable restraints of trade and monopolization.

_____ prohibits anticompetitive mergers, price discrimination, director interlock, and tying contracts.

_____ is selling products to a customer for less without a lower cost for serving the customer.

_____ is having a director serving on the boards of two companies that are in direct competition.

_____ require the buyer to purchase additional products as a condition of the sale.

_____ prohibits unfair competition and deceptive practices; it created the FTC to help enforce antitrust laws.

_____ requires premerger notification and approval, and it allows states to sue businesses for price-fixing.

_____ occurs when a larger company buys a smaller company.

_____ occurs when two relatively equally sized companies combine.

_____ combine two companies in the same industry.

_____ combine two companies at different stages of the supply chain.

_____ combine a company with a firm in an unrelated industry.

_____ require judges to follow decisions of superior or previous courts.

_____ are agreements reached by the litigants under the sanction of a court.

_____ consists of the precedents from the ruling in courts on cases brought by plaintiffs.

_____ is a judge who determines whether laws are legal under the Constitution or whether officials have exceeded their authority.

_____ are cases brought by the government against a person or group for breaking the law.

_____ are cases brought by a plaintiff against a defendant seeking compensation for damages.

_____ are cases brought by a plaintiff against the government for failure to act in accordance with its statutory obligations.

KEY TERMS (IN ALPHABETICAL ORDER)

KEY TERMS
10

acquisition (p. 378)
Antitrust Improvement Act (p. 377)
antitrust laws (p. 374)
civil lawsuits (p. 391)
Clayton Act (p. 376)
common law (p. 390)
conglomerate mergers (p. 381)
consent decrees (p. 389)
criminal lawsuits (p. 391)
director interlock (p. 376)
Federal Trade Commission Act (p. 376)

horizontal mergers (p. 378)
judicial review (p. 390)
legal precedents (p. 388)
merger (p. 378)
predatory pricing (p. 375)
price discrimination (p. 376)
price-fixing (p. 375)
public lawsuits (p. 391)
Sherman Act (p. 376)
tying contracts (p. 376)
vertical mergers (p. 380)

REVIEW QUESTIONS

REVIEW QUESTIONS
10

1 Who are the three groups protected by antitrust laws?

2 What are the three types of pricing antitrust made illegal?

3 Who benefits from and who is hurt by price-fixing?

4 Why is a monopoly prohibited under antitrust law?

5 Can a business charge any customer any price it wants to?

6 Why is director interlock illegal under antitrust law?

7 Tying contracts usually makes it cheaper to get multiple products than buying them separately, so what's the problem with them?

8 Which antitrust law created an independent executive agency to help enforce antitrust, and what is the name of the agency?

9 Which antitrust act allowed states to sue businesses for price-fixing?

10 Acquisitions and mergers are similar, so is it worth knowing the difference?

11 What is a hostile takeover?

12 Which stakeholders are generally the biggest winners and losers as a result of a merger?

13 Why does a company acquire another business that is not a direct competitor in the same industry?

14 What is the difference between backward and forward vertical mergers?

15 What is the most challenging part of managing a conglomerate?

16 What are the two main antitrust enforcement agencies?

17 How do government agencies prevent mergers?

18 How do government agencies approve mergers?

19 Who developed the merger investigation guidelines?

20 Where does most antitrust enforcement originate?

21 What types of laws does the United States have?

22 What is the courts' greatest power that serves as a check and balance against the legislative and executive branches?

23 What are legislative and executive branches' checks and balances with regard to the courts?

24 What are the functions of courts?

25 What types of lawsuits are there?

26 What are the three major federal and state courts?

27 What are the legal nonmarket strategies?

28 What is the difference between per se and rule of reason legal charges and defenses?

29 Why do companies file lawsuits against others?

30 Who are the plaintiffs and defendants in the four types of lawsuits that companies are commonly involved in?

DISCUSSION/ CRITICAL THINKING QUESTIONS

10

DISCUSSION/CRITICAL THINKING QUESTIONS

Be sure to give a detailed explanation for your answer to each question.

1 Antitrust laws were amended years ago: are they too outdated to be effective today?

2 With the global economy, business has changed dramatically. Do we still need antitrust laws?

3 Businesses undergo mergers that are in their best interest. Does society also benefit from mergers, or is it hurt by them?

4 Should any of the three types of mergers be allowed or not allowed?

5 Is it necessary to have both the DOJ and FTC involved in antitrust? If not, which one should enforce antitrust?

6 Should antitrust be enforced at both the federal and state levels? If not, which level should enforce antitrust?

7 Is the judicial system too complex? If yes, how can it be simplified?

8 In relation to the government system of checks and balances, does the judicial branch have too much or too little power over the legislative and executive branches?

9 Is it ethical for one business to file a lawsuit against another business?

10 Is it ethical for a business to file a lawsuit against the government?

APPLICATION EXERCISES

10.1 MERGER AND ACQUISITION

Find a business news story, online or offline, about a merger or acquisition. Report the details of the story; be sure to specify whether it is a merger or acquisition.

10.2 ANTITRUST CASE

Go to the Department of Justice's Antitrust Division at www.justice.gov/atr.

Select an antitrust case. Report the brief details of the antitrust case.

10.3 SUPREME COURT CASE

Visit www.supremecourt.gov. Select one of the "Recent Decisions" and report the results.

CASE 10.1

Is Toshiba Seeing the Big Picture? Alliances and Price-Fixing in the LCD Industry

"Toshiba products play an active role [in our lives], be it in computing, controlling, powering, or communicating—transporting, playing, or even just chillin'. The company's portfolio includes personal and professional computers (PCs, point-of-sale systems), telecommunications and medical equipment (LCDs for mobile devices, X-ray machines), industrial machinery (power plant reactors, elevators), consumer appliances (air conditioners, Blu-ray Disc recorders), electronic components (electron tubes, batteries), and semiconductors. Its portfolio also includes air traffic control and railway transportation systems. . . ."[129]

"[In order to grow their LCD operation] Toshiba bought out Panasonic's stake in Toshiba Matsushita Display Technology in 2009. . . . Renamed Toshiba Mobile Display, the company is a leading provider of LCDs used in mobile phones, in-vehicle displays, and portable computers. In 2012 Toshiba became part of a joint venture, named Japan Display, Inc. (JDI) that combined its small and medium-sized LCD panel business with those of Hitachi and Sony, along with investment by a Japanese government-backed fund. The [Japanese] government owns 70% of JDI while the three companies each hold 10%."[130]

"Toshiba, LG Display and AU Optronics (AUO) have agreed to pay a combined sum of US$571 million to settle a lawsuit over the price-fixing of liquid crystal display (LCD) panels. According to newswire Bloomberg, San Francisco attorney Joseph Alioto, who was the co-lead counsel representing consumers suing the companies, said US$543.5 million would be awarded to consumers in 24 states who overpaid for electronics because of the alleged price-fixing. Another US$27.5 million in civil penalties to eight states would also be paid out, bringing the total settlement to US$571 million, Alioto added."[131]

"The lawyer did not reveal how much each company would pay, but said a court document seeking approval of the settlement would be filed Thursday in a federal court in San Francisco, Bloomberg reported. The attorney told the newswire an earlier settlement with other panel manufacturers for US$553 million had been approved by a federal judge. Altogether, the two settlements totaled more than US$1 billion, setting a record for recovery in a class action lawsuit over price-fixing. The companies were alleged to have fixed prices for the LCD panels, driving up prices from 1999 to 2006, according to the class-action lawsuit filed in 2007. A separate report by Reuters said several companies also pleaded guilty to separate criminal charges and paid fines."[132]

In a separate Reuters report, a U.S. jury fined Toshiba US$87 million for conspiring to fix prices of LCD panels. "The class-action suit was brought against Toshiba, Samsung, Sharp and other LCD makers in 2007. It was filed by U.S. purchasers of LCD panels, both consumers and TV and computer manufacturers that incorporate the panels into their products. Toshiba has consistently maintained that there was no illegal activity on its part in the LCD business in the United States, and Toshiba continues to hold that view, the company said. 'While Toshiba appreciates the jury's time and effort, Toshiba believes that the jury's verdict is in error as to the finding of wrongdoing on Toshiba's part. Toshiba plans to pursue all available legal avenues to correct that finding.'"[133]

Questions

1. What antitrust legislation addresses price-fixing and alliances?
2. What are the responsibilities of the U.S. Department of Justice relative to price-fixing?
3. Why would Toshiba, Hitachi, and Sony, along with the Japanese government, have formed Japan Display, Inc., rather than merge and/or acquire the companies that are part of the alliance?
4. How does the existence of the alliance make a prima facie case for investigating Toshiba for price-fixing?
5. What nonmarket, and specifically judiciary, strategies were employed by Toshiba in light of the jury ruling?
6. What other strategies were available to Toshiba, and which ones would you have employed?

CASE 10.2

RockYou® Gets Rocked by the FTC: Online Gaming and Children's Privacy

Lisa Marino CEO of RockYou® has been rocking the online gaming world as of late. "RockYou® is ranked 4th amongst the largest social gaming companies on Facebook, with nearly 20 million monthly active users."[134] "RockYou® operates a website that allows consumers to play games and use other applications, many of which are arguably targeted to kids and tweens, such as Zoo World and Galactic Allies. In addition, the site allows users to assemble slide shows from their photos and share the content with other users. To save their slide shows, users are asked to enter their email address and email password. Further, to register on the site, the user is also asked to provide his or her birth year and gender."[135] "RockYou®is committed to defining the future of social gaming, creating products intended to serve players, advertisers, and developers alike. The company has dedicated itself to the development of high-quality games and the celebrated Zoo World™ franchise. With advertising products that offer brands more meaningful interactions with players, RockYou® creates an unmatched value-per-engagement for both brands and users. RockYou's® partnerships with world-class talent are part of their steadfast commitment to working with the next generation of social game developers."[136]

Yet RockYou® and Marino found themselves buried by a landslide of turmoil when the FTC "alleged the company's practices violated Section 5 of the FTC Act, as well as the Children's Online Privacy Protection Act of 1998 (COPPA). In particular, the FTC complaint alleged that RockYou® had failed to obtain parental consent when it collected data from children under the age of 13, which is a requirement of COPPA. Further, in its complaint, the FTC also pointed to security failures in the operation of the website, as well as statements in RockYou's® privacy policy that seemed inaccurate. . . . Specifically, it alleged that the RockYou® knowingly collected approximately 179,000 children's email addresses and associated passwords during registration without their parents' consent. Further, the website allowed children to create personal profiles and post personal information on slide shows that could be shared online without consent. In the complaint, the FTC pointed to a statement in RockYou's® privacy policy—which said that the company did not collect data from children under the age of 13—as evidence of RockYou's® failure to have a clear and recognizable policy with respect to the collection and use of data from children."[137]

"Finally, the FTC alleged that Rock You's® security features were not effective and put users' personal information at risk. In this regard, the FTC complaint pointed to a statement in RockYou's® privacy policy that promised visitors that it would provide 'commercially reasonable efforts to ensure the security of its systems' when, in fact, the company was not encrypting data or segmenting its servers. Also, the FTC noted that the company failed to address vulnerabilities in its system to address web-based application attacks, such as 'Structured Query Language' and 'Cross-Site Scripting' attacks. In the complaint, the FTC explained that such attacks were 'well-known and well-publicized forms of hacking attacks, and solutions to prevent such attacks were readily available and inexpensive.'"[138]

"In response, RockYou® agreed to settle with the FTC. The proposed settlement order prohibits future deceptive claims regarding privacy and data security and requires RockYou® to implement a data security program. It also requires the company to submit to security audits by independent third-party auditors every other year for 20 years. RockYou® must also delete information collected from children under age 13 in violation of COPPA, and pay a $250,000 civil penalty for the alleged COPPA violations."[139]

Questions

1. Under what general legal authority does the FTC have the right to interfere in any firm's operation of a website?
2. Assuming that RockYou® decided to fight the FTC ruling, what would be its legal recourse?
3. Given your answer to question 2, what would be the benefits and costs to these actions?
4. What legal actions could the parents of the children registered on RockYou® have taken in this matter?
5. If you were CEO Lisa Marino, what actions would you have taken to address parents' potential legal actions?
6. Assume Google or Microsoft wanted to purchase RockYou®. What objections might be brought under antitrust laws?

INTEGRATIVE CASE (Part 10)

"Lining" on DHR Construction, LLC[140]

This is a continuation case—please refer to Chapters 1–9 for further information.

"What do you mean we can't close on the Smith residence right now?" shouted Richard Davis, managing partner of DHR Patio Homes LLC. Richard Davis, the general contractor, David Smith, the buyer, and Marsh, the representative of the mortgage company, were all sitting around Marsh's conference room. Davis was opposite Smith, with Marsh at the head of the table. What had started out as a friendly meeting had taken a sudden turn for the worse.

"All of the arrangements were made weeks ago to do this closing on exactly this date at this time," continued Davis. "All the paperwork has been done, and everyone is in agreement with the terms of the contract.

The Smith family is ready, I'm ready, the house is ready, and you told me that the mortgage company is ready. What could possibly be the holdup?"

"That's right," chimed in David Smith. "I'd like to finally close on this house as well. First it was the mortgage company not getting my paperwork right, then I was sent out of town for two weeks by my company, and then the town made a mistake in issuing an erroneous certificate of occupancy. When will I finally own my home?"

To Close or Not to Close, That Is the Question!

"Well, you see Mr. Davis," stated Marsh, "the title company has done a thorough search of the property in question and has noted that a mechanic's lien has just been placed on the property by a local firm, Eddie O's Landscaping LLC. This encumbrance on the property title/deed filed with the local court must be paid or resolved prior to a sale. The lien acts like a mortgage or deed of trust because it is a recorded and/or filed claim against the property itself. It has the effect of preventing the owner from selling, financing, or refinancing the property. A mechanic's lien is caused by a failure to pay a contractor for services rendered on a property."

Davis was livid but tried to calmly explain the situation. "But I know absolutely nothing about this lien, and I have never heard of the company in question. In fact, I have purposely not landscaped the property so that the Smith family could work with my landscaper directly and decide how they want to allocate the landscaping budget I have set aside for the house. Mr. Smith mentioned that he might go over budget, which is fine with me as long as he pays for the overcharges. Secondly, if you knew that there was a lien on the property, why didn't you contact Mr. Smith and me to let us know that there was a problem prior to this meeting? Perhaps we could have solved the problem before we met!"

"That was not possible," replied Marsh. "I just received the updated title search 30 minutes before the meeting. Since I knew that the two of you would be here shortly, I thought that the simplest thing would be to just tell you both when you got here. I apologize for not contacting you sooner although I do not know how successful I would have been in trying to reach each of you." The air in the conference room turned heavy as Davis and Smith sat uncomfortably in their chairs. Neither Davis nor Smith said a word and allowed the silence to permeate the room. "Be that as it may," Marsh said finally to fill the void, "a lien is a lien, and I cannot grant a mortgage today on this property. . . . Unless, of course, either you, Mr. Davis, or you, Mr. Smith, were to put an amount equivalent to the lien in an escrow account. We have lawyers right here at the company who could quickly establish this account."

"Not a problem," responded Davis to Marsh's suggestion. "I'll take care of the lien. How much could it be? A few thousand dollars? I've got the corporate checkbook right here." A light seemed to appear at the end of a long tunnel, and relief spread on the faces of both Smith and Davis.

"Let's see," said Mr. Marsh "There it is—the lien amount is $450,000." A thick silence followed as if Marsh's statement was the equivalent of a death sentence. Both Davis's and Smith's jaws dropped simultaneously, their openings quite pronounced, as if both had seen a ghost.

The stillness was short-lived as Davis found both his voice and his anger. "The sales price of the house is $250,000; how in God's name could the lien be for $450,000? There's got to be an error somewhere!"

"There is no error, Mr. Davis, and I apologize for the inconvenience that this will cause both you and Mr. Smith. The lien amount is what it is, and only $450,000 placed in an escrow account will allow us to move forward today."

From the Frying Pan into the Fire

Davis and Smith both left the closing empty handed, with Davis first apologizing to Smith for the inconvenience and then vowing to get to the bottom of the situation. Davis filled in his business partner, Hodgetts, and Davis's wife, Adrienne, right after the meeting. Adrienne then called the landscaping company and found out what was behind the lien.

"The land development firm we purchased the property from, Florence Development, hasn't paid its landscaping company," commented Adrienne Davis. "The developer was served papers just this last Saturday. The landscaping firm filed a lien on all of the lots in the development, including our own, with each lien equal to the total amount of the outstanding bill. We should be receiving these third-party lien papers shortly. The landscape firm's owner said, 'Well, you can just pay the lien and go to closing!' After talking with the landscape firm, I called Milton James, the president of Florence Development. He said he'd have this settled in a week to 10 days and not to worry. I also spoke with James's lawyer, and he told me that everything should be settled in two weeks at the latest."

Hodgetts flew into a rage. "We have eight properties at Florence, four of them currently under construction. Are you telling me that we can't close on any of these properties until either the liens are removed or we put $450,000 per property into an escrow account? We've got over a million dollars already tied up in these projects; how are we going to operate if we can't free up some capital? Secondly, it is quite unfair that the lien was not apportioned as a percentage of the properties in question. How can the landscaper recover damages that are larger than the outstanding amount due?"

"I don't know the answer to your second question, but I do understand your feelings about the situation and I share them," retorted Richard Davis. "Let me call Milt to verify that this is just a minor glitch that will be quickly settled. If the closing for the Smith's house is delayed for a week or two, it won't be a major tragedy." Richard Davis then called Milton James and verified that there was a dispute between his firm and Eddie O's and that the dispute would be

resolved by next week. James assured Davis that everything was under control.

From Bad to Worse but then an Epiphany

Hodgetts called for a meeting to discuss the situation after two weeks because nothing had seemingly been done about the liens. When he and the Davises met, he was fuming.

"Hold that thought for a moment, Stephen. Let's see if we can, through our powers of deduction, try to piece this puzzle together before we confront the big question." A few moments passed as Davis deeply pondered the situation. "I should have known that something like this would happen," pronounced Davis. "Remember those properties up on the ridge that Milt originally showed us?"

"No," Hodgetts replied, "and what does this have to do with our problem?"

"You'll see in a minute; just hold on," retorted Davis. "Well, if you recall, when we first were dealing with Milt, he kept showing us these properties that he swore on a stack of Bibles would have a wonderful view of the mountains."

"Oh yeah, now I remember," snapped Hodgetts. "You're talking about those properties with the restricted fronts imposed by the local zoning board. The garages on those properties had to be set back 15 feet from the front of the house. Our preliminary architectural drawings on those properties produced a very small first floor, under a thousand square feet, and we concluded that only two story homes could be built on those lots in order to obtain decent sized homes. We also concluded that the market segment we were targeting much preferred ranch (one story) style homes, and therefore homes would not sell on these properties."

"Your memory," shot back Davis, "when not moderated by wine, women, and song, is remarkable." This jibe evoked several giggles from Adrienne and softened Hodgetts' overly foul mood.

"Again," Hodgetts grumbled, "what does this have to do with the situation at hand?"

"You're a smart guy," responded Richard Davis in his normal manner. "Let's see if you can put two and two together! You don't need to be Sherlock Holmes to solve this mystery."

"Indubitably, my dear Davis. It is as clear as the nose on your face that if we, mere beginners at the construction game, have concluded that these properties are of little value then evidently our competitors have reached the same conclusion. That being the case, Milt is the proud owner of over 50 acres of property, normally worth about $5 million, which he will have a very difficult time divesting."

"Exactly," chimed in Richard Davis. "I'm sure that his inability to sell off these properties is putting a real crimp in his cash flow. It is not hard to imagine that Milt would be very slow in paying some of his bills related to the Florence development given the fact that about a quarter of the development may remain 'au naturel' [as is] for a long while."

"So what you're saying," concluded Hodgetts, "is that Milt stiffed his landscaper because he can't sell off a good portion of his development."

Richard Davis allowed a small smile to emerge as he turned to his wife and said, "By George, Adrienne, I think he's got it."

Coda

"Oh I got it all right, right in the neck," barked Hodgetts. "His problems have become our problems. Milt's been stalling us for the past two weeks because he's not man enough or honest enough to just tell us straight out that he has a problem that he can't handle. 'Pride goeth before the fall,' but my fear is that we'll all be taking a fall with Milt."

"That's right," indicated Adrienne Davis. "We can't go to closing because of the third-party liens on our properties, but the liens won't be removed until Milt pays his bills or we handle the liens ourselves. Probably Milt can't afford to pay his bills, and I know we can't afford to cover the exorbitant liens on our properties. What do we do now, pray for a miracle or make a deal with the devil?"

Questions

1. What types of laws are being discussed in this case?
2. A lien acts like a lawsuit in that a claim is being made by one party against another. What type of lawsuit does a lien act like?
3. What judicial strategies are available to Davis and Hodgetts in order to settle this matter?
4. Which court system would deal with each of these judicial strategies?
5. What would be the role of the courts given these judicial strategies?
6. What other nonmarket strategies could Davis and Hodgetts employ in order to solve this problem?

REFERENCES AND NOTES

REFERENCES AND NOTES

10

1 http://premium.hoovers.com/subscribe/co/overview.xhtml?ID=ffffrcrtffxrcjjxcs (accessed June 23, 2006).
2 Ibid.
3 M. Jacoby, "Why Microsoft Battles Europe Years After Settling With U.S.," *Wall Street Journal* (May 5, 2006), A1.
4 Ibid.
5 Ibid.
6 Ibid.
7 Ibid.
8 http://en.wikipedia.org/wiki/European_Union_Microsoft_competition_case (accessed July 25, 2012).
9 S. Forbes, "Unneeded, Destructive," *Forbes* (May 7, 2012): 12.
10 C. Marquis and Z. Huang, "The Contingent Nature of Public Policy and the

Growth of U.S. Commercial Banking," *Academy of Management Journal* 52(6) (2009): 1222–1246.

11 D. P. Barron, *Business and Its Environment*, 6th ed. (Upper Saddle, NJ: Prentice Hall, 2010).

12 S. Forden and J. Bliss, "Google Gets Ready to Man the Barricades," *Business-Week* (July 4–10, 2011): 30–31.

13 J. Whalen, "Glaxo to Pay U.S. $3 Billion to Settle," *Wall Street Journal* (November 4, 2011): B3.

14 M. Orey, "Why Google Wants to Make Nice," *BusinessWeek* (May 11, 2009): 54–55.

15 "16 Years Later: Word v. WordPerfect," *Wall Street Journal* (November 22, 2011): B1.

16 M. Eckblad, "Pilgrim's Pride Tried to Manipulate Prices of Chicken, U.S. Judge Rules," *Wall Street Journal* (October 4, 2011): B2.

17 T. Catan, J. A. Trachtenberg, and C. Bray, "U.S. Alleges e-Book Scheme," *Wall Street Journal* (April 12, 2012): A1, A8.

18 M. Orey, "Why Google Wants to Make Nice," *BusinessWeek* (May 11, 2009): 54–55.

19 C. Forelle and D. Clark, "Intel Fine Jolts Tech Sector," *Wall Street Journal* (May 14, 2002): A1, A14.

20 K. J. Winstein and W. M. Bulkeley, "IBM Faces Justice Antitrust Inquiry," *Wall Street Journal* (October 8, 2009): B1.

21 T. Catan, "B&N Sought Microsoft Inquiry," *Wall Street Journal* (November 9, 2011): B5.

22 T. Catan and B. Kendall, "After AT&T: The New Antitrust Era," *Wall Street Journal* (December 21, 2011): B1.

23 S. Raice and J. Angwin, "Facebook Unfair on Privacy," *Wall Street Journal* (November 30, 2011): B1.

24 J. Whalen, "Glaxo to Pay U.S. $3 Billion to Settle," *Wall Street Journal* (November 4, 2011): B3.

25 D. P. Barron, *Business and Its Environment*, 6th ed. (Upper Saddle, NJ: Prentice Hall, 2010)

26 J. Whalen, "Glaxo to Pay U.S. $3 Billion to Settle," *Wall Street Journal* (November 4, 2011): B3.

27 B. Greeley and T. Shields, "Behind AT&T's Epic Lobbying Failure," *BusinessWeek* (December 12–16, 2011): 40–42.

28 D. Searcey and B. Steinberg, "SBC's Embraces of AT&T Brand Brings History—and Baggage," *Wall Street Journal* (October 28, 2005), B1.

29 M. Warner, "Icahn Says 55% of CVR Shares Are Tendered," *Wall Street Journal* (April 3, 2012), http://online.wsj.com/article/SB1000142405270 230381650457732144144871530 0.html?KEYWORDS=hostile+takeover.

30 D. Cimilluca, G. Chon, and D. Cameron, "UPS Near Deal to Buy TNT Express," *Wall Street Journal* (March 19, 2012): B1.

31 H. Sherman, D. J. Rowley, and B. Armandi, *Strategic Management: An Organizational Change Approach* (Lanham, MD: University Press of America, 2006).

32 R. N. Lussier, *Management: Concepts, Applications, Skill Development*, 5th ed. (Mason, OH: Cengage, 2012).

33 www.pepsi.com (accessed June 4, 2012).

34 T. Catan and B. Kendall, "After AT&T: The New Antitrust Era," *Wall Street Journal* (December 21, 2011): B1.

35 A. Troianovski, "AT&T Hangs Up on T-Mobile," *Wall Street Journal* (December 20, 2011): A1, A2.

36 T. Catan and B. Kendall, "After AT&T: The New Antitrust Era," *Wall Street Journal* (December 21, 2011): B1.

37 H. Sherman, D. J. Rowley, and B. Armandi, *Strategic Management* (Lanham, MD: University Press of America, 2006).

38 "Global 500," *Fortune* (July 25, 2011): 161, F1–F6.

39 "The World's Most Admired Companies," *Fortune* (March 21, 2011): 109–146.

40 www.ge.com (accessed June 4, 2012).

41 www.tyco.com (accessed June 4, 2012).

42 www.pepsico.com(accessed June 4, 2012).

43 www.tyco.com (accessed June 4, 2012).

44 http://dealbook.nytimes.com/2011/12/19/att-withdraws-39-bid-for-t-mobile (accessed July 26, 2012).

45 Ibid.

46 Ibid.

47 B. Kendall, "U.S. Scores Victory in H&R Block Merger Case," *Wall Street Journal* (November 1, 2011): B4.

48 T. Catan and S. E. Ante, "U.S. Sues to Stop AT&T Deal," *Wall Street Journal* (September 1, 2011): A1.

49 S. Forden and J. Bliss, "Google Gets Ready to Man the Barricades," *Business-Week* (July 4–10, 2011): 30–31.

50 D. P. Barron, *Business and Its Environment*, 6th ed. (Upper Saddle, NJ: Prentice Hall, 2010).

51 J. R. Wilke, "Internet-Law Expert Is Nominated as Antitrust Chief," *Wall Street Journal* (January 23, 2009): A1.

52 B. Kendall and J. Palazzolo, "FTC Hires High-Profile Lawyer to Help Lead Google Probe," *Wall Street Journal* (April 27, 2012): B3.

53 J. Whalen, "Glaxo to Pay U.S. $3 Billion to Settle," *Wall Street Journal* (November 4, 2011): B3.

54 D. Mattioli and M. J. Randall, "Reebok Stands Behind Its Claims As Toning Shoe Runs Afoul of FTC," *Wall Street Journal* (September 29, 2011): B1.

55 M. Orey, "Why Google Wants to Make Nice," *BusinessWeek* (May 11, 2009): 54–55.

56 T. Catan and B. Kendall, "After AT&T: The New Antitrust Era," *Wall Street Journal* (December 21, 2011): B1.

57 S. Forden and J. Bliss, "Google Gets Ready to Man the Barricades," *BusinessWeek* (July 4–10, 2011): 30–31.

58 A. Troianovski, "AT&T Hangs Up on T-Mobile," *Wall Street Journal* (December 20, 2011): A1, A2.

59 D. P. Barron, *Business and Its Environment*, 6th ed. (Upper Saddle, NJ: Prentice Hall, 2010).

60 Ibid.

61 Ibid.

62 M. Porter, *Competitive Advantage* (New York: The Free Press, 1985).

63 D. P. Barron, *Business and Its Environment*, 6th ed. (Upper Saddle, NJ: Prentice Hall, 2010).

64 Ibid.

65 K. Clark, "NBA Players File Antitrust Lawsuit," *Wall Street Journal* (November 16, 2011): B3.

66 www.americanantitrustinstitute.org (accessed June 5, 2012).

67 K. Mayo, "Etc. Hard Choices," *BusinessWeek* (January 9–15, 2012): 84.

68 B. Kendall, "Judge Allows Sprint Challenge to AT&T Deal Over Devices," *Wall Street Journal* (November 3, 2011): B3.

69 J. R. Wilke, "Internet-Law Expert is Nominated as Antitrust Chief," *Wall Street Journal* (January 23, 2009): A1.

70 T. Catan, "B&N Sought Microsoft Inquiry," *Wall Street Journal* (November 9, 2011): B5.

71 J. Whalen, "Glaxo to Pay U.S. $3 Billion to Settle," *Wall Street Journal* (November 4, 2011): B3.

72 www.naag.org (accessed June 5, 2010).

73 R. Parloff, "Uncle Sam's New Crusade Against Banks," *Fortune* (November 21, 2011): 22.

74 P. Davies and K. Scannell, "Guilty Verdicts Provide Red Meat to Prosecutors Chasing Companies," *Wall Street Journal* (May 26, 2006): A1.

75 D. P. Barron, *Business and Its Environment*, 6th ed. (Upper Saddle, NJ: Prentice Hall, 2010).

76 J. Eaglesham and S. Kapner, "SEC Cops Want to Fight U.S. Judge," *Wall Street Journal* (December 15, 2011): C1.

77 S. Forbes, "EPA All Wet," *Forbes* (April 23, 2012): 16.

78 M. Trottman, "Union-Organizing Rule Easing Votes Is Rejected," *Wall Street Journal* (May 15, 2012): A3.

79 www.family.org (accessed June 19, 2006).

80 http://www.uscourts.gov/FederalCourts/UnderstandingtheFederalCourts/FederalCourtsStructure.aspx (accessed June 6, 2012).

81 Information for Figure 10.6 taken from www.uscourts.gov (accessed June 5, 2012).

82 www.uscourts.gov (accessed June 6, 2012).

83 Ibid.

84 Ibid.

85 G. Colvin, "Business Paralysis: Regulatory Uncertainty Means That Leaders are Afraid to Act," *Fortune* (November 1, 2010): 65.

86 C. Marquis and Z. Huang, "The Contingent Nature of Public Policy and the Growth of U.S. Commercial Banking," *Academy of Management Journal* 52(6) (2009): 1222–1246.

87 A. Armenakis and J. Wigand, "Stakeholder Actions and Their Impact on the Organizational Cultures of Two Tobacco Companies," *Business and Society Review* 115(2) (2010): 147–171.

88 D. P. Barron, *Business and Its Environment*, 6th ed. (Upper Saddle, NJ: Prentice Hall, 2010).

89 K. Mayo, "Etc. Hard Choices," *BusinessWeek* (January 9–15, 2012): 84.

90 P. Schreck, "Reviewing the Business Case for Corporate Social Responsibility: New

Evidence and Analysis," *Journal of Business Ethics* 103(2) (2011): 167–188.

91 P. Roythorne, "Special Report–Public Relations: The Specialist Subject," *Marketing Week* (April 21, 2005), 37.

92 S. Forden and J. Bliss, "Google Gets Ready to Man the Barricades," *BusinessWeek* (July 4–10, 2011): 30–31.

93 J. Bravin and J. Cummings, "Nominee's Record Shows Backing of Business Interests, Contracts," *Wall Street Journal* (November 1, 2005): A1, A11.

94 Fulbright & Jaworski, sidebar note "45%," *Entrepreneur* (February 2009): 33.

95 T. McThenia, "A Crackdown on Patently Absurd Lawsuits," *BusinessWeek* (May 14–20, 2012): 33–35.

96 J. Whalen, "Glaxo to Pay U.S. $3 Billion to Settle," *Wall Street Journal* (November 4, 2011): B3

97 J. Eisinger, "Why Independent Research Is Drying Up," *Wall Street Journal* (March 8, 2006): C1.

98 "16 Years Later: Word v. WordPerfect," *Wall Street Journal* (November 22, 2011): B1.

99 T. Catan and S. Hughes, "Google Defends Dominance," *Wall Street Journal* (September 22, 2011): B1.

100 A. Armenakis and J. Wigand, "Stakeholder Actions and Their Impact on the Organizational Cultures of Two Tobacco Companies," *Business and Society Review* 115(2) (2010): 147–171.

101 T. McThenia, "A Crackdown on Patently Absurd Lawsuits," *BusinessWeek* (May 14–20, 2012): 33–35.

102 D. P. Barron, *Business and Its Environment*, 6th ed. (Upper Saddle, NJ: Prentice Hall, 2010).

103 Staff, "16 Years Later: Word v. WordPerfect," *Wall Street Journal* (November 22, 2011): B1.

104 D. P. Barron, *Business and Its Environment*, 6th ed. (Upper Saddle, NJ: Prentice Hall, 2010).

105 "16 Years Later: Word v. WordPerfect," *Wall Street Journal* (November 22, 2011): B1.

106 http://subscriber.hoovers.com/H/company360/fulldescription.html?companyId=161810000000000 (accessed July 26, 2012).

107 http://news.cnet.com/8301-1023_3-57411560-93/new-shareholder-lawsuit-targets-groupon-execs (accessed July 26, 2012.

108 Ibid.

109 Ibid.

110 Ibid.

111 "The Supreme Court Takes on Trial Lawyers," *BusinessWeek* (June 27–28, 2011): 34–35.

112 S. Carey and J. Nicas, "United Feeling Merger Pains," *Wall Street Journal* (September 27, 2011): B1.

113 M. P. McQueen, "Bloggers, Beware: What You Write Can Get You Sued," *Wall Street Journal* (May 21, 2009): D1.

114 www.riaa.org (accessed June 7, 2012).

115 "Microsoft Sues," *BusinessWeek* (June 29, 2008): 9.

116 "Apple: Sued for Price Fixings e-Books," *BusinessWeek* (April 16–22, 2012): 24.

117 "Did J&J Go Astray?" *BusinessWeek* (February 1–8, 2010): 6.

118 R. Parloff, "Uncle Sam's New Crusade Against Banks," *Fortune* (November 21, 2011): 22.

119 K. J. Delaney and R. A. Guth, "Google Calls Microsoft Lawsuit a Scare Tactic," *Wall Street Journal* (July 28, 2005): B4.

120 "Reebok: No Tebowing Allowed," *BusinessWeek* (April 16–22, 2012): 24.

121 J. E. Vascellaro and E. Ramstad, "Apple, Samsung Hold Patent Talks," *Wall Street Journal* (May 21, 2012): B3.

122 S. Prasso, "How Samsung Turned Up the Sizzle," *Fortune* (July 25, 2011): 28.

123 "Kodak Suffered," *Wall Street Journal* (May 22, 2012): A1.

124 T. McThenia, "A Crackdown on Patently Absurd Lawsuits," *BusinessWeek* (May 14–20, 2012): 33–35.

125 B. Kendall, "Judge Allows Sprint Challenge to AT&T Deal Over Devices," *Wall Street Journal* (November 3, 2011): B3.

126 M. Esterl, "Grisly Tobacco Labels Thrown Out by Judge," *Wall Street Journal* (March 1, 2012): A6.

127 G. A. Fowler, "Craigslist Sues Critic of Its Adult Ads," *Wall Street Journal* (May 21, 2009): B1.

128 T. M. Burton, "The Free Speech Pill," *Wall Street Journal* (November 3, 2011): B1.

129 http://subscriber.hoovers.com/H/company360/fulldescription.html?companyId=41888000000000 (accessed July 26, 2012).

130 Ibid.

131 Ibid.

132 http://www.zdnet.com/toshiba-lg-auo-settle-lcd-price-fixing-case-7000000755 (accessed July 26, 2012).

133 http://www.displayalliance.com/news-categories/2012/7/6/toshiba-found-guilty-of-lcd-price-fixing.html (accessed July 26, 2012).

134 http://rockyou.com/ry/about-us (accessed July 30, 2012).

135 http://www.arentfox.com/publications/index.cfm?fa=legalUpdateDisp&content_id=3659 (accessed July 26, 2012).

136 http://rockyou.com/ry/about-us (accessed July 26, 2012).

137 http://www.arentfox.com/publications/index.cfm?fa=legalUpdateDisp&content_id=3659 (accessed July 26, 2012).

138 Ibid.

139 Ibid.

140 Adapted with the permission of the authors from H. Sherman and D. J. Rowley, "Liening on DHR Construction, LLC," *Organizational and Management Journal* 2(3) (2005): 109–117.

Part 5

INTERNATIONAL BUSINESS, SOCIETY, AND GOVERNMENT

Chapter 11

COMPETING IN THE GLOBAL ECONOMY

Learning Outcomes

In this chapter, you will find out the answers to these key questions:

- What is globalization, and why is it important?
- What are the roles of business and government in the global economy?
- What strategies are used to compete in the global economy?

After studying this chapter, you should be able to:

1. Compare and contrast the types of businesses in the global economy
2. Contrast U.S. business ownership and government–business relations with those in the EU, China, and Japan
3. Discuss who benefits and who pays the cost of protectionism
4. Compare and contrast types of trade barriers and explain why they are not always successful
5. Compare and contrast the World Trade Organization (WTO), World Bank, and International Monetary Fund (IMF)
6. Describe the systems of free trade that the EU has in common with the United States
7. Compare and contrast grease payments, bribes, and offsets
8. Define the following key terms (in order of appearance in the chapter)

globalization	tariffs	International Monetary
international company	trade quotas	Fund (IMF)
multinational company (MNC)	trade bans	grease payments
free enterprise	trade deficit	bribes
central state control	antidumping	offsets
competitive advantage	World Trade	ethical impact statements
of nations	Organization (WTO)	
trade subsidies	World Bank	

■ Chapter Outline

What's This Chapter All About?

From Model 1.1 (p. 5), discussions throughout this textbook have covered the interrelationship of business, society, and government in the market and nonmarket environments. In the last part of the book, we broaden the discussion to include the global macroenvironment.

The focus has intentionally been on conducting business in the United States. Now it is time to progress to thinking about the complexity of managing a company that conducts business in many countries with a wide diversity of customers, laws, and regulations.

We begin with an overview of globalization, followed by a comparison of political and economic systems and then a discussion of trade laws and regulation. The fourth section presents organizations and agreements that facilitate global trade.

With the book's focus on stakeholder management, we include an entire section on ethics. As usual, we end with a discussion of the strategies business uses to meet its objectives, but with the emphasis on international business.

CASE

Bandai America and the United States: I Think We're Turning Japanese, I Really Think So

Go into any American home and you're bound to see younger children watching such live action adventure shows as *The Power Rangers* (with all of its differing versions) or cartoons, such as *Teen Titans, Zatch Bell,* or *Digimon.* Older children and teenagers have also been attracted to what is called Japanese anime, including such interesting titles as *Cowboy Bebop, Naruto, Gundam,* and *Witch Hunter Robin.* If they're not watching these shows incessantly, they may be playing Gundam or Naruto video games or playing trading card games of similar titles. And let us not forget the plethora of *Power Ranger* and *Thunderbirds* toys, full-length animated movies, handheld games, cell phone games, and manga (graphic novels). Masayuki Matsuo, director of Bandai America, a subsidiary of **Namco Bandai Holdings Inc.,** can't help but be proud of his firm's accomplishments in importing Japanese-style entertainment into the United States.[1]

"Bandai Co. Ltd. is a Japanese toy-making company, as well as the producer of countless anime, and tokusatsu programs [live-action productions that primarily feature the use of special effects]. It is the world's third largest producer of toys. After the merger with video game developer and producer **Namco,** Bandai Co. Ltd. is now under the management of Namco Bandai Holdings Inc."[2] "Namco Bandai was formed in 2005 when Bandai, Japan's largest toy maker and a developer of regionally popular game titles, acquired global computer games legend Namco to build market share in the gaming space domestically and abroad. Faced with formidable competition from the likes of Sony and Nintendo, the company develops games based on Bandai's catalog of toy and anime characters, using Namco's software gaming expertise. Namco made its name in the 1980s with such video arcade classics as *Pac-Man* and *Galaga.* . . . The firm is looking to extend its reach beyond its home market of Japan but hasn't made as much progress in recent years as it continues to square off against global toy-making stalwarts Mattel, Hasbro, and Disney that have a strong presence outside Asia. The economic downturn, particularly in the United States, has conspired to create dips in sales. Indeed, Europe and the Americas accounted for 22% of sales in 2010 vs. 17% in 2011."[3]

"Bandai America is the American distribution arm of Bandai that makes toy products for the U.S. market, distributes Bandai games, and distributes many of Bandai Visual's anime titles (in addition to animes licensed from other animation studios, such as *.hack//SIGN*) in the United States through its **Bandai Entertainment** arm headquartered in Cypress, California, and in Canada through **Bandai Entertainment Canada,** which is headquartered in Mississauga, Ontario."[4] A leader in introducing Japanese toy trends to the United States, Bandai's interests now encompass hobbies (toys, models, apparel, and sundries), amusement facilities, game content (home and arcade console gaming), mobile content, and visual and music content (including home entertainment).

"Bandai America is the manufacturer and master toy licensee of some of the most popular brands in children's toys and entertainment today. Bandai America consistently seeks opportunities to grow its brands by forging synergistic partnership with the leading licensors and entertainment companies in the industry. Bandai America's partners have included the Walt Disney Co./Disney Consumer Products, Warner

Bros. Animation/WB Consumer Products, Cartoon Network, WiZ Entertainment of Japan, and 4Kids Entertainment. . . . Bandai America's products, toys, and entertainment can be found at mass retailers, specialty shops, hobby stores, club stores, drug stores, and grocery chains nationwide."[5]

Yet fame and fortune have not come without at least some controversy. At times, fans of the *Power Rangers* series have complained about Bandai America seeming to dump some of their inferior versions of Japanese toys when brought to the United States. Other complaints stem from the sometimes sexist handling of the Power Rangers toy line. In nearly every season, Bandai makes "souped-up" versions of the male characters but not of the female characters. Most female villains and mentors get skipped over altogether.[6]

Some critics have objected to anime becoming an increasingly large part of American pop culture.[7] More specifically, the **American Family Association** (AFA), which has a conservative Christian political orientation, has objected to many of the anime characters, game cards, games, and story lines, claiming that "the story behind [some of] the cartoon series resemble[s] Eastern mythology."[8] The AFA appears to strongly object to any cultural message that has occult and mystical references, including those appearing in the popular British *Harry Potter* series. Objections aside, Japanese culture seems to have taken the United States by storm and infiltrated pop culture and U.S. consumer trends,[9] an excellent omen for chairman and director Masayuki Matsuo.

The following questions are related to the Bandai America case. Answers can be found within the chapter.

1. What are some of the pros and cons of globalization, specifically dealing with Bandai America?
2. Why would Bandai want to globalize its operations?
3. What type of international firm is Namco Bandai Holdings Inc.?
4. What political, economic, business ownership, and government–business relations would Namco Bandai Holdings Inc. find in its home country?
5. What competitive advantage of its nation might Bandai be exploiting in its strategy?
6. If the United States wanted to protect companies such as Hasbro and Disney from increased competition from Bandai, what trade barriers might it employ?
7. What previous actions by Bandai might change U.S. trade policy toward Japan and cause the president to impose sanctions and temporary safeguards to protect U.S. businesses?
8. What business regulatory agencies would have overseen the merger of video game developer and producer Namco, with Bandai Co. Ltd.?
9. Which world agency would handle a trade dispute between the United States and Japan if issues arose related to product dumping and imposing tariffs on Bandai products?
10. Gift giving is a long-honored tradition in Japan. What type of corruption might gift giving be construed as, and what organizations would monitor gift giving in Bandai's U.S. subsidiary?
11. What nonmarket strategies might Bandai America employ against the AFA to combat its attack on Japanese anime characters, game cards, games, and story lines?

GLOBALIZATION AND MULTINATIONAL COMPANIES

If you think it is difficult to manage a business in the United States, you are correct. But think about conducting business in more than 100 countries. **McDonald's** knows no boundaries; it has more than 32,000 locations in more than 100 countries around the globe.[10] **Coca-Cola** has more than 3,500 beverages, serving 1.8 billion per day, in more than 200 countries.[11] The **FedEx** worldwide network provides delivery access to more than 220 countries and territories worldwide.[12] Imagine dealing with activists in all these countries. Imagine the complexity of dealing with multiple political and regulatory systems and knowing and obeying the laws in a hundred countries, some of which conflict. CEOs cannot know and do it all, but they are responsible for global operations. This chapter expands our discussion to include how globalization affects business, society, and government. In this section, we discuss globalization concepts, arguments for and against globalization, the importance of globalization, and multinational companies.

Globalization Concepts

Globalization. Although many different definitions of globalization have been offered up, for our purposes it's about free trade that allows companies to conduct business in multiple countries without boundaries and with few trade barriers. *Globalization is the integration of national economies into one global economy.* Thus, the terms *globalization* and the *global economy* essentially are the same. What happens to business in the United States, the EU, China, and Japan has consequences in these countries and in the rest of the world. Several forces have led to the continual growth of globalization of business by increasing efficiencies while decreasing costs.

Globalization Forces. Among the forces are: the availability of *capital*, providing money to expand;[13] *technology*, making communication quick with low cost;[14] *transportation*, making travel and product delivery quick with low cost; and *standardization* of products with economies-of-scale, making it easier to sell the same product in many countries.[15] The *Internet*, which U.S. government funds created and continue to play a behind-the-scenes role in running, has also helped globalization.

On the society side, the **Global Policy Forum** (**GPF**, www.globalpolicy.org) is an independent policy watchdog that monitors the work of the **United Nations** (**UN**, www.un.org) and scrutinizes global policymaking. GPF works particularly on the UN Security Council, the food and hunger crisis, and the global economy. It promotes accountability and citizen participation in decisions on peace and security, social justice, and international law.[16] Global forces have made it difficult to "Buy American."

"Made in America" is blurred. Did you know that most U.S. ports are run by foreign companies?[17] Many unions and consumers subscribe to the idea behind "Buy American," but even for those who want to buy American, few people know the country of origin of the products they regularly buy. Did you know that although **Nike** is an American company, almost all of its clothes and sneakers are not made in the United States? Look at the labels in your clothes, and you will realize that most clothing is not made in America. *iPods, iPhones*, and *iPads* are made in China for **Apple**. So if you own a pair of Nikes or an iProduct, are you really buying American?

If you buy a **Nestlé** candy bar, **Samsung** TV, **Bayer** aspirin, fill up your tanks with **Shell** gas, or drink a **Bud Light** are you buying American?—all of these companies are foreign owned. If you buy a **Nissan** *Altima* or *Maxima* that are **Japanese** manufactured with **French** partner **Renault** (two global companies linked by cross-shareholdings with the same CEO **Carlos Ghosn**), made at a plant in Tennessee with **U.S.** employees, what is the real country of origin of the car? Are you getting the picture of the global economy, which is comprised of companies that have no boundaries? It is difficult for people to know whether they are buying products made in the United States.

Personal and Professional Applications

1. Do you make an attempt to buy "made in America" products?

2. Identify the country of origin of the products of your current or past employer.

Arguments For and Against Globalization

Those for globalization claim it has resulted in significant job creations, improved living standards, and a wide variety of cheaper consumer products. However, opponents question whether globalization's benefits outweigh the dislocations of downsizing that it causes. Four areas of debate include jobs, inequality and poverty, national sovereignty and cultural diversity, and the natural environment.[18] See Figure 11.1 for a list of some of the arguments for and against globalization. Read left to right, as each argument for globalization is matched with a response against. We briefly expand on these arguments.

Arguments for Globalization	Arguments against Globalization
Increases business sales and profits	Feeds business greed
Means greater productivity, economies of scale, and lower cost	Doesn't really benefit society, just business
Creates greater competition	Helps foreign companies
Leads to a net increase in jobs	Outsources jobs to other countries
Makes more variety of products available	Replaces U.S. products with ones that are foreign-made
Results in lower consumer prices	Lowers wages that don't offset lower prices
Increases standard of living in other countries	Exploits employees with low wages and poor working conditions (MNCs)
Improves human rights	Shows little care for human rights and even exploits them (MNCs)
Provides technology to improve environment	Destroys the environment (MNCs)

■ **Figure 11.1:** Arguments For and Against Globalization

Bandai America Case Question 1: What are some of the pros and cons of globalization, specifically dealing with Bandai America?

Bandai America is the American distribution arm of Bandai, which makes toy products for the U.S. market, distributes Bandai games, and distributes many of Bandai Visual's anime titles in the United States through its Bandai Entertainment arm headquartered in Cypress, California. By bringing Japanese entertainment to the United States, Bandai has provided greater choices to consumers, brought increased competition to American toy manufacturers (and thereby lower prices), and created numerous jobs in the United States through Bandai's California headquarters. On the other hand, increased competition from Bandai has undoubtedly negatively affected the U.S. toy industry, exported some wages and profits to Japan, and perhaps limited the types of toys and entertainment being offered; for example, U.S. firms like Walt Disney have formed partnerships with Bandai to offer Japanese-influenced products.

Personal and Professional Applications

3. Are you for or against globalization, and how has it affected you?

The Importance of Globalization

Recently, the pace of global integration has dramatically increased.[19] Do you believe in the importance of globalization? The CEOs of major corporations ranked globalization as the number-one challenge of business leaders in the twenty-first century. According to the late management guru Peter Drucker, there will be two kinds of managers—those who think globally and those who are unemployed.

Why Business Has Gone Global. Large companies want to continue to grow, increasing sales and profits. In the United States, how many people don't know about Coca-Cola and McDonald's? People can buy soft drinks and Big Macs just about everywhere; it's a saturated market. The United States has about 314 million people, and the EU, with its 27 countries, has a population of more than 500 million. The world, however, has more than 7 billion potential consumers, with about one-third of them in China (1.343 billion) and India (1.205 billion).[20] China will soon overtake the United States as the largest economy in the world.[21] In other words, 95 percent of consumers live outside the United States. By the year 2050, the world population will grow about 20 percent to 9 billion people.[22] So to continue to grow, big business must go global.

As global companies grow, they often obtain economies of scale, allowing them to cut costs and lower prices to be more competitive. So even to compete locally with global companies often requires doing business with global suppliers to stay competitive. Many MNCs have anywhere from 5,000 to 10,000 plus suppliers, emphasizing the value chain theme and antitrust material introduced in Chapter 10. Antitrust DOJ and FTC agencies have allowed big companies, such as Exxon and Mobil, to merge so that they can compete with big foreign companies, such as Royal Dutch Shell and British Petroleum (BP).

Globalization also helps companies maintain growth and profit levels. For example, Cisco gets 55 percent of its revenues from overseas and calculates that is where 70 percent of its growth will come from overseas.[23] Only 26 percent of Yum Brands (*KFC, Pizza Hut, Taco Bell*) profits come from the United States; with 40 percent coming from its 4,000 locations in China.[24]

Bandai America Case Question 2: Why would Bandai want to globalize its operation?

Bandai is Japan's largest toy maker and acquired global computer games legend Namco in 2005 in an effort to build market share (growth) in the gaming space domestically and abroad. Faced with formidable competition at home from Sony and Nintendo, the company has set out to broaden its global reach (the company wants to expand overseas revenue beyond the current 20 percent of total sales) as it squares off against global toy-making stalwarts Mattel, Hasbro, and Disney.

Your Career. Globalization will affect your career in one way or another. For example, you may end up taking a job in Europe working for a Japanese company. To advance to the top of some firms, it is important that you leave the country and work abroad.[25] You could take a job working in the United States for a foreign-owned company, such as Shell (gas) of The Netherlands, Nestlé (food) of Switzerland, Nokia (phones) of Finland, Samsung (TVs) of South Korea, Dalian Wanda Group (AMC Entertainment) of China, or Honda (cars) of Japan. Even if you work in America for a U.S. company, such as IBM, GE, or FedEx, it is likely that you will work with employees from other countries and deal with customers or suppliers from other countries. At the very least, in the corporate world, you will compete with foreign companies for business.

> **Personal and Professional Applications**
>
> 4.   How has or how will globalization affect your career?

> Learning Outcome 1: Compare and contrast the types of business in the global economy.

Multinational Companies

The three types of business in the global economy are shown in Figure 11.2, along with their definitions.

Domestic Companies	*International Companies*	*MNCs*
conduct business in one country	based primarily in one country but transact business in other countries—imports and exports	have significant direct investment operations in more than one country

■ **Figure 11.2:** Types of Business in the Global Economy

Domestic. A *domestic company* conducts business in one country. There are more than 27 million businesses in the United States, and more than 99 percent are small businesses with less than 500 employees.[26] Most of them are domestic companies that compete with international and multinational companies. Many domestic companies are not importers, but they do buy and sell foreign products locally. A local mom-and-pop convenience store most likely sells Swiss Nestlé candy and other foreign products it buys from its local wholesaler. A local car dealership may sell Japanese Hondas or Toyotas that are made in America.

International. *An international company is based primarily in one country but transacts business in other countries.* Internationals are commonly in the import and export business. Pier 1 Imports was founded in 1962 as a single store in San Mateo, California. It continues to sell home furnishings imported from all over the world.[27] An increasingly popular way to go international is *outsourcing* work to foreign companies. Over the years, more products have been made overseas. The use of the Internet has also helped international companies. In its first month of business, U.S. Amazon.com recorded sales in all 50 states and exported books to 45 countries.[28]

The U.S. government supports globalization with its **Export-Import Bank (Ex-Im Bank**, www.exim.gov). Ex-Im Bank is the official export credit agency of the United States. Its mission is to assist in financing the export of U.S. products to international markets. Ex-Im Bank enables U.S. companies, large and mostly small, to turn export opportunities into real sales that help to maintain and create U.S. jobs and contribute to a stronger national economy.[29]

Multinational. MNCs are important in the global economy, and they can be a private company, such as family-owned **SC Johnson**; a cooperative, like **Land O' Lakes**; or a **Chinese** state-owned entity, like **Shanghai Automotive Industry**. *A multinational company (MNC) has significant direct investment operations in more than one country.* A direct investment refers to owning operating facilities in other countries. **Amazon.com** has expanded from international exporting to become MNCs. MNCs have no boundaries. In fact, **P&G** relocated its top executives of its global skin, cosmetics, and personal-care units from its Cincinnati headquarters to Singapore. **GE**, **Halliburton**, **DSM**, and **Rolls-Royce** also have business units in foreign countries.[30]

Bandai America Case Question 3: What type of international firm is Namco Bandai Holdings Inc.?

Namco Bandai Holdings Inc. is an MNC because it has significant direct investment operations in more than one country (United States and Canada) and conducts approximately 20 percent of its business outside of its home country, Japan. It has modified its products, to a certain extent, for the North American market and has subsidiaries in California and Ontario.

Personal and Professional Applications

5.   What type of global business is your current or former employer, and/or a business it deals with; who are its major competitors; and how does it compete in the global economy?

COMPARATIVE POLITICAL AND ECONOMIC SYSTEMS

Among the 200 countries in the global economy[31] you will find much diversity in government systems and laws, product and ethical standards, cultures and customs, and socio-economic systems. In this section we compare political and economic systems, including business ownership and government–business relations.

Political Systems

We discuss three primary political systems: democracy, single-party, and military dictatorship.

1.   **Democracy**. About 70 percent of countries are considered to have a *democracy*. According to the **UN** (www.un.org), a democracy has:[32]

■ Fair elections with multiple party candidates

■ Independent media with freedom of political speech without fear of censorship or punishment

■ Separation of powers among the legislative, executive, and judicial government branches

■ An open society with independent organizations pursuing social, religious, and cultural goals.

2. **Single-party**. *Single-party* government systems run by Communist parties exist in **China**, **Vietnam**, **Cuba**, and the **Democratic People's Republic of Korea** (North Korea). Single-party governments have been accused of not being especially forceful at stopping people from violating patent and copyright laws. For example, many more illegal copies of software, music, and movies, rather than legal ones, are found in these countries.

3. **Military dictatorships**. *Military dictatorships* rule by total power and exist in **Burma (Myanmar)**, **Sudan**, **Uzbekistan**, **Liberia**, and **Eritrea**. The UN estimates that 106 countries still limit important civil and political freedoms. The right of citizens to organize in support of cultural and religious goals is restricted in a number of Arab states including **Iran**, **Syria**, and **Saudi Arabia**.

Human Rights. Political systems affect human rights, which vary widely globally. Generally, democracies do a better job of protecting human rights than other forms of government. The **UN** developed the "Universal Declaration of Human Rights," which includes the right to a decent standard of living, free speech, religious freedom, due process amongst others. Over half of the countries have ratified all of the UN human rights covenants, but serious human rights violations still occur. The United States and other countries have stopped trading with some countries because of their human rights violations.

Activist **Amnesty International** (**AI**, www.amnesty.org) is a global watchdog societal interest group for internationally recognized human rights. AI is independent of any government, political ideology, economic interest, or religion. Within the context of its work to promote all human rights, it envisions a world in which every person enjoys all of the human rights enshrined in the Universal Declaration of Human Rights and other international human rights standards that seem to prevent and end grave abuses of the rights to physical and mental integrity, freedom of conscience and expression, and freedom from discrimination.[33]

Conflict of Interest. In the **United States**, laws prohibit government officials from having ownership of business and making any money from speaking or consulting with business. However, in most other countries, few or no laws address conflicts of interest. For example, in **Japan**, government officials can own stock in companies, they can give and receive lavish gifts, and officials can be hired as business consultants. In **China**, the single **Chinese Communist Party** (**CCP**) pretty much has the power to do what it wants because it runs the government, which has ownership of many business enterprises. The CCP selects industries to support with heavy investments.[34]

Economic Systems

Although the way in which assets are controlled differs among the various economic systems, most countries operate somewhere between the two extremes of the continuum. At one end is free enterprise, and at the opposite end is central state control.

Free enterprise allows anyone to start a business, with open markets and essentially no government regulation of business. Open markets let businesses and customers voluntarily transact business through selling and buying products. Democracy and free enterprise tend to go together. **U.S.** business is close to free enterprise, but clearly, as discussed throughout this book, government does regulate business. The **Heritage Foundation** (www.heritage.org) compiles an *Index of Economic Freedom* ranking in which the top category of "free" has five countries, with **Hong Kong**, **Singapore**, and **Australia** at the top. The **United States** ranks tenth in the "mostly free" category. **China** ranks in the mostly "unfree" category at 138. The lowest category, "repressed," includes **Cuba**, **Zimbabwe**, and **North Korea** at positions 177–179.[35]

Central state control does not allow, or limits, private ownership of businesses, and markets are closed because only the government operates all business. So the government owns the production, distribution, and place of sale of products. Central state control is often associated with military dictatorships and has not been very successful economically for the people of those nations. With the collapse of the **Communist Party** rule in the former **Soviet Union** and its satellites in **Eastern Europe**, only a few real central state control systems remain, with the **Democratic People's Republic of Korea** being an example.

China is a Communist country with central planning and control, but it does have a market economy.[36] With the strong growth in China, some suggest that the U.S. model is not the only plausible model to emulate.[37] Others state that China's model is working, so why democratize?[38] Yes, China will be the world's largest economy, but it still will only be about a fifth of the size of the U.S. economy on a per capita basis because the gross national product (GNP) has to be distributed over a much larger population. So it is far from inevitable that China will become the dominant country.[39] Thus, it is moving more toward free enterprise but not democracy.

Learning Outcome 2: Contrast U.S. business ownership and government–business relations with those in the EU, China, and Japan.

Business Ownership and Government–Business Relations

Business Ownership. Democracies are generally more open to capitalism with free enterprise. **North America**, **Japan**, **EU** countries, and **India** are primarily free enterprise countries. **China** is not as free because it does not allow any non-Chinese business ownership, only joint ventures between the Chinese government or business and the foreign company. Chinese businesses are also acquiring U.S. companies, for example the **Dalian Wanda Group** bought **AMC Entertainment Holdings** (with 5,000 movie screens) to move into the Hollywood movie business.[40]

The U.S. government generally does not own any business enterprises, does not have joint business ownership, and doesn't even invest in company stocks. Yet, it did make an exception and temporarily took partial ownership of some banks and insurance companies, including **Citigroup**, **JPMorgan Chase**, and **AIG** during the financial crises. **Fannie Mae** and **Freddie Mac** are mixed government and private ownership and have had problems, prompting calls for them to be one or the other.[41] Most other countries' governments, however, do engage in business ownership. The **Chinese** government's 100,000 or so state-owned enterprises (SOEs) use its favored status and ready access to cheap land, loans, and energy to become ever more powerful in their competition with Chinese businesses and joint ventures.[42]

Some countries control certain industries and allow others to be privately owned. For example, the **Nigerian** government owns the oil industry, but it also has foreign partners including **Chevron** and **Shell,** and still other industries are privately owned. The **French** government owns some large companies and is fighting foreign acquisition takeover bids.[43] **France**, **Great Britain**, **Germany**, and **Spain** formed a consortium that founded **Airbus Industries** by providing billions of dollars in ongoing government aid to finance the development of commercial airliners to compete with the U.S. civilian jet airliner businesses, **Boeing**, **Lockheed**, and **McDonnell Douglas**. Airbus has been successful

---

Personal and Professional Applications

6.   Give examples of government-owned business enterprises in the global economy.

---

at taking a good percentage of the market share away from Boeing, the only major U.S. manufacturer today.

Government–Business Relations. Governments interact differently with businesses globally. For example, generally, the **U.S.** government acts more like a referee by setting and enforcing the rules of business impartially; it has no conflict of interests or real business ownership. But in most other countries (including **Japan**, **China**, and **EU** countries), the government has ownership in business, making it partial to what happens to business, so it generally gives more help and subsidies to business. With Chinese SOEs with government subsidies and the certainty of government purchases, like in solar energy, some question whether U.S. firms can compete.[44]

The **Netherlands**, **Sweden**, **Norway**, and **Denmark** have close relationships between government and large business. The **Japanese** government has a close working relation-

---

Bandai America Case Question 4: What political, economic, business ownership, and government–business relations would Namco Bandai Holdings Inc. find in its home country?

Namco Bandai Holdings Inc.'s (NBH) home country is Japan—a country that has a democracy, is capitalistic, and allows free enterprise and business ownership. Yet, unlike the U.S. government, the Japanese government may have some ownership of NBH and has a close working relationship to help NBH penetrate foreign markets while protecting NBH at home against foreign competition.

---

ship with MNCs as it helps them penetrate foreign markets while protecting them at home against foreign competition. So governments are more often owners of business and allies to business than simple impartial referees in most countries.

INTERNATIONAL TRADE

We know business is global, but it is difficult to determine which countries to invest in abroad.[45] In this section, we discuss the economics of international trade, the politics of international trade, trade barriers, U.S. trade policy and law, and global business regulation.

The Economics of International Trade

Competitive theory holds that international trade is based on gains from trade. When one country cannot produce a product that its citizens want to consume, the country gains by importing the product from another country, which, in turn, gains by exporting. When both countries have a product the other wants, both gain through international trade. Even when one country is more efficient at producing both products, gains are realized through trade.[46] Gains from trade result from the competitive advantage of nations.

Competitive Advantage of Nations. The theoretical foundation for trade is based on David Ricardo's theory of comparative advantage. The phrase was popularized by Professor Michael Porter. *Competitive advantage of nations means that a country has a cluster of similar companies in industries that give the country a special advantage over other countries.* For example, Brazil is a world leader in coffee, Switzerland in chocolate, and Italy in quality shoes. Japan is strong in the electronics industry, and the United States leads in computer information systems and technology.

In essence, a country needs to determine what it does best and capitalize on producing to its strengths while relying on foreign companies to provide products in its weak areas. For example, the United States has high labor costs and is capital intensive; whereas China has less capital and is more labor intensive. Therefore, the United States should import textiles and clothes and export machinery and high-tech products to China. Although China makes Apple and other U.S. products, they prefer iProducts, Starbucks, and Nike over their domestic competitors.[47]

ETHICAL DILEMMA 11.1 British Royalty and the Naked Ugly Truth: Disrobing Zara International's Sweatshops in Bangladesh

Catherine, Duchess of Cambridge, looked stunning in her Zara dress when heading off to her weekend honeymoon, yet who would have thought that this dame of fashion would wear anything from a Spanish high-end chain store rather than a famous designer dress? Certainly CEO Pablo Isla Álvarez de Tejera[48] did!

When most people think of fashion, they typically think of either France or New York, considered to be fashion capitals. Nobody would think that a large clothing manufacturer would come out of another European country, Spain. Zara Espana is a trendy and fast growing fashion retailer that sells everything, including women's, men's, and children's clothing. They even sell plus size and maternity clothing to accommodate a larger target market. Zara currently operates about 1,485 stores in major cities worldwide, as well as more than 200 Zara Kids shops in some 75 countries. It has spread into Mexico and the United States, with some 50 shops in each country.[49]

Some of the major competitors that Zara faces in Europe and around the world include other popular fashion retailers such as El Corte Ingles, H&M, and Gap.[50] The main difference that helps Zara differentiate itself and concentrate more on marketing through advertising campaigns rather than outsourcing of manufacturing is that Zara focuses more on the manufacturing and production of its products. Zara chooses this option to avoid the trouble that other companies have experienced via sweatshop accusations and problems with production. Jeffrey Ballinger, a Harvard researcher stated, "Zara, on the other hand, has turned control over garment factories into a competitive advantage."[51]

"However, the company has lately been under fire for working conditions in Bangladesh, with allegations of sweatshop labor and a scandal involving the death of two workers in Bangladesh. [In January 2012] workers staged a walkout in Dhaka, Bangladesh, wanting compensation for the families of two workers who died in the stampede when a water heater exploded. The publicity has been less than happy for Zara International"[52] and less so the Duchess.

"The National Garment Workers' Association in Bangladesh, which works in partnership with War on Want, a British charity, is calling the Duchess on her choices and says she has ignored the conditions in which her 'budget' fashion is made. They say that the Duchess of Cambridge should call for fair compensation and lobby the British government to protect overseas workers.

However, it is exactly the kind of political work that the Duchess of Cambridge cannot, as a member of the royal family, get involved in. Direct lobbying is out, period, and advisors will understandably be working to ensure the Duchess isn't exploited, too. While the Duchess of Cambridge might, in future, be able to represent the British government in business relations overseas, the only stance she can reasonably make at this point is to pointedly not wear Zara clothing anymore."

Questions

1. What type of international firm is Zara?
2. Why might Zara want to globalize its operation?
3. What is its competitive advantage over other major international retailers?
4. What is the ethical dilemma facing CEO Pablo Isla Álvarez de Tejera of Zara International?
5. What would you do if you were CEO de Tejera?
6. What would you do if you were the Duchess of Cambridge? Her advisors?

Bandai America Case Question 5: What competitive advantage of its nation might Bandai be exploiting in its strategy?

Because Japan dominates the electronics industry, and entertainment in the twenty-first century is based on the use of technology (anime, movies, and computer games), Bandai is capitalizing on the reputation of its own and other technologically driven entertainment firms (Sony and Nintendo) to export a unique resource to the United States: a westernized and modernized twenty-first-century Japanese culture.

Personal and Professional Applications

7. Identify the competitive advantage of national industries of foreign products you buy.

The Politics of International Trade

Although we do need government, economic disasters don't generally come from flaws in the free enterprise market system. Problems generally come from government policy mistakes.[53] Let's discuss some issues that affect global business trade.

Conflicting Laws Between Countries. Difficulties facing MNCs are not only the different laws in each country but are also the conflicts in laws between countries. For example, the U.S. *Sarbanes-Oxley Act* directed companies operating in America to set up whistleblower hotlines for employees everywhere to confidentially report potential corporate abuse. However, in the EU and under its country data-protection laws, anonymous accusations are not allowed. Thus, which law should the MNC obey, and which should it violate?[54]

The Need for International Business Regulation. As governments try to create a level playing field for domestic business, they must also do the same in the global economy. Customers in the global economy routinely buy products from other countries. Imported products are required by law to meet domestic standards. So in addition to protecting society from domestic business, governments need to regulate international business. Governments work to protect consumers from dangerous products and domestic business from unfair foreign competition. At the same time, countries want to ensure that their exports also meet standards. To protect national security, some governments make it illegal to sell technology products that have military applications that could be used against them. Thus, governments cooperate to develop the rules of international business. Countries also cooperate to set standards for using or affecting global resources that are not owned by any nation: standards have been created for ocean fishing and protecting sea mammals (dolphins and whales), as well as protecting the global environment by limiting land, water, and air pollution.

> Learning Outcome 3: Discuss who benefits and who pays the cost of protectionism.

Free Trade vs. Protectionism. All countries can gain through international trade because the benefits of free trade outweigh the cost for the country as a whole—society and its consumers. Although the global economy is moving toward more free trade, it is mixed with protectionism because international trade policy is driven by domestic politics. Politics to protect special interests often overrule free trade.[55] Politics is often driven by other barriers to globalization including cultural issues, customs, infrastructure, and language.

The Cost of Protectionism. Isolationism and protectionism tend to go together.[56] Protectionism doesn't work in the long run. Part of the reason for the Great Depression was the massive protectionist trade bill *Smoot-Hawley Tariff Act* of 1930 that placed a tax on imports.[57] Protectionism leads to decreased efficiency in the utilization of the country's resources because they are directed toward industries that are not efficient in the global economy, taking some resources away from the industries that have competitive advantages.

Protectionism also results in higher prices paid by consumers, with fewer product choices, in those protectionist countries. A study estimated that protectionism costs consumers more than $70 billion per year, or approximately $280 for every American. About 45 percent of consumer cost goes to business as additional profits. Protectionism does save some jobs, which is a major concern of union employees, but it costs consumers an average of $54,000 per job.[58] So special interest business and its employees have greater incentives to seek government protection from foreign competition.

Supporters of tariffs claim they help save jobs at home. However, others disagree. For example, the Tire Industry Association (TIA, www.tireindustry.org) found that tariffs have not created any more American jobs, but they have hindered commerce. In 2009, the United States put tariffs of 25–35 percent on tires from China. Employment was at 55,000, but three years later it fell to 51,700. Tariffs also add to the cost in other industries, for example, tariffs on steel raised costs to U.S. car makers and other steel-consuming companies struggling to compete on a global scale.[59] Although unions are concerned about jobs staying in the United States, free trade actually increases total net employment in the long run without subsidizing local jobs. Employees who lose their jobs in inefficient firms and industries that can't compete globally find other jobs, and new jobs are created in those industries that have competitive advantages.

Personal and Professional Applications

8. Are you for free trade or protectionism, and how has it affected you?

9. Has a business you work(ed) for, or producers of the products it sells, sought protection from foreign competition?

Learning Outcome 4: Compare and contrast trade barriers and explain why they are not always successful.

Trade Barriers

Governments sometimes use public policy trade barriers to protect domestic industries, to provide subsidies to business, and to stimulate demand for domestic products. See Figure 11.3 for common trade barriers.

Subsidies	*Tariffs*	*Quotas*	*Bans and Restrictions*
government funds given to business to lower its costs	a tax on imports to make them more expensive	limits set on imports and export	prohibition of the import and export of products; or limits on business activity

■ **Figure 11.3**: Common Trade Barriers

1. **Subsidies.** *Trade subsidies are government funds given to a business to lower its costs.* The **U.S.** government has subsidized agricultural products for years as some farmers are paid not to grow crops to keep supply down and prices up. Recall that **EU** countries subsidized **Airbus** so that it could compete with **Boeing**.

2. **Tariffs.** *Tariffs are a tax on imports and exports to make them more expensive.* Tariffs are also called *duties*. Tariffs are commonly used to protect domestic business by giving them a price advantage or equalizing their price disadvantage. Tariffs are far more commonly placed on imports than exports, but tariffs are a means of increasing tax revenue and slowing exports under pressure and threats of quotas from other countries. The **United States** slapped tariffs on **Chinese** wind-power turbine towers and solar panels based on a complaint to the **Commerce Department** from **Solar-World** and six other firms.[60]

3. **Quotas.** *Trade quotas set limits on imports and exports.* Limiting imports decreases supply and increases prices, helping to stimulate demand for domestic products that may be more expensive. Limiting exports also helps domestic business keep prices down at home while increasing prices overseas. For example, **China** has quotas on exports of rare-earth metals (copper, iron).[61] The **EU** put quotas on **Chinese** imports; and when making the deal, its trade minister stated that managing trade by quotas is bound to fail because of unforeseen consequences and the costs of protectionism.[62]

4. **Bans and restrictions**. *Trade bans prohibit the import and export of products.* Bans are the strongest barrier and provide the greatest protection to domestic business. The **EU** bans the import of some **U.S.** foods and drugs. A few countries temporally prohibited the import of **U.S.** beef after problems within the industry.

    Some countries, including China, have been resistant to opening their markets to foreign firms, so they place restrictions on their activity.[63] For example, China severely restricted **U.S.** banking firms' (e.g., **Citigroup, JPMorgan Chase, Wells Fargo**, and **Bank of America**) operations within China. After spending $60 billion over the past decade on building and acquiring franchises, these global banks have only earned about $10 billion.[64] China state-owned banks have nearly 66,000 branches, whereas China only allows all foreign banks combined to have 387 branches.[65]

Most governments allow companies within their country to export to other countries; however, some nations may be excluded, such as the U.S. ban on exports to **Cuba**. The **United States** also bans the export of weapons and products that have military applications that could be used against America.

Personal and Professional Applications

10. Has a business you work(ed) for, or producers of the products it sells, benefited or been hurt by trade barriers?

Retaliation. Public policy to protect domestic business and jobs sounds good in theory. However, protection often leads to retaliation by the foreign country, offsetting the intended benefits.[66] The Chinese have no problem saying, "If you're going to hit us, we'll hit you back."[67] **China** put tariffs on imports of some **U.S.**–made cars in retaliation for U.S. trade policies.[68] The **EU** extended its tariffs on Chinese shoes, and the next day China announced tariffs on EU carbon-steel fasteners. The United States put tariffs on Chinese solar cells, and two weeks later China investigated U.S. support for renewable power. The United States imposed tariffs on Chinese tires, and China put tariffs on U.S. poultry products. **Japan**, EU, and the United States challenge China's rare-earth export quotas, and China imposed tariffs on stainless steel tubes from the EU and Japan and anti-dumping tariffs on photographic paper imported from the United States, EU, and Japan nine days later.[69] In essence, both countries often end up losing (often referred to as "the *prisoner dilemma*"). Typically, the best way out of the dilemma is to negotiate a deal to limit or drop the public trade policy in both countries.

Trade Surplus and Deficit. *A trade deficit occurs when a country imports more than it exports.* Due to trade barriers, the United States consistently has high trade deficits with other countries. A trade deficit places a strain on the domestic economy when the country sends funds to foreign countries to pay for the imports. Conversely, a trade surplus occurs when a country exports more than it imports, stimulating the domestic economy. **Japan**

and **China** are two major U.S. trade partners that, intentionally, consistently run large surpluses with the United States to gain economic advantages. Running trade deficits can lead to pressure on the government to make retaliation trade policies. In April 2012, the U.S. international trade deficit was $50.1 billion.[70]

Bandai America Case Question 6: If the United States wanted to protect companies such as Hasbro and Disney from increased competition from Bandai, what trade barriers might it employ?

If the U.S. government determined, due to our trade deficit with Japan, that the benefits of free trade did not outweigh the cost for the country as a whole in terms of lost jobs and tax revenues (and perhaps lost culture), it could subsidize U.S. entertainment and toy manufacturers, place a tariff on Japanese imports, establish quotas on imports, or ban imports altogether. The government, however, should expect retaliation from Japan, who might possibly invoke its own trade barriers, as well as a backlash from U.S. consumers who would be negatively affected by these new policies.

U.S. Trade Policy and Law

The U.S. Constitution gives Congress the power to regulate commerce with foreign nations and to set and collect tariffs. U.S. trade law enables private parties to initiate foreign trade. Recall that the president has the power to negotiate international trade agreements (Chapter 8). Members of Congress have been concerned about protecting their constituents' interests. Congress has amended the trade laws to make it easier to initiate action to open foreign markets to U.S. products, and it has also provided protection for some industries from foreign competition.

The Executive Branch. Cabinet departments, regulatory agencies, Congress, and the Office of the President are involved in the politics of international trade. The executive branch, primarily the Departments of the Treasury, State, and Commerce, has responsibility for administering trade policy. The **International Trade Administration (ITA**, www.trade.gov) of the Department of Commerce and the independent quasi-judicial federal agency the **International Trade Commission (ITC**, www.usitc.gov) administer certain aspects of trade law. They participate in developing trade policy, provide congressional testimony, lobby for their policy objectives and the interests they represent, and interact with businesses in other countries.

Although we have discussed the merits of free trade and the high cost of protectionism, helping domestic firms prosper amidst competition is sometimes warranted. The U.S. trade laws come primarily from the *Trade Act of 1974*. Here are just a few of the many trade laws that help business in the global economy.

Temporary Safeguards. They provide for temporary relief for domestic industries seriously injured by increased imports without the need to prove unfair trade practices. The objective of the law is to give companies some limited time to improve their competitiveness. The *Trade Adjustment Assistance Act* provides help for those injured by imports by providing retraining programs to find new jobs, but it is not awarded very often.

Retaliation. The U.S. president can take tariff, subsidy, and quota action against countries that restrict U.S. imports or subsidize exports to America. The United States can also retaliate against countries that violate U.S. patents, copyrights, or protected trade secrets.

Antidumping. "*Dumping*" refers to the act of exporting goods and services to foreign countries at very low prices, sometimes even below cost, in order to increase market share and potentially leading to putting competitors out of business and then raising prices. The antitrust fear is that MNCs will sell a product in the United States at a lower price to drive out U.S. competition and then raise the price.

Antidumping allows tariffs on products that are imported at a price that is less than fair value. Note that the price can be less than fair value (LTFV) but above cost, as antidumping protects domestic business from foreign, not domestic, competition. The *Commerce Department* of **ITA** and **ITC** investigate dumping charges. They found several **Chinese** solar-panel companies guilty of dumping (selling at below-market prices) and slapped 31 percent tariffs on their products.[71] Decisions can be appealed to the **World Trade Organization (WTO)** and **U.S. Court of International Trade** and, like other government decisions, to the **court of appeals**.

Bandai America Case Question 7: What previous actions by Bandai might change U.S. trade policy toward Japan and cause the president to impose sanctions and temporary safeguards to protect U.S. businesses?

Dumping is the exporting of goods and services to foreign countries at very low prices, sometimes even below cost, in order to put competitors out of business. Fans of the *Power Rangers* series have complained about Bandai America's allegedly dumping some of their inferior versions of Japanese toys when brought to the United States. If the United States can determine that these items are being sold in order to undercut competitors, the president may impose antidumping tariffs on products imported at a price that is less than fair value.

Personal and Professional Applications

11. Has a business you work(ed) for, or producers of the products it sells, been affected by dumping from foreign competition?

Global Business Regulations

You need to quantify the rule-of-law in a given country and analyze its impact on business.[72] In the international business world, uniform regulations of business globally are needed. Important areas are antitrust law and how to set effective global business regulations, and the G20 (Group of Twenty) works toward this end.

Antitrust Laws. Antitrust laws are commonly referred to as *competition policies* in the global economy. The **U.S.** government prosecutes foreign firms for antitrust violations in the United States, as do others to U.S. companies in their countries. Because it is a global leader, many countries cooperate with **U.S.** antitrust laws.[73]

Over the years, the **U.S.** government has allowed mergers of large companies and joint research so that business can compete in the global economy to strengthen the national competitiveness of the United States. But at the same time, the government helps the U.S. economy. Under the *National Cooperative Research Act (NCRA),* with the permission of the **U.S. attorney general** and **FTC**, competing companies can share information and cooperate in ways that would otherwise violate antitrust regulations. The U.S. government now allows complex collaborations between domestic and foreign firms, such as between **GM** and **Toyota** and **Ford** and **Mazda**.

The **EU** is stricter with allowing mergers, requiring more concessions, and it is easier to sue to stop mergers in the EU than in the **United States.** For mergers that would affect the United States and EU, both regulators must approve the merger. In fact, the **DOJ** approved a merger between **GE** and **Honeywell**, but the EU rejected the merger of two U.S. companies to compete in the EU because it would be a monopoly for some products. **Google** and **Facebook** have faced antitrust charges in court in **India**, and Google has had legal problems in the **EU** and **China** as well.[74] **Coca-Cola** has encountered antitrust problems and was forced to scale back its acquisition of **Cadbury Schweppes** in the **EU**, and **France** blocked it from acquiring *Orangina* from **Pernod Ricard**. China's *Commerce Ministry* blocked Coke from acquiring **China Huiyuan Juice Group**.[75] **China** has also severely limited **U.S.** banking in China.[76]

Bandai America Case Question 8: What business regulatory agencies would have overseen the merger of video game developer and producer Namco with Bandai Co. Ltd.?

In Japan, the antitrust authority is the Fair Trade Commission. However, in the United States, the U.S. attorney general and FTC would also have oversight on this merger because it affected the U.S. entertainment market. In Europe, the EU would have authority; it is stricter than the United States in allowing mergers, requires more concessions, and makes it easier to sue to stop mergers, given its focus on protecting competition.

Personal and Professional Applications

12. Has a business you work(ed) for, or producers of the products it sells, been affected by global regulations?

Effective Regulation. A major challenge for governments is to develop effective domestic laws that don't conflict with trading partners and to develop common laws among countries with limited trade barriers. Although some countries have agreed on competition policies and the trend is toward unified global regulation, no common and clearly enforceable set of global regulations has emerged. In fact, the **United States** and **EU**, which have their differences, are working together to try to get **China** to follow their trade laws rather than create its own new set of regulatory hurdles.[77]

A **World Bank** study recommended five major steps to effective global business regulation: (1) simplify and deregulate competitive market business; (2) focus on enhancing property rights; (3) expand the use of technology; (4) reduce court involvement in business matters; and (5) make reform a continuous process.[78]

G20. The **G20** (www.g20.org) works to coordinate policy and regulations among the countries to promote global economic and financial stability and sustainable growth. In more detail, the G20 is the premier forum for international cooperation on the most important aspects of the international economic and financial agenda. It brings together the world's major advanced and emerging economies. The G20 includes 19 country members and the EU, which together represent about 90 percent of global GDP, 80 percent of global trade, and two-thirds of the world's population. The finance ministers and central bank governors meet to discuss and achieve the following G20 objectives: (1) to coordinate policy between its members in order to achieve global economic stability and sustainable growth; (2) to promote financial regulations that reduce risks and prevent future financial crises; (3) to create a new international financial architecture.[79] For a list of the 20 members, visit www.g20.org.

INTERNATIONAL ORGANIZATIONS AND TRADE AGREEMENTS

In this section, we discuss three NGOs that help countries trade in the global economy (see Figure 11.4) by setting the rules of international trade; then we discuss trade agreements in Europe and the United States.

World Trade Organization (WTO)	*World Bank*	*International Monetary Fund (IMF)*
administers trade agreements, develops trade rules, and settles trade disputes between member nations	is a lending institution that provides loans and technical assistance to poor countries so that they can conduct trade in the global economy	keeps track of the global economy and the economies of member countries, lends to countries with balance of payments difficulties, and gives economic and financial policy advice

▪ **Figure 11.4:** Nongovernmental Global Organizations

Learning Outcome 5: Compare and contrast the World Trade Organization (WTO), World Bank, and International Monetary Fund (IMF).

The WTO

The WTO (www.wto.org) deals with the global rules of trade between nations. Its main function is to ensure that trade flows as smoothly, predictably, and freely as possible. The WTO is an organization for trade administration, a forum for governments to negotiate trade agreements, and place for them to settle trade disputes. It operates a system of trade rules. Essentially, the WTO is a place where member governments try to sort out the trade problems they face with each other. So *the World Trade Organization (WTO) administers trade agreements, develops trade rules, and settles trade disputes between member nations.* The WTO was born out of negotiations, and everything the WTO does is the result of negotiations. The WTO is located in Geneva, Switzerland, and it has 155 member countries that have agreed to follow its trade rules and can use its negotiating and other services. Its major functions[80] include administering WTO trade agreements; forum for trade negotiations; handling trade disputes; monitoring national trade policies; technical assistance and training for developing countries; and cooperation with other international organizations.

Think about it. If you were the president or a trade representative and you wanted to negotiate a trade agreement with another country, or countries, or you were having trade problems with a country, wouldn't it be nice to have the WTO involved in the negotiations? And doesn't it help you to have a global set of trade rules to follow for international trade?

The WTO has also been involved over the years with **U.S. Boeing** and **EU Airbus** and their charges of illegal government subsidization against each other.[81] The WTO has been actively involved in helping the **United States** and **China** settle trade complaints against each other.[82] Intellectual property rights, including copyright, patents, trademarks, brand names and logos, industrial designs, and trade secrets are protected and are included in the WTO dispute settlement system. *Piracy* in China, and other developing countries, has been a big problem for U.S. business, but **China's Public Security Bureau** is cracking down on it. Microsoft said a court in China convicted 11 people of manufacturing and distributing counterfeit software valued at $2 billion.[83]

The World Bank and IMF

The World Bank and IMF were both created at an international conference convened in Bretton Woods, New Hampshire, United States, in 1944. The goal of the conference was to establish a framework for economic cooperation and development that would lead to a more stable and prosperous global economy. Today, the IMF and the World Bank are institutions in the **UN** system. They share the same goal of raising living standards in their member countries. Their approaches to this goal are complementary, with the IMF focusing on macroeconomic issues and the World Bank concentrating on long-term economic development and poverty reduction.[84]

The World Bank. Not a bank in the ordinary sense, the World Bank (www.worldbank.org) is a unique partnership to reduce poverty and support development. With headquarters in Washington, DC, the World Bank has more than 100 offices worldwide managed by 188 member countries. It is actually comprised of two institutions: (1) the *International Bank for Reconstruction and Development (IBRD)* and (2) the *International Development Association (IDA)*. The IBRD aims to reduce poverty in middle-income and creditworthy poorer countries, while IDA focuses exclusively on the world's poorest countries.

The IBRD and IDA are part of a larger body known as the **World Bank Group** with three other organizations: (1) the *International Finance Corporation (IFC)* provides loans, equity, and technical assistance to stimulate private-sector investment in developing countries; (2) the *Multilateral Investment Guarantee Agency (MIGA)* provides guarantees against losses caused by noncommercial risks to investors in developing countries; and (3) the *International Centre for Settlement of Investment Disputes (ICSID)* provides international facilities for conciliation and arbitration of investment disputes.[85] So keeping it short, the *World Bank is a lending institution that provides loans and technical assistance to poor countries so that they can conduct trade in the global economy.*

IMF. The IMF (www.imf.org) is an organization of 188 countries with headquarters in Washington, DC, working to foster global monetary cooperation, secure financial stability, facilitate international trade, promote high employment and sustainable economic growth, and reduce poverty around the world. In short, *the International Monetary Fund (IMF) keeps track of the global economy and the economies of member countries, lends to countries with balance of payments difficulties, and gives economic and financial* *policy advice.* In detail, the IMF's fundamental mission is to help ensure stability in the international system. It does so in three ways:

1. The IMF keeps track of the global economy and the economies of member countries. It oversees the international monetary system, monitors the financial and economic policies of its members, and consults regularly with member countries, providing them with macroeconomic and financial policy advice.
2. The IMF lends to countries with balance of payments difficulties. This financial assistance is designed to help countries restore macroeconomic stability by rebuilding their international reserves, stabilizing their currencies, and paying for imports. The IMF also provides concessional loans to low-income countries to help them develop their economies and reduce poverty.
3. To assist mainly low- and middle-income countries in effectively managing their economies, the IMF provides practical guidance and training on how to upgrade institutions and design appropriate macroeconomic, financial, and structural policies.[86]

When providing loans and other assistance, both the World Bank and IMF impose strict requirements on member-country governments to ensure the correction of economic and financial problems and the ability to repay loans. They faced real challenges in helping **EU** countries (Greece, Spain) in 2011–2012, and worked with them to help keep the EU and eurozone together. Critics of the World Bank and IMF claim they don't always give good advice, and policies have led to problems, including in **Latin America**, **Russia**, **Turkey** and numerous other places. In the mid-1990s, **China** ignored U.S./IMF advice and is doing well today.[87]

Bandai America Case Question 9: Which world agency would handle a trade dispute between the United States and Japan if issues arose related to product dumping and imposing tariffs on Bandai products?

The *World Trade Organization (WTO)* administers trade agreements, develops trade rules, and settles trade disputes between member nations. The United States and Japan are members of the WTO and therefore may not discriminate against foreign products for any reason, under the most favored nation rule. Import restrictions are illegal unless their basis is proven scientifically, such as in the case of unsafe products. The WTO can and has imposed sanctions against countries and could do so if it determined that tariffs or bans are unjustified.

ETHICAL DILEMMA 11.2 Clean Up Your Act or Taxation without Representation? EU Emissions Trading Scheme and the International Airline Industry

The EU took the first steps in January 2012 to control carbon discharge of planes by non-EU members by imposing fines on those airlines that exceeded EU emission standards. "The Emissions Trading Scheme (ETS) creates permits for carbon emissions. Airlines that exceed their allowances will have to buy extra permits, as an incentive to airlines to pollute less. The number of permits is reduced over time, so that the total CO_2 output from airlines in European airspace falls. European officials say the scheme could force airlines to add between €4 and €24 ($5 to $29; £3 to £19) to the price of a long-haul trip, the AFP reports.

"Nations opposed to the EU's controversial carbon tax on airlines met in Washington aiming to come up with an alternative plan. Delegates meeting at the U.S. Department of Transportation are exploring an alternative global solution that would include the EU. China, India, Russia, and the United States are among the countries opposed to the EU scheme, which took effect on 1 January [2012]. The United States says the EU's unilateral action could lead to a patchwork system if other countries impose their own tax. International airlines will begin receiving bills in April 2013, after this year's carbon emissions have been assessed.

A U.S. Senate committee voted to move forward a measure that would make it illegal to comply with the EU law. [Meanwhile] airline industry groups called for the Obama administration to challenge the EU law's application to foreign carriers. A letter from Airlines for America (A4A) and the U.S. Chamber of Commerce urged the United States to file an action under the UN's aviation body, the International Civil Aviation Organization. The BBC's Kim Ghattas in Washington says the looming deadline to pay up and the prospect of a trade war next year may motivate the delegates in that city to find a way out of the impasse, though no breakthrough is expected this week.

American officials have warned the EU's unilateral action could lead to a patchwork system around the world if other countries start imposing their own tax. U.S. Transportation Secretary Ray LaHood has denounced the EU tax as 'a lousy policy, a lousy law,' saying the EU 'should have done it in a more collaborative way.'

The EU has refused to back down and has expressed frustration that opposing countries have not come up with a serious, alternative proposal. The European Commission says Europe would be willing to join a global scheme run by the International Civil Aviation Organization (ICAO) if it matches the targets set by the EU scheme."[88]

Questions

1. Which international organizations might have an interest in the EU's imposition of emissions standards and penalties? Why?
2. What is the nature of the complaint against the EU by the United States and other trading partners?
3. Why did the United States and other nations bring in the International Civil Aviation Organization to handle this situation?
4. What is the ethical dilemma facing President Obama? The EU?
5. What would you do if you were President Obama? The EU?
6. Is the EU being unfair in its trading practices with the United States and other foreign countries' airlines?

Learning Outcome 6: Describe the systems of free trade the EU has in common with the United States.

Trade Agreements

Trade agreements are designed to eliminate trade barriers to create free trade between countries and groups of countries. Here we discuss trade agreements in Europe and the United States.

The EU

As this text was being written, the EU had 27 countries with one acceding and five candidates seeking to join. The union provides a system of free trade between member countries by forming a political and economic trade union with a unified regional market by dropping trade barriers. The EU 27 created the largest trading agreement in the world with more than 500 million people and a GNP greater than that of the United States. Getting 27 countries to agree on trade issues is not easy, and some barriers to free trade remain. For a map showing the EU countries go to http://ec.europa.eu/enlargement/countries/index_en.htm.[89]

Europe has changed over the years to become more like the United States by having independent state/countries join together as one market, which is similar to the U.S. system of free trade between its states. The EU has three important systems that improve trade for member countries, and those who conduct business in the EU.

1. It has EU law (all countries must follow) and state law (each country/state has its own laws) similar to U.S. federal and state laws. A single EU legal system makes adjudication easier than it would be if dealing with 27 or more separate countries.
2. It has a common currency, the euro, similar to the U.S. dollar. The euro is the official currency of the *eurozone* (also called the European Monetary Union—EMU), which consists of 17 of the 27 member states of the EU. It is also the currency used by the *Institutions of the European Union*. The euro makes it much easier and less expensive to conduct business among countries for its members and for MNCs headquartered in other countries to conduct business in the EU, and it is also easier for tourists visiting multiple countries.
3. It has a central banking system under the European Central Bank (ECB), similar to the U.S. Federal Reserve, making financial transactions easier. The ECB arranged the conversion of the currencies of the eurozone members to the euro.

The United States. Under the *Executive Office of the President*, the Office of the **United States Trade Representative (USTR**, www.ustr.gov) has principal responsibility for administering U.S. trade agreements, which involves monitoring our trading partners' implementation of trade agreements with the United States, enforcing America's rights under those agreements, and negotiating and signing trade agreements that advance the president's trade policy.

The United States has free trade agreements in force with 18 countries: Australia, Bahrain, Canada, Chile, Colombia, Costa Rica, Dominican Republic, El Salvador, Guatemala, Honduras, Israel, Jordan, Korea, Mexico, Morocco, Nicaragua, Oman, Peru, and Singapore. President Obama signed a free trade agreement with Panama on October 21, 2011, but the agreement has not been implemented when this book was being written. The United States was also in negotiations of a regional Asia-Pacific trade agreement, known as the *Trans-Pacific Partnership (TPP)* Agreement with the objective of shaping a high-standard broad-based regional pact.

Two of the U.S. trade agreements combine some of the 18 countries. The **North American Free Trade Agreement (NAFTA)** among the United States, Canada, and Mexico links 450 million people producing $17 trillion worth of goods and services. Trade between the United States and its NAFTA partners has soared since the agreement. The **Dominican Republic–Central America–United States Free Trade Agreement (CAFTA-DR)** with five Central American countries (Costa Rica, El Salvador, Guatemala, Honduras, and Nicaragua) and the Dominican Republic is the first free trade agreement between the United States and a group of smaller developing economies.[90] For more information on U.S. trade agreements, visit the USTR at www.ustr.gov.

Other Countries. To learn more about trade agreements among other countries, visit http://en.wikipedia.org/wiki/Trade_agreement.

Personal and Professional Applications

13. How have you been affected by NAFTA?

14. How has a business you work(ed) for, or the producers of the products it sells, been affected by the EU and NAFTA?

ETHICAL ISSUES IN INTERNATIONAL BUSINESS

Recall that we discussed ethics in detail in Chapter 5. The same basic ethical concepts apply globally. However, here we expand ethics internationally. Differences in cultures, business practices, and laws among countries in the global economy create difficult moral, ethical, and legal problems for MNCs.[91] For example, as **Google** pushed into **China** and **India**, it had to meet higher levels of censorship.[92] To conduct business in some countries, businesses may find it necessary to make a variety of payments considered illegal in the United States. In this section, we discuss corruption, improving global business ethics, and global codes of ethics.

Learning Outcome 7: Compare and contrast grease payments, bribes, and offsets.

Corruption

Different countries have different standards—ranging from small bribes to outright extortion—when it comes to corruption,[93] making any universally accepted definition of corruption nearly impossible in the global economy. A few examples include giving questionable political contributions, misuse of company assets, kickbacks, protection money, secret price-fixing agreements, and insider dealings to gain business advantage. The big questions are: What corruptions are acceptable? How much is excessive? When do you pay and when do you refuse? Unfortunately, easy answers to these abuses of power are not available, but MNCs need to understand the nature of corruption in a given country[94] See Figure 11.5 for three types of corruption in the global economy.

Grease Payments. *Grease payments involve small amounts of money paid to employees to facilitate the conduct of business.* This type of payment is commonly given to lower-level employees to induce them to do their jobs sooner, faster, and better: for example, to expedite the processing of paperwork, mail, permits, licenses, distributing products; to get

Grease payments	Bribes	Offsets
small amounts of money paid to employees to facilitate the conduct of business, usually paid to lower-level employees	payments or "gifts" given to business and government officials for the purpose of getting or maintaining business, usually paid to high-level officials	government requirements to fund nonbusiness projects as a prerequisite to conducting business

■ **Figure 11.5:** Types of Global Corruption

products to customers; and other routine business transactions. Grease may also be called honest grafts, tokens of appreciation, contributions, and lubricating payments.

Grease is illegal in the United States, but it is considered acceptable in many countries as a legitimate cost for services rendered. These payments are seen as offsets to low salaries paid in foreign countries. For example, when a telephone installer asked for grease, the business manager refused to pay, so the worker left. The business manager visited the phone company and complained to a manager who responded by saying, "For a fee, I will look into this matter for you." Do you pay, go without a phone, or keep fighting corruption?

Bribes. *Bribes are given to business and government officials for the purpose of getting or maintaining business.* Bribes are commonly given to high-level officials to buy products, but they are also given to avoid taxes, to stop unfavorable government intervention, and to gain favorable treatment. Bribes are clearly unethical and illegal in the United States and in many other countries. But they are legal in some countries, and bribes do occur in the United States and other countries. Unfortunately, it is not always easy to tell the difference between a gift, grease, and a bribe.[95] Many companies are trying to stop bribes; for example, oil giants **Eni**, **Chevron**, and **Lukoil** launched probes of bribery payments to **Kazakhstan** customs officials based on a whistleblower's tip, which they could have ignored.[96]

Offsets. *Offsets are government requirements to fund nonbusiness projects as a prerequisite to conducting business.* For example, the **United Arab Emirates** pressed **Boeing**, **Northrop Grumman**, and **Lockheed** to spend millions of dollars to build a shipyard and medical centers and to clean up their oil spills in order to sell military hardware to the government.

The Cost and Consequences of Corruption. Although grease payments, bribes, and offsets are generally considered corrupt, they are committed and are even legal in some countries. *Extortion* is also present in some developing countries and it's a new challenge faced by MNCs. Corruption is the biggest problem for developing economies,[97] and unfortunately, corruption is pervasive and rampant.[98] Corruption costs businesses revenue and efficiency, as well as distorting competition and undermining antitrust laws. Corruption distorts government allocation of expenditures and its efficiencies of services, and it undermines political legitimacy. It also slows the development of a free market because it discourages the investments needed for economic progress.[99] Ultimately, corrupt dealings create extreme inequity—both in markets and in societies.[100]

The **World Bank** Institute estimated the global cost of bribes to be $1 trillion a year.[101] Corruption goes far beyond the petty palm greasing that is common globally. **India's** telecom ministry took $30 billion from various projects over the past few years. **Russians** revealed $4 billion fraud in a state-run company's trans-Siberian pipeline project. In **China** a minister overseeing the new high-speed rail network is accused of skimming $152 million and maintaining 18 mistresses.[102]

Personal and Professional Applications

15. Have you ever witnessed corruption on an international level or do you know someone who has? Explain the situation.

Improving Global Business Ethics

Clearly, business ethics is more complex at the global level when dealing with great diversity among nations, making it difficult to have universal codes of ethics. But the global economy is slowly agreeing on a common basis for such laws. One of the difficult things about stopping corruption is that government officials who make and enforce these laws are sometimes the ones who are committing corrupt acts; therefore, they have an incentive to continue the corruption. Public disclosure of corruption helps prevent and enforce laws, but in many countries, corrupt government officials control the media, and it is dangerous to accuse people in power of corruption.

Although it is difficult to overcome corruption, **Hong Kong** and **Singapore** virtually eliminated corruption in a generation. One of the best predictors of decreasing corruption is free enterprise with strong property rights. So this is a good starting point.[103] Here we discuss laws and organizations that are fighting to combat corruption; Figure 11.6 provides an overview of FCPA law and five organizations that fight corruption.

Foreign Corrupt Practices Act (FCPA)	U.S. law making payments to foreign government officials to assist in obtaining or retaining business illegal
U.S. Department of Justice (DOJ) **United Nations Global Compact**	Responsible for enforcing FCPA law Has *10 Principles* for corporate participants to follow
Organization for Economic Cooperation and Development (OECD)	Somewhat like the UN 10 Principles, the OECD has the *Guidelines for Multinational Enterprises,* which also fosters global business ethics
Transparency International (TI)	Works so government, politics, business, civil society, and the daily lives of people are free of corruption; measures corruption with three indexes
Social Accountability Accreditation Services (SAAS)	Gives *SA8000* accreditation that certifies compliance with social standards for ethical working conditions

■ **Figure 11.6:** Law and Organizations that Fight Corruption

FCPA and DOJ. To help improve global business ethics, Congress passed the *Foreign Corrupt Practices Act* (FCPA) of 1977 and amended it in 1998 to clarify the original act to some extent. Under the FCPA, making payments to foreign government officials to assist in obtaining or retaining business is illegal. Grease payments are not illegal when conducting international business, but bribes are. It is illegal to offer compensation to anyone (either foreign or domestic) if it is known that any or all of the bribe will be used to influence a foreign official, politician, or political party. The law also requires accounting practices that reveal accurate and fair transactions. FCPA specifies a series of fines and prison terms for violations.[104] The problem is that it is not always easy to tell the difference between grease and bribes.[105] Thus, the courts often have to make the distinction.

The **Department of Justice (DOJ**, www.justice.gov) is cracking down on foreign bribery by enforcing FCPA. At least 120 companies, including **Sun Microsystems** and **Royal Dutch Shell**, are under review. Companies are working to figure out whether they are at risk of violating FCPA laws.[106] **Walmart** disclosed that it was voluntarily internally investigating whether some of its workers violated FCPA laws.[107]

The UN. The **United Nations Global Compact** (www.unglobalcompact.org) is a strategic policy initiative for businesses that are committed to aligning their operations and strategies with 10 universally accepted principles in the areas of human rights, labor, environment, and anticorruption. With more than 8,700 corporate participants and other stakeholders from 130 or more countries, it is the largest voluntary corporate responsibility initiative in the world. Principle 10 states that "businesses should work against all forms of corruption, including extortion and bribery."[108]

The OECD. The **OECD** (www.oecd.org) promotes policies that will improve the economic and social well-being of people around the world. Its headquarters are in Paris, **France,** and it has 34 member countries. It also has the *OECD Guidelines for Multinational Enterprises,* which contains far-reaching recommendations for responsible business conduct that 44 adhering governments—representing all regions of the world and accounting for 85 percent of foreign direct investment—encourage their enterprises to observe wherever they operate, which foster global business ethics.[109]

TI. TI (www.transparency.org) has a vision of a world in which government, politics, business, civil society, and the daily lives of people are free of corruption. TI works with these groups to put effective measures in place to tackle corruption. Now present in more than 100 countries, the movement works relentlessly to stir the world's collective conscience and bring about change.

The level of corruption varies globally, and TI measures corruption through three indexes to put pressure on corrupt countries to change their ways. The *Corruption Perception Index (CPI)* ranks countries for corruption. The vast majority of the 183 countries and territories assessed score below 5 on a scale of 0 (highly corrupt) to 10 (very clean). **New Zealand**, **Denmark**, and **Finland** top the list, while **North Korea** and **Somalia** are at the bottom. The *Global Corruption Barometer* surveys more than 100,000 people in 100 countries and territories, making it the only worldwide public opinion survey on corruption. The *Bribe Payers Index (BPI)* ranks the world's wealthiest countries by the propensity of their firms to bribe abroad and looks at which industrial sectors are the worst offenders. Rankings on these indexes and other research can be found at www.transparency.org.

Much remains to be done to stop corruption, but much has also been achieved, including the creation of international anticorruption conventions, the prosecution of corrupt leaders and seizures of their illicitly gained riches, national elections won and lost on tackling corruption, and companies held accountable for their behavior both at home and abroad.[110]

SAAS. SAAS (www.saasaccreditation.org) accredit and monitor organizations' compliance with social standards, including the Social Accountability *AS8000* standard for ethical working conditions. SAAS is structured and operates as an accreditation body. It manages and directs accreditation activities, including the granting, maintaining, extending, reducing, suspending, and withdrawing of accreditation for applicable social standards and verification codes, such as SA8000 and InterAction.[111]

Personal and Professional Applications

16. Does a business you work(ed) for, or producers of the products it sells, follow the global guidelines of the OECD and/or UN? Is it SA8000 certified?

17. Has a business you work(ed) for, or producers of the products it sells, been pressured by activist societal interest groups to change its business practices in another country?

Global Codes of Ethics

We have discussed global ethical standards set by the OECD, UN, and SAAS international organizations. Other global guides exist as well; visit **Good Money** at www.goodmoney.com/directry_codes.htm for a list of others. Each MNC can choose to voluntarily follow the guidelines. But in any case, each MNC has to determine its own code of conduct.

Ethical Quandary. As discussed in Chapter 4, most MNCs have codes of ethics for dealing with stakeholders while conducting business at home in the United States. For operations in other countries, they must decide whether to use the domestic (U.S.) ethics globally or to follow the foreign country's ethical standards, which are usually lower. Should employees, customers, suppliers, competitors, communities, environments, and governments be treated the same or differently at home and abroad? Sweatshops with poor health, safety, and working conditions are illegal in the United States, but not in many countries. So should the firm operate them overseas, and should it buy products from sweatshops to keep costs and prices down?

Ethical Imperialism vs. Cultural Relativism. *Ethical imperialism* says yes to MNCs using the ethical standards that they use in the United States for their global operations as well, because it is the ethically and socially responsible thing to do. However, *cultural relativism* says not to do this, because no culture's ethics are better than any others—there is no global right or wrong. The United States should not impose its ethical values on other countries and get them to stop their corrupt methods of conducting business. Who should determine what is considered corrupt anyway? Cultural relativists say that MNCs should follow the local cultural values and ethics of conducting business.

As with political systems, the two ethics perspectives are on the opposite ends of a continuum with most MNCs operating between the two extremes and following the adage, "Think globally; act locally." Many MNCs have no national boundaries tying them to only one set of ethical standards. MNCs may be more likely to exploit workers and the environment where the standards are lower. On issues such as health and safety, the MNC may be more likely to use global standards, but not for pay.

Personal and Professional Applications

18. Are you more in favor of ethical imperialism or cultural relativism? Where along the continuum would you place your sentiment?

Ethical Impact Statements and Audits. MNCs that are SA8000 certified and others are concerned about their impact on society globally. *Ethical impact statements assess the underlying moral justification for businesses' actions and the consequences of those actions.* Statements are developed through audits as a method of measuring company influence, and policy changes can result in ethical performance improvement. They usually appear in the annual report. For example, the **Mattel** toy company developed a monitoring system with an independent panel of commissioners that assesses the impact of its manufacturing facilities and contractors for annual audits. Based on audits, Mattel stopped doing business with three contractor facilities, one in **Indonesia** and two in **China**, for violating its *Global Manufacturing Principles* regarding underage workers and safety. **Gap** dropped contracts with 136 factories for violating its global standards.

Personal and Professional Applications

19. Does a business you work(ed) for, or the producers of the products it sells, conduct audits and develop ethical impact statements?

Global Ethics Code Trend. As already discussed, the global economy is slowly moving in the direction of global ethics because it makes conducting business easier when the standards are the same. Also, societal advocates support this trend as they pressure business and government for global standards. In fact, many MNCs have developed global codes of conduct, often as international sections, including **Allis Chalmers**, **Chiquita**, **Caterpillar**, **Johnson's Wax**, and **Rexnord**. However, they have been criticized because, in trying to be universal, they are usually too general, without providing the details necessary to know how to operate ethically in many countries.

Bandai America Case Question 10: Gift giving is a long-honored tradition in Japan. What type of corruption might gift giving be construed as, and what organizations would monitor gift giving in Bandai's U.S. subsidiary?

Gift giving to lower-level employees in order to get work completed in a timely manner may be construed as grease payments while gifts given to high-ranking government officials and top-level executives would be interpreted as bribes. This situation poses an interesting conundrum for Bandai America because the MNC firm is based in Japan yet the subsidiary operates in the United States. Ethical imperialism would, therefore, apply Japanese standards in the United States while cultural relativism would apply stricter U.S. standards.

Global ethical standards are set by agencies such as the OECD, UN, and SAAS, and each MNC has the choice to voluntarily follow the guidelines. The U.S. Congress passed the Foreign Corrupt Practices Act (FCPA) of 1977 and amended it in 1988 to clarify the original act to some extent. Under the FCPA, grease payments are not illegal when conducting international business, but bribes are. This law may apply to the U.S. subsidiary but not the holding company. The holding company must determine its own code of conduct for the entire organization, including its international subsidiaries, within the context of differing laws and cultural norms.

Personal and Professional Applications

20. Does a business you work(ed) for, or the producers of the products it sells, have a global code of conduct?

BUSINESS NONMARKET AND MARKET STRATEGIES AND ETHICS

The business market and nonmarket environments are different throughout the global economy as cultures vary.[112] Understanding and dealing with the differences is important in formulating both market and nonmarket strategies and integrating them. As products are adapted to local taste, nonmarket strategies must adapt to the issues, interests, incentives, and information to develop interaction strategies (5 Is analysis).

The strategies we discussed in Chapters 1–10 are the same strategies used in companies operating globally, except grease payments are not legal in the United States. However, strategies do vary in importance based on the country. **China** provides great market opportunities, but it also requires the careful integration of nonmarket strategies.[113] One other strategy that combines market and nonmarket strategies is direct investment; many MNCs and other businesses make direct investments in other countries to bypass trade barriers, such as in **China** with Chinese partners.

Information Strategies

When conducting business in other countries, communications strategies are critical to successfully marketing products. Many MNCs have learned this the hard way. For example, **Chevy** was surprised that its Nova car did not sell well in Mexico, until it later found out that nova means "no go" in Spanish. To gain trust, which is more difficult when conducting business in other countries, open and honest communications are essential. It is important to communicate ethical awareness, based on a strong ethics code, and to implement the code[114] as discussed in Chapter 5, but on a global scale.

It is essential to have outside local sources, research, expert testimony, and stakeholder support backed with facts and figures. One challenge for MNCs is implementing information strategies that facilitate sharing manager knowledge and practices among their various divisions or groups across nations and subcultures.[115]

Societal Strategies

Although ethics do vary globally, MNCs' management from the top level down must pursue market opportunities and compete in an ethically and socially responsible manner wherever they conduct business in the global economy.[116] Although complex, business leaders are responsive to stakeholders and trying to balance their interests with the business interest.[117] Many MNCs are striving to improve the quality of life globally.[118]

Many MNCs use the grand strategy of working with activists to gain community public sentiment for being ethically and socially responsible locally. MNCs are going beyond international law to provide humanitarian help. For example, **Starbucks** paid above-market price for coffee, with the extra money going to improve the lives of coffee workers. Being socially responsible tends to lead to positive media relations that fuel positive public sentiment for companies.

MNCs need to be prepared to deal with activists on a global level, but activists vary by country, requiring some variations in dealing with them. However, in some countries, local activists don't exist. Chinese law requires foreign firms to allow organized labor, but **Walmart** has resisted unions in the 15 countries it operates in, so Walmart is fighting union activists.[119] MNCs also use global coalitions.

Even though U.S. consumers pay the cost of protecting U.S. businesses and jobs, they are not aware of the cost of protectionism, so it would be difficult to implement a grassroots strategy to organize consumers to fight for free-trade policies. On the other side, unions are concerned about losing U.S. jobs, and they are well organized to fight for protectionism. Industries with large numbers of employees (such as the auto, farming, steel, sugar, and textile industries) have been successful at pressuring the government to provide protection to businesses to keep their jobs at home.

Political Strategies

Gaining access to foreign markets often takes time as it involves developing relationships with government officials to get them to break down trade barriers and open their markets, but the patience strategy might eventually pay off. To speed access, many MNCs develop alliances with local firms. Appealing to the U.S. government for help in gaining access to foreign markets has also helped decrease the time it takes to develop global business. With the help of the U.S. government, **Motorola** gained fast access to the Japanese market to sell telecommunications and semiconductor products.[120] **ExxonMobil**'s CEO must play the diplomat to extract oil that is under the control of sovereign governments in politically dicey places.[121]

Successful MNCs with access to markets tend to deal with foreign governments by working with them as their grand strategy. Depending on the form of government, lobbying, campaign contributions, grassroots, coalitions, and testimonies are commonly used nonmarket strategies. MNCs tend to belong to global and local business societal interest groups for support, especially in the **EU**. Lobbying is the primary nonmarket strategy used to convey information strategies to influence EU institutions, and, as in the United States, lobbying early in the government process is important. **Philips Electronics** has been one of the most active and successful lobbyists in the EU, gaining trade barriers against **Japanese** and **South Korean** products. Peak business interest groups are especially important in the EU, some 3,000 of them that employ 10,000 lobbyists, double the number in 1990. Building coalitions is also important in the EU.[122]

Strong stakeholder relationships are critical to success in many countries, including **Japan** and **China**.[123] In fact, the Chinese manage their transactions by personal and social relationships; not primarily by legal processes.[124] So global executives need a relational perspective.[125] **Johnson & Johnson** was patient, and Tylenol was finally sold in **Japan** 45 years after its introduction in the United States. As discussed, U.S. banks, including **Citigroup** are patiently working their way into **China**.

Legal Strategies

Legal strategies vary based on the type of government, but MNCs commonly operate within the law to avoid lawsuits. However, they can be sued by individuals, businesses, and government based on foreign law. Lawsuits are more common in some countries than in others. For example, **Japan** tends to like harmony and to settle differences without lawsuits and has one lawyer for every 9,290 citizens, compared to one for every 360 people in the United States. **EU** MNCs are less likely to engage the government in open confrontation and take issues to court than are companies in the United States.

In **China**, it is difficult to go to court, and the court system is not a separate branch of government as it is in the United States. The highest court is the *Supreme People's Court*, which is essentially run by the *Chinese Communist Party (CCP)*. China joined the WTO in 2001, requiring it to open major industries to imports and foreign investment and to strengthen legal protection of foreign MNCs in China, similar to other WTO members.[126] However, it is opening some markets very slowly in selected industries, such as banking.

Government policies and regulations establish the ground rules for conducting business internationally, which clearly influence business market and nonmarket strategies.[127] As this chapter illustrates, managing in a global economy is highly complex.

Bandai America Case Question 11: What nonmarket strategies might Bandai America employ against the American Family Association to combat its attack on Japanese anime characters, game cards, games, and story lines?

Bandai America must be prepared to deal with activists on a global level and therefore employ informational, societal, political, and legal strategies to protect its international economic interests. More specifically, Bandai must dispute AFA's claims that its products promote eastern philosophies, the occult, and mysticism through research, expert testimony, and gaining stakeholder support. Bandai must also reach out to the news media, rights activists, consumer groups promoting anime and game playing, and the community to build a coalition of organizations that support these types of entertainment. Bandai must also solicit political support by working with politicians (lobbying, giving donations, seeking grassroots support, coalition building, and testifying at hearings) and its U.S. business interest groups to counterattack the AFA. Lastly, Bandai must operate in a way to avoid lawsuits (e.g., do not give gifts to government officials) and be prepared to sue the AFA if necessary.

Personal and Professional Applications

21. Discuss the strategies used by a business you work(ed) for, or the producers of the products it sells.

SUMMARY

The chapter summary is organized to answer the learning outcomes for Chapter 11.

1. **Compare and contrast the types of businesses in the global economy.**

   The three types of businesses in the global economy are domestic, international, and multinational. They are similar in that they all compete for business in the global economy. However, a domestic company conducts business in one country. Many buy and sell foreign products locally. An international company is based primarily in one country but transacts business in other countries. Internationals are commonly in the import and export business. A multinational company (MNC) has significant direct investment operations in more than one country.

2. **Contrast U.S. business ownership and government–business relations with those in the EU, China, and Japan.**

   The U.S. government generally does not own any business enterprises, does not have joint business ownership, and doesn't even invest in company stocks. However, the EU, Chinese, and Japanese governments do engage in business ownership. Generally, the U.S. government acts more like a referee by setting and enforcing the rules of business impartially; it has no conflicts of interests. But in the EU, China, and Japan, the government has ownership in business, making the government sensitive to what happens to business, and it generally gives more help and subsidies to business. So EU, Chinese, and Japanese governments are more like allies with business than like referees as in the United States.

3. **Discuss who benefits and who pays the cost of protectionism.**

Protectionism benefits special interest business and its employees by providing profits and jobs that may have been lost through foreign competition. Society pays the cost of protectionism through decreased efficiency in the allocation and utilization of the country's resources by providing resources to inefficient industries while taking resources away from the industries that have competitive advantages. Consumers pay higher prices, with fewer product choices, to finance business profits and employee wages.

4. **Compare and contrast types of trade barriers and explain why they are not always successful.**

Trade barriers are similar because they protect domestic business from foreign competition so that domestic products can compete with imports. However, how the trade barrier protects business varies. *Subsidies* are government funds given to business to lower its cost. *Tariffs* are a tax on imports and exports, making them more expensive. *Quotas* set limits on imports and exports, driving up product prices. *Bans* prohibit the import or export of products. Trade barriers are not always successful because they result in increased costs to consumers or retaliation from the foreign country via their own trade barriers that offset the benefits.

5. **Compare and contrast the World Trade Organization (WTO), World Bank, and International Monetary Fund (IMF).**

The WTO, World Bank, and IMF are all similar in that they are all nongovernmental organizations that assist free trade in the global economy. However, they each do so in different ways. The WTO administers trade agreements, develops trade rules, and settles trade disputes between member nations. The World Bank is a lending institution that provides loans and technical assistance to poor countries so that they can conduct trade in the global economy. The IMF acts as a monitor of global currency exchange by helping to maintain a system of payments between all countries. Thus, the WTO sets and enforces trade rules without providing any financial services. The World Bank provides loans to poor countries, and the IMF provides currency exchange services and loans to help with the balance of payments between countries to pay for trade.

6. **Describe the systems of free trade that the EU has in common with the United States.**

The three systems of free trade the United States and the EU have in common are as follows. The EU has its laws (all countries must follow) and state law (each country/state has its own laws) similar to U.S. federal and state laws. The EU has a common currency, the euro, similar to the U.S. dollar. The EU has a central bank system under the European Central Bank (ECB), similar to the U.S. Federal Reserve.

7. **Compare and contrast grease payments, bribes, and offsets.**

Grease payments, bribes, and offsets are similar because, from a U.S. point of view, they are all generally considered to be acts of corruption. The acts of corruption are different. Grease payments involve small amounts of money paid to employees to facilitate the conduct of business, usually paid to lower-level employees. Bribes are given to business and government officials for the purpose of getting or maintaining business, usually paid to high-level officials to buy products. Offsets are government requests to fund nonbusiness projects as a prerequisite to conducting business. All three are considered illegal in the

United States. However, under U.S. law, grease payments are not considered illegal in foreign countries. Some countries do not believe any of these acts are corrupt, so they are legal in these countries.

8. **Fill in the blank with the appropriate key term (in order of appearance in the chapter).**

_____ is the integration of national economies into one global economy.

_____ is based primarily in one country but transacts business in other countries.

_____ has significant direct investment operations in more than one country.

_____ allows anyone to start a business, with open markets, and there is essentially no government regulation of business.

_____ does not allow, or limits, private ownership of business, and markets are closed because only the government operates all business.

_____ means that a country has a cluster of similar companies in industries that give the country a special advantage over other countries.

_____ are government funds given to business to lower its cost.

_____ are a tax on imports and exports to make them more expensive.

_____ set limits on imports and exports.

_____ prohibit the import and export of products.

_____ occurs when a country imports more than it exports.

_____ allows tariffs on products that are imported at a price that is less than fair value.

_____ administers trade agreements, develops trade rules, and settles trade disputes between member nations.

_____ is a lending institution that provides loans and technical assistance to poor countries so that they can conduct trade in the global economy.

_____ keeps track of the global economy and the economies of member countries, lends to countries with balance of payments difficulties, and gives economic and financial policy advice.

_____ involve small amounts of money paid to employees to facilitate the conduct of business.

_____ are given to business and government officials for the purpose of getting or maintaining business.

_____ are government requirements to fund nonbusiness projects as a prerequisite to conducting business.

_____ assess the underlying moral justification for business actions and the consequences of those actions.

KEY TERMS (IN ALPHABETICAL ORDER)

antidumping (p. 434)
bribes (p. 442)
central state control (p. 426)
competitive advantage of nations (p. 428)
ethical impact statements (p. 445)
free enterprise (p. 426)
globalization (p. 420)
grease payments (p. 441)
international company (p. 423)

International Monetary Fund (IMF) (p. 437)
multinational company (MNC) (p. 424)
offsets (p. 442)
tariffs (p. 431)
trade bans (p. 432)
trade deficit (p. 432)
trade quotas (p. 432)
trade subsidies (p. 431)
World Bank (p. 437)
World Trade Organization (WTO) (p. 436)

KEY TERMS

11

REVIEW QUESTIONS

1 What forces have contributed to globalization?

2 What is the competitive advantage of nations?

3 How is the meaning of "Made in America" blurred?

4 What are the three types of businesses in the global economy?

5 Should the U.S. government get rid of its strict conflict of interest rules to be more like Japan?

6 Is free enterprise or central control the better economic system?

7 What is competitive theory and competitive advantage of nations?

8 What are the four commonly used trade barriers?

9 Which two major U.S. trade partners intentionally and consistently run large surpluses with the United States to gain economic advantages?

10 Which country is at an advantage and disadvantage with an imbalance of trade between countries? Be sure to explain a trade surplus and deficit.

11 Which two U.S. government agencies are primarily responsible for international trade law?

12 What are other common terms for the U.S. words *tariffs* and *antitrust*?

13 What are the two unique development institutions owned by World Bank members?

14 Has the EU helped or hurt trade with the United States?

15 What are FCPA, OECD, UN, and SAAS acronyms for, and what is the goal of these organizations?

16 What major contribution does Transparency International (TI) make to reducing global corruption?

17 What is the difference between ethical imperialism and cultural relativism?

DISCUSSION/CRITICAL THINKING QUESTIONS

Be sure to give a detailed explanation for your answer to each question.

1 Are the arguments for or against globalization more convincing?

2 Should the U.S. government start or acquire some business enterprises?

3 Should the U.S. government buy business stock as an investment, such as by putting social security funds into the stock market?

4 Should the U.S. government change its relations with business to being less of a referee and more of an ally with business?

5 Do the benefits of protectionism outweigh the costs?

6 Should the U.S. government protect domestic business against foreign companies that sell products for less than their fair value but are priced above their cost, as is allowed with domestic competition?

7 Has NAFTA helped or hurt the United States?

8 Should grease payments, bribes, and offset payments be made illegal by all countries?

9 Should the U.S. government require all major MNCs to conduct global audits and make ethical impact statements?

APPLICATION EXERCISES

11.1 WORLD QUIZ[128]

Answer the following 10 questions.

1 How long did the Hundred Years War last? _____

2 Which country makes Panama hats? _____

3 From which animal do we get cat-gut? _____

4 In which month do Russians celebrate the October Revolution? _____

5 What is a camel's hair brush made of? _____

6 The Canary Islands in the Pacific are named after what animal? _____

7 What was King George VI's first name? _____

8 What color is a purple finch? _____

9 Where are Chinese gooseberries from? _____

10 What is the color of the black box in a commercial airplane? _____

Answers to The World Quiz Passing requires only 4 correct answers
1. 116 years; 2. Ecuador; 3. sheep and horses; 4. November; 5. squirrel fur; 6. dogs; 7. Albert; 8. crimson; 9. New Zealand; 10. Orange.

11.2 EXPORT-IMPORT BANK (EX-IM BANK)

Visit www.exim.gov to find out more information that relates to your career, or select things of interest to you. Report on at least three new things that you learned.

11.3 ITA AND ITC

Visit www.trade.gov and/or www.saasaccreditation.gov to find out more information that relates to your career or select things of interest to you. Report on at least three things.

11.4 WTO

Visit www.wto.org to find out more information that relates to your career or select things of interest to you. Report on at least three things.

11.5 UN, OECD, TI, AND/OR SAAS

Visit one or more of their websites to find out information that relates to your career or select things of interest to you. Report on at least three things.

CASE 11.1

Trying to Slay the Dragon: Foreign Banks Hit the China Wall

"Walt Disney Co. (DIS) had little trouble raising money for its $4.4 billion Shanghai theme park after winning approval in 2009, as a dozen Chinese banks offered $2 billion in loans and promised more. Foreign lenders, limited in how much funding they can provide [by the Chinese government], watched from the sidelines. The deal size was beyond their reach.

Five years after China said it fully met World Trade Organization obligations to open its economy to global financial firms, Citigroup Inc. (C) and HSBC Holdings Plc (HSBA) are among companies still largely shut out of the world's third-biggest banking market as they face government restrictions on adding branches and offering products. Foreign banks hold less than 2 percent of assets in China, the lowest share among major emerging markets, according to the International Monetary Fund.

'China is a huge market, but it's also a hard one to crack,' said Liu Yuhui, director of financial research at the government-backed Chinese Academy of Social Sciences in Beijing. 'Being huge means that you have to plow in billions and billions to build the franchise and customer base from scratch, not to mention that China's banking market is highly regulated and well-entrenched by big state-owned players.'

Global banks, long gung-ho on the promise of growth in a nation of 1.3 billion people, have struggled to expand retail and investment-banking businesses after spending $60 billion in the decade since China joined the WTO and said it would open its markets. Obstacles to building branch networks have made it difficult to gather deposits and issue loans. Restrictions on stock and bond sales have thwarted investment banks, including Goldman Sachs Group Inc. (GS) and France's BNP Paribas SA (BNP).

At the same time, state-owned banks such as Industrial & Commercial Bank of China Ltd., the largest in the world by market value, have been transformed from almost insolvent institutions into profitable firms with the help of more than $650 billion in government bailouts. That has forced global lenders to retool their China strategies. 'Foreign banks have been over-optimistic about their business outlook in China,' Ivan Li, deputy head of research at Kim Eng Securities Hong Kong Ltd., said in an interview. 'They can't make good money in China as the market is dominated by Chinese lenders.'

Overseas banks have 387 branches in China compared with about 66,600 operated by the five largest state-owned lenders. They held just 1.6 percent of the nation's 83 trillion yuan ($13 trillion) of deposits and made 1.7 percent of its 58 trillion yuan in loans as of December 31 [2011], according to the China Banking Regulatory Commission.

Foreign banks typically account for almost 50 percent of deposits, loans, and profits in emerging markets, according to the IMF. They hold 22 percent of banking assets in Brazil and 5 percent in India. In the United States, the figure is 18 percent. Global banks combined have earned about $10 billion in China over the past decade after spending $27 billion to build their franchises and $33 billion to buy stakes in local lenders, data compiled by the banking regulator show.

They've also missed out on a surge in lending over the past three years accounting for 45 percent of the nation's total outstanding loans denominated in yuan. China's banking system, with 114 trillion yuan in assets, is larger than the 30 other emerging markets tracked by Fitch Ratings combined and smaller than only the United States and Japan. 'Foreign banks have pretty much sat out a once-in-a-lifetime expansion opportunity in China,' said Liu, the Chinese Academy of Social Sciences researcher, who blames their lack of scale and relationships. Among the four largest U.S. banks, Citigroup is the only one building a retail-banking network. . . . HSBC, Bank of East Asia Ltd., Standard Chartered Plc (STAN), Hang Seng Bank Ltd., Citigroup, and DBS Group Holdings Ltd. (DBS), the six biggest foreign banks in China by number of branches, had fewer than 1 million retail customers combined, compared with 260 million account holders at ICBC alone, according to a June 2011 survey by PricewaterhouseCoopers LLP. . . .

China had promised in December 2006, five years after joining the WTO, to remove geographic restrictions on overseas banks and allow them to start yuan lending and deposit services, as well as issue credit cards. Before that, the firms concentrated primarily on currency-exchange services for foreigners. The banking regulator then imposed an additional requirement that global banks, including those based in Hong Kong, incorporate locally to take deposits and offer services. The firms have been permitted to open fewer than 10 branches a year and need approval to sell new products or appoint executives. It took Australia & New Zealand Banking Group Ltd. (ANZ) more than a year to obtain approval in March to accept yuan deposits from Chinese citizens. 'The problem is their branch expansion is limited by regulatory approvals,' said Dominic Chan, an analyst at BNP Paribas in Hong Kong. Chinese banks, meanwhile, have been encouraged to expand. China Construction Bank Corp. the country's second-largest lender, opened 166 outlets on the mainland last year and said in April it plans to add 2,000 more by mid-2016. Bigger rival ICBC added 421 locations last year. . . .

Even in a country with a personal savings rate of about 50 percent, retail banking has been the biggest profit drag [for foreign firms], according to data that banks started disclosing in 2009. HSBC's China unit reported a loss of 112 million yuan on personal banking and 22 million yuan on private banking last year. At Citigroup, the personal-banking losses in its China arm widened 66 percent to 375 million yuan in 2011 from a year earlier. Standard Chartered, with 85 branches, had a loss of about $100 million on its China consumer-banking business last year, according to its annual report. . . .

'It is a very competitive market,' said Mike Smith, CEO of Melbourne-based ANZ Bank, which announced plans to increase the number of outlets to 20 over the next decade from six now. [Yet] some banks have exited the retail market. Deutsche Bank AG (DBK), Germany's biggest lender, stopped taking deposits from most Chinese customers on April 1 [2012 while] . . . Royal Bank of Scotland Group Plc in December 2010 abandoned its Chinese retail and commercial-banking businesses, which had 25,000 clients and $900 million in deposits, giving the operations to Singapore-based DBS for free. Melvin Teo, DBS's China head, said at the time that RBS decided to get out after a U.K. government bailout and record losses. . . .

For a time, foreign banks tried to partner with local counterparts, seeking minority stakes to participate in their profitability. Goldman Sachs, Bank of America, Zurich-based UBS, Citigroup, and RBS were among global financial institutions that first bought into Chinese lenders and then sold about $24 billion in holdings in the past three years as they replenished capital to meet global regulatory requirements. . . . 'Some foreign banks may no longer want a stake in Chinese commercial banks as that doesn't fit in much to their strategy,' said Nicholas Yeo, head of China and Hong Kong equities at Aberdeen Asset Management Plc, which oversees $295 billion globally. 'They may want to focus more on their securities joint ventures, as that may be more useful to their investment-banking business. [The bottom line is] even as some foreign banks are running at full speed, the gap is too wide for them to catch up in the decades to come,' said Liu of the Chinese Academy of Social Sciences."[129]

Questions:

1. What type of international firms are HSBC and Citigroup?

2. What are the political, economic, business ownership, and government–business relations in China, and how do they affect foreign and domestic banks?

3. What is the most critical issue that affects foreign banks like HSBC?

4. What nonmarket strategies would you employ to deal with this issue if you were a foreign bank?

5. What advice would you give the board of directors of a firm like HSBC concerning plans for future investments in China?

CASE 11.2

Microsoft Hiring Foreign Workers: We Have Met the Enemy and the Enemy Is "U.S."!

"With a U.S. unemployment rate at 8.6% [in early 2012], one would expect that many of the high-paying job openings available domestically are a positive sign for jobless Americans. However, that has not been the case. According to data from the U.S. Citizenship and Immigration Services department, U.S. companies have hired foreign workers at an expeditious pace. U.S. companies have set a three-year record on the amount of time it took to reach the cap of 65,000 H-1B visas."[130]

"The H-1B visa program allows skilled immigrants to work in the United States on a supposedly temporary basis. The legal cap on H-1B visas dropped from 195,000 back to its original level of 65,000 on October 1, 2003. However that does not include an additional 20,000/year cap for individuals who fall under the 'advanced degree' exemption, or the uncapped admissions to governmental agencies and not-for-profit employers. Microsoft, the computer programming giant, continued its streak of hiring the most foreign workers again this year by importing more than 2,500 foreign workers [in 2010]. Nearly twice as much as the second highest H-1B user, IBM."[131] Microsoft Corporation has filed 33,934 labor condition applications for H-1B visa and 10,918 labor certifications for green card since 2001, ranked 1 among all visa sponsors. In 2011, Microsoft filled over 7,000 jobs with foreign employees, paying an average salary of over $97,000."[132]

The U.S. government did not stand idly by during this foreign worker invasion. "[The] U.S. Citizenship and Immigration Services announced [that], 'On June 11, 2012, USCIS received a sufficient number of petitions to reach the statutory cap for FY 2013.' . . . Some would respond: 'This is good, now more Americans will be hired.' [Or that] a 15 month morato-

rium on hiring new H-1B visa holders will hopefully at least lead to a moratorium on blaming skilled foreign-born scientists, engineers, and other professionals for economic problems in the United States. [Yet] preventing U.S. employers from hiring skilled foreign nationals, including recent graduate students in engineering and other tech fields, *inside* the United States encourages opening offices and expanding resources for placing foreign-born personnel *outside* the United States. It could also discourage more investment in the United States. Small employers unable to find the right skilled people may simply grow less."[133]

"In a study for the American Enterprise Institute and the Partnership for a New American Economy, economist Madeline Zavodny found a connection between companies hiring H-1Bs and overall employment: 'The data show that states with greater numbers of temporary workers in the H-1B program for skilled workers and H-2B program for less-skilled nonagricultural workers had higher employment among U.S. natives. Specifically: Adding 100 H-1B workers results in an additional 183 jobs among U.S. natives.'"[134]

Yet Chairman Bill Gates and Microsoft as the largest foreign employer in the United States disprove Zavodny's research. With all of its foreign hiring Microsoft has decided to let its American workers go home. "Citing 'the further deterioration of economic conditions,' Microsoft said it would ax 5,000 workers, including an unspecified number of highly skilled research and development employees, this year. 'We are not immune to the effects of the economy,' CEO Steve Ballmer said at the time. [Yet while announcing these] plans to lay off 5,000 U.S. employees, [Microsoft] said it needs to import more H-1B visa workers into the country to cope with what it says is a shortage of American tech workers."[135]

Why does Microsoft need so many foreign employees while firing American workers? "'The future success of Microsoft and every other U.S. technology company depends on our ability to recruit the world's best talent,' wrote Brad Smith, general counsel at Microsoft, in a blog post. 'While the vast majority of Microsoft's U.S. workforce is American, Microsoft hires foreign workers to bring specially needed skill sets to our U.S. operations and to fill roles when qualified American workers are not available,' wrote Smith, in his post. . . . The company blames its need to recruit immigrants on what it says is a shortage of Americans pursuing education in math and science. . . . Smith said a 'startling' 61% of all Ph.D. candidates at American universities are temporary residents. . . . 'Microsoft has invested millions of dollars in a wide range of K-12 and higher-education programs. But it will take time to reverse the past decade's decline in computer science graduation rates among U.S. citizens,' wrote Smith."[136]

Questions:

1. Why would the U.S. government limit the hiring of foreign employees?
2. What are some of the pros and cons of this form of protectionism?
3. From Microsoft's perspective, why hire foreign workers in the United States and risk bad publicity?
4. In your opinion, is it ethical for Microsoft to fire 5,000 U.S. employees while simultaneously hiring foreign workers?
5. What retaliatory actions might be taken by the U.S. government against Microsoft and other major employers of foreign workers who fire U.S. employees?
6. What nonmarket strategies should be taken by CEO Steve Ballmer in order to address Microsoft's need to hire foreign workers?

INTEGRATIVE CASE (Part 11)

DHR Construction, LLC and Morrison Homes Inc.: The British Are Coming; The British Are Coming!

This is a continuation case—please refer to Chapters 1–10 for further information.

The monthly meeting of the local Home Builders Association was just about to begin, and the president, Mark Kessler, was going around the room and doing his usual politicking. He and Richard Davis, managing partner of DHR Construction, had become quite friendly over the past year, as Mark had mentored Richard in the politics of the local home construction real estate industry. Mark had emphasized Richard's need to know all of the key players in the local real estate game (inspectors, developers, suppliers, competitors, and creditors), and Richard had become quite savvy at putting names with faces and titles. It was quite surprising then that Richard came across a face in the audience that he was unfamiliar with, and he immediately sought Mark's expert knowledge.

"Who's that guy in the corner Mark? You see over there, the guy wearing the plaid jacket. Never saw him before—what's his racket?"

"Hmmm," mumbled Mark. "I haven't seen Bob Walter at one of these meetings in a very long while. He's the senior VP of the Western Region for Morrison Homes Inc. They're a Georgia-based operation. According to Hoovers, 'the company primarily builds single-family homes which average about $227,000, although its range extends as low as $120,000 for smaller homes targeted at first-time buyers and empty-nesters to high-end homes in the $500,000s. The company sells about 2,700 homes annually. Its Morrison Financial

Services unit processes mortgages and provides financing for half of its homebuyers.[137] The company does about $1 billion a year in sales and has a 25 percent annual growth rate.[138] His competitors include KB Homes, Toll Brothers, and Beazer Homes."[139]

"This guy's a big player then in my book," replied Richard. "I wonder what he's doing here. We're predominately made up of small home builders, ma and pa operations, with the biggest small firm around these parts being Best Homes. They've been around here since 1985 and have built homes in eight different communities."

"Glad to see you know the market," responded Mark proudly. "Let's corner him after the meeting and see what's up. You always wonder when a shark is swimming in shallow waters with the small fish. Never know who might get eaten!"

The meeting was fairly uneventful, and Richard took the opportunity to call his business partner Stephen Hodgetts and alert him to what was going on with Morrison Homes. Stephen told Richard that he'd do some Net surfing and see what more information he could dig up on the firm. In the meantime, Richard and Mark, after mingling with the other builders, managed to get Bob Walter's attention. Bob was in a very jovial mood and talking in a highly animated fashion—something rare for home builders given the declining new home sales and the increasing home mortgage rates.

"What brings you back to these parts Bob?" queried Mark. "Thought you Georgia boys liked to stay close to home and settle your nest so to speak."

Mark's sly remark could not dent Bob's congenial manner, and he responded in kind: "You haven't changed a bit, Mark. Unless of course you discount that tire you're wearing around your waist. What's the matter? Being president of the HBA put you too much behind the desk and not out there using your muscle building homes?" This rebuttal brought great laughter from both Bob and Mark who proceeded to pat each other on the back in an overly friendly way.

Richard took this all in as he followed the conversation between Bob and Mark. Once they got past their pleasantries, they turned to Bob's "visit." It seemed that Bob's firm was looking for a new development to build and Bob kindly remembered this area as being builder-friendly with a strong HBA support. He and his firm were looking for about 100 acres of land on which to build a planned community that would include at least 100 single-family homes, about 200 condominiums, a retirement center, a park with a swimming pool and a lake, and a nine-hole golf course.

While Richard was all smiles on the outside, and added his own compliments to Mark's about the plan laid out by Bob, he was shuddering on the inside. A development of this magnitude in this market would clearly produce a glut of newly constructed homes—it was hard enough getting buyers for DHR Construction at the prices he and Stephen had set, but this development would put price pressure not only on his houses but on the entire home construction industry in his area. He decided to talk with Mark about this after he had talked with Stephen Hodgetts and seen what Stephen had scraped up from the Internet.

The Power Behind the Man

Richard and Stephen met the next day not only to go over the details of the HBA meeting but to discuss what Stephen had found out about Morrison Homes Inc. Mark had been right on target when he said that Morrison Homes was a huge corporation but he forgot to add one important point: They were a subsidiary of a British firm called George Wimpey PLC. Wimpey is a $6 billion dollar publicly traded company (London stock exchange) with a nearly 30 percent growth rate[140] and is one of the UK's largest home builders. "George Wimpey UK completes about 12,145 homes a year, with an average selling price of £182,000. In the UK, George Wimpey acquired Alfred McAlpine's home-building operations (which sell about 3,000 homes a year), as well as Laing Homes (about 1,290 homes). Across the Atlantic, its Morrison Homes unit builds about 3,200 detached homes a year at an average price of about $252,000. Morrison Homes builds in Arizona, California, Colorado, Florida, Georgia, and Texas and offers mortgage and title services."[141]

"We're about to be invaded; that's what it is," said Richard after the facts about Morrison Homes were revealed. "A firm that size and with such big pockets can easily buy land in this depressed market. Heck, I'd even sell them some of our land in the Florence development in a minute for the right price. They can easily build this new development while simultaneously undercutting us and the rest of the local builders."

"That's right," concurred Stephen. "They'd be the Walmart of home builders, and we'd go the way of the local hardware store—out of business."

The silence was deafening as Stephen and Richard let the bombshell they had just dropped mushroom and finally dissipate. Richard then picked up the phone and called Mark Kessler to let him know what he and Stephen had found. As always, Mark was way ahead of them. "Let me tell you something you guys may not know," Mark said in a gruff voice. "I made a few calls to several real estate agents and over to the tax assessor's office, and Bob has been checking out the neighborhood."

"And?" replied Richard.

"Well," started Mark, "you no longer have to worry about Morrison Homes coming here and buying up tracts of land in order to start their project."

Richard and Stephen took a sigh of relief, thinking that it was all over; however, Richard wanted this confirmed and therefore asked Mark, "Why not?"

"Because," Marked continued, "they already have."

Questions

1. What type of international firm is George Wimpey PLC?
2. What are some of the pros and cons of globalization that are specifically raised in this case?
3. How does this case highlight the blurring of "American" businesses?
4. Should the U.S. government, local governments, and the local Home Builder's Association take any actions to protect the local home builders? If so, what actions would you recommend?
5. What nonmarket actions should Stephen Hodgetts and Richard Davis take in light of the emergence of this new competitor?

REFERENCES AND NOTES

1 http://subscriber.hoovers.com/H/company360/people.html?companyId=53666000000000 (accessed August 1, 2012).
2 http://en.wikipedia.org/wiki/Bandai (accessed July 20, 2006).
3 http://subscriber.hoovers.com/H/company360/fulldescription.html?companyId=53666000000000 (accessed August 1, 2012.)
4 http://en.wikipedia.org/wiki/Bandai (accessed July 20, 2006).
5 http://www.bandai.com/about/corporate_story.html (accessed July 20, 2006).
6 http://en.wikipedia.org/wiki/Bandai (accessed July 20, 2006).
7 "Christopher Anderson '08 Researches Impact of Japanese Anime on American Audiences" (April 12, 2006), http://www.lafayette.edu/news.php/view/8617/ (accessed July 24, 2006).
8 "Was Cardcaptors Promo Pulled Due to 'Occult' Complaints?" (February 5, 2002), http://www.icv2.com/articles/news/1088.html (accessed July 24, 2006).
9 "Is Japanese Style Taking Over The World?" http://www.businessweek.com/magazine/content/04_30/b3893091.htm (accessed July 24, 2006).
10 www.mcdonalds.com (accessed June 8, 2012).
11 www.coca-cola.com (accessed June 8, 2012).
12 www.fedex.com (accessed June 8, 2012).

13 J. Tozzi, "China's Next Export: Venture Capital," *BusinessWeek* (May 21–27, 2012): 53–54; M. Kung and R. December, "A Geijing Ticket to Hollywood," *Wall Street Journal* (May 22, 2012): B1.

14 C. Rose, "Rose Talks to Cicso's John Chambers," *BusinessWeek* (April 23–29, 2012): 41.

15 UPS thenewlogistics.com/guide (accessed June 8, 2012).

16 www.globalpolicy.org (accessed June 8, 2012).

17 L. Mechler and D. Machalaba, "Port Deal: Not a Foreign Idea," *Wall Street Journal* (March 9, 2006): B1.

18 J. F. Preble, "Toward a Framework for Achieving a Sustainable Globalization," *Business and Society Review* 115(3) (2010): 329–366.

19 www.globalpolicy.org (accessed June 8, 2012).

20 https://www.cia.gov/library/publications/the-world-factbook/rankorder/2119rank.html (accessed June 8, 2012).

21 C. Kenny, "The Case for Second Place," *BusinessWeek* (October 17–23, 2011): 14–15.

22 R. Karlgaard, "Energy in 2050," *Forbes* (April 23, 2012): 34.

23 C. Rose, "Rose Talks to Cicso's John Chambers," *BusinessWeek* (April 23–29, 2012): 41.

24 K. Evans, "China Consumers Say Yum to Fast Food," *Wall Street Journal* (October 4, 2011): C1.

25 L. Kwoh, "Don't Unpack That Suitcase," *Wall Street Journal* (May 9, 2012): B10.

26 www.sba.gov/sites/default/files/sbfaq.pdf (accessed September 17, 2012).

27 www.pier1.com (accessed June 11, 2012).

28 www.amazon.com (accessed June 11, 2012).

29 www.exim.gov (accessed June 11, 2012).

30 E. Glazer, "P&G Unit Bids Goodbye to Cincinnati, Hello to Asia," *Wall Street Journal* (May 11, 2012): C1.

31 http://geography.about.com/cs/countries/a/numbercountries.htm (accessed June 11, 2012).

32 www.un.org (accessed June 11, 2012).

33 www.amnesty.org (accessed June 19, 2012).

34 J. Bussey, "Subsidy Nation: Can Firms in U.S. Compete with China?" *Wall Street Journal* (October 21, 2011): B1.

35 www.heritage.org/index/ranking (accessed June 11, 2012).

36 M. J. Chen and D. Miller, "The Relational Perspective as a Business Mindset: Managerial Implications for East and West," *Academy of Management Perspectives* 25(3) (2011): 6–18.

37 T. Khanna, "Learning From Economic Experiments in China and India," *Academy of Management Perspectives* 23 (2) (2009): 36–43.

38 Y Huang, "Debating China's Economic Growth: The Beijing Consensus or the Washington Consensus," *Academy of Management Perspectives* 24(2) (2010): 31–47.

39 B. Powell, "China's New Politics," *Fortune* (September 26, 2011): 85–88.

40 M. Kung and R. December, "A Beijing Ticket to Hollywood," *Wall Street Journal* (May 22, 2012): B1.

41 S. Forbes, "Taxes, Trade, Social Security and More-George Bush Speaks Outs," *Forbes* (May 21, 2012): 15–18.

42 D. Roberts, "The Hazards of Being China-Owned," *BusinessWeek* (May 21–27, 2012): 17–18.

43 J. Wrighton, "France to Protect Strategic Sectors From Foreign Deals," *Wall Street Journal* (August 30, 2005): A3.

44 J. Bussey, "Subsidy Nation: Can Firms in U.S. Compete with China?" *Wall Street Journal* (October 21, 2011): B1.

45 P. B. Prime, "Evaluating Risk in China: Does Location Matter?" *Academy of Management Perspectives* 23(1) (2009): 82–84.

46 D. P. Barron, *Business and Its Environment,* 6th ed. (Upper Saddle, NJ: Prentice Hall, 2012).

47 T. Doctoroff, "What the Chinese Want," *Wall Street Journal* (May 19–20, 2012): C1, C2.

48 http://subscriber.hoovers.com.cwplib.proxy.liu.edu/H/company360/fulldescription.html?companyId=109755000000000 (accessed August 1, 2012).

49 Ibid.

50 Ibid.

51 "Zara, a Spanish success story," *CNN Europe/ Business,* http://edition.cnn.com/BUSINESS/programs/yourbusiness/stories2001/zara (accessed June 15, 2001).

52 http://www.examiner.com/article/zara-international-duchess-of-cambridge-asked-to-lobby-over-fashion-slave-labor (accessed August 1, 2012).

53 S. Forbes, "Golden Rule for Prosperity," *Forbes* (June 25, 2012): 21–22.

54 D. Reilly and S. Nassauer, "Tip Line Bind: Follow Law in U.S. or EU?" *Wall Street Journal* (September 6, 2005): C1.

55 D. P. Barron, *Business and Its Environment,* 6th ed. (Upper Saddle, NJ: Prentice Hall, 2012).

56 S. Forbes, "Taxes, Trade, Social Security and More—George Bush Speaks Outs," *Forbes* (May 21, 2012): 15–18.

57 S. Forbes, "Golden Rule for Prosperity," *Forbes* (June 25, 2012): 21–22.

58 D.P. Barron, *Business and Its Environment,* 5th ed. (Upper Saddle, NJ: Prentice-Hall, 2006).

59 "Beware Politicians Bearing Election-Year Trade Deals," *BusinessWeek* (March 19–25, 2012): 41–43.

60 K. Johnson and C. Sweet, "Solar-Trade Fight Flares Up," *Wall Street Journal* (March 21, 2012): B1.

61 J. Freedman, "Flooding the System with Tit-for-Tat," *BusinessWeek* (June 11–17, 2012): 18–20.

62 A. Browne, "EU's Mandelson Belittles Quotas After China Deal," *Wall Street Journal* (September 7, 2005): A1.

63 J. Freedman, "Flooding the System with Tit-for-Tat," *BusinessWeek* (June 11–17, 2012): 18–20.

64 "Foreign Banks Hit a Wall in China," *BusinessWeek* (June 11–17, 2012): 56–57.

65 J. Freedman, "Flooding the System with Tit-for-Tat," *BusinessWeek* (June 11–17, 2012): 18–20.

66 Ibid.

67 Ibid.

68 N. Shirouzu, S. Reddy, and S. Terlep, "U.S.-China Trade Spate Escalates to Autos," *Wall Street Journal* (December 15, 2011): A15.

69 J. Freedman, "Flooding the System with Tit-for-Tat," *BusinessWeek* (June 11–17, 2012): 18–20.

70 http://www.census.gov/indicator/www/ustrade.html (accessed June 11, 2012).

71 K. Johnson and C. Sweet, "U.S. Imposes Tariffs on China Solar Panels," *Wall Street Journal* (May 18, 2012): B3.

72 S. Holt, "Building Law-Abiding Businesses," *Suffolk Business Magazine* (Fall 2011): 38–39.

73 A. Raghavan, "U.S. Gains More Antirust Cooperation Abroad," *Wall Street Journal* (December 22, 2005): A3, A11.

74 A. Sharma and R. J. Krishna, "Google Ad Business Faces Antitrust Inquiry in India," *Wall Street Journal* (May 8, 2012): C3.

75 V. Baueriein and G. Fairclough, "China Rejects Coke's $2.4 Billion Deal for Juice Maker," *Wall Street Journal* (March 19, 2009): B1, B9.

76 "Foreign Banks Hit a Wall in China," *Business-Week* (June 11–17, 2012): 56–57.

77 W. Echikson, "U.S., EU Unite to Fight China Over Regulations," *Wall Street Journal* (June 21, 2006): A9.

78 www.worldbank.org (accessed June 12, 2012).

79 www.g20.org (accessed June 15, 2012).

80 www.wto.org (accessed June 13, 2012).

81 J. W. Miller and D. Michaels, "Boeing Set for Victory Over Airbus in Illegal Subsidy Case," *Wall Street Journal* (September 3, 2009): A1, A14.

82 J. Freedman, "Flooding the System with Tit-for-Tat," *BusinessWeek* (June 11–17, 2012): 18–20.

83 Y. I. Kane, "Microsoft Lauds China Piracy Case," *Wall Street Journal* (January 2, 2009): A11.

84 www.imf.org (accessed June 13, 2012).

85 www.worldbank.org (accessed June 13, 2012).

86 www.imf.org (accessed June 13, 2012).

87 S. Forbes, "Golden Rule for Prosperity," *Forbes* (June 25, 2012): 21–22.

88 http://www.bbc.co.uk/news/world-europe-19060872 (accessed August 1, 2012).

89 http://ec.europa.eu (accessed June 12, 2012).

90 www.ustr.gov (accessed June 12, 2012).

91 B. Macnab, R. Worthley, and S. Jenner, "Regional Cultural Differences and Ethical Perspectives Within the United States: Avoiding Pseudo-emic Ethics Research," *Business and Society Review* 115(1) (2010): 27–55.

92 A. Sharma and R. J. Krishna, "Google Ad Business Faces Antitrust Inquiry in India," *Wall Street Journal* (May 8, 2012): C3.

93 S. O. Osaglie, "The Voluntary Environmentalists," *Academy of Management Perspectives* 33(2) (2008): 564–568.

94 P. Rodriquez, K. Uhlenbruck, and L Eden, "Government Corruption and the Entry Strategies of Multinationals," *Academy of Management Review* 30(2) (2005): 383–396.

95 D. Searcey, "U.S. Cracks Down on Corporate Bribes," *Wall Street Journal* (May 26, 2009): A1, A4.

96 C. M. Matthews and J. Palazzolo, "Oil Giants Launch Bribe Probes," *Wall Street Journal* (June 7, 2012): B1.

97 G. Colvin, "The Biggest Problem for Developing Economies: Corruption," *Fortune* (May 2, 2011): 48.

98 Y. Luo, "Strategic Responses to Perceived Corruption in an Emerging Market: Lessons from MNEs Investing in China," *Business & Society* 50(2) (2011): 350–387.

99 G. Colvin, "The Biggest Problem for Developing Economies: Corruption," *Fortune* (May 2, 2011): 48.

100 www.transparency.org (accessed June 14, 2012).

101 www.worldbank.org (accessed June 14, 2012).

102 G. Colvin, "The Biggest Problem for Developing Economies: Corruption," *Fortune* (May 2, 2011): 48.

103 Ibid.

104 www.justice.gov/criminal/fraud/fcpa (accessed June 14, 2012).

105 D. Searcey, "U.S. Cracks Down on Corporate Bribes," *Wall Street Journal* (May 26, 2009): A1, A4.

106 Ibid.

107 M. Bustillo and J. Palazzolo, "Wal-Mart Discloses a Corruption Probe," *Wall Street Journal* (December 9, 2011): B2.

108 www.unglobalcompact.org (accessed June 14, 2012).

109 www.oecd.org (accessed June 14, 2012).

110 www.transparency.org (accessed June 14, 2012.)

111 www.saasaccreditation.org (accessed June 14, 2012).

112 B. Macnab, R. Worthley, and S. Jenner, "Regional Cultural Differences and Ethical Perspectives Within the United States: Avoiding Pseudo-emic Ethics Research," *Business and Society Review* 115(1) (2010): 27–55.

113 D. P. Barron, *Business and Its Environment,* 6th ed. (Upper Saddle, NJ: Prentice Hall, 2010).

114 Y. Luo, "Strategic Responses to Perceived Corruption in an Emerging Market: Lessons From MNEs Investing in China," *Business & Society* 50(2) (2011): 350–387.

115 R. Lunnan, J. Lervik, L. Traavik, S. Nilsen, R. Amadam, and B. Hennestad, "Global Transfer of Management Practices Across Nations and MNC Subcultures," *Academy of Management Executive* 19(2) (2005): 77–80.

116 P. Schreck, "Reviewing the Business Case for Corporate Social Responsibility: New Evidence and Analysis," *Journal of Business Ethics* 103(2) (2011): 167–188.

117 M. J. Chen and D. Miller, "The Relational Perspective as a Business Mindset: Managerial Implications for East and West," *Academy of Management Perspectives* 25(3) (2011): 6–18.

118 C. H. Amato and L. H. Amato, "Corporate Commitment to Global Quality of Life Issues: Do Slack Resources, Industry Affiliations, and

Multinational Headquarters Matter?" *Business & Society* 50(2) (2011): 388–416.

119 M. Fong and A. Zimmerman, "China's Union Push Leaves Wal-Mart With Hard Choice," *Wall Street Journal* (May 13–14, 2006): A1.

120 D. P. Barron, *Business and Its Environment,* 6th ed. (Upper Saddle, NJ: Prentice Hall, 2010).

121 J. Ball, "The New Act at Exxon," *Wall Street Journal* (March 8, 2006): B1.

122 D. P. Barron, *Business and Its Environment,* 6th ed. (Upper Saddle, NJ: Prentice Hall, 2010).

123 J. Tozzi, "China's Next Export: Venture Capital," *BusinessWeek* (May 21–27, 2012): 53–54.

124 B. Powell, "China's New Politics," *Fortune* (September 26, 2011): 85–88.

125 M. J. Chen and D. Miller, "The Relational Perspective as a Business Mindset: Managerial Implications for East and West," *Academy of Management Perspectives* 25(3) (2011): 6–18.

126 D. P. Barron, *Business and Its Environment,* 6th ed. (Upper Saddle, NJ: Prentice Hall, 2010).

127 C. Marquis and Z. Huang, "The Contingent Nature of Public Policy and the Growth of U.S. Commercial Banking," *Academy of Management Journal* 52(6) (2009): 1222–1246.

128 Source unknown, passed around on the Internet.

129 http://mobile.bloomberg.com/news/2012-06-04/china-wall-hit-by-global-banks-with-2-market-share (accessed August 1, 2012).

130 https://www.numbersusa.com/content/news/december-7-2011/uscis-data-us-companies-hiring-foreign-workers-record-pace-despite-86-unemploym (accessed August 2, 2012).

131 Ibid.

132 http://www.myvisajobs.com/Visa-Sponsor/Microsoft/356252.htm (accessed August 2, 2012).

133 http://www.forbes.com/sites/stuartanderson/2012/06/13/no-hiring-new-h-1b-visa-holders-for-the-next-15-months (accessed August 2, 2012).

134 Ibid.

135 http://www.informationweek.com/news/global-cio/h1b/216402240 (accessed August 2, 2012).

136 Ibid.

137 http://premium.hoovers.com/subscribe/co/factsheet.xhtml?ID=ffffhkktjrcrxxyyxc (accessed July 25, 2006).

138 http://premium.hoovers.com/subscribe/co/fin/factsheet.xhtml?ID=ffffhkktjrcrxxyyxc&ticker = (accessed July 25, 2006).

139 http://premium.hoovers.com/subscribe/co/competitors.xhtml?ID=ffffhkktjrcrxxyyxc (accessed July 25, 2006).

140 http://premium.hoovers.com/subscribe/co/fin/factsheet.xhtml?ID=ffffsfrjctxsfxxryf&ticker =WMPY (accessed July 26, 2006).

141 http://premium.hoovers.com/subscribe/co/overview.xhtml?ID=ffffsfrjctxsfxxryf (accessed July 26, 2006).

Chapter 12

GLOBAL TECHNOLOGY, THE NATURAL ENVIRONMENT, AND SUSTAINABILITY

Learning Outcomes

In this chapter, you will find out the answers to these key questions:

■ How does technology affect the global economy?
■ How should we protect our natural environment?

After studying this chapter, you should be able to:

1. Describe the relationship between technology and productivity and the difference between production and productivity
2. Explain how the winner takes most of the market share
3. Discuss issues of managing technology
4. Describe issues of biotechnology and bioethics
5. Compare and contrast ozone depletion, global warming, and the endangerment of biological diversity
6. Discuss the major environmental laws and regulations
7. Compare sustainability concepts
8. Define the following key terms (in order of appearance in the chapter)

technology
productivity
information technology (IT)
e-commerce
m-commerce
online communities
chief information officers
   (CIOs)

biotechnology
bioethics
pollution
ozone
greenhouse effect
biodiversity
Clean Air Act
Clean Water Act

National Pollutant Discharge
   Elimination System (NPDES)
Solid Waste Disposal Act
Resource Conservation and
   Recovery Act
Pollution Prevention Act
sustainability
sustainable development

What's This Chapter About?

In this chapter, we continue our global focus, expanding to include technology and the natural environment. The global approach to these two topics joins them together, but they are primarily independent topics. Therefore, we first discuss technology, including strategies, followed by the natural environment.

We begin with a discussion of how technology has changed the way we live and conduct business. Next, we focus on being ethical when using technology, followed by nonmarket and market strategies business uses to compete in the global economy.

Our fourth section changes the focus to the natural environment and the global challenges we face. This is followed by how the government protects the environment through developing and enforcing environmental laws. Related to the environment, our sixth section is on the importance of sustainability. The chapter ends with a discussion of the strategies business uses to deal ethically with environmental issues for sustainability.

CASE

Wake Up and Smell the Coffee: Heaven on Earth or Highway to Hell at Starbucks?

Howard Schultz, founder of Starbucks, might refer to his stores as "the third place" (between home and the office), yet many people have found that they not only go to Starbucks for an excellent (but expensive) cup of java but because Starbucks represents to them how a mature, socially responsible, technologically savvy firm should behave in the twenty-first century. It all starts with Starbucks' mission,[1] which includes providing a great work environment, paying employees well, treating each other with respect and dignity, fostering enthusiastic satisfied customers all of the time, contributing positively to its communities and the environment, and last, but certainly not least, recognizing that profitability is essential to its future success.[2] Starbucks is serious about the environment—both that of the world around it and in its stores. "We share our customers' commitment to the environment and we believe in the importance of caring for our planet, working with and encouraging others to do the same. As a company that relies on an agricultural product, it makes good business sense. And as people living in the world, it is simply the right thing to do."[3] Starbucks believes that many customers would not feel at home and hang out in a business that did not subscribe to the same values and ethical considerations that they did—especially if they knew that the firm was socially irresponsible and contributed to polluting the environment.

While Starbucks maintains an apolitical stance on issues,[4] it has a strong position on social responsibility, especially when it concerns supporting greening businesses and the environment. Starbucks has gone further than most firms to make its customers not only feel good about their purchases but feel good about the business they purchased their products from. "The success of the farmers with whom we do business is a critical component of our own success. We are taking an integrated approach to building relationships with coffee communities. Components of Starbucks integrated approach are: Paying coffee farmers premium prices to help them make profits and support their families. Providing coffee farmers access to affordable credit through various loan funds so that farmers can invest in their farms and their success into the future. Purchasing conservation and certified coffees, including Fair Trade Certified™, shade grown and certified organic, to promote responsible environmental and economic efforts. Encouraging participation in Starbucks Coffee and Farmer Equity Practices (C.A.F.E. Practices), a set of socially responsible coffee-buying guidelines, by offering preferential buying status for participants that score the highest on verified reports. Investing in social programs to build schools, health clinics, and other projects that benefit coffee-growing communities. Collaborating with farmers through the Farmer Support Center, located in Costa Rica, to provide technical support and training that promotes high-quality coffee for the future."[5]

Starbucks is committed to minimizing our environmental impacts throughout our entire supply chain, from coffee bean to coffee cup. It's one of our guiding principles and part of the way we conduct business. Starbucks' approach to minimizing our environmental footprint is guided by our environmental mission statement, which was adopted in 1992. Starbucks Environmental Footprint Team guides the company's environmental approach and establishes initiatives aimed at minimizing our impact on the planet. Starbucks environmental efforts are visible throughout our supply chain, from working with farmers to preserving the natural environment in places where coffee is grown to recycling coffee grounds into nutrient-rich soil amendment. Starbucks examines the environmental performance of store design and operations and seeks to reduce waste and energy and water consumption—the major impacts of our stores.[6]

With all of this concern about social responsibility and the environment, as well as expense, you might wonder whether being a green business is profitable—for Starbucks it is! Although profits may be last on its mission statement list, Starbucks' Fiscal Second Quarter 2012 highlights are as follows:

- Total net revenues increased 15 percent to $3.2 billion.
- Global comparable store sales increased 7 percent, driven by a 6 percent increase in traffic and a 1 percent increase in average ticket.
- EPS (earnings per share) increased 18 percent to $0.40 per share, compared to $0.34 per share in Q2 FY (fiscal year) 11.
- Channel Development revenues increased 57 percent driven by sales of Starbucks- and Tazo-branded K-Cup® packs and the benefit of recognizing the full revenue from packaged coffee sales under the direct distribution model.
- Starbucks opened 176 net new stores globally, including its 3,000th store in the China/Asia Pacific segment, its first store in Norway, and the first Evolution Fresh™ store in Bellevue, Washington.

"Starbucks record [2012] Q2 performance demonstrates the strength of our business, the increasing power and global relevance of our brand and the success of our unique Blueprint for Profitable Growth business strategy. In Q2 we expanded our retail presence, recorded our seventh consecutive quarter of over 20% sales growth in China, introduced new products into multiple channels and more than offset high legacy commodity costs through increased efficiencies. I could not be more excited or more optimistic about the future of our company as we pursue disciplined, profitable growth all around the world."[7]

And where do these profits and business growth come from? It all starts for the customer with the in-store experience—the human connection is at the foundation of everything that Starbucks does. Schultz tries to make the store environment as much like home as possible and to make its stores neighborhood gathering places with free Internet and downloadable music.[8] By opening their browser at any Wi-Fi–enabled Starbucks to watch complimentary Wi-Fi content from Starbucks' own website "Hear Music," customers can listen to music clips or watch videos of artist interviews, recording sessions, and concerts all while enjoying a latte.[9]

Starbucks has moved this notion of home further through their "new global store design strategy, setting the stage for a reinvigorated customer experience. Inspired by Starbucks™ Shared Planet™, the company's ongoing commitment to ethical sourcing, environmental stewardship and community involvement, the new designs will reflect the character of each store's surrounding neighborhood and help to reduce environmental impacts. . . . 'We recognize the importance of continuously evolving with our customers' interests, lifestyles and values in order to stay relevant over the long term,' said Arthur Rubinfeld, president, Starbucks Global Development. 'Our new design approach will allow customers to feel truly at home when visiting their local store and give them opportunities for discovery at our other locations around the world. . . . Ultimately, we hope customers will feel an enhanced sense of community, a deeper connection to our coffee heritage and a greater level of commitment to environmental consciousness."[10]

Nevertheless, Starbucks is not without its cynics. Googling "hate Starbucks" will lead you to a plethora of websites and a Facebook page,[11] many of which will indicate that Starbucks: (1) kills independent coffee shops; (2) is homogeneous (looks the same wherever you go); (3) supports the corporate power structure; (4) is overly expensive; (5) tastes burnt;[12] (6) has suppliers who use underpaid coffee bean pickers; (7) is infiltrating the cultures of numerous nations; (8) uses predatory business practices; (9) sells "fake" corporate and environmental responsibility; and (10) has products that are surprisingly unhealthy.[13]

The following questions are related to the Starbucks case. Answers can be found within the chapter.

1. Starbucks seems more concerned with customer/employee satisfaction as well as contributing positively to its communities and the environment than with productivity. Is this really the case?
2. How does Starbucks typify the impact of technology on the environment and jobs?
3. How has Starbucks incorporated the Internet into its stores' operations?
4. How has Starbucks demonstrated a "winner-take-most" strategy?
5. What technology-based ethical issues might Starbucks have to deal with in terms of its retail store operations?
6. Which environmental issues is Starbucks dealing with and how?
7. How is Starbucks addressing sustainable development?
8. Why is Starbucks a role model for green business?
9. What nonmarket strategies is Starbucks employing to address environmental issues?

TECHNOLOGY AND BUSINESS

Throughout history, new technology has fueled business and reshaped society. Technology continues to change how we live, play, learn, work, and interact with others at home, in school, and at work throughout the global economy. The new industries of the future will continue to meet materialist–individualist Western values.[14] In this section, we discuss the effects of technology, information technology, and the winner-take-most markets concepts.

Learning Outcome 1: Describe the relationship between technology and productivity and the difference between production and productivity.

Technology Effects

Technology. Technology *is the process of transforming resources into products.* Again, products include services. Technology is often referred to as the application of science to business. For example, years ago, thousands of farmers planted and harvested crops by hand. Today, machines do most of this work. Also, before computers, thousands of clerical workers recorded financial transactions using ledgers with paper and pencil records. With today's technology, these workers have been replaced by computers using electronic ledgers.

The presence of high levels of technology makes more technology possible, and it has a ripple effect throughout our society. Thus, innovations continue to increase at a faster pace, and the pace will continue to increase as customers continue to buy the latest products that will improve their lives. However, new products can get so complex that they scare some people from buying them.[15] Every new generation is exposed to new technological products that were not available to the prior generation. Effective use of technology gives companies a competitive advantage over their competitors. For example, a major reason why **Walmart** can offer everyday low prices is its use of technology to manage its distribution system, which it continually updates with the latest technology.[16]

Personal and Professional Applications

1. How has technology changed the way you lived over the past five years?

2. How has your present or past employer changed how it conducts business over the past five years?

Productivity. Technology is the key to productivity gains and a continuing rising standard of living. *Productivity is a performance measure relating product and service outputs to resource inputs.* In simple terms, productivity is producing more with less. The goal is to increase productivity; however, a firm can increase its production (the number of units it produces) while decreasing productivity. Thus, business needs to focus on productivity.

See Figure 12.1 for a productivity illustration; a company has a motor vehicle and wants to know the productivity measured by miles per gallon (mpg) of gasoline. To increase productivity, the company may be able to replace the engine with a more fuel-efficient one, or it may be able to buy a new vehicle. Even sports and luxury cars, including **Ferrari**, **Porsche**, **BMW**, and **Mercedes-Benz** are coming out with hybrid technology to increase auto speed while cutting fuel consumption by up to 40 percent.[17]

Labor productivity is a common measure. As labor productivity increases, costs usually decrease, which results in lower prices for consumer products and benefits society. A major reason why jobs are going overseas is that the cost of labor is so much cheaper, which lowers the input costs and increases productivity. Without productivity gains, paying workers more when they don't produce more leads to higher wages that make the firm less profitable, with the wage increases offset by higher prices through inflation. For example, if you get a raise of 3 percent, and the cost of living increases by 5 percent, even though you have more take-home pay, your standard of living is actually decreasing. Productivity gains have come primarily at the expense of layoffs.

$$\frac{\text{Output}}{\text{Input}} = \text{Productivity} \qquad \frac{1{,}000 \text{ miles traveled}}{100 \text{ gallons of gas}} = 10 \text{ miles per gallon (mpg)}$$

▪ **Figure 12.1:** Productivity

Starbucks Case Question 1: Starbucks seems more concerned with customer/ employee satisfaction as well as with contributing positively to its communities and the environment than with productivity. Is this really the case?

Productivity is a performance measure relating product and service outputs to resource inputs. By providing excellent wages, treating employees with respect, and providing a very comfortable and friendly work environment, Starbucks is showing its concern for firm financial performance by providing motivating factors that will lead to in-store labor productivity. Its concern for productivity is indirectly evidenced through its global comparable store sales increase of 7 percent, driven by a 6 percent increase in traffic and a 1 percent increase in average prices coupled with their seventh consecutive quarter of over 20 percent sales growth in China.

Personal and Professional Applications

3. Have your wages increased more than the rate of inflation?

4. How is your present or past employer, and/or a business it deals with, attempting to increase productivity?

Internet. The Internet has clearly changed our lives. The **Pew Internet & American Life Project** (www.pewinternet.org) is one of seven projects that make up the **Pew Research Center.** It is an NGO "fact tank" that produces reports exploring the impact of the Internet on families, communities, work and home, daily life, education, health care, and civic and political life through surveys that examine how Americans use the Internet and how their activities affect their lives. The project releases 15–20 pieces of research a year, varying in size, scope, and ambition.[18]

Side Effects. Although society as a whole benefits from technology, it also has some negative side effects. A major criticism of technology is environmental pollution— air, water, soil, solid waste, and noise. Technology and pollution have been blamed for global warming. Another criticism includes the depletion of our natural resources. Around the globe, various areas have experienced fuel and power shortages based on the increasing use of technology. For example, although we love our automobiles, they are the number-one polluter and cause the depletion of oil, resulting in shortages and higher gas prices.

Technological automation has also been blamed for the loss of jobs (our next topic) and for creating simple boring jobs. To overcome some of the criticisms of technology, and to increase sales, automakers, especially **Toyota**, are focusing more on producing hybrid cars, and **Nissan** developed the *Leaf,* the first pure electric car.[19]

Personal and Professional Applications

5. Have you experienced any negative side effects of technology?

6. Has your present or past employer, and/or a business it deals with, experienced any negative side effects of technology?

Jobs. Although society benefits from technology, people who don't change with the times can be hurt by the negative effects of lost jobs. Jobs tend to change with the level of technology. The United States has gone from an agricultural, to a manufacturing, to, currently, a service and information society. Jobs in agriculture were replaced by jobs in manufacturing, and manufacturing jobs are being replaced by service and information jobs.

Although thousands of people have lost their jobs in farming, factories, and offices due to automation and computers, new jobs have been created. For example, the Internet continues to create millions of jobs that did not exist that long ago. In fact, the number of total jobs available has increased over the years, and the increases are projected to continue. Also, the number of manufacturing jobs has only decreased as a percentage of the total labor force; the actual number of workers with manufacturing jobs has held steady since 1950, while output has increased by 773 percent due to productivity gains.[20] So U.S. technological advances create new jobs requiring new skills that replace the older ones as our standard of living and life expectancy continue to increase—as we produce more with fewer workers.

> **Starbucks Case Question 2: How does Starbucks typify the impact of technology on the environment and jobs?**
>
> Starbucks, through its tremendous growth in its retail operations, produces waste while consuming energy and water resources, therein adding to global pollution. It offers predominately retail/service jobs, rather than manufacturing jobs; jobs that involve the use of food-processing technology.

Information Technology and Business

Throughout history, most of the technical advances benefiting society have come through business. Today, every aspect of business in the global economy is influenced by technology.[21] Information technology is primarily electronic and digital in nature, and it is heavily dependent on the computer and its semiconductor chip. *Information technology (IT) is the ability to process, store, and retrieve large amounts of information at great speeds through networks of linked systems.* Cloud computing on the Web has grown into a $58 billion industry, but brings privacy and security issues inherent to moving into public and community clouds. NGOs and governments, as well as private industry, are struggling to find integrative strategies to adopt and manage these threats.[22] MNCs are integrating the Internet into every aspect of their business. Startups and small companies are also using IT to run their businesses using e-commerce and m-commerce.

E-commerce. *E-commerce involves transacting business electronically through the Internet.* Computer networks link all employees, known as person to person (*P2P*—**Google** employees in different countries communicate), business with employees (*B2E*—**UPS** and delivery drivers), businesses with other businesses (*B2B*—**Ford** with **Firestone** to get its tires), business with customers (*B2C*—**Amazon** sells products to customers), and customer to customer (*C2C*—**eBay** connects individuals to buy and sell to each other).

M-commerce. *M-commerce involves transacting business through a mobile device.* Mobile cell phones, tablets (iPads and e-book readers), or other devices are being used as a method of conducting e-commerce as the number of consumers making mobile purchases increases. Have you made a mobile purchase yet?

Personal and Professional Applications

7. Have you purchased anything online with a computer, cell phone, and/or other mobile device?

8. How does your present or past employer use e- and m-commerce?

Online Communities. Some Internet companies have developed business models that focus on developing an *online community. Online communities interact with each other through a firm's website.* **AOL**'s instant messaging (IM) helped it attract subscribers as it increased the speed of Internet computer communications. **eBay** is in the business of bringing buyers and sellers together through its auctions. **Facebook** has created a tremendously popular online community to keep in touch with your friends. Do you have a Facebook account?

Starbucks Case Question 3: How has Starbucks incorporated the Internet into its stores' operations?

Starbucks offers wireless broadband Internet service. By opening their browser at any Wi-Fi–enabled Starbucks to watch complimentary Wi-Fi content from Starbucks' own website "Hear Music," customers can listen to music clips or watch videos of artist interviews, recording sessions, and concerts.

Learning Outcome 2: Explain how the winner takes most of the market share.

Winner-Take-Most Markets

Technology can provide competitive advantage,[23] and online business creates opportunities and market strategies that are different from traditional business operations in that technology provides the company a way to recap its initial cost to produce a product: as production increases, the cost of producing each additional unit decreases. Economies of scale create winner-take-most market situations. Furthermore, creating the industry standard and being the first-mover are important market strategies.

Industry Standard. Bill Gates understood that **Microsoft** would succeed by creating a shared common standard for its computer operating system with compatible software. Although developing the programs is extremely costly, it is cheap to reproduce and distribute once developed. So each additional program sold generates great returns. Also, the more people there are using the program, the better off they are because of the compatibility of communicating directly and sharing files. *MS Office* was so popular that **Apple** had Microsoft work with it to develop its office software to ensure compatibility between *PC* and *Mac* users.

First-Mover Advantage. Being the first to develop the technological standard creates a first-mover advantage to become the strong winner-take-most of the market share leader.[24] For example, in the United States, **Intel** dominates the computer chip microprocessor market. **Amazon.com** dominates online sale of books, and it has expanded to other products. **eBay** dominates the online auction business However, first-movers can lose market share to competitors. For example, **AOL** was once the Internet access provider with paid memberships. **Google** was not the first-mover but has taken the lead in the Internet search engine market away from **Yahoo! Microsoft** is fighting hard to gain market share in the Internet market.

Starbucks Case Question 4: How has Starbucks demonstrated a "winner-take-most" strategy?

Although Starbucks is not a technology-driven firm, Starbucks, by being the first-mover, has set the industry standard for creating a welcoming experience where customers are encouraged to stay as long as they like and are provided with all the amenities necessary to make them comfortable—creating that third place between work and home. Starbucks has added to its first-mover advantage by providing high-speed Internet access and its own website that offers music and videos and by redesigning its stores to fit the local communities.

Learning Outcome 3: Discuss issues of managing technology.

ETHICAL ISSUES IN MANAGING TECHNOLOGY

In this section, we expand on our discussion of ethics to include technology issues. Managers need to obey the laws and adhere to high ethical standards. However, the laws and perception of what is ethical varies globally.[25] We discuss privacy and information security, privacy versus monitoring employees, and biotechnology.

Privacy and Information Security

Technology also has to consider the human factor.[26] Technology has been used to benefit society, but it can also be used for unethical purposes. Technology is raising serious ethical questions regarding society's privacy and the security of information. Although we tend to think of hackers as the major threat when it comes to stealing information, often the thief comes from among the firm's own employees.[27]

Personal Information. It is collected, saved, swapped, and sold through e-commerce. Companies develop detailed profiles of their customers. More firms are tracking our browsing habits to sell us more products.[28] If you buy a product and give the company personal information, how should the information be used? How secure is your information from being stolen from the company and being misused? Here are two sources to help you protect your personal info online. The **Online Privacy Alliance** (www.privacyalliance.org) leads and supports self-regulatory initiatives that create an environment of trust and that foster the protection of individuals' privacy online and in electronic commerce.[29] **OnGuardOnline.gov** (http://onguardonline.gov) is the federal government's website to help you be safe, secure, and responsible online.[30]

Identity Theft. Identity theft by computer hackers is a growing concern as business faces the major challenge of managing information security. Cyber criminals hacked into **CardSystems Solutions** and nabbed 200,000 **Visa**, **MasterCard**, **American Express**, and **Discover** card numbers and potentially exposed tens of millions more.[31] Hackers can also crack into cell phones (and other mobile devices) to steal personal information.[32]

Chief Information and Privacy Officers. Security is its number-one priority.[33] *Chief information officers (CIOs) are responsible for ensuring privacy and information security.* Some companies (including **American Express**, **Citigroup**, **IBM**, and **Sony**) also have *chief privacy officers* (CPOs). CPOs need to balance their customers' right to privacy with the firms' use of information for profit purposes. They also need to keep the business out of privacy lawsuits, which can be very expensive. For more information visit the **CIO** at www.cio.com.

Privacy Policies. Privacy and information security raise many ethical questions. Is it ethical to send spam to people who don't want it or to put adware and spyware devices (cookies) on people's computers without their knowledge and consent? Is it ethical to sell customer lists and consumer information without customers' knowledge and consent? To address some of the issues of invasion of privacy, many businesses have developed privacy policy statements for a variety of stakeholders. The best privacy policies include an "opt-in" policy that requires the firm to notify the customer of how the information is being used, and it requires customer approval to share or sell the information to other businesses. **Apple** is a strong supporter of privacy, so it developed a detailed privacy policy that covers how Apple collects, uses, discloses, transfers, and stores your information.[34]

The **National Consumers League** (www.nclnet.org) created the **Internet Fraud Watch** (www.fraud.org), enabling the **National Fraud Information Center (NFIC)** to offer consumers advice about promotions and cyberspace and route reports of suspected online and Internet fraud to the appropriate government agencies.[35]

Federal Trade Commission (FTC). The government has been involved in helping set standards and laws regarding privacy and information security, and the **FTC** is responsible for protecting consumers. You can file a complaint with the FTC through its helpline (1-877-FTC-HELP) and its website (www.ftc.gov). *Social networking sites* face privacy challenges. **Google** and **Facebook** have had their privacy practices investigated by the DOJ. On a global scale, Google received more than 1,000 requests from governments worldwide to remove content.[36]

Personal and Professional Applications

9. Do you fear misuse of your 12' privacy and/or information security by a business? Has this actually happened to you?

10. Does your present or past employer, or a company it does business with, have a chief privacy officer and privacy policy?

Privacy vs. Monitoring Employees. Business pays its employees to work, and technology makes it easier to know whether employees are working. Employees have been caught using company and personal telephones and cell phones, e-mail, and the Internet for personal use during business hours. Business must balance employee needs for privacy with its need to monitor the quality and quantity of their work. Should firms use video cameras to see if employees are working? Should firms listen to employee telephone conversations, read their e-mail, and check what websites they visit? Should firms use global positioning systems (GPS) to track where employees drive? Should firms monitor employee use of cell phones and texting while driving during business hours to avoid accidents that hurt and kill people and damage property that can bring large lawsuits against the business?

ETHICAL DILEMMA 12.1 How Loving and Caring Was the Loving Care Agency? Reading Employee Personal E-mails

"Big Brother is watching. That is the message corporations routinely send their employees about using e-mail. . . . Many workers log in to personal e-mail accounts from the office. In a 2009 study by the Ponemon Institute, a Traverse City, Michigan-based data-security research firm, 52 percent of employees surveyed said they access their personal e-mail accounts from their work computer. Of those individuals, 60 percent said they send work documents or spreadsheets to their personal e-mail addresses.

Legal experts say that courts in some instances are showing more consideration for employees who feel their employer has violated their privacy electronically. . . . 'Computers are becoming recognized as being so much a part of the ongoing personal as well as professional life of employees and everyone else that courts are more sympathetic all the time to granting greater recognition to privacy,' said Floyd Abrams, a First Amendment attorney at Cahill Gordon & Reindel LLP. Employees often assume their communications on personal e-mail accounts should stay private even if they are using work-issued computers or smart phones. But in most instances when using a work device, e-mails of all kinds are captured on a server and can be retrieved by an employer.

In New Jersey, a worker on the brink of resigning from her job at the Loving Care Agency Inc. used a personal password-protected Yahoo! account on a work laptop to e-mail her lawyer to hash out the details of a workplace discrimination suit she was planning to file against the agency. After the employee, Marina Stengart, left her job and filed suit, her employer extracted the e-mails from the hard drive of her computer laptop.

A lower court found that the e-mails from Stengart were company property, because the company's internal policies had put her on sufficient notice that her e-mails would be viewed. But a New Jersey appellate court disagreed, ruling in her favor, ordering the company to turn over the e-mails to Stengart and delete them from their hard drives. The court's ruling went so far as to dissect the company's internal policies about employee communications and decided they offered 'little to suggest that an employee would not retain an expectation of privacy in such [personal] e-mails.' . . . Loving Care, which declined to comment, has appealed the ruling. The case is pending in the New Jersey Supreme Court."[37]

Questions

1. Why would a firm want to access employee personal e-mail accounts?
2. What expectation of privacy should an employee expect in terms of his or her personal e-mails? Why?
3. How might the use of company equipment (e.g., laptop or server) or company e-mail account impact this expectation?
4. If Loving Care had a chief information and privacy officer, what should have been his or her role relative to this case?
5. How might a detailed privacy policy have helped the firm and the employee better understand employer ownership and employee privacy rights?
6. If you were a member of the New Jersey Supreme Court how would you have ruled on this case? Why?

File Sharing vs. Copyright Infringement. Concerns over intellectual property infringement are ongoing.[38] What moral responsibility should scientists, engineers, and others have for the uses of their work? Was it ethical for software developers of **Napster**, **Grokster**, and others to design P2P file-sharing systems that would allow people to get digital goodies like music and movies without paying for them, in possible violation of copyright laws? Some conclude that the P2P file-sharing systems were actually designed for an illegal activity and that the systems aided their users in committing a crime of stealing copyrighted materials.[39] Some people, including college students, were sued for illegally downloading music.

Codes of Ethics. Some business associations have developed codes of ethics that businesses can use as guidelines See Figure 12.2 for some example organizational resources.

Personal and Professional Applications

11. Do you use business resources during working hours?

12. In what specific ways does your present or past employer monitor your work?

13. Does your present or past employer, or a company it does business with, balance privacy and monitoring employees?

Learning Outcome 4: Describe issues of biotechnology and bioethics.

Biotechnology

Biotechnology combines biology and technology to develop and produce business products. The new industry of biotechnology has created great entrepreneurial business opportunities for health care, pharmaceutical, and agricultural firms to profitably increase our natural lifespan. A great scientific breakthrough came when researchers gained a better understanding of human *deoxyribonucleic acid (DNA)*, which instructs cells to manu-

---

- Computer Ethics Institute (www.computerethicsinstitute.org) developed the "Ten Commandments of Computer Ethics."
- Computer Professionals for Social Responsibility (CPSR, www.cpsr.org) is a global organization promoting the responsible use of computer technology.
- Institute for Business, Technology & Ethics (www.ethix.org) promotes business, technology, and ethics.
- The Center for Information Policy Research (CIPR, www4.uwm.edu/cipr) studies the intersections of policy, ethical, political, social, and legal aspects of the global information society.
- Information Systems Society (www.informs.org/Community/ISS) seeks to foster, promote, and disseminate research on the use and impact of information technology in organizations.
- Ethics Resource Center (www.ethics.org) advances high ethical standards and practices in public and private institutions.

■ **Figure 12.2:** Codes of Computer Ethics Resources

facture proteins that carry out all of the functions of human life. Stem cell research and cloning have the potential to help conquer diseases and replace and regenerate our failing body parts. Two broad categories of genetic biotechnology include genetic engineering and genetically modified foods (GM foods).

Genetic Engineering—Stem Cells and Cloning. Two major issues of genetic engineering include *stem cell research* and *cloning*. Stem cell research is carried out in two areas: embryonic and adult. Stem cells are the basic building blocks of all other cells: that is, they are the raw materials on which our bodies are built. Embryonic stem cells are obtained for research as frozen (usually from fertility clinics where they have been obtained from couples who no longer need them to get pregnant), fresh (created for research, usually in a fertility clinic), and cloned (created by reproducing human cells) cells. Stem cells can also be grown into tissues for transplanting into people who need them for nerve cells, bone cells, and muscle cells. Stem cells offer potential future hope for developing treatments for diseases such as cancer, Alzheimer's, Parkinson's, and juvenile diabetes. Biologists are looking to mass produce stem cells to reduce the high-cost gene-based drugs and vaccines.[40]

Embryonic stem cell research raises ethical and moral concerns with regard to the status of an embryo as a human being. Although an embryo has life (after eight weeks the embryo becomes a fetus), stem cell research ends its life, causing ethical controversy. Using adult stem cells for research is not an ethical or moral issue, so many companies (**Abbott Laboratories**, **Eli Lilly**, **Johnson & Johnson**, **Schering**, and **Wyeth**) are conducting regenerative research using adult stem cells.

Personal and Professional Applications

14. How do you feel about stem cell research and cloning?

15. Should the government allow businesses to conduct stem cell research and cloning?

Genetically Modified Foods. To improve productivity, agribusinesses have been genetically modifying foods (also called GM foods, or biotech foods) for animal and human consumption. Genetic engineers alter the DNA makeup of a living organism by inserting virtually any gene into a plant to create a new crop or new species. GM foods use herbicides (weed killers that leave the desired crop relatively unharmed) and insecticides (bug killers) to improve crop yield. Most of the genetically engineered crops that are commercially available have been developed to carry herbicide-tolerant or insect-resistant genes. The **U.S. Department of Agriculture** (**USDA**, www.usda.gov) approves GM foods.[41] Farmers around the world use **Monsanto**'s innovative products (including *GM seeds* and *Roundup*) to address on-farm challenges and reduce agriculture's overall impact on our environment.[42]

Personal and Professional Applications

16. How do you feel about eating GM foods?

17. Should the government allow business to genetically modify food?

---

of business societal interest groups and built coalitions. Experts gave testimony in favor of increased support for stem cell research. People with diseases that may some-day be eliminated through stem cell research, along with their friends and families, got involved in grassroots campaigning. Part of the strategy was implemented using Internet technology. Although companies are operating in ways to avoid lawsuits, some are being sued or suing others over the use of technology, especially patent violations.[58]

BUSINESS IMPACT ON THE NATURAL ENVIRONMENT

There is clearly a link between technology and environment.[59] Business, society, and government all recognize the importance of environmental protection. Thus, the relationship between business, society, and nature are evident in the management literature.[60] The use and maintenance of the deteriorating natural environment are significant societal issues of our time.[61] Thus, some basic environmental literacy will aid you in making business environmental decisions. Although technology can hurt the natural environment, it can also be used to clean up pollution—cleantech.[62] In this section, we discuss some of the natural environmental issues and environmental responsibility.

Natural Environmental Issues

Many natural environmental issues require global business and government cooperation because all countries share many of the same resources, and pollution in one country affects other countries. Let's examine some natural environmental issues that affect global sustainable development. We begin with pollution, as most of the others are specific types of pollution.

> Learning Outcome 5: Compare and contrast ozone depletion, global warming, and the endangerment of biological diversity.

Pollution. Clearly, economic growth contributes to pollution and to the depletion of our natural resources, and global economic growth will continue to accelerate. *Pollution is a substance released into the environment that has a negative effect on the environment and on society.* Virtually all business contributes to some form of pollution or depletion of our natural resources. Many industries (such as logging and mining) have polluted and depleted the air, water, and land in their extracting, transporting, and processing of raw materials. The manufacturers of the raw materials also pollute and deplete natural resources, as do the retailers and consumers of their products, as they use and discard products. Because environmental issues are now a major social concern, companies in polluting industries face tighter government regulations, increased negative media attention, and strong activism from societal interest groups.[63]

> **Personal and Professional Applications**
>
> 20. How does your present or past employer, or a company it does business with, pollute the natural environment?

Unfortunately, economic growth occurs commonly at the expense of the natural environment. MNCs have been accused of simply exploiting underdeveloped countries for their resources. Foreign MNCs are also polluting in the United States. Part of the problem is government regulations regarding the environment and pollution vary globally.[64]

Ozone Depletion. *Ozone is an oxygen-related gas that floats in a thin layer in the stratosphere between 8 and 25 miles above the earth.* It acts as a strong oxidizing agent and is used in water purification. Near the earth, ozone is a pollutant, but it is vital in the stratosphere because it forms a protective layer that absorbs dangerous ultraviolet radiation emitted by the sun. Excessive ultraviolet radiation can cause skin cancer and damage the eyes and immune systems. Thus, always wearing sunscreen and sunglasses is recommended by doctors.

NASA scientists found a large decrease in ozone over Antarctica in 1985 and then a hole in the ozone layer larger than North America in 2000, letting in more ultraviolet light. The ozone layer has thinned by as much as 30 percent in high latitudes. The cause of the ozone problem was determined to be human-produced chemicals; primarily chlorofluorocarbons (CFCs) used in refrigeration, halons used in fire extinguisher systems, and other chemicals, such as propellants in spray cans. The global community set strict controls on the use of these harmful gases through the United Nations *Montreal Protocol.*

Global Warming. The atmosphere of the earth is heating up, causing potential danger through the greenhouse effect. *The greenhouse effect is the prevention of solar heat absorbed by the atmosphere from returning to space, creating global warming and climate changes.* Some scientists fear that the warming effects are being undesirably increased, causing climate changes. Warming of the earth's surface is the result of atmospheric pollution by gases, primarily the burning of fossil fuels (including, coal, natural gas, and oil), which release carbon dioxide. Other causes of global warming include deforestation (cutting down the trees that absorb carbon dioxide), increased population (breathing out carbon dioxide), raising cattle for beef and dairy products (cows release methane gas), and CFC gases.

On the other side, some scientific studies don't agree that global warming is even a problem,[65] and that the earth has been naturally rising in temperature for centuries. Others contend that cleantech can bring the pace of global warming under control.[66] Congress was considering climate change legislation, but many businesses and the **Chamber of Commerce** aggressively opposed new laws, based on outside research and also citing that business technology can reduce greenhouse gases without needing to legislate it.[67]

In 1997, many global nations met in Kyoto, Japan, to amend the *Convention on Climate Change* of 1992. They came to an agreement known as the **Kyoto Protocol** to reduce greenhouse gases. The nations have continued to meet over the years. By 2003, 110 nations ratified the Kyoto Protocol, which went into effect in 2005. Kyoto is the only international agreement that legally binds some countries to agreed reductions in their greenhouse gases emissions. The problem with Kyoto is that it binds none of the world's three largest polluters that are responsible for nearly one half of all emissions. The United States never signed the protocol, and India and China were exempted from emissions caps. Russia and some other countries did not ratify the protocol either. Kyoto expires in 2012 and during the 2011 meeting, a replacement agreement was not even discussed.[68]

Endangerment of Biological Diversity. *Biodiversity is the number and variety of species and the range of their genetic makeup.* Of the estimated 10 to 100 million species, some 1.7 million species of plants and animals have been named and described so far. Species used to live an average of 1 million years. The current rate of species extinction is between 100 to 1,000 times greater today, and new birthrates are also declining, mainly caused by pollution and the destruction of habitats.[69]

The richest biodiversity appears in rain forests, the number of which has been cut in half; the forests continue to be destroyed, killing species and eliminating sources of food, medicines, and fiber. The survival of 20,000 endangered animal species around the globe is threatened by overhunting and poaching. To help protect biodiversity, 187 countries ratified the *Convention on Biological Diversity*. The United States has not yet ratified the treaty.

Solid and Hazardous Wastes. U.S. business, society, and government produce more than 229 million tons of solid waste each year. Recycling has helped to reduce solid waste, but at the same time, people throw away more trash year after year. The trend toward bottled water has caused more solid waste because an estimated 80 percent of the bottles are not recycled and end up in landfills.[70] Landfills require land, and solid waste pollutes the land, water, and air. With technological advances in new chemicals, we may be developing hazardous waste that is dangerous to people and the environment without knowing it until the damage has been done.

Hazardous waste creates an even greater problem when it requires special handling to prevent harming people and the environment. Hazardous waste in the land, air, and water has been found to cause birth defects, cancer, and several other problems.[71] Some communities have tight controls over the disposal of hazardous waste. With the extra work and high cost of disposal, some people illegally dump hazardous waste in unauthorized areas, causing additional pollution problems.

Land Degradation. The **UN's** *Environment Programme* found multiple causes of land degradation, including land turning to desert, deforestation, overgrazing, salinization, alkalization, soil acidification, urban sprawl, soil sealing, and industrial soil contamination. Human-induced land degradation of soil has put the livelihood of nearly 1 billion people at risk. Each year, 20 million hectares of agricultural land become too degraded for farming or go to urban development. Global land degradation affects about 60 percent of Africa and Asia, 11 percent of Europe, and 8 percent of North America, and the problem is projected to increase.[72]

Deforestation. People depend on trees for building materials, fuel, medicines, chemicals, food, recreation, and jobs. However, cutting down forests without planting trees to replace them hurts our natural environment. Recall that trees absorb greenhouse gases, and burning them adds carbon dioxide to the atmosphere. Moisture and nutrient ecosystems are also damaged through deforestation. Tropical deforestation could result in a 25 percent decrease in the number of primates by the year 2030.[73] On the positive side, the pace of deforestation has slowed, and replanting has increased.

Marine Environment Pollution. Many of the pollutants of fresh water also affect marine (ocean) environments. Trillions of gallons of sewage and industrial waste are dumped into marine waters every year. Pollutants, including oil and plastics, have caused significant damage to a number of coastal ecosystems including salt marshes, mangrove swamps, estuaries, and coral reefs. Shellfish beds have been closed, fish populations have shrunk, people have caught seafood-related illnesses, and the shoreline protection from floods and storms has been damaged. Global warming of the waters is causing coral reefs to die. Toxic and nutrient runoffs are causing algae to grow rapidly in the sea, and the tide brings it in to pollute the shore. Fishing fleets are larger than the ocean can sustain, with fewer fish to catch, and trawling is damaging the bottom of the ocean. Overfishing has cut the variety of ocean predators such as tuna, marlin, and swordfish by as much as half over the past 50 years. U.S. beaches are closing more frequently because of higher levels of pollution.[74]

Freshwater Pollution. Although water pollution is a global problem, in America, more than one-third of the lakes, rivers, and their estuaries are not safe for swimming and fishing; they can't provide a healthy environment for fish and other wildlife. More than 40 percent of American waterways are polluted in violation of the Clean Water Act, yet millions of pounds of dangerous pollutants are legally dumped into our waters each year.[75] Our waters are polluted by sewage, industrial wastes, urban runoff, agricultural runoff, and atmospheric fallout. Dam sedimentation, deforestation, overharvesting, overgrazing, and overirrigation also harm our waters.

The global water supply is unevenly distributed, causing shortages in many countries. People in some developing countries face droughts, land turning to desert, waterborne diseases, and contamination of water. An estimated 1.5 million people (mostly children) died in 2007 from waterborne illness.[76] Some people have to walk great distances each day to get fresh water to survive. China has less water than it needs for its large population, and the Aral Sea in the former Soviet Union lost two-thirds of its water. It has been estimated that by the year 2025, two-thirds of the global population will be living in countries under water-stress conditions.[77]

Personal and Professional Applications

21. Which of the eight natural environmental issues is most relevant to you? Why?

22. Which of the eight natural environmental issues is most relevant to your present or past employer, or a company it does business with? Why?

Environmental Responsibility

Environmental problems are global in scope and too complex to assign simple blame and responsibility for correcting the problems. Here we discuss how people are passing the buck rather than taking responsibility for resolving environmental issues and how activists and other stakeholders are helping to solve our environmental problems.

NIMBY. "Not in my back yard" (NIMBY) illustrates attitudes and behaviors that deny responsibility for the misuse of our natural environment and for pollution. We throw out lots of trash, but who wants to live near the dump? People want good-paying manufacturing jobs, but who wants to live near the plant? Some activists fight against allowing the plant to locate in the community. Many people don't want to conserve energy; many even waste it. Yet, when a power plant wants to meet local electric needs, the community fights to keep the plant out of its town. Some companies pollute but don't want to pay the full cost of preventing the problems or cleaning up after the natural environment has been damaged by them. How would you categorize your business's responses to environmental issues?[78]

The NIMBY phenomenon is a complex societal issue. For example, many people and organizations are polluting and degrading the environment, but no one is the single cause of the problem, and most people want to do as little as possible to solve the problem, hoping someone else will do so. For example, in numerous cities, the personal automobile is the single greatest polluter (not business), as emissions from millions of vehicles on the road add up.[79] If you drive a car, you are part of the problem. What are you doing to solve the problem?

Starbucks Case Question 6: Which environmental issues is Starbucks dealing with and how?

Starbucks is taking anything but a NIMBY approach to environmental issues. Starbucks is committed to minimizing its environmental impacts throughout its entire supply chain, from coffee bean to coffee cup. It therefore deals with issues related to global warming, solid waste, and deforestation. Starbucks' approach to minimizing its environmental footprint is guided by its environmental mission statement, which was adopted in 1992. Starbucks Environmental Footprint Team guides the company's environmental approach and establishes initiatives aimed at minimizing its impact on the planet. Starbucks environmental efforts are visible throughout its supply chain, from working with farmers to preserving the natural environment in places where coffee is grown to recycling coffee grounds into nutrient-rich soil amendment. Starbucks examines the environmental performance of store design and operations and seeks to reduce waste and energy and water consumption—the major impacts of its stores.

Personal and Professional Applications

23. What attempts are you making to conserve energy and cut down on pollution?

Environmental Ethics. Living creatures, by their mere existence, pollute the environment. Animals expel carbon dioxide, urea, and fecal matter—pollutants that the environment has historically been able to absorb and reprocess, creating a natural balance. Humankind, due to the evolutionary development of advanced technology, has added to this environmental pollution, and as some would argue, to the point of offsetting nature's balance. So the question becomes, what level of destruction and pollution is acceptable from an ethics point of view? How clean should our air, water, and land be? Are people willing to share our limited natural resources or just pursue their own self-interests? How should we leave the environment for future generations?[80] Who should decide what environmental practices are ethical and unethical? Values are important, but actions speak louder than words. We need government to help protect our natural environment. How much should we pay to have a clean environment? Public sentiment is on the environment side, but not that many people per capita get involved as social activists to help the environment.

Societal Interest Groups. Numerous societal interest groups rally people to support their cause, which focuses on "greening" (maintaining and improving our natural environment), commonly called the environmental movement.[81] Green social activists are pressuring business to be greener.[82] They have successfully used picketing, demonstrations, boycotts, education, research, negative publicity, lobbying, and lawsuit strategies to get global business, society, and governments to better protect our natural environment. Figure 12.4 presents a list of two related governmental agencies followed by a list of societal Interest Groups.

Some economists are going green by opting to work for societal interest groups using economic arguments to persuade businesses to be greener.[83] Green advocates challenge specific businesses to be more environmentally friendly. For example,

---

Department of Energy—Green Power Network (www.eere.energy.gov/greenpower): Provides up-to-date information on green power providers, product offerings, consumer protection issues, and policies affecting green power markets. Green Power Network is operated by the NREL of the U.S. Department of Energy.

National Renewable Energy Laboratory (NREL) (www.nrel.gov): The only federal laboratory dedicated to the research, development, commercialization, and deployment of renewable energy and energy efficiency technologies.

Audubon (www.audubon.org): Conserves and restores natural ecosystems and biodiversity.

Earth Charter Initiative (www.earthcharterinaction.org): Sixteen principles; four (5–8) promote ecological integrity.

EnviroLink Network (www.envirolink.org): Provides access to thousands of online environmental resources.

Environmental Defense Fund (www.edf.org): Scientists, economists, and lawyers team up to solve environmental problems.

Greenpeace (www.greenpeace.org): Protects against threats to our planet's biodiversity and natural environment.

Intergovernmental Panel on Climate Change (IPCC www.ipcc.ch): The leading international body for the assessment of climate change.

Izaak Walton League of America (www.iwla.org): Defends soil, air, woods, waters, and wildlife.

National Resources Defense Council (www.nrdc.org): Working to curb global warming and create a clean energy future; improving our water and protecting wildlife and wild places.

Rainforest Action Network (RAN) (www.ran.org): Campaigns for the forests, their inhabitants, and the natural systems.

Sierra Club (www.sierraclub.org): Works to protect communities, wild places, and the planet itself.

Sustainable Style Foundation (www.sustainablestyle.org): Provides information, resources, and innovative programs that promote sustainable living and sustainable design.

UN Environment Programme (UNEP) (www.unep.org): Identifies and works to solve global environmental problems.

UN Global Compact (www.unglobalcompact.org): Ten principles; three (7–9) promoting environmental responsibility

World Resources Institute (wri.org): Works with governments, companies, and civil society to build solutions to urgent environmental challenges.

▦ **Figure 12.4:** Green Government and Societal Interest Groups

RAN pressured **Burger King** to stop selling rainforest beef, **Mitsubishi** to be more environmentally friendly in harvesting Asian rainforests, **Occidental Petroleum** to stop causing the harmful effects of planned oil exploration and development in Colombia rainforests, and **Home Depot** and **Lowe's** to be greener in general. **Greenpeace** pressured **Shell** to remove its petroleum platforms in the North Sea in an environmentally friendly manner.

Green Business Interest Groups. Figure 12.5 contains a list of some green business interest groups.

Other Stakeholders. Business also listens to green consumers, employees, and investor stakeholders. Consumers want to deal with green companies that produce environmentally safe products. They are more likely to buy environmentally green products than to volunteer to help green advocates. Green consumers are commonly young, well-paid,

---

Ceres (www.ceres.org): The Ceres Principles is a 10-point code of corporate environmental conduct.

Dow Jones Sustainability Indexes (www.dowjones.com/sustainability): Measure the performance of the world's sustainability leaders in multiple categories.

Global Environmental Management Initiative (GEMI) (www.gemi.org): *Business helping business achieves environmental sustainability excellence.*

Green Building Council (www.usgbc.org): Promotes buildings that are environmentally responsible, profitable, and healthy places to live and work—it rates and certifies buildings (LEED).

GreenBiz Group (www.greenbiz.com): Provides information, resources, and learning opportunities to help companies integrate environmental responsibility into their operations in a manner that supports profitable business practices.

International Chamber of Commerce (ICC) (www.ICCWbo.org): "Green Economy Roadmap;" sets out 10 conditions needed to drive growth in a resource-constrained world with strong demographic growth.

International Organization for Standardization (ISO) (www.iso.org): ISO 14001 environmental management systems standards certification.

Environmental Leader (www.environmentalleader.com): Daily trade publication that keeps corporate executives fully informed about energy, environmental, and sustainability news.

Sustainability Consortium (www.sustainabilityconsortium.org): Through multi-stakeholder global collaboration, participants are working to make the world more sustainable through better products and consumption.

Sustainable Businesses (www.sustainablebusiness.com): Provides global news and networking services to help green business grow.

World Business Council for Sustainable Development (WBCSD) (www.wbcsd.org): CEO-led organization that galvanizes the global business community to create a sustainable future for business, society, and the environment.

■ **Figure 12.5:** Green Business and Interest Groups

highly educated Internet users. Green employees are promoting environmentalism at work. They go beyond the traditional health and safety issues and work on pollution prevention, recycling, energy and environmental audits, and community projects. Many firms, including **Ace Hardware**, **Apple Computer**, **Eastman Kodak**, and **Goldman Sachs**, have "green teams" to promote their environmental values at work.

Green investors own stock in green companies. Similar to investing in socially responsible companies, investors can select from a growing number of mutual funds, stock and bond offerings, money market funds, and other financial instruments that include environmental components.

Personal and Professional Applications

24. Are you a green consumer, employee, and/or investor?

ENVIRONMENTAL PROTECTION REGULATIONS AND LAWS

In this section, we discuss government regulation, environmental laws, and cost–benefit analysis of regulation.

Learning Outcome 6: Discuss the major environmental laws and regulations.

Government Regulation

The role of the government is to protect its people and its environment. A single business has little incentive to incur additional costs that exceed those of its competitors to protect the environment. In fact, when a single firm operates in an environmentally responsible way, the result is usually greater cost, higher prices, and less business. Thus, government is needed to set a common standard for business so that all companies can compete on a level playing field. To this end, Congress passes environmental statutes; executive regulators set the standards and enforce the laws; and courts interpret the laws and determine the outcomes of lawsuits. The government can also offer incentives to reduce pollution and maintain our natural resources.

NEPA. In 1970, the U.S. *National Environmental Policy Act (NEPA)* was passed. The act requires all federal agencies to prepare *environmental impact statements (EISs)* for any proposals for legislation and other major federal action that would significantly affect the quality of the human environment. Business consultants are hired to prepare EISs. Firms wanting to secure licenses and permits to conduct timber, grazing, mining, highway, dam, and nuclear construction operations will need EISs. Businesses with federal government contracts usually must participate in EISs. NEPA is often the model for state governments, so businesses with significant state and local contracts usually are involved in the EIS process.

EPA. The Environmental Protection Agency (EPA, www.epa.gov) is the primary U.S. regulatory body responsible for administering environmental laws and for coordinating our federal, state, and local efforts. The EPA works to develop and enforce regulations that implement environmental laws enacted by Congress. When Congress passes an environmental law, EPA regulators write specific rules to be followed to obey the law.

The EPA was also established in 1970 to enforce the NEPA as an independent agency to research pollution problems, aid state and local government environmental efforts, and administer many of the federal environmental laws. The mission of the EPA is to protect human health and the environment (air, water, and land). The EPA is responsible for researching and setting national standards for a variety of environmental programs, and it delegates to states and tribes the responsibility of issuing permits and monitoring and enforcing compliance. When national standards are not met, the EPA can issue sanctions and take other steps to assist the states and tribes in reaching the desired levels of environmental quality.[84] Under the Obama administration, the EPA got tougher on environmental rules and enforcement, which some industries and businesses fought, including **GM**.[85] The EPA developed new rules curbing drilling methods for fracking oil underground.[86]

Pollution-Control Enforcement Methods. The two major approaches to pollution control are command-and-control and incentive. Under *command-and-control*, the government sets environmental standards and specifies how all business will control pollution, such as the specific types of equipment that must be used. This one-size-fits-all approach often leads to excessive costs for some firms and allows others to pollute excessively.

The *incentive system* sets pollution goals, but it allows the businesses flexibility on how to reach the goal. One incentive approach is the *tradable permit program* that allows businesses to buy and sell the right to pollute. For example, each company has a set amount it can pollute—its tradable permit. If a firm is efficient and pollutes less than its allocation, it can sell its permit to an inefficient company. Thus, the inefficient companies pay more to pollute and have the incentive to voluntarily cut back pollution. The government gradually cuts back the amount of allowable pollution, leaving businesses to determine how they will meet the goals. Another incentive system is for the government to charge a fee (green tax or eco-tax) based on the amount of pollution. Thus, business has an incentive to pollute less. The government also gives consumers tax incentives to conserve energy.

Environmental Laws

Environmental protection laws are commonly categorized into three areas: air, water, and land. However, specific environmental issues often involve more than one category.

Air. The primary air quality law is the Clean Air Act, amended in 1990. *The Clean Air Act requires the EPA to set national standards that limit pollution harmful to people and the environment without regard for the cost.* The EPA sets standards to control six substance emissions, known as *criteria pollutants* that are the primary air quality threats (see Figure 12.6).[87]

1. Carbon monoxide (primarily from vehicle emissions)
2. Nitrogen dioxide (primarily from vehicle exhaust and fuel combustion in industry)
3. Sulfur dioxide (primarily from electric utilities burning coal and oil—contributes to acid rain and particle pollution)
4. Ozone (primarily from vehicle emissions and industry)
5. Particulates (primarily from industry—the dust particles are commonly raised by vehicle travel and the wind, and they are the greatest health risk)
6. Lead (primarily in areas around lead processing, such as lead smelters and battery plants)

■ **Figure 12.6:** EPA Criteria Pollutants

In addition to the six criteria pollutants, the Clean Air Act specified controlling *hazardous air pollutants* or *toxins*. The EPA identified many air toxins and it set standards for 187 air toxins. About a quarter of toxins come from large industry, including electric utilities, oil refineries, paper mills, and chemical plants. Smaller sources include dry cleaning, gas stations, and diesel exhaust.

Other damaging air pollutant problems include acid rain, indoor pollution, ozone, and greenhouse gases. *Acid rain* is primarily caused by burning fossil fuels, which release harmful amounts of nitric and sulfuric acids, causing chemical reactions in the atmosphere. Americans spend 80–90 percent of their time indoors, so *indoor pollution* is another problem. Indoor air is polluted by a mix of harmful substances, including asbestos, radon, tobacco smoke, combustion by-products from cooking, chlorine gas released from chlorinated water, biological contaminates such as mite dust and vapors from insecticides, glue, and paint. We have already discussed the problems of *ozone* and *greenhouse gases* and their relationship to global warming.

Water. The primary water quality law is the Clean Water Act (or the Federal Water Pollution Control Act). *The Clean Water Act sets broad environmental quality goals and an implementation system for the federal and state governments.* The primary purpose of the act is for water quality to be consistent with protecting fish, shellfish, and wildlife and with safe conditions for people, including use for recreation. The act cut back, but did not eliminate, the level of pollutants discharged into U.S. rivers, streams, and lakes, and it required a permit to release polluted factory discharge into waterways. *The National Pollutant Discharge Elimination System (NPDES) was created to specify maximum permissible discharge levels and timetables for installing state-of-the-art water-pollution control equipment.* Each factory is analyzed to determine the effluent levels of a substance the water can absorb before unacceptable deterioration and the ability of equipment to remove the pollutant.

The *Marine Protection, Research, and Sanctuaries Act* of 1972 sets standards to control the discharge of pollutants within U.S. coastal ocean waters. The *Safe Drinking Water Act*, amended in 1996, sets minimum standards for various contaminants in both public water systems and aquifers that supply drinking-water wells. The *Pesticide Control Act* restricts the use of dangerous pesticides that can pollute groundwater. Recall our prior discussion of marine environment pollution and freshwater pollution.

Although the EPA controls direct effluent into water, a major water pollution problem is indirect effluent—*runoff.* Agricultural runoff (animal wastes, pesticides, and fertilizers) is now the primary cause of water pollution. Thus, the EPA has placed several thousand large farming operations under pollution permits allowing a set amount of pollution. Urban runoff is another major pollutant, and the EPA is now requiring that cities prevent water from flowing through their streets causing polluted water to be used by the greater population.

Land. Recall our discussion of solid and hazardous wastes and land degradation. Land pollution and degradation are more visible and more locally focused than air and water pollution. The two primary land acts are the Solid Waste Disposal Act of 1965 and the Resource Conservation and Recovery Act of 1976. *The Solid Waste Disposal Act gives regional, state, and local governments the main responsibility for nontoxic waste management.* The EPA assists them with research and other projects. However, the *Resource Conservation and Recovery Act created a federal system for the responsibility of hazardous waste.* It is a (cradle-to-grave) system for tracking and reporting the generation, transportation, and eventual disposal of hazardous wastes by those firms generating the waste.

The *Toxic Substances Control Act* of 1976 requires manufacturing and distributing businesses in the chemical industry to identify any chemicals that pose substantial risks to people and the environment. The act also requires chemical testing before commercialization with potential denial of use of the chemical. With new chemicals being developed each year, the EPA primarily focuses on controlling chemicals that may cause cancer, birth defects, or gene mutations.

The *Comprehensive Environmental Response, Compensation, and Liability Act* of 1980 (*CERCLA*), better known as the *Superfund*, is another toxic waste initiative to clean up more than 2,000 hazardous waste dumps and spills around the United Sates. The Superfund comes from taxes on chemicals and petroleum. The Superfund has an EPA National Priorities List for cleanup. Legal and financial responsibility for the cleanup is assigned to the polluters when they can be identified, and the Superfund pays when they can't. New unauthorized hazardous waste spills must be reported and cleaned up. An amendment to the law was the *Emergency Planning and Community Right-to-Know Act* of 1986. It requires manufacturers to present an annual report of their released chemicals. Reports are available online from the EPA (www.epa.gov/triexplorer).

Trend. The government is currently taking a more proactive approach, trying to prevent pollution rather than clean it up after the damage. To this end, Congress passed the Pollution Prevention Act of 1990. *The Pollution Prevention Act provides guidelines, training, and incentives for companies to reduce pollution.* The trend is also toward the use of environmental incentive systems rather than command and control.

Costs and Benefits of Environmental Regulation

As with everything the government gets involved with, the question of whether the benefits outweigh the costs can be debated at great length. Some believe that the costs of reduced capital investment, lost jobs, and lower productivity outweigh the benefits. Others believe that having a clean environment improves the quality of life and outweighs the costs. At the center of this debate is the EPA.

The EPA is a large federal agency with an $8.4 billion budget for 2012 and more than 17,000 employees.[88] The total annual cost of the EPA is estimated at $900 per person in the United States.[89] Business spending to meet regulations can divert funds from investing in new plants and equipment, research and development, and other business activities. The cost of using substitute products for banned pollutants can also be expensive. Some plants have been unable to meet pollution standards and have gone out of business, and workers have lost their jobs. Environmental standards and costs are higher in the United States than in other countries; this hurts businesses' global competitiveness and can lead to outsourcing production and jobs to plants in other countries with lower costs and environmental standards.

On the other hand, environmental regulation stimulates some business sectors. Business activity and jobs are growing in the environmental service and pollution control industries, such as environmental consulting, recycling and reuse, waste management, and pollution control products. Keeping our environment clean maintains property values, fishing and recreation facilities and their employees, and tourism, which helps the local economy. Without government control, our environment would continue to deteriorate at an increasing rate. More people would become ill, and health–maintenance costs would rise.

Again, it is easier to put a price on the costs than the benefits. How do we put a price on the health and life of a person and the other nonquantifiable benefits of a clean environment? Actually, recall that the government must do a cost–benefit analysis to justify new regulation, and the assumptions are subjective. Ultimately, the decision about how much to spend and how clean the environment should be is made by society through the political process. Each year, the EPA develops goals (Annual Performance Plan) and a budget (Congressional Justification) that must be approved by Congress, which is submitted by the president.[90]

Out of the White House Office of Management & Budget, the **Office of Information & Regulatory Affairs (ORIA)** sits in judgment over most proposed government rules, especially those for environment, health, and safety.[91] ORIA is critically important because it is the only real gatekeeper in Washington. Business feared that the Obama ORIA would enact many new environmental regulations, but its head has blocked some green rules based on the costs being greater than the benefits.[92]

ETHICAL DILEMMA 12.2 BP PLC and the U.S. EPA—Is BP Trying to Cleaning Up Its Act or Just Its Image?

BP PLC is "is the world's #3 publicly traded integrated oil concern, behind Exxon Mobil and Royal Dutch Shell. BP explores for oil and gas in 30 countries and has proved reserves of 17.8 billion barrels of oil equivalent. BP is the largest oil and gas producer in the United States and a top refiner, with 16 refineries processing 4 million barrels of crude oil per day; it is also a major producer of petrochemicals. BP operates 21,800 gas stations worldwide."[93] With a net income in 2011 of nearly $26 billion dollars and an annual sales growth rate of nearly 28 percent one would think that CEO Robert W. Dudley would be relaxing on easy street, yet BP is cleaning up more than just at the bank; it is trying to clean up its image along with oils spills.[94]

How so? BP is promoting their publicly circulated 2012 Code of Conduct. "Safety is good business. Everything we do relies upon the safety of our workforce and the communities around us. We care about the safe management of the environment. We are committed to safely delivering energy to the world. . . . We operate in hazardous environments, and we are committed to excellence and to the disciplined management of our operations. Our leaders have the responsibility of being role models for safety leadership and creating the right environment for people to be comfortable living the value of safety. Our health, safety, security and environment (HSSE) goals are no accidents, no harm to people, and no damage to the environment."[95]

However, public relations aside, the code does not seem to have fueled its operations. Responsibility for the 2010 disastrous blowout and gas explosion on BP's leased Deepwater Horizon offshore drilling rig in the Gulf of Mexico are a long way from being determined. Yet already BP's actions are facing unprecedented scrutiny, thanks to a years-long history of legal and ethical violations that critics, judges, and members of Congress say shows that the London-based company has a penchant for putting profits ahead of just about everything else. Over the past two decades, BP subsidiaries have been convicted three times of environmental crimes in Alaska and Texas, including two felonies. It remains on probation for two of them.

"It also has received the biggest ever fine for willful work safety violations in U.S. history and is the subject of a wide range of safety investigations, including one in Washington State that resulted last week in a relatively minor $69,000 fine for 13 'serious' safety violations at its Cherry Point refinery near Ferndale, Washington. While BP has said it accepts responsibility for the spill, it denies that it's guilty of a systematic pattern of safety and environmental failures. 'We are a responsible and professional company,' said BP Alaska spokesman Steve Rinehart. 'We work to high standards. Safety is our highest priority.' A review of BP's history, however, shows a pattern of ethically questionable and illegal behavior that goes back decades. BP's best-known disaster took place in 2005, when an explosion at its refinery in Texas City near Galveston killed 15 workers, injured 180 people, and forced thousands of nearby residents to remain sheltered in their homes."[96]

Questions

1. What natural environmental issues are raised by the BP oil spill?
2. How might NIMBY impact this situation?
3. Which societal and business interest groups might take an interest in this situation? Why?
4. Which environmental laws might apply when investigating the oil spill?
5. What is the ethical dilemma facing CEO Robert W. Dudley?
6. What would you do if you were Robert W. Dudley?

Personal and Professional Applications

25. Do the personal costs to you outweigh the benefits of a clean environment?

26. Identify some of the major costs and benefits of a clean environment to your present or past employer, or a company it does business with.

SUSTAINABILITY

Learning Outcome 7: Compare sustainability concepts.

Sustainability is about repairing and maintaining our natural environment. The issue involves a human dimension.[97] *Sustainability is meeting the needs of today without sacrificing future generations' ability to meet their needs.*[98] Sustainability is now a business buzzword, and it is an important topic for all countries.[99] Society expects sustainability and for managers to use resources wisely and responsibly; protect the environment; minimize the amount of air, water, energy, minerals, and other materials found in the final goods we consume; recycle and reuse these goods to the extent possible rather than drawing on nature to replenish them; respect nature's calm, tranquility, and beauty; and eliminate toxins that harm people in the workplace and communities.[100] This section describes sustainable development, the World Business Council for Sustainable Development (WBCSD), Sustainability Consortium, codes of environmental conduct, and business green management initiatives.

Sustainable Development

Environmental issues are now a major social concern,[101] and sustainable development has become one of the foremost issues facing the world.[102] Sustainability, or multifaceted long-term quality of life, may be the most complex yet vital phenomenon of our time. Environmental, social, and economic sustainability are interconnected from the local to global scale. How we use our natural resources impacts business and society and its natural environment on a global basis, as we sometimes are destructive. In other words, if China and India pollute the air and water, it will affect people and society in the United States. Being aware of this crisis, business, society, and governments are working to support our environment through sustainable development.[103] Growth shouldn't occur at the expense of the environment. *Sustainable development balances the need for economic growth with the need to maintain our natural environment.* However, getting global businesses and governments to cooperate is difficult.

Starbucks Case Question 7: How is Starbucks addressing sustainable development?

Starbucks works with farmers to preserve the natural environment in places where coffee is grown by recycling coffee grounds into nutrient-rich soil amendments. It supports sustainable growth by paying coffee farmers premium prices to help them make a profit and support their families; providing coffee farmers access to affordable credit through various loan funds so that farmers can invest in their farms and their future success; and purchasing conservation and certified coffees, including Fair Trade Certified™, shade grown, and certified organic, to promote responsible environmental and economic efforts. It also encourages participation in Starbucks Coffee and Farmer Equity Practices (C.A.F.E. Practices), a set of socially responsible coffee-buying guidelines, by offering preferential buying status for participants that score the highest on verified reports. Furthermore it invests in social programs to build schools, health clinics, and other projects that benefit coffee-growing communities, and it collaborates with farmers through the Farmer Support Center, located in Costa Rica, to provide technical support and training that promotes high-quality coffee for the future.

WBCSD, Sustainability Consortium, and Codes of Environmental Conduct

World Business Council for Sustainable Development (WSCSD). One of the leaders in the global effort to promote sustainable business practices, the **WBCSD** (www.wbcsd.org), is listed in Figure 12.5 and described in greater detail here. WBCSD's motto is "business solutions for a sustainable world." Its mission is to provide business leadership as a catalyst for change toward sustainable development, and to support the business license to operate, innovate, and grow in a world increasingly shaped by sustainable development issues. The WBCSD is a CEO-led global association of about 200 companies from more than 35 countries and 20 different industries, including **IBM**, **Nokia**, **Deutsche Bank**, **Honda**, **Infosys**, and **Cemex**, dealing exclusively with business and sustainable development.

The WBCSD challenges businesses to manufacture and distribute products more efficiently, to consider their lifelong impact, and to recycle components. It believes that more eco-efficient companies are more competitive and more environmentally sound. *Eco-efficiency* is a management philosophy that encourages business to search for environmental improvements that yield parallel economic benefits, which means adding the most value with the least use of resources and pollution.[104] For more information about WBCSD, visit its website www.wbcsd.org.

Sustainability Consortium. *Sustainability Consortium* (www.sustainabilityconsortium.org) is also listed in Figure 12.5. Through multistakeholder global collaboration, participants are working to make the world more sustainable through better products and consumption. The Consortium develops and promotes science and integrated tools that enable stakeholders to improve informed decision making for product sustainability throughout the entire product life cycle across all relevant consumer goods sectors. Its mission is to design and implement credible, transparent, and scalable science-based measurement and reporting systems accessible for all producers, retailers, and users of consumer products.[105] Unfortunately, rating products on sustainability is difficult and many companies are complaining about their ratings.[106]

Codes of Environmental Conduct. In line with codes of conduct, organizations also develop codes of environmental conduct, which are helping sustainability.[107] Many companies have developed their own codes or follow the codes developed by other organizations. Review Figure 12.5 for a list, especially **ISO 14001** certification, the **International Chamber of Commerce**, and **U.S. Green Building Council**. Industry-specific organizations also have codes of environmental conduct.

Green Management

Should businesses undertake activities to ensure sustainability, which are referred to as *green management?* The term *green management* came from people's expectations of how managers should conduct their business to protect the environment.[108] Some people state that businesses should only engage in green management activity that complements the business and pays for itself.[109] Green management pays for itself when the expense of the activity reduces costs and/or boosts efficiency.[110] Business saves money by reducing energy and waste.[111] On the other side, some people state that business has a moral obligation to go green; whether it pays is only partly relevant.[112] In another approach, some entrepreneurs have started business ventures to help firms go green.[113] The question is, is a green business a sustainable business?[114]

Today, most businesses view the green of the environment and the green of economics and financial returns as going hand in hand, so they embrace green management.[115] Within the last few years a new title has emerged—*chief sustainability officer (CSO)*. Linda Fisher is the CSO of **DuPont**, and her job is twofold. First, to keep operations in compliance with the law and to go beyond that to reduce the company's footprint—to increase efficiency and reduce cost. The second part is to find market opportunities that are evolving through societal needs—new ventures.[116] Many firms, including **Intel**, are including "*Sustainability Reports*" in their annual reports.[117]

Green products are increasing,[118] but businesses also need sustainability going from natural resource extraction through manufacturing and service delivery processes to material and energy reuse.[119] Organizations have advanced sustainability by implementing the following green management activities: reducing energy consumption, conserving water supplies, improving air quality, and preserving ecosystems and other community ills. Firms are going "green" by constructing energy-efficient buildings, installing or upgrading recycling systems, using renewable energy, purchasing environmentally preferable equipment and supplies, and working with one another and with surrounding communities to advance sustainability values.[120]

Here are a few company-specific examples of green management practices.

▪ **Walmart** has been building green stores for a while now. The Sustainability Consortium actually came about through Walmart bringing together retailers, suppliers, and research groups to develop a sustainability index to track suppliers. The Consortium rates most items sold in Walmart for more than 50 product categories.[121] Its new "green" environmental labeling program for the products it carries could redefine the design and makeup of consumer goods sold around the globe. The rating will boost costs for suppliers and customers. Customers will see the ratings alongside prices for everything from T-shirts to televisions.[122]

▪ **Amazon.com** is going green in many ways with: frustration-free packaging, reducing packaging waste, environmentally friendly packaging, Earth Kaizens, eco-friendly building designs (LEED-certified), and the sale of green products.

▪ **3M Company** is known for adopting a comprehensive proactive environmental policy as a competitive advantage. Its life cycle management programs are designed to minimize environmental impact from product design to consumer disposal.[123]

▪ **Dell Computer** has designed its PCs with many recyclable parts and offers free recycling to its customers. Many old computers are taken apart, rebuilt, and sold as refurbished machines.[124]

▪ **Volkswagen** designs cars for eventual disassembly and reuse. Old cars can be taken apart in just three minutes. Plastics, steel, precious metals, oil, acid, and glass are separated and processed. Many materials are used again in its new cars.[125]

▪ **Nike** is working to make its supply chain and products greener; for example, the sole of its new *Air Jordan* is made with ground-up bits of old Nike sneakers.[126]

▪ **Nissan** CEO Carlos Ghosn hopes to be a first-mover by leapfrogging the hybrid cars with its all-electric battery-powered *Leaf*.[127] "Are people willing to pay more for more sustainable products? By and large the answer is no."[128] So will drivers buy the Leaf? Nissan has invested more than $5 billion in the first version of the Leaf, with sales starting in December 2010. Ghosn expects the Leaf to be profitable with global sales of 500,000 in 2013.[129] Only time will tell whether the Leaf will turn into a green profit opportunity or red losses.

Personal and Professional Applications

27. Select a business and identify some of its green management activities.

Starbucks Case Question 8: Why is Starbucks a role model for green business?

Starbucks, through its strong financial performance and commitment to sustaining businesses and preserving the environment, has demonstrated that a business can minimize its impact on the environment while achieving financial success. It is successful because it has tapped into green consumers (Generation Yers) who are willing to pay more for an excellent cup of coffee knowing that, through their purchase, they are supporting sustainable development and environmental protection.

BUSINESS NONMARKET AND MARKET ENVIRONMENTAL STRATEGIES AND ETHICS

In this section, we discuss information, societal, political, and legal strategies, and environmental sustainability strategies. The current trend is to integrate sustainability into strategic management,[130] as we are doing here. As a manager, you should take a profit-maximizing approach to green management by adapting strategic green activities in which the benefits outweigh the cost.[131] Even small companies are profiting by adapting sustainability strategies.[132] The MNC green management activities listed in the sustainability section are all strategies, and we will give some more examples in this section.

Crisis, issues, and stakeholder management (Chapter 2) all apply to the natural environment. Crisis management is important to prevent and deal with environmental accidents. Issues management includes staying on top of natural environment trends to deal with problems in the early stages of product life cycles.

Information Strategies

Companies often have to present their side of the environmental issue through effective information strategies.[133] The growth of bottled water slowed due to green backlash when most water bottles were ending up in landfills. Thus, companies are using green management.[134] For example, the label on **Pepsi**'s Aquafina water bottles says they are made with 100 percent recycled material, including caps and labels.[135] Many corporations now provide more information about their environmental activities. Homebuyers are going green to cut bills,[136] while **GE** and **Whirlpool** are making greener more-profitable products and informing buyers of the savings on energy that comes from using energy-efficient appliances.[137] Many MNCs are setting environmental goals and conducting environmental audits that are then included in their annual reports.

Societal Strategies

MNCs are becoming more active in pursuing strategies to achieve sustainable solutions to environmental problems.[138] *Social entrepreneurs* focus their companies on addressing environmental issues.[139] Through operating a global supply chain in a sustainable manner by engaging in socially responsible green management activities, businesses can also increase sales, decrease costs, and increase profits.[140] Recall that many companies' annual reports include a section on social responsibility. Some companies are now using *triple bottom line (TBL)* reporting—financial, social, and environmental.[141]

Thousands of companies follow business interest group guidelines and ISO 14000 standards that require triple bottom line reporting. They use business codes of environmental ethics or develop their own written codes of conduct. Having a code of ethics can promote a positive image. **GE**'s general code of conduct includes a statement of environmental ethics (Chapter 5, Figure 5.5).

Depending on the issue, many MNCs are using the grand strategy of working with societal green interest groups, called environmental partnerships. For example, under pressure from **Citizens Clearinghouse for Hazardous Waste**, McDonald's converted from polystyrene containers and plastic nonbiodegradable packaging to biodegradable paper products. **McDonald's** established a joint task force that worked with the **Environmental Defense (ED)** to reduce McDonald's solid waste.

As discussed earlier, business coalitions of interest groups are cooperating in becoming more environmentally friendly. Businesses that are environmentally friendly get positive news media coverage and gain favorable public sentiment for being ethically and socially responsible. Research supports that being green enhances a company's reputation to the benefit of its marketing and its subsequent financial performance.[142] Patagonia founder started the **Patagonia Music Collective**—musicians who give back to the environment program. The program features about 100 artists donating $.99 benefit per track on **iTunes**. All proceeds go to the environmental groups of the artists' choosing.[143]

Political and Legal Strategies

Business must interact with a variety of regulatory officials to obtain permits, to influence regulation, to receive guidance on meeting standards, and to inspect facilities, which is complex for MNCs facing different standards in various countries.[144] Sometimes MNCs' grand political strategies are to oppose environmental regulation that is overly burdensome, but they also commonly work with regulators to suggest new ways of achieving environmental goals in a more efficient manner. Companies have worked with the EPA, such as through project XL (eXellence and Leadership), to relax regulations in order to try innovative lower-cost methods. Companies that sign up for voluntary cooperation keep records and report results to the EPA but are not penalized for missing their goals. **Georgia-Pacific** tried using a new steam gasification technology rather than simply installing a new incinerator.

Political constituency-focused strategies are common.[145] Business commonly donates to politicians and lobbies them to influence environmental regulations. Companies often use their supply chains for grassroots campaigning to politicians. Corporations may build coalitions, frequently with the help of business interest groups, to develop new innovative solutions to pollution problems. Executives give testimony at hearings to explain how regulations do and will affect business and the natural environment.

Companies must meet the legal environmental requirements to avoid costly fines, liability, lawsuits, and even criminal charges. In addition to defending themselves against lawsuits, in their own defense, businesses may also sue individuals, societal interest groups, and the government. Activists tried to stop the Yucca Mountain nuclear-waste repository through a lawsuit, but the court ruled in favor of the business.[146] As discussed previously, successful companies are proactive environmentally and go beyond the legal minimum to be ethical.

Starbucks Case Question 9: What nonmarket strategies is Starbucks employing to address environmental issues?

Starbucks has used the social strategy of adopting a comprehensive proactive environmental policy as a competitive advantage. It carries out this strategy by setting voluntary standards that exceed legal environmental requirements, developing an environmental mission statement, and implementing programs that attempt to minimize environmental degradation, from bean growth to store operations. Starbucks' information strategy is to provide more information about its environmental activities to customers and stockholders, as well as informing the public at large.

Environmental Strategies

Here are a few strategies:[147]

■ **Revenues**—driving revenues by designing and marketing products that are environmentally superior and meet customers' desires.
■ **Costs**—cutting operational costs and reducing environmental expenses such as waste handling and regulatory burdens throughout the value chain.
■ **Risks**—identifying and reducing environmental and regulatory risks in the operations, especially in the supply chains to avoid costs and increase speed to the market.
■ **Intangibles**—creating intangible brand value by marketing the overall corporate greenness.

Personal and Professional Applications

28. What strategies does your present or past employer, or a company it does business with, use to deal with environmental issues?

SUMMARY

The chapter summary is organized to answer the learning outcomes for Chapter 12.

1. **Describe the relationship between technology and productivity and the difference between production and productivity.**

   Technology is the process of transforming resources into products, and technology is used to increase productivity. Production is a performance measure indicating how many products were produced whereas productivity is a performance measure that relates outputs to inputs. The goal is to increase productivity; however, a firm can increase production while decreasing productivity. Thus, business needs to focus on productivity.

2. **Explain how the winner takes most of the market share.**

   Technology and online business create opportunities and market strategies that are different from traditional business operations in that technology provides the company a way to recap its initial cost to produce a product, because as production increases, the cost of producing each additional unit decreases. Economies of scale create winner-take-most market situations. Furthermore, creating the industry standard and being the first-mover are important market strategies that go hand in hand to dominate a market. Being the first to develop the standard creates a first-mover advantage to become the strong winner-take-most of the market share leader.

3. **Discuss issues of managing technology.**

   Issues of managing technology include protecting the privacy of consumers, employees, and other stakeholders and providing security to prevent information from being misused. Companies use chief privacy officers to develop and implement privacy policies and to ensure privacy and information security. Managers also need to balance employee privacy with the need to use technology to monitor employees and ensure their performance meets the company's standard. To this end, business is developing codes of computer ethics.

4. **Describe issues of biotechnology and bioethics.**

   Issues of biotechnology include genetic engineering and genetically modified (GM) foods. Two major issues of genetic engineering include stem cell research and cloning. Embryonic stem cell research raises ethical and moral concerns over whether a human embryo is actually a human being. GM foods alter the natural makeup of a living organism to increase productivity. Controversy persists in the matter of safety, ethics, and labeling of GM foods. Along with biotechnology comes the field of bioethics to deal with ethical questions related to new procedures and products. Business, society, and government are debating ethics in this field as they determine how the government should support biotech research. Some biotech businesses are using bioethics advisory boards.

5. **Compare and contrast ozone depletion, global warming, and the endangerment of biological diversity.**

All three of these problems are similar because they are natural environmental issues that have been caused primarily by pollution. However, each is a different problem. Ozone is an oxygen-related gas that floats in a thin layer in the stratosphere between 8 to 25 miles about the earth. Ozone is vital in the stratosphere because it forms a protective layer to block dangerous ultraviolet radiation from the sun, which causes health problems. The atmosphere of the earth is heating up, causing potential danger through the greenhouse effect—the prevention of solar heat absorbed by the atmosphere from returning to space, creating global warming and climate change problems. Biodiversity is the number and variety of species and the range of their genetic makeup. The current rate of species extinction has increased dramatically, cutting our global sources of food and medicine.

6. **Discuss the major environmental laws and regulations.**

The major environmental protection laws are categorized into three areas: air, water, and land. The *Clean Air Act* requires the Environmental Protection Agency (EPA) to set national standards that limit pollution harmful to people and the environment. The *Clean Water Act* sets broad environmental quality goals and an implementation system for the federal and state governments. The *National Pollutant Discharge Elimination System (NPDES)* was created to specify maximum permissible discharge levels and timetables for installing state-of-the-art pollution control equipment. The *Solid Waste Disposal Act* gives regional, state, and local governments the main responsibility for nontoxic waste management, with the EPA assisting them with research and other help. However, for dealing with hazardous waste, the *Resource Conservation and Recovery Act* created a federal (cradle-to-grave) system. The EPA is the primary U.S. regulatory body responsible for administering environmental laws and coordinating federal, state, and local efforts. The regulatory trend is to prevent pollution through the use of incentives under the *Pollution Prevention Act.*

7. **Compare sustainability concepts.**

Sustainability is meeting the needs of today without sacrificing future generations' ability to meet their needs, while sustainable development balances the need for economic growth and the need to maintain our natural environment. Green management refers to the activities businesses engage in to ensure sustainability and sustainable development.

8. **Fill in each blank with the appropriate key term (in order of appearance in the chapter).**

_____ is the process of transforming resources into products.

_____ is a performance measure relating product and service outputs to resource inputs.

_____ is the ability to process, store, and retrieve large amounts of information at great speeds through networks of linked systems.

_____ involves transacting business electronically through the Internet.

_____ involves transacting business through a mobile device.

_____ interact with each other through a firm's website.

_____ are responsible for ensuring privacy and information security.

_____ combines biology and technology to develop and produce business products.

_____ is the application of ethics to the field of biotechnology.

_____ is a substance released into the environment that has a negative effect on the environment and on society.

_____ is an oxygen-related gas that floats in a thin layer in the stratosphere between 8 and 25 miles above the earth.

_____ is the prevention of solar heat absorbed by the atmosphere from returning to space, creating global warming and climate changes.

_____ is the number and variety of species and the range of their genetic makeup.

_____ requires the EPA to set national standards that limit pollution harmful to people and the environment without regard for the cost.

_____ sets broad environmental quality goals and an implementation system for the federal and state governments.

_____ was created to specify maximum permissible discharge levels and timetables for installing state-of-the-art water-pollution control equipment.

_____ gives regional, state, and local governments the main responsibility for nontoxic waste management.

_____ created a federal system for the responsibility of hazardous waste.

_____ provides guidelines, training, and incentives for companies to reduce pollution.

_____ is meeting the needs of today without sacrificing future generations' ability to meet their needs.

_____ balances the need for economic growth and the need to maintain our natural environment.

KEY TERMS (IN ALPHABETICAL ORDER)

KEY TERMS
12

biodiversity (p. 480)
bioethics (p. 477)
biotechnology (p. 475)
chief information officers (CIOs) (p. 473)
Clean Air Act (p. 487)
Clean Water Act (p. 488)
e-commerce (p. 470)
greenhouse effect (p. 480)
information technology (p. 470)
m-commerce (p. 470)
National Pollutant Discharge Elimination System (NPDES) (p. 488)

online communities (p. 471)
ozone (p. 480)
pollution (p. 479)
Pollution Prevention Act (p. 489)
productivity (p. 468)
Resource Conservation and Recovery Act (p. 488)
Solid Waste Disposal Act (p. 488)
sustainability (p. 491)
sustainable development (p. 492)
technology (p. 467)

REVIEW QUESTIONS

REVIEW QUESTIONS
12

1 Employees produced 6,000 products at a cost of $9,000. What was their rate of productivity?

2 What is the difference between e-commerce and m-commerce?

3 What are online communities?

4 What is biotechnology?

5 What are stem cells?

6 What is the current title for the manager responsible for privacy and information security?

7 What is bioethics?

8 What is ozone?

9 What is the greenhouse effect?

10 What does the acronym NIMBY stand for?

11 What is Ceres?

12 What U.S. regulatory body is primarily responsible for administering environmental laws?

13 What is the difference between command-and-control and incentive systems of pollution control?

14 What are the three categories of environmental protection laws?

15 What is the triple bottom line?

16 Why are so many companies improving their environmental responsibility?

17 What are sustainable development and the WBCSD?

DISCUSSION/ CRITICAL THINKING QUESTIONS

12

DISCUSSION/CRITICAL THINKING QUESTIONS

Be sure to give a detailed explanation for your answer to each question.

1 Does technology help or hurt the job market?

2 Is privacy and information security really all that important to business?

3 Should businesses leave employees alone in privacy, or should they monitor employee performance more closely?

4 Is business abusing its power through the use of technology?

5 Can bioethicists who are paid by the company really be neutral, or is there a conflict of interest?

6 Does business really care about the natural environment?

7 Do you agree that the natural environment is one of the most significant societal issues of our time?

8 Are MNCs trying to help underdeveloped countries, or are they just exploiting them for their resources?

9 Is sustainable development possible?

10 Should we be concerned about endangered species?

11 Do the benefits of environmental protection outweigh the costs?

12 Can a single business really be socially responsible with the natural environment and also be profitable?

13 Are you optimistic or pessimistic about the future of our natural environment at the local, national, and global levels?

14 Is sustainability just a fad or is it here to stay?

15 Should all businesses engage in green management?

APPLICATION EXERCISES

12.1 COMPUTER ETHICS INSTITUTE

Go to the Computer Ethics Institute (www.computerethicsinstitute.org). Review the "Ten Commandments of Computer Ethics." Do a self-assessment to determine which commandments you do and do not keep.

12.2 GREEN SOCIETAL INTEREST GROUP

Using Figure 12.4 select an environ-mental societal interest group and visit its website. Report what you found out about the environment and the societal interest group.

12.3 GREEN BUSINESS INTEREST GROUP

Using Figure 12.5, select an environ-mental business interest group and visit its website. Report what you found out about the environment and the business interest group.

CASE 12.1

Bayer AG and Genetically Modified Food: Buying Much More than What They Bargained For or Wanted!

Aventis seemed like a simple purchase at the time, thought Manfred Schneider, chairman of Bayer AG, a German-based firm that focuses "on the fast-growing, innovation-driven health care, nutrition and high-tech materials businesses in line with its mission statement: 'Bayer: Science For A Better Life.'"[148]

"Bayer is a global enterprise with core competencies in the fields of health care, nutrition and high-tech materials. Our products and services are designed to benefit people and improve their quality of life. At the same time we want to cre-ate value through innovation, growth and improved earning power. . . . We believe our technical and commercial expertise entails a duty to contribute to sustainable development—a principle we wholeheart-edly endorse, mindful of its social, ethical and environmental elements. In aware-ness of our responsibilities as a corporate citizen, we define economy, ecology, and social commitment as objectives of equal rank."[149]

"Bayer's growth measures its two core segments, MaterialScience and Crop-Science . . . the CropScience division . . . [has] expanded its German and U.S. pro-duction facilities in 2010. The unit has also picked up U.S.-based biotech company Athenix, for which it paid about $365 mil-lion in 2009, and Hornbeck Seed, a maker of plant breeding products, in 2011. To bol-ster the growth of its fruits and vegetables business in 2012, the company agreed to acquire AgraQuest, a Davis, California-based supplier of biological pest manage-ment solutions based on natural microor-ganisms, for $425 million (plus milestone payments). Bayer places a significant amount of focus on R&D efforts within its MaterialScience and CropScience divisions to be able to provide a broad range of crop solutions based on seeds, traits, chemical crop protection, and biological pest and disease control."[150]

"All of the company's growth measures paid off when Bayer's sales rose in 2010; however, declining income levels over the last few years—caused by economic diffi-culties, competitive conditions, and other factors—have led Bayer to conduct some cost-control and restructuring measures.

Such measures also include efforts to integrate a number of purchases made during a period of heavy acquisitive growth from 2005 through 2008."[151]

The problem began back in 2001, when Bayer acquired **Aventis CropScience** for €7.25 billion, making it a world leader in crop protection.[152] Part of this deal included buying experimental rice strains developed in the United States that made crops more resistant to the firm's own weed killers.[153] Yet this purchase would come back to haunt CEO Schneider and Bayer for it seemed that some of the rice crops it had purchased were "genetically modified" long-grain rice [that] had been released through an unknown method and showed up in very low levels in storage bins in Missouri and Arkansas. . . . [In reaction], trading partners abroad began tightening their controls on American-grown rice after the discovery of an accidental release of [this] genetically modified variety unapproved for sale by U.S. regulators. Prices of rice futures contracts sank as countries such as **Japan** and **South Korea** moved to prevent the genetically modified rice from coming into their markets from the United States, which counts on foreign customers to buy roughly half of its annual production. **EU** officials said they were requesting more information from the United States and Bayer AG of Germany, the maker of the accidentally released long-grain variety, before deciding whether to ban imports of U.S. long-grain rice. The European environmental group **Friends of the Earth** was already calling on **Brussels** to restrict U.S. rice.

"Farmers in the United States—which has been more accepting of genetically modified crops than those in many other nations—have been pestered by accidental releases in the past, as some genetically modified products have been inadvertently mixed in distribution or as pollen of modified crops fertilizes crops intended to be sold as nonmodified. Development of new crops often outpaces both consumer acceptance or regulatory approval. . . . Some consumers are leery of the safety of the modified-crop technology, despite government assurances. The rice industry, which is heavily dependent on foreign consumers, had been avoiding the use of genetically modified crops until they received consumer acceptance, both domestically and abroad. 'Basically, we don't want to produce, modified rice,' said David Coia, a spokesman for **USA Rice Federation**, a rice trade group."[154]

"Two Missouri farmers in 2010 sued Bayer for contaminating their crop with modified genes from an experimental strain of rice engineered to be resistant to the company's Liberty-brand herbicide. The contamination occurred in 2006, during an open field test of the new rice, which was not approved for human consumption. According to the plaintiffs' lawyer, Don Downing, genetic material from the unapproved rice contaminated more than 30 percent of all rice cropland in the United States. 'Bayer was supposed to be careful,' Downing said. 'Bayer was not careful and that rice did escape into our commercial rice supplies.'"[155]

"The plaintiffs alleged that in addition to contaminating their fields, Bayer further harmed them financially by undermining their export market. When the U.S. Department of Agriculture announced the widespread rice contamination, important export markets were closed to U.S. producers. A report from Greenpeace International estimated the financial damage of the contamination at between $741 million and $1.3 billion. Bayer claimed that there was no possible way it could have prevented the contamination, insisting that it followed not only the law but also the best industry practices. The jury disagreed, finding Bayer guilty of carelessness in handling the genetically modified crops. The company was ordered to pay farmers Kenneth Bell and Johnny Hunter $2 million. 'This is a huge victory, not only for Kenny and me, but for every farmer in America who was harmed by Bayer's LibertyLink rice contamination,' Hunter said. According to

Hunter, the company got 'the wake-up call they deserved.'"[156]

Questions:

1. What is the role and importance of biotechnology for Bayer AG?
2. How is this technology used to make farmers more productive?
3. What is Bayer's policy toward sustainable development?
4. What is the main issue confronting Manfred Schneider, chairman of Bayer AG?
5. What nonmarket strategies would you employ, if you were Schneider to address the issue?

CASE 12.2

The Economic Rollercoaster and the Environment: Is China Paying the Price for Its Slowing Prosperity?

The sleeping dragon has not only awakened, it seems to have taken flight and then started to nose dive. "[In 2012] China's annual economic growth slowed to 7.6 percent in the second quarter, just above the government's 7.5 percent full year target and the weakest quarter since Q1 2009 when the global financial crisis choked world trade flows and saw 20 million Chinese jobs axed in a matter of months. . . . 'China's job market could turn for the worse and the government needs to step up efforts to create more jobs,' Premier Wen Jiabao said, underscoring official concerns about an economic slowdown. 'Currently and in the future, China's employment situation will become more complex and more severe.'"[157]

Despite the dip in the economy China's continued growth and prosperity is being hindered by the by-product of its own economic growth: pollution. Since China operates a socialist market economic system where government employs macrocontrol systems through which it steers the economy, the government, and not private business, is in charge of China's continued economic prosperity[158] as well as the country's environmental condition.

"China's environment minister warned that pollution in the country poses a threat to long-term economic growth. In remarks posted on the ministry website, Environment Minister Zhou Shengxian said,

'Natural resources are shrinking, degenerating and drying up. Ecological and environmental decay has become a bottleneck and a serious obstacle to our economic and social development.' Zhou is pushing for environmental protection to be a key component of China's new Five Year Plan (2011–15) to be debated during the National People's Congress set to begin Saturday. 'If our homeland is destroyed and we lose our health, then what good does development do?' Zhou wrote."[159]

"In January [2011], for example, staterun news agency Xinhua reported that 200 children in eastern China had elevated lead levels. While there are laws prohibiting factories from being located within 1,600 feet of residential areas, the affected children lived close to battery factories. 'Environmental concerns will play a major role in massaging the way the economy is going to grow in the 12th five-year plan,' said Zhang Jianyu, head of China's environmental defense fund, the *Financial Times* reports. China, the world's top emitter of greenhouse gases, emits 6.5 billion metric tons of carbon dioxide each year, U.N. statistics indicate."[160]

"The country's new five-year plan is expected to include targets for reducing energy intensity and carbon dioxide intensity as well as to address a wider range of pollutants than previous plans. Zhang said the plan would be a challenge because China will be moving from an export and investment-oriented approach toward 'a more stable, balanced, sustainable approach.' [In 2011] Chinese Premier Wen Jiabao lowered the target for average gross domestic product growth to 7 percent from 7.5 percent, saying there was a need for slower, cleaner growth.

'We must not any longer sacrifice the environment for the sake of rapid growth and reckless rollouts, as that would result in unsustainable growth featuring industrial overcapacity and intensive resource consumption,' said Wen in an Internet chat reported on by state media."[161]

"While China's previous five-year plan had a growth target of 7.5 percent, the economy actually grew 11.1 percent from 2006–10. Under that plan, China sought to reduce energy consumption per unit of gross domestic product by 20 percent compared with 2005 levels by the end of 2010. But as a last-ditch effort to achieve those pollution-reduction targets, some local governments had resorted to enforced blackouts."[162]

Questions:

1. What specific natural environmental issues apply to this case?
2. How might NIMBY impact this situation?
3. How does this case exemplify the relationship between pollution and sustainable growth?
4. What U.S. environmental laws might assist China in dealing with its pollution problems? Why?
5. Given China's centralized government and social economy, what actions would you suggest that the Chinese government take in order to deal with this problem?

INTEGRATIVE CASE

12

INTEGRATIVE CASE (Part 12)

DHR Construction, LLC Technology and the Environment: Using Hi-Tech and "Green" to Get the Gold

This is a continuation case—please refer to Chapters 1–11 for further information.

Although the sun was shining brightly, it seemed like another dark, dingy, and downcast afternoon to Richard Davis as he drove up once again to DHR Construction, LLC's work site. Richard, a college professor who had started a real estate management firm back in 2002 with his friend and colleague, Stephen Hodgetts, was now the managing partner of their baby conglomerate and served as contractor for the firm's home construction operations. Richard chatted with several of the subcontractors and checked in with his foreman, James Kennison, while he blankly gazed past the picturesque snow-covered mountains. After Richard toured the work site and took a long look at the scenic view, he sighed heavily, got back into his SUV, and drove toward his office.

Why was Richard so glum? Changes in the home construction industry had taken what was a booming industry just months ago and quickly made it into a bust market. The Federal Reserve's Beige Book Report noted that residential real estate markets continued to cool across much of the country—with most districts reporting a slowdown in home building and sales of existing homes.[163]

Why the slowdown? From Richard Davis's discussions with Mark Kessler, president of the Home Builders Association, it was all tied to the cost of capital, as set by the Federal Reserve (see "Integrative Case Part 9"). The Federal Reserve had continued to increase the Federal Funds Rate from 1 percent in June 2003 to 5.25 percent as of June 2006.[164] This resulted in raising the 30-year fixed home mortgage rates from 5.43 percent (June of 2003) to 6.83 percent

(June 2006) and 1-year adjustable variable rates from 3.75 percent (June 2003) to 6.08 percent (June 2006).[165]

The rise in interest rates caused an increase in personal bankruptcy and foreclosures, which were linked to the increases in homeowners' adjustable rate mortgage payments. Personal bankruptcy rates soared from the average monthly filing rate of 130,183 in 2004 to nearly 500,000 in March of 2006.[166] Furthermore, "in January [2006], 103,540 homes were in foreclosure, up 27% from 81,290 in December and 45% above last year [2005]. January's foreclosure total was the highest level since RealtyTrac began releasing monthly reports in May 2005. . . . January's 27% increase in foreclosures is consistent with the increasing foreclosure trend seen throughout 2005. In total, nearly 847,000 properties entered foreclosure in 2005, representing 0.7% of total households."[167]

The Federal Reserve reacted by then dropping the rates after the "bust" of 2008 down to historic lows of .25 percent (2008), which led to significantly lower home adjustable mortgage rates (2.5 percent),[168] yet the damage had already been done. The glut on the market of foreclosed homes or homes advertised as distressed sales was unprecedented.[169] Many potential home buyers had poor credit ratings[170] and did not have the cash on hand to meet lenders' now more stringent "money down" requirements (i.e., 20 percent versus no money down).[171]

The New Market Niche: Go Hi-Tech and Green

Back in his office, Richard knew neither he nor the Home Builders Association could do anything about the slowing housing market, yet he was not the type to just sit on his hands and lament his fate. He called a meeting with his business partner Stephen Hodgetts and invited their real estate agent, Robert Moss, to join them. Robert started the meeting by describing what he perceived as the changes in the market. "His-

torically, we have defined our target population as those people living within a 100-mile radius of the area. It seems that the 'locals' cannot afford or are not interested in Snowy Mountain or any other development in the area. If they are looking for a nicer home, they are also willing to travel, that is move, in order to be in a new neighborhood and a new region."

Stephen Hodgetts shook his head incredulously. "So what you are saying, Bob, is that people who want the type of home that we build who live in our area would rather move out of the area to live in a similar development? That sounds crazy—how do you know this?"

Robert, used to Stephen's questioning style, took this in stride and continued, "I conduct focus groups for the agency every month in order to get a better feel for the local market. We also track hits on our website and the websites of our clients, property inquiries, local sales, new construction applications, and interestingly enough, business openings and closings. Most of the inquiries and sales are coming from people outside of the area. In fact, they're predominantly from people who live out-of-state and out of the region entirely. These people are looking for showcase energy-efficient maintenance-free homes using supplies that are environmentally friendly, like a low-toxic floor finish or 100-percent recycled-fiber carpeting.[172] They are also looking to live in areas that they have never experienced before—those who are land-locked want the ocean; those on the beach want the mountains. They want to own several homes, usually a summer and a winter residence, in areas where they can have all the amenities of a vacation community. The Internet has made location less of an issue for them because many are teleworkers, working out of their homes, and also do a lot of traveling. Also, many of them are semiretired and economically well-off enough to work when they want to work and where they want to work."

"That's right," chimed in Richard Davis. "Our market niche has narrowed, and we're now dealing predominately with well-to-do Generation Yers and DINKS (dual income no kids). DINKS are often the target of marketing efforts for luxury items such as expensive cars and vacations.[173] Our custom-built patio homes fit their lifestyle, because they require less maintenance than a typical home and are in a fashionable neighborhood. These homes, although running upwards of 4,500 square feet, are on no more than half-acre plots with lawn care, garbage removal, and snow removal handled by the homeowner's association (HOA). The homes are part of a gated community, which provides each homeowner membership in the local golf club and pool club, discounted meals and merchandise at the clubhouse and pro shop, and numerous walking paths."

"So what does this mean for us?" queried Stephen Hodgetts.

"What this means," replied Robert, "is that your homes and your operation have to be perceived as hi-tech, green, and sustainable—that your homes blend into the surrounding environment while providing upscale amenities. Use feng shui (the art of arranging your home or workplace to enhance your health, wealth, and happiness) in your building and interior designs.[174] This will appeal to not only a national audience but an international one as well."

"International?" asked Richard Davis.

"Sure," responded Robert. "Besides offering the usual advertising like multiple listings, video tours, and listings in real estate magazines, my agency is part of an international real estate brokerage firm, and therefore, your homes are in a worldwide database. This means that people using search engines like Google and Bing can find our listings by doing a search for real estate in this area. I'm sure you've used these sites yourself to check on your competition—you type in the area, the type of home you want, the price range, and boom, a list of homes pops up that lets you read the fact sheet and take a virtual tour of the house. More importantly, I can track hits on your homes, read the cookies of people who have visited our sites, get information about what other sites they've visited, and perhaps even get some background information, and therefore, get a better idea about people interested in your homes. You've heard the term 'data mining'; well that's what we do best! We use potential clients' own data to tailor-make our marketing messages to fit their needs."

Stephen, who had been listening intently to all of this banter between Richard and Robert had heard more than enough. "Now wait a second. I understand that Robert is a wordsmith and a spin doctor. Heck, that's what marketing people do, but I hope you're not saying what I think you're saying, which is that we spy on visitors to our websites and steal information off their computers. Next you'll be telling me that we sell this information to third parties for a handsome profit." On this last comment, Robert's face turned red while Stephen started to fidget in his seat.

"Also," continued Stephen, "regarding this business about being green—using environmentally friendly material and feng shui in our designs is all well and good for future construction, but we can't change our show homes, which are none of the above. I hope you're not proposing that we advertise ourselves like greenhomebuilding.com, people who actually advocate for sustainable architecture; their first principle is think small,[175] not exactly the type of homes (4,500 square feet) DINKS want." Both Robert and Richard were sinking deeper and deeper into their chairs while Robert's face had morphed into a deep cherry red. Richard and Robert looked at each other as if they were pleading for help, yet no cavalry was coming to the rescue.

Questions

1. How has information technology affected how DHR Construction, LLC markets its homes?

2. How might this technology be incor-

porated in the design and features of a new home?

3. What are the issues relating to privacy and information security in this case?

4. How do the issues of sustainable devel-

opment and environmental responsibility relate to this case?

5. If you were Richard Davis, how would you respond to Stephen Hodgetts' comments?

REFERENCES AND NOTES

1 http://www.starbucks.com/about-us/company-information/mission-statement (accessed July 12, 2012).

2 http://www.starbucks.com/aboutus/environment.asp (accessed August 21, 2006).

3 http://www.starbucks.com/responsibility/environment (accessed July 16, 2012).

4 http://www.starbucks.com/aboutus/pressdesc.asp?id=668&rumor=true (accessed August 21, 2006).

5 http://www.starbucks.com/aboutus/origins.asp (accessed August 21, 2006).

6 http://www.starbucks.com/responsibility/environment (accessed July 16, 2012).

7 http://news.starbucks.com/news/corporate+news/financial (accessed July 16, 2012).

8 http://www.starbucks.com/retail/wireless.asp (accessed August 21, 2006).

9 Ibid.

10 http://news.starbucks.com/article_display.cfm?article_id=232 (accessed July 16, 2012).

11 http://www.facebook.com/pages/I-hate-starbucks/119766841380780 (accessed July 16, 2012).

12 "Urban Snobbery, or Why I Hate Starbucks," http://shae.typepad.com/followingthebrush/2005/04/urban_snobbery_.html (August 21, 2006).

13 http://www.ihatestarbucks.com/why.php (accessed July 16, 2012).

14 B. Dyck, K. Walker, F. Starke, and K. Uggerslev, "Addressing Concerns Raised by Critics of Business Schools by Teaching Multiple Approaches to Management," *Business and Society Review* 116(1) (2011): 1–27.

15 D. Pringle, "In Mobile Phones, Older Users Say, More Is Less," *Wall Street Journal* (August 15, 2005): A1.

16 K. Hudson, "Wal-Mart's Need for Speed," *Wall Street Journal* (September 26, 2005): B4.

17 T. Ebhardt, "Supercar Makers Seek a Dif-

ferent Shade of Green," *BusinessWeek* (May 28–June 3, 2012): 22–23.

18 www.pewinternet.org (accessed June 18, 2012).

19 A. Taylor, "The Great Electric Car Race," *Fortune* (September 26, 2011): 33.

20 G. A. Steiner and J. F. Steiner, *Business, Government, and Society,* 11th ed. (Burr Ridge, IL: McGraw-Hill/Irwin, 2006).

21 T. A. Jenkin, L. McShane, and J. Webster, "Green Information Technologies and Systems: Employees' Perceptions of Organizational Practices," *Business & Society* 50(2) (2011): 266–314.

22 Reviewer J. D. Kerr Harris-Stowe State University.

23 C. Dibrell, J. Craig, and E. Hansen, "Natural Environment, Market Orientation, and Firm Innovativeness: An Organizational Life Cycle Perspective," *Journal of Small Business Management* 49(3) (2011): 467–489.

24 D. P. Barron, *Business and Its Environment,* 6th ed. (Upper Saddle, NJ: Prentice Hall, 2010).

25 B. Macnab, R. Worthley, and S. Jenner, "Regional Cultural Differences and Ethical Perspectives Within the United States: Avoiding Pseudo-emic Ethics Research," *Business and Society Review* 115(1) (2010): 27–55.

26 J. Pfeffer, "Building Sustainable Organizations: The Human Factor," *Academy of Management Perspectives* 24(1) (2010): 34–44.

27 M. Totty, "The Dangers Within," *Wall Street Journal* (February 13, 2006): R1.

28 J. Angwin, "Online Tracking Ramps Up," *Wall Street Journal* (June 18, 2012): B1.

29 www.privacyalliance.org (accessed June 19, 2012).

30 http://onguardonline.gov (accessed June 19, 2012).

31 D. Bank and R. Richmond, "Where the Dangers Are," *Wall Street Journal* (July 18, 2005): R1.

32 A. Sharma, "Hackers vs. Hand-Helds," *Wall Street Journal* (May 15, 2006): R1.

33 P. W. Tam, "The Word From the Front," *Wall Street Journal* (April 5, 2006): C1.

34 www.apple.com (accessed June 18, 2012).

35 www.nclnet.org, and www.fraud.org (accessed June 18, 2012).

36 "Google Received," *Wall Street Journal* (June 18, 2012): A1.

37 http://online.wsj.com/article/SB125859862658454923.html (accessed July 17, 2012).

38 C. K. Ajemian and D. M. Reid, "Preventing Global Warming: The United States, China, and Intellectual Property," *Business and Society Review* 115(4) (2010): 417–436.

39 L. Gomes, "Ethical Responsibility, At Issue With Grokster, Applies to Others, Too," *Wall Street Journal* (June 27, 2005): B1.

40 L. Gomes, "Biologists Are Looking to the Chip Industry for Production Models," *Wall Street Journal* (August 9 2006): B1.

41 www.usda.gov (accessed June 19, 2012).

42 www.monsanto.com (accessed June 19, 2012).

43 Presidential Commission for the Study of Bioethical Issues, http://bioethics.gov (accessed June 19, 2012).

44 C. K. Ajemian and D. M. Reid, "Preventing Global Warming: The United States, China, and Intellectual Property," *Business and Society Review* 115(4) (2010): 417–436.

45 M. Orlitzky, D. S. Siegel, and D. A. Waldman, "Strategic Corporate Social Responsibility and Environmental Sustainability," *Business & Society* 50(1) (2011): 6–27.

46 C. H. Amato and L. H. Amato, "Corporate Commitment to Global Quality of Life Issues: Do Slack Resources, Industry Affiliations, and Multinational Headquarters Matter?" *Business & Society* 50(2) (2011): 388–416.

47 J. P. Bonardi and G. D. Keim, "Corporate Political Strategies for Widely Salient Issues," *Academy of Management Review* 30(3) (2005): 555–576.

48 R. Van der Merwe, L. F. Pitt, and R. Abratt, "Stakeholders Strength: PR Survival Strategies in the Internet Age," *Public Relations Quarterly* 50 (Spring 2005): 39–49.

49 www.monsanto.com (accessed June 20, 2012).

50 www.gefoodalert.org (accessed June 20, 2012).

51 B. Dyck, K. Walker, F. Starke, and K. Uggerslev, "Addressing Concerns Raised by Critics of Business Schools by Teaching Multiple Approaches to Management," *Business and Society Review* 116(1) (2011): 1–27.

52 Y. Luo, "Strategic Responses to Perceived Corruption in an Emerging Market: Lessons from MNEs Investing in China," *Business & Society* 50(2) (2011): 350–387.

53 A. F. Buono, "Stuart Cooper. Corporate Social Performance: A Stakeholder Approach," *Personnel Psychology* 58 (Autumn 2005): 811–816

54 C. Marquis and Z. Huang, "The Contingent Nature of Public Policy and the Growth of U.S. Commercial Banking," *Academy of Management Journal* 52(6) (2009): 1222–1246.

55 J. P. Bonardi and G. D. Keim, "Corporate Political Strategies for Widely Salient Issues," *Academy of Management Review* 30(3) (2005): 555–576.

56 "2009 Trends to Watch," *Entrepreneur* (December 2008): 57–60.

57 J. P. Bonardi and G. D. Keim, "Corporate Political Strategies for Widely Salient Issues," *Academy of Management Review* 30(3) (2005): 555–576.

58 S. Prasso, "How Samsung Turned Up the Sizzle," *Fortune* (July 25, 2011): 28.

59 Reviewer M.A. Govekar, Ohio Northern University.

60 J. Marcus, E.C. Kurucz, and B.A. Colbert, "Conceptions of the Business-Society-Nature Interface: Implications for Management Scholarship," *Business & Society* 49(3) (2010): 402–438.

61 S. Sndhu, "Shifting Paradigms in Corporate Environmentalism: From Poachers to Gamekeepers," *Business and Society Review* 115(3) (2010): 285–310.

62 C. K. Ajemian and D. M. Reid, "Preventing Global Warming: The United States, China, and Intellectual Property," *Business and Society Review* 115(4) (2010): 417–436.

63 P. Berrone and L. R. G. Mejia, "Environmental Performance and Executive Compensation: An Integrated Agency-Institutional Perspective," *Academy of Management Journal* 52(1) (2009): 103–126.

64 S. O. Osaglie, "The Voluntary Environmentalists," *Academy of Management Perspectives* 33(2) (2008): 564–568.

65 S. Forbes, "Bearable Truths," *Forbes* (May 7, 2012): 12.

66 C. K. Ajemian and D. M. Reid, "Preventing Global Warming: The United States, China, and Intellectual Property," *Business and Society Review* 115(4) (2010): 417–436.

67 J. Sasseen, "Who Speaks for Business?" *BusinessWeek* (October 19, 2009): 22–23.

68 C. Kenny, "Kyoto Protocol: Dead Letters," *BusinessWeek* (December 12–18, 2011): 16–17.

69 E. Wilson, "Vanishing Before Our Eyes," *Time*—Special Edition on How to Save the Earth (Spring 2000): 29–34.

70 "Aquafina," *Fortune* (July 25, 2011): 130.

71 www.unep.org (accessed August 11, 2006).

72 www.unep.org, Strategy on Land Use and Soil Conservation (accessed August 11, 2006).

73 E. Check, "The Silence of the Woods," *Newsweek* (November 13, 2000): 65.

74 "Overfishing Has Cut," Wall Street Journal (July 29, 2005): A1.

75 www.uspirg.org, Clean Water Fact Sheet (accessed August 11, 2006).

76 P. L. Thompson, "Economically Sustainable Safe Drinking Water Systems for the Developing World," *Business and Society Review* 115(4) (2010): 477–493.

77 United Nations Press Release, "Commission on Sustainable Development Holds First of Four Dialogues," (April 24, 2000).

78 S. Sndhu, "Shifting Paradigms in Corporate Environmentalism: From Poachers to Gamekeepers," *Business and Society Review* 115(3) (2010): 285–310.

79 www.epa.gov (accessed June 21, 2012).

80 B. Dyck, K. Walker, F. Starke, and K. Uggerslev, "Addressing Concerns Raised by Critics of Business Schools by Teaching Multiple Approaches to Management," *Business and Society Review* 116(1) (2011): 1–27.

81 S. O. Osaglie, "The Voluntary Environmentalists," *Academy of Management Perspectives* 33(2) (2008): 564–568.

82 P. Berrone and L. R. G. Mejia, "Environmental Performance and Executive Compensation: An Integrated Agency-Institutional Perspective," *Academy of Management Journal* 52(1) (2009): 103–126.

83 J. E. Vascellaro, "Green Groups See Potent Tools in Economics," *Wall Street Journal* (August 23, 2005): B1.

84 www.epa.gov (accessed June 21, 2012).

85 S. Power, "Obama's EPA Move Likely to Spur Fight," *Wall Street Journal* (January 27, 2009): A3.

86 T. Tracy, "First Fracking Rules Unveiled," *Wall Street Journal* (April 19, 2012): A3.

87 www.epa.gov (accessed June 21, 2012).

88 Ibid.

89 D. P. Barron, *Business and Its Environment,* 5th ed. (Upper Saddle, NJ: Prentice Hall, 2006).

90 www.epa.gov (accessed June 21, 2012).

91 www.whitehouse.gov (accessed June 21, 2012).

92 J. Carey, "Greener, Yes, But Not at Any Price," *BusinessWeek* (March 9, 2009): 58–59.

93 http://subscriber.hoovers.com/H/company360/overview.html?companyId=58872000000000 (accessed July 17, 2012).

94 http://subscriber.hoovers.com/H/company360/overview.html?companyId=58872000000000 (accessed July 17, 2012).

95 http://www.bp.com/liveassets/bp_internet/globalbp/STAGING/global_assets/downloads/C/Code_of_Conduct_2011.pdf (accessed July 17, 2012).

96 http://www.mcclatchydc.com/2010/05/08/93779/bp-has-a-long-record-of-legal.html (accessed July 17, 2012).

97 C. Fritz, C. F. Lam, and Gr. M. Spreitzer, "It's the Little Things that Matter," *Academy of Management Perspectives* 25(3) (2012): 28–39.

98 Definition developed by the Brundtland Commission. Cited in Colvin Interview of Linda Fisher, *Fortune* (November 23, 2009): 45–50.

99 A. Nadim and R. N. Lussier, "Sustainability as a Small Business Competitive Strategy," *Journal of Small Strategy* 21(2) (2012): 79–95.

100 A. A. Marcus and A. R. Fremeth, "Green Management Matters Regardless," *Academy of Management Perspectives* 23(3) (2009): 17–26.

101 P. Berrone and L. R. G. Mejia, "Environmental Performance and Executive Compensation: An Integrated Agency-Institutional Perspective," *Academy of Management Journal* 52(1) (2009): 103–126.

102 S. Ambec and P. Lanoie, "Does It Pay to Be Green? A Systematic Overview," *Academy of Management Perspectives* 22(4) (2008): 45–62.

103 "Sustainability in Management Education," *Academy of Management Learning & Education* 8(3) (2009): 312.

104 Information in this section taken from www.wbcsd.org (accessed June 22, 2012).

105 www.sustainabilityconsortium.org (accessed June 25, 2012).

106 P. Keegan, "The Trouble With Green Product Ratings," *Fortune* (July 25, 2011): 130–134.

107 S. O. Osagie, "The Voluntary Environmentalists: Green Clubs, IO 14001, and Voluntary Environmental Regulations," *Academy of Management Review* 33(2) (2008): 564–568.

108 J. Pfeffer, "Building Sustainable Organizations: The Human Factor," *Academy of Management Perspectives* 24(1) (2010): 34–44.

109 D. S. Siegel, "Green Management Matters Only If It Yields More Green: An Economic/Strategic Perspective," *Academy of Management Perspectives* 23(3) (2009): 5–16.

110 R. Plant, "How Green Should My Tech Be? It Depends on the Tech," *Wall Street Journal* (January 25, 2010): R6.

111 P. Keegan, "The Trouble With Green Product Ratings," *Fortune* (July 25, 2011): 130–134.

112 A. A. Marcus and A. R. Fremeth, "Green Management Matters Regardless," *Academy of Management Perspectives* 23(3) (2009): 17–26.

113 J. Wang, "3 Steps to Being Green from the Get-Go," *Entrepreneur* (February 2009): 70.

114 A. C. Cosper, "Green Bubble or Green Opportunity," *Entrepreneur* (April 2010): 14.

115 J. Bennett, "Are We Headed Toward a Green Bubble?" *Entrepreneur* (April 2010): 51–54.

116 Colvin Interview of Linda Fisher, *Fortune* (November 23, 2009): 45–50.

117 "Who's the Greenest of Them All?" *BusinessWeek* (November 28–December 4, 2011): 59–61.

118 "Eco-Friendly Growth," *BusinessWeek* (May 4, 2009): 5–6.

119 H. M. Haugh and A. Talwar, "How Do Corporations Embed Sustainability Across the Organization?" *Academy of Management Learning & Education* 9(3) (2010): 384–396.

120 "Sustainability in Management Education," *Academy of Management Learning & Education* 8(3) (2009): 312.

121 "Who's the Greenest of Them All?" *BusinessWeek* (November 28–December 4, 2011): 59–61.

122 M. Bustillo, "Wal-Mart to Assigning New 'Green' Ratings," *Wall Street Journal* (July 16, 2009): B1.

123 www.3M.com (accessed June 26, 2012).

124 A. T. Lawrence and J. Weber, *Business and Society,* 13th ed. (New York: McGraw-Hill, 2011).

125 Ibid.

126 R. Jana, "Nike Goes Green, Very Quietly," *BusinessWeek* (June 22, 2009): 56.

127 M. Ramsey, "Ghosn Sees Electric Cars Taking Off," *Wall Street Journal* (May 25, 2010): B4.

128 Colvin Interview of Linda Fisher, *Fortune* (November 23, 2009): 45–50.

129 M. Ramsey, "Ghosn Sees Electric Cars Taking Off," *Wall Street Journal* (May 25, 2010): B4.

130 L. K. Audebrand, "Sustainability in Strategic Management Education: The Quest for New Root Metaphors," *Academy of Management Learning & Education* 9(3) (2010): 413–428.

131 D. S. Siegel, "Green Management Matters Only If It Yields More Green: An Economic/Strategic Perspective," *Academy of Management Perspectives* 23(3) (2009): 5–16.

132 A. Nadim and R. N. Lussier, "Sustainability as a Small Business Competitive Strategy," *Journal of Small Strategy* 21(2) (2012): 79–95.

133 R. Van der Merwe, L. F. Pitt, and R. Abratt, "Stakeholders Strength: PR Survival Strategies in the Internet Age," *Public Relations Quarterly* 50 (Spring 2005): 39–49.

134 C. Palmeri and N. Byrnes, "Coke and Pepsi Try Reinventing Water," *BusinessWeek* (March 2, 2009): 58.

135 P. Keegan, "The Trouble With Green Product Ratings," *Fortune* (July 25, 2011): 130–134.

136 J. Carlton, "Homebuyers Go Green to Cut Bills," *Wall Street Journal* (February 12, 2009): D1.

137 A. Athavaley, "Paying $1,299 for a Washer in Order to Save $90 a Year," *Wall Street Journal* (February 12, 2009): D1.

138 H. M. Haugh and A. Talwar, "How Do Corporations Embed Sustainability Across

the Organization?" *Academy of Management Learning & Education* 9(3) (2010): 384–396.

139 P. A. Heslin, "Social Entrepreneurship," *Academy of Management Learning & Education* 10(1) *(*2011): 164–166.

140 R. N. Mefford, "The Economic Value of a Sustainable Supply Chain," *Business and Society Review* 116(1) (2011): 109–143.

141 H. M. Haugh and A. Talwar, "How Do Corporations Embed Sustainability Across the Organization?" *Academy of Management Learning & Education* 9(3) (2010): 384–396.

142 M. Miles and J. Coving, "Environmental Marketing: A Source of Reputation, Competitive, and Financial Advantage," *Journal of Business Ethics* (February 2000): 299–311.

143 "The Sounds of Sustainability," *Entrepreneur* (May 2011): 21.

144 S. O. Osaglie, "The Voluntary Environmentalists," *Academy of Management Perspectives* 33(2) (2008): 564–568.

145 J. P. Bonardi and G. D. Keim, "Corporate Political Strategies for Widely Salient Issues," *Academy of Management Review* 30(3) (2005): 555–576.

146 "Nevada Lost," *Wall Street Journal* (August 9, 2006): A1.

147 Reviewer M. Chowdhury Lincoln University.

148 http://www.investor.bayer.com/1275_schwerpunkte/schwerpunkte.php (accessed August 23, 2006).

149 http://www.investor.bayer.com/15416_unternehmenspolitik/unternehmenspolitik.php (accessed August 23, 2006).

150 http://subscriber.hoovers.com/H/company360/fulldescription.html?companyId=41808000000000 (accessed July 18, 2012).

151 Ibid.

152 http://www.bayer.com/bayer-group/history/1996-2006/page8711.htm (accessed August 23, 2006).

153 S. Kilman and J. V. Reppert-Bismarck, "U.S. Rice Prices Are Stunted by Concerns of Biotech Controls," *Wall Street Journal* (August 22, 2006): A2.

154 Ibid.

155 http://www.naturalnews.com/028585_GMOs_Bayer.html (accessed July 18, 2012).

156 Ibid.

157 http://articles.chicagotribune.com/2012-07-17/news/sns-rt-us-china-economy-jobsbre86h040-20120717_1_china-s-wen-job-creation-job-market (accessed July 18, 2012).

158 http://english.gov.cn/2006-02/08/content_182584.htm (accessed August 23, 2006).

159 http://www.upi.com/Business_News/Energy-Resources/2011/03/01/Pollution-a-threat-to-Chinas-growth/UPI-94781299004853/ (accessed July 18, 2012).

160 Ibid.

161 Ibid.

162 Ibid.

163 http://interactive.wsj.com/edition/resources/documents/bbbeige.htm (accessed July 10, 2006).

164 J. J. Miller, "FOMC Makes it 17 at 5.25% and Seems to Get it About Housing," http://matrix.millersamuel.com/?p=723 (June 30, 2006) (accessed July 10, 2006).

165 http://www.hsh.com/mtghst.html (accessed July 10, 2006).

166 "Bankruptcy Filings Up Despite Reforms," http://money.cnn.com/2006/06/12/pf/personal_bankruptcy.reut/?section=money_pf (June 12, 2006) (accessed July 10, 2006).

167 http://bigpicture.typepad.com/comments/2006/02/home_foreclosur.html (accessed July 10, 2006).

168 http://online.wsj.com/article/BT-CO-20120717-712181.html (accessed July 18, 2012).

169 http://www.charlotteobserver.com/2012/01/01/2889998/housing-glut-looms.html (accessed July 18, 2012).

170 http://www.thinkmoney.com/banking/bad-credit-bank-accounts/what-causes-a-bad-credit-history-0-4364.htm (accessed July 18, 2012).

171 http://bucks.blogs.nytimes.com/2011/06/29/whats-a-reasonable-home-down-payment (accessed July 18, 2012).

172 http://www.environmentalhomecenter.com/learn.shtml?Directory_Code=topicsmain&Page_Code=budget (accessed August 24, 2006).

173 http://www.investopedia.com/terms/d/dinks.asp (accessed July 11, 2006).

174 http://thegeomancer.netfirms.com/fengshui.htm (accessed August 24, 2006).

175 http://www.greenhomebuilding.com/small.htm (accessed August 24, 2006).

Appendix

CASE ANALYSIS APPROACHES

> ### What's This Appendix About?
>
> When conducting a case analysis, analysts can use any of at least four approaches. And more than one method can be used for the same case. The first approach is to simply answer the questions at the end of the case. The second is the generic approach, an approach that could be used for analyzing a case for any course. The third approach is to follow a procedural strategic analysis. The fourth approach uses the Business, Society, and Government Case Analysis Table. We discuss the four approaches in this introduction, but your professor will inform you of his or her preferred case analysis approach.

INTRODUCTION TO CASE ANALYSIS

The use of case analysis in the study of business, society, and government is the primary method of learning how the various tenets of the subject matter we describe throughout this book work in practice.

Benefits of Case Analysis

Case analysis is valuable in that it shows how market and nonmarket strategies work in the real world, which aids you in mastering the subject matter. Through the study of actual business nonmarket practices, you are able to see how many of the theoretical underpinnings of the discipline affect the course of business growth, prosperity, and survival.

Cases take theory and test it in practice. Frequently, theory and practice coincide, making it is easy to see how a determined strategic approach resulted in an intended result. However, periodically, the theory does not lead to the expected result, or it fails completely. Here, it is important to examine why—what went wrong, what was overlooked, or what happened beyond the control of the strategic planners and managers that resulted in the unanticipated outcomes.

Case analysis provides you with the opportunity to answer the questions, What would I do in these circumstances? What decisions would I make that, hopefully, would make a positive difference? How would I know if I were doing the right thing or not? Second-guessing real-world decision makers is not merely an *interesting* process, it is also a valuable *educational* process. You can examine the pros and cons of what actual decision makers have done (or are doing) and use this as a forum to conduct an in-depth examination of the decision-making processes and come up with creative alternatives.

The analysis of case studies involving real companies brings the subject matter to life. This active learning approach has many benefits over other methods of learning the subject matter (such as pure lecturing) and gives you the opportunity to engage the material on a first-person basis.

All in all, case analysis is an important part of the study of business, society, and government. It cements the learning process, and makes the tenets of the discipline more real. In order to conduct a meaningful analysis, however, certain case analysis approaches are more helpful to follow; we present four of them.

The Role of the Professor

The professor's primary role in case analysis is one of facilitator. The instructor helps to keep the class focused on the key issues, creates a classroom environment that encourages classroom discussion and creativity, bridges "theory to practice" by referring to key concepts learned in this or prior courses, and challenges students' analyses in order to stimulate further learning and discussion. Several variations of the aforementioned approach include written assignments, oral presentations, team assignments, structured case competitions, and supplemental fieldwork. Regardless of the variation employed, most professors will evaluate and grade a case analysis as partial fulfillment of the course's requirements. We will now discuss four approaches to analyzing a case.

ANSWER CASE QUESTIONS

All of the cases in this book have questions at the end of the case. Whether an instructor assigns questions for you to analyze with the case is usually a matter of his or her educational philosophy and your readiness. The simplest case method approach your professor may employ is to have you simply answer the case questions.

Each chapter starts with an introductory case with answers to the case questions embedded in the text after the related chapter material. These answers can serve as examples of how you should be answering the questions posed in the end-of-chapter cases, in chapter ethical dilemmas, or in other case material assigned by your instructor. When you answer the questions, be sure to refer back to the chapter outline and chapter content to know what text concepts relate to the case. When you write and/or discuss your answers, be sure to apply the text concepts to the case; that is, the concepts should be part of your answer. Your professor may grade your discussion or written answers based on how well you apply the text concepts because, in essence, they provide the fundamental knowledge required to answer a question that goes beyond simply asking for your opinions.

Your professor may require you to answer case questions, add pertinent questions, or have you use one or more of the other case analysis approaches.

THE GENERIC CASE APPROACH

Although you may have already been exposed to the case method in your other classes, let's review the case method of analysis. In the traditional case method, case questions do not accompany the case. You assume the role of a manager or consultant by taking a generalist approach to analyzing and solving the problems of an organization. This approach requires you to develop your own case questions so to speak, in that you utilize all of your prior learning in the subject area, as well as in this course, to analyze the case without receiving specific directions from the instructor. It is therefore strongly suggested that you prepare for the case prior to class discussion, using the following recommendations: allow adequate time in preparing the case, read the case thoroughly, focus on the key issues, adopt the appropriate time frame, and draw on all your knowledge. You should also reread the case during and after doing your case analysis before finalizing it. You will be surprised how often you find that you missed something.

The Case Analysis

Consider the case study report as a task assigned to you by your employer because the problems lie within the scope of your responsibilities. This task, which is a part of your job, will result in a report that will have an effect on your boss's opinion of how well you do. Your rate of pay (grade) and your chances for advancement are often influenced by your efforts.

It is essential in problem solving that the problem be clearly recognized and understood. If a problem or issue is not defined, how can it be solved? To assist you, the following four steps may help you think through the problem in a logical manner and then help you in preparing your report.

1. **Recognize the real problems or issues**. Read the entire case to get an overall impression of what it is about. Read it again and list in brief form all the key facts, assumptions, and sentiments (as described in Chapter 2 and later in this Appendix). Next, examine the key facts and isolate symptoms, which call attention to the problem or issue and its possible causes. For example, customer complaints are a symptom that may be triggered by numerous factors described in the case, such as product failure or poor customer service that are causing those complaints. Make sure to separate symptoms (effects) from the actual sources (causes).

2. **Determine what principles of business, society, and government are involved.** Ask yourself what material from the text, and this specific chapter, apply to this case. Your analysis of that case should focus on using the material in that chapter, plus prior chapters, especially Chapters 1 and 2. Material from other courses you have taken as well as personal experience may also be applicable.

3. **Evaluate the causes and the principles (as in step 2) and then plot possible courses of action available to you to correct the situation.** List *all* possible actions that occur to you—even the ones that seem downright impractical; Figure 1.4 provides nonmarket strategies to consider. Then go back and study each possible action, asking the following questions: What are the chances that this action will cure the problem? How will it solve the problem? Can I really put this action into operation? What hurdles do I face in putting it into operation? Where does it leave me if it fails? Does it bring in new problems of its own even if it succeeds?

4. **Make your final selection of the action or actions you intend to use.** Not every problem has a "complete" or single solution. It is also possible that any one of several solutions may work. So first list your alternative strategies, and then select one or a combination.

Writing the Case Analysis Report

Everything done thus far has been "think" work with notes. You have tackled your problem and you have a recommendation to make. Your problem now is to present your analysis and solution strategy in such a manner that it will be given careful attention. Above all, you want to have the wisdom of your decision recognized so make your report neat, clear, and easy to read.

A suggested format (though by no means the only one) is:

1. State the basic problem in terms of what has been happening and the principles involved. Avoid telling or repeating insignificant details.
2. Indicate briefly the possible approaches you considered.
3. Indicate in detail the steps you choose to take. Tell exactly what you intend to do. Tell why you believe this action will solve the problem. Point out the difficulties you anticipate and the actions planned to deal with those issues. Wherever possible, relate the actions you take and the reasons you give to the principles of business, society, and government as per this text.

In short, telling what you intend to do is only half of the task—the story. The other half requires you to explain why you think it makes sense to do so, based on the text concepts.

STRATEGIC ANALYSIS APPROACH

Many professors use a procedural method to thoroughly analyze a case. In Chapter 2, we present the 5 Is Strategic Analysis process. However, as previously stated, no single method is universally accepted. Your professor may have you use the 5 Is process in the book or may tell you his or her preferred strategic method. More than likely, it will include parts of the 5 Is, as the generic approach does. Your professor will tell you if you are to use a strategic analysis process, and if so, what the process is.

The common written and/or discussion process is to give answers to each of the parts of the strategic analysis. For example, with the 5 Is, you state the issue, who the interested strategic stakeholders are, and the incentives of stakeholders. Then, you write an objective to deal with the issue, and you state information you will use to present the business side of the issue. Finally, you state the strategic action you will take to deal with the issue.

Again, you may be asked both to answer the questions and to follow a procedural strategic analysis. Actually, it is to your benefit to at least read the questions because they often deal with some aspects of the strategic analysis process, and they may provide information that helps you with the analysis.

THE BUSINESS, SOCIETY, AND GOVERNMENT CASE ANALYSIS TABLE

The Business, Society, and Government (BSG) Case Analysis Table is based on the 5 Is strategic analysis discussed in Chapter 2. The table format walks you through each of the five stages to analyze the case using a structured method. Your instructor may require you to use this table/form. Your instructor may also use an adapted version of the form; he or she will explain the requirements. If your professor requires you to use some other form of case analysis, you may still use the BSG case form as a *worksheet*.

In this section, we discuss the BSG Case Analysis Table format, presenting a blank form that you can copy and use, and a completed form that explains what to write in each column, with a simple case analysis example. You can make copies of the blank table for your use and write your answers in the columns, or make the table template and then input your answers as described next.

Making BSG Case Tables to Input Your Analysis

All you need to do is make a table. These are the steps using MS Word:

1. Open a Word document.
2. To begin, type in the case name, your name, the chapter, and the date, or provide this information in whatever format preferred by your instructor.
3. Click Insert and then Table (usually found in the toolbar).
4. When you click Insert Table, a dialog box will ask you to indicate rows and columns.
5. For page 1 of the table, select 4 columns and 2 rows.

6. Click OK.
7. For the second page, repeat the process, making the table contain 5 columns and 2 rows.
8. Click OK.
9. Put the cursor in the portion of the table where you want to type and get started. Don't worry about column/row size. When you type within the column, it will enlarge to accommodate what you type.

The default for the table format is portrait, but it is better to use the landscape format, which allows for wider columns than portrait, which is what we prefer, but the choice is yours or the professor's. To change your default portrait page setup to landscape:

1. On the tool bar, click on Page Layout.
2. Click on Orientation.
3. Click Landscape.
4. If you click Margins, you may choose Custom Margins, which gives you a dialog box and allows you to choose .4 on all four sides, which will provide more typing space in your table.
5. Click OK.

Conducting a BSG 5 Is Strategic Analysis Using the Table

The best way to explain how to use the table is to type what goes in each column of the table and to show you how to complete a table by typing in a simplified case analysis, which we did. Your professor may go over the answers and indicate what goes in each column in class. Again, the nine-column table guides you though each of the five stages, so let's go past the blank table, which you can copy for your use, and go to the completed table.

BLANK TABLE

BSG 5 Is Strategic Analysis: CASE _____   Ch. _____ Name _____   Date _____

Issue Identification [1 Write the problem issue {One issue per sheet} [Ch. 2]	Interested Strategic Stakeholders [2 {Bus, Soc, & Gov} For (+) or Against (−) Business or Neutral (=) {Model 1.1, p. 5} [Ch. 2, 1–10]	Incentive of Stakeholders [3 What can they gain or lose that will get them involved? Cost vs. Benefit (C > B, B > C) [Ch. 2]	Objective for issue and Information to be [4 used to meet objective Fact (F), Assumption, (A) {#s, outside sources} [Ch. 2]
Stage of Life Cycle {Figure 2.4 p. 53]			

Interaction Strategies:

Alternative strategic action [5 to meet the objective {Figure 1.4 p. 22} [Ch. 2, 1–10]	*Market analysis* [6 Market reactions (+, =, –) [Ch. 2]	*Nonmkt analysis* [7 Nonmarket reactions (+, =, –) [Ch. 2]	*Select strategic action* [8 Is it legal and ethical? Selected? (Y/N/Wait) [Chs. 1–10]	*Implementation actions for each strategy* [9 Urgency? {policies, procedures, rules} *Evaluate results* [Ch. 2, 1–10]

COMPLETED TABLE

Remember, you are a top manager of the business taking its side using the stakeholder approach to management, unless your professor says otherwise.

BSG 5 Is Strategic Analysis: CASE _____ Ch. _____ Name _____ Date _____

Issue Identification [1] Write the problem issue {One issue per sheet} [Ch. 2]	*Interested Strategic Stakeholders* [2] {Bus, Soc, & Gov} For (+) or Against (−) Business or Neutral (=) {Model 1.1, p. 5} [Ch .2, 1–10]	*Incentive of Stakeholders* [3] What can they gain or lose that will get them involved? Cost vs. Benefit (C > B, B > C) [Ch. 2]	*Objective* for issue and *Information* to be [4] used to meet objective Fact (F), Assumption, (A) {#s, outside sources} [Ch. 2]
As shown in the *title*, this is the first stage of the 5 Is strategic analysis. Refer to Chapter 2 for details.	As shown in the *title*, this is the second stage of the 5 Is strategic analysis. Refer to Chapter 2 for details.	As shown in the *title*, this is the third stage of the 5 Is strategic analysis. Refer to Chapter 2 for details.	As shown in the *title*, this is the fourth stage of the 5 Is strategic analysis. Refer to Chapter 2 for details.
The two major questions that you must answer during this step of the analysis are: (1) What is the issue? (2) At what stage of the life cycle is the issue?	The two questions you must answer here are: (1) Who are the specific strategic stakeholders? (2) Will they be for or against your firm's stance on the issue?	The two important questions now are: (1) What does each stakeholder have to gain or lose by helping or opposing your business? (2) Will the stakeholders take action to help or oppose the business on the issue?	The questions to answer are: (1) What do we want to accomplish, or what is our objective? (2) What are the facts and assumptions regarding the issue, interest, and incentives? (3) What supportive information should we get, or do we have, from the case to use in presenting our side of the issue?
(1) Type/write in the issue problem faced followed by a brief explanation of what it is about.	(1) Refer back to Model 1.1. For each triangle stakeholder group (Bus, Soc, & Gov), list only the *strategic* stakeholder. Then, be precise by naming the specific subgroups.	(1) Briefly state what each stakeholder has to gain or lose by helping or opposing your business.	(1) Review your information in Q 2+3 above, and then write your objective(s) for the issue at the top of the column. (To + action verb + specific-measurable result to be achieved + target date—when appropriate)

(2) Here you select which of the five stages of the life cycle the issue is in, with a brief explanation of why you believe it is.	(2) Be sure to state whether they will be for (simply indicate with +) or against (use –) the business or neutral (=) for the issue.	(2) You conduct your own cost–benefit analysis to predict which stakeholders will take action on the issue. Use a separate cost–benefit analysis for each stakeholder listed in column 2—on the same line/row.	(2–3) Then in the column, put the supportive information you will use to present your side of the issue. Be sure to try to use facts and figures and outside sources.
Note that it says only one issue per sheet, unless your instructor says otherwise.		The C > B indicates that the stakeholder will likely not take action because the cost is greater than the benefit for taking action.	Info can be placed in two ways. Just list general info under the objective. And/or put specific info for each stakeholder in its row. This information should be labeled with Fact (F) or Assumption (A) next to each source.
Stage of Life Cycle [Figure 2.4, p. 53]	One example BSG (there could be several under each category)	The B > C indicates that the stakeholder likely will take action.	To stop an increase in emissions standards.

For example, YOU are the president of Chrysler U.S.A. The issue is: requiring autos to pollute less—emissions. Stage 4 legislation and reg.	Business
	  Competitors
	    GM + ……
	    Ford +
	Society
	  Interest groups
	    Friends of the Earth –
	    Alliance of Auto. Manufacturers
	Government
	  Executive/Regulation
	  Environmental Protection Agency (EPA) –
		Continuing our example from column 2 rows
		B > C They don't want increase either.
		B > C They don't want increase either.
		B > C We know they are pressing EPA.
		B > C It helps auto industry with such issues.
		B > C We know it is working to increase standard.
			List facts and figures supporting your side, from the case and other sources, from inside and outside the business (F). For example, how much will it cost the firm, its customers and its consumers (F/A?)? How much will the higher standards actually help the environment—cost vs. benefit (F/A?)?

Interaction Strategies: This is the final stage of strategic analysis. As you can see by the headings, these are the five parts of strategy

Alternative strategic action to meet the objective [5] {Figure 1.4 p. 22} [Ch. 2, 1–10]	Market analysis [6] Market reactions (+, =, –) [Ch. 2]	Nonmarket analysis [7] Nonmarket reactions (+, =, –) [Ch. 2]	Select strategic action [8] Is it legal and ethical? Selected? (Y/N/Wait) [Chs. 1–10]	Implementation actions for each strategy [9] Urgency? {policies, procedures, rules} Evaluate results [Ch. 2, 1–10]
The question is: What strategies can we use to meet the objective?	The market and nonmarket analysis are done at the same time for each alternative, or you go from column 5 to 6 and 7 for each alternative. When analyzing strategies, consider the stage of the life cycle. The question is: Are the strategies any good for meeting the objective?		The two questions are: Is each alternative legal and ethical? Yes or No? You can answer these questions in later chapters.	Now you give the details of how you will implement the strategy(s) you selected using text concepts.
Brainstorm several alternatives without evaluating them. Just list them for now.

Strategies may come from:
■ The case
■ Figure 1.4 (strategies: information, societal, political, legal)
■ Other sources | The key market question is: Will the strategy help us in the market environment?

Will our strategic stakeholder: owners/stockholders, employees/managers, customers, suppliers, and/or cooperative competitors support the strategy? (+, =, –) If not, how powerful are they?

What are the consequences of each alternative strategy in the market? How | The key nonmarket question is: Will the strategy help us in the nonmarket environment?

Will our society strategic stakeholders: institutes, public sentiment, and news media support the strategy? (+, =, –) If not, how powerful are they?

Will our government strategic stakeholders: legislative/congress, executive/regulatory agencies, and judi- | Will each strategy be used? Yes or No? This is based on cost vs. benefits

Again, double check to make sure you believe the alternative will achieve the objective. If not, don't select it. If none seem to work, go back and develop more alternatives that will.

You also need to review all selected strategies to make sure they don't conflict or offset each other in some way. If they do, drop one or somehow combine them. | Urgency refers to how quickly you will get started—target dates.

When you write multiple actions, sequence them, as shown below.

You may need to develop some policies, procedures, and rules to make the plan standard operating procedure.

The last stage is to evaluate the results. In real life, you can do this, but when conducting a case analysis you really can't. You can, however, state how you would evaluate the results to know whether you have indeed resolved the issue. |
| Example continues (limited #) | | | | |

Strategy	Will the strategy affect sales and profits? You can conduct a cost-benefit analysis for each and simply list +, =, −.	Will the [so]cial/courts support the strategy? (+, =, −) If not, how powerful are they? What are the consequences of each alternative strategy in the nonmarket? You can conduct a cost-benefit analysis for each and simply list +, =, −.		
(1) Do nothing, wait and see if the EPA changes standard.	(1) Customers, suppliers, and competitors can be hurt with increased prices (−), which could reduce sales and profits. C > B	(1) Friends of the Earth (FE) and EPA will be pleased to have no opposition (+), and EPA will likely raise standard. C > B	(1) Yes, but Not selected	
(2) Lobby EPA regulators.	(2) Could help meet objective of not raising standard, market. (+) B > C	(2) FE will oppose us (−) and do their own lobbying against us. EPA will expect it and may be willing to work with us to at least minimize loses. (=) B > C	(2) Yes, and Yes selected	(2) Search for inside and outside sources of supportive info. Contact Alliance of Auto Manufacturers for info and help. Contact Ford and GM to form a coalition and share info. Get expert testimony, especially if a hearing is held. Meet with EPA to lobby, presenting your side info.
(3) Lobby president and/or Congress to pressure EPA regulators not to increase the standard.	(3) Might help, but they may not think it's appropriate to ask and not help, and it could hurt ongoing relations with them. (−) Could be expensive and not meet objective. C > B	(3) Likely to be opposed and used against us, which could hurt. (−) Could be expensive and not meet objective. C > B	(3) Yes, but Not selected When you have multiple strategies, you can skip the yes for ethical and legal unless it is not. In that case, say so: NO.	

INDEX

Note: 'F' after a page number indicates a figure; 't' indicates a table.